Tammarniit (Mistakes)

Between 1939 and 1963, the federal government embarked on a program of relocation and relief in the Eastern Arctic that would dramatically alter the lives of Inuit living there. This book documents how the development of the Canadian welfare state coincided with attempts to assimilate Inuit and organize their lives according to Western ideas about the family, work, and community. This policy resulted in many 'tammarniit' (mistakes) that led to social disruption, cultural disintegration, and even contributed to death among Inuit.

Tammarniit begins with an account of the debate over which branch of government should be responsible for the Inuit. It then considers the impact of the postwar liberal welfare state on Inuit. This is followed by a detailed account of one attempt to deal with emerging concerns: relocation of Inuit from the east coast of Hudson Bay to the high Arctic. Subsequent chapters deal with tragic events taking place in the Keewatin region in the late 1950s, including deaths from starvation at Henik and Garry lakes. The authors examine the subsequent relocation of the survivors and further attempts to assimilate Inuit with mainstream Canadian society. Throughout the book, the themes of responsibility, relief, and relocation emerge as central concepts in understanding this unique and often troublesome period in Canadian history.

The authors have made extensive use of archival documents, many of which have not been available to researchers before, among them the Alex Stevenson Collection, which was stored in the Archives of the Northwest Territories. They have also interviewed many key individuals who were involved with events during the period. The result is a compelling and sobering look at the evolution of Canadian policy in the North and its tragic effects on Inuit.

Frank James Tester is a professor in the School of Social Work at the University of British Columbia. *Peter Kulchyski* is a professor and chair of the Department of Native Studies at Trent University.

Frank James Tester and Peter Kulchyski

Tammarniit (Mistakes):
Inuit Relocation in the
Eastern Arctic, 1939-63

UBCPress / Vancouver

ISBN 0-7748-0452-1 (hardcover)
ISBN 0-7748-0494-7 (paperback)

Canadian Cataloguing in Publication Data

Tester, Frank J.
  Tammarniit (Mistakes)

  Includes bibliographical references and index.
  ISBN 0-7748-0452-1 (bound). – ISBN 0-7748-0494-7 (pbk.)

  1. Inuit – Canada – Government relations. 2. Inuit –
Northwest Territories. 3. Northwest Territories – History – 1905*
I. Kulchyski, Peter Keith, 1959- II. Title.

E99.E7T47 1994 323.1′197107192 C94-910201-6

This book has been published with the help of a grant from the Social Science
Federation of Canada, using funds provided by the Social Sciences and Humanities
Research Council of Canada.

UBC Press also gratefully acknowledges the ongoing support to its publishing
program from the Canada Council, the Province of British Columbia Cultural
Services Branch, and the Department of Communications of the Government of
Canada.

UBC Press
University of British Columbia
6344 Memorial Road
Vancouver, BC V6T 1Z2
(604) 822-3259
Fax: (604) 822-6083

ᐃᑕᖅᓂ ᐊᕐᕆᑎᖕᓄᑦ

Contents

Figures and Tables

Tables

Preface

The 1990s are witness to a fundamental re-examination of the Canadian liberal welfare state which developed following the Second World War. The attack on liberal welfare values comes not only in the form of a neo-liberal agenda that emphasizes the development of a global economy unimpeded by national boundaries, as well as a restatement of competitive individualism. But, among those committed historically to the central tenets of Fabianism and the welfare state, there is also a growing tendency to question the extent to which the welfare state could ever achieve its stated ideal of equality, while respecting diversity among Canadian citizens. Recent history also suggests that the welfare state has ultimately failed to act as an effective 'buffer' against the excesses of capitalist enterprise. Social workers and others are coming to understand that the welfare state is not the benevolent purveyor of egalitarian and humanitarian social values it was once held to be. Rather, it is increasingly recognized as something quite different – a source of oppression and racism, a regime which, because of its structures and biases, has often discriminated against women, children, and other marginalized groups.

In the case of First Nations and aboriginal peoples, the racism inherent in the welfare state takes an assimilationist form but has been couched, historically, in liberal humanitarian language. Thus, those developing and delivering services within the precepts of welfare liberalism argued, as was consistent with liberal discourse on rights, that they were committed to extending the privilege of citizenship developed by the Canadian state to all Canadians. It was argued that aboriginal peoples were entitled to the same levels of schooling, social security, and health care as other Canadians. These commitments were genuine and consistent with what was seen to be the dominant and progressive discourse of the day. But this discourse was also about nation-building – about creating a country of shared values, in the belief that the end result would be social harmony, as well as proficiency and efficiency in the capitalist development of Canada's economic base.

This book explores the application of the precepts and norms of welfare liberalism to the Inuit of the eastern Arctic in the period following the Second World War. It commences with a review of the 1939 Supreme Court decision which concluded that Inuit, at a constitutional level, were in effect 'Indians.' It follows the development of welfare liberalism, as applied to the Inuit, through the period of high modernism, until 1963. By that time, the consolidation of Inuit in settlements throughout the eastern Arctic was virtually complete.

The idea for the text originated with Frank who, in the early 1970s, spent several years working and travelling in the high Arctic as a graduate student at the University of Calgary. Subsequently, between 1977 and 1979, he coordinated a social, economic, and environmental impact assessment of the proposed Polar Gas Pipeline, in the District of Keewatin, under a joint agreement with Indian and Northern Affairs Canada, Inuit Tapirisat of Canada, and the Keewatin Inuit Association. It was through these experiences that he first became aware of the many relocations of Inuit following the Second World War. During the 1980s this interest culminated in the research that informs this text. Both of us worked for a short period during 1984 at the Arctic Institute of North America and subsequently at the same campus at York University, where we first considered writing this book. Peter discussed this research project, in its earliest stages, with Frank and eventually agreed to be a co-investigator. At the time, Peter was a graduate student in the Department of Political Science, completing a doctoral thesis on political theory and aboriginal politics. Peter's work has taken him primarily to the western Arctic, where he is known for his commitment to popularizing aboriginal history in Canada.

Writing this book has been a truly exciting and rewarding experience for both of us. The result is a genuinely collaborative effort and a blending of the various pieces for which we took prime responsibility. Frank drafted the Preface and Chapters 2, 3, and 4, while Peter drafted the Introduction and Chapters 1, 5, 6, and 7. Chapter 8 was a collaborative effort. Chapters drafted by one of us would be substantially rewritten by the other, and drafts of whole sections were sometimes moved from one chapter to another. It therefore makes sense to say that the text is truly ours and can be cited as Kulchyski and Tester, or Tester and Kulchyski.

The research for this book relies predominantly on the RG 85 series of the National Archives of Canada (NAC), supplemented by material from other series and other sources. This is because RG 85 contains material related to the day-to-day workings of the departments responsible for Inuit affairs during the period in question and has thus afforded us the opportunity to detail the historical processes we wanted to explore.

Another major source of material was uncovered at the Prince of Wales Northern Heritage Centre, which contains the Northwest Territories (NWT) Archives, in Yellowknife. The papers of Alex Stevenson, a major figure in the events documented in this book, were turned over to the archives following his death. At the time, the NWT Archives were without a chief archivist, and the papers – some thirty-six cases of material – were stored away. Frank first became aware of the possibility of this collection while interviewing Nigel Wilford of the Department of Indian and Northern Affairs, formerly an Anglican priest in the eastern Arctic. The trail eventually led to the NWT Archives, where the collection was still in storage, uncatalogued and unknown. We found this to be one of the most interesting and valuable collections of material dealing with the contemporary history of the eastern Arctic, and we have relied extensively upon it throughout the book. The collection was still being catalogued as this book was being written. Therefore, the specific locations of documents are unspecified.

Throughout the text we have referred to 'Inuit' and 'Indians.' Both are aboriginal peoples. To use the term aboriginal would thus include Inuit and confuse the reader when we are making distinctions between Inuit and other aboriginal people. We realize that the use of 'Indian' is not ideal, but neither the term 'aboriginal' nor 'First Nations' allowed us to make the distinctions necessary for the book.

The years of research that have gone into this effort have brought us into contact with dozens of people throughout Canada. All have enriched our understanding of this period – to the point where we sometimes felt that we were actually living and acting inside it. Our most obvious thanks go to the communities of Resolute Bay and Grise Fiord, which Frank visited in the summer of 1991. Special thanks go to Elizabeth Allakariallak, Paul Amarualik, Simeonie and Sarah Amagoalik, Ludy and Dora Pudluk, Meeko Nastopoka, Minnie Allakariallak, George Eckalook, and Allie Salluviniq from Resolute Bay, and to Lydia Nungaq, Etuk Noah, Mary Akulukjuk, Zipporah Ningiuk, Seegollk Akeeagok, Looty Pijamini, Rynie Flaherty, Johnny Flaherty, Peepeelee Pijaminimi, and Syla Pijamini of Grise Fiord; to Jimmy Quappik, who helped set up the historical documents that were used as the basis for discussion in Grise Fiord; to Ellen Bielawaski, who shared many of our research interests and travelled to Resolute and Grise Fiord at the same time; and to longtime friends Cathy and Buster Welch of Winnipeg and Resolute Bay, with whom Frank sometimes stayed in the early 1970s and whom he had the pleasure of visiting again.

In Ottawa, special thanks go to Rosemarie Kuptana, president of Inuit Tapirisat of Canada (ITC), who has shown particular interest in the development of this work, and to Jack Hicks, who has been a very helpful and pleasant point of contact for us within ITC. On the title, we first consulted Kayrene Nookooguak, but also talked with Okalik Eegeesiak and others.

Sincere thanks go to Richard Valpy, who gave us special permission to examine the Alex Stevenson Collection before it had been processed. The entire staff of the NWT Archives was most helpful. We are grateful to John Poirier for help in dealing with photographs and audiotapes contained in the collection. Similarly, without exception, the staff of the National Archives of Canada was outstanding in the service they provided. We wish to recognize the importance of both the staff and a badly underfunded institution in making efforts such as this possible.

We also interviewed a few key informants in southern Canada and have relied extensively on their assistance in compiling the text. Our thanks go to Father Charles Choque of Ottawa; the late Ross Gibson, former RCMP constable; Ben Sivertz, former northern administrator and commissioner of the Northwest Territories; Doug Wilkinson, former northern service officer; Dr. H. Ewart, former administrator of the Mountain Sanatorium, Hamilton, Ontario; Walter Rudnicki, the first social worker hired by the Arctic division in 1955; and the late Harold Serson and Geoff Hattersley-Smith, both formerly with the Defence Research Board. We are particularly grateful to Dr. Otto Schaefer of Edmonton, who was not only a conscientious reviewer of parts of the text, but who, along with Dr. Gordon Hodgson, professor emeritus at the University of Calgary, inspired much of Frank's original interest in Arctic Canada.

The text has been reviewed both by people involved in the events outlined in the book and by others familiar with the period in question. Ben Sivertz and Ross Gibson suffered many phone calls seeking clarifications and did extensive reviews of Chapters 3 and 4. Alan Marcus of the Scott Polar Institute has also researched and written about the 1953 relocations to the high Arctic, and we appreciated our contacts with him. Professor Shelagh Grant of Trent University, who has also written about the high Arctic relocations, was meticulous in her review of drafts of these same chapters. She also provided some documents we did not have at the time. We have acknowledged this contribution wherever appropriate in the references and extend our thanks. Doug Wilkinson provided helpful comments on Chapters 5 and 6, as did Dr. 'Buster' Welch of Winnipeg.

Frank would like to acknowledge Dr. Glenn Drover, who has made a number of outstanding contributions to our understanding of social welfare in Canada and provided critical comment on the Introduction as well as on Chapters 7 and 8. Professor Michael Yellow Bird and Jack MacDonald, professor emeritus, School of Social Work, University of British Columbia, also provided critical comments that helped us refine key portions of the text. Thanks to Stan de Mello and Colleen Kasting for support and encouragement. Other comments on various chapters from Dr. Tim Tyler, professor emeritus, Faculty of Social Welfare, University of Calgary, and Dr. Gordon Hodgson, former editor of *Arctic*, the journal of the Arctic Institute of North America, were especially helpful. Dr. Julia Emberley of the University of Northern British Columbia gave very useful advice after her reading of several chapters, and we are grateful to her. Audrey Panter, Runa Loeb, and Gladys Simard provided much appreciated assistance with indexing. Eleanor Tao provided administrative support in Vancouver.

Peter would like to thank Kate Jennings and Joyce Miller for research and administrative support in Peterborough. Thanks as well to Mose Aupaluktuk, Jose Awa, Janice Mathewsie, Stephen Inukshuk, Aluki Koherk, Andrew Qaunaq, and Andrew Tugak for guidance and inspiration.

In putting together the book, Jean Wilson of UBC Press was extremely helpful and a pleasant contact. To Carolyn Bateman, our copy editor, goes our thanks for outstanding work on a very difficult task; and to Holly Keller-Brohman and Stacy Belden, our appreciation for seeing the book through the final stages of production.

The research for this text was funded by a grant from the Social Sciences and Humanities Research Council of Canada.

The book is the culmination of a long journey. We have been richly rewarded by the many people who have inspired, assisted, and supported us. To them goes much credit for a book we hope will increase our understanding of ourselves – Inuit and Qallunat alike – as people both shaping and being shaped by a very rich and sometimes troubled history.

Frank James Tester
Peter Kulchyski
November 1993

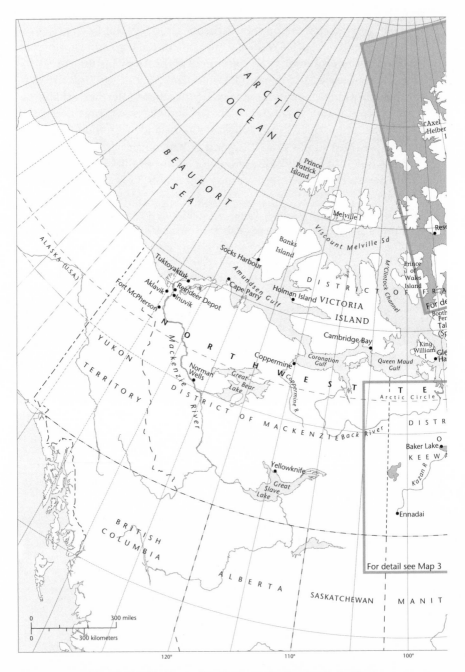

Map 1 The Northwest Territories (including Arctic Quebec)

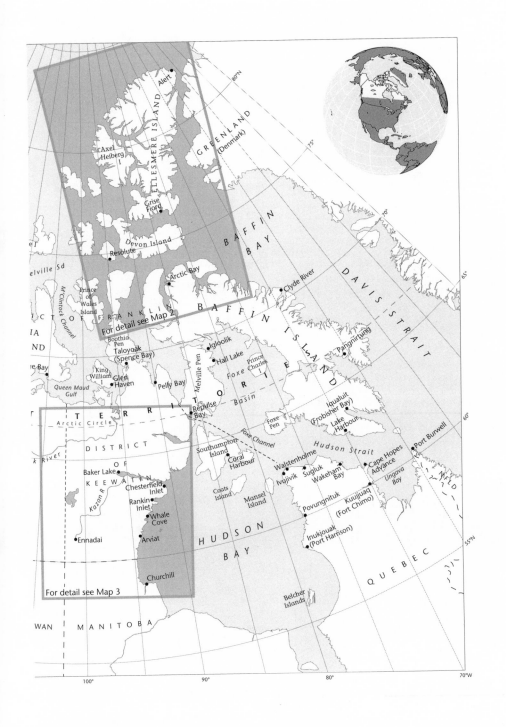

Alert

Axel
Heiberg
I

ELLESMERE ISLAND

GREENLAND
(Denmark)

Grise
Fiord

Devon Island

Resolute

BAFFIN

BAY

DAVIS STRAIT

Melville Sd

M'Clintock Channel

Prince
of
Wales
Island

Arctic Bay

Clyde River

FRANKLIN

BAFFIN

For detail see Map 2

ISLAND

Pangnirtung

IA

ND

Boothia
Pen

Taloyoak
(Spence Bay)

Igloolik

Hall Lake

Foxe

Prince
Charles

DISTRICT OF

e Bay

King
William
I

Glen
Haven

Queen Maud
Gulf

Pelly Bay

Melville Pen

Basin

Repulse
Bay

Foxe
Pen

Iqaluit
(Frobisher Bay)

Lake
Harbour

T
E
R
R
I
T
O
R
I
E

Arctic Circle

k River

DISTRICT

OF

KEEWATIN

Baker Lake

Kazan R

Chesterfield
Inlet

Rankin
Inlet

Whale
Cove

Ennadai

Arviat

Churchill

For detail see Map 3

WAN

MANITOBA

Foxe Channel

Southampton
Island

Coral
Harbour

Coats
Island

Mansel
Island

HUDSON

BAY

Walstenholme

Ivujivik

Sugluk

Wakeham
Bay

Povungnituk

Inukjouak
(Port Harrison)

Belcher
Islands

Hudson Strait

Cape Hopes
Advance

Port Burwell

Ungava
Bay

Kuujjuaq
(Fort Chimo)

QUEBEC

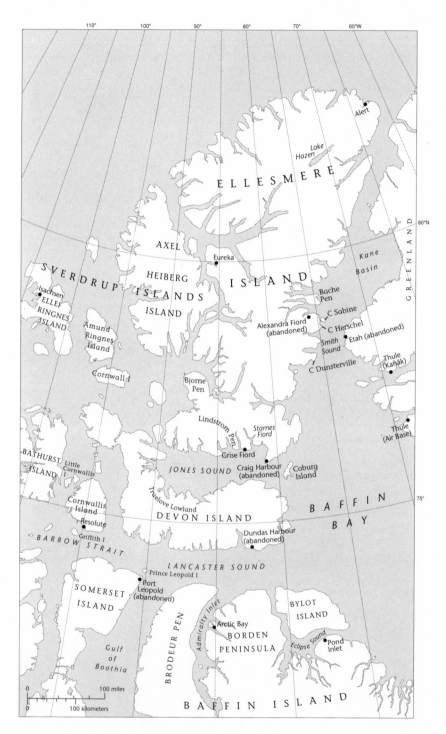

Map 2 High eastern Arctic

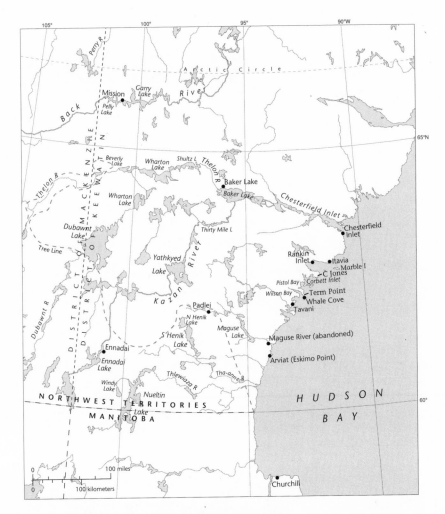

Map 3 District of Keewatin

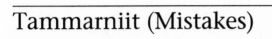

Tammarniit (Mistakes)

Introduction

Between 1939 and 1963, the lives of Inuit people in Arctic Canada changed dramatically. This change represented a crucial phase in a longer historical process, commencing with whaling in the eighteenth century, which saw self-defined and self-reliant Inuit drawn into a vastly different network of social relations. By the mid-1960s, nomadic Inuit family groupings had settled into communities where attempts were being made to organize Inuit life according to Western ideas about the family, work, community, and social relations.

During the period in question, the major agent of change was the Canadian state, which was undergoing a structural shift as it entered a period of welfare state reform. That reform had grown out of the trauma of the depression, which had fuelled fears that the aftermath of the Second World War – like that of the First World War – would be characterized by recession and unemployment. Inuit were profoundly affected by the changes that accompanied the introduction of a Canadian version of the welfare state. During this period, they were portrayed by the popular media as 'innocent and malleable children.' On the contrary, Inuit increasingly resisted attempts to assimilate them within the dominant Canadian culture.

The line of contact between Inuit and non-Inuit in the North had been largely economic in the 1920s and '30s and organized around the exigencies of the white fox fur trade. Coastal trading posts were established, and Inuit adapted to them. Some settlements, usually consisting of a trading post and a mission, resulted from this relationship. Similar relationships, based on the beaver fur trade, had influenced Indian and non-Native relations in the period between the seventeenth and the late-nineteenth centuries. As Arthur Ray has demonstrated, a credit system that developed during the fur trade was transformed, in the late nineteenth and early twentieth centuries, into a welfare system.[1] This occurred when the state began to assume control over the line of contact between Natives and non-Natives. Through the credit system, aboriginal trappers would obtain supplies on credit and return to posts with furs a year later, paying their bills and gaining more credit for the coming year. The system benefitted the fur trading company because it encouraged Native peoples to participate in the fur trade and thereby helped the traders to secure a more reliable supply of furs.

As prices dropped and the fur trade bottomed out, the credit system became difficult for companies to carry on their books. They asked the government to intervene. Slowly, credit was transformed into relief, and reliance on an exchange economy changed to reliance on the state. This happened in sub-Arctic Canada roughly in the period between 1870 and 1930. In Arctic Canada, a similar process was taking place much later, well into the 1950s. What this means is that an era of neglect of Inuit affairs on the part of the state (which was preceded by a short burst of involvement in the 1920s) slowly came to an end in the 1940s and '50s.

This book documents two waves of expansion of state involvement in the lives of Inuit. One of these occurred in the late 1940s. In this period, Inuit were still actively involved in the fur trade and were living more or less traditional lives. However, the presence of the military, resource exploration, and missionary activity took its toll. Serious medical problems, including epidemics of tuberculosis and polio, could no longer be ignored. As the value of furs declined, 'relief' and family allowances became essential to survival. Against the background of a hunting and trapping culture, the problems experienced by Inuit, especially in Arctic Quebec, were seen as a matter of 'overpopulation' – of too many people and too few resources. Thus the second wave of state involvement was characterized by relocation and renewed efforts to integrate Inuit within the norms and precepts of Canadian culture and society.

Inuit history is, therefore, characterized by something almost unique: the central historical dynamic that came to link Inuit to non-Inuit society politically was put in place during the period of high modernism. Unlike Indian affairs, where a pre-welfare state employed largely coercive measures, in Inuit affairs it was a liberal form of welfare state, which gave the appearance of having a more benign face and which employed a greater reliance on ideology, that became the means for attempting assimilation.

The changes that took place in the lives of Inuit in the period in question can be understood in terms of 'totalization.' The state became a critical agent in the struggle to incorporate Inuit into the dominant Canadian society. This was a struggle to totalize a social group that had previously remained marginal and largely outside the sphere of dominant social relations. While a totality 'is defined as a being which, while radically distinct from the sum of its parts, is present in its entirety, in one form or another, in each of those parts, "totalization" is a developing activity.'[2] So wrote Jean-Paul Sartre, whose work on totalization informs our analysis of these historical events. It is important to emphasize that we are using the concept of totalization to describe a moment in a broader historical process. This always contested historical process begins with the development of capitalism in Europe – a process that set in motion the dynamic of capitalist expansion. It is a dynamic that has come to dominate the globe. For this reason, the study of attempts to assimilate and to 'modernize' Inuit culture has broader implications. Much of what is observed in this book closely parallels present-day attempts to bring indigenous and local cultures around the world into a web of international capitalist relations.

We have also used the concept of totalization in another way. Totalization is a process of consciousness, a way in which consciousness apprehends the world. For example, the apparent minutiae of human behaviour – details such as the instructions regarding 'ladies' in the North, found in Chapter 8 – are of significance, not only to the construction of this history at every level, but to creating a sensibility that may allow the reader to live inside this particular historical period and experience it as a developing and intimate moment of consciousness. In other words, history cannot be understood merely in terms of large or small events and structural change: if it can be understood at all, it must in some way be experienced, a feeling must be provoked, whether it be empathy or distaste, even at a moment distant from that in which the events under examination occurred. For this reason, the sensibilities revealed by the words of those involved – Inuit and Qallunat alike[3] – are essential to making this history.

In the beginning of the period in question, the dominant social order perceived Inuit as a marginal social group. They were an outside, an 'Other,' an excess, an unincorporated remainder, and a reminder of the limits of Canadian 'dominion.' The Canadian Dominion was founded on an economic logic that placed the accumulation of capital at its centre; this economic logic was dynamic in the narrow sense that it could not (can not) stand still. Growth lies at the heart of its dynamic. It was, then, inevitable that Canada would eventually turn its attention to the high Arctic, or to any region outside its totalizing control. What was not inevitable was the historical moment for totalization, the form it would take and the kinds of resistance that would be encountered. That the welfare state would be the locus of totalization in this context meant that the process had (and has) a specific, regional dynamic.

It is only recently that social theorists have come to pay close attention to the state as a totalizing instrument. Nicos Poulantzas and Anthony Giddens have separately, in the last two decades, begun to think seriously about this role of the state. As a totalizing force, the state operates in very particular fashion. Its goal is the establishment of a material and social reality conducive to the accumulation of capital. The social reality effectively means the creation of people who are prepared to sell their labour power in a marketplace of labour relations. This implies a process of dispossession: of separating people from their means of subsistence, which, in most cases and for most cultures, is the land. The material reality involves the transformation of space and time or, in political theorist Nicos Poulantzas's words, the construction of temporal and spatial 'matrices' whose central principle is the logic of seriality. The series is the order of the sequential line – 1..2..3..4..n – that is conducive to the instrumental form of rationality associated with dominant forms of Western thought.

As Sartre writes: 'There are serial behaviour, serial feelings and serial thoughts; in other words a series is a mode of being for individuals both in relation to one another and in relation to their common being.'[4] Crucial to seriality, and worth noting in this context, is the fact that it implies the surrender, by social actors, of their ability to make choices based on qualitative, internal factors. This ability is surrendered to an external and impersonal logic. Poulantzas's contribution was to observe how states attempt to construct histories and territories on the same basic principles. It is important to emphasize that both marginalization and absorption can serve as totalizing instruments of the state. Giddens, meanwhile, has focused on how surveillance has become a critical dimension of state power.

The state does not automatically get its own way everywhere and at every time. People find different ways of resisting and subverting the mechanisms and policies of the state. The state itself, particularly the welfare state, is also not a block, inherently and at every turn attempting to impose forms of domination and to quell resistance. The state is itself a site of struggle. Hence the process of totalization is a complex one, subject to resistance at every turn. In the Arctic, totalization remains an incomplete project, the continued battleground of struggle, as Inuit attempt to negotiate a path through the modern world – a contemporary element of which is the creation of Nunavut in the eastern Arctic and other attempts by Inuit in the Beaufort, James Bay, and Labrador regions to negotiate self-government agreements. The concept helps us understand the intelligibility of historical processes at work in Arctic Canada between 1939 and 1963.

As noted, in an earlier period of Arctic history, economic forces were the main mechanisms of totalization. The process was characterized by a degree of voluntarism because these mechanisms were underlying and implicit. Thus Inuit were 'free' to follow more or less traditional pursuits in terms of lifestyles, culture, and cosmology. However, in the 1940s and '50s, the liberal welfare state became the crucial locus of totalization in the North. This locus included, but was far more expansive than, economic means. The focal point for this expanded means of totalization, and the resistance and struggle that accompanied it, became Arctic settlements. Earlier settlements had developed around missions and trading posts, sometimes placed where Inuit could be found in traditional locations and sometimes placed where non-Inuit traders and missionaries had relatively easy access to communication or transportation networks to the south. In the '40s and '50s, settlements were developed by state planners. Inuit were moved, as often as not, rather than moving themselves. The fact and nature of settlement, frequently associated with projects involving the relocation of large numbers of people, became a site of totalizing struggle.

A shift in attitudes can be detected within the bureaucracy in the period under consideration. In the 1940s and through the early 1950s, the dominant approach was to promote traditional economies because it was thought this would avoid the creation of dependency. This logic lies behind the creation of communities in the high Arctic – Resolute Bay and Grise Fiord. While remote, these communities could be justified on the grounds that they were believed to afford Inuit an opportunity to pursue their traditional lifestyle under the surveillance of state officials – especially the RCMP. Factors other than welfare concerns have made these relocations the source of ongoing controversy and interest. However, in terms of the overall historical period, other events, which will be described in subsequent chapters, are at least as significant. Administrators wanted to learn from the mistakes of their predecessors in the field of Indian affairs. They did not want to create Arctic reservations and the dependency that they associated with the reservation system. In the late '40s and early '50s, this policy led to a kind of strategic neglect of Inuit at a time when the fur trade was failing miserably. A slow shift took place in the minds of administrators. They began to take a more interventionist approach and to expand the social services network to the Arctic.

Instead of reservations, they wanted 'northern suburbs.' They wanted Inuit citizens who would be self-reliant, but integrated into a broader Canadian social reality. They wanted a material infrastructure that could provide Inuit with a degree of material security and well-being that, they believed, had not existed previously. As will be shown in this book, the outcome was quite contrary. The housing, sanitary, and other conditions in Arctic settlements at this time were appalling. The state moved to integrate Inuit with Canadian society, believing that the old hunting and trapping economy could not support them. New settlements were created and older ones expanded. Rational principles and serial logic dominated their creation. This meant that settlements would be located in areas accessible to the South rather than areas occupied in the past by the Inuit. And the communities that resulted, almost always situated in the most accessible areas for southerners, allowed a new generation of northern 'helpers' – teachers, welfare officers, social workers, and service officers – to 'guide' the integration of Inuit into Canadian society.

No analysis that looks at history exclusively in terms of totalization is complete. This is because, as noted, people – whether in feminist collectives, British trade unions, or Inuit hunting camps – find different ways of resisting and of struggling against totalizing logic. Therefore, because this is a book about totalization, we must also acknowledge that we have not written anything like a full history of this period (if such a project is even possible, it would itself fall into the logic of totalization). We have produced a history focusing on one side of a historical process. Our focus is the state and its attempts at totalization. While we have, at specific points, illustrated forms of implicit and explicit Inuit resistance, the book should not be seen as a history of that resistance. It was necessary to develop our understanding of the specific logic of totalization in this specific geographical and historical context before we could follow the logic of resistance – something that merits detailed and future consideration.

To understand why the fact of settlement became so important, it is crucial to understand something of the nature of the different societies that confronted each other in Arctic Canada. Marshall Sahlins has characterized, at a very abstract level, a fundamental difference between hunting societies and modern societies as embodied in forms of thought: what he calls the 'locus of symbolic production' in a society is the way in which it sees the world, the defining realm that conditions all others or to which all others refer: 'One can thus speak of a privileged institutional locus of the symbolic process, whence emanates a classificatory grid imposed upon the total culture.'[5] In modern society, according to Sahlins, a practical reason – or economic or material logic – organizes how we assess and understand people and events. It might also be called, following the work of the Frankfurt School of critical theory, an instrumental rationality. Among hunting peoples, kinship relations – the bonds between people – are the locus of symbolic production. If this is true, it says something about the profound social and cultural impacts of Canadian Arctic policy in the 1940s and '50s. This was policy that located people on the basis of the costs of access, servicing, and proximity to resources – the relevance of which was decided by the state. Thus people who had relied on caribou were expected to survive on fish. All of this logic is essentially economic. This logic divided and re-divided extended families and groups based on kinship, with a casual disregard for elaborate networks of reciprocity – networks which formed the basis of Inuit economic, as well as social, systems.

An example from one sphere of social existence is illustrative here. Gathering and hunting peoples are also frequently nomadic. Inuit were nomadic. This does not mean they travelled every day of their lives, but they did make seasonal use of different resources across a wide geographic terrain. In the tradition of Western thought, we have only begun to understand the differences involved in nomadic cultures. In the context of this book, one of these differences is particularly worth closer examination. How do we look at objects? How do we see the things around us? For a gatherer or hunter, objects may often be viewed with suspicion: any object found will have to be carried, therefore it is seen first in terms of weight. For people from agricultural or settled societies, objects are seen first in terms of desire: any object found may have a value and, after all, even if it isn't worth anything, why not take it since there is a place to put it. Hunting peoples do not tend to accumulate material goods. Saving for the long term has little meaning. Industrial society is based on a logic of capital accumulation, served by processes of totalization. Accumulation of material objects is so deeply rooted as an individual motivation in Western thought that it has been constructed as an aspect of 'human nature.' And, of course, one only need survey a random half-hour of television to realize that a cognitive relation of desire towards objects is constantly being provoked. This example is intended evocatively and we need not pursue it with the rigour it deserves: the change from nomadic to settled existence has extraordinary and unforeseen consequences, not least on our way of seeing, our way of looking at objects.

Settlement – the fact of settlement – involves a cultural shift of extraordinary significance that we can only begin to examine here. The fact that settlements were needed in the eastern Arctic was rarely an explicit policy: it was an assumed necessity that would allow various policies to be implemented. Thus, the creation of high Arctic Inuit communities solved several problems at one time. It is therefore no surprise that addressing the costs of 'relief' relative to concerns about state expenditures in support of capitalist accumulation, and a concern for Arctic sovereignty – both considerations relevant to a totalization function – played an active part in these moves. In this instance, administrators had found a single solution to two pressing policy problems.

Settlement was one of the tools of a logic of totalization. That, in the material establishment of settlements, kinship bonds were weakened and a serial logic imposed, only contributed to their effectiveness. The processes we examine, relating to the determination of government responsibility, the development and application of a policy of relocation, and the establishment of a relief and welfare regime, were also the mechanisms of totalization. Finally, while the logic of seriality dominates this invasion of the Arctic by state officials – most of whom were well-intentioned – it does not pervade every aspect of social being: Inuit were, and remain, able to draw on their traditions and culture to carve out a social space where a different logic is operative. The struggle against totalization continues.

We have told the story of this historical period through the reconstruction of a variety of texts, primarily of government origin. Our method has been to treat texts respectfully. We have quoted extensively so that the reader may feel the grain of history, the personalities, the logics, the uncertainties, the unspoken, the assumptions, the writings, and the recordings of the social actors in their own context. Although it is true that our text frames, selects, organizes, and comments on this material, we hope enough is offered to allow readers to live inside this period and to evaluate, from their own perspectives, the sensibilities applied to Inuit at the time. We have included recorded comments of Inuit people in this period that, almost without exception, stand in counter-distinction to the perspectives applied by 'Others.' Thus, we are hopeful that the text can be treated, as Michel de Certeau puts it, 'like a rented apartment.'[6] De Certeau notes that texts are habitable, and that, just as renters organize an apartment in line with preferences, the reader furnishes the text with unique acts and memories, messages, turns of phrase, desires, and goals. We have also tended to stay away from elaborate theoretical arguments and language; having relied on the reader's indulgence to this point, we had no desire to exhaust their patience completely. We return to review a few theoretical concerns in the concluding chapter.

The story we have reconstructed is not a progressive narrative, and we have not written an epic history in the style that informs so much of what is written about northern Canada. Our approach is somewhat episodic, and the narrative does not always make for smooth, straightforward reading. As well, northern history is often almost exclusively a history written about and for men. What may seem like digressions to male-centred realities have been for us occasions to explore those instances when the archival material revealed an overlay between ethnocentric and patriarchal assumptions. Our hope is that these dislocations suggest the complexity of events and the contradictions inherent in an imposed social and political order. The development of Arctic policy and practice during this period was anything but smooth and straightforward. We have not dealt with the construction of the DEW Line, the establishment of Frobisher Bay as a regional centre, the development of education and health delivery apparatuses, or the evolution of territorial governmental forms. Some of these topics are dealt with in other texts. Our approach was to use events to illustrate patterns of decision-making, control, and power relations. Although totalization appears inexorable, particularly in the guise of progress, the process is carried by historical agents who may be insecure and indecisive, or who lack knowledge, resources, or skills. Totalization took place with fits and starts, structures evolved and fell apart, and plans were made and never carried through. This too – the debris of history – merits our attention.

Finally, it is easy to judge history and its actors. History gives rise to new processes, new insights, and new forms of understanding. Many of the players in the dramas described in this book were born early in this century and received their schooling just prior to, during, and after the First World War. Still others were confronted with the depression as a context for much learning and experience. One of the people interviewed extensively for this book is Ben Sivertz, former Arctic administrator and commissioner of the Northwest Territories. We respect his candour and openness, while recognizing that he – and others – will not necessarily be sympathetic to the perspectives used to interpret these events. One of Sivertz's observations during one of these interviews sticks with us. He talked openly of the depression and its terrible impact on the consciousness and attitudes of a generation of Canadians – many of whom played a role in the events outlined in this book. He noted how the depression contributed to a certain 'meanness,' a fear of material realities and social circumstances that both divided people and, in some cases, gave them impetus to struggle to create other forms by which these circumstances might be overcome. The introduction of the cooperative movement to the North reflects this experience – as do many other contradictory initiatives of this period. Our book – despite its tones of amazement and occasional disapproval – is not intended as a condemnation of any individual. It is, rather, a comment on what the American sociologist George Herbert Mead described as 'the role of the generalized other.' We are, after all, products of different historical moments and the insights to which they give rise. Our hope is to offer an examination of a specific historical moment through the lens of what we understand to be pervasive features of the social and economic systems within which Canadian society has developed.

We have divided our text into a number of stories. We begin with the debate over which branch of government had control and responsibility for Inuit, a debate that developed because of the costs of delivering relief and that reached the Supreme Court of Canada, which rendered a decision in 1939. Chapter 2 deals with the first wave of expansion of government interest in the North, an expansion coterminous with the development of the liberal welfare state in the postwar era. It also corresponds to the development of other social programs, like family allowances and pensions for Inuit. The provision of these welfare programs had a dramatic impact on Arctic affairs. Chapter 3 examines the policy level debates that would lead to a decision to relocate Inuit from relatively southern communities on the east coast of Hudson Bay to the high Arctic. Chapter 4 follows the implementation of this decision, examining the on-the-ground movements of people and materials. Chapter 5 examines the Henik Lake famine that occurred in the Keewatin District in the late 1950s. This is a story already told by Farley Mowat in his book *The Desperate People*, but, unlike Mowat's rendition, our narrative is reconstructed from archival sources. Chapter 6 examines the Garry Lake famine, which took place at almost the same time. Chapter 7 discusses the establishment of the coastal community of Whale Cove in response to the inland famines in the Keewatin. Finally, Chapter 8 looks at a second wave of state expansion in the late 1950s and the emergence of a new dynamic of intervention. The themes that run through these disparate but related processes and events are relocation, 'relief,' and government responsibility.

1

Are Inuit Indians? Relief, Jurisdiction, and Government Responsibility

In the early part of the twentieth century the legal status of Inuit was uncertain. Little or no legislation existed defining who Inuit were, which level of government had jurisdiction over them, and what their rights were. There was no Inuit policy that corresponded to the well-established, evolving Indian policy. Inuit of the Northwest Territories were a concern for the federal government, which had overriding authority for all matters within the vast expanse of the eastern Arctic.

As the prosperity of the 1920s gave way to the economic conditions of the 1930s, the cost of 'relief' for Inuit of Arctic Quebec made the question of Inuit status an important one. The struggle over whether Quebec Inuit were a federal or provincial responsibility eventually moved from a political to a legal forum. Inuit status was yet another example of bureaucratic infighting arising from that most typical of Canadian conflicts – federal versus provincial jurisdiction. In the first few decades of the twentieth century, Inuit occupied an ambivalent social position at the extreme margin of Canada's territorial limits. Therefore, the basic starting point in the totalizing incorporation of Inuit into Euro-Canadian culture and economy was the question of which level of government had jurisdiction. But this was only a place to start. Once this question was settled, definitions, policies, structures – the full range of totalizing mechanisms – could develop. Inuit, it was believed, could successfully be assimilated into Canadian society.

The British North America Act of 1867 made no mention of Inuit (or Eskimos, as they were called at the time). Section 91(24) of the BNA Act ensured that 'Indians and lands reserved for Indians' were a federal responsibility. This had wide-ranging implications for the administration of Indian affairs. For example, the federal government passed the Enfranchisement Act of 1869 under the jurisdiction granted to it by the BNA Act. This eventually evolved into the Indian Act of 1876. Section 91(24) can also be interpreted to imply that the federal government has a special fiduciary or trustlike relationship with the Indians of Canada and must act in a manner appropriate to the legal responsibilities of such a relationship.

However, at the drafting of the BNA Act, no explicit mention was made of responsibility for Inuit. At the time, Canada was not in possession of the Arctic islands and Canada's northern borders did not include large numbers of Inuit citizens. Therefore, the oversight was understandable. When the British transferred authority for the Arctic islands to Canada by an order-in-council in 1880, no one had the foresight to raise the issue of the status of its aboriginal inhabitants. In fact, Morris Zaslow notes that 'Canada took no overt step until 1897 to proclaim its authority in the region itself'[1] and in general moved very slowly to assume its new responsibilities or to assert its new authority. This was in spite of Canada's explicit desire to assert its sovereignty over the region.

During this period, jurisdiction for Inuit affairs was uncertain and lodged with different governmental authorities at different times. In 1905, the Canadian government divided up the huge area over which it had assumed control in 1870, creating the provinces of Saskatchewan and Alberta. The Northwest Territories Act gave authority over the North to a commissioner who remained in Ottawa with little or no direct contact or experience with northern Native peoples. In effect, the territory was governed by the Royal North-West Mounted Police, with Lieutenant-Colonel Fred White acting as commissioner of the Northwest Territories until his death in 1918.[2] Aboriginal northerners were an administrative headache for southern bureaucrats, whose main concern was 'showing the flag' to ensure Canada's claims over this territory were established.

In the late 1800s and early 1900s, the government's central concerns in the Far North were clearly with sovereignty. Whalers, primarily from the United States and operating in the Beaufort Sea and in the eastern Arctic, represented one kind of challenge to Canadian claims. Explorers from countries other than Canada represented another. A third challenge was Inuit from Greenland, who were hunting across Smith Sound on Ellesmere Island.

Whaling ventures in the late nineteenth century may have represented the most pressing concern. In the last two decades of the nineteenth century, the price of whalebone did not fall below four dollars a pound. As Zaslow notes, 'A full-grown whale, carrying 2,000 pounds of baleen in its jaw, became a very valuable quarry indeed.'[3] Scottish whalers from St. John's, Newfoundland, began establishing summer trading camps. While whaling in the eastern Arctic declined, it underwent a remarkable expansion in the Beaufort Sea to the west. By the end of the nineteenth century, the Herschel Island whaling base in the western Arctic had become a hub of activity, with disastrous consequences for the Mackenzie Inuit of the region.

In addition to the activity of whalers, the government was also concerned about British, American, and Scandinavian explorers, adventurers, scientists, and others who made voyages of 'discovery' in the region. There was no assurance that the 'discoverer' would not claim territory for his homeland. Of these, the 'most serious [were] the attempts of Peary and Cook to reach the North Pole and Otto Sverdrup's discovery of three large, uncharted islands to the west of Ellesmere.'[4]

As a direct result of these two challenges to its position, the government of Canada established, in 1903, three police posts: at Herschel Island, Fort Macpherson, and Fullerton Harbour. The government also sent the ship *Neptune* on an expedition, showing the flag around Baffin and Ellesmere islands.[5] This is a pattern that would repeat itself in the next few decades, when the Royal North-West Mounted Police, later renamed the Royal Canadian Mounted Police, acted as Canada's only official representatives in the Far North.

A third challenge to Canadian sovereignty emerged a few years later when it was found, in 1919, that 'the Inuit of north-western Greenland, which was a possession of Denmark, had been accustomed to travelling across Smith Sound from Thule to hunt musk-oxen on Ellesmere Island.'[6] The diplomatic incident was aggravated when the Danes were advised by the well-known Arctic explorer, Knud Rasmussen, that the region was, in effect, a 'no man's land.' Subsequently, in 1922 the Canadian government started sending ships for regular summer trips into the eastern Arctic and established an RCMP post at Craig Harbour.[7]

This relatively limited activity did not establish any clear responsibility for Inuit affairs. If, as Diamond Jenness argued, 'to receive international recognition, possession demands the acceptance of two responsibilities: continuing interest in the territory, and a concern for the welfare of its inhabitants,'[8] then the former was ignored until the beginning of the twentieth century, and the latter until much, much later. The government was quite prepared to act, and act quickly, when its territorial claims in the North were challenged. It was not prepared to act, or even to contemplate acting, when it came to accepting responsibility for the welfare of indigenous inhabitants of the North.

Jenness has also noted that 'the Northwest Territories Act of 1905 had omitted to provide any special administration of Eskimos affairs,'[9] and that it did not distinguish between Inuit and other northerners in its ordinances until at least 1930. Ostensibly, the Inuit had the full rights of other citizens, although in practice this was not the case. This is glaringly obvious from an examination of the government's treatment of Inuit under the Old Age Pensions Act of 1927, which will be discussed in Chapter 2. The Department of Indian Affairs had spent some money on health and education for Inuit in the Mackenzie area,[10] but, for the most part, 'between 1905 and 1920 the then Royal Northwest Mounted Police were the main administrators of the NWT.'[11] This state of affairs would change dramatically in the next few decades. Inuit jurisdiction would become an issue of at least some concern to politicians, before it would be settled by the highest court in the land.

Inuit Status and Arctic Administration, 1920-30

In 1920, with the discovery of oil in the Norman Wells area of the western Arctic, the government made important changes to the administration of northern affairs. It revised the Northwest Territories Act, creating a council to support the commissioner that would have a more active role in northern affairs. It also created a Northwest Territories and Yukon Branch within the Department of the Interior. Once again, however, no specific mention of Inuit was made in the legislation.

The commissioner-in-council had powers designated by the minister of the interior and subsequently by the minister of mines and resources when the department was reorganized in 1936. These powers were somewhat more expansive than those of a local or municipal administration.[12] Commencing in 1921, the commissioner of the Northwest Territories was the deputy minister of the department responsible for territorial administration. This pattern lasted until 1963 when Ben Sivertz, former head of northern administration within the Department of Northern Affairs and National Resources, was made commissioner.[13] Until 1947, when a mine manager from Yellowknife was appointed to the council, members were federal bureaucrats drawn from related departments.[14]

While the responsibility for governing the Northwest Territories lay with the territorial council, the administrative responsibilities belonged to the Northwest Territories Branch of the Department of the Interior. The branch, created in 1921 and renamed the Northwest Territories and Yukon Branch in 1922, was headed by O.S. Finnie until it was eliminated by R.B. Bennett's Conservative government in 1931, and Finnie took early retirement. Bennett had tried unsuccessfully to deal with the depression by cutting government expenditures. Finnie was, for his day, a progressive administrator, not entirely convinced of the benevolence of the Hudson's Bay Company and a strong advocate of government taking a more active role in its responsibilities for the health and welfare of Inuit. He left the branch rather than taking another assignment.

During the 1920s, Finnie had appointed physicians to serve on the CGS *Arctic* during the Eastern Arctic Patrols. He also located physicians at Chesterfield Inlet, Pangnirtung, and Coppermine in the central Arctic and at Aklavik in the Mackenzie Delta. However, as Mark Dickerson notes in *Whose North*, the general attitude of the government was to stay out of the

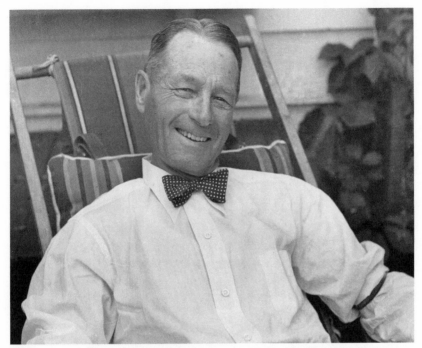

Figure 1 O.S. Finnie, director, Northwest Territories and Yukon Branch, Department of the Interior, 1921-31. Finnie was a progressive administrator concerned about Inuit health and welfare. His branch was eliminated as part of cost-cutting measures undertaken by the government of R.B. Bennett in 1931, and Finnie took early retirement.

hospital business and encourage the private sector to provide for the health care needs of its employees. The Anglican and Roman Catholic churches were to meet the health, education, and welfare needs of Indians and Inuit in the Northwest Territories, with some government support.[15] These needs were developing rapidly in relation to the commercial activities in the region, including the fur trade, which was supported and encouraged by the government. The sentiments that health was a matter for private sector initiative and that welfare was a matter of charity and philanthropy were reinforced with the election of the Conservative government of R.B. Bennett in August of 1931.

The budget and staff of the Northwest Territories and Yukon Branch had never been significant. In 1921-2, its inaugural year, the government, through the branch, spent $1,500 on school subsidies and $7,040 on relief throughout the entire Northwest Territories. Among the first initiatives of this new northern administration was the establishment of the Eastern Arctic Patrol to 'show the flag.' When police posts were established at Craig

Figure 2 Frederick Banting aboard the CGS *Arctic* in 1927. Banting created a 'stir' upon his return to southern Canada by publicly criticizing the Hudson's Bay Company for its treatment of the Inuit.

Harbour on Ellesmere Island and at Pond Inlet on Baffin Island, 'to give evidence of "occupation" as well as the presence of authority, several Inuit families were moved to these previously uninhabited locations.'[16]

The problem of Inuit status, meanwhile, was raised by Finnie in his capacity as director of the Northwest Territories and Yukon Branch of the Department of the Interior. According to Shelagh Grant, Finnie argued that 'territorial rights carried obligations and that the government should not relegate the responsibility for Inuit education and welfare to the fur traders and missionaries.'[17]

It is likely that Finnie's concern was provoked by Rasmussen's observations during the Danish expedition of 1921-3 in the Hudson Bay area. Apparently, Rasmussen 'had been shocked by the deplorable condition of the Eskimos along its western shores and in the hinterland.'[18] However, Finnie's proposal backfired when responsibility for Inuit affairs was transferred to the Department of Indian Affairs. An amendment to the Indian Act in 1924 read: 'The Superintendent General of Indian Affairs shall have charge of Eskimo affairs.'[19] This amendment was subject to intense debate in the House of Commons.

In its original form, the amendment was far-reaching. It would have given the superintendent general 'control and management of the lands and property of the Eskimos in Canada,' ensured that 'the Indian Act shall apply to the Eskimo' and that 'the Department of Indian Affairs shall have the management, charge and direction of Eskimo Affairs.'[20] Arthur Meighen argued from the opposition benches that 'the best policy we can adopt towards the Eskimos is to leave them alone.'[21] After considerable debate, the Liberal government of the day revised its proposal to reflect Meighen's concern. Meighen stated that he had 'no objection to one of the Department's having charge of Eskimo affairs, and I have no doubt that the Indian Department is the right one.'[22] Essentially, the proposed amendment was revised in accordance with Meighen's wishes and the Indian Act was not applied to Inuit.

Meighen's attitude was typical of the day. The concern that Inuit policy not follow the same path as Indian policy, and that a reserve and dependency regime not be established, would influence Inuit affairs for more than three decades. The consequences would ultimately be disastrous, for not only was government prepared to ensure that Inuit policy not develop in the same way as Indian policy, it was also unwilling, for decades, to accept any active responsibility for Inuit welfare. By the end of the Second World War, it was forced to act. By then, the social and economic crises in the region were considerable. Internally, the government was torn between those who continued to advocate minimalist or residual approaches to dealing with welfare concerns and others who actively sought to intervene in the growing social and economic problems faced by Inuit.

In the 1920s and '30s, 'Leaving the Eskimos alone' was a fine slogan, but

Inuit had already been closely connected to non-Natives through the fur trade, the work of missionaries, and contact with whalers. Inuit economic strategies had become linked with outsiders. Diseases were already devastating them, and they were being integrated into the region's trading and trapping economy. Meighen's attitude amounted to neglect. The state was willing to promote economic and commercial activity but unwilling to assume responsibility for the consequences. When it finally moved, as will be documented in subsequent chapters, attempts to totalize Inuit within the Canadian state and Euro-Canadian culture would be fraught with controversy and plagued by many mistakes.

Problems with the 1924 arrangement, which gave Indian Affairs jurisdiction over Inuit, emerged very quickly. The Indian Affairs Branch was not really prepared to manage Inuit affairs, having little experience in the Arctic. Finnie continued to oppose the jurisdiction of the Indian Affairs Branch. On 31 August 1927, Inuit affairs was transferred by order-in-council to the commissioner of the Northwest Territories.[23] In a change to the Indian Act in 1930, the amendment giving control of Inuit affairs to the superintendent general of Indian Affairs was repealed. Inuit in the Northwest Territories were clearly under the jurisdiction of the commissioner of the Northwest Territories. The question of which branch of the federal government would have jurisdiction had, for the time being, been settled.

Inuit Relief, 1920-40: The Need

By the 1920s, the government had firmly established a policy of providing 'relief' to Inuit in distress. This was certainly connected to the Hudson's Bay Company's unwillingness to continue to carry outstanding debts and outfitting on its books. As Arthur Ray has argued with respect to the sub-Arctic fur trade, the company deliberately developed a debt system to create dependency among aboriginal fur producers. In the late nineteenth century, the 'good' company could no longer afford this system and began to pass the responsibility over to government. The northern trade system developed into a welfare system.[24] In other words, the Hudson's Bay Company then – as is true of many private sector interests now – increasingly attempted to pass the social costs of its activities on to the state. The same process was taking place in the Arctic in the early part of the twentieth century.

It is interesting to note the manner in which the government linked the provision of relief to Inuit with Arctic sovereignty. A memo to Duncan Campbell Scott, dated 6 October 1922, refers to the original establishment of relief estimates: 'In 1906, "to establish the principle that these aborigines are also under our control," on your recommendation a small sum was placed in the estimates.'[25] Government files over this period reveal an

interesting debate between governments, private companies, and missionaries over the provision of relief.

That some measure of relief was needed is evident even on cursory
examination of the documents found in government files from the period.
The following two stories illustrate the difficulties experienced by Inuit in
the 1920s. The first story comes from a report by A.W. Joy of the RCMP,
posted at Pond Inlet. The report is dated 26 May 1923.

> I have the honour to report that Eskimo Oo-mee arrived here from Igloolik
> via Admiralty Inlet and Lancaster Sound on the evening of the 24th inst;,
> bringing the news of the death by starvation of ... thirteen souls. Oo-mee
> with another Eskimo named Kolnak made the gruesome discovery while
> travelling on Admiralty Inlet a few days ago. They first observed komatik
> tracks on the inlet going between a patch of open water and the land, which
> were followed to the shore line and for some two miles inland, where they
> terminated at a snow igloo. Outside the igloo Oo-mee and Kolnak found
> the dead bodies of Koud-noo, a boy and girl both about fourteen years of
> age, and a second girl about seventeen, and inside the igloo they found the
> bodies of three women, the wives of Edineyah, Pannikpah and Koud-noo,
> all in a sitting position and frozen stiff. Their surroundings and the condi-
> tion of the bodies indicated that the whole party, with the exception of
> Koud-noo, had died of starvation and cold. Those of the women, girls and
> boy were nothing more than skeletons, whilst Koud-noo's carried consider-
> ably more flesh, which would indicate he had died of sickness. Oo-mee states
> there was positively nothing in the way of food or fuel in or about the igloo,
> neither was there any dogs dead or alive, although dog bones were in
> evidence in the igloo, which would suggest that the party had eaten their
> dogs ... There were four small children in the party when they were last seen
> at the commencement of the winter ... Nothing was seen of these, however,
> by Oo-mee and Kolna.[26]

Oo-mee and Kolnak try to follow the tracks of Edineyah and Pannikpah.
They find a rifle and a few other items, but the 'tracks were immediately
obliterated by the falling snow.' Ahteetah, Edineyah's brother, passes
through Pond Inlet and, hearing the story, goes out in search of his brother's
body but is equally unsuccessful. The RCMP officer does not seem to
undertake any kind of search.

A second story has a somewhat happier ending. A report from Inspector
C.E. Wilcox, dated 23 September 1926, deals with illness among a camp of
Inuit near Igloolik. On 9 May, an Inuk woman, Sonia, arrives at Pond Inlet
with the news that there is serious sickness in two bands of Inuit, which
required medical assistance. On travelling to the first camp, Wilcox reports:

I found about twenty igloos at this camp, and of their numbers fifteen were ill with a form of pneumonia. The conditions were pitiful in the extreme. The weather was getting warm, with the result that during the day the interior surface of the igloos was thawing and then freezing at night. As a consequence the interior of the igloos was a mass of icicles. The floors were covered with about six inches of slush, and to add to their discomfort they were without oil for their lamps. I found three of the women were running temperatures of 105 and 106 and their bodies were covered with sores. As can readily be understood their spirits were very low, they were thoroughly disheartened and feared the worst. I immediately made hot tea and gave all a ration of tea and biscuit, and treated those that were sick with Dover powders, poulticed their chests and gave them a laxative. It was very noticeable how their spirits rose after my arrival. I visited all and tried to assure them of their recovery. One instance is typical, in one igloo I found a young married woman in a very low state of health. Her temperature was around 106, and the natives all told me it was no use doing anything for her. However I told them she would certainly get better and I treated her as I did the others. To my surprise in a few days she was well and around again. It was to my mind quite illuminating what effect a cup of tea, a little laxative, coupled with a lot of faith, would have on the natives.[27]

The story basically repeats itself at the second Inuit camp. Wilcox 'respectfully recommends,' at the end of his report, 'that sufficient canvas to construct ten tents be sent to Pangnirtung and Pond Inlet to issue to destitute natives.'

These two stories illustrate the clear need for some form of social assistance in the North at this time. Furthermore, the tone of Wilcox's report and the manner in which he 'respectfully recommends' relief depicts the strictures placed on police reporting. The police were to obey and to follow policy. Evaluating policy and recommending action was something with which most officers, given their discipline, were clearly uncomfortable. Moreover, to recommend 'relief' was to go against the prevailing attitude that Inuit were to 'fend for themselves.'

The stories recounted above do not suggest that Inuit cultural and economic strategies were impoverished or even that those strategies had become in some way outdated. In fact, it is a mistake to interpret these stories – as is often done – as indicative of a culture clinging to survival in a hostile environment. Rather, changes in economic strategy brought on by trade and other contact with non-Natives had already disrupted Inuit culture. Some form of social assistance was clearly required. Where such assistance was not provided, tragedy was often the result. Nevertheless, commencing in the 1920s, a debate emerged among those with responsibility for the

North over whether assistance should be provided. In almost the same terms, the debate would continue through to the 1950s.

The basic language of this debate was established by 1922. In the memo of 6 October 1922 to Scott, Inspector Canku advances the following argument.

> It would, undoubtedly, be a great mistake to inaugurate a broad system of assistance through relief issues. Charity, even in such places will lead to pauperization as quickly, if not more so, than in civilization. It would be equally irrational to attempt to change their mode of life or their habitat. Rather should they be encouraged to follow their natural, healthy nomadic life, teaching them, if necessary, to develop their native handicraft, or other means of obtaining food from the countries [*sic*] natural resources.[28]

He goes on to note that 'the question of cost also enters,' and he commends the attitude of Moravian missionaries who 'encourage the Eskimos to live as natives – eating native food and wearing native clothing.'[29] This approach, in Carku's view, 'appears to have been found successful in establishing authority and improving conditions without the mistaken idea of civilizing them.'[30]

Field officers seemed to have a particular concern about creating 'indigence' among the Inuit. For example, a Corporal Petty, reporting from Chesterfield Inlet on 31 January 1926, noted that, 'except in bad years and in some exceptional cases, there is no real reason why the natives of this country should have to rely on the Government at all. They will however on the slightest encouragement stay in our settlements and live on our food, which they accept as their due and without thanks.'[31]

A 1928 report on the situation of Inuit living on the east coast of Hudson Bay and James Bay, quoted in a 1938 memorandum, illustrates what government officials feared would result from prolonged contact with settlement life.

> These natives have long been in contact with the trader and are now dependent upon many imported commodities. It would be a doubtful benefit to attempt to re-establish them in their original mode of living. They no longer have the admirable independence of the aboriginal Eskimo, having degenerated until they are little more than slaves of the trade posts. They should be good subjects for any experiment as their outstanding characteristic is to work industriously under the direction of a white man.[32]

Government officials consistently singled out the more southern, Quebec Inuit as being on the road to 'indigence.' The reference to this group in this

1938 memo as 'good subjects for any experiment' is ominous in light of future events, particularly the relocation of Inuit to the high Arctic in 1953. Referring to the Inuit north of Fort George, the report noted: 'They draw far too heavily on the store rations which are as in other areas, very poorly balanced. Each year their demands for imported foods increase but it is doubtful if this is due to any decrease in the local supply of native foods. While the physical condition of these people is not yet too seriously affected they appear to be losing the spirit which formerly prompted them to get out and hustle.'[33] Over the next few decades, similar attitudes would prevail. Relief was seen as something that produced indigence. Under a rhetoric of supporting independence, relief could be withheld and officials had a convenient rationalization for limiting the resources they spent on Inuit welfare.

Inuit Relief, 1920-40: The Conflicts

Coinciding with the debate over whether or not to provide relief – except in the direst circumstances where such assistance might already be too late – was a debate over who would accept financial responsibility and who would accept control. This debate took place at a number of levels between missions of different faiths, between different trading companies, and between different levels of government, as well as among each of these parties.

In a letter dated 28 March 1927, Donald Marsh, newly appointed Anglican missionary at Arviat (Eskimo Point), complains bitterly about the Catholics' control of medical supplies. Marsh's antipathy for Catholics would become legendary in the years to follow. In this instance, an Inuk named Echinak had sustained a gunshot wound. Over the course of two years the wound was never properly treated and continued to fester. Marsh reports that he treated the wound and that Echinak was 'on a fair way to recovery' but left for his winter camp with minimal medical supplies provided by the Catholics.

> As a result of this meagreness of medical supplies given him which necessarily ran out very soon, suppuration spread over his body not long after he left the Post, and he was soon unable to move without help. Consequently he could not provide himself and family with food. That this man could not hunt, was known by the settlement at Christmas time last year, and yet no relief was sent by your Agents here. It was later heard at the settlement that he was entirely destitute, and I sent him relief in the form of food and medical supplies and promised that if he was brought in, I would feed and attend to him. He was brought in three days ago by his father, completely unable to walk, and only then did your Agents come forward with food and

medical relief, and so it was I discovered that the Roman Catholic priests
were in possession of relief to the Eskimos.[34]

Marsh goes on to suggest that relief be handled by some neutral party, such
as the Hudson's Bay Company. The department responds by clarifying the
issue of who is responsible for relief and by clearing up Marsh's misconcep-
tions about how much responsibility the Catholics actually had.

Missionaries were not only unhappy with each other; many did not see
the trading companies in such a favourable light either. In a personal letter
to Major McKeand, superintendent of the eastern Arctic, written in 1938,
one missionary notes: 'I certainly feel that the Commercial Interests have
far too much control over the Natives, often to their detriment, as many of
the men employed in trading have no personal interest in the Eskimo or his
welfare, the main incentive being in profit and balancing the books, while
the Native is regarded as the instrument for production of Fur, while the
Human side of the bargain is not taken into account.'[35] This was an attitude
also held by many RCMP officers.

Meanwhile, the government was having its own difficulties sorting out
who was responsible for relief among the trading companies. Responding
to Marsh's concerns, Duncan Campbell Scott wrote: 'The Roman Catholic
priests are not our "Agents,"' and, 'This department acts through the R.C.M.
Police, who are the government representatives in that district.'[36] He went
on to say that 'at a considerable number of points where no Police Detachment has been established, relief is issued by this Company or by Messrs
Revillon Frères, and accounts for same are submitted to this department.'[37]
However, the department was actually attempting, with some difficulty, to
ensure that where there was no RCMP post, the companies assumed full
responsibility for relief.

The rationale for this policy and the difficulties of enforcing it are revealed
in a memo, dated 31 October 1924, by Sergeant Clay of the Chesterfield
Inlet detachment.

I think in the event of destitution amongst these 'Post Natives' that the
Trading Company responsible for keeping these people from their hunting
grounds for commercial purposes should in future be asked to provide them
with food and other necessities, instead of allowing them to become a
charge on the Government. I mention this as I understand last winter
considerable supplies were given to destitute Eskimos at Baker Lake, for
which the Company expect the Government to pay.[38]

'Post Natives' can be regarded as an Inuit equivalent to the 'homeguard
Indians' of the sub-Arctic fur trade.[39] They largely abandoned subsistence

economies for trade economies. While in the sub-Arctic, the two may have been more compatible – trade activities acting as an adjunct to earlier, subsistence lifestyles[40] – in the more demanding northern environments, the choice of trading or subsistence was likely more mutually exclusive. Maintaining a dog team and other equipment necessary to service an Arctic trapline required a considerable expenditure of time and energy in an environment where energy was a critical factor in survival. It seems likely that, under these circumstances, a trapping and trading economy had severe implications for subsistence hunting, it being impossible to carry out subsistence hunting and maintain a trapline at the same time. Dependence on supplies from the Hudson's Bay Company was essential.

Many government employees felt, with some justification, that where companies were inducing Inuit to adopt a trade-based economy the company should absorb the cost of occasional relief. It was in the government's interest to take this position since it allowed the government to reduce relief expenditures. Nevertheless, this view seems to have been enforced sporadically at best, though Territorial Council minutes from a meeting on 9 February 1937 state clearly that 'the stand that had been taken by Council and generally accepted by the Hudson's Bay Company was that where the Company had no competition they would look after Eskimo relief.'[41]

As will be discussed in subsequent chapters, the transition from company administration of a credit-relief regime to state administration of a relief-welfare regime was not a smooth one. The arguments advanced above by Sergeant Clay were quite cogent in recognizing the effect fur trapping could have on subsistence economies. He was of the opinion that under these circumstances, the companies should bear responsibility.

Much of the confusion and conflict over the administration of 'relief' resulted from the simple fact that government presence in the North was so small. Furthermore, RCMP posts, trading posts, and missions were scattered and isolated. A 1937 memo to Roy Gibson, deputy commissioner of the Northwest Territories, from Major D.L. McKeand, superintendent of the eastern Arctic, explained the procedure for inspecting trading posts in Quebec: 'Owing to the difficulties of transportation and communication, inspections are only possible by komatik in spring and boat in summer. Both inspections occur after the relief has been issued, consequently the government representative can only report on the amount of relief issued during the previous winter and must rely on the judgement and co-operation of the missionaries and post managers as to the need in each individual case.'[42]

However, the effectiveness of these inspections was, even at the time, subject to question. One correspondent provides a different glimpse of the annual visits: 'The annual visitation by the Police is regarded in the light of a joke by the Eskimo and the H.B.Co., as he usually walks around looking important and accomplishing very little good. A Summer Policeman can do little more than accept the statements of the H.B.Co. employees which may be correct or incorrect according to the sobriety of the man being questioned, and if the Policeman is of the wrong calibre according to his own sobriety.'[43] The procedure certainly left room for conflict, aside from the quality of the individuals who carried it out. Each of the parties – government, traders, and missionaries – had their own interests and their own perspective on events. They struggled to form alliances or to discredit each other, as the circumstances and personalities demanded. Relief was clearly one small bargaining chip in the struggle.

The 1920s and '30s were a crucial period, as the consequences of non-Native expansion in the Far North were being felt by Inuit. The health and welfare of Inuit in the Keewatin and Mackenzie districts had already been seriously affected by whaling and trading activities, while at the same time government, missionaries, and fur traders were busy arguing about who would bear the cost of social assistance. The parties argued with each other and among themselves. The objective was to force one or the other of these agencies to assume responsibility.

The opinion of almost all who worked in the North about the effects of such relief on Inuit 'morale' are relatively consistent. For example, Corporal Covell of the Moose Factory detachment, while reporting on the conditions of Inuit in the Belcher Islands and at Great Whale River, notes that 'they have probably been treated a little too easily in the past and been given out help for nothing which has a demoralising influence on them.'[44] He goes on to commend the new manager of the HBC post there, who

has had much experience with the more northern eskimo and it is his opinion that these natives could be more productive and self-supporting if they could be roused and show the same spirit as the more northern eskimo. He is doing his best to put them on a better footing, and whilst the natives think him a little hard in comparison with his predecessor, it will be found that he is doing much more to put the natives on a self-supporting basis. He believes in giving out ammunition rather than food for relief, except in special cases to keep the native on country foods as much as possible and is much against indiscriminate issuing of direct relief.[45]

Even faced with the shocking sight of starved, frozen bodies in igloos, there was a stubborn and financially convenient attitude that resisted facing the need for social assistance.

The most serious conflict over who would be responsible for the costs of assistance was between levels of government, and, as noted earlier, it emerged because of the lack of constitutional definition regarding the status of Inuit. The context was the issue of relief payments to Quebec Inuit. This conflict led to a 1939 Supreme Court of Canada decision on the status of Inuit known as *Re: Eskimos*.

The Legal Challenge, 1933-9

When administration of Inuit affairs was transferred from Indian Affairs to the territorial commissioner's office in 1927, the question of Quebec Inuit status was raised. According to a memo from the Dominion Land Commissioner's Office dated 4 January 1928, 'the Department of Justice expressed the opinion that the Eskimos residing in the Province of Quebec and Manitoba were not covered by this authority.'[46] That is, Quebec Inuit were not covered by the terms of the 31 August 1927 order-in-council.

The Department of Indian Affairs continued to cover the costs of relief until the 1928-9 fiscal year, when the office of the Northwest Territories commissioner took over. A meeting was arranged between the commissioner and the premier of Quebec:

> The question of jurisdiction of the Quebec Eskimo was raised departmentally and on the 11th of January, 1929, there was a conference between the Commissioner of the Northwest Territories and the Premier of Quebec, in the latter's office at Quebec. Although it was pointed out that the Department of Indian Affairs had been looking after relief and the Department of the Interior proposed doing the same for Eskimo advancement, Premier Taschereau seemed unaware of the fact that there were any Eskimo in Quebec and thought the conference had been called for the purpose of discussing the plight of Eskimo on the Labrador.[47]

Having been caught unprepared, the premier was then presented with a map indicating the estimated Inuit population in Canada, a copy of the order-in-council, and a copy of the Department of Justice's written opinion on jurisdiction. In these circumstances, 'it was agreed that for the present, at least, the federal government would carry on as formerly and that the provincial government, on the presentation of proper vouchers, would reimburse the Department of the Interior for all expenditures made on Eskimo relief.'[48]

Interestingly, an earlier memo suggests another chain of events, one that served federal government interests somewhat better. In this version, Inuit status 'was questioned by the provincial authorities. The Quebec government claimed the Eskimo as citizens of Quebec and insisted upon assuming responsibility for any relief necessary.'[49] In light of the events that followed, and the clear evidence of the justice department's written opinion, this version of events seems highly unlikely.

What is clear is that almost as soon as Quebec agreed to accept responsibility for relief payments, conflict arose over payments that had been made in the past. The Province of Quebec declined to refund about $1,800 worth of relief payments that had already been made by the Department of the Interior in the year 1928-9. However, over the next few years, Quebec quietly paid up.

A letter, dated 29 March 1933, from the deputy minister of the interior, H.H. Rowatt, to Charles Lanctot, deputy attorney general for Quebec, summarizes in some detail the growing conflict that eventually developed. Until 1931, the Department of the Interior paid accounts submitted to it by the various parties distributing relief. Rowatt writes:

> These accounts were then transmitted to you in order that at the end of the fiscal year we might be reimbursed for the amount expended. The reason for this arrangement was that this Department was familiar with Eskimo affairs throughout Canada and greater uniformity might be obtained if the distribution of relief to Eskimos in Quebec was supervised by our officers, on the understanding that the Provincial Government was in no way relieved of financial responsibility.[50]

Relief would be distributed by missionaries, traders, or RCMP officers in the field; they would submit their accounts to the government, which would pay them and then bill the provincial authorities for their share. The provincial government had no role in assessing whether the accounts submitted by the federal government were valid. This was left to the federal officials who had greater 'familiarity with Eskimo affairs.'

By early 1931, R.B. Bennett's strategy for dealing with the depression by drastically reducing federal expenditures was felt by government departments. The federal government no longer wanted to assume the cost of administering relief in Arctic Quebec. It wanted Quebec to assume the full responsibility for providing relief to Quebec Inuit. On 17 March 1931, the minister of the interior wrote to the premier of Quebec requesting he begin to pay relief accounts directly. Quebec refused and the two parties squabbled over it for the next year. On 12 March 1932, the premier of Quebec wrote: 'There is no objection to payment being made to the amount voted but what we object to is making payment direct to the purveyors with whom you do business in this connection, considering that this procedure is contrary to the convention which actually exists between the two governments.'[51] However, by pressuring and irritating Quebec over the method of payment, the federal government was overplaying its hand.

By July, the government of Quebec, also looking for ways of cutting government expenditures, began to re-examine the question of the status of Quebec Inuit. Charles Lanctot, deputy attorney general of Quebec, sent a wire to the federal government on 5 July 1932 inquiring about how the federal government 'bases its contention that the Province is responsible for the matter.'[52] On 7 July, Deputy Minister Rowatt responded: 'Eskimo not classed with Indian in British North America Act and Indian Act does not apply to Eskimo. Eskimos own property and operate businesses in their own names and have all rights of citizenship. Debates in Dominion House show contrary intention with respect to Indians. Eskimo is not ward of Crown.'[53] The attorney general's response was equally definitive: 'We cannot find the authorities you cite establish[ing] that Provinces are responsible for Eskimos. We think on the contrary that the word 'Indians' in number twenty four of section ninety one B.N.A. Act includes all aboriginal inhabitants of Canada.'[54]

Rowatt telegraphed back on 24 July: 'Your interpretation of word Indian submitted to Department of Justice who do not agree with view expressed.'[55] The matter now had some urgency attached to it since the Hudson's Bay Company ship SS *Ungava*, carrying government officials on the Eastern Arctic Patrol, was due at Wakeham Bay on the 25th and, as Rowatt pointed out, they needed 'immediate authority to issue relief as there is no means of communicating with that post or others in Hudsons [*sic*] Strait and Bay after that date.'[56] Inuit had become pawns in a struggle over jurisdiction and responsibility. Rowatt added: 'This Department unable to accept responsibility in matter of relief to Quebec Eskimos [stop] suggest you communicate with company.'[57]

The crisis was averted when Lanctot responded: 'We still maintain our interpretation. We are ready however [to] continue for another year arrangement which existed.'[58] Both sides had staked out irreconcilable positions. Once again, as the next summer approached, the threat of discontinuing relief was used as a chip in this federal/provincial squabble. In his letter to Lanctot dated 29 March 1933, which summarized the conflict to that point, Rowatt states that 'under this head I may say that the Law Officers of the Crown have advised that relief for destitute Eskimo in Northern Quebec is purely a Provincial responsibility and, therefore, there does not appear to be any reason for further intervention by the Dominion Government in a matter which solely concerns the trading companies and the Government of Quebec.'[59]

In January 1933, the Quebec government had attempted to press its claim that Inuit were Indians and therefore a federal responsibility by requesting that its bill for relief be charged to an outstanding account the federal government had with Quebec respecting Indian lands. Rowatt noted that 'there does not appear to be any connection between these two questions' and that the federal account in the other matter was about to be covered by a separate appropriation. In conclusion, he asked 'that your Government will take immediate steps to reimburse this Department for the sums paid for relief in 1930-31.'[60]

Once again, Inuit welfare was jeopardized by the intransigent positions adopted by both levels of government as the July 1933 sailing date for the Eastern Arctic Patrol approached. On 22 June 1933, the acting federal minister of finance stated: 'I think it should be made absolutely clear that the Dominion accepts no responsibility for the payment of accounts in respect of relief given to destitute Eskimos' in Quebec.[61] In late July, Quebec paid the accounts for 1930-1, per Rowatt's request, but indicated it would go no further. On July 24, the premier wrote to the solicitor of the Hudson's Bay Company to the effect that this was 'the last payment that we shall make until this question of Indians is definitely settled with Ottawa. We cannot consider that the Eskimos are not Indians according to the terms of the British North America Act who from that authority are under the jurisdiction of the Dominion Government.'[62]

The company responded quickly, first pointing out the urgency of the situation, since the 'last opportunities of communicating with Cape Smith Povungnetuk, Port Harrison and Great Whale river will be August first and with other Quebec posts August fifteenth.'[63] The telegram continued: 'While we are prepared to render all reasonable assistance to relieve sick and destitute natives we cannot assume any responsibility for consequences of the two governments refusal to give us necessary authorization to relieve destitution. Surely, human beings will not be left to die from starvation because there is a conflict of views between the two governments on the question of jurisdiction.'[64] The company was also prepared to abdicate any responsibility it might have for the welfare of Quebec Inuit, whose well-being – and in some cases lives – were at risk because of conditions created by the company and its involvement in the Arctic economy. Obviously frustrated at being caught in the middle of the squabble, the company asked for a guarantee that 'whichever government is responsible for the Eskimos or has them under its control, will reimburse the company as it has always been done in the past.'[65]

The matter had gone too far to be resolved through diplomacy. In a letter to Premier Taschereau dated July 29, the minister of justice, H. Guthrie, announced that 'this Government will take the necessary action in the near future to cause to be referred to the Supreme Court of Canada, for hearing and consideration, the question whether the term 'Indians,' as used in head 24 of sec. 91 of the British North America Act, 1867, included the Eskimos resident within the Province of Quebec.'[66] Regarding the more immediate matter of Quebec Inuit relief, the minister wrote:

Since humanitarian considerations obviously require that *destitute Eskimos resident within the Province of Quebec should not be left to die pending the determination of the constitutional question involved,* I am to inform you that this Government has taken the necessary action to request the trading companies to arrange, through their posts in the northern parts of Quebec, to afford necessary relief to destitute Eskimos (not beyond absolute necessities nor by way of relieving the companies from their practice of grub staking hunters) in the same manner as they have in the past.[67]

The minister went on to indicate that such payments were not to prejudice the federal government's position on the issue and they would expect full reimbursement should the Dominion's position be upheld.

The archival record does not leave room for much sympathy with any of the actors in this drama. All of them – the federal government, the provincial government, and the Hudson's Bay Company – played a game of brinkmanship with the welfare and the lives of Quebec Inuit. The drama then moved to another forum – the Supreme Court of Canada.

Re: Eskimos

The question would not reach the Supreme Court of Canada until 2 April 1935. The formal question the court was asked to answer was: 'Does the term "Indians," as used in head 24 of section 91 of the British North America Act, 1867, include Eskimo inhabitants of the province of Quebec.'[68] As in *St. Catherine's Milling*, the 1888 case which determined the nature of aboriginal title in Canada, Inuit had no voice in the Supreme Court deliberations about their status. *Re: Eskimos* heard no evidence or arguments directly from any Inuit. The judgment was rendered on 5 April 1939.

The decision is an interesting one and worth more than the generally cursory treatment it has been accorded by northern and legal historians. For example, a note accompanying a reprint of the case in the *Dominion Law Review* explains that the editors found the case interesting not for any intrinsic value the decision might have but, rather, as an example of how the court arrives at decisions. The decision, nonetheless, had far-reaching implications for Inuit status in Canada.

The federal government argued that Inuit were a different 'race' than Indians and, therefore, not covered by Section 91 (24) of the British North America Act. This section said that 'Indians and lands reserved for Indians' were a federal responsibility. Furthermore, the federal government noted that in 1867, at the time of the British North America Act, there were no Inuit living within the borders of what was then Canada. Therefore, in the Dominion's view, Inuit could not have had their status decided or even contemplated by the legislation. The Dominion placed great weight on the fact that Inuit had been treated differently from Indians, noting the lack of a treaty with Inuit, the fact that the Indian Act had not been applied to Inuit, the absence of Inuit reservations, and the Inuit's different experience with liquor regulations. This position was quintessentially liberal. Rather than recognize special status for Inuit, they were considered Canadians – no different from any other. The problem was how to 'make' them Canadian. It was the same position taken by Pierre Trudeau in defending the 1969 white paper on Indian affairs thirty years later. By comparison, politicians at the time of Confederation had relatively less trouble with the idea of creating classes of people – Native, in this case – with less status than other Canadians.

Quebec argued that these claims were irrelevant, maintaining that, prior to 1867, the term 'Indian' had often been applied to Inuit and that the two groups were aboriginal inhabitants who should be governed by the same constitutional authority. As far as Quebec was concerned, the Indian and Inuit 'races' were the same. The question of absence of Inuit within the boundaries of Canada, as it existed in 1867, was immaterial. Many other groups of Indians had lived outside those boundaries but subsequently had Section 91(24) applied to them. Similarly, there were other Indian groups not covered by treaty.

The anthropological experts were clearly divided on the question. As Dominion anthropologist, and employee of government, Diamond Jenness helped the federal government prepare its case. He might have easily been persuaded that an argument about the distinctiveness of Inuit culture could save them from what he knew by then to have been the serious conse-quences of the Indian Act. On the other hand, another internationally respected anthropologist, Franz Boas, while giving a series of lectures at McGill University, publicly expressed the opinion that 'there is no more difference between the Eskimo and the Indian than there is between the Swede and the Southern Italian.'[69] Boas noted the linguistic differences between the many Indian cultures, suggesting that the Inuit were just another of these variations, who had migrated in a later period but were 'closely related racially to the Indians.'

The Supreme Court justices all emphasized the application of the term 'Indian' to Inuit. For example, Chief Justice Duff argued that 'it appears to me to be a consideration of great weight ... that ... the Eskimo were recognized as an Indian tribe by the officials of the Hudson's Bay Company which, in 1867 ... exercised powers of government and administration over this great tract; and that, moreover, this employment of the term 'Indians' is evidenced in a most unequivocal way by documents prepared by those officials.'[70] The chief justice went on to examine the terms used to describe Labrador Inuit in particular, noting that in a 1762 official report by General

Murray, governor of Quebec, 'the Eskimo are classified under the generic term Indian. They are also called "Savages," it is true, but so are the Montagnais and so also the Hurons settled at Jeune Lorette. It is useful to note that he speaks of the Esquimaux as "the wildest and most untamable of any" and mentions that they are "emphatically styled by other Nations, Savages."'[71] A great number of documents using the terms 'Indians,' 'savages,' 'Esquimaux,' and 'Esquimaux Indians' were examined by the justices.

More critical, however, was what the chief justice, in particular, had to say about the Royal Proclamation of 1763. The Royal Proclamation has been characterized by contemporary legal scholars as an aboriginal Magna Charta and the most important early recognition of aboriginal rights. Of continued debate among scholars and academics is the question of how far the Royal Proclamation's jurisdiction extends. For example, the governments of British Columbia have consistently maintained that because the province was virtually terra incognita to Europeans in 1763, the proclamation did not apply.

The federal government argued, during *Re: Eskimos*, that Inuit were not 'connected' with the British in 1763 and therefore excluded from its provisions. Chief Justice Duff noted, however, that he found

> some difficulty in affirming that the Eskimo and other Indians ruled by the Hudson's Bay Company, under either charter or licence from the Crown, were never under the protection of the Crown, and in understanding how, especially in view of the Proclamations cited, that can be affirmed of the Esquimaux of northeastern Labrador. I cannot give my adherence to the principle of interpretation of the British North America Act which ... would impose upon that term in the British North America Act a narrower interpretation by reference to the recitals of and the events leading up to the Proclamation of 1763.[72]

This is a crucial statement because it implies that the Royal Proclamation does have jurisdiction in the Far North (and the West). This in turn implies that in applying Section 91(24), the federal government must exercise a 'protective' responsibility towards Inuit. On this critical legal question, Chief Justice Duff was not unambiguous. Later in the decision he wrote: 'Nor do I think that the fact that British policy in relation to the Indians, as evidenced in the Instructions to Sir Guy Carleton and the Royal Proclamation of 1763, did not contemplate the Eskimo (along with many other tribes and nations of British North American aborigines) as within the scope of that policy is either conclusive or very useful in determining the question before us.'[73] In effect, Chief Justice Duff makes the commonsensical argument that while Inuit, and many Indians, were not contemplated by the Royal Proclamation, its terms and the rights it confers were meant to apply as the British colony expanded. Expansion of territory implied expansion of policy. Therefore the Royal Proclamation and Section 91(24) of the BNA Act would apply in the Far North.

As a (not insignificant) aside to these questions, the prevalence of a clear ethnocentrism and, at many points, racism throughout these proceedings is notable. The question of 'race' was central to the debate: it was, in effect, an attempt to determine whether Indians and Inuit were the same 'race.' 'Race' seemed to imply some affinity beyond language and culture, a biological or natural affinity that cut deeper than social bonds.

But beyond the category of 'race' itself was an ethnocentric paternalism that positioned Inuit in the most derogatory of fashions. For example, among the sources the chief justice referred to was an 1849 report from the bishop of Newfoundland, who, on visiting some Indian (Inuit) 'huts,' made this comment: 'A strange group, or crowd, we were. Indians will compress into the smallest possible compass; but still we were brought into painfully close proximity.'[74] This is passed over by the chief justice, who quoted it merely as another sample of the term 'Indian' applied to Inuit. Of course, the lawyers from both sides, the justices, indeed all the bureaucrats involved, spared themselves from anything like a 'painfully close proximity': Inuit had no voice and no place in this legal forum that was deciding their status and future.

The question of whether the term 'Indians,' as used in 91 (24) of the BNA Act, included Inuit was answered 'in the affirmative.'[75] It was a unanimous decision. Like many legal decisions, it would create almost as many problems as it was intended to solve.

Implementing *Re: Eskimos*

The immediate reaction of federal civil servants was to suggest an appeal of the decision. In 1939, the option of appealing Supreme Court decisions to the Judicial Committee of the Privy Council in London remained open. In fact, acting on the advice of counsel for the Dominion, 'a memorandum ... was reviewed by the members of the Northwest Territories Council and a resolution was passed requesting the Minister of Mines and Resources to urge that an appeal be taken.'[76] The war intervened and no appeal was launched.

In late 1944, the issue of an appeal was raised again, this time by the minister of mines and resources, who wrote to the minister of justice on December 26 asking for a decision on whether or not an appeal could go forward. The deputy minister of justice responded by suggesting that 'it did [not seem] desirable to proceed with an appeal involving a dispute with one of the [provinces] pending a fresh mandate being obtained from the electors.'[77] First a war, then an election interfered with the case's appeal.

Other considerations also affected the matter of an appeal. The whole question of the status of the Privy Council as a final arbiter in Canadian jurisprudence was then being debated. When the question of an appeal was raised after the federal election of 1945, it was noted that 'it is not likely the Minister of Justice would agree'[78] until after the question of the status of the courts was resolved. By 1947, there was a further difficulty because 'the former officers of the Department of Justice who dealt with the submission to the Supreme Court and were familiar with the various aspects of the problem have now left the Department and the whole subject will have to be studied anew.'[79]

There were also substantive difficulties in finding grounds for an appeal, as J.W.K. Lock from the Bureau of Northwest Territories and Yukon Affairs noted on 25 June 1947: 'It would appear that the only argument which could be advanced is that the Indian Act is not applicable to the administration of Eskimo Affairs and Mr. T.L. Cory has dealt with this very fully in his memorandum of November 8, 1946.'[80]

Thus delays and confusion prevented an appeal from going forward. The merits of such an appeal, not to mention its viability, were in any case dubious. The possibility of an appeal disappeared after 1949, when a series of negotiations, court cases, and legislation culminated in the Supreme Court of Canada establishing its position as ultimate arbiter of Canadian law.

However, the vexing problem of Inuit status did not disappear as easily. If the court-imposed solution remained unsatisfactory to some, there was still room to develop a political solution. The problem remained of where, within the federal government, administration of Inuit affairs would lie. Subsequently, the question of Inuit jurisdiction became more an interdepartmental one than an ongoing debate between the federal government and the province of Quebec, although the possibility that this would once again become an issue had not been eliminated. For example, the Supreme Court decision led to a situation in which the governing council of the Northwest Territories became financially responsible for the education of Inuit living in northern Quebec. As in the 1920s, there was also a struggle between the northern administration and the Indian administration over who would have responsibility.

In 1950, as part of the extensive overhaul of the Indian Act, which would lead to a new act in 1951, it was suggested that Inuit become the responsibility of the new Citizenship and Immigration Department. Indian Affairs had been transferred to it from the Department of Mines and Resources when this ministry was reorganized in 1950. However, opposition to the transfer of Inuit affairs was strong within the bureaucracy in the old Department of Mines and Resources. As a result, Inuit affairs was retained by the new Department of Resources and Development by order-in-council on 27 June 1950. Late in 1953, the department was again reorganized and became the Department of Northern Affairs and National Resources.

Revisiting the Question of Jurisdiction

Re: Eskimos created confusion in the minds of administrators and did not, in the end, settle the question of Quebec Inuit jurisdiction. In a memorandum written in 1954, James Cantley, a service officer in the Arctic division of the Department of Northern Affairs and National Resources (which now had responsibility for Inuit affairs), wrote to Ben Sivertz, the newly appointed head of the Arctic division, summarizing the situation. By then, there was no question of appealing the Supreme Court decision. Noting that the Supreme Court had interpreted Section 91(24) of the BNA Act to include Inuit but that 'the subsequent Indian Act expressly excluded Eskimos,' Cantley wrote: 'Consequently, the responsibility of Canada for the Eskimo race residing in the Canadian Arctic, has never been clearly defined, nor has there been a clear statement made as to who may or may not be regarded as "Eskimo."'[81]

Administrators wanted to distinguish between jurisdictional authority on the one hand and responsibility on the other. Cantley noted that since Quebec had 'repudiated any responsibility for Eskimo residents in northern Quebec on the strength of the Supreme Court ruling,' the federal government 'had to assume a moral responsibility which it has endeavoured to discharge mainly through the Department of Northern Affairs and National Resources.'[82]

Cantley then summarized departmental policy respecting Inuit and dealt with the question of the desirability of an 'Eskimo Act.' The general feeling he expressed was that it would not be wise to repeat Indian policy with Inuit: 'I think it would be preferable to do everything in our power to make the Eskimo realize they are free and responsible citizens, without special privileges and to devise means whereby they will be able to accept this responsibility and to retain native self-reliance.'[83] Effectively, the goal of both Indian and Inuit policy was the same: assimilation into the dominant culture.

However, Arctic administrators had decided that the wardship policy developed for Indians was not working. They could then justify their relative neglect towards Inuit as a policy of promoting 'native self-reliance.' Later, they would use the same term to justify a much more active involvement in Inuit affairs. The general spirit of the Arctic administration's approach is conveyed in the following: 'If an Eskimo Act were to be enacted, there would be a need for a definition of the term "Eskimo." If, however, we accept the fact that the Eskimos are not wards of the Canadian Government, but simply a small, under-privileged group, living in a very difficult environment, then there does not seem to be any need to define the term any more than there would be to define what is meant by a French-Canadian, Chinese-Canadian or any other ethnic group.'[84] No one was prepared to suggest that Section 91(24) of the BNA Act conveyed anything more than jurisdictional authority; obligations, including respect for aboriginal title, were not the order of the day.

Ironically, this approach would lead to the renegotiation of the question of Quebec Inuit status a mere ten years later. But by the early 1960s, the roles of the participants had reversed; Quebec began to actively lobby for control over Inuit affairs within its territory. This round of negotiations involved the federal minister Arthur Laing and, for Quebec, René Lévesque, at the time the Liberal minister responsible for northern affairs in the province.

Quebec's overtures met with a relatively favourable response because they accorded with the overall direction of federal Inuit and Indian policy. This was stated as a situation where, as Arthur Laing noted, 'while Canada has the sole jurisdiction over Eskimos as such and Quebec has jurisdiction to provide services to all residents in the Province, what we are faced with here is a transition period from the primitiveness of the aborigines to their incorporation (say twelve years hence) in the normal provincial structures.'[85]

In mid-April, 1964, Arthur Laing, minister of northern affairs and national resources, wrote to Prime Minister Pearson explaining that 'it is the social policy of this Government to integrate the indigenous people of Canada over a period of time into the programme of services maintained by the Federal and Provincial Governments for all Canadians and to terminate the wardship concept by creating conditions under which Canadians will accept these indigenous people on a basis of social equality.'[86] Giving the provinces responsibility for Inuit affairs clearly dovetailed with this policy. However, when the federal government, as part of the Trudeau white paper, attempted a similar approach to Indian affairs five years later, an enormous struggle between First Nations and the Canadian government ensued, eventually leading to formal withdrawal of the policy proposal.[87]

It is interesting to note that a concern for health and welfare services was clearly articulated by Inuit confronted with the possibility that responsibility for their health and welfare would be assumed by the province of Quebec.

Furthermore, there is evidence of Inuit opposition to the transfer to the provincial government. A report by northern administrator P.J. Gillespie, written in April 1966, reviewed the 'attitudes' of Inuit to the proposal. According to Gillespie, Inuit from Great Whale River, attending a meeting in 1964 with Quebec minister René Lévesque at Fort Chimo to discuss the transfer, left feeling 'deeply suspicious and antagonistic toward Quebec.' At a second meeting with two other officials from Quebec, people were mollified with the notion that if they were dissatisfied with the transfer the Inuit could ask for the return of Northern Affairs, and that this would be done. In 1966, it was reported that

> there was unanimous agreement among the Eskimo representatives of Arctic Quebec to a gradual and complete takeover of N.A. & N.R. [Northern Affairs and National Resources] and I.N.H.S. [Indian and Northern Health Services] responsibilities by Quebec. It is quite clear that this agreement was made on the basis that they had nothing to lose as [they] could always ask for the return of Northern Affairs and I.N.H.S. It is also clear that they are not convinced that Quebec can do a better job. They would like to see for themselves, and then decide.[88]

However, uncertainty remained. The nature of this concern was clearly expressed by Inuit who considered relocating from Arctic Quebec to the Belcher Islands if the province of Quebec took over. A report on a meeting held in March 1966 noted that 'apparently a number of the Eskimos are considering moving to the Belcher Islands should Quebec take over. This has come to the point where the Eskimo co-operative is seriously thinking of dissolving its membership here and re-establishing itself on the Belcher Islands.'[89]

In the March 1966 meeting, 'unanimous agreement among the Eskimo' to a 'gradual and complete takeover' was, according to Gillespie, secured. There was in fact some dissent. The key Inuit representatives seem to have been Tasumi Quma and Simiuni Taqulialu of Povungnituk and George Koniak of Fort Chimo. Their questions at the end of the meeting all had to do with specific community and welfare needs, and whether Quebec would accommodate them. For example, Tamusi Quma asked 'that false teeth be provided by the Quebec Government when necessary' when it was noted that 'Quebec said that a dentist may visit all the settlements.' Most of the answers from Quebec were vague assurances rather than firm commitments. Simiuni 'asked whether a nurse or teacher could be provided to reside at his camp, because he was not in favour of the camp children having to live in the settlement hostels, away from home. Mr. Gourdeau, negotiating the transfer for the Province of Quebec, said that this matter would be investigated.'[90]

Clearly the question of jurisdiction had not been entirely resolved by the 1939 Supreme Court decision. Much of the confusion continued. In 1966, a report to the minister of the new Department of Indian Affairs and Northern Development said:

> In the case of the Eskimos the legislative authority is quite clear based upon the British North America Act and the interpretation of the Supreme Court judgement in 1939. However, according to Gourdeau there is no responsibility since no specific legislation has been enacted; there have been no treaties with the Eskimos; there are no Eskimo lands corresponding to the reserves and Eskimo status has never been defined. He claims that neither the reference to Eskimos in the Indian Affairs and Northern Development Act nor the annual appropriation acts of Parliament is sufficiently specific to establish, by legislation, a federal prerogative with respect to provincial type services on behalf of Eskimos.[91]

This was the rationale, in the view of Quebec administrators, for the transfer. They could argue 'that the Province in extending services to Eskimos does so as a matter of right and as a principal not as an agent.'

Nevertheless, Quebec also insisted that it be transferred funding, in amounts that would approximate at least the then current federal levels, in order to bear this responsibility. In the early 1960s, as in the early 1930s, who would pay the costs was the paramount concern of both levels of government. Eventually, a funding formula was developed and an agreement on transferring the administration of programs in Arctic Quebec was negotiated, for a ten-year period, based on 'recognition of the exclusive federally legislative authority.' The jurisdictional pendulum had completed its swing.

Implications for Government Responsibility

The debate over jurisdiction essentially involved the question of how best to incorporate Inuit into the existing legal and political order. It became a debate because financial costs were involved. At the centre of the debate was the question of welfare: who was responsible? The two levels of government scrambled to marshall arguments that would shift the financial costs of relief in ways that suited them at different historical moments. Although the legal debate did not directly involve northern Inuit, it affected them because it determined that all Inuit have the same constitutional status as Indians and are a federal responsibility.

In the context of his review of the 1922 debate over which federal department should have jurisdiction for Inuit affairs, Duffy has argued that 'the Canadian government had, even if unofficially and unconstitutionally, assumed responsibility as guardian of the Inuit.'[92] In fact, it struggled for the next decade to unburden itself of that responsibility. Had Quebec lost the 1939 case presented to the Supreme Court, the federal government would have been in a position to argue that it had no legal responsibilities to Inuit beyond those it had to ordinary citizens. In effect, the whole notion of legally enshrined Inuit aboriginal rights depended on the outcome of *Re: Eskimos*, a case largely ignored by aboriginal rights scholars and northern historians.

From the 1880s on, the Dominion of Canada was determined to assert its sovereignty over the northern Arctic islands. It was not, however, prepared to assume any responsibility for the indigenous inhabitants of the area. The Hudson's Bay Company struggled to free itself of the social costs of a debt system devised to create dependency and tie Inuit to the fur trade. The government of Quebec struggled to ensure that it not bear the costs of relief created by this situation, and the government of Canada acted to ensure that it bore as little responsibility for Inuit as possible. Government agents used a rhetoric of independence to justify providing the bare minimum. Missionaries argued among themselves over who would save the souls of those whose lives and welfare were threatened by bureaucratic squabbling and an economy built on one commodity – white fox furs.

The Supreme Court, based on the most trivial of evidential bases, decided that Inuit were indeed Indians according to Section 91(24) of the BNA Act. This meant legal recognition that Inuit had aboriginal rights. It meant legal recognition that Inuit had aboriginal title. It meant that the federal government had a fiduciary, trustlike responsibility for Inuit. If it wanted control over land and resources occupied and used by Inuit, it would have to accept responsibility for what happened to them. However, at the time, no one was prepared to accept the notion of aboriginal rights and no one was prepared to accept this broad level of social responsibility.

Following the war, the attitudes of the public and of government towards social welfare underwent some significant changes. However, within the bureaucracy and the general public, debates continued about the role of the state versus 'self-reliance' in addressing the social costs of a rapidly changing Canadian context. These perspectives were mirrored in the attitudes towards Inuit welfare that characterized Inuit administration.

By the early 1970s, in the context of its Quiet Revolution, Quebec had forcefully asserted administrative jurisdiction over Inuit affairs in Quebec – a jurisdiction it had struggled with equal force to deny a few decades earlier. However, in the interim period to which we now turn our attention, clear federal jurisdiction and control set in place a structure that allowed the federal government to use northern, high Arctic territories to 'solve' problems of social welfare in northern Quebec, while at the same time using northern Quebec Inuit to address issues of sovereignty in the Canadian high Arctic. Moral responsibility in the context of a deeply colonial administrative apparatus became the basis for a specific kind of paternalism.

2

Social Welfare and Social Crisis in the Eastern Arctic

Few decades have produced more fundamental change in Canadian society than the 1940s. The Second World War brought about technical innovations in communications, transportation, and resource development – including atomic energy and weapons. Their impact proved to be dramatic and enduring. But changes were not restricted to material aspects of society. Socially and culturally, the country underwent transformations that created struggles within Canadian society in general, the federal civil service in particular, and within Inuit culture as Inuit were drawn into new relationships with the state.

The limited welfare reforms introduced by the Liberal administration towards the end of the war broke the dominance of laissez-faire liberal economic and social policy in the presence of a burgeoning and short-lived sympathy among many Canadians for socialist ideals. The impact of these developments on the Inuit of the eastern Arctic was unique. The cold war was focused on the Arctic. Northern airfields constructed during the Second World War acquired considerable commercial importance on routes to Europe flown by aircraft incorporating technologies originally intended for military purposes. The entire Northwest Territories was increasingly seen as a 'new frontier,' a region to be settled and 'colonized' just as the Prairies had been exploited in the 1890s.

The language of the administration incorporated these sensibilities. The North was seen as the key to Canadian prosperity and development – an indelible part of the Canadian psyche. These images were increasingly exploited by politicians, the most successful being John Diefenbaker in his 1957 defeat of the Liberal administration of Louis St. Laurent.

The 1940s produced changes in the eastern Arctic that influenced nearly every aspect of Inuit culture and society. Attempts by the administration to deal with these changes led to further impacts on the Inuit and produced additional problems. For example, medical evacuations to deal with tuberculosis disrupted family life and structures while contributing to a rapid decline in the incidence of the disease.

The Inuit response to these changes developed gradually during the 1940s and 1950s. By the 1960s, the creation of settlement councils, Inuit demands for greater control over local affairs, continued resistance to externally imposed hunting regulations, and other insights into the impact of the Qallunat on Inuit culture provided the foundation for Inuit demands. By the 1970s, these included the settlement of land claims and calls for self-determination.

The idea that relocation offered a solution to rising relief bills was an old one. Initiated in the 1930s, it was a persistent solution invoked for the next forty years. But it was not only a solution to the problem of relief. Inuit were relocated to southern sanatoriums to deal with the tuberculosis epidemic following the Second World War. They were relocated to take advantage of employment opportunities at air bases and facilities operated by the American and Canadian military. This was true of employment offered Inuit at Fort Chimo, Arctic Quebec.

Inuit were also relocated by the Hudson's Bay Company in an attempt to exploit the potential of Arctic fox in regions not inhabited by Inuit. This was the motive behind the relocation of Inuit to Dundas Harbour, Devon Island, in 1934. The move proved to be a disastrous experiment, ultimately resulting in the permanent dislocation of Inuit from Baffin Island to the Boothia Peninsula. Consistent with the notion that welfare was a corporate responsibility, the government supported and encouraged the move with the provision that the Hudson's Bay Company would be solely responsible for the welfare of those relocated.

As the 1940s turned into the 1950s, children were moved for schooling. Their families often went with them. This led to the development of a permanent Inuit settlement at Chesterfield Inlet on the west coast of Hudson Bay. As the fox fur trade collapsed, Inuit relocated to this and other settlements that had formerly been little more than Hudson's Bay Company posts and RCMP stations. With the collapse in fox fur prices in the late 1940s, sustaining oneself through trapping was increasingly impossible. Welfare and family allowances became major sources of income. Finally, during the 1950s, Inuit were relocated for training to cities like Edmonton, Winnipeg, and Churchill, and within the Territories to take advantage of employment in Yellowknife and in Rankin Inlet on the west coast of Hudson Bay.

During the 1940s, Inuit, who still occupied hunting and trapping camps structured around extended family groupings, were introduced by the military to rudimentary housing. The collapse of fur prices, changes in education, dramatic changes in the welfare system, the pressing medical needs of a generation exposed to tuberculosis, polio, outbreaks of flu, typhoid and other contagious diseases, medical evacuations, and possibilities of wage employment put pressure on Inuit culture to conform to the foreign social relations characteristic of permanent settlements.[1] By 1965, the transformation from traditional hunting and trapping camps to permanent settlements was virtually complete throughout much of the eastern Arctic,[2] while the social relations and cultural forms this implied were increasingly resisted. Inuit struggled to preserve hunting and trapping practices, language, artistic forms of expression, cosmologies, and collective social and economic organization.

As noted in Chapter 1, the 1939 Supreme Court decision had its origins in disputes over relief bills in Arctic Quebec. In the 1940s, welfare matters and attempts by the Arctic administration to address the deplorable economic and social conditions in the eastern Arctic played a prominent role in shaping Inuit policy. In these transformations the churches, the RCMP, the Hudson's Bay Company, and the northern administration played significant roles.

Many of the forces affecting Inuit lives had their origins in Canadian society in general. The Liberal government of Mackenzie King, returned to power in 1935, was forced to address conditions that had developed and persisted throughout the 1930s. The pressure for welfare reform in Canadian society came from the political left, as it had done since J.S. Woodsworth and A.A. Heaps, two labour members of parliament, forced Mackenzie King to adopt the Old Age Pensions Act of 1927 in return for their support of his minority government.[3] By the 1940s, the sensibilities of Woodsworth and Heaps had been formalized in the creation of the Co-operative Commonwealth Federation (CCF) at a convention of political organizations made up of labourers, socialists, and farmers held in Calgary in 1932. Industrial unionism, which developed during the 1930s, put further pressure on the Liberal administration. The strength and role of Canadian Communists in organizing labour and in influencing union politics served notice on the Liberal administration that the interests of capital were seriously challenged by the demands of organized labour.

By the early 1940s, the pressure for social reform was mounting rapidly. On 9 February 1942, in the 'forever Tory' riding of York South in Ontario, federal Conservative party leader Arthur Meighen was defeated by a CCF high school teacher named Joe Noseworthy. Party memberships in the CCF soared. By July 1942, a deliberate attempt to affiliate labour unions with the CCF was initiated by a CCF-trade union conference. In Saskatchewan, the CCF was the official opposition. In British Columbia, it threatened a Liberal-Conservative coalition trying desperately to keep the 'socialist hordes' from power. The Liberal government of Ontario went to the polls in August 1943. It was swept from office and replaced by the Conservatives. The victory was a narrow one. The CCF captured four seats less than the Conservatives and walked away with 32 per cent of the popular vote.

During the same month, the Liberals lost four seats in federal by-elections, two of them to the CCF, one to the Communist-controlled Labour Progressive party, and one in Quebec to the antiwar Bloc Populaire.[4] But the most solid indication of the mood for reform came a year later in Saskatchewan. The CCF, inspired by the oratorical genius of Tommy Douglas, became the first socialist government elected in Canada. Fear that a recession would follow the Second World War further contributed to government intervention in an uncertain economy.[5]

Among the welfare reforms subsequently introduced, the Family Allowances Act of 1944 and revisions to the Old Age Security and Old Age Assistance acts in 1951 had particular significance for Inuit in the eastern Arctic. But other reforms were also important. To administer family allowances, and in anticipation of other innovations in the health care field planned by the government, the Department of National Health and Welfare was created in October 1944 to replace the old Department of Pensions and Health. Brooke Claxton, its first minister, was one of the 'reform Liberals' challenging the laissez-faire liberalism that had previously dominated party policy.[6] In 1947, he became minister of defence and was replaced by Paul Martin – another reform Liberal.

The administration of family allowances and of welfare in the eastern Arctic presented public officials with dilemmas unique in the history of Canadian public administration. The measures taken to adapt the Liberal version of the welfare state to the situation of Inuit in the eastern Arctic reveal the forces shaping Canadian social values at the time. They also reveal conflicting values and ideas about the role of the state in shaping Canadian society in general and the future of Native peoples in particular. These ideas and values are relevant to ongoing struggles over aboriginal self-government.

It was expected that the new Department of National Health and Welfare would acquire responsibility for other health and welfare-related measures proposed by the government. Proposals for health insurance and public health contained in the Heagerty Report of 1943 underwent considerable revision before being presented to the provinces in a series of 'Green Book Proposals' in 1945. Negotiations over the proposals broke down and finally they were shelved.

However, while some measures to deal with the health of Canadians were abandoned, the new department soon acquired responsibility for Indian and Inuit health. This was transferred (by order-in-council, 12 October 1945) from the unwieldy Department of Mines and Resources, which contained the Indian Affairs Branch as well as the Northern Lands, Parks and Forests Branch which was responsible for the administration of Inuit affairs.[7] The Department of Mines and Resources' budget was subsequently reduced by $3 million.[8]

The Social Construction of Health and Welfare

The change in jurisdiction was significant. The new department, with Montreal lawyer Brooke Claxton as minister, embodied the reformism adopted by the Liberal administration as a pragmatic response to the country's growing support for social democratic ideals and to changes in Canadian society which had developed during the 1930s. However, in administering the health and welfare of the Inuit, its reformist posture was severely muted. For political reasons, many of them to do with the ultra-conservativism of Quebec, the government had to address the values of Canadians who still embraced a Tory worldview. These inclinations were particularly hard on government programs affecting the Inuit.

The year after its inception, the department placed an X-ray machine on the *Nascopie,* which was making its annual patrol of the eastern Arctic. More than 1,500 chest X-rays gave conclusive evidence that the incidence of tuberculosis in the region had reached epidemic proportions.

Yet, press reports of the medical work done on the RMS *Nascopie* by officials of the newly created department painted an entirely different picture. For example, on 7 November 1946, the *Calgary Albertan* used the headline, 'Find Eskimos Healthy' to report on the work done by National Health and Welfare personnel. Based on government press releases, this and other articles covering events in the Arctic perpetuated the socially con-structed myths Canadians held of a happy, 'furry' people, living blissful and innocent lives in a land of perpetual ice and snow. 'Cancer, nervous, mental and heart diseases, common among Canada's civilized population, were not in evidence, according to Dr. H.W. Lewis, medical superintendent for the Eastern Arctic.'[9]

Headlines like, 'Daily Paper Only Thing Missed in the Arctic: Life Among Eskimos More Pleasurable and Placid Than South's "Civilization,"' and reports from physicians such as Major N.R. Rawson, who dealt with a typhoid epidemic in Cape Dorset that killed forty people, fed these myths. Rawson, awarded the Order of the British Empire for his efforts, reported that he regretted leaving his post because 'you never see women pulling each others hair, nor did the Eskimo quarrel or steal – though he occasionally knifed a rival quietly – and they were the smilingest and happiest people in the world.'[10]

The physician as hero, rather than social neglect and the impact of a trapping economy on Inuit health and culture, was to become the way

Canadians saw northern medical problems. The official reports upon which such articles were based obscured what was actually happening. In the eastern Arctic, epidemics of flu, typhoid, and, in the winter of 1948, an outbreak of polio, all took their toll.

On rare occasions alternative reports of conditions reached the general public, including the following one on the findings of Dr. Trevor Lloyd. Lloyd conducted a survey of northern conditions for the Canadian Institute of International Relations in 1945. He reported that 'Canadians would be shocked if they ever discovered the disgraceful job we have done in the Arctic. Health of the Eskimos in the eastern Arctic is very bad and in the last three years there have been three serious epidemics that killed a lot of them.'[11] Such claims were vehemently denied by government officials. Rather than take seriously the statements made by Dr. Lloyd, such articles focused on the official response. Everything was under control. Doctors, nurses, and public officials were risking their lives to do everything possible for these poor, deserving people.

It was not until the 1950s that the use of drugs became commonplace in the treatment of tuberculosis. The immediate solution was relocation to southern sanatoriums. The resulting disruption of families, communities, and traditional lifestyles irrevocably changed Inuit society and presented the administration with welfare issues entirely foreign to its experience.

Family allowances were another initiative of the Liberal administration. The timing of their introduction was, in many respects, fortuitous. The collapse of the trade in Arctic fox pelts in the late 1940s had a devastating effect – especially in Arctic Quebec where Inuit were more dependent on trapping than elsewhere in the eastern Arctic. Without family allowances, the deprivation and starvation found in some regions would have been even more extreme. Nevertheless, in the late 1940s and '50s, Inuit in the eastern Arctic died of starvation and disease. These were the cumulative effects of years of cultural change and neglect by a state and society that only grudgingly, and after nearly 100 years of commercial activity in the eastern Arctic, took seriously its responsibility for the social costs to the Inuit of whaling, mineral exploration, trapping, and militarism.

The images of the conditions experienced by Inuit during this period were, in some cases, deliberately distorted beyond all recognition by photographers and journalists. Many of them had their own peculiar biases about the limited welfare reforms introduced by the Liberal government at the end of the war. One of these journalists was Charles Lynch, who, until he retired in the 1980s, was a well-known columnist for Southam News. An article he published in *American Weekly* in 1946 is illustrative. Lynch saw no problem mixing the development of oil at Norman Wells during the Second World War with the experience of Inuvialuit living about 600 kilometres to the north in the Mackenzie Delta. Not only had Inuit of the Delta never seen Norman Wells, none of them had, at the time, ever benefited from the discovery of oil and gas. The exploration for oil and gas in the Mackenzie Delta was still decades away.

In 'Eskimos Sitting on Top of the World,' Lynch, writing under the pseudonym 'Homer Croy,' vents his own biases against welfare reforms in what might be one of the most racist and inaccurate pieces of journalism ever published about Inuit:

> It didn't seem possible there would be oil two jumps from the North Pole; it didn't make sense. But it turned out to make cents. The latter is what the Eskimos now have more of than ever before in all their born days.
>
> Not only oil but they're also getting mineral money! And not one cent of income tax do they pay. It's true. No income tax forms to fill out. No housing shortage. No set of relatives sleeping in the best beds. I tell you it's heaven! Of course, a little on the frosty side, but still a mighty nice place to be.
>
> Here's the way the new oil-rich Eskimos escape the housing shortage. They just get out their knives and shovels and build themselves a house. No janitor tipping. No having to buy a set of old furniture at fabulous prices. It's a place to look into.
>
> ... There's even more good news. The Canadian Government supplies the Eskimos with vitamins. The Eskimos get it from the cod, halibut and from seal oil, but now and then they run out. So the Canadian government loads up some concentrated vitamin preparations, puts them into an airplane and flies them to the Eskimos.
>
> No Eskimo in all northern Canada ever has to go down to the drug store and pick through a mess of bottles and packages with cellophane faces to get the vitamins he wants. No. He just goes down to the airplane and says 'Me need F-4.' Then he gets it. But this is not all. He doesn't have to pay a cent for his vitamins. The Eskimos take a lot of vitamins.[12]

Lynch's tirade against the supplying of vitamins and other benefits, which were part of the family allowance system introduced at the time he wrote the article, was only an extreme version of the attitude prevalent among some civil servants and the general public. In this view, Inuit (not unlike Indians) were freeloaders taking advantage of ordinary Canadian taxpayers. Nothing could have been further from the truth.

An epidemic of polio that struck the southern Keewatin District in the winter of 1948-9 illustrates the medical problems experienced by Inuit. The disease originated in Churchill, an active port shipping grain internationally as well as supplies to northern settlements during the summer months. At the time, Churchill was also a major military establishment. On 8 July 1948, a member of the military was flown to Winnipeg where a diagnosis of poliomyelitis was confirmed.

On 14 September, an Inuk by the name of 'Tootoo' apparently left Churchill for his home camp at Pistol Bay near Tavani, north of Arviat (Eskimo Point). On the way, he visited camps at Nuella, north of Churchill, and at Arviat.[13] This was one possible route by which the disease was transmitted to an unsuspecting population. The other may have been via boat crews taking supplies from Churchill to Arviat. By early October, eight cases of the disease were reported. These resulted in five cases of paralysis. Poliomyelitis spread quickly. In late November, at a camp south of Chesterfield Inlet, five adults died suddenly from the disease.[14] Early in December, Constable Carey of the RCMP at Arviat and special constable Jimmy Gibbons travelled to camps in the Padlei region, 200 kilometres inland from Arviat. The special constable had contracted the disease in the fall and had still not entirely recovered. He apparently had a residual paralysis of the shoulder girdle. In a group of fifty Inuit at this location there were, within two weeks of the constable's visit, two deaths and ten cases of paralysis. The Padlei area was subsequently visited on February 1 by two Inuit from the Kazan region to the north. Two Inuit from Padlei travelled back with them. Within a week, two Inuit in the camps near the mouth of the Kazan River were ill and, ultimately, two Inuit died while another four were paralyzed.

Meanwhile, poliomyelitis may have been spread from Arviat to Chesterfield Inlet by a Roman Catholic priest:[15]

> On January 28th, Father Dionne of the R.C. Mission at Eskimo Point arrived at Chesterfield for a visit remaining until February 9th. Throughout his visit, Father Dionne had a room in the hospital, visited and mingled freely with patients of the hospital, inmates of the Industrial Home, and with all the other natives on the settlement at the Mission and in their snow houses, as well as visiting two or three times at the homes of all the white inhabitants of the settlement ... Within a day or so of the termination of Father Dionne's visit, the first reports of illness among the natives were heard.[16]

Following Father Dionne's visit, approximately sixty people contracted the disease. The outbreak resulted in fourteen deaths and twenty-five Inuit left paralyzed.[17]

This is how the Toronto *Globe and Mail* reported on the epidemic. The headline read: 'Germ-Carrying Eskimo Blamed for Death Toll, Paralysis in Northland.' It carried a subtitle: 'Tutu Dangerous.' It went on to report:

> Canada's white population may some day find they owe a debt which can never be paid to the gregarious child-like Eskimo, again ravaged by the white

man's disease. Thirteen dead Eskimo, 36 more paralysed and 11 others who have shown symptoms of poliomyelitis since the outbreak around Chester-field Inlet got under way last month are opening a new field of research which could save thousands from the disease in years to come ...

The Eskimo sleep in bunches in their igloos on a small raised platform indiscriminately, visitors with families, as many naked bodies as can be squeezed under one skin. Through the dark day they crawl in and out of one igloo after another, leaving a trail of infection.[18]

While Inuit sleeping habits were portrayed as the reason for the spread of the disease, many of the infected Inuit were resident in a mission hospital and industrial home at the time, where their sleeping habits were no different than those of any Qallunat living in southern Canada. Neverthe-less, Inuit themselves were, to the greatest extent possible, held responsible for their own demise.

A theme consistent with the attitude held by many administrators and, at the field level, by the RCMP, was restated by Inspector Cronkhite in explaining the epidemic. He also used the occasion to illustrate the conflicts between the various interests implementing policy in the North:

It was unanimously agreed the chief reason was the same old question about which countless reports have been written in the past, and which has and will probably always be a controversial issue on this settlement, namely the unwarranted congregation of natives on the settlement when they should be at their camps inland or along the coast hunting, trapping, and making some effort at self support. I do not know what report the doctors will make on this matter and having already made several reports myself last year, I am not going to repeat myself other than to say the situation will never be corrected as long as one organization on the settlement continues to encourage unlimited visiting and entertainment in their buildings, allows the natives to build snow houses, erect tents, and live in close proximity to their buildings, and over sympathizes with them in the smallest adversity.[19]

Inspector Cronkhite had no need to worry. In reaching a professional and scientific conclusion as to the causes of the epidemic, the doctors who dealt with the epidemic wrote an article for the *Canadian Medical Association Journal*. They parroted his remarks almost exactly.[20]

Fighting for Souls
The 1939 decision of the Supreme Court had few immediate implications for the federal government and the administration of Inuit affairs. The Second World War diverted Canadian attention and resources to other

aspects of northern development.[21] The North received attention as a route for transferring planes and equipment to the European allies. The western Arctic and the oil resources at Norman Wells acquired sudden and critical importance with the bombing of Pearl Harbour. The American presence in the North grew dramatically. Airfields and weather stations were built. In the western Arctic, the Canol Pipeline between Norman Wells and Alaska was completed by 1943. This followed Japanese occupation of the islands of Attu and Kiska in the western Aleutians of Alaska in June 1942. The Alaska Highway, 2,580 kilometres from Dawson Creek to Fairbanks, Alaska, was built in the summer of 1942.

The war brought the Canadian and American military to the North; by the late 1940s, the machinations of the cold war had returned them to the region. These military developments provided a few Inuit with wage employment for the first time. At some military installations, such as Fort Chimo, Inuit were provided with rudimentary housing. The rivalry between the Catholic and Anglican churches, which had developed in the 1920s, escalated as they fought for 'souls' and for government funds to run schools and hospitals. The hatred and bigotry characterizing these skirmishes further disrupted community life and social relations. With these developments came the cultural confusion and disintegration that Canadians are more inclined to associate with the impact of western culture on so-called Third World countries than they are with the Canadian social landscape.

The feuding between the Anglicans in the eastern Arctic under the tutelage of Bishop Marsh and the Catholics, as illustrated by the examples that follow, was intense and contributed to the assault on the culture, norms, and cosmology of Inuit in the eastern Arctic. This feuding had a notable impact on Inuit who were increasingly migrating to the settlements being developed in the region. In these small communities, social relations and feuding among non-Native administrators and clergy had serious implications for how Inuit were treated and, as documented in subsequent chapters, were sometimes relevant to their very survival.

In August 1942, Donald Marsh, at the time a missionary located at Arviat, reported to the RCMP that the Roman Catholic priests in the community, Reverend Father Paul Dionne and Reverend Thibert, were making subversive statements to the Inuit about the possibility of Germany winning the war. The RCMP were instructed to investigate the complaint and interviewed the Inuit reportedly being influenced by the Catholic priests. One of those interrogated claimed that one of the fathers had suggested it would be better if the Germans won the war. The others, when questioned, said they had been told nothing. In the end, the author concluded that everyone was thoroughly confused: 'The Eskimo language is very hard to understand, and it is the opinion of the writer that Father Dionne could not explain [the war] in a way that the natives could understand, and it it [*sic*] quite likely that the same thing happened when this information was being given to Mr. Marsh.'[22] For the next thirty years, until his death in 1974, Marsh hounded the department with a righteous indignation about government policy and a hatred of Catholics unparalleled in Canadian history. He constantly complained about 'favours' shown the Catholic Church and was never short on reminding the government that the vast majority of Christians in the Arctic were Anglicans.

In notes he penned for new workers in the Arctic while he was still an archdeacon working out of the mission at Eskimo Point, Marsh was very clear about how 'Romans' should be regarded.

> The Roman Church and conjurors are alike; both rule with fear and both give charms and amulets, in one case of skin and in the other, pieces of saints's clothes, medals, etc. Christ gives life. Any Roman native will tell you that this is true. If you are at a mission where the Roman Church has not yet come, then a little teaching along Biblical lines as to where the Roman Church is wrong would be of great value, for there is no doubt that the Roman Church intends to spread through the whole of the North.[23]

The Catholic Church was not, however, beyond a little aggression of its own. The following was reported from Baker Lake in October 1944 after Father T. Choque acted violently towards Thomas Tapati of Baker Lake. Tapati had arrived at the Roman Catholic mission to request that another Inuk, Arseevuk, accompany him to see Reverend James at the Anglican mission. Father Choque had previously told Arseevuk not to go to the Anglican mission. He 'again commanded Arseevuk not to go to the Anglican Mission and at the same time followed Thomas Tapati outside the R.C. Mission house, shook him in a violent manner, and ordered him off the Mission grounds.'[24] Throughout the period, such feuds were common. Competition for funds to run schools and hospitals was fierce and was gradually eliminated in the 1950s when the state took on increased responsibility for both.

Ironically, while the social relations between the denominations in the eastern Arctic were contributing to the destruction of Inuit culture, the presence of church-run hospitals at Chesterfield Inlet and Pangnirtung on Baffin Island allowed for the treatment, in the North, of infectious pulmonary tuberculosis and helped to prevent Inuit from being sent South for treatment. This southward movement of Inuit, which amounted to about 10 per cent of the population of the eastern Arctic by 1957,[25] was a further contributing factor in the disruption of Inuit lives, language, and culture with long-lasting implications for contemporary social conditions.

While the church was encouraging Inuit to come to the settlements to attend mass and to have their children attend church-run boarding and day schools, the RCMP and some administrators were encouraging Inuit to spend time on the land, hunting and trapping for a living. The overwhelming fear of many government officials and the RCMP, responsible for the delivery of welfare services, was that Inuit would become dependent on social assistance in the settlements; that they would dwell permanently in locations where the Hudson's Bay Company and other traders were located, thus becoming 'post Eskimos.'

Their fears were well-founded, while their analysis of the situation and their subsequent actions were often remarkably shallow and inappropriate. Rather than openly attributing the problem to the vagaries of participation in a single-resource economy in which fur was in and out of fashion, vulnerable to market substitutes, and an unreliable source of income, Inuit were often credited with being 'naturally lazy'; with developing the attitude that the government would 'take care of them' – of always looking for 'handouts.' On the contrary, economic conditions became so bad in the eastern Arctic that by the end of the 1940s, relying to some degree on social assistance was a necessity, not an option.

The role of the churches, the Hudson's Bay Company, and other traders in creating conditions of dependency was increasingly the subject of controversy and debate within the Arctic administration as the crisis intensified following the Second World War. The debate increased as reform-minded administrators took over the Arctic administration from a generation of bureaucrats schooled as the sun was setting on the last remnants of the British Empire. It was under these circumstances that the federal government's responsibility for the welfare of Inuit residing in Arctic Quebec took on considerable significance.

The Inuit population of Arctic Quebec added a substantial number of people to the responsibility the federal government had for Inuit welfare. Allowing for problems in data collection, the federal census of 1941 indicated that the Canadian Inuit population was about 7,700. Of these, it was estimated that 1,965 were living in Arctic Quebec.[26] The 1939 Supreme Court decision had increased the number of Inuit for which the federal government was responsible by about 25 per cent.

However, mere numbers are deceiving. Quebec Inuit had participated in the fur trade far longer than Inuit in other parts of the eastern Arctic. Posts were located to facilitate transportation and supply, not subsistence hunting by Inuit. The rivalry that developed between the Hudson's Bay Company and the Revillon Frères fur trading company was something Inuit trappers often used to their advantage. They were consequently more integrated into the operations and logic of the trade and were more vulnerable to the

Table 1

Direct relief costs, eastern and western Arctic, 1945-6 – 1949-50

	Estimated population	1945-6	1946-7	1947-8	1948-9	1949-50	Total
Eastern Arctic							
Quebec	2,465	$6,858	$8,658	$13,892	$30,915	$48,329	$108,652
NWT	3,930	3,219	3,552	4,748	7,878	14,922	34,319
Subtotal	6,395	10,077	12,210	18,640	38,793	63,251	142,971
Western Arctic							
Eastern Section	1,035	421	1,010	830	3,371	7,585	13,217
Mackenzie Delta	1,007	337	529	1,165	5,318	13,844	21,195
Subtotal	2,042	758	1,539	1,995	8,689	21,429	34,410
Total Eskimo relief	**8,437**	**10,835**	**13,749**	**20,635**	**47,482**	**84,680**	**177,381**

Source: from NWT Archives, Alex Stevenson Collection, N92-023, 'Memorandum for Mr. Wright, [from] J. Cantley, Arctic Services, Ottawa,' 12 February 1951.

collapse in prices that recurred in the late 1940s. Throughout the 1930s and '40s, the bills for relief in Arctic Quebec were higher than in any other region of the eastern Arctic. After the Second World War they climbed dramatically (Table 1).

By the early 1950s, these conditions and circumstances caught up to the federal administration. It floundered in dealing with the social, economic, and medical problems facing the region. An active intervention in Inuit lives was increasingly seen as essential to solving these problems. Within the administration, colonial attitudes and resistance to the welfare state clashed with humanitarian and philanthropic ideals to produce contradictory results. Relocation and resettlement for economic, social, and medical reasons developed as a response to welfare concerns, medical problems, and, coincidentally, issues of Arctic sovereignty.

The Administration
The problems of the 1940s gave momentum to new frameworks for dealing with northern issues. In introducing the bill establishing the Department of Northern Affairs and National Resources in 1953, Prime Minister Louis St. Laurent made an often-quoted observation that Canada had administered her northern territories 'in an almost continuing state of absence of mind.'[27] The prominence given to northern administration in the newly created department was intended to correct the problem. St. Laurent's remarks were generous. With the exception of military and commercial matters, primarily mining and exploration, the Inuit had been largely ignored by the administration, especially prior to 1945. And expenditures related to their health and welfare were often, in keeping with the parsimony and residual attitudes to welfare characterizing Canadian society at the time, an expendable luxury.

However, by the late 1940s many different factors were conspiring to make government initiatives imperative: the internal bickering between Catholic and Anglican faiths; the rate at which social and material circumstances were changing; and the inability of private sector interests (notably the Hudson's Bay Company) and the churches to meet educational, health, and welfare needs. If nothing was done, Canada would be embarrassed over its treatment of indigenous people on an international stage, where, under the tutelage of Lester Pearson and his colleagues, it was trying to play a leading role in world affairs. As it turned out, the administration would ultimately be embarrassed despite its interventions.

The publication in 1952 of *People of the Deer*, in which well-known Canadian author Farley Mowat claimed that the Ahiarmiut, a group of Inuit in the interior of the Keewatin, were approaching extinction as a result of government incompetence and neglect, set the Arctic administration on edge. As the book was serialized and published internationally, the minister and the department were swamped with letters from outraged readers, not only in Canada but in Britain, Europe, New Zealand, Australia, and the United States. This, and related problems, had their origns in a historical attitude of pessimism and neglect.

In 1936, the newly elected administration of Mackenzie King attempted to reduce administrative costs by creating a huge department integrating the Department of Mines and the departments of the Interior and Indian Affairs into the Department of Mines and Resources. Dr. Charles Camsell, the former deputy minister of mines, became the deputy minister of the new department with T.A. Crerar as the minister. Camsell was to retire in 1946, and his position as deputy minister and commissioner was assumed by Hugh Keenleyside. Keenleyside brought to the northern administration a visionary and socially progressive perspective. He had opposed, for exam-ple, the internment of the Japanese by Mackenzie King's government during the Second World War. Keenleyside arrived as deputy minister from Exter-nal Affairs, where he had been Canadian ambassador to Mexico. He was an internationalist, humanitarian, and like his colleague Lester Pearson, com-mitted to the work of the United Nations. In his memoirs, Keenleyside cites his determination to do something about 'the appauling [sic] conditions existing among Indians and Inuit' as one of his reasons for accepting the appointment of deputy minister.[28]

Within the department created in 1936, responsibility for the administra-tion of the Northwest Territories was given to the Northwest Territories section of the Lands, Parks and Forest Branch of the department. The director of the branch from 1936 until 1950, when the department was dismantled and northern administration was given to the Department of Resources and Development, was Roy Gibson. Gibson is described by Morris Zaslow as a colourless, single-minded bureaucrat given to frugality and a conscientious attention to detail.[29] In his memoirs, Hugh Keenleyside describes Gibson as, 'a rotund, industrious, tough and not universally popular administrator.'[30] He had previously been the assistant deputy minister of the Department of the Interior, commencing in 1921. Unfortu-nately for Keenleyside, who was also commissioner of the Northwest Territories, Gibson was also his deputy commissioner. Two more different minds within the Arctic administration would be hard to imagine.

Within the Northwest Territories section, administrative responsibilities were divided between the western and eastern Arctic. The superintendent for the eastern Arctic, appointed in 1936, was Major D.L. McKeand. McKeand was another 'old Arctic hand,' having joined the Department of the Interior in the 1920s. McKeand had been in charge of many of the Eastern Arctic Patrols, beginning in 1927, and appears not to have shared the parsimony of Roy Gibson, Minister of Mines and Resources Crerar, and his deputy Charles Camsell.[31] McKeand retired in 1945.

St. Laurent's statement about the lack of attention paid to northern administration is perhaps best illustrated by the size of the Bureau of Northwest Territories and Yukon Affairs at the end of the Second World War. The bureau had a staff of forty.[32] However, with Hugh Keenleyside appointed as deputy minister in 1947, and given the accumulation of welfare issues neglected by the department since the early 1930s, the bureau expanded rapidly. Keenleyside's appointment, while only lasting three years, was significant. It broke the traditional, parsimonious, and 1930s-style conservativism within the bureaucracy, setting in place something of a contest between reform-minded bureaucrats with social democratic leanings, and those with well-entrenched traditional values. Expenditures of the Northwest Territories section doubled between fiscal year 1945-6 and 1946-7 from $926,000 to $1,865,000 and continued to grow thereafter.[33]

By order-in-council, 12 October 1945, responsibility for the health of Inuit and Indians was transferred from the Department of Mines and Resources to the newly created Department of National Health and Welfare. Further reorganization of the department was carried out in 1947. In November, the Lands, Parks and Forests Branch was abolished and the Northwest Territories and Yukon Services located within a newly created Lands and Development Services Branch that also included the National Parks Service, the Dominion Wildlife Service, the lands division, an engineering and construction division, and an administrative division. In its annual report of 1948-9, the department openly acknowledged for the first time its responsibility for the welfare of the Inuit of Quebec. Expenditures for the Yukon and Territorial division amounted to $3.5 million.[34]

The creation of the Department of Resources and Development in January 1950, with Robert Winters as minister, reflects the extent of the social crisis in the eastern Arctic that had developed following the war, the growing strategic importance of the region in the face of the cold war, the realization that the Soviets had their own nuclear bomb, and, as the title of the new department suggests, a growing perception that the North was a source of mineral resources waiting to be developed.

Within conventional wisdom, Winters was the right man for the job as long as resource development was a major concern. When it came to dealing with the social and welfare problems plaguing the Inuit, a more inappropriate minister would have been hard to find. Winters was the most conservative of the four ministers to deal with northern affairs between 1945 and 1950 and given to private sector solutions to public welfare problems.[35] Keenleyside describes his inclinations as follows:

As was to become somewhat clearer in his later career, particularly as a major participant in the work of such multinational corporations as Rio Tinto, he believed that the only sure way to promote development in the poor and backward countries was to strengthen the practices of private enterprise and to introduce modern methods of resource development under the aegis of capitalistic institutions. He believed strongly in the trickle down principle.[36]

In five years, the administration of northern affairs had gone from a minuscule branch in a huge department to a department in its own right. Roy Gibson, who had been with the northern administration since the 1920s, retired in 1950. The Development Services Branch was then headed by G.E.B. Sinclair, the former head of the lands division. It appears that Sinclair did not represent a serious change from the sensibilities of Gibson, and he has been described as 'a thoroughly difficult man who had no interest in Indians or Eskimos, except as nuisances.'[37]

The Development Services Branch of the new department included three divisions, one of which was northern administration, responsible for the administration of the Northwest Territories, the Yukon, and the Eastern Arctic Patrol. In 1951, the size of the Territorial Council was increased from six to eight members, with three being elected from the Mackenzie District. By 1951, responsibility for lands – meaning all non-renewable and timber resources in the North – had been added to the Northern Administration Branch. By 1952-3, branch expenditures were almost $5 million.[38]

In December 1953, the Department of Resources and Development was replaced by the Department of Northern Affairs and National Resources. The new minister, Jean Lesage, was given additional responsibilities for coordinating the activities of all federal government departments in the Northwest Territories. Gordon Robertson, who was to remain deputy minister of the department for a decade, replaced Major Hugh Young. The North was emerging as an important focus within a government that had finally recognized its commercial potential and the seriousness of the military, social, and administrative difficulties that developed following the war.[39]

Within the new department, the Northern Administration and Lands Branch was divided into the territorial, Arctic, and lands divisions. Ben Sivertz became director of the Arctic division. By fiscal year 1956-7, the branch had expenditures of more than $12 million.[40]

Following the Second World War, the administration of the eastern Arctic became a microcosm of tensions existing within Canadian society in general. These tensions come into sharp relief when focused on the fate of the Inuit. At the political level and within the bureaucracy were conservative personalities committed to the laissez-faire liberalism of the 1930s. These included Charles Camsell, the deputy minister until 1946, Roy Gibson, deputy commissioner and head of the Arctic administration, his successors, G.E.B. Sinclair and F.J.G. Cunningham, Robert Winters, minister from 1950 until 1953, and, at the field level, James Cantley, a former superintendent of Eastern Arctic Posts for the Hudson's Bay Company and an independent trader in the eastern Arctic, appointed by Gibson in 1949 to review the northern economy.

The appointment of Hugh Keenleyside as deputy minister in 1947 created space within the department for many of the reform-minded bureaucrats who later joined the department. These included Ben Sivertz, who joined Keenleyside from External Affairs as a special assistant in 1950, and, in 1955, Walter Rudnicki, later head of the welfare division. Rudnicki, a social worker and native of Winnipeg, was to bring the most critical bent to the administration in its history. At the field level, the northern service officers hired after the 1953 reorganization gave further impetus to the reform element within the department. While men like Henry Larsen, the head of the Arctic division of the RCMP, and Alex Stevenson, a field officer with the department, can be seen as somewhat sympathetic to the reform-minded bureaucrats, their dispositions were closer to that of philanthropic Tories given to benevolent, yet colonial, approaches to dealing with the policy issues that plagued the department.[41] This disposition also seems to have been somewhat characteristic of Hugh Young, the deputy minister at the time. Larsen, Stevenson, and Cantley were to become the initiators of the 1953 relocation of Inuit from Inukjuak (Arctic Quebec) and Pond Inlet (Baffin Island) to the high Arctic.

Thus, between 1936 and 1953, the attention and resources directed at the administration of Inuit affairs grew considerably. This was reflected in the increasing importance of the Arctic Administration Branch and in the activities of National Health and Welfare and the Indian and Inuit Health Services Branch. Furthermore, the election of three members to Territorial Council in August 1951 initiated a process of extending the franchise that would later encompass the Inuit of the eastern Arctic.

In May 1952, a meeting of a committee on Eskimo affairs resulted in a permanent committee to deal with issues affecting the Inuit and a separate committee to deal with education. In February 1953, the advisory committee on northern development established by Hugh Keenleyside and Arnold Heeney (clerk of the Privy Council in 1948) to coordinate government policy and to provide advice to the minister was reactivated. As participation in these initiatives was gradually extended to Inuit representatives, they were increasingly used by Inuit to dissent from and to resist many of the decisions supposedly being made for their benefit. Ultimately, they provided a base from which demands for land claims and self-government developed in the 1970s.

Figure 3 Alex Stevenson aboard the RMS *Nascopie* in August 1946. The vessel sank in the summer of 1947 after striking a reef at Cape Dorset.

A Finger in the Dike: Welfare Administration in the Eastern Arctic

The end of the depression did not bring about a decline in the need for relief (social assistance) in the eastern Arctic. On the contrary, the disruptions brought by the war and, in the late 1940s, a declining price for Arctic fox to levels lower than those during the depression increased the need. Throughout the entire Northwest Territories, the value of fur production declined dramatically (Table 2). It was reported at a special meeting of the Northwest Territories Council on 27 October 1949, 'that under the present depressed state of the long-haired fur trade the Eskimo receives about $3.50 for white fox which in 1946 brought him $20.'[42] While the average price paid for Arctic fox in 1949 was ultimately somewhat higher, the trend in prices being paid by the traders was obvious (Table 3). The eastern Arctic economy, almost totally dependent on the trapping of Arctic fox, was in serious trouble.

During the war, with the 'old guard' firmly entrenched in the administration

Table 2

Value of fur production and pelts taken in the Northwest Territories, 1941-2 – 1950-1

Year	Number of pelts taken	Value
1941-2	445,336	$2,840,701
1942-3	385,440	3,165,107
1943-4	297,633	2,199,132
1944-5	258,931	1,743,710
1945-6	565,065	2,750,183
1946-7	488,039	1,658,754
1947-8	482,420	1,872,302
1948-9	922,136	1,535,461
1949-50	561,400	909,504
1950-1	643,579	2,038,339

Source: from NWT Archives, Alex Stevenson Collection, N92-023, 'The Fur Trade in the NWT, 1952, Resources and Development, Editorial and Information Division,' p. 1.

Table 3

Number and value of Arctic fox pelts taken in the Northwest Territories, 1941-2 – 1950-1

Year	Number of pelts taken	Average value Value	per pelt
1941-2	50,970	$1,317,575	$25.85
1942-3	60,521	1,694,588	28.00
1943-4	28,310	912,998	32.00
1944-5	16,765	603,540	36.00
1945-6	20,854	448,361	21.50
1946-7	57,750	779,625	13.50
1947-8	53,227	585,497	11.00
1948-9	31,317	275,590	8.80
1949-50	9,989	64,929	6.50
1950-1	39,739	455,806	11.47

Source: from NWT Archives, Alex Stevenson Collection, N92-023, 'The Fur Trade in the NWT, 1952, Resources and Development, Editorial and Information Division,' p. 3.

of northern affairs, little was done to change the arrangements that had inadequately handled the problem of relief throughout the 1930s. The department's policy was simple, as expressed in the following correspondence from 1933:

As a matter of Departmental Policy, very little, if any, relief will be advanced in cases where there seems to be no reason why the half-breed or native should not be able to maintain himself and family. This also applies to indigent whites. It is not desired that any steps should be taken that would lessen in any way the sense of responsibility on the part of the native towards their aged and helpless brethren, and we do not wish to encourage these natives to congregate in settlements away from hunting and trapping areas ...

The necessary relief will be distributed sparingly and in such fashion that those capable of earning sustenance otherwise (for themselves and their dependents) will not be encouraged to settle down comfortably under relief conditions and continue to live on charity. Wherever feasible, the equivalent in work will be required for the relief advanced.[43]

The arrangements for handling relief in the early 1940s were straightforward and deliberately punitive. In settlements where the RCMP had no permanent presence, relief was handled by the Hudson's Bay Company. The company was expected to grubstake capable hunters – to advance them credit in hard times. The policy contributed to creating an underclass in Inuit communities. Inuit regarded as good hunters and trappers, or who were thought likely to trade back at the same post later in the season, were extended credit. Inuit regarded as poor or 'inefficient' trappers – something that could be explained by a myriad of factors beyond individual control – were given limited or no credit. Not unlike any other society, many Inuit had skills and interests accommodated within a culture based on subsistence hunting but which had no place in the economy that developed after the First World War. Inuit who did not participate with enthusiasm were labelled 'unproductive' and 'layabouts.' The new economy was devoted solely to trapping Arctic fox.

Capable hunters were also expected to look after relatives who, for any reason, were incapable of providing for themselves. In instances where Inuit could not care for themselves and where relatives were not available to look after them, the company, in communities where it had a trading monopoly, was expected to provide relief at its own expense. This policy was, however, never strictly enforced. By 1940, in many instances, conditions were so desperate in some areas that the RCMP simply issued relief and charged the department – taking great pains to justify their decisions and to reassure Ottawa that they were being as miserly in its distribution as possible. As the price of fox furs declined and the costs to the company of relief increased, so did pressure on the government to assume all of the costs for 'widows, the indigent and the infirm.'[44] At locations where more than one trader was present, the government openly assumed the costs of relief.

At Inukjuak (Port Harrison), Arctic Quebec, the costs of relief paid by the HBC were remarkably high in comparison to other locations.[45] In 1947-8 and in 1948-9 they were $3,280.76 and $3,361.13, respectively. This fact provided much of the impetus for the relocations of 1953. Similar increases were noted at other Quebec posts (Table 4). In Inukjuak, where the HBC had competition from the Baffin Trading Company until 1948, the government was responsible for paying relief. However, with the closure of the Baffin Trading Company in 1949, the HBC became responsible for relief, a cost it was increasingly unwilling to assume.[46]

Therefore, the 1953 relocations from Inukjuak to the high Arctic – detailed in the next two chapters – were, in part, a concession to the HBC to ensure that responsibility for relief did not erode the company's profits to the point where they might consider leaving the region. In 1942, the company had abandoned its unprofitable posts in Labrador (Table 4). There was fear in the department that they might do the same in Arctic Quebec.

An examination of the cases reported by the RCMP in the early 1940s reveals not only the government policy in practice but the extreme conditions of deprivation experienced by Inuit families. Furthermore, the impact of an imposed trapping economy on the ability of hunters to provide food and the use of relocation as a solution to the welfare problem in the case of individuals – as well as entire groups of Inuit – becomes obvious. The following case illustrates this use of relocation:

1. Mamayak is an aged widow with one grandson and she has been on destitute rations for some time as her grand son, [sic] Wallace, was not old enough to provide for her ...
2. Wallace, her grandson, is now 17 or 18 years of age and should be able to do more towards looking after her than he has done in the past ...
3. In view of the above Mamayak was interviewed in late July and asked if she would like to go to Holman Island with Tom Goose as Wallace was now old enough to hunt for himself and *she would have to be cut off rations to make him get out and work if she stayed around Coppermine.* She agreed that it would be a lot better for him to be with an older man and asked for arrangements for transportation to be made.[47]

It was also obvious that integration into the trapping economy affected the ability of Inuit hunters to obtain food. Henry Larsen, who was later to become superintendent of the Arctic or 'G' division of the RCMP, was strongly of this opinion and consequently, throughout his career, a detractor of the Hudson's Bay Company. The following quote from an RCMP constable in the field further illustrates welfare policy in practice:

Table 4

Relief paid by the HBC at posts in the Northwest Territories and Labrador, 1936-7 – 1948-9

Post	1936-7	1937-8	1938-9	1939-40	1940-1	1941-2	1942-3	1943-4	1944-5	1945-6	1946-7	1947-8	1948-9
Tuktoyaktuk													
Aklavik													
Povungnetuk								$1111.50	$396.32	$430.71	$341.84	$1088.27	$1050.30
Cape Smith								97.98	125.29	173.88	211.70	905.86	406.12
Wolstenhome											109.55		
Sugluk											220.88	1041.06	559.09
Stupart's Bay				(1940)									
Payne Bay								461.23	99.18	38.89	317.03	732.49	480.65
Broughton Island									115.94	31.83			85.82
Repulse Bay									1225.30	82.44	90.46	60.28	155.40
Baker Lake									4.88				
Chesterfield Inlet											184.51	60.57	318.56
Tavane													3.35
Padley										408.98	503.80	186.85	41.55
Nueltin Lake							(1942)						
Eskino Point													
Igloolik								(1943-8)					200
Dundas Harbour (1936)													
Cambride Bay													
Fort Ross							(1948)		76.17	20.47		22.86	
Hebron							(1942)						
Nutak							(1942)						
Nain							(1942)						

continued on next page

Table 4 continued

Post	1936-7	1937-8	1938-9	1939-40	1940-1	1941-2	1942-3	1943-4	1944-5	1945-6	1946-7	1947-8	1948-9
Davis Inlet							(1942)						
Hopedale							(1942)						
Makkovik							(1942)						
Bathurst Inlet													
Reid Island													286.73
Holman Island													
Coppermine													931.02
George's River								205.65	279.40	159.39	430.72	575.09	830.71
Fort Chimo								3.80			229.01	351.92	572.69
Great Whale River													
Arctic Bay										10.00			
Pond Inlet								350.86	11.18				33.55
Clyde									40.91	90.71	203.07	179.47	17.85
Pangnirtung										73.30		2300.00	173.35
Frobisher Bay									37.39	14.00	2.54	44.21	76.72
Lake Harbour									51.55	3.30	8.66	107.49	2.31
Cape Dorset									84.84	15.60	184.27	186.09	154.18
Port Harrison								1330.61	529.77	319.19	1182.63	3280.76	3361.13

Note: numbers in parentheses indicate year post was closed.
Source: from records of the Hudson's Bay Company, NWT Archives, Alex Stevenson Collection, N92-023, 'MEMORANDUM TO THE CABINET: CANADIAN SOVEREIGNTY OVER THE ARCTIC ARCHIPELAGO, CONFIDENTIAL.'

6. KAWICK. This Eskimo is also from Back River. He had little meat reserved for the winter and when this became exhausted he was able to obtain some from another member of the camp. During the latter part of the winter all meat in the camp had been used and, there being no game in the district, the people were unable to get enough food. Fur was also extremely scarce and so much time was spent in hunting that the natives were unable to trap effectively. Consequently, few furs were obtained. In this case it was found necessary to issue an order for the following provisions: – 48 lbs. Flour, 50 lbs. Biscuits, 24 lbs. Rolled Oats, 10 lbs. Sugar, 2 lbs. Baking powder, 3 lbs. Tea, 1 doz. Matches, small boxes. Total cost of the above was twenty-one dollars and forty-three cents ($21.43).[48]

When the Hudson's Bay Company was no longer willing to extend credit to Inuit families, the situation often became desperate.

8. AMEETNAK ... Ameetnak is the sole support of his aged parents and their two small grand-children, whose parents are dead. Another dependent is a badly crippled Eskimo who is suffering from spinal trouble, and who is unable to contribute anything toward the support of himself or his family. In all, there are fourteen people in this camp, with only one active hunter. This spring the people became short of food and had no means of obtaining any. Their credit at the trading company had become exhausted, and the only alternative was to ask for destitute relief. Amount of the order is sixteen dollars and forty cents ($16.40).[49]

In 1937, two 'mission' or industrial homes had been established in the eastern Arctic, one at Chesterfield Inlet and the other at Pangnirtung. The idea was that Inuit who were crippled, too old to look after themselves, or without anyone to care for them would be relocated to these two facilities and cared for by the Catholic and Anglican churches. The government would provide some financial support for the facilities, and the overall cost of relief would be reduced. However, in a 1940 memo to deputy commissioner Gibson, A.L. Cumming of the Bureau of Northwest Territories and Yukon Affairs noted that this innovation had not affected the amount spent on relief. He suggested that the government control the price of fur and of staple goods and that 'when a hunter has a good catch some credit should be carried over to the next year, preventing him from wasting any surplus he may have by buying unnecessary articles.'[50] Under the circumstances, and given the way Hudson's Bay Company posts were stocked, it is difficult to imagine what waste and which unnecessary articles he was referring to. However, as illustrated later in the text, in a few instances Inuit were encouraged to purchase goods of questionable value.

Throughout the war period, these and other suggestions fell on deaf ears. While appearing to call for investigations into solutions to the mounting welfare problem, Gibson, director of the bureau and deputy commissioner, was committed to a strongly residual approach to welfare and to holding departmental costs at an absolute minimum.

Relief was given out in kind, with credits being issued for use at a designated trading post. This system further contributed to the ongoing struggle of the Hudson's Bay Company for monopoly control of trading in the eastern Arctic. The company took its competition seriously. Following the dismantling of the Revillon Frères in 1937, one of the company's district inspectors decided to remain in the eastern Arctic as a free trader. The Hudson's Bay Company gave the job of putting him out of business to three employees, one of whom was Alex Stevenson. Stevenson and his colleagues chased Jean Berthe, the French independent trader, with a mobile store based out of a Peterhead boat. Berthe abandoned his trading activities several years later.[51]

This rivalry also affected the administration of relief. In December 1940, James Cantley, then manager of the Baffin Trading Company and a former Hudson's Bay Company employee, wrote a letter to Roy Gibson asking the department to reimburse his company for relief it had issued at Inukjuak and seeking clarification of government policy:

At the present time, there seems to be a great deal of uncertainty on the subject, the Hudson's Bay Co. apparently taking the attitude that they will not issue relief to people who have any dealings with us.

Naturally I quite appreciate the Department wishes to keep these relief costs at a minimum, but on the other hand you will appreciate that it would be rather unfair to expect us to carry the full burden of the relief we issue, if our competitors are to have theirs paid, particularly as we are only starting up.[52]

Paradoxically, in 1950 Cantley would become an employee of the Department of Resources and Development, a participant in the relocations of the 1950s, and a strong advocate for the monopoly of the Hudson's Bay Company.[53] On this occasion he was rebuffed by Gibson, who informed him that only the Hudson's Bay Company was authorized to issue relief in Inukjuak. Cantley responded:

Although I quite agree that the logical course is to have only one relieving officer at each place, I discovered last year, that the authority given was being gravely abused by the H.B.C. manager at Port Harrison. The natives there complained to me of the dangerously high-handed attitude taken by the H.B.C. manager at that point and his repeated threats throughout the year that anyone who dared trade *anything* with us would, among other grave penalties, be permanently deprived of any relief or assistance in any way.

... The natives at Port Harrison are being deliberately terrorized and that can sometimes have rather dangerous consequences.[54]

This system of providing relief thus contributed to factionalism and division within both the Inuit and the Qallunat population of small Arctic communities.

There were other ways in which the administration of relief through the Hudson's Bay Company was inappropriate. Post managers were responsible for the profitability of their stores. At the same time, in locations where the HBC was the only operator, the company was supposed to absorb the costs of relief. Keeping such relief to a minimum was clearly the only option for a manager whose job depended on the state of his post's books. On the other hand, the company was faced with increasing criticism from missionaries and, as noted, from some government officials who suggested that the government take over trading operations or place ceilings on the price of dry goods and a floor beneath the price paid for furs. Military personnel stationed in the Arctic were also not always impressed with what they saw. In a letter to Gibson dated 10 June 1943, R.H. Chesshire, manager of the fur trade department, addresses these complaints: 'We were somewhat surprised to learn that Lieut. Manning and some U.S.A. army officers have been critical of what they call "the way the traders have been allowed to exploit the Eskimos in the Eastern Arctic." Unfortunately, it seems to be a weakness of many temporary visitors to the North to make sweeping and general criticisms and comments which do not hold water when they are put up against the test of plain facts.'[55]

As investigations into the administration of family allowances later in the decade were to reveal, the plain facts were that the HBC was more than willing to take advantage of the added income that government relief and family allowances provided the Inuit.

As criticism mounted, the company took steps to counter it. These are reflected in a memorandum to post managers dated 13 July 1944:

One point is always to be stressed, and to a very large extent quite rightly so, namely, that in regard to relief measures nothing should be done which could in any way undermine the native's self-reliance and initiative. However, a too literal interpretation of this objective has, I know, often resulted in a procedure being followed which merely amounted to supplying such meagre rations that it was all the native could do to keep body and soul together ... Doubtless a great deal of sickness and epidemics which result from under-nourishment could be avoided if a more humane and common-sense attitude was used in looking after the native basic life necessities during poor times.

To my mind, where our men fall down is in their failure to distinguish between relief requirements arising from conditions imposed on the native through no fault of his own as compared with hardship resulting from the indolence and indifference of the individual.[56]

Chesshire then went on to outline the conditions under which relief was to be granted, including hardship from natural shortage of fur in the lean years, failure of the walrus hunt, and shortage of seals and other natural food products. He warned that rations, clothing, equipment, etc., 'issued in this way for relief to able-bodied natives is not to be handled as an advance which can be collected when conditions have improved. This is a legitimate relief charge and regarded as a part of the normal operating costs of the post.'[57]

Far from being illustrative of company altruism, as Duffy claims in his book *The Road to Nunavut*,[58] the policy directive was intended to address criticism. In practice, it was inoperable, placing post managers in a conflict of interest position between maximizing the returns for their posts on the one hand and being benevolent distributors of relief on the other. In the face of these problems and the hardship brought by disease and declining fur prices, the government continued with exactly the same welfare policy that had been in place for twenty years, taking care after 1945 to distinguish between family allowances that were intended to raise the standard of living of the children and the issuing of relief.[59] However, in many instances, what this distinction meant in practice is debatable. As noted below, family allowances were treated as another welfare program.

Wherever possible, the government encouraged traders and the RCMP to issue relief in the form of ammunition or fish nets, a practice consistent with the notion of preventing the indolence to which Inuit were seen to be prone. In 1948, Gibson distributed a memo that again reinforced the existing policy but included a revised list of recommended monthly rations from National Health and Welfare. The list was the same one used for Indians in the Territories and was applied as a result of conflicts that arose over the administration of relief and family allowances in the Mackenzie Delta, where Inuit and Indians trading at the same posts were given different rations. He suggested that the list be used as a guide for officers issuing relief. It included four pounds of rice, four pounds of dried beans, two pounds of dried prunes, and seven cans, size 2½, of tomatoes.[60] One can only speculate on how these items fit with Inuit food preferences – if they were available.

However, it is not difficult to imagine what the canned tomatoes looked like after several hours of transport on a *komatik* at -30°C!

In 1948, the HBC also took steps to further cut its responsibility for welfare by refusing to support inefficient trappers, meaning those who failed to bring in an average of ten foxes a year over the previous five years.[61] In fact, as the price of furs collapsed in the late 1940s, the company faced the prospect of losing money on many of its operations. The motivation for this change in policy was obvious.

Family Allowances: A New Form of Welfare

On 1 August 1944, 'An Act to Provide for Family Allowances' was passed by the House of Commons and assented to on 15 August. The act made a variable amount of money available to parents of children up to sixteen years of age for the purposes of 'the maintenance, care, training, education and advancement of the child.'[62] The amounts to be paid varied from five to eight dollars, depending on the age of the child, and were reduced in families with more than four children. These amounts were available to parents as a right and were not subject to a means test.

The act contained a clause providing that, at the discretion of the governor in council, 'in the case of Indians and Eskimaux payment of the allowance shall be made to a person authorized by the Governor in Council to receive and apply the same.'[63] At the time, the possibility of challenging the 1939 Supreme Court decision was still likely. The legislation allowed for the possibility that Inuit might, like Indians, be treated as wards of the Crown.

The regulations drafted by the Department of Health and Welfare under the act included special provisions for handling the registration of Inuit beneficiaries and for payment of benefits.[64] Registration was essential to receive the allowance, and the disc numbers issued to all Inuit in the Arctic were used for this purpose. The disc numbers had been issued earlier in the decade as a way of keeping track of Inuit, most of whom, at the time, had no Christian names and whose identities were, subsequently, a problem for non-Inuit administrators. A letter and number identified the person and the region he or she was from. The discs were typically worn as neck tags. 'White' Canadians were registered on a white form and Indian and Inuit on a pink one!

District registrars were appointed throughout the eastern Arctic, RCMP in most cases, with provisions for subdistrict registrars to perform duties designated to them. In recognition of the problems to be encountered in registering children scattered in remote hunting and trapping camps over one of the largest and most sparsely populated areas in the world, the department suggested registering children by 'wireless' in order not to delay payments. This didn't work. Inuit were still scattered in remote camps, and the RCMP had to visit each one to complete the registrations. Having a wireless located at a post did little to solve the problem of having to travel hundreds of miles under extreme conditions to do the job. By 1948, there were still many Inuit children who had not been registered.

It was agreed that payment of allowances would be in the form of supplies from a list of items approved for distribution as family allowance. Retroactive payments were authorized where a delay in registration was no fault of the parent. Under the circumstances, this eventually led, in many cases, to the accumulation of considerable family allowance accounts. The fear that access to these credits would create dependency and would make it possible for families to purchase 'luxury' items led the department to introduce an amendment to the regulations, effective 1 April 1949. Back-payments were limited to one year from the date of registration. The registrar was authorized to issue orders for supplies to the traders so that they could then provide the beneficiary with the designated items. The Hudson's Bay Company clearly had a new and substantial source of revenue at a time when the profitability of its operations was in serious decline.

The allowances also affected Inuit families and culture in unanticipated ways. In Inuit society, children are not regarded as narrowly belonging to a particular nuclear family, but rather, the responsibility of a large extended family network. Under traditional adoption, children often moved extensively within the extended family unit. With the advent of family allowances, children became a source of income in a situation where income was very scarce. As a result, children were often consciously shared with childless and older couples who otherwise had no or very restricted means of support. In the 1950s, this prompted the state to consider ways of regulating traditional Inuit adoption.

> After a careful study of all the factors involved in present adoption methods practised by the Eskimos, it has been decided that for the welfare of the children concerned there should be some supervision given to all cases of adoption whether they be official or native-custom ... For the protection of the children concerned, therefore, it is requested that some supervision at least be given to all unofficial native adoptions and the Eskimos encouraged where feasible to discuss any proposed native adoptions with the District Registrar or his representative, or failing this at least to report accomplished adoptions.[65]

Registrars were to determine whether or not the placement was 'a satisfactory one for the child.' In addition to families 'suffering from tuberculosis and those treating children as a servant,' registrars were warned to be on the lookout for:

(a) an elderly widow who adopts a child to care for her in her old age – especially to do her heavy menial work ...
(b) A single woman who adopts a child in order to receive Family Allowances, and an increased relief ration as well as help in later years ...
(c) An inefficient trapper or poor hunter with a number of children [who] may wish to adopt still another child.[66]

The gender implications of this policy should not go unnoticed. Adoption – whether within a traditional framework or as a response to the new economic opportunity represented by family allowances – may have provided a means of support for Inuit women with primary child care responsibilities. However, the state moved to ensure that this means would be restricted by intervening in the customary adoption network.

The Family Allowances Act also contained a provision related to schooling. Section 4(2) contained a proviso that terminated the allowance of a child 'when, being above the age of six years and physically fit to attend school, he fails to attend school or to receive equivalent training as prescribed in the regulations.'[67] The clause caused some concern, as it did not make any explicit provision for Indians or Inuit who could not attend school. Consequently, Section 37 was added to the regulations, making it clear that equivalent training meant, in the case of Inuit or Indian children, training in traditional hunting, trapping, sewing, or other pursuits where no possibility existed of attending school.[68]

However, Section 4(2) was later to be used in the settlements to ensure that children attended – and more important – stayed in school. This affected the normal patterns of periodic movement to and from traditional trapping and hunting areas. Combined with general economic conditions, the family allowance system clearly facilitated the relocation to settlements that developed in the 1950s. This movement off the land and into settlements was virtually complete in most areas by 1965.

As the family allowance system was created, recognition of the extent to which children moved about within the extended family unit led officials to create separate ledger sheets for each child, rather than use one form for each family as was done with non-Native registrants. A system was put in place whereby the registrar could check to ensure that only authorized supplies were issued and, in turn, the Department of Mines and Resources was supposed to check all receipts to ensure that prices charged conformed to lists submitted to Ottawa by the traders. District registrars were authorized to deviate from the approved list of supplies if warranted by special circumstances.

In the 1940s, the infant mortality rate among Inuit in the eastern Arctic was discovered to be considerably higher than for the Canadian population as a whole. Between 1936 and 1943, the infant death rate for the eastern Arctic was estimated at 170 per thousand live births, compared with about eighty per thousand for the Canadian population for the period 1936-1940.[69] The problem, given the conditions experienced by Inuit in the 1940s, was multifaceted. In any epidemic, children – especially young infants – and the elderly are the most vulnerable. The health of young children is much dependent on maternal health and the ability of mothers to breast-feed. Family allowances were intended for children, not for their mothers.

However, when first implemented in 1945, the allowances were directed at parents 'with the main objective of assisting [them] to provide more country produce for their children.'[70] This was changed in 1947 because, 'observations by medical officers in recent years have shown that even in more primitive groups who live the most completely off the land there is often malnutrition, particularly amongst the small children.'[71]

The Department of Health and Welfare responded by promoting the use of milk and Pablum among infants. The milk, which was commonly distributed in powder form, was accompanied by wire whippers to assist in its preparation.[72] Neither milk nor Pablum were a normal part of the Inuit diet. The Department of National Health and Welfare was optimistic it could change this. As of 1947, it suggested to the Department of Mines and Resources that registrars should authorize the issuing of milk and Pablum as part of family allowance, and that every effort should be made to teach the Natives the use of milk.

Other items to be issued as family allowance were the same as those issued to Indians in the Territories and included flour, rolled oats, sea biscuits, sugar, corn syrup, jam, eggs (fresh or powdered), canned or fresh meat when game was scarce, peanut butter, cheese, fruit, canned tomatoes and tomato juice, green or dehydrated vegetables, rice and beans, salt, cocoa, baking powder, and lard. Children's clothing and other items were also listed, including shirts, caps, mitts, towels, footwear, yarn, thread, soaps, sun glasses, feeding bottles, baby powder, and baby oil. In addition, a special list allowed for the issuing of rifles, ammunition, gasoline, stoves, and other hunting equipment. Family allowances introduced goods seldom stocked previously by the HBC and ushered in a dramatically new dimension of culture change. Many of the items listed were unavailable (especially fresh eggs) and others too impracticable to be distributed.

While it was likely true that malnutrition existed even among children living a primitive lifestyle, attributing this to a traditional diet was foolish. The inability to obtain country food under the circumstances was part of

Figure 4 Poster designed to educate Inuit parents in the use of family allowances in 1947. Allowances were given out 'in kind.' The items which could be obtained are listed on the poster. Officials feared that family allowances would be used to support entire families rather than just the children.

the problem. Hunting for food while trying to run a trapline under Arctic conditions was not entirely practical. Supplying meat to the large dog teams needed to cover the ground was problem enough. The diet available through the Hudson's Bay Company in trade for fox furs was anything but adequate for such a cold, demanding climate. Integration into the trapping economy was the cause of poor health and malnutrition. Anything that facilitated hunting for food – as opposed to trapping for furs – was likely to help. Those in the administration who suggested this, including Henry Larsen, were seen as hopeless romantics, harbouring outdated images of self-sufficient Inuit.

It took more than two years to complete the registration of children in the eastern Arctic – a job that proved to be an impossible headache for the RCMP. Therefore, little family allowance was actually paid out between 1945 and 1947 and credits accumulated. The initial policy of using family allowances to assist Inuit in obtaining country or local foods was a good one. As research conducted much later (by Dr. Otto Schaefer, working for National Health and Welfare at Camsell Hospital in Edmonton) revealed, traditional diets were vastly superior to anything that could be introduced in supplying the basics needed for human health.

The policy of assisting in obtaining local foods clearly never had a chance to work. Before children were even registered, the medical profession had pronounced it a failure and suggested a dramatic intervention in the traditional Inuit diet. The result was to suggest that Inuit, and especially Inuit women, were part of a culture that didn't know how to properly look after and feed its children and to perpetuate the myth of the Qallunat as a benevolent 'saviour' of poor, starving (and unknowledgeable) people. 'It is confidently expected that proper use of the credits will ultimately result in a general improvement in the diet not only of the children but of the natives generally, particularly of those who are seriously influenced by the increasing availability of "white man's" food.'[73]

These interventions were misguided. Infant bottle feeding, encouraged by Health and Welfare nurses who issued bottles under family allowances, was later demonstrated by Dr. Schaefer to be linked to the incidence of otitis media (inner ear infection) in children. This insight was to have international significance in campaigns against transnational food companies like Nestlé's and their attempts to introduce Third World women to bottle feeding and the use of baby formulas. Ultimately, 'white man's' food was to contribute to a phenomenal increase in dental caries, obesity, and other health problems.

Many Canadians had difficulty with the idea that family allowance payments were available to Canadians as a right. In a rather nasty, pejorative article published in January 1945, the *Vancouver Sun* drew the reader's attention to the fact that the governor general's children were eligible for family allowance, and that while the allowances were offset by income tax, the governor general paid no such tax. Furthermore, 'Japanese children born in Canada are eligible, or the children of other enemy aliens if born in this country.'[74] The article also suggested that the payments would be of little use to Inuit as the amount was too trivial to purchase anything significant at Arctic prices. However, for Inuit with little or no other source of income, the amount, even in the presence of higher prices, was anything but trivial.

The *Vancouver Sun* wasn't the only institution having trouble with the idea. For the Hudson's Bay Company, the family allowance was a double-edged sword. On the one hand, the increased purchasing power of Inuit meant extra income; on the other, allowances were seen as undermining the self-sufficiency of Inuit and as likely to be yet another source of indigence. The possibility of withholding allowances was entertained in a letter to Roy Gibson in May 1945:

> Another point I would like clarified has reference to the with-holding and accumulating of benefits if conditions do not appear to warrant payment ... With reference to the with-holding of payments in periods of relative prosperity, I gathered from our recent talks that, since the fox will reach its regular peak this coming season, it was not the intention of your Department to make any payments under the scheme during this period, but rather allow values to accumulate for ultimate distribution in harder years.[75]

Chesshire, manager of the fur trade department of the HBC, continues in his letter to express concern that Inuit may have access to the foods listed during difficult years when family allowances are issued but might not voluntarily purchase these same items when family allowances are not being distributed. In other words, his perception of family allowances was that it was another welfare scheme. He goes on to ask if 'milk, fruit juices, rolled oats etc., are essential to the good health of the Eskimo children or whether their "natural diet" when obtainable in adequate quantities is not better for them.'[76] However, in making this suggestion he was not reflecting an enlightened attitude towards Inuit health. Rather, he had commercial considerations in mind. He suggests limiting the foods given out to cod liver oil and perhaps dried milk.

Chesshire's concerns were clearly with the problems of stocking northern stores to provide the items suggested on the distribution lists. If, as Chesshire believed, family allowances were to be doled out as another form of welfare, then considerable stock, which would not voluntarily be purchased by Inuit, would have to be held over. Another of his concerns was that family allowances, given out at times when the Arctic fox was at the peak of its cycle, would negatively affect the willingness of Inuit trappers to pursue them.

Chesshire's perception that the family allowance program was another welfare scheme was not without foundation. What was a universal program for non-Native Canadians was anything but for Indians and Inuit whose benefits were given, in trust, to the Department of Mines and Resources. Clause 36 of the regulations covered the matter: 'The allowance payable in respect of an Eskimo or Nomad child registered in accordance with the provisions of this Part, shall be paid to the Bureau of Northwest Territories and Yukon Affairs to be disbursed by such Bureau on behalf of the child in respect of whom the allowance is paid, in accordance with the provisions of agreements from time to time made between the Director of Family Allowances and such Bureau.'[77] This clause is of considerable significance. While the 1939 Supreme Court decision had made it possible for Inuit to be placed under the Indian Act and made wards of the Crown, the government had refused to do so. However, with this provision in the regulations approved under the Family Allowance Act, 1944, Inuit were formally treated, for the first time since the 1939 decision, as wards of the Crown. In responding to Chesshire, Gibson makes it clear that the wardship was to be exercised by treating what was for other Canadians an important universal program as a means-tested welfare scheme.

In a letter dated 18 June 1945, Chesshire indicates that Gibson had verbally stated to him that 'it was not the intention of the Northwest Territories Bureau to make any payments under this scheme in good years.'[78] He further suggests that the Hudson's Bay Company would be more than happy to indicate to the government 'the degree of prosperity likely to be enjoyed by the natives, although naturally the decision, as to whether or not benefits would be paid, must originate from Ottawa.'[79] Two days later, Chesshire sent out to his post managers instructions on how administration and accounting procedures for family allowances were to be handled, noting that goods were to be supplied under the scheme at regular retail prices.[80] The matter of withholding allowances was not addressed in the instructions.

By February 1946, 876 children had been registered but only 392 of these were receiving payment, with a further 321 pending. A total of $18,801 had been paid out in allowances to Inuit in the Northwest Territories and northern Quebec. Most of these children – 729 – were from the eastern Arctic.[81] By 31 October, the number of children registered had increased to 2,089 in the eastern Arctic and $101,383 was available for distribution as credits.[82] This, however, did not mean that the amount was actually distributed. Rather, much of it was held in trust to be doled out by district registrars as it was needed. The available credits peaked in 1948-9 (Table 5).

The RCMP were experiencing considerable difficulties. Registering children required patrols of all the camps found within districts for which they were responsible. Furthermore, at places like Cape Dorset, Inukjuak, and Sugluk, where more than one trader was operating, the matter of which

Table 5

Family allowance credits, including transfers by financial year to date (as of 31 March 1952)

	1945-6	1946-7	1947-8	1948-9	1949-50	1950-1	1951-2	Culmulative to 31 March 1952
Eskimo Point	$4,929.00	$15,027.00	$10,994.00	$19,932.00	$16,241.75	$8,597.87	$11,431.93	$87,253.55
Churchhill	5,121.73	2,716.07	7,837.80					
Baker Lake	1,526.00	16,436.00	12,569.00	14,673.00	14,743.00	13,546.04	14,479.20	87,972.44
Chesterfield	14,275.00	21,280.00	22,980.20	10,239.65	15,963.41	12,885.19	97,623.45	
Southampton Island	3,589.00	9,024.00	7,937.00	7,596.80	8,798.00	7,750.70	8,596.22	53,291.72
Spence Bay	38,230.06	19,978.62	15,744.04	73,952.72				
Pond Inlet	479.00	38,026.00	48,679.00	27,357.95	32,230.06	32,147.13	35,185.35	214,658.08
Pangnirtung	252.00	29,289.00	17,953.00	18,172.00	18,964.00	19,221.00	19,768.00	123,619.00
Lake Harbour	42,436.00	35,587.00	3,718.00	23,462.70	23,814.00	23,735.80	152,753.50	
Frobisher Bay	34,549.00	11,223.00	10,137.00	9,943.20	63,852.20			
Fort Chimo	2,764.00	26,952.00	22,810.00	24,750.00	22,980.25	22,975.15	22,721.00	145,952.40
Moose Factory	7,703.00	14,484.00	14,524.00	13,067.13	12,854.00	12,923.00	12,576.40	88,131.53
Fort Harrison	1,590.00	36,722.00	54,521.00	35,403.87	32,733.05	33,693.85	32,565.60	227,229.37
Cambridge Bay	768.00	15,286.00	9,792.00	34,325.30	10,524.91	8,069.22	17,704.92	75,420.53
Coppermine	16,605.00	23,241.00	19,790.05	19,363.60	16,920.28	7,787.03	103,706.96	
Aklavik	33,432.00	32,576.00	31,010.70	29,824.00	28,636.00	28,636.00	12,179.55	167,658.25
Tuktoyaktuk	16,628.50	16,828.50						
Arctic Red River	206.00	606.00	392.00	204.00	1,408.00			
Rae	162.00	419.00	579.00	1,160.00				
Total	**23,968.00**	**309,019.00**	**313,019.00**	**307,530.00**	**281,916.00**	**279,595.00**	**276,648.00**	**1,792,110.00**

Source: from NWT Archives, Alex Stevenson Collection, N92-023, 'Family Allowance Credits Including Transfers by Financial Years to Date.'

trader would be a sub-registrar created major headaches.[83] In the process of registering children for family allowances, it was discovered that the discs issued to all Inuit during the 1941 census gave an inaccurate account of the population of the eastern Arctic. As there was no necessary correspondence between the discs and other documentation identifying a person, it became clear that disc numbers could be shared and that many people were unregistered. A decision was made to recall all of the discs issued in 1941 and to reissue them along with a birth certificate in order to exercise better control over the family allowance system.[84] The RCMP were given additional responsibilities.

The matter of withholding allowances quickly became an issue. In April 1946, the *Vancouver Sun*, consistent with the enlightened approach it had already demonstrated when reporting on family allowances, ran a headline; 'Girls Welcome in Igloo Now; Eskimos Get "Baby Bonuses."'[85] The article suggested that female infants, formerly shoved out of the igloo and left to die during difficult times, were now welcome. A Hudson's Bay Company factor, on leave to the south, was quoted as saying: 'It hasn't taken them long to realize that with four or five children, they draw enough in allowances to live without bestirring themselves to hunt or fish ... Some of the Eskimos are developing the habit of spending their time sitting around trading posts, drinking tea, smoking, and gossiping.'[86]

The article attracted attention from the Ottawa press gallery and the British press and generated a letter from Gibson to Chesshire of the Hudson's Bay Company suggesting that traders out on holiday should 'exercise a bit more discretion when trying to make the front pages.'[87] Furthermore, an inquiry from James Cantley of the Baffin Trading Company a few days later made it clear that administering family allowances – addressing the possibility that traders might use the program to their own advantage and dealing with the fear and perception that the program would lead to Inuit 'indigence' – was not going to be easy.

Cantley inquired about whether Inuit could draw their full back allowances for 1945-6, as well as what they were entitled to for 1946-7. Gibson, realizing that traders who knew Inuit had credits might encourage them to spend as much as possible on anything available, responded to Cantley by articulating a clear policy of withholding credits and of means-testing family allowances.

In the north there are regularly recurring cycles of plenty and scarcity. In periods when any parents have good credits with the traders and are able to provide extra benefits for the children on their own account, the paying of Family Allowances would, in most cases, be wasteful and likely to tend to impair the industry of the natives and develop a class of people who would spend their time in the vicinity of the trading posts waiting for government aid.[88]

He included a list of points concerning the administration of the act in the case of Inuit, which contained the following: 'The natives are not entitled to draw any definite monthly allowances either retrospective or current. The allowance will take the form both as to time and quantity of such articles and supplies as the Sub-Registrar considers will be of assistance in raising the standards of the children.'[89] The paternalistic policy of issuing family allowances in kind through the traders clearly had its limitations. Rather than address this issue, Gibson turned a universal social program into a means- tested welfare scheme.

In many instances, Inuit were not prepared to passively accept decisions made by registrars and sub-registrars as to what they were entitled. The actions of eight Inuit at Inukjuak are illustrative. These Inuit – who included some of those later relocated to Resolute Bay and Craig Harbour – approached Corporal Stewart of the RCMP detachment, seeking to use their family allowance credits to pay down the balance of $2,200 owing on a Peterhead boat they had purchased the previous year from the Hudson's Bay Company for $4,000. Tommy Pallisser, the HBC interpreter, helped convey their request to the corporal. He wrote to 'G' division in Ottawa seeking advice.

However, in a separate and confidential report, he advised Ottawa against approving the payment for this purpose, citing a multitude of reasons. These included: his contention that the boat was too large and expensive to operate, that it was only used by some and not all of the Inuit supposedly involved, that it had been a poor year for fur and that the credits would be better used for what they were intended, and that the HBC had sold the Inuit the boat knowing it might never be paid for in full and that they should live with their decision. The corporal also provides two other reasons, which reveal both the paternalism characteristic of administration at the field level and that fears about traders maximizing their profits and transferring the resulting social costs to the state were well-founded. He reported that 'the natives do not know what Family Allowance credits they have or what can be done with them, to have thought of the matter themselves.'[90] Furthermore:

The traders never attempt to curb foolish trading by the natives. I know of one native, who is rather a poor specimen and who seldom makes a good hunt, but when he got six foxes this winter – after it was known that this was not going to be a good fur year, he was sold a second hand cabinet model Victor gramophone, that the HBC had had in the store for years. It cost the native $45.00 (4 foxes at that time). A week later he was asking for debt at the HBC. If one can imagine a Cabinet model gramophone in an igloo or damp tent, one can see the foolishness of the sale.[91]

The request to use family allowance credits to help pay for the boat was subsequently refused.

The treatment of family allowances as a means-tested form of welfare did not sit well with Dr. Percy Moore of National Health and Welfare, the assistant superintendent of the Indian Health Services. In March 1947, he called J.G. Wright, the acting superintendent for the eastern Arctic, and Colonel Craig, in charge of family allowances for the department, to his office. Moore had two concerns. He was of the opinion that family allowances should be available at all times, and that milk and Pablum should be given out as a matter of course. He also noted that treating family allowances as welfare was causing major headaches for the traders, who didn't know what to stock from year to year. It was agreed that steps would be taken to ensure that traders had at least a supply of milk and Pablum on hand and that National Health and Welfare would prepare a pamphlet for Inuit mothers encouraging them to purchase the same for their children under seven years of age.[92]

Discussion of the issue had also been prompted by a note from the Treasury Board, which observed that while $200,000 had been handed over to Mines and Resources for family allowances, the board's records as of February 1947 indicated that less than $1,000 had actually been paid out to Inuit families.[93] It seems likely that the figure was based on very early returns recorded before children had been registered to any great extent. Therefore, while the department's records indicated the funds that were available to Inuit children, this did not mean the funds had actually been paid out. The department appears to have been severely applying its policy of treating family allowances as welfare, something it was entitled to do given its position of 'trust.'

Moore persisted with his concerns. Deputy Commissioner Gibson was suspicious. He was of the impression that Dr. Moore was being 'leaned on' by R.H. Chesshire of the Hudson's Bay Company and was leery of 'The Bay's' motives. He conveyed these concerns to J.G. Wright, the acting superintendent for the eastern Arctic, on the same day that Moore called a meeting in his office of all senior personnel involved in the delivery of family allowances and health care in the eastern Arctic to discuss the matter. The letter to Wright suggested that 'it is evident that [Chesshire] urged upon Dr. Moore and upon the Commissioner of Police his company's point of view that as fine fur is becoming less abundant in many places and prices are being sharply reduced all down the line, the company would like to see the government a little more generous with the Family Allowance expenditure on behalf of the natives.'[94]

At the meeting Dr. Moore stated that he

felt that Eskimo children were physiologically similar to any other children in that they should be given nourishing food during the period in which they are weaning. He felt very young children are definitely undernourished, falling easy prey to illnesses which ordinarily would be considered of a trivial nature but which these children cannot combat due to their malnutrition. Dr. Moore stated that he had grave doubts as to the advisablity or wisdom of the general plan of withholding F.A. credits from Eskimo families until a period of poor hunting; that such has caused considerable distress among the natives.[95]

Moore went on to suggest that the family allowances should be given out as they were for other Canadians. In a curious bit of medical speculation, reflecting the notion that a non-Native Canadian's diet was likely superior to the traditional Inuit one and his own lack of understanding of Inuit mothers' feeding habits, he added: 'Any child's health would be adversely affected by such a radical change as being fed seal meat directly after having been taken from the breast.'[96] Dr. Moore was apparently unaware that Inuit mothers masticated food before transferring it orally to Inuit children as well as providing them with blood soups and broths. He went on to note that most infant deaths occurred in February and March when food supplies were at their lowest.

J.G. Wright of the Northwest Territories and Yukon Branch of Mines and Resources, having been advised by the deputy commissioner as to who was influencing Dr. Moore, was having none of this. He countered Dr. Moore by blaming infant deaths on European culture and the tendency of Inuit to live off the white man's food rather than to rely upon their own Native resources. He noted that 'a large proportion of the Eskimo who have high mortality rates are the two thousand odd in Northern Quebec who, for the most part, are living on bannock and tea.'[97] Wright had a point, while failing to see the role the fur trade had in creating these conditions. Rather, his concern was to ensure that family allowances did not get distributed as Dr. Moore preferred, believing the problem was that Inuit were 'naturally lazy' and would take full advantage of the allowances, thereby undermining their willingness to trap for a living. Wright wanted Inuit to both trap for a living (embrace European culture) and hunt for food (remain independent of the state). The likely impossibility of this combination was not something he was willing to entertain.

This exchange between Moore and Wright is a clear illustration of the policy mess that prevailed at the time. Moore's advocacy of a universal approach to family allowances can be seen as a progressive one: treating Inuit with a sense of justice and a concern for their health and welfare. On the other hand, his advocacy of a non-Native Canadian's diet was ill-informed. By comparison, Wright's support for a residual approach can be recognized as a traditional punitive approach to welfare, but his argument that the white man's diet was responsible for many of the problems had considerable merit.

What neither Moore nor Wright were willing to entertain was the possibility that the private sector behaviour of the Hudson's Bay Company lay at the bottom of many Inuit health problems. The presence of the HBC and the logic behind the accumulation of wealth by the company, with Inuit bearing the social costs of this accumulation, was taken as a given. The task of those formulating government policy was to accommodate 'The Bay.' The result was distorted policy that couldn't begin to deal with the serious problems of Inuit health and welfare developing at the time.

The solution agreed upon was not a change in the policy. Rather, education was evoked with uncommon enthusiasm as the answer to Dr. Moore's concerns.[98] Circulars outlining a program of education for Inuit were to be prepared.

> It was suggested that these circular letters to the nurses might be drawn up in such a manner as to be suitable for the use of and instruction to district registrars and post managers. They would not only be instructive but inspiring – stimulating the nurses, R.C.M.P, and even post managers to expend every effort to decrease the death rate among this group of children. Everyone considered that the drafting of such a letter of instruction would be most valuable and that this should be produced just as quickly as possible.[99]

The material subsequently produced for Inuit mothers was a delightful piece of colonial gibberish (Figure 5). Not to be outdone by the Department of National Health and Welfare, the Department of Mines and Resources undertook to produce educational material of its own. The task was given to Alex Stevenson, who already had a considerable command of Inuktitut.

The result was the publication and distribution in 1950 of the *Book of Wisdom*. It directed the 'kitchen culture' being created for Canadian women in the late 1940s and early '50s at the Inuit. The *Book of Wisdom* contained sections dealing with clean camps, clean igloos, clean air, clean water, clean bodies, clean pots and pans, clean everything. It also contained sections on caring for babies, lung sickness, family allowances, caring for rifles, conservation of game, and 'planning for periods of scarcity.'[100] According to

---

TO ALL MOTHERS WITH SMALL CHILDREN

Our King has made a law that all mothers of children will get help in seeing that these children grow up to be strong and healthy.

One way this help will be given is by bringing to them good baby foods. All the traders will have these foods at the stores and will let you have them. These foods are for small children up to three years old.

These foods are like flour and will not get bad unless they get wet. Keep them dry. They do not need to be cooked. All that you need is clean water.

There are two foods, Dry Milk and Pablum.

Here is how to get them ready to eat.

MILK
Boil water and let cool
In a bowl put 1 cup of warm water
Add 1 dessert-spoon (2 small spoons) of dry milk
Beat well with whipper till all lumps are gone
This milk is a good drink.

PABLUM
In a bowl put (1) cup of Milk.
Add 1 dessert-spoon (2 small spoons) of Pablum
Mix well by stirring.
This is a good baby food.

Figure 5 Notice to Inuit mothers regarding family allowances. [NAC, RG 85, vol. 1125, file 161-3, vol. 1B, April 1947]

Marjorie Hinds, the welfare teacher at Inukjuak when the book was released, the paternalistic section on 'conservation of game' was the least appreciated.[101] However, for colonial cackle, the section on family allowances was unparalleled.

The King is helping all the children in his lands. He is giving aid to the White and Indian children and He wishes to help the Eskimo children also and has instructed His servants the Police to proceed this way ... The traders are working with the Police to help you and your families and the King has instructed them to issue goods only when it is necessary. He does not wish you to become lazy and expect to receive goods any time. You are to continue to work hard at hunting and trapping, teaching your children to be good hunters and workers.[102]

The *Book of Wisdom* was not appreciated by all those involved in the administration of Inuit health and welfare. Father Joseph Buliard of Garry Lake wrote Alex Stevenson to complain that it ignored the work of the missionaries among the Inuit. In addressing these criticisms, Stevenson noted that the book was 'designed as an experiment in order to convey to the Eskimos in very simple language information on subjects which are of importance in their daily lives,' and that it was not intended to deal with any religious aspects. The word 'experiment,' used to describe the offering, had, with regard to all Arctic policy matters, acquired considerable currency.

Despite Marjorie Hinds's comments on the section dealing with the conservation of game, Stevenson noted that the book had been 'received with enthusiasm by the Eskimos themselves.'[103] As would later prove to be the case, Alex Stevenson had a proclivity for seeing the world as he believed it ought to be. His presumptions were frequently at odds with what was actually happening. However, the implications for government policy were to be important because Stevenson's command of Inuktitut, his affable personality, and his northern experience gave him a credibility not afforded other government personnel.

With family allowances, the Hudson's Bay Company had found a new source of revenue. As profits from the sale of furs were declining, it was determined to take full advantage of the situation. A few days after the meeting in Dr. Moore's office, Chesshire wrote to Gibson complaining that a Catholic priest had been appointed a sub-registrar at Wolstenholme, rather than 'The Bay' manager, and that this could lead to a situation where the Anglican Church would expect similar treatment. He also complained about Sergeant Stewart's unwillingness to consider the purchase of Peterhead boats under the family allowance scheme.[104]

A few weeks later, the Northwest Territories Council responded to Chesshire's concerns by authorizing the purchase of a small dory, a whale boat, and several replacement engines for Peterhead boats under the family allowance scheme with seventy-five to ninety per cent of the cost coming from the allowances and the balance from the Inuit themselves.[105]

In July 1947, S.J. Bailey of National Health and Welfare made a trip down the Mackenzie River and to the Delta region to check on the administration of family allowances. While confined to the eastern Arctic, his observations confirmed that the Hudson's Bay Company was taking full advantage of the system and that the RCMP were having a terrible time administering it.

Bailey, from independent reports of his trip, appears to have been an incredibly thorough investigator of the administration of allowances and a man genuinely interested in Indian and Inuit people. In Fort MacPherson, he took the time to meet with the entire community and, according to a report written by Dorothea Dewdney, a field matron with Indian Affairs, Bailey listened carefully to Indian reports of how family allowances were working, joked with local people, and was meticulous in his investigation of all aspects of the program.[106] As a result, Bailey became convinced that the family allowance scheme was very helpful to Indian people and serving the purposes for which it was intended. This was in contrast to the opinion of D.J. Martin, superintendent and officer commanding the Arctic division of the RCMP at the time. In responding to Bailey's report on family allowances, he reported:

> I wish to say however that on my recent Inspection Patrol this year to the MacKenzie District I found that the Indians were loitering and wasting their time at the various posts waiting for and depending on Family Allowances. They have thus lost or are loosing [*sic*] all inclination to hunt and trap ... Employers have found it difficult to hire Indians, such as on River Transportation, even at the wage rate of $1.00 per hour ... Laziness comes natural to an Indian as compared with White men.[107]

Bailey discovered many problems with the administration of family allowances, which was being handled by the RCMP. His reports revealed that family allowances were being used instead of grubstaking trappers and as an alternative to relief.

The cost of grubstaking trappers was borne by the Hudson's Bay Company, as were the costs of relief in settlements where no other trader was present. Lard and baking powder were not included on the list of items to be distributed to Indians, while other provisions, including canned tomatoes, eggs, and other food items, were. At the time, the items on the Inuit list included lard and baking powder. The logic was that lard and baking powder were essential items to making bannock, and that if an Indian could not afford them, he or she was clearly in such dire straights that these items should be issued as relief. Rather than do this and absorb the cost, HBC traders were issuing them, contrary to regulations, under the family allowance program and 'cooking' the vouchers to hide the evidence. Thus they received remuneration for something they would otherwise have been financially responsible for as 'relief.'

Inuit were not allowed canned tomatoes, dried fruit, eggs, etc., because, as previously noted, when the family allowance program was first established it was felt that Inuit would be better off hunting for country foods, and that family allowances should be used to assist in this. Given that in some cases in the Delta region, Inuit and Indians were dealing with the same trader, the difference in goods available to these two groups was causing considerable difficulty. Traders had abandoned the Inuit list and, without authorization, were issuing Inuit with the same goods available to Indians. They then 'fixed' their books to hide the practice.

Bailey also noted that the RCMP were having a difficult time administering the program. In Tuktoyaktuk, credits received by the detachment at Aklavik had not been forwarded to the HBC trader. People had gone without benefit of the allowance for some time. Furthermore, many people were still not registered. When credits had built up, traders were giving them to Inuit in a lump sum rather than dispensing them gradually. When queried about this, they indicated that it was impossible to encourage Inuit to save their credits.

However, the records indicate that Inuit were not prepared to be dictated to, and for good reason: 'According to the R.C.M.P. it is very seldom that their advice regarding accumulation of credits has been followed and the majority of those few who do, return to the officer in a few days asking for the remainder of their credit ... The R.C.M.P. feel that trying to accumulate credits is a useless procedure and certainly to refuse to grant the Eskimo his entire credit on request is beyond their jurisdiction.'[108] Inuit were well-advised in their practice of receiving all their credits at the time they became available. Bailey later uncovered evidence that some credits, left to accumulate on the books of the HBC, disappeared.

As a result of Bailey's investigation, the Inuit list was changed on 20 March 1948 to include items formerly available on the Indian list. As considerable credits had been accumulated, a policy of allowing the purchase of items from the special list was pursued. The special list included, among other things, items useful for hunting – with the exception of gasoline, which was deleted. However, once the credit level reached thirty-five dollars, it could no longer be used for items from this list. In issuing these instructions, Gibson once again warned against the development of the 'dependency complex' and noted that things would improve once 'the natives were seriously influenced by the increasing availability of 'white man's food.'[109]

In the eastern Arctic, similar problems existed. However, as noted by Bailey as part of his inspection tour of the area in the summer of 1948, the HBC also charged different prices for the same goods, depending on whether they were being issued as family allowance or purchased privately. Prices under the family allowance program were controlled in that the Northwest Territories and Yukon Branch in Ottawa had master lists of company prices against which they could check the items being issued under family allowances. In Baker Lake, evidence from the RCMP and the Catholic priest confirmed that the trader charged fifty cents a pound for powdered milk if purchased as part of family allowance and sixty cents a pound otherwise – unless it was being bought by a non-Native, in which case the lower price was charged. Furthermore, Inuit reported that they were afraid to leave credits on the books unspent because, if left, they mysteriously disappeared.[110]

These reports prompted the department to suggest to Chesshire of the HBC that a system allowing Inuit to keep track of their debts and credits be implemented.[111] The response of the HBC was not very enthusiastic, noting that since Inuit could neither read nor write, any system would be of limited value.

By 1949, some difficulties in the administration of the family allowance system appear to have been solved. It was, however, still a residual program. In the eastern Arctic, there were glowing reports of the quantities of powdered milk being consumed. The HBC manager in Baker Lake reported that prior to the advent of family allowances, he had stocked about 350 pounds of powdered milk a year. By 1949, he was carrying 3,000 pounds.[112] Family allowance credits that had accumulated were being used for the purchase of small boats. Gibson's overwhelming concern had not changed. Anything that might contribute to 'loitering around the posts,' such as the suggestion by Arctic Bay Inuit that they use their collective credits to build a community hall, was strongly resisted.

Increasingly, family allowances were used to coerce children into school attendance, as the following case from Tuktoyaktuk illustrates. While there were not many similar cases in the early 1950s, as Inuit gravitated towards settlements and as more schools became available, the use of the family allowance system to force school attendance became more common.

In June 1950, the RCMP at Tuktoyaktuk reported on the situation of a young Inuk boy whose school attendance while his family was in the settlement was very irregular. The welfare teacher, Dorothy Robinson, noted that the boy's irregular attendance was starting to have a bad effect on other pupils. The RCMP took the matter in hand and paid the boy's father a visit. 'According to the father, he would like the boy to go to school, but does not wish to force him to go. In other words, the boy does just as he wants. It was explained that this might have a bad effect on the boys' [sic] character, as if he was not taught discipline and obedience when he is a child, he would later grow into a headstrong, self-centred man.'[113] The officer advised the father that family allowance payments would be withheld if a child, without sufficient reasons, did not attend school. He concluded by observing that: 'The parent's [sic] idolize this child, and hate to force him to do anything against his wishes. They also became so lonesome for him while he was in school in Aklavik, that they sent for him to return. This is a good example of lack of discipline in Eskimo homes, which later is a prime factor in the moral laxness of the adolescent natives.'[114]

Apart from noting that, from the constable's own spelling and grammar, he could have used a few more years of schooling himself, the report is entirely revealing of the attitudes and values that dominated the federal civil service. It was 1950. The colonialism, racism, and attitudes of moral and cultural superiority that had driven the northern administration for thirty years still dominated the Arctic's social landscape.

In the 1950s, changes were slowly introduced to the way family allowances were administered. Much of the impetus for these and other important changes in programs run by the northern administration were initiated, not by federal bureaucrats, but by Inuit themselves.

By 1952, a council had been formed by Inuit in the Mackenzie Delta. At a meeting, held at the Reindeer Station in the Delta in December, a number of issues were addressed that council then placed before the Council of the NWT. Charlie Smith, the Inuk leader of the council, dealt with complaints from Inuit parents in the Delta to the effect that they were cut off family allowances when their children were sent to boarding school in Aklavik. The allowances were given to the church-run schools to support the children while at school. The policy was, he noted, not likely to encourage parents to send their children to school. Another Inuk resident of the Delta spoke to the matter before a request that the policy be changed was put to a vote and carried unanimously. In seconding the motion, Herbert Allen was reported in the minutes as stating: 'It is a good subject to put children to school because he had no opportunity to attend school himself. And that he finds it very hard to speak or write. As those that have attended school and he would like to this enforced so the children have an opportunity to better themselves by attending school.'[115]

Council also dealt with a problem familiar to departmental officials: the matter of encouraging people to save money for times when they had little or no income. The chairperson observed that young people working for the Department of Public Works during the summer did not end the season with any money to account for their work. It was noted that they received seventy-five dollars a week. When asked how much they needed to live on, 'the boys' stated that forty-five dollars was sufficient. It was suggested that the balance be put away for their benefit in a 'frozen fund': 'Therefore as leader I asked the young men whether or not we should put this suggestion into the hands of our council member to be brought up at the next N.W.T. council meeting to the rest of the members of the council. And now several of the boys answered us and gave us the consent that the suggestion was very favourable and should be enforced.'[116] Finally, Kenneth Peeloolook brought up a matter that had apparently been discussed among Inuit residents of Aklavik since 1948.[117] The suggestion was made that a cooperative store, owned and run by Inuit, should be opened somewhere in the Delta, preferably at a site other than Aklavik. The chairperson seemed to be quite knowledgeable about cooperatives and commented on their success in Saskatchewan and Alberta.

Before adjourning, council discussed the idea of constructing a fish trap or series of traps for the benefit of the elderly in the Delta, noting that prices for furs were so low and the cost of goods so high that many people were suffering. Council expressed some concern that fishing was currently benefitting whites and not the Inuit.[118]

The minutes of this council meeting are significant. They effectively counter the colonial attitudes and perceptions that existed among many Arctic administrators, both in Ottawa and at the field level, that Inuit were like children, incapable of understanding policy issues and of acting on their own behalf. On the contrary, it is obvious that their initiatives and ideas were progressive, practical, and far in advance of many ideas held by those supposedly responsible for their welfare.

The population of the Mackenzie Delta was a mixture of Indian, non-Native, and Inuit. As was true in the administration of welfare, this increasingly caused problems in administering family allowances. Non-Native residents received their payments in the form of a cheque mailed directly to them. By 1953, the Indian Affairs Branch of Department of Northern Affairs and National Resources had started to do the same for Indians living in the region. Inuit in the Delta complained that they were being treated differently and requested that they be paid the same way.

The matter was not an easy one for the northern administration, which still harboured fears that Inuit would become dependent on the dole. These fears persisted despite what was, by now, abundantly clear: family allowances and relief, given the collapse in the price of Arctic fox, were the only means by which Inuit could survive. As Table 6 reveals, by 1951 in northern Quebec, family allowances, old age pensions, and government relief accounted for 61 per cent of annual Inuit income. For Baffin Island the figure was 46 per cent while in the western Arctic, by comparison, it was 18 per cent.

Donald Marsh, by now 'Donald The Arctic,' Anglican bishop of the Arctic, contributed to fears that the family allowance system and public relief were being abused. His criticisms of government welfare programs were tireless. In a story published in the 19 January 1953 issue of *Time* magazine, he was quoted as saying that 'government doles are ruining the morale and undermining the health of the Eskimo,' and, further, that 'many Eskimos have

Table 6

Analysis of Hudson's Bay Company sales for the year ended 30 June 1951

Sections	Southern Baffin Island	Northern Baffin Island	North Quebec	Western Hudson Bay	Western Arctic	Totals
Estimated no. of families	250	380	585	385	540	2,140
Furs	24,892 (100)	51,340 (135)	40,977 (70)	80,011 (208)	231,909 (429)	429,129 (200)
Other producer HBC wages, etc.	19,441 (77)	11,355 (30)	24,325 (42)	14,847 (39)	4,759 (9)	74,727 (35)
Wages from other sources and sundry other income	10,283 (41)	10,793 (28)	21,700 (37)	27,138 (70)	10,796 (20)	80,710 (38)
Cash	6,962 (28)	1,068 (3)	5,909 (10)	3,480 (9)	6,886 (13)	24,305 (11)
Total	**61,578 (246)**	**74,556 (196)**	**92,911 (159)**	**125,476 (326)**	**254,350 (471)**	**608,871 (284)**
Family allowances	42,454 (170)	58,222 (153)	64,905 (111)	49,513 (129)	49,656 (92)	264,750 (124)
Old-age pensions	257 (1)	1,882 (5)	344 (1)	96	206	2,785 (1)
Government relief	9,112 (37)	3,862 (19)	77,117 (132)	8,875 (23)	5,204 (10)	104,170 (49)
Total	**51,823 (208)**	**63,966 (168)**	**142,366 (244)**	**58,484 (152)**	**55,066 (102)**	**371,705 (174)**
HBC relief	588 (2)	200 (1)	14,664 (25)	3,024 (8)	405 (1)	18,881 (9)
HBC unpaid debts	663 (3)	962 (3)	2,494 (4)	1,743 (5)	531 (1)	6,393 (3)
Earned	61,578 (246)	74,556 (196)	92,911 (159)	125,476 (326)	254,350 (471)	608,871 (284)
Unearned	51,823 (208)	63,966 (168)	142,366 (244)	58,484 (152)	55,066 (102)	371,705 (174)
Total	**113,401 (454)**	**138,522 (364)**	**235,277 (403)**	**183,960 (478)**	**309,416 (573)**	**980,576 (458)**
HBC relief at sales	785 (3)	265 (1)	19,550 (33)	4,030 (10)	540 (1)	25,170 (13)
Total	**114,186 (456)**	**138,787 (365)**	**254,827 (436)**	**187,990 (488)**	**309,956 (574)**	**1,005,746 (471)**

Note: Numbers in parentheses indicate the average per family.
Source: from NWT Archives, Alex Stevenson Collection, N92-023, 'Analysis of Hudson's Bay Company's Sales for the Year Ended June 30, 1951.'

given up hunting and fishing to live on the white man's dole, often squandering their $5 baby bonuses and $40 old-age pensions on such foibles as electric clocks, to be used merely as decoration on igloo walls.'[119] A 'man of the cloth' or not, Bishop Marsh was not above stretching things a bit to give colour to his rigid values. George Davidson, deputy minister of National Health and Welfare, was livid. He pointed out to 'Donald The Arctic' that, at the time, not one cheque for old age pensions had yet been paid to any Inuit and furthermore that 'we have never, since its inception in 1945, permitted family allowance monies paid on behalf of Eskimos to be spent on items other than very carefully selected lists of foods, clothing, etc., which certainly do not include alarm clocks.'[120]

Cheques were finally issued to Inuit living in the Mackenzie Delta, prompted by complaints from the region and a change in the regulations governing family allowances authorized by order-in-council, 5 March 1953. The new regulations made it possible for the director of family allowances, Department of National Health and Welfare, to be directly responsible for the issuing of allowances to Inuit in agreement with the Northwest Territories and Yukon Services.[121] Formerly, the responsibility for all Inuit had been placed in the trust of the department.

This apparently progressive move was not without problems. These are illustrated by the case of a hunter, living about 112 kilometres from Aklavik, who came to the settlement to receive foodstuffs with the family allowance cheque held for him by the RCMP. His wife was the designated payee. 'In view of the fact that there are small children in the Family his wife the designated payee couldn't accompany him. As a result HARRY had to take his cheque back to his camp get his wife to sign it and then return to Aklavik for the foodstuffs he came for the first time, thus travelling twice as far as was necessary had his wife been able to travel.'[122]

In the eastern Arctic, the struggle to remove the power of officials in doling out benefits under the family allowance scheme had only begun. But the need was pressing, as illustrated by the situation of Jimmy Koodlooalook of Inukjuak. Following his arrival at Inukjuak from the Belcher Islands in August 1953, he was interviewed by Marjorie Hinds, the welfare teacher. Koodlooalook and his camp had nearly starved to death and had eaten all of their dogs. At the time, several prospectors were on the islands, and they also ran into difficulty. 'The white people would have starved if the Eskimos hadn't looked after them when they ran out of food. Whenever Eskimos killed a seal they shared it with the white people just the way they share among themselves. The Eskimos often talked among themselves wondering why white people were there without food.'[123] Hinds was not given to the RCMP's style of reporting on such incidents, and her interviewing skills were considerable.

QUESTION: What did you get from Family Allowances?
ANSWER: Very little, the least I have ever had from F.A. Some cottonade to make pants for the three children, 2 yards of duffle and 5 lbs of milk to last all winter. I also got one sweater, but I put it back so as to get more milk. I didn't even get flannelette to make shirts for the children. I also had 2 bags of oats with 6 lbs in each bag, that was for three children to last all winter.
QUESTION: How much money was to your credit on F.A. at this time?
ANSWER: I don't know. But I've never got so little when I've asked for Family Allowances.
QUESTION: Did you get cod liver oil and vitamin pills for the children from the nurse before you left last fall?
ANSWER: No, we got no cod liver oil at all and no vitamin pills. She wouldn't hear of it. We wanted medicine but the first time we went to ask she wouldn't give us any, so we went again and that time we got some cough medicine and aspirin. About one-third of a Winchester bottle of cough medicine, (i.e. approximately 24 ounces) and quite a lot of aspirin. We know how to use the medicine if there is a label on the bottle with it written in syllabic. We should like to take medicine back with us this time.[124]

The message was subtle but obvious. If Inuit were so generous in hard times, why were white people so incredibly stingy? Subsequently, for the remainder of the 1950s, the issue of paying family allowances directly to Inuit parents was to become a major issue for the Northern Administration and Lands Branch. Koodlooalook's implied question was well placed.

Old Age Pensions: A Question of Entitlement
The 1939 Supreme Court decision also caused considerable confusion about the eligibility of Inuit for old age pensions. Commencing in 1927 with the passage of the Old Age Pensions Act, Canadians were eligible for a means-tested pension. The act contained a Section (8) that explicitly excluded Indians from the provisions of the legislation.

In 1948, the Indian Affairs Branch within the Department of Mines and Resources started to pay eligible Indians a pension of eight dollars a month. The payment was made, provided that the applicant was not in receipt of income in excess of $400 per year. Shortly after the Indian Affairs Branch had initiated this practice, the Northwest Territories Council authorized the same for aged Inuit.[125] The initial payment of this amount was made effective 1 April 1949 and was paid in kind. The payment was restricted to someone who had attained his or her seventieth birthday and was not in receipt of income of more than $400 per year. Again, the RCMP were enlisted as registrars for the purpose of administering the scheme, although little work was involved. A year after the plan was initiated, only sixty-four Inuit over seventy years of age had been identified as eligible for pensions under the plan.[126]

However, a year later and following the dismantling of the Department of Mines and Resources, the minister of citizenship and immigration, who now had responsibility for Indian affairs, announced his intention to pay eligible Indians a pension of twenty-five dollars per month. The twenty-five-dollar payment was to include relief payments. In other words, the amount received by Indians would be considerably less than twenty-five dollars in most cases. This payment was also subject to a means test. The maximum income, after which the twenty-five dollars was reduced by an equivalent amount, was set at $120 for a single person and $300 for a couple. In other words, the payment did not, in most cases, represent any increase in pension to Indians, despite appearances to the contrary.

The Arctic administration had considerable difficulty with the idea of increasing Inuit pensions from eight dollars to twenty-five dollars per month. The reasons were familiar. On the one hand, they did not feel that twenty-five dollars, as a replacement for relief in the case of elderly applicants, was sufficient income for someone living under Arctic conditions. The second reason replayed an old theme. 'Secondly, where aged Eskimos are being maintained without outside assistance (apart from the present eight dollars per month for minor purchases of a personal nature) it would be unfortunate to increase the regular cash income for it would tend to encourage whole groups to move farther away from their hunting localities and move closer to the posts.'[127]

The suggestion was made that the amount be held at eight dollars. Since concern was expressed that in the Mackenzie Delta a different rate of pension for Indians and Inuit might cause problems, it was recommended that the age of qualifying for Inuit be dropped to sixty-five as compensation. However, events quickly overtook such suggestions. At a meeting of the Northwest Territories Council, 23 June 1950, it was noted that the question of whether or not Inuit were eligible for the same means-tested pension of other Canadians had been raised and that the Department of National Health and Welfare had put the question to the Supreme Court. Council decided to defer from taking any action on the pension issue until council had become familiar with the decision.[128]

The decision of the Supreme Court was somewhat surprising. The court ruled that Inuit were eligible for pensions, reasoning that the clause in the 1927 Old Age Pensions Act excluding Indians did not apply.[129] They were also found to be eligible for blind persons pensions under the same legislation. Contrary to the 1939 Supreme Court decision, for purposes of the Old Age Pensions Act, Inuit were not Indians. 'An Eskimo cannot be said to be a "male person of Indian blood reputed to belong to a particular band" as the word "band" is defined in section 2(b) of the Indian Act, and he would, therefore not be an "Indian as defined by the Indian Act" within the meaning of section 8 of the Old Age Pensions Act.'[130] At the time, the maximum pension payable to non-Native residents of the Northwest Territories from National Health and Welfare was forty dollars per month less income over $120 per year.[131]

If Inuit were, for pension purposes and contrary to the 1939 decision, not Indians, it appeared that they might also not be Indians for other purposes as well. In fact, it seemed that the Supreme Court was prepared to rule that Inuit were Canadian citizens with a status no different from any other Canadian. Recognizing this, the federal government granted Inuit a right not held by Indians. In 1949, Inuit were given the right to vote in federal elections. However, the right was only exercised in the Mackenzie Delta region. Inuit in the Keewatin, Baffin, and Franklin regions of the eastern Arctic were not included in any existing electoral district under the Canada Elections Act and, consequently, could not vote until the federal election of 1962, which created one riding for the entire Northwest Territories.

The 1949 ruling created major problems, for to be eligible for a pension under the Old Age Pensions Act applicants had to present conclusive proof of age. This hardly existed in the case of potential Inuit beneficiaries, and National Health and Welfare made it clear that it was adopting a 'hard line' by applying to Inuit the same criteria it applied to non-Native Canadians. This was revealed in July 1951, when the northern administration tried to get a pension for an elderly Inuk woman who, not surprisingly, had no birth certificate. As evidence, the department submitted testimony from a priest that had baptized her to the effect that, at the time of baptism, the woman appeared to be of a certain age. The Department of National Health and Welfare responded:

> The evidence submitted in the case of Marguerite Kralalak seems to me to be similar to evidence given in affidavits. The priest who baptized her had no way of knowing her age and therefore had no alternative but to reach his own conclusion, no doubt based on her appearance and possibly on what she told him at that time. The information may, of course, be reasonably accurate but if the evidence submitted in this case is accepted it seems to me that we will be accepting evidence which is not considered as satisfactory proof of age in the case of white persons.
>
> The difficulty I see in dealing with this case is that it may establish a precedent for future cases and I feel that it would be a mistake to set up rules to be applied to Eskimos which had been found to be unsatisfactory in dealing with applications from white persons.[132]

Nevertheless, Inuit were officially eligible for the same means-tested old age pensions as any other Canadian. What is important to note is that it appears, from the archival evidence, that they had been eligible since 1927 when the Old Age Pensions Act was first passed. Given the income levels of Inuit, it is likely that they would have received full benefits under the legislation. The problem for the administration would have been proof of age. However, even in 1927, conclusive proof of age was a problem for many non-Native Canadians. Despite being eligible, not a single Inuk over seventy received a cent of pension money under the provisions of the legislation until 1950. Even then, attempts to provide pension benefits were hampered by the strict requirement of proof of age.

The means-tested nature of the pension also caused considerable difficulty. In fact, given the number of Inuit involved, the administrative provisions of the act likely cost the government more than the total paid out in pensions. Determining the income received by Inuit over seventy became an absurdly punitive exercise. In the provinces, income included income in kind – notably food and shelter provided to the applicant. What was the equivalent rent on the average Inuit igloo or skin tent? How much was a hind quarter of caribou provided for an elderly relative worth? The image of bureaucrats and administrators trying to make such determinations is more pathetic than amusing. The responsibility for reporting the amount of income in kind being received by Inuit over seventy fell, as usual, on the shoulders of the RCMP. Again, reducing the amount received by Inuit elderly so as to prevent them and their extended families from becoming 'post Eskimos' was a major concern.

When it came to means-tested pensions for Inuit, the administration was soon put out of its misery – almost. In 1951, two new pieces of legislation were introduced by the Liberals. The Old Age Security Act replaced the means-tested pension with a universal one and extended the benefits to Indians. It made forty dollars a month available to all Canadians over seventy years of age. However, the second piece of legislation, the Old Age Assistance Act, provided additional pension funds of up to forty dollars a month on a means-tested basis to persons over sixty-five.[133]

The program, whose cost was shared on a fifty-fifty basis with the provinces, was administered in the case of Inuit by the Department of Resources and Development on behalf of the NWT Council. However, by January 1953, nothing had yet been paid to any Inuk in the NWT. The requirement for proof of age was presenting the department with considerable headaches.[134] The administrative problems associated with dealing with a population born before any administration had taken the Canadian North seriously were not over. The federal bureaucracy had spent thirty years trying to ensure that Inuit did not get the same benefits from social programs as did other Canadians. It persisted in its contention that these would interfere with 'self-reliance' and create 'post-Eskimos.' The introduction of yet another universal social program was, for many Arctic administrators, a disappointment. The tide was clearly moving in a direction other than the one they favoured. However, in their own area of jurisdiction they did all they could within the emerging new welfare state structures to ensure that their conventional ideas still influenced policy.

Inertia and Initiative: Trying to Steer Another Course

For the few administrators who saw the necessity of changing directions within the bureaucracy, the administration of Inuit affairs was moving like a large tanker. Its momentum was enormous and nothing short of a bureaucratic disaster seemed likely to change its direction. Disaster was in the making.

By 1950, the economy of the eastern Arctic was virtually in complete collapse. The idea that people could make a living from the land with fox prices lower than they had been in the entire history of trapping in the region was absurd. Roy Gibson's perpetual fears of people becoming dependent were, to put it graciously, utterly ridiculous. Without alternatives, Inuit were increasingly dependent upon relief and family allowances for income. There were few other options.

Relief costs soared from $10,077 for the eastern Arctic in 1945-6 to $63,251 in 1949-50.[135] The value of fur production in the Northwest Territories plummeted from $3,165,107 in 1942-3 to a mere $909,504 in 1949-50.[136] But the figures for the entire North are somewhat deceiving. The variety of pelts available in the western Arctic, to some extent, protected Native people from the vagaries of a single-resource based economy. In the eastern Arctic, virtually the only pelt of commercial significance was the white fox. In 1942-3, 60,521 fox were taken with a value of $1,694,588. The average value per pelt was twenty-eight dollars. In 1949-50, 9,989 pelts were taken with a total value of $64,929 and an average price of $6.50 per pelt. In 1945-6, $23,968 had been paid out in family allowances. By 1949-50, the figure had risen to $281,916.[137] In Arctic Quebec the situation was particularly desperate. The Hudson's Bay Company granted $2,867 relief in Inukjuak and $991 at Povungnituk.[138]

To address the problem, the Arctic administration hired James Cantley in 1949. Cantley, in the face of the complete collapse of the fox fur market, had retired his Baffin Trading Company and sold the assets to the HBC. Cantley's inclinations found favour with Roy Gibson, who was on the verge of retirement. However, his approach to the problems proved to be consistent with the ideals of the new minister, Bob Winters, appointed in 1950.

In April 1950, Cantley produced his report. A wordy, sixty-five-page document, the report rambled through the same tired arguments and observations that had been around the department for years. Cantley recommended against doing what some in the department had suggested – establishing government-operated and monopoly trading operations parallel to those created by the Danish government in Greenland.

As an alternative, Cantley suggested closer cooperation with the Hudson's Bay Company. He argued against placing more administrative responsibility in the hands of the RCMP. In a strange bit of logic, he suggested that the cost of feeding the dog teams required to take the RCMP and social workers around to the camps could not be justified by the value of the services they provided.[139] Rather, Cantley recommended that all economic and social matters be supervised directly by the Arctic Services Branch of the department in close cooperation with the Hudson's Bay Company and that the RCMP be relieved of all administrative responsibilities.[140] Cantley had no other concrete solutions for dealing with the huge social and economic crisis that had developed.

By some accounts, the eastern Arctic was a complete disaster. Henry Larsen's observations and his analysis were among the most cutting:

> The Eskimos generally have drifted into a state of lack of initiative and confusion. Conditions are generally appalling. Never has there existed so much destitution, filth and squalor as exists today, and in the opinion of some people, the conditions under which some natives live is a disgrace to Canada, surpassing the worst evils of slum areas in cities. Bad sanitary and economic conditions are gradually undermining the health of these people and if not checked will ultimately result in their extermination.[141]

The very title of Larsen's memo, 'Responsibility, Care and Supervision of Eskimos,' provides ample evidence of his Tory worldview. Nevertheless, the conditions he described existed, and Larsen laid responsibility squarely at the feet of the HBC, the churches, and the northern administration.

> Fundamentally, the trouble goes back very many years, actually to the time that traders first went into Eskimo territory and changed the whole way of life of the Eskimos, that is, changed them from primarily hunters of meat to primarily trappers of fur ... Year by year the natives become more poorly clad in store bought clothes which are quite inadequate to withstand the rigours of the far north climate and which do not begin to compare with native skin clothing, that is, caribou skins and seal skins ... Rubber boots are being substituted for seal skin footwear. The Eskimos sell their seal skins to

the traders and in some cases make up seal skin clothing in substantial quantities and donate it to the missions or dispose of it to other white residents for some very small remuneration perhaps in the way of tobacco and cigarettes or some trinket ... many Eskimo habitations are made from discarded box boards, odds and ends of burlap, canvas, and other waste material, and the accumulation of filth inside these habitations is indescribable.[142]

Larsen's observations were not appreciated by the administration. James Cantley was given the task of responding. This he did on 20 November 1951 in a memo to J.G. Wright, the chief of the northern administration division. Cantley, quick to recognize Larsen's dislike of traders, disagreed with everything he had to say, point by point.

On page 1 Inspector Larsen states that 'food supply and clothing are extremely unsatisfactory at all Eskimo camps,' yet on page 4 he says 'There are still sufficient quantities of sea food, such as white whale, walrus, seal and also fresh fish to sustain Eskimos *if they will get after them.*' It seemed to be inferred here that the whole trouble cannot be attributed to the white man but that part of the blame may lie with the Eskimos themselves.[143]

The one recommendation that Larsen had made, and with which Cantley concurred, was that a meeting be convened of all persons concerned with Inuit administration. The meeting was held on May 19 and 20, 1952, and was presided over by Major General Hugh Young, the deputy minister.

Two recommendations that came out of the meeting are worthy of note. One was that a general committee should be formed to review suggestions made at the May meeting. The other was that 'the movement of Eskimos from over-populated areas to places where they can be assured of being able to make a better living' be considered.[144] The first meeting of the newly created Committee on Eskimo Affairs was held in October of the same year.

By then, as already discussed, Farley Mowat's *People of the Deer* was creating a considerable amount of trouble for the administration. *The Atlantic* serialized the book in its January, February, and March editions of 1952. By midsummer, A.E. Porsild and Douglas Leechman, both of the National Museum of Canada (and both in attendance at the May meeting) had prepared scathing reviews of Mowat's work.[145] Many of the criticisms were deserved, for Mowat was a storyteller not given to a dull account of the facts. Nor would he refrain from serious exaggeration where it contributed to narrative drama. Nevertheless, combined with internal criticism, the department was on the defensive. The minister was having to address

Mowat's claims in the House. For the time being, something clearly had to be done to avert a potential disaster in the region of the Arctic suffering the most from the demise of the fur trade. Attention focused on Arctic Quebec. Unbeknown to Inuit at Inukjuak, a significant portion of the rationale for their ultimate relocation to the high Arctic was already firmly in place.

3

Planning for Relocation to the High Arctic

On 19 November 1990, Tom Siddon, minister of Indian affairs and northern development, rose in the House of Commons to table a report responding to requests from the House standing committee on aboriginal affairs. The committee had asked the government to apologize to Inuit who were moved to the high Arctic in 1953 as part of a government resettlement program. The minister was also requested to recognize the contribution to Canadian sovereignty made by the residents of Grise Fiord and Resolute Bay. He was asked to compensate them for their service to Canada and for wrongdoing inflicted upon them. The committee, following testimony before it on 19 March 1990 and again on 19 June, had concluded that considerable wrong was inflicted on those who were relocated. Lawyers for Makavik Corporation, representing the Inuit of Inukjuak, Arctic Quebec, had argued before the committee that Inuit were 'used' in the early 1950s by the federal government to strengthen Canadian sovereignty over the Arctic Archipelago.

In response to the standing committee report, the federal government contracted an Ottawa consulting firm – the Hickling Corporation – to investigate the charges and to report to the minister. The Hickling Report, compiled primarily by 'Bud' Neville, a former welfare officer and long-standing employee of the department (whose role in the development of the emerging Inuit welfare regime is discussed in Chapter 7), absolved the government of any wrongdoing. It argued that, based on archival evidence, Inuit had been relocated for humanitarian purposes and had volunteered to move. In addressing the House, Tom Siddon echoed the findings of the report: 'The decisions by the federal government, in the early 1950s, appears [sic] to have been solely related to improving the harsh social and economic conditions facing the Inuit at Inukjuak at that time.'[1]

The editor of the *Toronto Star* responded in dramatic fashion, noting the minister's claims as well as an article by historian Shelagh Grant, published by the Canadian Arctic Resources Committee, which maintained that 'concern for sovereignty was the primary motive in determining when and where resettlement should occur.'[2] In a headline proclaiming: 'Arctic Self-exiles Canada's Shame,' the editorial went on to describe the relocation as a 'gruesome experiment with human lives' and called upon the minister to apologize on behalf of Canadians and to consider appropriate compensation.[3]

However, this was far from the end of the matter. Inuit approached the Canada Human Rights Commission and asked it to investigate the matter. The commission gave the task to Professor Daniel Soberman of the Faculty of Law, Queen's University. In his report, submitted December 1991, Soberman claimed there was evidence that the government of Canada did have concerns about Arctic sovereignty at the time but suggested that it was not a primary concern in the relocation.[4] However, he concluded that, at the time, the government did regard the two high Arctic settlements as making a tangible contribution to Canadian sovereignty. He further noted that Inuit had been promised that they would be returned to Inukjuak within three years of the relocation if they desired, and that this promise was not honoured. Finally, he concluded that Inuit had suffered as a result of inadequate preparation and implementation of the project.[5]

The report of the Human Rights Commission and the criticisms directed at the original Hickling Report, commissioned by the Department of Indian and Northern Affairs, generated yet another report and another response from the federal government. This time, the department contracted Professor Magnus Gunther of Trent University, Peterborough, Ontario, to produce a report[6] addressing the claims and charges made by Inuit and academics, including Professor Shelagh Grant,[7] also of Trent University; Keith Lowther, who had written a thesis on the topic while a student at the University of Calgary;[8] Andrew Orkin, a lawyer and assistant professor of family medicine, McGill University;[9] and Alan Marcus of the Scott Polar Research Institute, Cambridge, England.[10] The struggle over what had actually happened to Inuit relocated in 1953 had increasingly become a contest among academics defending their reputations in the face of criticism from other academics. In this 'contest,' Inuit voices were increasingly lost. In writing his report, Gunther chose not to consult any Inuit involved in the issue.

Gunther's findings were in sharp contrast to those of other researchers studying the event. He concluded that the relocation had been carried out with humane intentions based on the government's desire to help Inuit remain self-sufficient by hunting and trapping. Noting Gunther's report, Tom Siddon stated: 'It would, therefore, be inappropriate for the government to apologize for having initiated and carried out the relocation.'[11] The government also refused compensation except to pay for housing and transportation should the Inuit from Inukjuak remaining in the high Arctic decide to return to Arctic Quebec.[12]

In the summer of 1953, seven families from Inukjuak and three from Pond Inlet on the northern tip of Baffin Island were moved to two locations in the high Arctic: Craig Harbour on the southern tip of Ellesmere Island and, 400 kilometres to the southwest, Resolute Bay, the site of a military base and Department of Transport weather station on Cornwallis Island.[13] The relocation reveals the attitudes many Canadians held towards an emerging and incomplete welfare state. These attitudes affected Inuit considerably, as they were translated into concerns about Inuit welfare and concerns about Arctic sovereignty. Two areas of totalization converged: the state's concern for establishing territorial integrity and its concern for managing Inuit within the norms of Canadian society and economy. Furthermore, the relocation can be seen as a state response to the ability of Inuit in Inukjuak to adapt provisions of the welfare state to their own unique circumstances – and to conditions which have their genesis in the Hudson's Bay Company's move into the eastern Arctic.

What actually happened? How could lawyers for the Inuit, and the Inuit themselves, claim they were mistreated and relocated for purposes of sovereignty, while the minister, backed by research reports that included letters written by Inuit subsequent to the move, claimed they were relocated for humanitarian purposes?

The Historical Precedence

The 1953 relocation was not the first time Inuit had been moved to the high Arctic. It was also not the first time RCMP posts had been opened in the region. What is remarkable about the relocations of 1953 is the extent to which the rationale and the circumstances surrounding the move parallel events that took place in the same region nearly twenty years earlier. These events are important because they contribute to circumstances that, in turn, explain the controversial relocations in the summer of 1953.

In 1922, the federal government was confronted with questions about Canadian sovereignty over the Sverdrup Islands. These were raised by Norway after a fishing dispute between Norway and Denmark involving Danish claims to the northeast part of Greenland. The federal government sent the ship *Arctic* north under the command of its seventy-year-old captain, J.E. Bernier. This was the first of what became annual patrols of the eastern Arctic. These patrols were conducted between 1922 and 1969. They supplied northern communities with provisions, carried mail, brought a doctor and dentist for their annual visits, and performed medical surveys of the Inuit population. Inuit were moved by ship from community to community and often to the South for treatment of tuberculosis, returning to the North during the annual patrols of the eastern Arctic carried out by government or Hudson's Bay Company ships.

In 1922, J.D. Craig of the Department of the Interior, after whom Craig Harbour is named, was the officer in command. His mission was to reinforce Canadian claims to the Arctic Archipelago. The government was ill-prepared to deal with its claims as the ship CGS *Arctic* had not been north since before the First World War. On these trips, Bernier had been captain. The presence of American whalers in eastern Canadian waters was one of his concerns. Built in Germany in 1898 and purchased by the Canadian government in 1904, the *Arctic* had been relegated, during the First World War, to the status of a lightship among the shoals of the Lower Traverse at the eastern end of Isle d'Orleans near Quebec City. It required a refit before heading north once again.[14] Two police posts were established: Craig Harbour on the southern coast of Ellesmere Island and Pond Inlet on the northern tip of Baffin Island. A year later, two Inuit families from Etah on the west coast of Greenland were hired to assist the police at Craig Harbour. Canadian anthropologist Diamond Jenness asserts that the Etah Inuit were knowledgeable about the area, having hunted musk-ox on Ellesmere Island for years.[15] This tacit approval of Greenland Inuit on Canadian territory was later to become a major concern and a consideration in relocating Inuit from Inukjuak and Pond Inlet to Ellesmere Island in 1953.

In 1924, another police post was opened at Dundas Harbour on the southeast corner of Devon Island. Craig Harbour, Dundas Harbour, and Pond Inlet were all strategic locations that controlled passage into the Arctic Archipelago from the east. The same year, an attempt was made to open an additional post on the Bache Peninsula, halfway up the eastern coast of Ellesmere Island and north of the settlement of Etah across Smith Sound on the Greenland coast. However, pack ice blocked the passage of the *Arctic* – a frustration to be repeated when the icebreaker *d'Iberville* attempted to reach the same location in August 1953. The two Inuit families that had been picked up at Etah to serve at this post were subsequently taken to Dundas Harbour. In 1926, another attempt to open a post on the Bache Peninsula was successful, and the post at Craig Harbour was temporarily closed.

In the meantime, additional questions about Canadian sovereignty had been raised by American interests. In 1925, an American educator and explorer, D.B. MacMillan, had teamed up with Lieutenant-Commander Byrd of the U.S. Navy to search the Arctic Ocean north of Alaska for new lands. The plan involved caching supplies on Canadian territory. Despite being asked to request official Canadian government permission, the expedition proceeded without it. The British ambassador in Washington was subsequently asked to register a strong protest against the American government on Canada's behalf.[16] The United States did not apologize for the event. In fact, the United States refused to formally acknowledge Canada's claims to sovereignty over the region.

Another event that was to influence the decision to relocate Inuit to the high Arctic in 1953 took place in 1926. O.S. Finnie, director of the Northwest Territories and Yukon Branch of the Department of the Interior, was increasingly concerned about the depletion of game in the Northwest Territories, especially musk-ox. The musk-ox had been driven to near extinction on the mainland. In the 1880s and '90s, musk-ox skins, with long thick hair, were valued as winter robes for European and American sleds and carriages. Finnie persuaded the Council of the Northwest Territories to declare the Arctic islands, where herds of musk-ox were still reasonably healthy, a game preserve. This was done by order-in-council, 19 July 1926, in the belief that unless the area was protected for the 'sole use of the aboriginal population of the Northwest Territories, there [*is*] a grave danger that these natives will be reduced to want and starvation through the wildlife being driven out of said preserves by the exploitation of the same by white traders and other white persons.'[17] Finnie's division was, however, soon to be the victim of the restraint measures of R.B. Bennett's administration. In 1930 it was eliminated. The Arctic was not an item of priority spending for the Bennett government. Finnie subsequently took an early and disheartened retirement from the civil service.

While preservation of musk-ox was a consideration in establishing the Arctic Islands Game Preserve, the ordinance also addressed the issue of sovereignty. In fact, the creation of the Arctic Islands Game Preserve is one document cited in a 1960 'Memorandum to Cabinet' dealing with sovereignty over the Arctic Archipelago. This move is held as an example of Canada asserting its claim to the Arctic islands.[18] The order-in-council establishing the preserve was rescinded in 1939 and replaced with far more detailed regulations affecting the same geographical area.[19] These new regulations affected licensing and made enforcement a more demanding and specific task than the order establishing the original preserve.

Within the preserve established in 1929, hunting and trapping were restricted to Canadian Native people resident in the area. The order-in-council also restricted the operation of fur trading posts in the region. Writing in *Eskimo Administration*, Jenness indicates that, subsequently, posts at Arctic Bay, Baffin Island, and at Port Leopold, Somerset Island, were closed in 1926 and 1927, respectively.[20]

However, a private and confidential report, submitted to the Department of the Interior by Dr. Frederick Banting of the University of Toronto, contradicts this claim.[21] Banting joined the Eastern Arctic Patrol on the *Beothic* in 1927 to accompany his friend, artist A.Y. Jackson, on a voyage around the eastern Arctic. The *Beothic* left Halifax on the afternoon of 16 July and first proceeded to Godhaven, Greenland, before visiting Canadian Arctic settlements. The *Beothic* arrived at Port Leopold on Somerset Island on 8 August and visited Arctic Bay on 12 August.[22] As the ship arrived, wireless messages were received by post managers that both posts were to be closed. Furs and post managers were taken on board.

Banting, a physician, was not one to sit around while his friend put paint to canvas and captured the novelty of the northern Canadian landscape. In addition to doing some painting of his own, he examined and wrote about the conditions of Inuit in the communities they visited. Upon his return to southern Ontario, Banting submitted a report to O.S. Finnie of the Department of the Interior, but not before he had talked to a reporter from the *Toronto Star*.[23] He was scathing in his criticism of the treatment of Inuit by the Hudson's Bay Company. Banting reported on cases of tuberculosis at Arctic Bay and on an influenza epidemic that had killed a considerable proportion of the population at Port Burwell in 1926.[24] The article that resulted from Banting's conversation with the *Star* reporter generated a detailed reply to every sentence of the story by the governor and council of the Hudson's Bay Company, headquartered in London, England.[25]

In his official report to Finnie, Banting observed that

it was our opportunity to visit two isolated Hudson Bay posts where there were no R.C.M.P. representatives, namely Arctic Bay and Port Leopold. Since the Hudson Bay supply boat could not call at these places this year, Mr. MacKenzie received word to bring out traders and their skins. At Arctic Bay alone there were twenty-three bales of fox furs taken aboard the *Beothic*. Since the number of skins taken by any trading company is maintained secret, I was unable to ascertain the exact number, but there are said to be at least one hundred skins per bale. The estimated values of skin from this port from this one post would therefore be in the neighbourhood of $100,000. The total native population of Arctic Bay consisting of about fifty men, women and children, came aboard, and it was pitiable to see them wearing cheap, dirty, print dresses, sweaters, sailor caps, for which they had no doubt given valuable white and blue fox skins.[26]

Banting's observations capture what many northern officials, including RCMP officers, often observed but upon which they did not often feel free to comment. His observations also provide important insight into the dependency that developed between the Hudson's Bay Company and Inuit throughout the eastern Arctic. It was a troubled relationship during the best of times and created particular hardship for Inuit trappers when fox fur prices and volumes declined.

The gravest danger which faces the Eskimo is his transfer from a race-long hunter to a dependent trapper. When the Eskimo becomes a trapper he becomes, to a large extent, dependent on the white man for food and clothing. Instead of wearing warm, light native clothing which time has taught him is most suitable for the climate, he is given cheap woollen and cotton, which the white man would not wear himself under the same conditions. His native food is seal, walrus, whale, fish, clams, bear, caribou, rabbit, eggs, duck, geese and ptarmigan. His only vegetable is the occasional sea weed. In exchange for his furs he is given white flour or sea biscuits, tea and tobacco, which do not provide sufficient fuel to keep his body warm and nourished.[27]

This observation is interesting when one looks at the food supplies available through the government store created in 1953 to serve the Inuit on the Lindstrom Peninsula near Craig Harbour. As will be discussed in the next chapter, they were not much more extensive than those available from the HBC in Arctic Bay in 1927. This is not entirely surprising as the 1953 order for the Resolute Bay and Craig Harbour communities was the responsibility of James Cantley, the former HBC trader who was, at the time, employed by the federal government.

Fur prices had always played a role in the relocation of Inuit. In the 1930s, fox pelt prices declined to a low of about twelve dollars. By 1937, the number of Hudson's Bay Company posts in northern and western Canada had been reduced from 334 to 230.[28] In 1929, before the depression set in, there was a brief period when fox pelts traded as high as fifty to sixty dollars.[29] With this dramatic decline in prices, Inuit trappers and their families, caught in a web of dependent relations, were devastated. A decline in fur prices was to have a similar impact on the well-being of Inuit at the time of the 1953 relocation. As noted in the previous chapter, by 1946, the price paid for fox pelts had risen to about twenty-five dollars. By 1949, they had declined in some cases to an incredible low of $3.50 – far below even the lowest price experienced during the depression. By 1952, the year before the high Arctic relocation, they had increased marginally to about six dollars.[30]

The observations of men like Banting, and the personal experiences and observations of many RCMP officers and other officials, created conflicting attitudes towards the Hudson's Bay Company within the civil service and the RCMP. For example, Henry Larsen did not look favourably upon the way 'The Company' treated Inuit.[31] Larsen was an important figure in the administration of the eastern Arctic during this period. The captain of the RCMP vessel *St. Roch*, Larsen patrolled the western Arctic in the late 1920s and '30s and ventured through the Northwest Passage after leaving Vancou-

Figure 6 The RCMP police vessel *St. Roch* in Burrard Inlet, Vancouver, in the late 1920s.

ver on 23 June 1940.[32] The *St. Roch* arrived in Halifax two years later. By the time of the relocations to Craig Harbour and Resolute Bay, Larsen was superintendent of the Arctic division – division 'G' – of the force. On the other hand, James Cantley, a government employee and another key figure in the 1953 relocations, was a strong defender of the Hudson's Bay Company. Cantley, like Alex Stevenson, was a former HBC employee and had been superintendent of Eastern Arctic Posts until 1940, when he founded the Baffin Trading Company. Until it closed in 1949, it operated posts alongside those of the Hudson's Bay Company in some communities of the eastern Arctic, including Inukjuak.

The debate over HBC's role in creating the welfare conditions the government had to address was ongoing within the civil service commencing in the 1920s. At various times throughout this period it was suggested that the government take over trading operations in the eastern Arctic as a way of addressing what some officials and RCMP officers saw as the company's gross exploitation of Inuit. These suggestions were countered by others within official circles who saw such suggestions as dangerous and as 'creeping socialism.' Nevertheless, in the climate of the reform-minded federal

Liberal government following the Second World War, government stores were created to service resettled Inuit at Resolute Bay and Craig Harbour. In the late 1950s, cooperatives emerged as an appealing 'third option.'[33]

Inuit presence in the high Arctic had previously been associated with Canadian efforts to show the flag. Prior to 1930, the Canadian government feared claims to the high Arctic by Norway. But in 1930 Norway's claim to the Sverdrup Islands was settled when the Canadian government compensated the Norwegian explorer Otto Sverdrup by the amount of $67,000 for the 1900-02 exploration of the islands in the eastern Arctic Archipelago that bear his name. In 1933, following a series of spectacular police patrols over incredible distances and in extremely harsh conditions across the high Arctic by officers stationed at the post on the Bache Peninsula, the post was closed and the officers relocated to Craig Harbour. While the credit for these patrols, in standard Arctic histories, is given to the RCMP, it is clear that without Inuit guides and assistance, such patrols would never have been possible. In 1940, the Craig Harbour post was closed. Thus Inuit had previously played a role in demonstrating Canadian sovereignty in the high Arctic.

Welfare concerns had also previously played a role in high Arctic relocations. In the 1930s, with the price of fox pelts in decline, government officials became interested in the possibility of reducing relief costs by dispersing some Inuit from areas where it was believed they could not make a living (because game had been depleted) to areas where it was believed resources were plentiful and unexploited. Clearly, however, the presence of the HBC, the relationship between Inuit and the HBC, and the inherently unstable nature of the fur trading economy, offers a more intelligible explanation for the problems Inuit experienced than do the references to Inuit 'overpopulation' found in many government documents. These texts illustrate the relationship between the state and corporate interests and the subsequent role of texts in socially constructing 'realities' to suit these interests.[34]

In 1933, the same year the RCMP vacated the post at Dundas Harbour, the government suggested to the Hudson's Bay Company that it would welcome an application to open a trading post at the same location. The company applied for the opportunity. In a letter to the Hudson's Bay Company written 15 March 1934, the deputy minister of the Department of the Interior granted the company a permit and made it clear that the company was responsible for the well-being of any Inuit it transferred to the post. It also specified that 'in the event of the company withdrawing from Devon Island the company agrees to return the natives to their homes at its own expense or to transfer them to such other trapping grounds as may be designated by the Department.'[35]

In 1934, the Hudson's Bay Company supply vessel *Nascopie* took twenty-two Inuit from Cape Dorset, twelve from Pangnirtung, and eighteen from Pond Inlet to Dundas Harbour. The so-called 'experiment' to see whether the Inuit could make a living at this location was a disaster. The harbour, while abundant in seals, whales, and walrus, was choked with so much rough ice that they were impossible to catch. Similar problems were encountered along the coast, and the shore ice also made it very difficult to set fox traps. In 1936, the *Nascopie* relocated most of the Inuit to Arctic Bay. Dundas Harbour was not reopened as a police post until 1945.

A year after being moved to Arctic Bay, Inuit were moved again, this time to Fort Ross at the south end of the Somerset Peninsula. This was a region with unexploited fox trapping potential and was seen as a connecting link between Hudson's Bay Company operations in the eastern and western Arctic.

However, supplying the post was a major problem due to ice conditions. The *Nascopie* could not reach the settlement in 1942 or in 1943. In November 1943, the two HBC employees were removed from the post by a U.S. military plane, which also left food for the Inuit. The post was reopened the following summer but finally closed in 1947. Inuit were then moved south to Spence Bay on the Boothia Peninsula. Unhappy with this outcome, Cape Dorset Inuit requested for years to be returned to their home community.[36] To this day, Cape Dorset people live in Spence Bay and the dynamics of the community reflect the presence of two populations who have barely inter-married.[37] In the cases of the relocations to Dundas Harbour, Arctic Bay, Fort Ross, and, finally, to Spence Bay, the Inuit were clearly an economic asset – a source of labour and of furs for the Hudson's Bay Company. Their relocation was clearly in the company's interests.

In 1930, the government relaxed its short-lived prohibition against trading posts on the Arctic islands. According to Jenness, the idea of relocating Inuit to Craig Harbour was discussed in 1935 by the secretary of the Northwest Territories Council in approving the reopening of the posts at Arctic Bay and Port Leopold. 'There was also the probability of establishing posts at Craig Harbour and on other islands in the Archipelago to facilitate the general plan of northern migration and settlement where game is abundant.'[38]

The idea of resettling Inuit on the Arctic islands was again suggested by Jenness in an address given in Toronto ten years later. Jenness reveals the attitude towards Inuit migrations that prevailed at the time of the 1953 relocations:

> There can be no doubt that Canada would immensely strengthen her claim to sovereignty over the uninhabited islands in her Arctic sector if she established either Eskimo settlements or (and) scientific research stations

on those islands that are most readily accessible by sea or by air. I say Eskimo settlements, not settlements of white men, because no ordinary white man is content to make his home and raise his family in a land where the usual amenities of civilized life can find no place, and where medical, educational, and other facilities are either non-existent or totally inadequate. The eskimos, on the other hand (whether from ignorance or not, makes no difference) prefer their Arctic home to any other, and they will gladly settle in any part of it provided they can kill enough seals and caribou and muskoxen to provide them with food and clothing, and can trap enough foxes to trade for guns, ammunition, and a few other articles they require from our civilization.[39]

Jenness, the leading Canadian anthropologist at the time whose fieldwork had been with the Copper Inuit, exhibited a shocking disregard for the nuances of Inuit ecological and economic strategies. One might have expected him, at least, to have some sense of the variability in Arctic conditions. His promotion of a relocation scheme here simply lends greater weight to the plan, though it is based on the same ethnocentric assumptions of other government officials.

Writing in *Eskimo Administration* (1964), Jenness makes it clear that concerns for sovereignty as well as welfare played a role in the decision to open a Hudson's Bay Company post at Dundas Harbour. In the book, he reproduces an article that cites a 'high official in the government service' as saying: 'In addition to the placing of the Eskimos in new regions where game is more abundant and work more regular, there is the angle of occupation of the country, now that aerial routes, mineral developments, and other reasons make possible the claims of other countries to part of Canada's Arctic, which now reaches to the North Pole.'[40]

The Dundas Harbour experience was not unknown to any of the originators of the 1953 relocation, which included Inspector Larsen of the Arctic division of the RCMP and Alex Stevenson of the Department of Northern Affairs and National Resources. At the time of the Dundas Harbour relocation, Stevenson was an employee of the Hudson's Bay Company in the eastern Arctic. Larsen regarded his Arctic patrols of the 1930s and '40s as upholding and enforcing Canadian sovereignty in the Arctic islands.[41] For example, in a memo to the deputy minister of the Department of Mines and Resources on 24 November 1944, S.T. Wood, who was then commissioner of the Northwest Territories, listed all the cairns set up by Commander Larsen during his 1944 visit to the Arctic on the *St. Roch*. The memo was entitled, 'British Sovereignty in the Arctic.'[42]

Thus the idea of relocating Inuit to the high Arctic did not suddenly occur to government officials in the spring of 1953. It was an old idea that had existed among civil servants and other northern 'experts' for nearly twenty years. The notion that Inuit were pliable, happy to live anywhere seals, snow, and foxes could be found, and that this was a solution to the problem of their welfare (portrayed as problems of overpopulation and scarce game), had already been well established through historical precedence.

Sovereignty, Welfare, and the 1953 Relocation

What role, then, did concerns for Arctic sovereignty piay in the 1953 relocation? The question is a critical one. The claim that sovereignty was the central and perhaps the sole reason for the move was the basis upon which the relocated Inuit and their descendants developed their claim against the federal government in the 1980s. They argued that 'there is overwhelming evidence to suggest that the central, if not the sole, reasons for the relocation of Inuit to the High Arctic was the desire by Canada to assert its sovereignty over the Arctic Islands and surrounding area.'[43] In 1987, the relocated Inuit and their descendants sought $10 million in compensation from the federal government. Their claim made front-page news.[44]

The circumstances and concerns outlined in the previous chapters make it clear that by 1953, federal officials were very concerned about welfare conditions – or at least the cost of relief payments – throughout the entire eastern Arctic and especially in Arctic Quebec. Furthermore, the attention given Arctic Quebec can be understood in light of the 1939 Supreme Court decision. This was not a region for which the federal government had previously accepted responsibility. The 1939 decision gave the federal government added administrative and financial responsibility it clearly did not wish to accept. Therefore, there is little doubt that these concerns – specifically the fear of recreating a dependency that government officials believed already existed between the Crown and other Native people – played a significant role in the relocation decision.

Government documents reveal that at the time of the 1953 relocations, the Liberal administration of Louis St. Laurent was also very concerned about sovereignty and the enforcement of Canadian law in the Arctic Archipelago. After the issue of relocation for purposes of sovereignty was raised by Inuit in the 1980s, these concerns in relation to the actual relocations became a major source of conflict between the government and the Inuit pursuing compensation.

Arctic sovereignty is an issue that has always attracted the attention of Canadians. The subject contributes to a romantic and passionate response to the Canadian North that has become part of the Canadian identity. The identity of Canadians as a northern and northward-looking people was successfully manipulated by John Diefenbaker during the 1957 federal election, a few years after the 1953 relocations. Canadian sovereignty over the Arctic islands and the waters that surround them is an issue that, historically, has attracted attention from the press, academics, and many institutes established to address northern issues.[45]

Sovereignty considerations have since arisen over the unauthorized passage of the American supertanker *Manhattan* through the Northwest Passage in 1970 and the American icebreaker *Polar Sea* in the summer of 1985. In January 1988, an agreement between Canada and the United States allowed the U.S. to send icebreakers through the Northwest Passage with Canadian permission and without prejudice to Canadian and American claims in law. The historical evidence is overwhelming that Canadian sovereignty over the islands and waters of the Arctic Archipelago has been, throughout most of this century, a matter of concern to the federal government and of considerable interest to the Canadian public.

Dealing with sovereignty as a lawyer is to be engaged in the prestigious field of international law. For all these reasons, the idea that Inuit were moved north to act as human 'flagpoles' and to strengthen Canada's claim to the Arctic islands during the cold war has attracted considerable attention and generated a passionate response from the Canadian public, from researchers, and from the legal community since Inuit claims were advanced in the 1980s.

The exact nature of the role played by sovereignty considerations in the 1953 relocations is therefore, of considerable importance. There are, and were at the time, legal and human rights implications to risking people's health, safety, and welfare for such reasons. The claim by Inuit and others has been that political leaders and senior officials deliberately risked the lives of Inuit to achieve national security objectives. The debate over the 1953 relocations became particularly heated in 1991. On 28 September 1991, a Montreal professor, Andrew Orkin, suggested on a CBC program *Quirks and Quarks* that Inuit lives were deliberately put at risk as part of a social 'experiment' to determine if Inuit could survive under extreme conditions, thus setting a precedent for moving other Inuit north. He argued that the experiment should be evaluated using the Nuremberg Code, which was created in 1947 following the trials of Nazis accused of war crimes – including conducting experiments on Jewish people. Despite Orkin's subsequent claims that no comparison with the medical experiments to which Jews were subjected in the Second World War was intended, it was impossible not to draw such comparisons given the manner in which the issues were framed.[46]

Government officials responded by claiming they were initiating a project – referred to in much of the government documentation as an 'experiment' – which they believed would improve the welfare conditions of Inuit. Not surprisingly, what actually happened – and why – is far more complex than many of the claims made and conclusions reached by those involved in the issue.

Contrary to the images suggested by Andrew Orkin when he used the Nuremberg Code in evaluating the 1953 relocation, the notion that people were relocated with a sense of malice, cruelty, or calculated disregard for their welfare is not substantiated by the historical record. However, this does not mean that people did not suffer or that the relocation was well planned or executed. Furthermore, evaluating these events is complicated by a familiar problem: regarding the norms, values, worldviews, and practices of the early 1950s with contemporary hindsight, norms, and values. While this does not excuse certain practices, it does affect how historians interpret the intent of those people involved. It is these problems of interpretation that make the 1953 relocations and the related historical evidence both interesting and problematic.

The social norms, values, and attitudes towards Native people that prevailed at the time are, it is hoped, not those most widely held today. However, there is little doubt that attitudes prevalent in the early 1950s still exist among many Canadians. Addressing the matter in 1987, Jacques Gerin, deputy minister of Indian affairs and northern development, claimed that he could not excuse what happened, but that the relocation was not carried out with any dark purpose.

> We cannot deny that living in Port Harrison and Resolute are two very different things. But there was no ulterior motive.
>
> This was not a police measure. While they were not forceably moved, it is also true that it is not the kind of thing the Government could get away with today without a lot of consultation ... Rightly or wrongly, at that time the Government moved all the Inuit great distances to settlements so they could be near health services.[47]

This statement typifies the problem. The claim made in the last sentence is preposterous. The health services available in Inukjuak at the time were infinitely better than those at Craig Harbour and certainly no worse than those available through the military base in Resolute Bay. Such claims have generated considerable controversy, fuelling the idea that the other claims in Gerin's statement are part of a cover-up, and that the real reasons for the relocation were indeed sinister.

The attitudes and values that help explain both why and how the relocation took place include paternalism, convictions about the superiority of European and North American culture, cultural norms, and notions of civilization, faith in progress and modernization, and fears about the systemic implications of welfare on the economy of the Inuit. This is not to say that at the time such values were singularly applied. Within the civil service and the Canadian public there were intense debates about whether Inuit should be left to make a living from trapping and traditional pursuits or introduced to education and wage employment.

However, both of these positions on the future of Inuit were commonly held with considerable paternalism and particular convictions about the nature of European culture relative to that of the Inuit.[48] Assimilation, then as now, was commonly seen as a humanitarian position that included the notion that Native people should be treated no differently from other Canadians – that they should have the same education, the same welfare and health services, and the same rights and privileges, with no special status. These are liberal perspectives of social justice and racial equality, increasingly questioned by many non-Native Canadians since the late 1960s. This questioning was, in large measure, inspired by the Native-led criticisms of the Trudeau administration's 1969 white paper on Indian affairs.

Canadian government concerns for Arctic sovereignty prior to 1950 have been detailed by Shelagh Grant in *Sovereignty or Security* (UBC Press, 1988). The Americans had never clearly recognized Canada's claims to the islands of the Arctic Archipelago. In fact, as discussed previously, a number of events prior to the Second World War were enough to confirm Canadian suspicions that ownership of the Arctic islands was still an open question in the minds of the American administration.

During the Second World War, the American military presence in the Canadian North was considerable and shocked some government officials once it was detailed. Of critical importance in raising the alarm was a report in the spring of 1943 on American activity in the Canadian North prepared by Malcolm MacDonald, the British high commissioner. MacDonald toured the Arctic in late February and March of 1943 and met Prime Minister Mackenzie King at the Ottawa airport upon his return. King recorded the event in his diary: 'A long talk with Malcolm MacDonald who had just returned from Edmonton. Says Americans sending 46,000 workers to construct another highway along Mackenzie river. I said to him that we were going to have a hard time after the war to prevent the U.S. attempting control of some Canadian situations.'[49] The response to this and other reports was a policy of 'Canadianization.' The federal government moved to compensate the American government for infrastructure constructed on Canadian soil as part of the war effort. This was an attempt to ensure that no questions arose about Canadian sovereignty and to ensure that the American presence in western and northern Canada did not give rise to ideas that the future of these regions lay in incorporation into the United States.

Agreement was reached with the United States government on the disposal of the Canol pipeline by an 'Exchange of Notes' on 7 June 1944. Further agreements were reached that affected American-built airfields, weather stations, port facilities, and telephone/telegraph lines. Plans were made to have the Department of Transport and the RCAF take over all northern weather stations and airfields constructed by the United States as part of the war effort.[50]

The period following the Second World War was one of intense interest in the North. These interests were propelled by recognition that major air routes to Europe, made possible by the developments in aviation during the war, would be across the eastern Arctic. Therefore, the region – including the Arctic islands – acquired new commercial importance. Arctic weather stations had been built for military purposes during the war and, in the case of the eastern Arctic, played a role in the movement of aircraft across the north Atlantic to Britain and to the European allies. While agreement had been reached that these stations would be turned over to Canadian control following the war, the lack of trained Canadian personnel meant that in many instances the Americans retained control.

New weather stations were planned for the Arctic. One of these was a jointly operated weather station and airfield at Resolute Bay, Cornwallis Island, constructed in the summer of 1947. By the summer of 1948, more than 200 American military personnel were at Resolute.[51] Supplies for Resolute were handled by American planes and ships as part of an annual resupply exercise named operation 'Nanook.'

In 1947, the Hudson's Bay supply ship *Nascopie*, with Alex Stevenson aboard, struck a rock and sank off Cape Dorset. The government had rented space aboard the Hudson's Bay Company ship SS *Ungava* in 1932 and had used the HBC ship *Nascopie* for the Eastern Arctic Patrols since 1933 when the Bennett government, desperately and unsuccessfully trying to slash government spending during the depression, had ceased to charter the SS *Beothic* for the annual patrols. The loss of the *Nascopie*, at a time when a more obvious government presence in the high Arctic was considered important, resulted in the construction and launch of the government vessel *C.D. Howe*. The ship became available for service to the eastern Arctic in the summer of 1950. In planning its maiden voyage, the government's concerns with sovereignty over the high Arctic were made clear. Resolute Bay was the focus of attention.

At the fifth meeting of the advisory committee on northern development in December 1949, it was suggested the *C.D. Howe* visit Resolute Bay as part of its schedule. 'The Northwest Territories Administration were of the opinion that in the interests of Canadian sovereignty, a token visit to Resolute Bay should be included in the proposed itinerary.'[52] The committee decided that, given the low volume of freight that could be accommodated on the trip, such an exercise should be delayed until the following year. The committee concluded that 'in view of the national importance of maintaining all evidences and acts of Canadian sovereignty, the question should again be considered as soon as the Transport ice-breaker is available to accompany the *C.D. Howe*.'[53]

In the late 1940s, Canadian military activity had increased significantly throughout the Arctic, with Canadian planes conducting aerial surveys of both land and ice conditions. At the same time, American interest in the region was intense. Writing in *Sovereignty or Security*, Shelagh Grant notes an article published in the 9 March 1944 issue of the American *Journal of Commerce*, which demonstrated a common American attitude towards Canadian claims.

> Interest in the area has been stirred by the need for clarification of post-war controls over air routes which will extten [*sic*] over the top of the world.
>
> According to airline methods of mapping the world, it is claimed that the shortest air routes from New York to Asia or to the East Indies, India and even Moscow lie directly over Arctic territories claimed by Canada.
>
> The claim is based on the 'sector principle' which many countries, including the United States, do not recognize as valid. This principle implies a declaration of ownership of lands without exploring or policing them. The United States does not recognize other claims to the area.[54]

Despite the open question about sovereignty over the Arctic islands, Grant concludes that the policy of Canadianizing military installations in the North was reasonably successful: 'Although there was still a heavy reliance on "paper sovereignty," Ottawa appeared to have retained a surprisingly good measure of control in the Arctic.'[55]

However, in 1949, the detonation of an atomic bomb by the Soviet Union changed the tone and direction of the cold war. Once again, the Arctic became a source of concern. American military personnel were convinced that the threat to North America now lay in Soviet bombers armed with nuclear weapons launching an attack on North America via polar routes.

As these military considerations were developing in the high Arctic, the welfare situation of Inuit in northern Quebec became more desperate, fuelled by the collapse in the price of Arctic fox pelts previously noted. That the problem was especially serious in Arctic Quebec is no surprise. Fur traders had established themselves at Port Harrison in 1909, with fierce rivalry developing between the Hudson's Bay Company and the Revillon Frères Trading Company after the former also located a post there in 1920. Revillon Frères was finally absorbed by the Hudson's Bay Company in 1937.[56]

However, in the 1940s, the Baffin Trading Company continued to put pressure on the Hudson's Bay Company in the community.

As a result of this confluence of concerns, the idea of relocating Inuit received new attention. In 1949 and again in 1950, the idea of relocating Inuit as a partial solution to the problem was discussed by the Northwest Territories Council.[57] By the fall of 1950, consideration was being given to conducting economic surveys of the Eureka area of Ellesmere Island.

In a memo to J.G. Wright of the Arctic division dated 13 October 1952, J.W. Burton of the Department Services Branch proposed a study of the resources in the vicinity of the weather station at Eureka near the northern tip of Ellesmere Island. 'Considering it will be necessary in the very near future to move a number of Eskimos from their presently poor productive hunting gounds [sic] to more favourable locations, it is considered that the Eureka area should be considered.'[58]

A week later, Wright replied to the request for funds to carry out the research: 'In the case in point [Eureka] I do not think we should stress any immediate requirement for Eskimos. In any mass movement of Eskimos we shall use more accessible areas first. However, if these Arctic weather stations prove to be a continuing project we may find it advisable to place one or two Eskimo families at certain stations. In such an event a knowledge of the local wild life of the land and the sea would be most valuable.'[59]

What started out as a concern for the deteriorating welfare conditions of Inuit in Arctic Quebec was to became entangled in the minds of some officials within the Department of Resources and Development and the RCMP with concerns about sovereignty and the enforcement of Canadian law in the Arctic Archipelago, both of which were fuelled by cold war fears, Soviet atomic capability, and American military paranoia.

The Relocation as an 'Experiment'
The use of the word 'experiment' in documents describing the 1953 relocation and other activities in the eastern Arctic at the time requires explanation. This use of language, which, as noted, has for some conjured up images of Nuremberg-style experiments, can only be understood when placed in a historical context. Part of this context includes the notion of 'nation-building' and the considerable optimism about Canada's future and its development following the Second World War. Federal civil servants saw themselves participating in the opening up of the North in a manner parallel to what had happened on the Prairies following Confederation and the building of the Canadian Pacific Railway.

Some insight into the pattern of language and expression used to describe the 1953 move of Inuit to the Arctic islands is to be found in earlier discussions of the same phenomenon. For example, in an article entitled

'Eskimos Advised to Go Northward,' published in the *Montreal Gazette* in 1943, Major McKeand, then superintendent of the eastern Arctic, employs the same logic and language when referring to the relocation of Inuit to Fort Ross: 'The Eskimos have a habit of sending messages to their friends in the south, asking them to come along to join them, and they talk as enthusiastically about the Far North as white pioneers used to speak of the far west.'[60]

The notion that relocated Inuit were happy and excited pioneers exploring new frontiers was an old one, and it had found expression in the federal administration for years. Of course, McKeand's statement in relation to the movement by the HBC of Inuit to Fort Ross obscures the real reason for their relocation. As noted, Inuit were moved by the company for commercial reasons, and the notion that they agreed to the relocation in the same sense as a non-Native person doing so under similar circumstances is highly suspect. The same is true, as we shall see, of the notion of consent in the case of the 1953 relocations.

The 1950s were, in many ways, a golden age for science and the idea of science in Canadian society. The Second World War had been won by science: the atomic age, the jet engine, the four-wheel drive vehicle. The 1950s saw the commercial introduction of plastics and electronics to Canadian homes. Serious questioning of the benefits of this postwar scientific boom had not yet occurred. Scientists were powerful people, and to be involved in something scientific was to be involved in something important. To be involved in 'experimental work' was to be involved in something important and legitimate. Consequently, such language was ubiquitous throughout the federal administration and within civil society.

For example, in the mid-1950s, the Catholic Church in discussing its boarding school at Chesterfield Inlet also invoked the notion of science and experimentation:

> In the first place, there are real inconveniences in the living-in system. But if this system was adopted it was because it is the most practical. The nomadism of the great majority of the central Arctic Eskimos and their dispersal in small and scattered camps would permit the usual day schools to serve but a few privileged pupils, or else oblige the parents to gather in large settlements, which in the present circumstances could have disastrous results on the Eskimo economy.
>
> We need hardly add that the present experiment is but the first groping step and in such matters, perfection is seldom attained at the initial attempt.[61]

Expressed pejoratively, and in the context of attempting to address the many problems of the eastern Arctic, the relocation 'experiment' was a matter of 'let's try this and see if it works,' which was true of many other things done by church and state. While questions can be raised about what happened and why, suggesting that a social science experiment, which deliberately endangered human life, was under way is to interpret the language used to describe the move without reference to the historical or social context of the period. Such expressions were part of a pattern of language already well established within the bureaucracy. The use of terms such as 'experiment' are best seen as attempts to socially construct particular images about what was happening and the worthiness of those involved.

Moving North – Again
Early in 1950, plans were made to transfer the RCMP detachment at Dundas Harbour, Devon Island, to Craig Harbour. However, the decision to move the detachment was delayed for a year because there would not be enough freight to justify sending the *C.D. Howe* into the high Arctic. On board the *C.D. Howe* during the patrol of 1950, the idea of not only relocating the RCMP detachment but also groups of Inuit took on more significance. Furthermore, the wording of Alex Stevenson's report on the 1950 patrol reveals how innocently the idea of addressing both welfare and sovereignty concerns had developed in his mind.

> If the R.C.M.P. close Dundas Harbour and reopen Craig Harbour I still think some natives should be left on Devon Island and others established on Ellesmere Island, spreading out along the East Coast as far north as Bache Peninsula. If Bache was well stocked, plus a radio transmitter, the police could make a patrol back and forth visiting camps en route. It would even be possible to go up from Craig in the spring – spend the summer at Bache – then return south in the fall or early winter.
>
> There is no doubt that country produce is plentiful in the aforementioned regions and Baffin Island Eskimos could easily live off the country. In this regard I understand that there is evidence that the Greenland Eskimos are hunting on Ellesmere Island and vicinity. Why not give the natives a chance to cover this country and also if it is considered necessary help improve the position regarding sovereignty rights.[62]

Much of the controversy over the role sovereignty concerns did or did not play in the 1953 relocations has centred about statements such as this, made by Alex Stevenson and others who were not, at the time, senior bureaucrats. However, dismissing them is a mistake.[63]

At the time, the department had only a handful of people dealing with the eastern Arctic. Many others concerned with the region knew little of it, having never been there. Alex Stevenson, like Henry Larsen, was held to know the region well and, furthermore, was fluent in Inuktitut. Despite being a junior officer – a 'fourth level public servant' as Gunther describes him,[64] Stevenson's impact on the thinking of the department, as revealed by the paper trail related to the 1953 relocations, was considerable. The same was true of Henry Larsen, whose role within the RCMP gave him considerable clout in the making of policy, not only within the RCMP but within the Department of Resources and Northern Development. Furthermore, Larsen's Arctic experience gave him influence even in departments like National Health and Welfare, where he was later to play a significant role in affecting policy on the payment of family allowances to Inuit. In other words, unlike the practices that subsequently developed, in the early 1950s policy was often developed at the field level by persons who, like Stevenson, while officially junior in rank, were incredibly influential by virtue of their considerable Arctic experience. Similar circumstances also help explain James Cantley's 1949 appointment to investigate the Arctic economy and his considerable influence in departmental policy thereafter, while still a comparatively junior officer of the department.

By the fall of 1950, clear and pressing reasons for relocating the RCMP detachment from Dundas Harbour to Ellesmere Island were presented. On 11 October 1950, Henry Larsen wrote to the commissioner of the RCMP in Ottawa and passed on to him observations made by Inspector Lee while he was with the joint U.S. and Canadian scientific expedition to establish weather and other stations in the Canadian Arctic. Inspector Lee indicated the following in a report to Larsen: 'To Bache Pen. Detachment via helicopter at 8.45 p.m. Buildings checked and found in poor repair. Detachment quarters filthy as Eskimos had been using same for skinning seal, otherwise in fair shape ... Indications are that Greenland Eskimos are using this point as a base as large cache of seal, walrus, white whale, fox and a musk-ox skull located by another Canadian Observer on Cape Camperdown in same area.'[65] In turn, the commissioner of the RCMP, S.T. Wood, forwarded the information to the deputy commissioner of the Northwest Territories at the Department of Resources and Development, Ottawa, suggesting that the Department of External Affairs should raise the matter with the Danish government to prevent Greenland Eskimos from hunting on Ellesmere Island.[66]

In 1951, Alex Stevenson again found himself in charge of the Eastern Arctic Patrol. The detachment was moved from Dundas Harbour to Craig Harbour on the southern tip of Ellesmere Island, with two Inuit families also moved to assist the RCMP. On 2 September, Stevenson sent a telegram to Ottawa announcing the successful reopening of the post. His description of the event, and the handing over to the detachment of the Canadian flag by

Figure 7   Re-establishing the RCMP Post at Craig Harbour, Ellesmere Island, in 1951.

Inspector Larsen, breaks ranks with a Canadian proclivity for modest expressions of patriotism. Stevenson's enthusiastic telegram reads:

SERVICE INCLUDED APPROPRIATE ANTHEMS [STOP] SHIP PASSENGERS COMMA ESKIMO FAMILIES IN ATTENDANCE [STOP] SNOW CLAD MOUNTAINS COMMA ICEBERGS COMMA GLACIERS TUNDRA AND WHITE CARIBOU FORMED BACKDROP FOR IMPRESS- IVE OCCASION [STOP] FILM BOARD UNIT COVERAGE [STOP] SOVEREIGNTY NOW IS A CINCH.[67]

While the white caribou paint a pleasant postcard image of the scene, there is little doubt that not one white caribou was near Craig Harbour on the day of the event, given the absence of caribou in the region. The reference to sovereignty is one many researchers have pointed to as a clear indication of government intentions. And there can be little doubt that sovereignty – something of concern to Henry Larsen and something challenged by Greenland Inuit hunting on Canadian soil – was the immediate reason for reopening the Craig Harbour detachment.

Of particular interest is the press release prepared by the department based on Alex Stevenson's telegram. It was a word-for-word duplication of the telegram, with one exception. The last line was omitted.[68]

Unbeknown to the party re-establishing the post at Craig Harbour, a

French scientist, J. Malaurie, had visited Ellesmere Island with a party of Greenland Inuit several months earlier between June 2 and 9. This was revealed to the secretary of state for external affairs in a memo sent by the Canadian embassy in Paris on 19 October 1951, a copy of which was forwarded to the commissioner of the RCMP in Ottawa. He, in turn, passed the memorandum on to Inspector Larsen of division 'G.'[69] The visit raised a number of issues. The embassy note indicated that Malaurie believed an agreement existed between Canada and the Danish government permitting Greenland Inuit to cross over to Ellesmere Island at any time. Malaurie's unauthorized presence on Canadian soil was clearly of concern. The RCMP, charged with enforcing Canadian law, had a problem on their hands. And this at a time when the ability to enforce Canadian law, given the presence of many American military personnel in the region and American refusal to clearly recognize Canadian claims, was also a consideration in strengthening Canadian sovereignty.

A number of laws were relevant to these concerns, including the Immigration Act, regulations prohibiting hunting by non-residents without a licence, and an Ordinance Respecting Scientists and Explorers made by the commissioner of the Northwest Territories in 1926 and requiring all scientists working in the territories to also obtain a licence. Malaurie's party included eleven people, nine sleds, and 110 dogs, which had to be supplied with meat. Canadian laws were being broken with no one in a position to enforce them.

Consequently, the deputy commissioner of the Northwest Territories, F.J.G. Cunningham,[70] was asked by J.A. Peacock, the commissioner of the RCMP, to establish whether an agreement allowing Greenland Inuit to visit Canada existed.[71] J.G. Bouchard of the public services section of the department looked into the matter. He responded to J.G. Wright, secretary of the council, on 17 January 1952. Bouchard discovered that an exchange of notes between Canada and Denmark, dated 14 October 1949, permitted such visits. However, visitors still required a visa issued by the Canadian consular authorities in Denmark. The suggestion was made that the matter be shelved until a visit to Canada by the governor of northern Greenland, scheduled for May 1952. The deputy minister of the Department of Resources and Development, Major General Hugh Young, was advised, as was the RCMP commissioner.[72]

The RCMP reaction to Greenland Inuit hunting on Canadian soil was to consider moving the Craig Harbour detachment up the coast of Ellesmere Island to the vicinity of Cape Sabine, near the post that had been closed in 1933. On 11 February 1952, L.H. Nicholson, recently appointed commissioner, wrote to General Hugh Young, the deputy minister, indicating that the RCMP was considering the move. The correspondence is worth examining at length, for it reveals a concern for the enforcement of Canadian law and the proposed relation of Inuit to that undertaking.

> The advantages of placing our Detachment directly across from Greenland would be that we then would have full control and supervision of Greenland Eskimos and others travelling back and forth, and over hunting activities they may engage in. As you already know, we had a Detachment established at Bache Peninsula in 1926 primarily for the maintenance of sovereignty.
>
> ... I believe one mistake in connection with the Ellesmere Island Detachments in those days was the hiring of Greenland Eskimos exclusively (accompanied by their families) to act as hunters and guides for our Detachments. People in those days were under the delusion that Canadian Eskimos were incapable and unsuited to live and travel in the islands north of Baffin Island on account of the longer dark period. This belief that only Greenland Eskimos were suitable was no doubt based on the fact that the American Explorers PEARY and MacMILLAN, hired exclusively large familites [*sic*] for their various expeditions in the area and for their many attempts to reach the North Pole. On the other hand, Captain Otto SVERDRUP in the Norwegian 'Fram' expedition spent the years from 1898-1904 in the same area and travelled quite as extensively without any Eskimo help whatever, and he spent his first winter in the neighbourhood of Cape Sabine ... and, as SVERDRUP describes it, the country around there at the time was teeming with game both on the land and in the sea. Therefore, if we could get a Detachment established here, we should, in addition to the two native families employed permanently by the Police, endeavour to recruit three or four good Eskimo families from the Pond Inlet area to be transported up there for the purpose of trapping, hunting, etc., and thereby in a general way improve their economic circumstances.[73]

It is clear from the letter that Nicholson had developed the idea in consultation with Henry Larsen who, in turn, had previously discussed the idea with Alex Stevenson. The idea of addressing the welfare problems of Inuit by relocating them to an area plentiful in game, and having them assist the RCMP in the maintenance of Canadian law (and hence, sovereignty), is clearly evident from the wording of the correspondence.

Elsewhere in the letter he includes a quote from Larsen on ice conditions at Craig Harbour. These comments suggest that Craig Harbour was not a good location for a post because of ice conditions and that 'conditions were much more favourable for establishing and supplying a Detachment in the vicinity of Cape Sabine than Craig Harbour.'[74] Nothing could have been further from the truth. In fact, prior to opening Craig Harbour, the deputy commissioner of the Northwest Territories Council had noted to the previous commissioner of the RCMP that in all the years the Craig Harbour detachment had been open, there had never been a problem in supplying it.[75]

These observations and contradictions raise questions about the actual knowledge of the men who conceived the relocation and whose ideas and opinions were respected because of their years of Arctic experience. The impression that the area around Cape Sabine/Bache Peninsula was 'teeming in game' later proved to be highly questionable, as did the notion that ice conditions were more favourable up the coast of Ellesmere than they were at Craig Harbour. Thus, 'experts,' who appear to have known considerably less than was attributed to them and who tended to rely on anecdotal information, played a vital role in making decisions that would significantly affect the lives of Inuit. Problems arose for similar reasons when Inuit were relocated to Resolute Bay. By all accounts, Henry Larsen was a pleasant and well-respected RCMP officer, with decades of Arctic experience. At Resolute Bay, Inuit were dropped off late in the summer of 1953 with the expectation on Larsen's part that they would be able to hunt walrus. Unbeknown to Larsen, it was late in the season and few walrus were left in the region.[76]

Nicholson's letter of February 1952, addressed to the deputy minister, also suggests, for the first time in detail, the trading and commercial arrangements to be used in meeting the needs of relocated Inuit.

> The Family Allowances which might be due to these people could be supplied by Northern Administration and Lands Branch, shipped up on the supply vessel with our own supplies and placed in our warehouse to be issued by our men as required. A small stock of necessities such as ammunition, tobacco, tea, sugar and some food could also, if found advisable, be stored at our Detachment and handled by our men for the benefit of the native trappers. The fur obtained by these native trappers could either be retained by the natives themselves, or stored in our warehouse until the arrival of the supply vessel and be handed over to the Officer in Charge of the Eastern Arctic Patrol ... to be disposed of on arrival in Montreal at the fur auction sales and the respective hunters credited with the proceeds.[77]

It is likely that these ideas were conveyed by Henry Larsen to Nicholson, who had just taken over the position of RCMP commissioner. As already discussed, Larsen was not a supporter of the Hudson's Bay Company, and the idea of the RCMP operating a store for the government would have appealed to his sensibilities. What Nicholson suggests in his letter is close to what was eventually created to meet the trading needs of those Inuit relocated to both Craig Harbour and Resolute Bay. Despite these intentions, the late arrival of the *C.D. Howe* in the high Arctic meant that ice conditions had deteriorated; this stopped any attempt to relocate the Craig Harbour detachment north to the Bache Peninsula in the summer of 1952.

Between 1950 and 1952, a number of incidents occurred in the eastern Arctic that involved the United States and violated Canadian sovereignty in the region. The Canadian government was fearful that these events would become public, thus raising the issue of Canadian sovereignty and focusing attention on what the Liberal government of the day was or was not doing to protect Canadian interests in the high Arctic. This concern is revealed in a note from the Privy Council Office to the clerk of the Privy Council dated 29 December 1952. The clerk of the Privy Council at the time was Jack Pickersgill. In his memo, R.A.J. Phillips notes a number of 'unfortunate incidents' and goes on to express his concerns. 'One or two of the incidents have come very close to being made public. The first listed, for instance, appeared in a manuscript written by Peter Inglis, which he agreed to suppress at the request of Mr. Claxton.'[78] Brooke Claxton was, at the time, the minister of national defence.

The incidents listed included an occasion on 5 March 1952 when an RCAF Lancaster on a photography mission was asked by Americans based at Thule, Greenland, to cease its operations off the coast of Baffin Island and land at Thule until authority was granted to proceed. The aircraft refused the order. Another incident involved a request from the United States government to use the air base at Alert to supply a research project on ice islands north of Ellesmere. The Americans requested Canadian permission on 21 March 1952[79] but proceeded with the mission before receiving clearance.[80]

Of particular interest is the response of Hugh Young, deputy minister of the Department of Resources and Development, to the request. In stating that the department had no objections, he emphasized that American personnel were not to disturb or remove any objects of archeological or historical importance.[81] One of the other incidents noted in the list provided to the clerk of the Privy Council was the destruction, that same year, of an archeological site on Banks Island in the western Arctic by American personnel on the icebreaker *Burton Island*. There was clearly a reason to be concerned about American personnel in the high Arctic who, because of the lack of enforcement capability, could break Canadian laws with impunity. The enforcement of regulations affecting hunting and archeological sites later becomes a reason, suggested by Alex Stevenson in his 1952 report on the Eastern Arctic Patrol, for locating an RCMP officer at Resolute Bay.

At the moment, there are no means of enforcing the Game Regulations, the protection of archaeological sites or any of the other ordinances affecting the Northwest Territories. To obtain any assistance at all, it would be necessary to write to three separate O.I.C's [Officer-in-Charge] i.e. of the meteorological and radio stations, the ionospheric station and the R.C.A.F. If all these men co-operate in enforcing the regulations – well and good. If one of them refuses, however, there is nothing the others can do about it and the outcome may well be that everyone in the place does as he sees fit. This situation is further aggravated when outsiders visit the area and may appear to violate some of the regulations. Criticism was heard of the number of specimens taken by R.F. Jasse when he was there last summer. Rightly or wrongly, the senior men at the stations felt he had abused his privileges and taken much more than he needed for scientific purposes. He was also reported to have killed a muskox in 'self-defense.'[82]

This suggestion is parroted a few months later in the memorandum of 29 December 1952 from the Privy Council Office to the clerk of the Privy Council.[83]

Records for this period reveal that towards the end of 1952 and into 1953, government concern for Canadian sovereignty in the high Arctic was considerable. By this time, plans to relocate Inuit to Ellesmere Island were already under active consideration in light of the activities of hunters from Greenland, and J.G. Wright of the Eskimo research section of the Department of Resources and Development claimed that Inuit at Inukjuak had indicated their 'willingness to emigrate.'[84] The Privy Council Office expressed concern about American plans to develop airstrips at weather stations on Ellesmere Island suitable for the heaviest of freighters and jet aircraft. The office went on to say that 'at these two joint Arctic weather stations, there is now a total of seven Canadians. If the airfields were developed, the installations would probably assume the character of small U.S. bases, and Canadian control might well be lost.'[85] In the same report, American requests to survey Ellesmere and Coburg islands with the idea of establishing radar stations to protect its base at Thule are noted. Coburg Island is a short distance from Craig Harbour. The number of American personnel relative to the few Canadians in the region is noted again.[86]

The Privy Council Office memorandum, cited above, then goes on to make the extent and nature of this concern abundantly clear:

It is government policy to attach importance to the maintenance of Canadian sovereignty in the Arctic. Until now the main activity in that area has been the weather station programme. We have maintained our tenuous position by providing half the staff, but in the entire Archipelago we have less than 50 men. This figure is now matched by the United States. Any new U.S. activity is bound to change the delicate balance of manpower in the northern Arctic. This in itself, of course, is not necessarily serious, but I think that our experiences since 1943 have indicated the extreme care which we must exercise to preserve Canadian sovereignty in remote areas where Canadians are outnumbered and outranked.

About a year ago Mr. Pearson remarked in private that he wondered how good our claim was to some areas of the Arctic. If it must rest on discovery and continous [sic] occupation, it may well be in future that our claim to some relative unexplored areas will be shaky indeed. I am not worried by formal claims, because the U.S. Administration has been eminently reasonable during the past years that we have been working together in the Arctic. Probably of much greater concern is the sort of *de facto* U.S. sovereignty which caused so much trouble in the last war and which might be exercised again.[87]

One of the recommendations contained in the summary which follows the above memo supports a proposal to have the RCMP reopen their post at Resolute.[88] The RCMP had maintained a post at Resolute until 1951 and apparently closed it because there was not enough work to justify the detachment.[89]

On 31 December 1952, a memorandum was sent from the under-secretary of state for external affairs, L.D. Wilgress, to Lester Pearson, the secretary of state for external affairs. In the memo, he warns Pearson of requests likely to come from the United States for the development of defence-related facilities in the high Arctic, including those noted above. He then proceeds to recall the policy of Canadianization initiated at the end of the war to deal with the American presence in the North and notes that it was carried out by the advisory committee on northern development, which had not met since 1949. Wilgress suggests that he write General Hugh Young, the deputy minister of resources and development and the chair of the committee, suggesting that the advisory committee urgently consider 'a vigorous policy in all Canadian Arctic services including communications, transportation, aids to navigation, meteorology and police.'[90]

Pearson followed up with a memorandum to the clerk of the Privy Council, Jack Pickersgill, dated 15 January. In it he identifies the threat to Canadian sovereignty posed by all the developments indicated in memos from Phillips and Wilgress.

One of the most important questions facing us now is this one of Arctic development and the danger of being excluded from such development on our own territory by U.S. penetration. I would like to have a talk with the Prime Minister about it as soon as possible preparatory to a full consideration of the question, either in Cabinet or by a Committee of the Cabinet. It is difficult to view with equanimity some of the things that are going on in the north to which reference is made in Phillips report. In general I am not so critical of United States action as I am our own inaction.[91]

But sovereignty concerns based on the presence of Americans in the high Arctic were not the only ones receiving attention in late 1952 and early 1953. As already noted, it was discovered in the fall of 1951 that a French scientist had visited Ellesmere Island with a group of Inuit in June of the same year. In the fall of 1952, it was discovered that a group of Greenland Inuit were actually living on the Bache Peninsula. This was noted when the officer-in-charge of the Department of Transport weather station at Eureka sent a telegram on 13 October to the RCMP 'G' division in Ottawa informing them that they had been visited by Greenland Inuit camped at Bache Peninsula.[92]

On 16 October 1952, J.A. Peacock, assistant director of the criminal investigation branch of the RCMP, notified Colonel F.G.J. Cunningham, director of the Northern Administration and Lands Branch of the Department of Resources and Development, that Greenland Inuit were living on the Bache Peninsula. The same day, Cunningham attended a meeting of the special Committee on Eskimo Affairs. At the meeting, 'consideration was given to the possibility of assisting natives to move from over-populated areas to places where they could more readily obtain a living. It was agreed that Craig Harbour and Cape Sabine on Ellesmere Island should be investigated as possible localities where Eskimos could be placed under the care of the R.C.M.Police detachments and arrangements made to enable them to obtain supplies through the loan fund.'[93] The meeting was chaired by the deputy minister, Hugh Young, and attended by Inspector Larsen, with James Cantley acting as secretary to the committee.

The matter of damage to an archeological site on Banks Island, previously noted, was also dealt with in January 1953. Writing to Hugh Young, L.D. Wilgress of External Affairs made it known that he was going to raise the issue with the United States embassy. In his letter he reveals the thinking of the deputy minister, thinking that appears to have already been in place and which likely accounts for the eventual decision to locate an RCMP officer at Resolute Bay.

I am in accord with your observation that incidents such as this raise the question as to whether there should not be supervision of all U.S. activities in isolated areas where there are no permanent Canadian representatives. This Department has always been anxious to insure that there should be opportunity for Canadian personnel to accompany any U.S. official group operating in Canada, and I should very much like to see full advantage being taken of these opportunities.[94]

The deputy minister was clearly of the opinion that a greater Canadian presence in the high Arctic was desirable. In response to Pearson's initiatives, cabinet dealt with the matter of Canada-U.S. relations in the Arctic at a 22 January meeting. It directed that the advisory committee on northern development (ACND) should 'consider and report immediately, and periodically thereafter, on all phases of development of the Canadian Arctic and on the means which might be employed to preserve or develop the political, administrative, scientific and defence interests of Canada in that area.'[95] At a subsequent meeting of the cabinet on 30 January, the membership of the ACND was expanded to include the deputy ministers of finance and mines and technical surveys and the commissioner of the RCMP as well as representation from the Defence Research Board.

At the advisory committee meeting of 16 February 1953, Jack Pickersgill, the secretary to the cabinet, 'reviewed the background of the Cabinet's concern about the Canadian north. Ministers had a genuine feeling of interest in this area but, unfortunately, incomplete knowledge of northern activities. There was also an apprehension of seeming encroachment on Canadian sovereignty.'[96] The overall tone and direction of this meeting is significant. It is clear from Pickersgill's comments and from those of the military personnel that a difference of opinion existed over the extent of the threat to Canadian sovereignty posed by the American presence in the high Arctic. General McNaughton, chairman of the permanent joint board of defence, 'expressed the view that there was nothing sinister about US activities in Canada.'[97] Pickersgill seems to have been less than convinced. He suggested a 'need to ensure that the civilian activities in the North were predominantly Canadian.'[98]

The idea that Inuit might play a role in Canadianizing the Arctic is then put forth by the RCMP commissioner and the deputy minister of resources and development. Commissioner Nicholson asks if 'any thought had been given to the potential of the inhabitants of the North – training, development or adaptabilities and so forth.'[99] General Young suggests that 'use could be made of the Eskimo, as they had considerable latent ability which could be developed gradually.'[100] This was also not a new idea. Within the military, some officers felt that Inuit were ideally suited to take over defence-related positions. Other officers, as later became clear in the Resolute relocation, were opposed to the idea.

In reviewing these events, Magnus Gunther in his 1992 report to the federal minister of Indian affairs and northern development, appears to have overlooked the comments made by both Commissioner Nicholson and

General Young at the ACND meeting of 16 February.[101] He concludes that 'had the primary or secondary purpose of sending Inuit north been sovereignty, this would have been the perfect place for Young to indicate what his Department was doing with respect to Pickersgill's concern, since at this point in the discussion, each department was listing activities that strengthened Canada's presence in the North in support of sovereignty.'[102]

However, this was far from the appropriate place to raise the matter as there was considerable disagreement between the military and others about the exact nature of the threat posed by the American presence. Announcing that Inuit were being relocated to the high Arctic where they would make a tangible contribution to Canadian sovereignty would have likely met with stiff opposition from the military. Given that the project was deemed important for a variety of reasons – including addressing the welfare problem in Arctic Quebec and giving an RCMP constable at Resolute sufficient responsibility to warrant the expense of locating one there – to jeopardize it by pointing out that Inuit would also make a contribution to Canadian sovereignty would have been entirely foolish. When the military did find out Inuit were being relocated to Resolute Bay, as noted in Chapter 4, they were opposed. As it was, the statements from both Nicholson and Young were likely intended to 'feel out' the situation to see if the idea might be taken up by others. However, the discussion shifted to matters of transportation.[103]

Even within the military, there were different ideas about the importance of Inuit to Canadian sovereignty. For example, in a secret memo to AMOT (Thru DASS)[104] dated 7 January 1950, S.E. Alexander of the Canadian Armed Forces suggested Inuit be used to secure the Canadian Arctic, especially against the supposed threat posed by the USSR. After reviewing developments in the USSR following the 1926 establishment of an Institute for Peoples of the North in Leningrad, the author advocates a more prominent role for Inuit in the development and defence of the Canadian North. He also reveals the mentality of the time regarding the threat posed by the USSR:

It would seem very obvious that in the 24 years that have elapsed since the inception of the Institute, an imposing number of natives have been thoroughly trained in various sciences and also thoroughly indoctrinated with the Red virus of future world domination.

... Anyone who has knowledge of the Eskimos know them to be most ingenious, of outstanding integrity, loyalty, patience and industrious far beyond the average whiteman in the Arctic. Given half a chance the Eskimos would prove beyond any doubt the ideal race for staffing Armed Service Units, meteorological Stations, hospitals, schools and scientific bases in the far North ... The undersigned spent considerable time in Alaska during the summer of 1949 and has been visiting there since 1935. There appears to him no reason why throughly [*sic*] trained University educated Eskimos acting as Red agents from Siberia cannot infiltrate into Alaska and on to Canada at the present time, if indeed, they have not done so already. On the other hand, properly educated and indoctrinated Eskimos in Canada would be a definite and positive bar to such a movement. It has been most noticeable in latter years, especially in the Mackenzie Delta, that the Eskimos are most unhappy with their lot and it would be well to examine the source or sources of such agitation.[105]

The author summed up his observations as follows:

The comparison is made: the USSR is doing much to assimilate the Eskimo and proving that this is not only feasible but profits the country as a whole. On the other hand, the Eskimo in Canada with exactly the same possibilities is rapidly becoming more and more dissatisfied, a ready and fertile ground for the seeds of Communism, and with the decline of the fur industry, is moving closer and closer to being a direct liability on the government. Something should be done to remedy this in the immediate future.[106]

Thus the idea that the presence of Inuit in the high Arctic might address Canadian concerns for sovereignty was inextricably linked to welfare concerns, expressed not only in terms of 'overpopulation' but as a fear of Inuit becoming dependent on the state. At the 16 February meeting, Jack Pickersgill's obvious desire to Canadianize operations in the region through a mix of military and civilian activities was clearly in the minds of both the commissioner of the RCMP and the deputy minister of resources and development.

Subsequently, the Department of Resources and Development was asked to prepare a report detailing Canadian activities in the North, to be submitted to cabinet through the minister of resources and development. Furthermore, Pickersgill suggested that one person be responsible for coordinating the needs and activities of all departments operating in the North. R.A. MacKay, assistant under secretary of state for external affairs, leaves the impression that Resources and Development should play this role. He suggested that the department not only coordinate a report to cabinet, but that 'all other departments should keep Resources and Development fully informed respecting their activities in the North and of any new developments that were being considered.'[107] Subsequently, in March, the secretariat of the ACND was placed under the Department of Resources and Development to which it reported.

By late 1992, the historical records on the Arctic relocations had been thoroughly combed by a number of researchers. No edicts or directives from Privy Council, the Prime Minister's Office, or from the Department of External Affairs supporting the notion that Inuit were relocated as part of a deliberate, high-level scheme to strengthen Canadian sovereignty in the Arctic had been found.[108] However, the idea that Inuit could make a contribution to Canadian sovereignty clearly existed at the field level within the department and had successfully combined with time and circumstances to find favour at senior administrative levels – including that of the deputy minister. The idea of combining the perceived need to address the growing welfare problems in Arctic Quebec with the need to provide the RCMP on Ellesmere Island with Inuit assistance in enforcing Canadian law was firmly in the minds of both the RCMP commissioner and the deputy minister of resources and development at the time of the February meeting. Furthermore, the idea that Inuit might be trained to take over civilian responsibilities in the area is clearly implied in the comments of the RCMP commissioner and the deputy minister. It was made obvious from the meeting that Resources and Development was to have an enhanced responsibility in dealing with 'seeming encroachment upon Canadian sovereignty,' which was in fact the subject of the meeting. The subsequent actions of the department can thus be seen as a response, in part, to this enhanced responsibility.

Relocating Inuit to the North was an established idea that had previously been invoked in the interests of the Hudson's Bay Company. These interests were often considered synonymous with concerns for Inuit welfare. In the case of the 1953 relocations, the Hudson's Bay Company was not involved. The notion of relocating Inuit to the Arctic to assist the RCMP, to make a tangible contribution to Canadian sovereignty, and to provide Inuit with a chance to continue in their hunting and trapping traditions in regions relatively unexploited belonged to Henry Larsen and Alex Stevenson. The idea that such relocations could solve the extensive and persistent welfare problems the department faced in Arctic Quebec appears to have belonged to James Cantley, who had clearly documented the problem in his 1950 economic survey. These men were operating within a well established precedent. Stevenson, with his passion for Arctic history and geography, was also well aware that the Inuit had occupied the high Arctic as recently as the sixteenth century and had abandoned it in the face of global cooling. It made sense to him that, with the climate changing again, northern migrations were more than possible.

The emerging concerns for the enforcement of Canadian law in the early 1950s gave impetus to the idea and ensured the support of Deputy Minister

Hugh Young. He was placed in a critical position of addressing the sovereignty issues identified at these meetings. It is no surprise that his department hastened to develop an idea that had been discussed at the field level within his ministry and the RCMP for years. Inuit from Arctic Quebec and from Pond Inlet were heading north.

4

Recolonizing the Arctic Islands: The 1953 Relocations to Resolute Bay and Craig Harbour

The Eskimo Loan Fund

The decision to relocate Inuit to the high Arctic was facilitated by the creation of the Eskimo Loan Fund within the Department of Resources and Development. While the fund, as well as the idea of sending Inuit north, had been discussed in the department since the previous October, it required the approval of the federal Treasury Board. It did not, therefore, come into existence until the end of the fiscal year. The fund was, in part, a response to the Cantley report of 1950 and to other indications in the early 1950s that the economic base upon which Inuit were increasingly dependent was in serious trouble.

On 16 March 1953, a memorandum was sent to the deputy minister by departmental officials in anticipation of the fund's approval. Four relocation projects were proposed for the high Arctic, including a project for Resolute Bay, one for Craig Harbour, another for Cape Herschel, and a fourth for Banks Island. The memorandum outlined in detail the plans for the high eastern Arctic and the rationale for implementing them. It is quoted in full because it provides a 'snapshot' of the southern administrator's perceptions of the high Arctic relocations at the planning stage:

Loan Project No.1
Cape Herschel
The R.C.M. Police will establish a detachment at Cape Herschel on the east coast of Ellesmere Island to police a region where Greenland natives have from time to time been hunting on Canadian territory. Native food supplies are reported to be plentiful. There are no Canadian Eskimos in the region and it is planned to move in five Eskimo families from overpopulated depressed areas and establish them in the native way of life under the direction of the R.C.M. Police. It is estimated that the cost of moving these Eskimos and equipping them to live at Cape Herschel will not exceed $200

per family or $1000 in all, which will be charged to the time in the estimates – Transportation of Eskimos – and to Relief.

As there is no trading post at Cape Herschel a year's stock of supplies for the natives will have to be provided in care of the R.C.M. Police. It is proposed to finance the purchase of these supplies under a loan issued to a leading Eskimo in the group. These goods will be held by the R.C.M. Police as security for the loan and will be dispensed by the Police on behalf of the loanee in return for payment in money or in kind and the proceeds will be credited to the loan. When goods for relief or Family Allowances are to be issued, the R.C.M. Police will make out the vouchers to show the order as being filled by the loanee who for this purpose will be acting as a trader. When the vouchers are approved for payment the amounts will be credited to the loan.

The exact cost of supplies will not be known until the families are selected and the purchases made. It is estimated that the cost should not exceed $1000 per family. The loan to the leader of the group should, therefore, be for an amount up to $5000.

Loan Project No. 2
Craig Harbour
This project is similar to Project 1. Five Eskimo families would be established under the R.C.M. Police to live off the country where native food supplies are reported to be good. The amount of the loan would be up to $5000.

Loan Project No. 3
Resolute Bay
It has been tentatively agreed with the R.C.M. Police that if we will move five Eskimo families to Resolute Bay they will reopen their detachment there to supervise the Eskimos and maintain law and order in a settlement where there are four different organizations, each with its own senior officer, and many transient visitors.

The Meteorological Service could offer permanent employment to at least one Eskimo to learn to replace one of their mechanics and might employ one or two others on semi-skilled jobs. All could be employed on menial jobs but, except in summer, we prefer at least part of the group to hunt and trap after the native way so that the children of employed Eskimos can learn the native way of life with them. The details as to terms of employment and rotation of labour will be carefully worked out for the guidance of the R.C.M. Police.

As there is no trading post at Resolute Bay this project would operate on the same principle as Project 1. The amount of the loan would be up to $5000.

The above three projects have as their object:

(a) Relief of population pressure in distressed areas.
(b) A pioneer experiment to determine if Eskimos can be induced to live on the northern islands which, relics indicate, once supported a native population.
(c) An experiment to work out a method by which Eskimos may be trained to replace white employees in the north without the Eskimo children losing touch with the native way of life.
(d) If these projects warrant it, more natives can be moved north both to these pioneer points and to other points to be selected later.[1]

As this memorandum makes clear, the well-developed plan called for the establishment of three high Arctic communities.

Choosing 'Volunteers'

A few days after the memo on the financing of the relocations was sent to the deputy minister, another report of Greenland Inuit camping in the vicinity of Bache Peninsula was received by the department. In a letter to L.D. Wilgress, under-secretary of state for external affairs, Deputy Minister Hugh Young suggests that 'the present would be an opportune time to bring this matter to the attention of the Danish Government and to ask for their co-operation in preventing natives from either country crossing over without complying with the usual immigration requirements.'[2] External Affairs proceeded to raise the matter with the Danish government. However, by June, all of the Greenland Inuit had left Ellesmere Island.

The creation of the Eskimo Loan Fund by the government in its budget appropriations for the fiscal year 1953-4 set in place the means for carrying out the relocation. The government then moved to identify Inuit who would be relocated, referring to them as 'volunteers.' Initially, some consideration was given to relocating Inuit from Fort Chimo Quebec, as well as from Pond Inlet and Inukjuak. At Fort Chimo, Inuit had been employed by the U.S. military as truck drivers, tractor operators, and as general labourers. They had been living in housing on the base. By 1953, the base had been closed and they needed employment.

The idea of employing Inuit at the Resolute base occurred to the department. The Canadian Air Force was approached about the possibility.[3] However, as the Fort Chimo Inuit had adapted to living in houses and none were available at Resolute Bay, and as a reply from the air force was not forthcoming in time to accommodate the departure and schedule of the *C.D. Howe*, it was decided not to relocate Inuit from Fort Chimo.[4]

The matter of consent is of concern in understanding the 1953 relocation.

As noted, in government records, relocatees are often referred to as 'volunteers.' In defending the actions of government, the Hickling Report, commissioned by the minister of Indian and northern affairs and tabled in September 1990, largely avoids the issue of consent. It concludes that every attempt was made to fully explain the project to Inuit and implies that they were volunteers.[5]

How were Inuit chosen? Were they 'volunteers'? Do the ideas of consultation and choice make sense given the historical period and the historical relationship between Inuit and white administrators and given the perception of white authority figures held by Inuit? Interviewed in 1992 about the process of selecting volunteers, former Constable Ross Gibson had this to say:[6]

I went out to the camps and chose the people. He [Constable Webster] threw the whole thing in my lap. Tommy Pallisser went with me on those patrols. Webster just said that this was being proposed and to pick seven or eight families and so on, and – ah –further information would be arriving.

... But anyway, we were having a cup of coffee in the office and he said, 'This is for you.' And he shoved the wire across to me. So I said, 'Where are we going to start? What are we going to do about this?' And of course, this is where ... well, it was all just out of the blue and something had to be started. So I called the school teacher and the Hudson's Bay and so on, and I said that I had received this thing and that I was going to be the one to bear the brunt of this thing and I asked for their cooperation.

Marjorie [Marjorie Hinds, the welfare teacher] wasn't too happy about that one, but I guess maybe it was the way I expressed myself. I might not have been up to standards – or her standards. I don't know. But anyway, – ah – this is when I encountered Tommy Pallisser and Roop said you can take Tommy Pallisser and Willya out on patrol.[7]

... It wasn't difficult choosing people because Tommy Pallisser was an excellent traveller. He was Labradorian – from Nain – and he knew the Native people and he knew the situation and how serious it was. So he had no problem because he'd been working with the company for years and he was set, you know. And everybody respected him and so I had nothing but everything on my side.

... I took the message – I took the wire right along with me and I just read the thing out. And I said this is it and they're going to move further up into the North and in fact they were going up into Twin Glaciers and Alexandra Fiord – which is where they were all going to go ... This was the original thing. They were going to open up a new detachment at the Bache Peninsula. So I was telling them all this. But little did I know that I was going to be the one who was going to take them.

... In fact, [the Inuit] were all approached and some were indifferent, some thought it was a good idea. And no Eskimo in my experience has ever given me a direct answer right off the bat. They wouldn't say, 'No – look, so and so ...' They have to have time to think about it you know. And after they'd thought about it they might change their minds, even while they were talking to you.

... I told them that it was going to get dark and I knew pretty well what it was like on Ellesmere Island. I never had been there, but I could read and was interested in what I'd heard, and from my own common sense I couldn't see that the conditions up there where they were going were that much different than where they already were, because they already lived in igloos. They already lived in skin tents. They already lived in canvas tents. They already hunted seal. The only thing I stressed and I stressed very much was the fact that it was going to get dark; that they were going to have three months of darkness, but that it wasn't going to get that dark – that we were going to be able to travel and be able to hunt but that it wasn't going to be that bad. You must remember that in Port Harrison they only had a couple of hours daylight. But this didn't matter. They only shrugged their shoulders and said, 'Iamungnuk' – which means 'it can't be helped' and – well – it couldn't be helped.[8]

Gibson further elaborated on the process of selection:

When we went out on that patrol, we travelled to all the camps between Port Harrison and Povungnituk and as far as Sugluk. But it was too late in the season to go any further. It was my decision. We had records and we knew who the good, bad, and indifferent hunters were, and you could see it in how they handled their camps. In the end, they all wanted to go ... We had records to go by and you can pretty well size things up from these. We were looking for – well – I guess the word I'd use would be 'resourceful' trappers ... Fatty wanted to go. He was always pulling fast ones and he was a real 'bum' in some ways and we thought that all he needed was a good environment and he would do well.[9]

From this account, it appears that at the time Inuit were consulted, the impression was that they were all to be relocated to Twin Glaciers on Ellesmere Island.[10] It also appears that the 'volunteers' were to be a chosen or selected group rather than a self-constituted group.

Furthermore, the last lines of the telegram received by the officer-in-charge at Inukjuak read: 'The heads of families should be good energetic hunters stop Families will be brought back home at end of one year if they so desire.'[11] Given that Constable Gibson read this telegram verbatim to the

Inuit whose camps he visited, it is clear that a promise that they would be returned in one year if they were not satisfied was given to all prospective relocatees. However, the telegram also makes it clear that families were to be distributed to 'Craig Harbour, Cape Herschel and Resolute Bay.'[12] According to Constable Gibson, Inuit were given the impression that they were all going to Twin Glaciers (which is in the vicinity of Cape Herschel). It is not surprising, then, that they were astonished to find themselves separated from each other and distributed to three (or, as it turned out, two) locations in the high Arctic. They indicated this in testimony before the House of Commons standing committee in 1990.

There were good reasons why Inuit were promised that they would be returned home at the end of a year if they were not satisfied in their new locations. Not the least of these would have been a concern in the minds of some government officials that if they did not successfully adapt to the new conditions, their reliance on social relief might increase. In any event, the promise was inserted in the telegrams sent to both Pond Inlet and Port Harrison by Henry Larsen and was communicated to the Inuit. It was not a promise that had been agreed upon by any other government officials. Nevertheless, as a promise made by the head of the RCMP Arctic division, the commitment was official.

The same day that he sent out the telegrams to his detachments at Pond Inlet and Inukjuak, Larsen wrote the director of the Northern Administration and Lands Branch of the Department of Resources and Development, clearly explaining his rationale:

Please note the reference in the messages to the Eskimo families being brought back to their homes. I considered it advisable to make that promise. I have in mind the sad experiences of those families of Eskimos (I believe eleven families) who were taken from Cape Dorset to Dundas Harbour in 1934 by the then Northern Administration and after being there with the Hudsons Bay Company for two years were taken to Arctic Bay and Fort Ross. They suffered hardships and asked, from time to time to be taken back to Cape Dorset. They never were taken back and the survivors and their descendants are still in the Fort Ross – Spence Bay district, under the supervision of our Spence Bay Detachment.[13]

In light of the history of this relocation, Larsen's concerns are easily understood. However, it was not a promise the department appeared to take seriously.

In testimony before the House of Commons standing committee in March of 1990, the Inuit witnesses all recalled that they had been promised they could return to their home communities if they so desired, but that when they inquired, they were discouraged from doing so and were, in fact, encouraged to have their relatives move to the high Arctic to join them.

> We were also told that we could return if we wanted to do so. So after one year elapsed, in 1954, my father went to the police and told them, 'This land is no good for us, it is too different, too harsh, too dark and too cold. We therefore cannot carry on here. We also have our relatives in Inukjouac to consider.' This is what they told the policeman, but they were refused, turned down. Instead, the policeman proposed to ask our people to send for the other relatives still in Inukjouac while we stayed in the High Arctic. When we were told this, my father and his group were given no more choice in the matter.[14]

In its investigation of the relocation, the Hickling Corporation appears to have missed the telegrams and Henry Larsen's letter altogether. Therefore, while agreeing that a promise to return the Inuit was made, the researchers focus on departmental understandings of what the promises were. The fact that Henry Larsen's promise, made in the telegrams, was not taken seriously is evidenced by the varying interpretations within the department of what was promised. Both Alex Stevenson and Ben Sivertz, who became the chief of the Arctic division following the 1953 reorganization of the department, later recalled that some sort of promise that Inuit would be returned within two or three years, if they were dissatisfied, had been made.[15]

The physical conditions at Resolute are very different from those on Ellesmere Island. So were the hunting opportunities. The following account of how Inuit were chosen for relocation to the high Arctic was offered to the House of Commons standing committee on aboriginal affairs by Markoosie Patsauq on 19 March 1990:

> Firstly, in 1953, we were approached by the Police (RCMP) when we were yet still living in our traditional camp. The policeman came to tell us that they required Inuit to go to the High Arctic. Our grandmother and all my cousins were going to move to the High Arctic, and he said my father had to come along with them. We were told this. We have always found this approach unacceptable because we ourselves did not initiate anything to ask to be moved elsewhere. We did not say 'Help us and move us out to a new land.' We were told that in the High Arctic, wildlife was very plentiful. That in our land, animals were too scarce, this was the reasoning that was put to us when they wanted us to move away. My father eventually agreed to this, because in those days, police were feared, their authority unquestioned. This applied to any Qallunaat (white men). They were all feared in those days. So my father gave in to the pressure of the Qallunaat, as did all

my other relatives. White men were authoritative and fearsome then, especially policemen.

So then we were sent away to a place they told us abounded in wildlife. We would never be hungry again, they told us. The Government carried out this move, even though we did not consent to being sent away.[16]

... In those days, Inuit were not educated and did not understand the meaning of written documents, nor how government worked and operated. We were also not aware of all Canadians' freedom to live where they so chose. We did not know of our right to refuse to be moved to the High Arctic, when we could have done so. Since we were not knowledgeable about this, though, our fathers gave in and agreed to move. They mostly feared the awesome authority of the Government.[17]

While Inuit may have agreed to the relocation, there were obvious misunderstandings about what this meant, about the possibilities of returning to Inukjuak, and even where they were actually going. Noting the deference for authority that characterized Inuit in their relations with non-Native authority figures at the time, it is clear that those relocated were not strictly 'volunteers.'

The Relocation
In the summer of 1952, the *C.D. Howe* was supposed to visit the east coast of Ellesmere Island in the vicinity of Cape Herschel to select a site for an RCMP post. In February of 1952, plans were made to reopen a post in the area and a scouting patrol to Ellesmere Island was to be part of the Eastern Arctic Patrol in the summer of 1952. However, the *C.D. Howe* was damaged by ice off Inukjuak and returned to Montreal for repairs. These were delayed by a strike. The scouting trip to Ellesmere Island was subsequently dropped from its 1952 summer schedule. Therefore, the intent in the summer of 1953 was to locate a site for a new police post, to construct the post, and to relocate Inuit from Pond Inlet and Port Harrison, Quebec, to the area.

On 28 July 1953, the *C.D. Howe* picked up the seven Inuit families from Port Harrison destined for Resolute Bay, Craig Harbour, and Cape Herschel. Clearly, it had not been decided which families would be located in the new communities to be established in the high Arctic: 'He [Sublieutenant O'Neil of the RCAF] asked how many families would be going to each of the three settlement areas. Mr. Cantley stated that this would be decided on the boat taking the Eskimo to their destination. It was not desirable to break up family groups if possible.'[18] What constituted a 'family group'? Like other indigenous cultures, Inuit society is based on extended family groupings. Being in the vicinity of uncles, cousins, second cousins, and so on, has, historically,

Figure 8 Inuit being loaded aboard the *C.D. Howe* at Inukjuak for the trip to the high Arctic in the summer of 1953. The woman in the centre, outfitted in a mink coat, is Marjorie Hinds, the welfare teacher in the settlement.

been vital to the functioning of Inuit cultural norms and behaviour. Travelling many miles for a cup of tea at a relative's camp was not unusual.

Speaking before the House of Commons standing committee on aboriginal affairs in 1990, John Amagoalik described what happened later when it was learned that the group on the *C.D. Howe* was to be broken up between Craig Harbour and Resolute Bay.

Figure 9 Inuit from Inukjuak aboard the *C.D. Howe* at Churchill, Manitoba, in the summer of 1953. The ship was being loaded for its trip to the high Arctic.

We had been promised that our whole group would stay together, that we would not be separated. But when we got near Craig Harbour on Ellesmere Island, the RCMP said to us, half of you have to get off here. We just went into a panic because they had promised that they would not separate us. That was the first broken promise. And when we realized it, I remember we were all on the deck of the *C.D. Howe*. All the women started to cry. And when women start to cry, the dogs join in. It was eerie. I was six years old then, standing on the deck of the ship. The women were crying, the dogs were howling, and the men had to huddle to decide who is going to go where.[19]

Thus the *C.D. Howe* left Port Harrison without anyone having a clear idea of who was to be relocated to which community. The ship then proceeded to Churchill where it spent a week loading. During this time, the Inuit camped near the old Hudson's Bay Company post at Fort Prince of Wales to the east of Churchill.[20]

Meanwhile, the *d'Iberville* was supposed to call at Pond Inlet and rendezvous with the *C.D. Howe* at Clyde River on the east coast of Baffin Island, where the Inuit from Port Harrison would be transferred to the *d'Iberville*. It was then to take Inuit from Pond Inlet and Port Harrison to Craig Harbour, Cape Herschel, and Resolute Bay.[21] However, the *d'Iberville* was unable to rendezvous with the *C.D. Howe* because it first went north to Cape Herschel to scout a site for the police post and settlement. There it encountered difficulties with ice conditions and couldn't return south in sufficient time to complete the rendezvous. Consequently, the *d'Iberville* did not call at Pond Inlet on the northern tip of Baffin Island. It was decided that the *C.D. Howe* would journey all the way to Craig Harbour, disembark the Inuit who were to be relocated to that community and transfer to the *d'Iberville* those Inuit destined for Cape Herschel and Resolute Bay.

The *C.D. Howe* called at Pond Inlet on 28 August, where three Inuit families, including twelve women and children, joined the others from Port Harrison. It also picked up Doug Wilkinson, a Canadian filmmaker who was working on what would become a well-known film entitled *Land of the Long Day*. The film featured a skilled Inuk hunter and trapper by the name of Idlout. Idlout would later move to Resolute Bay where his life would end tragically; by some accounts, in suicide.[22]

The *C.D. Howe* then proceeded to Craig Harbour. Wilkinson was to film the landings for the National Film Board, and his camera and film had been placed aboard the *d'Iberville* in Montreal. Also on board the *d'Iberville* was Fred Doucette, a photographer hired by the Department of Transport to record the ship's first voyage.

The *d'Iberville* had travelled first to Resolute Bay, where Inspector Henry Larsen had chosen a site for the Inuit village.[23] Next, the ship proceeded on to Craig Harbour, arriving on 12 August. It had unloaded supplies and, as previously noted, headed north to do what had not been accomplished the previous summer – locating a site for the new RCMP post. On 15 August, the *d'Iberville* anchored off Cape Herschel. Fred Doucette, the ship's photographer, describes what happened:

> Although we had arrived at our goal, all we could see was the floating ice surrounding the ship. To the officials in Ottawa, Cape Herschel seemed like a good location. It was at the narrowest point of Smith Sound, within 30 miles of the Greenland settlement of Etah. The RCMP detachment with a permanent eskimo settlement would help establish Canadian sovereignty on Ellesmere Island.
>
> As the visibility improved, RCMP Superintendent Henry Larsen made four flights by helicopter over the area, scouting for a site for the new detachment and settlement. On his return just after midnight, we learned that he thought conditions at the Cape did not look good ... We left Cape Herschel and steamed slowly southward in loose drifting pan ice.[24]

Following another attempt to reach the Cape, the *d'Iberville* headed even further north up the east coast of Ellesmere Island to the site of the old post abandoned in 1933. Again, the ship was blocked from shore by ice. Finally, the decision was made to create a new post to the south, between the Bache Peninsula and Cape Herschel at Alexandra Fiord. Because of this delay, the *d'Iberville* was unable to rendezvous with the *C.D. Howe* at Clyde River as originally planned.

Supplies were ferried to shore by helicopter and construction was begun. On 26 August, the *d'Iberville* weighed anchor and headed south to Craig Harbour to rendezvous with the *C.D. Howe*, leaving behind a carpenter to finish the job of constructing the new post. By the time the *C.D. Howe* reached Craig Harbour on 29 August, the *d'Iberville* was already at anchor. However, all was not well. While riding at anchor, the ship had been struck broadside by an iceberg. A 4 1/2 metre gash had been torn in the hull and Fred Doucette's bunk had moved a metre to starboard. Fortunately, the gash was well above the water line. It was an omen of things to come.

The *C.D. Howe* disembarked the Inuit families destined for Craig Harbour and departed. The *d'Iberville*, with families destined for Resolute Bay and Alexandra Fiord, headed up the east coast of Ellesmere Island where it encountered severe ice conditions. After drifting for about five hours, and following several helicopter flights to try to find a route into Alexandra Fiord some sixty-five kilometres to the north, the captain decided to return to Craig Harbour. The stranded carpenter, facing a rather unpleasant winter isolated on the coast of the island, got lucky. He was taken out of the settlement by the U.S. icebreaker *Staten Island*, returning from Alert on the northern tip of the island in September. It was one of the few trips that an icebreaker had ever been able to make that far north.

On 4 September, the *d'Iberville* off-loaded the families originally destined for Alexandra Fiord at Craig Harbour. However, neither these Inuit nor those who had arrived earlier remained at the police post for long. By 10 September, they had all been transported to a site on the Lindstrom Peninsula to the west of Grise Fiord. The site was 72 kilometres of open water from the RCMP post at Craig Harbour. The rationale for the move is found in police reports of the transfer: 'It was thought best to have the natives away from Craig Harbour at least by one day's sled travel. Being encamped at Craig Harbour might have given these natives the tendency to look for handouts when not absolutely necessary.'[25] There were actually three different locations of significance near Craig Harbour: the RCMP post at Craig Harbour itself; the original camp of relocated Inuit on the Lindstrom Peninsula, 72 kilometres away; and finally, the present-day community of Grise Fiord, which is located east of the original camp site on the Lindstrom Peninsula. Historical documents refer to the Inuit camp established at the time of the relocation as Craig Harbour.

The *d'Iberville* left Craig Harbour at 5:50 A.M. on 5 September and arrived

Figure 10 The Canadian icebreaker *d'Iberville* in pack ice near Resolute Bay in August 1955.

at Resolute Bay on 6 September, anchoring about five kilometres offshore. Four families, twenty-seven dogs, and equipment were off-loaded. Three of the families were from Port Harrison/Inukjuak and one was from Pond Inlet. The Inuit families included eleven children between one and sixteen years of age, eight of whom were less than eight years of age and four of whom were two years old or younger.[26] The group also included an eighty-year-old woman. They were left at a site on a tip of land several miles to the south of the military base and airstrip and on the west side of Resolute Bay, facing Griffith Island. Inuit on the Lindstrom Peninsula near Craig Harbour were in the hands of RCMP constable G.K. Sargent, while at Resolute Bay, Constable Ross Gibson was in charge. Doug Wilkinson, who was aboard the *C.D. Howe* to film the landing, recalls:

> There was stuff piled everywhere, and I saw a couple of tents put up for temporary shelter ... The whole thing was a smozzle from beginning to end. On the other hand, I think you have to remember that back in those days, no one really knew differently about that sort of thing. Everyone thought the Eskimo could live in their land anywhere. No one gave much thought to what really went into what it took to get this kind of knowledge to exist in an Arctic land – even as a hunter. As far as Alex Stevenson – even Alex,

as far as he was concerned I think – but certainly as far as Jim Cantley and the rest of the people in Arctic Services were concerned, all you had to do was get a hold of the RCMP and the Department of Transport to arrange for these people to be on the boat at a certain time, walk them off the other end and everything would be fine.[27]

Who went where?[28] At Resolute Bay, the Amagoalik family from Pond Inlet had been included to assist the Inukjuak Inuit in hunting and trapping. This family grouping included Amagoalik, his wife Kanooinoo, a son Ekaksak, daughter Merari, and another daughter Seepohrah, who was to die of pneumonia the following year at Mould Bay. From Inukjuak, the Sudlavenick family included Sudlavenick, his wife Sarah, a son Alle, and daughter Louisa. The community included Simeonie and his wife Sarah, both from Inukjuak, who also came to use the surname Amagoalik. Not included on the lists prepared by the department of those to be transferred was a son, Paul, born on the *C.D. Howe* and apparently named after the captain, Paul Fournier. Jaybeddie accompanied his brother Simeonie to the Resolute settlement. Simeonie and Sarah's household also included Jeannie, a woman who was no relation. Another family grouping included Alex, his wife Edith, and three sons, Markosie, Johnnie, and Jimmie, and a daughter Lizzie. Another child born to the Sudlavenick family, Martha, died of pneumonia despite the attempts of Dr. Otto Schaefer, aboard the *C.D. Howe*, to save the child – including the use of an oxygen tent made with a plastic raincoat. The community also included an elderly woman, Nellie, who had raised Simeonie and his brother Jaybeddie. Nellie was to die in 1956.

On the Lindstrom Peninsula, the community consisted of Fatty, his wife Mary, and children, Minnie and Larry. Sam Willie, who had been a special constable at Port Harrison, was accompanied by his wife Anna, and children, Elijah, Joalamee, Ikomak, and Lydia. Philapushie, his wife Annine, and children, Pauloosie and Elipsapee made up another family. Thomassie, who was to become the titular operator of the government store following the death of Fatty, was accompanied by wife Mary and children, Alle, Josephie, and Charlie. The largest family relocated to Craig Harbour was that of Angnakudlak, his wife Kowmayoo, and eight children, Damaras, Rhoda, Killiktee, Akjaleeapik, Tataga, Ootootee, Tookahsee, and Muckpa.

Life on a Gravel Beach
By the time the Inuit were landed on the Lindstrom Peninsula, Ellesmere Island, and at Resolute Bay, Cornwallis Island, winter was returning to the high Arctic. At Resolute, it snowed immediately after their arrival. It was still too early in the season for travel by dog team. Travel in the high Arctic is mostly on the sea ice. At the time of their arrival and for some considerable

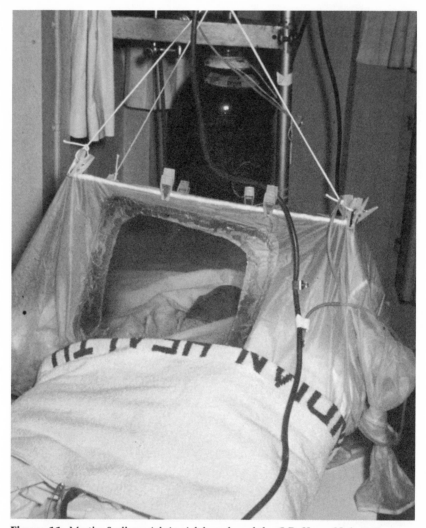

Figure 11 Martha Sudlavenich in sick bay aboard the *C.D. Howe*, 23 August 1955. The newborn was suffering from bronchial pneumonia and died a few hours after this photo was taken. Note the oxygen tent made from a plastic raincoat.

time thereafter, there was still-open water. Contrary to common Canadian images of the high Arctic, much of the land area, excepting gullies and river valleys, is windswept, bare, and devoid of snow most of the year. Travel over land, other than by foot, was difficult.

None of the Inuit had boats that would have permitted extensive travel on the still-open water. The RCMP in Craig Harbour had a boat at their disposal. This small powerboat was loaned to the Inuit living on the Lindstrom Peninsula, along with forty gallons of gasoline and oil, in the form of destitute relief.[29] At Resolute Bay, the boat supplied to the community and off-loaded from the *C.D. Howe* was missing its propeller and was virtually useless.[30]

Hunting, especially in the case of the Resolute Bay Inuit, was thus restricted. Furthermore, contrary to the idea that Inuit would be happy and successful anywhere, hunting requires intimate knowledge of an area – something that only time and experience can teach. While the Inuit at Grise Fiord had the benefit of the experience of the Inuk special constable and the RCMP stationed there, the Inuit at Resolute Bay were in for a much more difficult time. No prior knowledge of hunting conditions or possibilities existed in the community. Ross Gibson, the constable in charge of the move to Resolute, explains:

The man who saved the day and the whole project was Amagoalik from Pond Inlet. The Natives in Port Harrison had never set nets under the sea to catch seal. They had never hunted polar bear. And they were set in their ways and they weren't about to be told. And poor old Amagoalik was sweating himself to death making these nets. I'd never even seen the like! He even made them out of seal skin you know. And he put them under the ice. And those darn Port Harrison Natives wouldn't even give him ... they would stand around and watch him and they wouldn't even help him unless I asked them to help him. It was – well – if it hadn't been for Amagoalik or myself, those Port Harrison people would have sat on their fannies and they would have starved to death. They would have just given up and said again, 'It can't be helped.' And then they would have eaten the dogs and they would have died.

But they couldn't have died. The air force was behind us – only about three miles behind us. And this is the point where they came out and said they starved.[31] But they never starved because I had access to everything the air force had. I made a list and gave it to the commander in charge and that was no problem.

... You couldn't live off the land very easily at Resolute. We found this out. Half the time – the water – there were open leads. That lake up behind the camp – there were fish but when we caught them they were full of worms. So I bundled one up and I sent it out to Ottawa to have the thing analyzed and I got an urgent message back that the food was not even to be boiled or cooked – that the fish were not for human consumption if it wasn't absolutely necessary. So that really threw a wrench into the food business because the Eskimos do like their fish![32]

There were no caribou. There were lots of polar bear but you don't eat polar bear.[33] When we got there, the walrus had gone. And I told Henry Larsen. This was the only time Henry Larsen and I locked horns. He must have wondered what kind of an Irishman he had! But I said to him – and Craig Harbour had just had a successful hunt when we first arrived there – and I piped up and said, 'What the devil is going to happen to me if I'm going to Resolute Bay and there's not going to be anything there?' And Henry says, 'There will be all kinds of walrus there.' Well, there wasn't. They had all gone. They'd headed south.[34]

Differences between the two newly established communities, based on the quite different environmental circumstances and the presence of an air force base at Resolute Bay, quickly emerged.

The relationship between the Inuit at Resolute and the air base, a few miles to the north, soon became an issue. This issue was quickly identified by Ben Sivertz, administrative officer with the Arctic division of the Department of Resources and Development. He made a hasty trip to several communities in the eastern Arctic between 8 and 13 September 1953. Reporting on Resolute Bay, Sivertz noted: 'I think there is danger these people will become camp fringe dwellers, combing refuse dumps and looking for handouts. If they are to be hunters they should live away from the base. If they are to live near the base they should be made part of it.'[35] Appearing before the House of Commons standing committee on aboriginal affairs in March 1990, almost forty years after the relocation, John Amagoalik seems to confirm Sivertz's worst fears:[36]

'I remember being very excited when any military airplane arrived in Resolute, because we knew that the people on those airplanes had box lunches, food. We used to rush to the dump five miles away in the middle of winter to get those boxes of half-finished sandwiches. The two trays of sandwiches we had here – those were our treasures.'[37] The image this evokes is that of Inuit children and teenagers raiding the air force dump under the nose of the RCMP and other officials, becoming the 'camp fringe dwellers' about which Sivertz was so concerned.

As a remedy, Sivertz suggested complete integration of the Inuit into operations at Resolute Bay, with Inuit being trained to replace white workers whom he noted as giving 'indifferent service.' He advocated that Inuit be given the means to construct proper housing for themselves and that they receive the benefits of an Eskimo school.[38] This opinion was shared by other members of the administration, including G.W. Stead of the Department of Finance and a member of the ACND. Stead was part of a tour, by plane, of the Arctic islands between 8 and 12 September. He reported on his visit to Resolute:

An Eskimo family had just been put down a few days before by the sea supply at this place and an RCMP post established. The Eskimo family came from

Figure 12 RCMP constable Ross Gibson in Resolute Bay in 1954. Gibson did not learn of his transfer to the high Arctic with the Inuit until just before the loading and departure of the *C.D. Howe*. He died in Victoria in 1993.

Port Harrison on the east coast of Hudson Bay where the increasing Eskimo population has been outrunning the food supply. Eskimos lived at Resolute some 300 years ago and I can only presume that they moved away owing to a decline in the availability of food which now appears to be restored. As soon as the Eskimo family arrived problems of their relationship to the Military encampment began to appear. Where Military camps and Eskimo villages are adjacent, the Eskimos tend to be turned into 'camp followers.' The different moral bases of the two societies tend to exercise a harmful influence on both: junior members of the Armed forces attempt to get a corner on the output of handicrafts and so forth.[39]

In isolating Inuit women on the beach at Resolute, and forbidding them to come to the base, there was potential for other problems to emerge. It was the 'and so forth' that was of most concern to the department. Stead went on to express an opinion somewhat parallel to that of Sivertz.

> My opinion at the moment is that we should gradually drop the assumption that the Eskimo culture should be maintained. The process can be gradual, starting with the present points of contact between the cultures and extending it as further contacts demand or opportunity offers. Whether we like it or not these contacts are occurring and I think we should endeavour to fit the Eskimos for them. Beginning with the present younger generation training should be provided so that Eskimos can be made welcome in the present Military establishments as truck drivers, junior technicians and the like ... the key to the problem is the raising of living standards which will give reason to the training and will make demands upon the Eskimo so that he is obliged to develop steady work habits which alone will make him acceptable to the Military. This is not always the case now, the Eskimo being regarded as lazy, when after two or three days he feels the cash acquired to be sufficient for his present needs and goes fishing.[40]

A more clear statement about entirely different cultural values and which ones – by implication – were superior and were to prevail, is hard to imagine. However, the rate at which the cultural integration suggested by Sivertz and Stead was to proceed was a matter of some disagreement among department officials.

Asked to respond to Sivertz's memo, James Cantley of the department was less than enthusiastic. He argued that it would not be advisable to effect a complete change from the primitive way of life, as suggested by Sivertz: '[The Inuit] went north on the understanding that they would continue to live as hunters and trappers and that if they were satisfied to settle there permanently we would provide the trading facilities. On the other hand, if they did not like the country, they would be returned to their home again.'[41] Cantley then goes on to note the lack of enthusiasm among other government departments that the Department of Resources and Development encountered when it first considered the idea of relocation to the high Arctic.

> At the time these arrangements were made, we inquired into the possibilities of some of the people finding employment, but nobody was interested. As

a matter of fact, most of those we approached were quite lukewarm to the idea of transferring Eskimos to the high Arctic at all. However, we felt that the experiment was worth while. Faced with the problem of having too many people in northern Quebec for the resources available, it was felt that if we could encourage people to move to virtually virgin territories where there seemed to be every prospect that they could at least obtain sufficient food, it would be a step in the right direction.[42]

In effect, a policy of using the air force base as a vehicle for establishing systematic integration of Inuit workers would have implied failure of the relocation project because the project was developed on the assumption that Inuit would be more able to be self-sufficient in this 'virgin' territory.

Food, Fuel, Clothing, and Shelter

Given the circumstances, surviving the first winter in a completely foreign environment quickly became a problem, especially at the Resolute Bay settlement. In addition to being very different terrain, the species available at Resolute were limited compared to those at Inukjuak. At Inukjuak, Inuit were used to many different species of birds and their eggs, fish, whales, seals, and walrus. Caribou could be hunted to the south at Richmond Gulf.

However, even at Inukjuak, hunting was not particularly easy. This is not surprising, as the location of such settlements was determined historically by the fur trade. Locations for what became Arctic settlements were chosen for the trading of fox pelts and not necessarily for Inuit subsistence hunting. The essential criterion for posts – mostly established after the First World War – was that they be accessible by ship. Ross Gibson describes conditions at Inukjuak:

> Port Harrison wasn't that greatly endowed with ... well, we were on a flyway so in the spring and fall we had lots of birds. But we had to go way out onto the Sleeper Islands and to the Belcher Islands for walrus. And the only thing that was plentiful around there were the harbour seals. We had to go south for caribou. We had to go down to the Richmond Gulf for caribou; down to the tree line. And certainly there were no polar bears; Arctic fox, and, as I say, ptarmigan, but Lord ... we had to go out to the islands to go hunting. Good fish though. Good Arctic char.[43]

Caribou are few in the high Arctic. They are more plentiful on the southern tip of Ellesmere Island and in the Jones Sound/Truelove Lowland area between Ellesmere and Devon islands to the south than on Cornwallis Island where the Resolute settlement was located. Therefore, while the biological resources in the vicinity of Resolute Bay were limited, the resources available to the Inuit at Craig Harbour, which included those of Jones Sound, Devon Island – including the Truelove Lowland – and Coburg Island were among the richest in the high Arctic.

The idea of the Arctic as a frozen wasteland is a popular myth in Canadian culture. However, generalizations about the conditions faced by these two communities are difficult to make. The settlement on the Lindstrom Peninsula was certainly isolated, particularly in the early 1950s. The only means of travel out of the community was once a year on the supply ship or by dog team on the sea ice – a journey of 400 kilometres to Resolute Bay. On the other hand, Resolute Bay, with its air base, was not as isolated. However, it was not an area where there was an abundance of the resources to which Inukjuak Inuit were accustomed. While Resolute Bay Inuit were deprived of much of their traditional foods, the Inuit on the Lindstrom Peninsula fared somewhat better. Both locations are subject to perpetual darkness for much of the winter.

Inuit on the Lindstrom Peninsula, near Craig Harbour, apparently took twenty caribou within two weeks of their arrival. They were advised not to take any more in the area for fear of depleting them.[44] Thereafter, some restrictions were placed on the amount of game that could be taken. According to Ross Gibson, they also succeeded in hunting walrus immediately after their arrival.[45] By mid-October, the four Inuit families at Resolute Bay had taken one polar bear, five square-flipper seals, thirty-five silver jar seals, and eighty ptarmigan.[46]

The variety and number of species available to Inuit on the Lindstrom Peninsula were not so limited. In his annual report on game conditions in the vicinity of Craig Harbour, Corporal Sargent reported in August 1954 that in the year since they had arrived, the Inuit camped on the Lindstrom Peninsula had taken 26 caribou, 38 polar bear, 544 white fox, 9 blue fox, 35 ermine, 1 wolf, 80 rabbits, 300 ptarmigan, 35 eider ducks, 5 geese, 26 walrus, 7 narwhal, and 208 seal.[47]

Hunting had to be conducted without the benefit of any daylight between November and December. This long period of darkness was not something to which the Inuit from Inukjuak were accustomed and, by their own accounts, it affected their morale considerably: 'We discovered there were three months of total darkness. We had never been told that. One of the most devastating experiences we ever had was when we discovered that there was no sun from November until February.'[48] Some indication of the problem can also be gleaned from the wording of one of Constable Gibson's reports from Resolute Bay. Commenting on the small wooden building they had managed to build from discarded packing crates, he notes: 'The writer intends to occupy part of this building during some of the dark period to instruct the native children in simple schooling and to keep the

Figure 13 First polar bear hunt at Resolute Bay in 1953. Inuit from Inukjuak had never eaten polar bear. Inuit from Pond Inlet were transferred with them to help them adjust to living in the high Arctic.

camp active as the Port Harrison Natives have never experienced a dark period.'[49]

This was not a consideration overlooked by authorities in moving Inuit from Inukjuak. Writing to Commissioner L.H. Nicholson of the RCMP in April 1953, prior to the move, F.J.G. Cunningham of the department provided the rationale for moving Pond Inlet Inuit and noted concerns about the dark period: 'I think it would be most desirable, at the outset at least, to have one family at each place from the Pond Inlet area. These northern people are accustomed to the long darkness and could do a great deal to encourage and assist the newcomers in adjusting themselves to strange conditions.'[50] However, it appears that in the final analysis, little else was done to address the problem.

The same letter contains a specific reference to Idlout. At the time, the department considered him a prime candidate to go north with Inuit from Inukjuak. However, Idlout was working with Doug Wilkinson on the film *Land of the Long Day*. When approached about moving, Idlout declined. According to Doug Wilkinson, it was then intimated that he could have a job with the department if Idlout could be persuaded to move. Wilkinson declined. Wilkinson claims that there was subsequently some resentment towards him by departmental officials when he accompanied the *C.D. Howe* and then the *d'Iberville* to Ellesmere and Cornwallis islands to film the landing of the Inuit in these locations.[51]

Snow conditions and temperatures were also considerably different in the high Arctic. Not only are temperatures colder at Resolute Bay, but snow conditions at Resolute Bay and at the Lindstrom site, Grise Fiord, made it difficult to build igloos.[52] Therefore, the relocated families had to stay in canvas tents in a much colder climate for considerably longer than would have been the case in Arctic Quebec. Corporal Sargent of the Craig Harbour detachment reported on 31 December 1953, that 'all families are living in tents due lack [*sic*] of suitable snow for snow houses, but the difference in warmth has been compensated by the use of the buffalo skins as an outside covering.'[53]

Corporal Sargent's year-end report of 1953 reveals other problems. The location chosen on the Lindstrom Peninsula was inappropriate for landing a boat. The Inuit were using a boat loaned to them by the RCMP. Furthermore, the location appears to have been unpleasant for Inukjuak Inuit: 'The natives or majority of the same wish to move a little further west. Apparently it is the custom of the Port Harrison natives to reside in a valley where they can see a long way, whereas now they have a high cliff immediately at thier [*sic*] back.'[54] Not only was the landscape unusual for the Inuit from Inukjuak, at Resolute Bay it was particularly uninviting in some very practical ways. Cornwallis Island is essentially a very large, windswept pile of gravel with sparse vegetation cover, dominated by rocky beaches. Walking on such a terrain in sealskin *kamiks* is extremely hard on the feet. The women in the community, who carried children in their parka hoods, or *amautik* – as is the Inuit custom – found walking about to be particularly difficult.

Furthermore, while the men were encouraged to go out hunting and, in some cases, were able to do some work for the base, the women were strictly confined to the settlement in bitterly cold tents at temperatures as low as minus forty degrees Celsius in twenty-four-hour darkness, with virtually no source of light. Inuit recall that as children, they were cold and hungry.[55] It is obvious that women and children suffered considerably under these conditions.

Constable Ross Gibson confirms this confinement in a report filed the following summer: 'The natives have had little or no contact with the air base, particularly the women and children who have not left the camp site since their arrival.'[56] Gibson was apparently following orders and responding to the fear on the part of authorities that contact between Inuit women and servicemen at the North Camp base would result in sexual relationships becoming a problem. However, the confinement was particularly hard on

Figure 14 Erecting a Quonset hut on a beach ridge at Resolute Bay in September of 1953. The skin tents in the foreground, typical of those found historically in northern Quebec, were inappropriate for the high Arctic conditions.

the women, as one very strong Inuit habit in traditional camps was to travel – sometimes great distances – to visit relatives in other camps or, as already mentioned, just to have a cup of tea.

Fuel was a major problem for Inukjuak Inuit, who were used to burning wood. With no trees available, Inuit in Resolute scrounged the dump for wood scraps from building projects at the base and from packing crates to burn in handmade barrel stoves.[57] On the Lindstrom Peninsula, where no such source of wood existed, the most that could be burned were small willow branches. Eventually, seal-oil lamps, to which Inukjuak Inuit were not accustomed, had to be used.[58]

The clothing as well as the personal equipment with which Inuit arrived in Grise Fiord and Resolute Bay was quite inadequate. Corporal Sargent, in his year-end report, makes it clear the Port Harrison Inuit were used to 'whitemen's food stuffs and clothing.'[59] However, problems existed at both Grise Fiord and Resolute Bay in this regard. As will be discussed shortly, it appears the clothing supplied to the trading posts at Resolute Bay and Grise Fiord was inadequate and that supplies of non-Native foodstuffs were severely limited.

Sargent's comments make it clear that the food situation was complex. At Resolute Bay, the community included Nellie, an elderly woman in her eighties. For older people, the absence of traditional country food was a considerable problem, whereas for younger people, more accustomed to the provisions available from the Hudson's Bay Company, the problem would not have been so serious. Older Inuit have a particularly difficult time adjusting to a strange diet and have indicated they would go hungry if they could not get their traditional foods.[60] For example, as anyone living in another country and compelled to eat a diet different from their own realizes, being hungry is a matter of what one is used to and the *kind* of food available, not just quantity. Given the report that some Inuit were scrounging in the Resolute dump for sandwiches,[61] it appears that both kind and quantity were issues in the Resolute relocation. Given the importance of traditional foods – those indigenous to the region in which Inuit had been living – it is not hard to understand why officials, then and now, have difficulty understanding the reports of relocated Inuit that they were hungry.

A complete list of all the supplies available at the government trading store run by Thomassie at Craig Harbour in 1955 provides some indication of the foods available in Resolute Bay and Craig Harbour at the time. The list appears to be no better than the meagre supplies criticized by Dr. Banting in 1927 as he observed conditions at Arctic Bay. The food supplies available at Craig Harbour were: salt, baking powder, raisins, flour, sugar, rolled oats, pilot biscuits, jam, molasses, peanut butter, lard, tea, cocoa, coffee, Pablum, butter, and dried milk.[62]

The supplies available from the trading store established in Resolute Bay at the time of the move appear to have been grossly inadequate. On 9 November 1953, C.J. Marshall, a member of the government's advisory committee on northern development (ACND), in a confidential report to Graham Rowley, the secretary of the ACND, outlined the findings of a trip he had made to Resolute Bay with an RCAF resupply mission. Parts of Marshall's report are superficial. He reports that 'the settlement is a happy one because hunting has been very good.'[63]

While Marshall's observations on hunting conditions were limited, detailed notes on the supplies left for the Inuit are worthy of attention. Among the supplies he lists:

96 lbs. of butter at $1 a lb. but only 124 lbs. of lard at 25¢ a lb.
60 yds. of cheap cotton print.
24 towels at $1 each.
144 yds. of llama braid for decorating parkas – enough for about 30 parkas.
24 pairs of men's work pants although there are only 4 men in the group.

These pants are in sizes 36 to 38 which make them much to big for the Eskimo.

12 pairs of boys' pants although there are only 2 boys in the settlement.

5 lbs. of putty.

200 gals. of gasoline at approximately 70¢ a gal. and 2 Hot Shot batteries although the Eskimo have no internal combustion engine of any kind.

36 pairs of wool mitts which I understand the Eskimo can easily make for themselves.

12 pairs of men's braces for 4 men.

12 coat sweaters of poor quality and $7 each for 4 men.[64]

It is clear that among the supplies there was inadequate material to suitably clothe people for the climate and under the living conditions in question – a situation made all the more desperate by the absence of an adequate supply of caribou skins.

If caribou were scarce around Craig Harbour/Grise Fiord, they were even more scarce at Resolute Bay. Eventually, caribou had to be hunted across Lancaster Sound on Somerset Island, a location not accessible the first winter. In fact, from the records, it appears that even a trip, in the winter of 1954, around Griffith Island, lying immediately offshore to the south of the settlement, was a major undertaking for Corporal Gibson and the Inuit who accompanied him.[65]

At Craig Harbour, things were hardly better. Writing about Inuit conditions as of 31 December 1953, Corporal Sargent notes that 'the clothing of all natives, in the opinion of the writer, is not adequate at present in the form of skin clothing. All hunters have been provided for in the form of skin clothing, but the children have little or none at all.'[66] This passage is followed in the report by a restatement of a message sent to 'G' division of the RCMP requesting 200 clothing skins, which the RCAF was then to drop for the community.

Transportation appears to have been a serious problem in the case of the Lindstrom settlement. The open water in the summer and the shifting ice pack in the winter made travel between the police post at Craig Harbour and the camp on the Lindstrom Peninsula hazardous. Corporal Sargent describes one such incident: 'On October 16th several natives arrived at Craig Harbour by sled under very poor travelling conditions. They departed Craig Harbour on the seventeenth, but the ice had left the shore near thier [sic] camp. The provisions they were carrying were transported from the ice edge to land by samll [sic] boat in rough water which caused some of the supplies in being lost. The natives returned towards Craig Harbour and went to shore near Fieldup Point. They encamped there about four days and ran out of dog feed.'[67] Corporal Sargent then goes on to describe how a musk-ox killed one of the dogs and how the Inuit, in turn, shot two of them. However, the management of game and, especially, laws prohibiting the killing of musk-ox, even in the case of the Ellesmere Island community where game was more plentiful, limited hunting. 'Undoubtably if these natives were granted permission to hunt caribou as and when desired, the herds would soon be depleted. It is regretted that two musk-ox have been shot, but under the circumstances the writer advised the natives concerned they were perfectly in the right and that they would hear no more about the incident.'[68] Restrictions on the hunting of game and especially the killing of musk-ox were clearly an issue for relocated Inuit who had been told they were being moved to an area where game was more plentiful than it had been in Arctic Quebec:

> At the time of being moved my adoptive father was ... told only good things, such as ... the availability of caribou ... In regard to the promise of caribou, it sounded abundant. But in reality he was restricted to killing one caribou a year, being told it was to be enough. He was also told of abounding musk oxen. But it turned out to be: If you kill a musk ox, you can be fined $5000.00 or be arrested. This turned out to be an enticement, a lure, and a false one at that.[69]

Food and clothing were not the only items in short supply. Marshall, in his report of 9 November 1953, continued to describe other inadequacies in the equipment left at Resolute Bay. No rifles were included among the supplies, and the rifles brought from Inukjuak were apparently in poor condition. Marshall notes that Constable Gibson was 'attempting to borrow a rifle from the R.C.A.F. so that one of the Eskimos can continue to hunt.'[70] This and other concerns had been addressed in a memo to Alex Stevenson from James Cantley prior to the departure of Inuit from Inukjuak: 'It will also be necessary for you when you arrive at Craig Harbour, Cape Herschel and Resolute Bay, to check the rifles and shotguns owned by the families that are landed at each place and to see that they have the right ammunition for these rifles and guns.'[71] Gibson also reported that there was no duffle – essential for making warm Arctic clothing. However, the missing duffle was apparently eventually located by Constable Gibson among the supplies.[72]

The supplies sent for the government-run store included only three lanterns and no oil lamps for four families in a region where it is perpetually dark from November until February. There was no material sent for repairing tents, and from all accounts the Inuit tents were in terrible condition. Also missing were first aid supplies, fish hooks, and snow knives appropriate for building igloos.[73] Under such circumstances, it is hard to believe that the conditions endured during the first winter by those relocated were anything but extremely hard, bordering on the unbearable.

Marshall's observations on the inadequacy of the supplies have raised questions about the planning that went into the relocation. Historian Shelagh Grant suggests that incompetency on the part of government officials was to blame.[74] While incompetency was probably in evidence, there were other factors compounding the supply problems. Historical attitudes towards Inuit (such as those exhibited by James Cantley who prepared the order), thefts (most likely by stevedores aboard the *d'Iberville* and the *C.D. Howe*), and private sector suppliers taking advantage of government contracts were also contributing factors.[75]

One of the items missing from the boat supplied to the community at Resolute was its brass propeller. Consequently, Inuit were left without a functioning boat until an RCAF officer at the base was able to determine the correct pitch required to replace the missing propeller so that one could be ordered the following year.[76]

The order prepared by Cantley did not reflect the fact that the Inuit were farther north than any post with which he had previous experience. Given the low numbers of caribou near Craig Harbour and their complete absence at Resolute Bay, it is not surprising that both food and clothing shipped north was subsequently inadequate. It is also not surprising that the fuel and lamps provided were inadequate for a location of perpetual winter darkness. Finally, as Ben Sivertz has noted, the quality of goods supplied to government at the time was definitely inferior, and the systems for ordering supplies of the sort required for the relocation were woefully inadequate.[77]

The Arctic services division of the department was not about to let Marshall's criticisms pass without comment. F.J.G. Cunningham, the director of the division, received Marshall's 9 November report on Resolute Bay from Graham Rowley, the secretary of ACND. On 12 November, he directed James Cantley to respond to Marshall's criticisms. Cantley, the reader will recall, was a departmental employee with extensive experience ordering supplies for Hudson's Bay Company posts and for the Baffin Trading Company dating back to the 1930s and early 1940s.

It is particularly interesting to compare the final confidential communiqué, in which Marshall's observations are addressed by Cantley, with the original draft. Cunningham sent the final version to Rowley on 15 December 1953. An earlier draft of Cunningham's reply was produced by Cantley on 7 December. In it, he claims the order 'was confined to standard articles that many years of experience in trading posts in the Arctic has shown would be in greatest demand.'[78] However, Cantley's experience in ordering supplies was seven or eight years out of date. Furthermore, there was nothing 'standard' about the conditions and circumstances faced by Inuit in the high Arctic – the perpetual winter darkness and subsequent need for lamps being one of the uncommon conditions they faced.

In this draft letter, Cantley tacitly admits to the hasty planning that took place:

> Although the Port Harrison detachment had been informed of the proposal long before this and it had been discussed with the welfare teacher from Port Harrison in January, we had no definite decision until after the 1st of April. I might also say that Miss Hinds did inform the Constable at Port Harrison of the proposal on her return from Ottawa in January ... It is difficult to understand how the alleged short notice to the Constable has had any effect on the operations as the selection of the people had been made before the end of May and all necessary arrangements completed before the end of July.[79]

And, later in the same draft letter: 'To have the supplies at Churchill it was necessary to place an order before we were fully informed as to the numbers of Eskimos who would be moved, what they already had in the way of equipment, or what they would wish to buy when they had commenced to earn an income.'[80] These lines were removed from the final version sent to Rowley, as was the last sentence in the following comment addressing Marshall's observations on the condition of tents and the absence of any material with which to repair them: 'As the Eskimos had quite evidently been living in the same tents before they went to Resolute, it is not considered that the conditions they met with there were any more unpleasant than those they left. They are quite capable of looking after themselves and of carrying out their own tent repairs, etc.'[81]

With regard to the absence of lamps, Cunningham noted that 'Mr. Cantley reports that very few Eskimos use lamps, that they are accustomed to darkness in their homes during the winter period and use only the ordinary Eskimo stone lamp. An oil lamp is considered a luxury as few Eskimos can afford to buy coal oil or gasoline to operate them.'[82] Any attempt to operate such a lamp with gasoline would have produced more than just a little light. Cunningham, in paraphrasing Cantley, was clearly not well- versed in their operation.

Among the families relocated, a considerable number of Inuit had earned some income in Port Harrison from soapstone carving. However, no soapstone was sent north with the relocated Inuit. In the case of Grise Fiord, the Inuit took to carving whale bone, which they found lying on the beach.

Figure 15 Inuit tent village at Resolute Bay, 1955.

This was soon exhausted, and in a letter of 29 December 1953, Henry Larsen, the officer commanding division 'G,' requested that the director of the newly created Northern Administration and Lands Branch of the Department of Northern Affairs and National Resources quarry stone in Port Harrison for shipment, along with badly needed lumber for building, to Craig Harbour the following summer.[83]

Planning for the relocation had obviously been hurried. As noted, to send Inuit north, the department needed access to the Eskimo Loan Fund, created by the Treasury Board and available commencing fiscal year 1953-4. As the fiscal year runs from 1 April until 31 March, it was not until late in the fiscal year that the department was assured it would have a source of funds for the trading posts it proposed to operate as part of the relocation. Operations were also restricted by the short and fixed nature of the season that permitted the operation of the Eastern Arctic Patrol.

The following lines, illustrative of the extremes to which Cantley was prepared to go in rationalizing the supplies sent north, were also severely edited in the final version of the letter sent to Graham Rowley of ACND. Along with his suggestion that lamps were a luxury item, the following comment on washbasins reveals the austerity and residual welfare mentality dominating much public and official thinking at the time.

Eskimos do not practice washing in the winter time. No source of water is available and they could only melt down snow which would take an unconscionable [*sic*] amount of fuel. There are wash basins and pails available, if an Eskimo wishes to wash. Had tubs been supplied it is doubtful if they would have been used. Here again is an instance of a man who is experienced in the Arctic ordering only utensils which he knows are necessary and will be used.[84]

Northern experience seems to have occupied a sort of 'iconic' status among southern administrators. The senior level Arctic administrators were dependent for the most part on less senior bureaucrats, who often came from the private sector trade system where they had developed attitudes towards social welfare that served their objective interests. They relied instinctively on an ideological construction that assumed that relief creates dependency. When brought to government, these attitudes were given weight by their experience. Subsequently, officials quite low in rank had influences on departmental policies and practices not associated with their rank as civil servants.

The Government as Shopkeeper
As part of the relocation scheme, the government operated trading posts in both settlements. In each case, $5,000 taken from the newly created Eskimo Loan Fund was used to purchase supplies and equipment. These were shipped north on the *C.D. Howe*, having been loaded at Churchill.

The stores were to operate in the following manner. While the loans were given to an Inuk in each settlement, in fact, Inuit were titular traders only. The stores were, in effect, the responsibility of the RCMP. Wages paid to individual Inuit, as well as money from the sale of furs and other credits like family allowances, were supposed to be entered on the books of the trading store as credits against the account of the individual earning them. The individual could then take full payment in kind from the clerk of the store. The credit notes were forwarded to the department, which collected the funds from the organizations issuing the credit note. The funds were then applied against the loan. Ben Sivertz, who became head of the Arctic division of the newly created Department of Northern Affairs and National Resources in December 1953, explained the arrangement:

The amount of such a credit order is entered as a credit in the account of the Eskimo concerned ... In due course these credit notes are forwarded to this Department. We collect from the organization issuing the credit note and apply the money to the Resolute Bay Eskimo trading account. At present this account is in debt to the Crown because of an Eskimo loan with a substantial amount outstanding. Therefore, any credits received here are used to reduce the loan. You will understand that this still permits the individual Eskimo who earned the wages, sold the furs or received the family allowances to take full payment in kind from the clerk in the store at Resolute.[85]

The goods transferred to Resolute Bay and to Craig Harbour were marked up by an average of 25 per cent. Thus the $5,000 order had a market value of about $6,800 by the time it reached Resolute Bay. Inuit purchases not only paid back the loan fund but were also to generate a profit for the government. James Cantley explains why: 'The attitude we took in these operations was that a reasonable profit should be allowed for both on merchandise and furs. Whatever profit is made can be used to reduce the amounts of future loans required, or be prorated in the form of a dividend to the Eskimos themselves.'[86] In his criticisms of the operation at Resolute Bay, Marshall of the ACND suggested that as much as 40 per cent of the order was wasted and that, given the quality, the prices charged for the goods were too high.[87]

Constable Ross Gibson was also not impressed with the prices charged for goods. In a report dated 14 April 1954, he comments on the prices for rifles, presumably flown into the community to compensate for those not shipped with the relocated Inuit in the fall of 1953.

2. Recently the three 30-30 Winchester Rifles were received at this point for sale to the Eskimos. The purchase order received states the cost price of the rifles to be $64.65 each making a total of $193.95. The marked price for sale of these rifles is $90.00 thus making a difference of $25.35.
3. The writer does not wish to interfere with the prices set by the Department concerned but it is felt that a profit of $25.35 is in excess of the original cost per rifle. Could a check be made on these prices and those stated confirmed.[88]

The terms and conditions laid out by the Treasury Board in establishing the Eskimo Loan Fund are interesting. Section 3(3) of the conditions reads: 'Subject to Section six all loans shall be repayable within five years insofar as is possible, in equal annual instalments with interest on the unpaid balance at the rate of five per cent per annum, and all monies repaid on account of principal shall be deposited to the credit of the Fund and monies received on account of interest shall be deposited to the credit of the Consolidated Revenue Fund of Canada.'[89]

Section 6(b) of the agreement is particularly striking. One has to use a vivid imagination to relate the syllabic signatures of the Inuit on the agreement to the terms and conditions outlined by this section. It reads:

> The Minister ... may require that the principal sum of any loan with accrued interest, shall be repayable on demand, or if default in payment is made of any loan, or if the said Minister should consider any note given for such loan or any renewal thereof insecure, of which the Minister shall be the sole judge, he shall have full power to declare such note and all other notes made by the Eskimo in favour of the said Minister due and payable at any time, and suit therefore may be forthwith entered and tried in any court having jurisdiction and he may take possession of said goods or any of them and hold the same until such note or any renewal is fully paid, with interest and costs of taking and holding the said goods, or sell the same at public or private sale.[90]

The work of a characteristically keen legal mind, the above is likely one of the longest, barely understandable, and culturally inappropriate sentences in the entire history of the Arctic administration. Its purpose was to ensure the administration had recourse to expropriate goods to ensure loans were paid, a fairly draconian measure under the circumstances.

Thus, the Inuit of Craig Harbour and Resolute Bay were loaned money at 5 per cent to set up stores in both communities. The principle and interest was repayable to the government. However, the amounts charged for goods sold was clearly more than cost plus 5 per cent. Over time, the government made a profit from the operation. This profit went back into the loan fund to replenish it.

The extent and nature of the profit is illustrated by the following situation documented by Alan Marcus in *Polar Record*. 'In 1960, RCMP Asst. Supt. W.G. Fraser learned that during the previous trapping season, the Inuit at Grise Fiord received $6140 in credits for 379 white fox pelts. He further learned that the fox pelts were sold at auction by DNANR for $17,953. The balance of $11,800 in profit never reached the Inuit hunters.'[91] Shelagh Grant notes a 1960 memo from Glenn Warner of the RCMP, which indicates that the price set per pelt was between ten and fifteen dollars less than that paid by the Hudson's Bay Company.[92] In the case of furs sold to the store, it appears that the profit was comparable to profits that the Hudson's Bay Company typically received from its operations. The loans to the two stores were likely paid off quickly. However, other loans made under provisions of the fund did not always perform as well. The department was in an awkward position, operating stores for the benefit of Inuit that were turning a profit for the government.

Problems quickly arose with the bookkeeping. In a letter to Superintendent Larsen of the RCMP dated 23 November 1953, Cunningham noted a
discrepancy between the number of furs sold at auction in Montreal from
the Resolute Bay store, operated under the name of Salluviniq, and those
purchased by the store from the Inuit hunters and trappers. Two hundred
and ninety-five white foxes were purchased by the store, but only 279 of
these had been sent to Montreal. In total, 16 white foxes, 2 blue foxes, and
24 polar bear were unaccounted for.[93]

Furthermore, the accounts of three Inuit, Salluviniq, Simeonie, and
Jaybeddie, did not balance and required further credits to make up the
difference. Handicrafts had been purchased from a number of Inuit but no
record of the disposal of the handicrafts was found on the ledgers submitted
to Ottawa. There was no cash to cover them and no accounts for collection
for such items were sent in. Finally, Cunningham noted that $385.40 in
goods had been purchased by Constable Gibson, but his account had
apparently not been settled.[94]

Cunningham also observed that $270 in charges for labour from the
Meteorological Office had not been paid, and that Constable Gibson had
not submitted this account until the *C.D. Howe* had arrived for the 1954
sea lift. He complained that the delay in settling the account was not in
the interests of Salluviniq, who was paying interest on the money
borrowed to set up the store. Cunningham also noted that when an
inventory of the store was taken on 17 August, $154.11 worth of goods
was unaccounted for.[95] Constable Gibson was admonished to keep better
accounts.

On 23 December, H. Kearney of RCMP headquarters in Ottawa filed a
report with the force on his visit to Constable Gibson at Resolute. Kearney
had flown in on an RCAF plane on December 21 and had departed two hours
later. He reported that:

> It was ascertained that the 16 white foxes, 2 blue foxes and 24 polar bear
> skins, not previously accounted for by Cst. GIBSON ... had been sold locally
> by Cat. Gibson [*sic*] at $10.00 each for the 16 white foxes, $10.00 each for
> the 2 blue foxes and $20.00 each for the 24 polar bear skins, making a total
> of $560.00. Cst. Gibson had that sum and the undersigned took it into his
> charge and brought it out to Ottawa with him.
>
> 2. ... it was found that Cst. Gibson had sold Eskimo handicrafts for a total
>   sum of $189.00. He had that amount in cash and the undersigned
>   brought the cash out with him to Ottawa.
>
> 3. ... it was found that Cst. Gibson had purchased, for his own purposes,

stock from the Eskimo Trading Store to the value of $385.40. He had that
amount in cash and the undersigned brought it to Ottawa with him.[96]

Kearney confirmed that Gibson had up-to-date records of the store but had
not put them into record form. He added: 'In respect to his having kept the
above mentioned cash, rather than sending it out immediately, he said that
he did not know what he was supposed to do with the cash.'[97]

However, problems persisted with the accounting for the Resolute Bay
store. In August 1955, Alex Stevenson, aboard the *C.D. Howe*, contacted Ben
Sivertz to indicate that the ship was caught in pack ice and he was concerned
about being able to off-load at Resolute. The community was, however,
accessible to him by helicopter. In his communiqué he commented on the
accounting for the Resolute store.

> As requested by Mr. Cantley, I discussed the matter of accounting and books
> relating to the Eskimo Loan Fund at Resolute Bay with Constable Gibson.
> He advised me that he has recently sent out the complete record of all
> transactions in reply to your wireless message of July 15th requesting the
> quantities of fur, total amount of cheques, cash, etcetera. I told him that in
> the future he should make up a statement of each Eskimo account, listing
> the credits and debits ... Furthermore he was to follow the instructions given
> him last year dealing with casual labour, etcetera, and this should also be
> listed on the counter slips ... However, for this year I presume you will be
> able to check his accounts from the material he has sent out, including cash
> and a listing of the stock on hand.[98]

That accounts could be checked from this material was apparently wishful
thinking. By February 1956, Ben Sivertz was back to Ross Gibson with a host
of accounting problems.

> Since they came in, we have been endeavouring to make up the necessary
> accounting records from them but find that the information you have given
> is not nearly sufficient to enable us to do this. In some cases, the names of
> the people concerned are not given. In most cases the credits for furs, labour,
> etc., are not shown, nor any amounts entered for them. In some cases it is
> impossible for us to determine from the counterslips whether the entries
> should be made to the debit or credit of an account.[99]

It is obvious from these documents that accounting problems existed with
the Resolute Bay store. Ross Gibson was not an accountant and not only
had never had any training in keeping such books or records, in fact, he had
never had any official training as a police officer – other than a few days of

orientation in Ottawa, prior to being sent to Inukjuak from British Columbia, where he had been employed by the provincial police force. Subsequently, Corporal Sargent, who was in charge of the Craig Harbour detachment, went over the books of the store in Resolute with Corporal Gibson and, on 16 April 1956, submitted a balance statement for the trading store.[100]

In fairness to Constable Gibson, it appears that the troubles he encountered in keeping books for the store were not entirely of his making. The department was responsible for forwarding to the Resolute Bay trading store any credits earned by Inuit working for other government departments, expeditions, or other interests in the area. These credits were to be entered to the accounts of the Inuit who had earned them. It appears that the department failed to do this. In his report of 6 April, Corporal Sargent requested that such credits be forwarded for 1954-5.

Furthermore, he noted that Amagoalik had worked on a geological survey in the Mould Bay area in 1954 and that his wages for the period in question had not been credited to his account. As a consequence, his account was in the red. The practice would have been for the Geological Survey of Canada to reimburse the department for the work done, and the department, in turn, would forward a credit for the amount earned to Ross Gibson at Resolute. He would then enter it as a credit to the account of the Inuk earning the credit. Sargent requested that these credits be forwarded to Resolute Bay so that they could be carried on the balance statement for the store, making it clear that this had not been done.[101]

With this in mind, it is interesting to turn to the 1990 testimony of the Inuit before the House of Commons standing committee on aboriginal affairs. John Amagoalik stated: 'There is evidence of slave labour. It can only be labelled as slave labour, because my father and other relatives spent months at a time taking government surveyors around the high Arctic, mapping the islands and collecting mineral samples. And they were never paid for it.'[102] As a result of the standing committee's hearings, the RCMP was asked to investigate the charge that Inuit were used as unpaid labour in some situations. They concluded that the charges were unsubstantiated.[103] Their report further noted that the ledger sheets (cited above) were destroyed long ago and that this hampered their investigation. It appears likely that the bookkeeping practices used to operate the trading operation were a serious problem for the department, that Inuit did not always receive credit for their labour, and that such credits went to the general account of the federal government. In the available records, there is no indication that the problems noted above were ever rectified or that the Inuit in question ever received the monies owed to them. It appears that the internal investigation conducted by the RCMP failed to make some important connections and, subsequently, reached a false conclusion.

At first glance, the reference to 'slave labour' made by John Amagoalik in his testimony may seem to be extreme. However, in piecing together information from different sources, it becomes clear why such a phrase would come to mind.

In a master's thesis entitled 'Out in the Cold: The Legacy of Canada's Inuit Relocation Experiment in the High Arctic, 1953-1990' completed at Cambridge University in June 1990, Alan Marcus discusses a specific instance of accounting problems, similar to those noted above. His observations are noted in the July 1991 RCMP report into allegations of RCMP misconduct related to the relocation.

> For example, a Department of Transport receipt dated April 23, 1954, showed that 'Alex Simeonie, Salluviniq and Amagoalik earned $13.75 each and Jaybeddie earned $10.00 from wage employment at Resolute Bay.' An attached receipt issued from the Department of Resources and Development treasury office then grouped the five wages together forming a total sum of $65.00. This receipt was made out to the Eskimo loan fund and not to the individuals themselves.[104]

In fact, it seems likely from the timing of this receipt that it was for work done by these Inuit in repairing a broken pipeline. When one considers the conditions under which they worked, as described by Ross Gibson, it is not hard to understand why Inuit were more than concerned that their accounts were not credited with the money earned. Subsequently, 'slave labour' does not seem to be an extreme use of language. 'The native men were employed by the Department of Transport to uncover a broken pipeline. The writer set the hourly wage at one dollar twenty five cents. The reason being weather conditions of drifting snow and low temperatures where no white man would undertake the job, and further in some places the snow had drifted seven and eight feet thus making the work difficult.'[105] The RCMP were also asked to investigate other claims made before the House of Commons standing committee on aboriginal affairs, including the claims that women were forced to trade sexual favours for food and that Inuit mail was tampered with and dumped in the tip at Resolute Bay. They determined that these accusations were unfounded,[106] conclusions that should be noted in light of the questionable results of their investigation into the charge that Inuit did not receive remuneration for their labour, especially at Resolute Bay.

The problems with the government-run stores were, very simply, sloppy bookkeeping and the fact that, over time, the operations not only generated enough funds to pay back the loans and interest, but to create an embarrassing profit for the government.

This situation had not been overlooked by Ben Sivertz, executive assistant to Deputy Minister Hugh Young. The death in 1954 of Fatty, the titular trader operating the store at Grise Fiord, provided him with an opportunity. As Fatty had been the signatory to the loan for this operation, some legal matters had to be taken care of to wind up his estate and to deal with the fact that had his widow been cognizant of the law and the terms under which the stores operated, she could have made claims against the government for any profits that had accumulated. It appears that the government had established Fatty as the sole holder of a loan for the store at Craig Harbour, rather than a trustee for the operation.

Sivertz, who wanted to see cooperatives developed throughout the North, became head of the Arctic division on 1 March 1954. He contacted Father Coady of Antigonish, Nova Scotia, and Ralph Staples of the Co-operative Association of Canada. The association offered to assist. Clearing up the legal problems created by the loan to Fatty apparently took some time, as did developing a case for cooperatives. Sivertz raised the idea carefully from time to time. His most obvious attempt to get the idea considered was at a branch meeting within the department in May 1956. While not using the term cooperative, he proposed that, to avoid the problem created by the death of Fatty, partnerships be established and that 'a side agreement, in no way part of the loan agreement, should be made by the members of the partnership recognizing that any profits should be divided among the persons doing business with the partnership in proportion to the total of both purchases and sales of each individual compared to the grand total of purchases and sales.'[107] He went on to note: 'One of these days we shall probably need the machinery of a co-operative corporation for some Eskimo project. Development seems always to be outrunning us, and I would suggest that the Council be asked that an early date to consider a Co-operative Ordinance along the lines of legislation which I believe exists in most if not all provinces.'[108] Unfortunately, Sivertz was dealing with Frank Cunningham, the director of the Northern Administration and Lands Branch. He regarded cooperatives as 'communistic.' Sivertz recalls Cunningham saying: 'We're all liberal here and co-ops are socialistic – if not communistic – and we'll have nothing to do with it!'[109] Sivertz was not to get another chance until Alvin Hamilton became minister in the 1957 Diefenbaker administration.

Cunningham responded to the situation by having bank accounts established for each of the Inuit trading at the government stores. The accounts were created at the Billings Bridge Branch of the Canadian Bank of Commerce, Ottawa, in April 1957.[110] At almost the exact same time – 11 April 1957 – Sivertz replaced Cunningham as the director of the Lands and Administration Branch. Cunningham became the assistant deputy minister of northern affairs and national resources and R.A.J. Phillips, who had been an executive officer in the department, became chief of the Arctic division.

Alvin Hamilton, the new minister of Northern Affairs and National Resources, was a prairie Tory and sympathetic to the idea of northern cooperatives. However, there was still considerable resistance within the department, and it was not until 1960 that the government stores were finally converted to cooperatives. Was less paternalism exercised in their formation and operation than had been characteristic of the government as shopkeeper? Not entirely, as the following quote reveals:

> In election of the President, the same difficulties in nomination were experienced ... The first round did not produce results for each member of the Board received one vote. On the second balloting Simeonie – janitor at the Federal Day School – received 3 votes, Oolateetah – 2 votes. Cst Gordon's and my feelings were that Oolateetah was much more suitable for the office and we both tried to influence the Board that way by giving descriptions and requirements of the office before the election but – majority is what counts! Oolateetah was elected Vice-President. Constable Gordon was unanimously appointed Secretary-Treasurer but again it took time before the Directors or at least some of them could grasp the necessity for such decision. 'Why do they have to say that they want Constable Gordon – he is already running the store?' After the Board of Directors meeting, we asked the newly elected President to be around the next day to sign some cheques and also some papers related to takeover, but next morning it turned out that he had gone hunting.[111]

Between 1959 and 1962, fourteen cooperatives were created in the eastern Arctic – a movement that has been hugely successful. The largest was the West Baffin Eskimo Co-operative created at Cape Dorset with the assistance of James Houston. In 1961, the cooperative marketed more than $176,000 worth of carvings and prints.[112]

Relations with the Military

On 15 June 1953, as the relocation was being planned, Deputy Minister Hugh Young wrote to Brigadier Drury, deputy minister of national defence, to inform him of the department's intent to transfer some Inuit families to Cornwallis Island. He stated:

> While, primarily, our aim is to find out how Eskimos from the southern areas can adapt themselves to conditions in the high Arctic as hunters and trappers, we have also in mind the possibility that some of them, particularly those being placed at Resolute Bay, may be able to find employment. Local officers of the R.C.A.F. and of the Department of Transport at Resolute have

intimated that Eskimos could be used to advantage for a variety of jobs, either temporarily or on a permanent basis.

My reason for writing to you at this time is so that you may be informed of what we are proposing to do in these areas and to suggest that you might be good enough to pass on the information to your local officers at Resolute Bay. We would be very glad if they would co-operate with the R.C.M. Police in arranging for the Eskimos in this area to be given an opportunity to take any employment that may become available. The constable in charge will be able to make all arrangements and to deal with payments to the Eskimos.[113]

The *C.D. Howe* left Montreal for the eastern Arctic on 27 June 1953. On 6 July, the Department of National Defence in Ottawa received an opinion on the suggestions made by Deputy Minister Drury from the Air Officer Commanding, RCAF Transport Command, Robert Ripley.

Commander Ripley was responsible for RCAF operations at Resolute. He was not impressed with the idea of Inuit relocating to Resolute and with the idea of employing them at the base. He had a number of points to make.

1. The general principle of establishing Eskimos under proper surroundings where their standard of living can be improved and where they can be usefully employed cannot be argued against. However, casual information picked up by myself through various channels would indicate that the present proposal has not been discussed at the proper levels nor has the plan been formalized in a way that would guarantee some success ...
2. We now have considerable experience with Eskimos at Frobisher. Over a period of years, some of these people have become very useful, but the Majority have not, because their living and health standards make them unpredictable, unreliable and unemployable.
3. No mention is made of housing or support of the Eskimos. Because of the necessity of holding all present buildings for overflow of personnel during operations, no accommodation has been allocated for either the RCMP or Eskimo families. Similarly the question of food arises. Cornwallis Island cannot be expected to support Eskimos on a scale that would make them suitable for manual or other labour. They must have a properly balanced diet, clean healthy living accommodation and proper clothing will have to be supplied to them. Medical attention is not possible on Cornwallis other than the simplest first aid.[114]

This letter was forwarded by the deputy minister of the Department of National Defence to Major General Hugh Young on 20 July 1953, after the *C.D. Howe* had picked up the Inuit from Port Harrison. The letter suggested that an interdepartmental meeting be held to discuss the relocation.[115]

In a 'rear-guard action' to deal with this criticism, the department set about to organize the meeting for 10 August. F.J.G. Cunningham, director of the Lands and Administration Branch, also invited representatives from the RCMP, the director of the Indian Health Services, and personnel from the Department of Transport. Two statements made at this meeting are worthy of note. They are recorded in the minutes as follows: 'S/L O'Neil stated that he was afraid that there was not sufficient wildlife in the Resolute area to provide for the proposed Eskimo population. Mr. Cantley replied that he had reason to believe that there was sufficient marine life to support the Eskimo families concerned. No one could say for sure that this was the case and, consequently, the experiment was being staged.'[116] This statement by Cantley is probably one of the most callous in all those found in the records regarding the relocation.

Sivertz, drawing upon the rationale circulating within the department, was reported to have said that 'the Canadian Government is anxious to have Canadians occupying as much of the north as possible and it appeared that in many cases the Eskimo were the only people capable of doing this.'[117] Taken in context, this statement was clearly an attempt by Sivertz to give the department's project a more general sanction, in an attempt to win over the support of the air force. However, as noted previously, it was more than a ploy. There was considerable truth to it.

Later in the meeting, Sivertz attempts to smooth troubled waters and ensure the military that Inuit would not become a burden: 'The Eskimo's prime purpose in going to the High North was to see if it were possible for them to adapt themselves to conditions there and secure a reasonable living. Steps will be taken to see that the Eskimo are provided for in case the experiment is not successful and that every effort will be made to see that the R.C.A.F. is not inconvenienced.'[118] The rationale Sivertz presented to the military is echoed several months later by Graham Rowley, secretary to the advisory committee on northern development.

> One of the most sensitive areas for the maintenance of Canadian sovereignty is the Arctic Archipelago, where the main installations are the five weather stations. For effective occupation, permanent Canadian installations are highly desirable. Joint stations, in which another nation plays an equal part, do not provide the type of sole occupation that is desirable to demonstrate our sovereignty. It is known that doubts have been expressed as to the validity of our title in the archipelago.
>
> ... If Canada is to maintain and develop its position in the north, it must, even at considerable cost, build a growing corps of men, both civilian and service, who know the Arctic.[119]

He went on to note: 'As a longer term proposition, attention should be given to the possibility of training selected Eskimos to take over a part of the work. To the extent that this could be accomplished a permanent saving of manpower problems in the extreme north might be achieved.'[120]

Given the timing of these documents, it is clear that the Department of Defence had no prior knowledge that such a transfer was going to take place. This further supports the conclusion that the initiative for the relocation lay entirely within the Department of Resources and Development rather than at a more senior level of government. It is inconceivable that such an important decision, taken at a more senior level, such as cabinet, would have been unknown to the military who were seen to be playing a key role in protecting Canadian Arctic sovereignty.

Proof that the first winter was a difficult one and that, as already discussed, Constable Ross Gibson had to approach the military for help, comes from another letter sent from the office of the deputy minister of defence to Gordon Robertson, recently appointed deputy minister of northern affairs and national resources in February 1954.[121] Writing about the relocation to Resolute, James Sharpe of the Department of National Defence noted: 'It has been reported that these families have become, more or less, wards of the R.C.A.F. Detachment at Resolute Bay. It is perhaps possible that this state of affairs could have been avoided if a representative of the responsible Department had been posted to the R.C.A.F. Detachment, Resolute Bay, for the purpose of administering and directing the Eskimos involved in the experiment.'[122] Interviewed in 1992, Ross Gibson indicated that the military were not at all pleased with the presence of Inuit at Resolute Bay: 'They [the air force] felt that Resolute Bay was no place for them [the relocated Inuit]. Vice Marshal Ripley was in command, and he wasn't in favour of it. In fact, he would have flown them all out. Though in the end, he came around to thinking that it was a good idea.'[123]

Gordon Robertson replied to Sharpe on 18 February 1954, noting the meeting held with the air force the previous August. Robertson notes that Constable Gibson had recently visited the department in Ottawa and had reported that 'the four families in that area were camped about four miles from the base and had been very successful in their hunting and trapping. They had been able to obtain all the food they needed and had obtained sufficient fur and other produce to purchase their other requirements from the native store.'[124] This comment and Gibson's presence in Ottawa are extremely interesting for a number of reasons. Who was 'minding the store' while Constable Gibson was in Ottawa? What sort of scrounging and other events occurred in his absence, as presumably no one with Gibson's determination to keep Inuit separated from the base was carrying out his duties?

Second, it is obvious that Ross Gibson was in an impossible situation. He was on his own and responsible for patrolling other sites in the high Arctic. This left no one in charge while he was away. It was not as if he had any formal training for this kind of work as an RCMP officer. As observed earlier, he had little or none. He had been transferred from a posting near Vancouver to Inukjuak and now found himself in Resolute Bay. He spoke virtually no Inuktitut. He was determined to prove himself by being a good police officer and ensuring that the relocation was a success. Under the circumstances, this was virtually impossible without seeking the assistance of the air force. But Gibson also knew the attitude of the air force to the relocation and what the department and Henry Larsen, his officer in command, expected. The situation he presented to Robertson appears to have been one he was desperately trying to create – and, in fact, may have believed he had achieved.

In defending the department's actions to the deputy minister of defence, Robertson continues: 'In brief, they had been living their native life, had little or no contact with the base, and were so happy in their new surroundings that they were already talking of having some of their relatives from Port Harrison join them.'[125] Gordon Robertson's reply to the Department of Defence was copied to Commissioner Nicholson of the RCMP, who committed himself to verifying that everything at Resolute was 'okay.' By way of confirmation, Nicholson did nothing more than talk to Gibson once again and received the same reassurances that had been given Deputy Minister Robertson in the first place.

> Cst. Gibson advises that from his personal knowledge, the natives have had little or no contact with the air base, particularly the women and children who have not left the camp site since their arrival. With the exception of Christmas time when a small supply of fresh fruit was obtained for the native Christmas party, no foodstuffs have been obtained from the base, all necessities having been purchased under the supervision of Cst. Gibson.
>
> Upon their arrival at Resolute Bay, the Eskimos were given strict instructions that they were not to carry away any articles found in the base dump, however, packing boxes which would eventually have been destroyed, were removed by the natives and used for flooring and other purposes.[126]

Understating things seems to have been the deputy minister's specialty. In fact, Inuit used the packing boxes to build entire houses, as the department had provided them with none. Of even greater significance is the celebration of the fact that women and children had not left the camp since they had arrived.

Finally, Robertson's correspondence does 'double duty.' While attempting to convince the deputy minister of defence that the community was a

Figure 16 Resolute Bay in 1962, displaying numerous homes built with scrap lumber from the military base and Department of Transport weather station located north of the settlement.

happy, self-sufficient one, Gordon Robertson also attempted to convince the military that they should consider offering employment to Inuit from the village. Hunting and trapping could not on its own sustain Inuit relocated to Resolute Bay.

> In making these arrangements, we have not overlooked the possibility of some of the Eskimos at least finding employment, temporary or permanent. Just recently, we have been asked by the Meteorological Division of the Department of Transport for the assistance of the Eskimos in handling cargo during the spring and fall airlifts. Similar assistance could also be given in unloading operations from the sea-supply ships. Such casual employment will not interfere greatly with the natives present way of life and will enable them to add to their income during seasons when they have little else to do.
>
> The Meteorological Division is also considering the possibility of offering permanent employment to natives who can be trained for special jobs, and

possibly your Department might be inclined to consider this too. If so, we shall be glad to explore the possibilities with you and co-operate in any way possible.[127]

The difference between the emphasis on the separation between Inuit and the base noted in Robertson's defence of departmental actions and the content of the above quote is not insignificant. It reflects the conflict within the department over the future of Inuit. Should they, as Ben Sivertz had earlier suggested, be assimilated into a wage economy? Should they be encouraged to continue making a living hunting and trapping? Fear over the implications for welfare – for producing a situation in which Inuit might become dependent upon the state if introduced to wage employment and weaned away from traditional trapping pursuits – appears to have been paramount in the minds of administrators faced with the situation developing in Resolute Bay.

Despite realities that are obvious from the many reports, letters, and documents available on Resolute Bay, the police reports submitted by Corporal Ross Gibson continued to paint a rosy picture of how the 'experiment' was proceeding. The following line is typical of his descriptions: 'There has been no illness reported by the natives and all appear happy and content at this time.'[128] And Graham Rowley, secretary to the advisory committee on northern development, added to the picture, following a very brief visit: 'While at Resolute Bay I went down to the Eskimo camp where everybody appeared very cheerful.'[129]

In the case of Resolute Bay and the community near Craig Harbour, Alex Stevenson adds to the impression Ottawa officials had of how things were going in a message sent from the Eastern Arctic Patrol at Craig Harbour on 26 August 1954: 'Both projects Resolute and Craig huge success stop all natives happy with no desire to return home.'[130]

Upon his return to Ottawa, he furthered the impression.

I might say briefly at this time that both the projects at Resolute Bay and Craig Harbour have been a huge success during the past year. The Eskimos are all quite happy and contented, and were eager to advise us that they had never fared so well in their lives, particularly the Eskimos from Port Harrison, Quebec. In fact, they are so enthused with their new environment that they gave us the names of some of their immediate relatives who they would like to have come north to join them next year.[131]

It appears from the records that Inuit in both Pond Inlet and Port Harrison were intent on joining relatives in Resolute Bay and Grise Fiord. However, it also appears that some Inuit at Resolute Bay (and presumably Grise Fiord), despite the bravado about how contented they were, would have been quite happy to return to Inukjuak. This was not a message the department wanted to hear – or, in fact, heard. Not only did those examining the relocation have a vested interest in the outcome, but Inuit themselves, in deference to people they saw as having considerable power over them, were likely given to telling authorities and apparently important visitors what they wanted to hear.

However, some of their feelings did find their way into one of Ross Gibson's reports filed in November 1956. Gibson also suggests what is likely, in retrospect, one of the most intelligent ideas for dealing with the Resolute population ever received by the department.

> The matter of increasing the population at Resolute Bay by settling in more natives. To date the present natives have enjoyed virgin country surrounding Resolute Bay and have grown to be a part of it taking pride in their every undertaking. They do however from time to time express their desire to return to friends and relations at Port Harrison. They wish only to return to Harrison for one year. The writer believes they were promised by the Department they could return at the end of a given time. Rather than increase the population for the time being a rotation programme could be brought into effect by letting those who wish return to Port Harrison and have them replaced at Resolute by other keen and interested settlers.[132]

The suggestion went no further.

That conditions at Resolute were not pleasant – even years after the move. And that they were considerably different from those at Craig Harbour/Grise Fiord was confirmed by Bob Pilot, a former RCMP officer stationed at Craig Harbour (and at Grise Fiord after the police post was moved in the spring of 1956). Pilot testified before the House of Commons standing committee on aboriginal affairs in June 1990.

> In my opinion, the situation at Resolute Bay was undoubtably more severe than the situation in Grise Fiord. When we travelled, as we did each year from Grise Fiord to Resolute Bay by dog sled, the Inuit people who went with me and guided me across the ice and the islands to get to Resolute Bay were happy to leave Resolute Bay and come back to Grise Fiord. They found Resolute Bay to be extremely depressing, and I believe and I saw that the Inuit people there were living in a poorer environment and conditions than the people at Grise Fiord, albeit that the people in Grise Fiord were still living in sod huts. The people at Resolute Bay had made houses out of packing cases and out of any kind of old lumber they could get their hands on. They

were not properly insulated and they were not properly heated, whereas the sod huts, although it may not have been a very hygienic situation to be living in, did provide warmth and shelter and were far superior.[133]

Speaking before the House of Commons standing committee investigating the relocation in 1990, Sarah Amagoalik of Resolute Bay described conditions this way:

We were landed on a bare shore ... There was no other place possible. It started snowing just as we went about pitching our tents. The autumn had already arrived, it was bitterly cold and already freezing. There was not much water. We could not fetch water from anywhere. We had to melt ice for water, and this was an entirely new burden. Then when winter came, we had to settle into igloos. We moved into them as we were already accustomed to doing so when it was winter.[134] Then when spring came, we gathereed [sic] wood scraps from the dump, the dump of the qallunaat. We gathered this scraps [sic] all winter and spring. There was lots of wood at the dump, and they transported what they collected by dogteam. Then when summer came around, they started to build houses from the wood from the dump. Thus they collected scraps. There was not much to insulate these houses with. They even insulated them with cloth rags ... So when we got these houses, they were actually one room shacks with no other rooms. We had stoves, old drum stoves that we made ourselves. There was also a lot of coal discarded at the dump. So we went there to scrounge coal that we would use in our home made stoves. There was no other light. Old coal was our only source of heat all winter. After another winter went by, we were allowed one small light.[135]

The correspondence between Gordon Robertson and the Department of National Defence in the spring of 1954 appears to have ended any debate between the military and the department as to conditions at Resolute Bay. All parties seem to have been convinced that Inuit were fully satisfied in their new circumstances.

Late in December 1954, a CBC camera crew arrived in Resolute Bay to film Christmas in the high Arctic. They were particularly keen on filming the Inuit in the community built on the beach ridges to the south of the military base – not an easy thing to do in temperatures well below zero, twenty-four-hour darkness, and no electricity. The Inuit were subsequently invited to a party at the base so that the filming could be done there. Ross Gibson agreed to the arrangement. The footage made headline television viewing across the country. Ben Sivertz and others in the department watched with concern. The newsworthy event warranted a letter to Constable Gibson:

'From the television program we gathered that the Eskimos had been brought to the base just of [sic] this occasion and, presumably, also at Christmas time. We assume therefore that there has been no change in the arrangements which were made to have the people live at some distance from the base and to visit the base only when it is necessary for them to do so.'[136]

Gibson's reply was understandably defensive:

> The Eskimos at Resolute Bay visited the Air Force camp at the invitation and request of the Officer Commanding the base. This was the first time since the arrival of the natives at Resolute that the women have visited this base and the men only when employed here. Persons from the Canadian Broadcast Company attempted to photograph the natives at their camp but due to low temperatures and poor lighting this was impossible. Every effort was made to accomplish their mission without bringing the natives to the air base. The writer is aware that surroundings would appear that the air force were responsible for the welfare of the natives. It will be further noted that a party was later held at the Eskimo camp on December 24th, when the writer personally presented the children and adults with presents totalling forty five dollars. The writer felt this was a good investment and would assist in the general morale of the camp for the Natives to be given extra consideration at this time.[137]

By this time, the women and children had been virtual prisoners in the camp for nearly a year and a half. Gibson's response is that of a well-conditioned police officer, attempting to carry out orders without criticizing government policy. However, his sentiments could not be kept under wraps entirely. Later in the same report, Gibson responds to Sivertz's inquiry about sending more Inuit north. In doing so, he implies – without actually saying so – that Resolute Bay is not a good location and that the relocation was badly planned:

> Probably more natives should come to the area as it is felt there is plenty of game about. Should these steps be taken to settle more natives the writer respectfully suggests that a camp at Intrepid Bay or Assistance Bay would be satisfactory ... The complete removal of the present camp might be most satisfactory to either of these sights [sic] ... The persons chosen should not be aged as only too soon would they become a burden with only a few efficient trappers in the area. Should it be decided to move more natives to this area the writer suggests the Detachment where they are to come from be informed at the earliest possible date and the Detachment to where they are going. The writer feels that more time and thought could have been applied to the Resolute Bay Project.[138]

While the idea of relocating Inuit to the high Arctic may have been around for years prior to 1953, it is obvious that the planning of the actual event was, in Constable Gibson's opinion, inadequate, the location questionable, and the circumstances he was expected to address – political and otherwise – nearly impossible.

New Arrivals

By the spring of 1954, the department was considering adding more members to the high Arctic communities, including four families to Resolute Bay.[139] The RCMP at both Resolute and Craig Harbour were consulted. Corporal Sargent suggested that, in light of the number of animals taken by hunters at Craig Harbour, two or more additional families could be sent to the community.

However, there was one potential relocatee in which the department was not interested. In the spring of 1954, following the collapse of the white fox prices and upon completion of his role in Doug Wilkinson's film, *Land of the Long Day*, Joseph Idlout decided that he wished to move his family to Resolute from Pond Inlet. Despite their initial interest in relocating Idlout, the department was no longer keen on the idea. Amagoalik and his family had already been relocated from Pond Inlet to help familiarize the Inukjuak Inuit with hunting conditions in the high Arctic, and Idlout was not needed for this purpose. F.J.G. Cunningham wrote Henry Larsen of the RCMP with his opinion on Idlout's request to move: 'Idlout has never had any difficulty in making a satisfactory living for himself and his followers, and there is not immediate need in his case for a transfer. If we do increase the native population at Resolute Bay, it would be of greater benefit to move natives from overcrowded areas where they have great difficulty in getting sufficient food.'[140]

Idlout was discouraged from moving to Resolute and, consequently, he and his family did not move until the summer of 1955. However, in addressing Idlout's possible move in the spring of 1954, Constable Gibson contributes to our understanding of the conditions under which the original group had been relocated: 'The Eskimo family (Amagoalik) that arrived at Resolute Bay last year was very poorley [sic] outfitted for life in the high Arctic. The tent was unliveable and equipment in general very poor. The writer suggests a check be made of Idlout's equipment and if possible as many necessary articles be purchased for him prior to his arrival at Resolute.'[141] Clearly, considerable pressure was put on Idlout to remain in Pond Inlet. In May 1954, Constable Cooley of the Pond Inlet detachment of the RCMP requested permission to move Idlout and his family to Resolute Bay. The transfer was apparently agreeable to Superintendent Larsen of the RCMP and to James Houston, who was employed by the department at

Figure 17 Idlout and his family on Curry Island in July 1951. From left to right are Idlout, daughter Ruthee, wife Kidlak, daughter Leah, and sons, Noah and Pauloosee.

Igloolik. However, when approached for permission, departmental officials in Ottawa declined. They cited the fact that Idlout had the only serviceable boat in the Pond Inlet area and many other Inuit depended on him.[142]

It is clear from this exchange that 'voluntary' movement of Inuit was not something practised by the department. By one means or another, they obviously controlled who would relocate where – and when. Idlout was still insisting on being moved and the department was left with little choice but to accede to his wishes. It is apparent that the Hudson's Bay Company was concerned about further movement of Inuit from Inukjuak and Pond Inlet to the high Arctic. The company believed that if relocations were extensive, the economic viability of their posts in these settlements would be affected. 'The Bay' derived no benefit from the relocation of Inuit to the high Arctic, where they operated no trading posts.

Ben Sivertz of the Arctic division dealt with the issue. His correspondence to Henry Larsen, division 'G' of the RCMP, reveals the influence the Hudson's Bay Company had on government policy:

> The possibility of transferring Eskimos from northern Quebec or other places where conditions are not too favourable to Pond Inlet and Arctic Bay has been discussed with you from time to time, but no decision was ever

reached. If you think there would be advantages in increasing the population of northern Baffin Island by transfers from other places, we would be
glad to go into this with you when you are here at the end of the month.
... We do not wish to increase the colonies at Resolute Bay and Craig Harbour
much beyond their present size unless, as may possibly happen at Resolute
Bay, there are opportunities for the Eskimos finding steady employment
other than hunting and trapping. We do think, however, that northern
Baffin Island could support a larger population than is there now.[143]

This use of the term 'colonies' to describe the settlements at Resolute and
the Lindstrom Peninsula may strike the reader as odd. However, it was a
term used within the ministry since the 1930s, and its use did not disappear
from government documents until the 1960s. By then, a generation of
senior civil servants, which had entered the public service in the 1930s and
regarded itself as re-creating the pioneering work done on the Prairies in the
previous century, had retired.

While bowing to Idlout's insistence that he be moved, Sivertz, in correspondence to Superintendent Larsen, is careful not to reveal the real reasons
for holding back on the planned relocations from Pond Inlet and Inukjuak
– mainly that the Hudson's Bay Company was becoming concerned about
the loss of trappers, particularly in the Pond Inlet area. Sivertz was well aware
of Larsen's attitude toward the venerable 'Bay' and was not about to 'ruffle
any feathers':

> We have come to the conclusion that the number to be transferred this
> summer should be reduced. In this, we have taken into consideration the
> problem of transportation and the supplies that have been ordered for
> Resolute Bay and Craig Harbour, which cannot be increased at this late date.
> We are also rather perturbed about the number of people leaving Pond Inlet,
> where the population is already relatively small and where hunting condi-
> tions are by no means unfavourable.[144]

However, P.A.C. Nichols, of the company, was still concerned about Idlout's
move to Resolute Bay. Writing to Sivertz, he expressed his concerns:

> It is indeed unfortunate that Idlout and his group are leaving Pond Inlet for
> Resolute Bay. Idlout is, as you know, the mainstay of a large camp at Pond
> Inlet which has always made a good living due largely to his leadership.
> What will happen at this camp after he leaves is the question as Kudluk, one
> of the remaining men and the one man likely to succeed Idlout, may not
> be so successful as a camp boss.
> ... Should this migration continue I can foresee the danger of this area,

though abundant in food resources, being reduced in population to the
point where it will be difficult from an economic standpoint to operate a
trading post.

... We have tried on a number of occasions to interest the Sugluk Eskimo
in moving to a more productive area in Baffinland but without success. I do
not believe that this particular group will ever voluntarily leave their home
base.[145]

The letter affirms the role that the company's economic interests played in
the movement of Inuit. However, it is evident that government officials
leaned heavily on Idlout not to relocate to Resolute Bay. While they were
obviously successful for a year, in the end they relented.

Idlout was, of course, a strong, independent, and assertive Inuk with
considerable experience in dealing with government and other officials.
This is evidenced by Alex Stevenson's reports on his conversations with
Idlout aboard the *C.D. Howe* as he was being transferred: 'I have talked to
Idlout and explained to him the purpose of this experiment of moving
Eskimo so far north, and requested his co-operation in helping to make the
project a success. I bring this to your attention for I have known Idlout for
many years and although an excellent organizer, he is inclined to be
officious and I wanted to make it clear to him that there should be no
dissension with the Port Harrison natives.'[146] However, Idlout was not the
only Inuk to refuse to accede to government wishes about where he should
live. The resistance of Inuit at Sugluk, noted in the quote above, makes it
clear that other Inuit were not passive in dealing with attempts by the
Hudson's Bay Company and other parties to relocate them as they saw fit.

Idlout's determination to relocate to Resolute was driven by one of the
same concerns driving the government relocation of Inuit from Port Harrison. A remarkably successful hunter and trapper, Idlout had been severely
affected by the collapse of fox fur prices in the early 1950s. It seems likely
that he saw Resolute Bay as an opportunity to be part of something
important – something that would put him into closer contact with a
community of white people who, in some respects, he had come to emulate.
Idlout was determined to be successful and recognized. He was so determined to be relocated in the summer of 1955 that he and his family travelled
to Arctic Bay from their camp on Bylot Island north of Pond Inlet to board
the ship, as the *C.D. Howe* was not calling at Pond Inlet that year prior to
landing at Resolute Bay. Idlout's father was in Arctic Bay, and Idlout
apparently quarrelled with him over relocating to Resolute. As the ship
carrying Idlout and his family left Arctic Bay, Idlout's father shot and killed
himself.[147]

Idlout's experience at Resolute was not entirely pleasant. His expectations of being better recognized and connected to the non-Inuit community were not fulfilled, especially in light of the tight control exercised over relations with the base. Idlout had been a camp boss all his life. At Resolute, Salluviniq from Port Harrison was the titular trader and had a leadership role in the community, as did Amagoalik, also from Pond Inlet. There was little room for Idlout's ambitions, and Constable Gibson often found him a difficult man to accommodate.[148]

Nevertheless, Idlout, probably with his daughter Leah's assistance, was soon able to assert himself about matters in the Resolute community that were not to his liking. In a letter to Ben Sivertz, who had visited the community in October 1955 and had spoken with Idlout, he addressed 'the boss.' Idlout complained about his isolation in the village and the lack of ammunition at the store: 'Resolute Bay is very nice country only to [sic] bad we are Eskimo is not visits to whit [sic] peoples in Resolute ... my two rifle 222 and 270 ____ did not have any ammunition.'[149] On 18 December he wrote again to complain about the lack of ammunition and his confinement to the village. This time, he apparently sent a similar letter to his friend Doug Wilkinson, the filmmaker who had lived at his camp near Pond Inlet. Wilkinson tried to intervene with Ben Sivertz on his behalf. Sivertz was absent from his post, recovering from an operation, and James Cantley, acting chief of the Arctic division, responded:

> I can understand your desire to personally help Idlout in matters of this kind, but it does raise complications in so far as the conduct of affairs at Resolute Bay is concerned ... Idlouk, [sic] because of his association with whites and ability to speak some English, may feel that he should be free to visit the base when he feels like it, but I think you will understand that it is not possible to make any exceptions among the small group of Eskimos that are there.[150]

Even Idlout's influence had its limits.

In the fall of 1956, the first government houses were shipped to Resolute, and the community was connected by a power line running from the meteorological station at South Camp. Problems quickly arose with the prefabricated buildings. They had been confused with building materials for the base, and by the time the problem was corrected it was winter and the season too advanced to permit construction. However, time, weather, and general bungling were not the only problems.

> Cst. Gibson has advised that there was a rumour that one of these buildings was especially intended for Idlout. He felt that if there was any truth in this rumour that there might be some cause for dissatisfaction as there are nine

other families at Resolute Bay who are deserving equally as Idlout. Further, he considered that if the buildings were intended for occupancy by the Eskimos that the first four families that proceeded to Resolute Bay should be given the first consideration, as it was they who suffered the first winter in snow houses and had the real problem of adjusting to the new surroundings.[151]

The last line of the above quote should not be overlooked. Once again, Constable Gibson appears to have conveyed his real sense of the experience.

The problem was solved when Constable Gibson created different uses for the buildings. The '512' design houses were used for a community hall, a store, a warehouse, and a school.[152] The idea received the enthusiastic support of Sivertz who had himself, for a period in the late 1930s, been a teacher in British Columbia. There was no teacher at Resolute Bay at the time. School was taught by Leah, Idlout's sixteen-year-old daughter, who had spent time in a southern sanatorium and had learned to speak English and to read and write.

In the fall of 1956, Idlout became concerned about his son Paniloo, who was, at the time, living in Spence Bay.[153] Paniloo's situation is illustrative of the treatment many Inuit suffered during this period – as people who could be moved about and moulded to suit the ideas another culture held about how and where people should live, and what would be good for them. While in many cases those planning individual and mass movements of people truly believed they were acting benevolently toward the Inuit, sometimes motives were mixed with other values and beliefs that often did not well serve Inuit interests.

Idlout wrote to Sivertz asking that his son Paniloo come from Spence Bay and requesting that twenty-five dollars of his money be sent to the RCMP to help bring him to Resolute. Before his move to Resolute Bay, Idlout had offered Paniloo's services to Reverend Whitebread of the Anglican Church, who wished to make a trip from Pond Inlet to Spence Bay by dog team. Paniloo was accepted as a helper to Whitebread and they arrived at Spence Bay in April 1955.

In Spence Bay, Paniloo reportedly had no further means to make a living. Whitebread decided that he would undergo training as a catechist for the Anglican Church, and that he would be looked after by the church. Paniloo was apparently paid for his work for the Anglican mission with food rations.[154] However, in June 1956, Paniloo decided to marry Annie Kanayook, who was expecting their child. 'The marriage was according to Native Custom and registered as such. There was disappointment on Paniloo's part when Reverend Whitebread refused to conduct a church ceremony for this marriage. This refusal had to do with a clause in Paniloo's contract as an apprentice Catechist which stated that he could not become married ... the Reverend Whitebread from that time on, had nothing to do with him.'[155] The report went on to make it clear that Paniloo was subsequently living with his father-in-law and having a difficult time, as there was a shortage of food in the family. This prompted Idlout to announce, in a letter to Ben Sivertz of 18 December, that, come spring, he would likely go to Spence Bay to trade his fox skins.[156] He was disuaded from going. Shortly thereafter, Paniloo was evacuated from the settlement for medical reasons.

Idlout was clearly restless and unhappy with his circumstances. Yet in letters to Ben Sivertz, he indicated, with characteristic deference, how completely happy he was. However, his behaviour strongly suggests that this was not true. In February 1958, Idlout went to Churchill, Manitoba. While there, he purchased $300 worth of merchandise at prices much lower than those at Resolute Bay. Impressed with the facilities and opportunities at Churchill, Idlout decided that it was the place to be and approached Bob Kennedy, the northern service officer, with the idea of moving his family.[157]

Some idea of the control officials exercised over the movement of Inuit – while acknowledging Canadian law – can be taken from the following memo from Bob Kennedy: 'Eskimos are, of course, free to travel where they wish and to settle where they can, but we are able to exercise some control over movements to Churchill, since we own the houses in which they live.'[158] Social housing also had some potential as a means of social control. Idlout returned to Resolute Bay where RCMP Constable Moodie was given the task of convincing Idlout not to move.

This he did, suggesting that Idlout would have to pay for housing, that he and his wife would have five small children to look after without the help of his older daughter Leah, who was by this time in Frobisher Bay (Iqaluit) attending school, and his son Oolateetah, who wished to stay in Resolute Bay. Constable Moodie also convinced Idlout that his services would be needed in training armed forces personnel the following summer.[159] Relations in the Resolute Bay community were not good, and there were indications that Idlout did not enjoy the respect among other Inuit that government officials attributed to him. 'It is felt that one of the reasons Idlouk [*sic*] would like to leave is because of the hard feelings between Port Harrison eskimos and the Pond Inlet eskimos. When the writer first arrived one year ago, this was greatly noticed, they would not visit one another, would not inter-marry and in fact, they lived like two separate communities. However the writer has shown no favouritism and this matter has now been practically eliminated.'[160] Idlout settled into the routine of the Resolute Bay community. While respected by the Qallunat who knew his history, he does not seem to have gained the esteem of the Inuit community, something he had certainly enjoyed as a camp boss living on the land near Pond Inlet.

This is illustrated by his role in settling a dispute about a boat for the Resolute community.

During March and April of 1958, a dispute ensued between government officials and Inuit at Resolute Bay. By this time, the Inuit group at Resolute Bay had managed to acquire considerable credits on the store books and decided they wanted to buy a boat. A whale boat from Lake Harbour was to have been shipped to the community the previous summer, but due to an outbreak of measles on the *C.D. Howe*, the boat was not landed. The Inuit at Resolute Bay decided they wished to purchase a larger boat, a Peterhead, somewhat like the decked RCMP boat at Grise Fiord. At this point, Bob Williamson, a project officer employed with the department, attempted to convince the Inuit that the whale boat that had been ordered but not delivered the previous summer was a better choice. He enlisted Idlout to assist, claiming that Idlout's opinion was respected in the community. Some insight into Idlout's posture and attitude towards the rest of the community is captured by the reference to 'migrant group' in Bob Williamson's report on Idlout's efforts: 'He said that he had spoken at length with the migrant group, attempting to dissuade them from buying the larger boat, but with no success.'[161] Idlout, in trying to please the Qallunat, did not likely endear himself to the other members of the Resolute Bay settlement.

The matter, however, did not end there. In April, Ben Sivertz intervened with a letter to Henry Larsen of the RCMP. Sivertz was, by this time, director of the Northern Administration and Lands Branch. 'I think you will agree that even if the Eskimos have sufficient funds, a Peterhead boat in the hands of this Eskimo group, in an area well known for poor harbours and improper beaching facilities, would be a danger to life and a financial loss. Therefore, would you please ask Cpl. Moodie to review this whole matter with the Eskimos concerned, telling them that the whale-boat they ordered is being shipped this year.'[162] Officials were not beyond putting significant, repeated pressure on Inuit to do what the officials 'knew' was best. Inuit who persisted in wanting to do things their own way encountered problems, delays, and questions when they tried to get social assistance, housing, transportation, and so on. And these Inuit would find themselves being 'persuaded' or 'convinced' over and over again until – exhausted, exasperated, or fed up – they consented to the wishes of the non-Natives.

By the early 1960s, the prohibitions against Inuit visiting the base had disappeared.[163] Inuit acquired access to the Arctic Circle Club, a bar run at the base for service personnel. By all accounts, Idlout became an alcoholic – one of many Inuit from the village on the beach who spent evenings drinking with military and other personnel. Idlout was depressed by the death of his wife and likely realized that the recognition he sought from the white community at Resolute would never be what he expected. He tried to remarry a woman from a respected family in Pond Inlet but was apparently rebuffed by the woman's father, who knew Idlout was no longer the strong hunter and camp boss he had once been. He then married a woman much younger than himself.

On 2 June 1968, Idlout and his wife had been drinking at the Arctic Circle Club until past one o'clock in the morning. This was not unusual behaviour, and Idlout had travelled between the village and the base countless times under similar circumstances. Idlout's snowmobile had broken down so his wife accepted a ride back to the village. Idlout repaired his snowmobile. Then, between the base and the village, away from the normal and heavily travelled route to the community on the beach, Idlout drove it into a deep gully where he died.

Putting a Happy Face on a Sad Experiment

Idlout may have been the best documented relocatee to Resolute Bay, but in the five-year period following the establishment of Craig Harbour and the community on the Lindstrom Peninsula (both relocated later to Grise Fiord) as well as Resolute Bay, many other families were transferred from Pond Inlet and Inukjuak. Some families were returned to Pond Inlet. There was, however, little movement to Inukjuak. Relocating Inuit from the high Arctic back to Port Harrison/Inukjuak was very difficult, since it required a major diversion of the *C.D. Howe* back into Hudson Bay on the return trip to Montreal.

The transfer of Inuit to the high Arctic created problems. The provision of supplies and medical attention to the settlements proved to be a complicating factor in their operation. It seems that government officials found it difficult to admit that the two communities were less than a success. On the one hand, the RCMP, responsible for ensuring the success of the operation, not given to criticising government policy, and having no special training for reporting on social considerations in anything but the most superficial way, continued to give the impression that there were relatively few problems in the communities. And, as already discussed, the characteristic deference of Inuit in the presence of the authority of the RCMP and other government officials contributed to the image that everyone was happy and the so-called experiment was working well. Clues to the contrary come from some secondary observers as well as indirect comments contained from time to time in Constable Ross Gibson's correspondence.

By December 1954, Corporal Sargent at Craig Harbour was recommending that an additional native camp be established in the area to accommodate more families from Inukjuak. The suggestion was predicated on an exceptionally good year for fox trapping, during which 233 fox were taken.[164] His enthusiasm did not seem to reflect the fact that cycles of Arctic foxes – and of other game – meant that such conditions were temporary. One year later the harvest of foxes dropped off considerably. Subsequently, the department seemed to become more conscious of the limitations of game when resettling Inuit and turned to the Canadian Wildlife Service for help.[165]

Relations within the two communities and connections with families and friends in Inukjuak also created some problems in finding marital partners. For example, in the spring of 1955, Pauloosie, an Inuk from Grise Fiord, was requesting a wife from Inukjuak and had someone in mind whom he wanted moved to the high Arctic settlement. However, within a few months of making the request, he had married Anna Nungak, a woman at Grise Fiord.

In the summer of 1955, plans to move families from Inukjuak were changed. In April, Sivertz suggested to Henry Larsen that this was because it was impossible to change the order for supplies so that the stores to accommodate them.[166] However, as noted, it seems that the real reasons were more related to the concern of the Hudson's Bay Company that populations were being moved, thus jeopardizing their trading operations.

Other problems contributed to an eventual reconsideration of developing Inuit communities in such remote locations. Ice conditions in the high Arctic created problems for the Eastern Arctic Patrol in 1955. At Resolute Bay, the family of Josephie and his wife, Rynee, were put on shore as a temporary measure while the ship was being unloaded. However, as the ice moved in, the ship had to make a hasty retreat offshore. The result was that a family destined for Grise Fiord was in danger of being left at Resolute Bay. Alex Stevenson travelled back and forth to the ship by helicopter.[167] In typical fashion, he reported that 'the Eskimos presently residing at Resolute Bay are very happy and contented. As they did last year, they were eager to advise me that they had never fared so well in their lives, particularly the Eskimos from Port Harrison.'[168] Ice conditions finally permitted Josephie and his family to be transported to Grise Fiord. However, they presented a familiar problem on arrival. They had no money, no dogs, no traps, a torn and dirty tent, few accessories, and little clothing.[169]

Sivertz's decision not to move families from Pond Inlet also caused some problems at the other end. By December 1955, the family of Akpaleeapik had decided to return to Pond Inlet the next summer because Akpaleeapik's brother and family had not arrived the previous summer. Other families also requested that their relatives join them. It appears that the department was rapidly moving toward a policy crisis – attempting to control migration to please the HBC on the one hand, while satisfying relocatees by joining them with their extended families on the other.

In the spring of 1956, the unthinkable happened. Dundas Harbour was, once again, considered for Inuit resettlement. The history of attempts to settle Dundas Harbour has already been discussed. The idea appears to have originated with Commissioner Nicholson of the RCMP. Why he considered the possibility is a mystery, but it appears that Commissioner Nicholson was not well-versed in the history of his own force. In responding to a memo from Ben Sivertz on the matter, James Cantley, acting chief of the Arctic division, reveals the impact that the DEW Line was starting to have on departmental policy. The DEW Line was being constructed to the south of the high Arctic communities, and Cantley questioned the wisdom of relocating Inuit farther north when it appeared that employment opportunities were developing near existing and more southerly communities. He agreed with Sivertz that any attempt to conduct such a move in the summer of 1956 was unrealistic. He went on to introduce new cautions.

> With all the changes that are taking place in the Arctic now, we should perhaps be cautious in our approach to setting up new communities in the far north. At least, I think, we should make a careful survey of the present distribution of the population with a view to determining which areas are over-populated and which groups would benefit most by being transferred, provided they are willing to move ...
>
> We must also keep in mind possible developments in the areas from which such groups may be drawn. Apart from the Mid-Canada Line operations at Great Whale River, I am thinking of possible mining developments on the Belcher Islands and in Ungava Bay in northern Quebec and also at Rankin Inlet in Keewatin. If these developments come about, as they very well may, there is a possibility that quite a few Eskimos may find wage employment which might appeal to them more than going north to hunt and trap.[170]

James Cantley, who a few years earlier had been committed to preserving Inuit as hunters and trappers, was now bowing to the possibility of industrial employment.

On 10 May 1956, R.G. Robertson, the deputy minister of the department, wrote Nicholson noting that the history of Dundas Harbour did not support the idea. However, he also noted that the success of Grise Fiord and Resolute Bay suggested that more communities should be established in the high Arctic, contingent on a survey of possible locations conducted by the Canadian Wildlife Service.[171] Robertson also hints that all was not well in the communities by observing that 'sociological problems have not yet been entirely worked out. We do not know what proportion, if any, of the Craig Harbour Eskimos and those at Resolute Bay may wish to return to their former homes after a stay of, say, three or four years in the high Arctic.'[172] With a touch of irony, it was later noted that Dundas Harbour had been chosen by the United States Air Force for photoflash bombing by the Strategic Air Command.[173]

Figure 18 Grise Fiord in 1961 was the most northerly settlement in Canada.

The spring of 1956 saw the return of a familiar problem when Greenland Inuit were discovered hunting on Ellesmere Island. In May, five families from Greenland visited the detachment at Alexandra Fiord. Subsequently, W.J. Fitzsimmons of the RCMP suggested that game conditions in the area had improved since 1953, and that the area could support 'three or four native families.'[174] A familiar problem required a familiar solution: relocation. However, while departmental officials declared that all was well in the high Arctic, their hesitation indicated that some doubts existed about the wisdom of further transfers.

In the summer of 1956, the detachment at Craig Harbour was moved east to Grise Fiord, a location much closer to the Inuit camp on the Lindstrom Peninsula. While two Inuit families lived at Grise Fiord, the remainder stayed on the Lindstrom Peninsula until a federal day school was provided to the community in 1961, and the remainder of the Inuit moved to the new location. In October 1956, the director, F.J.G. Cunningham, directed Ben Sivertz to prepare a report on the settlement projects outlining the objectives and methods and appraising the results. He also requested that the report 'make specific recommendations for the next few years handling of economic and social problems in these two settlements [emphasis added].'[175]

By spring of 1957, Angnakadlak, his wife Kowmayoo, their six children, and Angnakadlak's grandmother wished to return to Pond Inlet, reportedly to help his aging parents.[176] Angnakadlak was the Inuk originally transferred to assist Inuit from Port Harrison/Inukjuak. At the same time, Pauloosie, the son of the special constable working at Alexandra Fiord, asked to be transferred back to Pond Inlet. Apparently, Pauloosie was looking for someone to marry. Arrangements were made for his transfer but, before he left, he married a 'young eskimo girl Minnie' and decided to stay in Grise Fiord.[177] Both of these situations illustrate the difficulties Inuit encountered in being isolated from their original communities and extended families.

In Resolute Bay, Leah, daughter of Idlout, wanted desperately to leave the community because her father was apparently keen on seeing her marry someone in whom she wasn't interested. The RCMP became involved when Leah asked to be sent out of the community for training. R.A.J. Phillips, who, at the time, was the chief of the Arctic division, reveals his attitude towards women by his response:

> We do not see how any planning can be done to bring Leah out, without her father being brought into the picture, otherwise we would be encroaching on parental rights ...
>
> If some solution to the marriage problem can be reached that would be satisfactory to all concerned and Leah still desires to go out for training and her father consents to it, then we would have to know more about her education, intelligence and capabilities in order to determine the type of training for which she might be suited.[178]

Leah's movement from the Resolute community was clearly blocked by conditions that were never imposed on any Inuk male who wished to leave for training. To help, Phillips sent along an outline to assist in evaluating Leah. Corporal Moodie was asked to evaluate her health, maturity – especially her self-confidence – her intelligence, manual dexterity, mathematical ability, and work history.

The isolation of Resolute Bay became obvious when the *C.D. Howe* arrived in August 1957. An epidemic of measles had broken out among the passengers, and they were moved ashore to a camp separated from the Inuit village. The separation of the camps didn't help, and soon people in both locations were contracting the disease. The presence of the air base was of limited benefit. While the base provided basic necessities such as water, electricity, and oil to make the camps habitable at the outbreak of the disease, there were limits to this aid, and other necessities had to be flown in from Churchill, including a welfare officer and serum. The *C.D. Howe* could not wait for the epidemic to pass before continuing on. Consequently, two families destined for Grise Fiord had to be left at Resolute with the idea that they would later be flown to the settlement.

In the meantime, the difficulties in dealing with the disease were many and reveal the problems of Resolute's remote location. The fifty-two Inuit and two non-Natives removed from the ship placed incredible strain on a limited food supply. Although they had initially made rations available to the camps, the RCAF and DOT refused to supply food on an ongoing basis because they believed they had no authority to do so. The children in the group were inadequately clothed for the winter weather that started to develop at the end of August. The Hudson's Bay Company in Churchill was wired for additional garments. One of the Inuit undertook to cook for the camp, assisted by three men and three women, but their pay became an issue. Water was a problem. F.J. Neville reported that 'thanks to the Air Force a 1000 gallon tank has been installed, a discarded bath tub and washing machine have been reclaimed from the base dump and Eskimo children are getting baths.'[179]

The epidemic was costly. Indian and Northern Health Services attempted to bill the department $2,364.42 for the charter of an aircraft from Winnipeg to Resolute Bay to deliver serum to the community. Sivertz declined to accept the invoice, arguing that the decision to send the serum was primarily a medical matter and that Indian and Northern Health Services should consequently assume the costs.[180]

The same year, following the visit of the *C.D. Howe*, there was an outbreak of impetigo at Grise Fiord, which was only successfully dealt with because the HMCS *Labrador* was in the vicinity and the medical party on board provided assistance.[181] As the outbreak of measles demonstrated, far from being in a location where medical attention was vastly superior to that available at Inukjuak (a claim made by Jacques Gerin, the deputy minister of Indian and northern affairs, in 1987), the Inuit of Resolute and Grise Fiord were in a location where serious medical problems were costly and difficult to address.

By the spring of 1959, one of the families – Pilipoosee's – trapped in Resolute Bay by the measles outbreak, had decided to stay. The other family – Aeesak's – was anxious to leave, as they were living in crowded conditions with one of the Resolute Bay families. Pilipoosee's decision prompted a response from Bob Pilot, who was, by now, the officer in charge of the Grise Fiord detachment. 'Constable Pilot complained about potential Grise Fiord "natives" being seduced by the comforts of Resolute Bay. Cpl. Moodie replied that if he felt strongly about this, he would order Pilipoosee to go to Grise Fiord. I suggested gently that this might be considered at variance with present-day policies regarding the freedom of individuals, and the matter was dropped.'[182] However, the matter was not to go away. In subsequent years, the desire of people to move from Grise Fiord to Resolute Bay and the desire of additional families to be united with their relatives in Resolute Bay was to cause the department considerable concern, as employment opportunities were limited and the land clearly could not support a large population.

Furthermore, the Hudson's Bay Company was still concerned about the profitability of its posts at Inukjuak and Pond Inlet. In a telegram to RCMP headquarters, Ross Gibson, who had been transferred back to Inukjuak following his stint at Resolute Bay, suggested that the HBC was not happy with the depletion of good hunters from the Inukjuak area and that only young people of marriageable age should be sent north. Gibson clearly had doubts about the long-term viability of the high Arctic experiment. He noted that the opportunities for people in the Grise Fiord community were considerably less than for those Inuit living in communities farther south.[183]

Nevertheless, in a memorandum to the deputy minister, Sivertz approved the removal of three more families, Jacka, Lucy, and Levi, from Inukjuak to Grise Fiord but noted that work by the Canadian Wildlife Survey, put off for budgetary reasons the previous year, was essential to assisting the policy decisions of the department.[184] Sivertz moved to set up a committee to study future relocations of Inuit from depressed areas to the high Arctic (discussed in Chapter 8).

However, by this time, life was not entirely pleasant in Grise Fiord. A report submitted as part of the Eastern Arctic Patrol on 27 August 1958 made it clear there were problems in the community that were likely to draw Inuit away from the community to Resolute Bay or back to either Pond Inlet or Inukjuak. The problems were many. About one ton of soapstone quarried on Broughton Island and brought into the community for carvers was virtually useless, being hard and unworkable. Operating the store had been made difficult because lists indicating the selling price of all goods sent to the community had been unavailable since 1953. Consequently, essential goods were being sold at cost and luxury items marked up 10 per cent. However, Inuit were unhappy with the goods available. The store was clearly a serious local concern:

> Shortly after the 'Howe' arrived at Grise Fiord, Thomassie ... who was estensibly [sic] the operator of the trading store came to see me regarding this problem. He said that the Eskimos had come to Craig Harbour five years before and although the hunting had been good there and at Grise Fiord, there had never been enough tea, coal oil, tobacco, flour, sugar, milk, 30-30 ammunition and duck for their tents at the store. He said that when the store ran out of food, heating and hunting supplies, the Eskimos did not like leaving the camp to go on hunts, because of the hardship cause [sic] to their wives and children by the food shortages and because of the cold in their houses. He said that although the game was good their children still needed white man's food and he pointed out that the Eskimos were obeying

white man's game laws as they had been asked, but because there was not enough white man's food at the store they were going hungry as a result. He said that if the police did not give them more food this winter that they would all wish to leave Grise Fiord next year.

The author of the report goes on to state:

When I was in Resolute Bay I was talking with two Eskimos who had been at Grise Fiord and who were going back there on the 'Howe.' They did not wish to return but as there was no space for them at Resolute and they had been transported on the 'Howe' last year from Port Harrison specifically at their request to go to Grise, we told them that they would have to go. They were most unhappy about this, not because they disliked the situation as far as the community, or the game resources were concerned, but because they could not buy the things they needed at the store.[185]

This report by Thomassie is probably the most accurate picture of how Inuit in Grise Fiord actually felt about many aspects of the relocation experience. It is likely that similar feelings prevailed at Resolute early in its history. The reports by Inuit testifying in front of the House of Commons standing committee on aboriginal affairs in March 1990 that they were cold and hungry are confirmed by this report from Thomassie, which was made to someone other than one of the RCMP officers responsible for ensuring the successful operation of the community.

The RCMP version of this situation is very different:

After the sudden death of Thomassie's two children, morale was at a very low ebb at the native camp. These natives still have their superstitions and several men stated they wished to move from this area. Also at this time staple food articles such as flour, rolled oats, sugar, milk and tobacco were depleted in the trading store, so that the natives were not to [*sic*] happy to start with. However with the arrival of the *C.D. Howe* and trading store supplies and especially the arrival of two new families to the area, old superstitions were soon forgotten and the natives were quite happy again.[186]

The dismissal of Inuit complaints and rationalization of their concerns is further evidenced by the following:

Any complaints the natives might have are usually voiced and often easily remedied. This native camp is lacking a camp leader, the two older men have not got the initiative to lead the younger men, but this has not presented any serious problems in the camp with the exception that a camp boss could help handle minor [*sic*] complaints amongst themselves. The natives enjoy these meetings and it has definitely helped to raise the morale of the men and to date the camp, as a whole, seems very happy and active.[187]

With a pen, Constable Pilot had reduced the Inuit of Grise Fiord to a very common stereotype – happy, smiling children whose problems were related to their 'superstitions' or inability to find a camp boss – anything but the very real problems created for them by government policy and its execution by the Force. Stocking the store was clearly a responsibility of government personnel and the RCMP. Unlike Thomassie's report given to the personnel on the *C.D. Howe*, no mention is made of women or children other than their arrival or departure from the community.

The RCMP version of events, when placed alongside Thomassie's recorded comments, reveal how the RCMP reports were inclined to portray the status of the settlements in the most favourable light. It also suggests that the Inuit response to the police was one of deference to the authority they represented.

Consequently, the images that police officers acquired about how pleased Inuit were with their surroundings were distorted. The inability of officers, within the norms of the Force, to openly criticize government policy, contributed to the false notions of what was actually happening in the communities. It is also evident that in many cases, paternalistic and racist attitudes towards Inuit, combined with conventional ideas about work, welfare, and dependency relations, further compounded the problems. Demands to stock more food at the store would suggest to many officers that Inuit were becoming lazy and dependent on store-bought rations rather than relying on hunting to provide food. The struggle to communicate some idea of what was really happening is most evident from the reports of Constable Ross Gibson at Resolute Bay. However, even his communications are muted. As the department depended heavily on the RCMP for information upon which to base policy, it is not surprising that government policy was warped accordingly.

Constable Pilot's reports that all was well at Grise Fiord – that everyone was more or less happy and smiling with only minor problems that could easily be remedied – was as false as it was glib. By early 1960, Constable Jenkins was reporting that Inuit were again wanting to be relocated to Resolute Bay, something greatly feared by the department, which was already having difficulty providing housing and dealing with employment there.

Constable Jenkins suggested that the department communicate with the Inuit, in their own language, the reasons why they should not move to

Resolute Bay. The notice, prepared by the department and signed by C.M. Bolger, administrator of the Arctic, speaks for itself.

> As you will know many years ago Eskimos used to live in your part of the country. Then for a long time nobody lived there. During that time the wildlife increased owing to the absence of any extensive hunting and trapping. Because of this, you and your families returned to the area and have trapped foxes and hunted the sea mammals and other animals and have had plenty of food.
>
> There is a lot we do not know about migration, and the reproduction of sea mammals and animals and the number that can be taken for food and still be enough for many years. Until we study this and have more information, we do not think it wise to bring any more Eskimos into the region because the additional hunting might deplete the game and there would not be enough for everyone.
>
> We hope it will be possible next year to have a team of scientists who, with your help, will do research and decide the number of Eskimos your area can support.
>
> If more Eskimos become engaged in wage employment, possibly a few more people could live in Resolute Bay.
>
> For the reasons we have given you and because we want you to remain successful and have plenty of food, we prefer that you do not encourage your relations and friends to come to Resolute Bay at this time. If you wish to have someone join you for a special reason, would you bring it to the attention of the R.C.M. Police or write to me.[188]

Despite the prohibitions against Inuit relocating to Resolute Bay, a number of families applied to be moved. One of these was Isa Smiler of Inukjuak, the other was Amagoalik from Iglpolik. Isa was apparently convinced by government officials that moving to Resolute Bay would not be in his best interests.[189] Such was perhaps the case. The problems of supplies at the stores at Resolute Bay and Grise Fiord persisted and were undoubtably a factor in the government ridding itself of the headache by turning them into cooperatives late in 1960.

Writing about the Resolute Bay store, Constable Jenkins reported in July 1960 that

> the Resolute Bay Trading Store is not capable to meet the requirements of non-hunting Eskimos. If this employment is to advance whereby most of the Eskimos will be affected the store buildings, stock of goods, and the staff will have to be enlarged considerably ... This aspect of permanent employ-

ment must be closely considered because it will not be the Eskimo employed male who will suffer as they receive their daily meals in the R.C.A.F. mess, but the families of these men. In the writer's experience this sort of situation developed on the eastern sector of the Dew Line in 1956 whereby the men were eating well but their families were doing without adequate food.[190]

Things were apparently no better at Grise Fiord despite the problems noted the previous year. Early in October it was revealed that some of the supplies destined for Grise Fiord had not been unloaded at the community and had found their way back to Montreal. The Department of Transport claimed that as the supplies had arrived late in the loading process, they had been placed in a hold separate from the bulk of materials being sent to the settlement. They were subsequently missed and not off-loaded. In suggesting an airlift of the supplies, Bolger was blunt: 'Any hardship that might occur to these people through the lack of essential supplies would not only be distressing and undesirable, but might be most embarrassing to our Minister and this Department.'[191]

Meanwhile, another familiar problem developed. Grise Fiord was hit with an outbreak of whooping cough, originally thought to be diphtheria. A radio blackout prevented the RCMP from reaching Resolute Bay with a message, which was picked up by the United States Air Force base at Thule. The Americans then attempted to air-drop medical people into Grise Fiord. They were unsuccessful. Finally, a doctor was flown from Ottawa to Resolute Bay and on to Grise Fiord by a charter plane.[192] The isolation and problems of servicing northern communities were, once again, more than obvious.

Despite these difficulties, Inuit from Inukjuak did request to join their relatives in Grise Fiord and in Resolute Bay. Furthermore, relatives in these communities requested that their relatives from Inukjuak come north to join them. This has been cited as evidence that life in the high Arctic was not as unpleasant as Inuit have since claimed. The fact that Inuit were lonely and missed their extended families is a more likely explanation. However, if life in the high Arctic was not pleasant, it appears that it may have been no better in Inukjuak. In fact, some of the same attitudes and some of the same roles played by the non-Natives sent north, supposedly to help Inuit, were at work in both places. In the summer of 1957, Constable Gibson, who had been in charge at Resolute, was returned to Inukjuak. By November, Inuit were requesting his removal from the community. RCMP Special Constable Willya wrote:

I am writing about my colleague, the policeman. It is not a nice thing to do, but I'm doing it ... This man is always sore at us. Here is an example, we get rations but they are not sufficient. On two occasions I asked him for more sugar, he just got sore at me. Also I had occasion to ask him for some radio batteries. He said that the radio was the property of the police boss and should be given to him ... He uses the name of the police boss as an excuse all the time.

The Eskimos here have been in habit of receiving their family allowance orders at the beginning of each month and coming to the barracks to receive them. This is not the rule here now. The Eskimos are to be pitied for being treated like this and do not deserve to have a policeman of this type. Policemen who have been here over the years past have never acted like that, they were all nice people. This man was here in 1952 and he wasn't nice then. Now that he is the boss here and married, he is worse than before ... I have related this so his boss can tell him how to behave or send another man.[193]

In spite of all these problems, through the 1950s it became a truism among Arctic hands that the relocations to the high Arctic were a strikingly successful venture. This truism had a great deal of influence on government policy and led, in part, to further relocation ventures such as that documented in Chapter 7 (the Keewatin relocation project). In 1958, Ben Sivertz, who was by this time director of the Lands and Administration Branch of the department, moved to set up a committee to study further relocations of Inuit.[194] Walter Rudnicki, chief of the welfare division, responded with observations on Resolute Bay and Grise Fiord. These are not the only observations on social relations and conditions in the communities at this time. Other reports substantiate Rudnicki's observations.[195] From Rudnicki's reports, it is obvious that problems existed in the communities from the outset.

The Resolute Bay experience exemplifies the possible danger of being guided by preconceived notions and the risk of overlooking the sociological aspects of such a move ... In actual fact, what has happened is the establishment of a community in which there is an extraordinary amount of animosity and bickering between the two groups, each representing a waring [*sic*] faction. It is significant that after living together for seven years, there has been not one instance of intermarriage between the Pond Inlet and Port Harrison groups. To this date, moreover, the two groups hunt separately, maintain separate caches, and generally prefer to stay out of each other's way.[196]

Furthermore, Rudnicki's report makes it clear that, contrary to the impressions created by police reports, Inuit in these communities wanted to return to Pond Inlet and Inukjuak. 'It is known for example, that many of these resettled Eskimos still speak of returning to their original settlements though they have been gone for seven years.'[197]

Rudnicki's observations on the government stores are also worthy of note.

> After seven years there is not one Eskimo in either Grise Fiord or Resolute Bay who knows even the most elementary thing about running the store. This responsibility is retained entirely by the R.C.M.Police, in one place even to the extent of being the only person in the community who knows the prices of goods on the shelves. The prices apparently are not marked. In other words, in transferring Eskimos to a new location, we merely transferred the former 'Boss-Eskimo' relationship that existed in the more established communities.[198]

Finally, Rudnicki's comments on the conditions that prevailed within the department at the time of the move north are revealing of why life in these communities was, initially, so difficult for those relocated. 'At the time [the relocations] occurred, the Department was ill-equipped for anything but the most rudimentary effort and in any case it is often difficult to foresee many of the problems until one or more pilot projects have been attempted.'[199]

By the 1960s, a series of important changes to the emerging complex of Arctic social structures, the most important being the growing presence and strength of Inuit political representatives, led to questioning the viability of further high Arctic relocations. By 1963, in fact, the idea was finished. The end of the Diefenbaker regime brought with it a new minister and new ideas about northern development. The problem of families wishing to be reunited persisted. A game survey of the Queen Elizabeth Islands clarified little as to what sort of population the region's resources might support.

The 1960s broght about many significant changes. No longer could native people be moved about at the behest of northern administrators and Hudson's Bay Company officials. No longer were Inuit willing to defer to the Qallunat, who had, at one time, seemed almost omnipotent. Northern native people were finding strong voices of their own. Canada's northern 'colonies' were in the early stages of a process of decolonization, ultimately demonstrated by Inuit demands in the 1980s, and before the House of Commons standing committee on aboriginal affairs in 1990, that their unique experience, role, and contribution to Canadian sovereignty in the high Arctic be recognized.

5

The Ennadai Lake
Relocations,
1950-60

It is, of course, comparatively easy to get a temporary acquiescence from the
Eskimos to any suggestion put to them.

– Graham Rowley, 1958

By the mid-1950s, the state had developed a comparatively elaborate
infrastructure to address the crises that seemed to plague the Inuit and the
northern economy. Inuit were receiving family allowances, though the
debate about the consequences of providing too-easy access to relief
remained lively and the form of payment for family allowances remained a
credit on account or payment in goods rather than by cheque. As noted,
family allowances were often provided as relief when the situation
demanded it. Northern service officers joined the ranks of fur traders,
missionaries, and police officers who monitored and/or controlled the
communities developing in the region. The transportation and communication network in the Keewatin made possible more regular contacts with
Inuit of the area. In spite of this, in three separate areas of the region, many
Inuit starved to death in the winter of 1957-8.

The emerging complex structure of institutions, values, and practices
surrounding Inuit relocation and the provision of social welfare reached a
climax of sorts in the 1950s. Particularly in the Keewatin region, events
crossed the threshold of tolerance with the famine experienced by Inuit at
Henik and Garry lakes in the winter of 1957-8. The actions and events
leading up to the starvations, as well as the government reaction, bring the
network of policies associated with relocation and social welfare into sharp
relief.

What is striking in reviewing the records of these events is how little
government officials of the day understood the desires, values, and motives
of their Inuit 'wards.' In the reports produced immediately after the starvations, government officials placed blame on the irrationality or laziness of

Inuit involved. Inuit were obviously operating within a completely different cultural context, yet over and over again government officials were perplexed by their values and actions and were critical of what they perceived as an Inuit 'lack of reason.'

This latter problem, the cultural blindness and ethnocentrism of well-intentioned officials at all levels, can be clearly seen in the lack of attention to the development of serious consultation processes in the larger communities and in the lack of respect that was given the fledgling indigenous advisory committees that did exist in some settlements. Smaller, semi-nomadic groups were seen as even less capable of making rational decisions and so were encouraged – sometimes badgered – into agreeing to do what was already planned for them. Ironically, this approach was developed in the context of trying to discourage dependency – in the interest of reducing government costs.

And so people were moved. They were moved in large groups, as communities. They were moved again. Groups were divided and reconstructed. Inuit in the southern Arctic were moved north, inland peoples to the coast, families were divided and kinship networks ignored. Families and individuals were relocated – ostensibly in response to crisis – with the details and rationale for such relocations depending on the whims of southern planners, the latest theories of economic development, and the biases of field-workers. And out of these moves? Certainly courageous efforts to struggle and survive. But also dislocation, disorientation, economic disaster, social conflict, famine, death.

The two famine stories of 1957-8, reconstructed in this and the subsequent chapter, are of two distinct Inuit groups living inland in the Keewatin region. One group had been relocated to Henik Lake in the summer of 1957; the other group had gathered around a Roman Catholic mission at Garry Lake some years earlier. In both cases, the immediate cause of disaster was the failure of the caribou hunt. Both stories reveal a great deal about the state, welfare, relocation, and Inuit/non-Native interaction in the 1950s.

The Ennadai Lake Inuit
The Inuit relocated to Henik Lake in the summer of 1957 had been resisting relocation for more than a decade. They had already been the victims of one failed relocation experiment. They were generally known as the Ennadai Lake Inuit because they were located at a camp on the Kazan River quite close to Ennadai Lake and lived primarily from caribou, hunted in the territory between the Kazan River and Nueltin Lake. In the summer of 1956, government documents show that there were thirty men and women and twenty-five children (twelve of whom were under the age of five).[1]

The story of the famine at Henik Lake is relatively well known, thanks to

Farley Mowat's *The Desperate People*. The story is reconstructed here, based on archival documents, largely without reference to Mowat. There are reasons for this. Mowat did not provide sources for his narrative. Although he did talk to many of the people involved and probably had access to at least some of the same sources used here, he does not make it clear from where he derived the general story and specific aspects of that story. There are at least some details where our sources indicate a story different than Mowat's; we do not suggest that we have told the 'truth' in these instances and that Mowat has not, but, rather, that what we have written is based on an identifiable document in the archive. It is worth noting that while Mowat may have had access to some of the same sources, much of the material used in this chapter was classified and not available to the public until recently. Mowat's presence 'on the ground' means his narrative may be as, or even more, reliable than ours. As narrative, Mowat's story has already won both acclaim and criticism. Our narrative of these events is structured around identifiable documents and oriented towards illustrating patterns of behaviour between different historical agents in the region, rather than provoking the kind of moral outcry that was necessary in the late 1950s. We have followed the practice of the documents in referring to the people involved as 'Ennadai Lake Inuit' rather than Mowat's 'Ihalmiut.'

Government reports on the Ennadai Lake Inuit often commented on their 'backwardness' and 'primitiveness.' A 1952 report on the failed relocation to Nueltin Lake emphasized this, noting that 'these people are the most primitive of all the Canadian Eskimos.' The report went on: 'Their wants are few and generally they are interested more in following their traditionally nomadic hunting ways than in trapping or earning money. Their existence depends almost entirely on the caribou and failure to obtain and properly cache sufficient meat during the northern and southern migrations of these animals inevitably means privation and occasionally starvation.'[2] In the discussion of the proposed move to Henik Lake, it was noted that 'the Ennadai Lake natives had many taboos, particularly as regards hunting and fishing which adversely affected their livelihood.'[3] From a critical perspective, it would seem that the government's own reports indicate that the Ennadai Lake people's culture and spiritual beliefs remained relatively intact. These values and beliefs were to constantly interfere with the rational plans for their economic well-being conceived by government officials.

The 1952 report quoted above had some interesting things to say about the history of these people's interaction with non-Natives. The report notes that 'what little contact this small group has had with civilization was through white trappers and small traders who penetrated into their country during the earlier years when white foxes were valuable ... apart from coming to depend on rifles and ammunition for hunting, these people never

Figure 19 Ennadai Lake landscape in the early 1950s. The area around Ennadai Lake, unlike much of the Keewatin, has small trees which were an essential source of fuel and heat for the Ennadai Lake Inuit.

became accustomed to the use of much of the white man's equipment or food.'[4] A report produced after the 1958 starvation added some important details, noting that 'at one time Revillon Frères had a trading post at Ennadai Lake which was abandoned in the early 1930's. The Hudson's Bay also conducted a trading post as Neulltin Lake [*sic*] which they, too, abandoned in 1941.'[5] After the HBC abandoned the area, it was left to independent traders and individual trappers. There may have been hostility between these trappers and Inuit; Doug Wilkinson, a northern service officer in the area at the time, remembered being told that 'some of the white trappers who had trap lines that ran inland from the west coast of Hudson Bay between Churchill and Tavani had actually threatened Inuit not to come near their camps on pain of being shot.'[6]

In any event, the later report noted that

these trappers have related how they had to organize caribou hunts for the Ennadai Eskimos and personally supervise them so that the Eskimos would have sufficient meat for the winter. This was done more for economic reasons than philanthropic ones as the trappers had learned by experience that Eskimos, in the district of a white man, showed little tendency to provide for the future, evidently on the assumption that in case of want the white trapper would supply succour from his food supplies.[7]

A curious detail: white trappers organizing Inuit caribou hunts to ensure sufficient stocks of food. This detail merits some attention. It seems that for at least one or two decades, the larger fur trading companies had trading posts in the area. It is quite possible – indeed likely – that they used the credit system to induce the Inuit to trade, and tried to create dependency. We cannot know how successful they were, but it is worth noting that the hunting of fox furs to exchange for store-bought goods would have involved a significant shift in the subsistence strategies of the Ennadai Lake Inuit. There was enough of a transition that, by all accounts, the Ennadai Lake Inuit were relying on European hunting technologies in the late 1940s. Had the Inuit genuinely come to believe that they could rely on outside provisions in times of difficulty, an attitude that in earlier years may have been encouraged by trading companies? Had they come to lose some of the knowledge necessary to their subsistence ecological strategies? Were they so confident in their ability to provide for themselves that they took a remarkably casual approach to the fall caribou hunt? Perhaps the trappers exaggerated the degree to which they became responsible for organizing caribou hunts. It seems especially difficult to relate this latter claim to what we are told about the many 'taboos' the Ennadai Lake Inuit had about hunting and to possible hostility between the two groups.

The most likely scenario is that the people of Ennadai were encouraged for more than ten years to adopt a system where they de-emphasized hunting caribou in favour of trapping the valuable white fox in exchange for food. As noted elsewhere, traders outfitted the Inuit and encouraged them to rely on the trader's food stores. All was well as long as fox furs were plentiful and prices were high. As prices declined, the traders had to worry about carrying the costs of sustaining the Inuit. So they began to encourage Inuit to re-emphasize caribou hunting. And, some time later, they told government officials they had become responsible for organizing Inuit caribou hunts – an action made necessary, in their view, because of Inuit indigence.[8]

In the period following the Second World War, non-Native independent trappers and traders also moved out of the area. The 1952 report noted that 'as restrictions were placed on white trapping and white fox prices declined, most of the trappers and traders pulled out of the interior and this Eskimo group was again left largely to depend on its own resources.'[9] Meanwhile, another presence began to make itself felt in the area: 'In the middle 1940's the Department of National Defence established a Radio Station at Ennadai Lake, operated by the Royal Canadian Corp of Signals. The Eskimos then

Figure 20 Inuit at the weather station at Ennadai Lake in the early 1950s. They were later to be relocated to Henik Lake, where some died under tragic circumstances in the winter of 1957-8.

congregated at this point. Fish and caribou were plentiful in the adjacent district but the Eskimos preferred the occasionally received "hand out" from the personnel of the Radio Station to fending for themselves farther afield.'[10] As trappers and traders left, they were replaced by government officials – initially radio operators.

The Nueltin Lake Move
By the latter part of the 1940s, the Ennadai Lake Inuit came to represent a problem for the authorities: 'In 1947 ... the withdrawal of the traders made it evident that steps would have to be taken to provide these people with means of obtaining essential supplies and also of benefitting by the payments of Family Allowances, which had begun to be made.'[11] Some organized social welfare benefits were provided. Dr. Robert Yule visited the group twice in 1947, each time arranging for food and ammunition to be provided for the relief of the group.

But for the government, this only created a problem. Relief supplies were sent in 1948 and in 1949. In 1948, two old and two young people died, possibly of starvation, and the Ennadai people were reported to be destitute. The people were about to become dependent on government handouts and to make the transition to the status of permanent indigence that so frightened officials. What was to be done? The answer for those in charge seemed obvious – move them.

That these people did not want to be moved, then and later, was clear. The 1952 report stated that 'there is one small isolated group in the area lying between Nueltin Lake and Kazan River who have persisted in remaining there despite repeated hardships and all attempts made to move them to a more accessible region.'[12] The report went on to note that, in spite of the dangers of destitution and starvation, 'in their stoical way they still prefer to live in familiar surroundings rather than move to other areas where they could be at least as well off and where they could obtain assistance when they needed it.'[13] The sentiments expressed in this report make it clear that the issue, in the minds of officials, was not settled. Sooner or later these Inuit would come to realize – or be made to realize – that a move was in their best interest. The reference to stoicism, a common ideological attribute of so-called 'primitives,' only served to strengthen the notion of their innate irrationality.

The question of 'accessibility' and the idea of moving them to a 'more accessible region' is also worthy of note. Accessibility obviously did not matter to isolated Inuit; it mattered to the bureaucrats who had to plan for the provision of social welfare and to monitor its delivery. Inuit had to be moved so they could more easily be reached by the state, but it had to be made clear to them that this was in their own interest.

Consequently, in 1950, the Inuit of Ennadai Lake were moved to nearby Nueltin Lake. Two reasons were given: 'the unreliability of the animal resources in the area, primarily the caribou, and the fact that they lived almost 200 miles from a trading post which could be a source of food in case of emergency.'[14] In the spring of 1950, as officials debated what to do about the problem, they received a message from two traders, Sigurson and Martin, who had a post at Nueltin Lake: 'We are in position to feed and put to work all who can reach new post. Suggest your department fly them down immediately.'[15] The 1952 report attributes the suggestion of moving the Inuit to the RCMP: 'The Police recommended moving this group to Nueltin Lake where they could obtain sufficient food, be near a trading centre and probably obtain employment at a commercial fishery being opened there.'[16] Subsequently, '47 people were moved by plane but by December 1950, they had all made their way back to the Kazan River.'[17] What happened in the intervening period is quite revealing.

A 1956 report on this incident, the 'Fishing Experiment at Nueltin Lake,' reveals what happened. Apparently, 'it was taken for granted that the department's responsibility would be limited to providing transportation for the natives from Ennadai Lake to Nueltin Lake.'[18] It was assumed that the traders at Nueltin Lake would oversee and organize the commercial fishing venture.

> There seems to have been no consideration given to issuing the natives with clothing, fishing gear, or other equipment to help them to fish when they arrived there. They were simply picked up as they were, transported to Nueltin Lake and left there ... The commercial fishing was not successful, and had a very short life. Sigurson and Martin found that they did not have the capital to finance the project and when a request for a government loan was turned down the whole idea was dropped.[19]

After the 1957-8 starvation, the government found it convenient to tell a different story: 'The Ennadai Lake Eskimo were transported to Nueltin Lake in 1950 by aircraft in an attempt to have them engage in a fishery that had commercial potentials. They were adequately outfitted for the venture but within a short time they drifted back again to Ennadai Lake.'[20]

The Ennadai Lake Inuit did not like being relocated to Nueltin Lake. There is no reference in any of the documents to their having been consulted about, or having consented to, the move. But moved they were. So they took matters into their own hands: 'They did not take to fishing and in any case they did not have any boats or other equipment to fish properly. There were reports that they wished to return to the Kasan [*sic*] River area and in November the department was just preparing to charter an aircraft to investigate the situation at Nueltin Lake when a wire was received from the Army Signal Station at Ennadai Lake saying that forty Eskimos had returned to that area from Nueltin Lake.'[21] In an assessment of the venture, it was noted that, 'there is no doubt that the department had the best interests of the Eskimos at heart,' but that 'it was probably expecting too much of Eskimos, who had been caribou hunters for generations, to become successful fishermen almost overnight, when they were not given the equipment or the guidance necessary.'[22]

It is possible to read the actions of the Ennadai Lake Inuit as resistance. They had a very close bond to their home territory, one which they were strongly opposed to breaking. This makes a good deal of sense in the context of the gathering and hunting cultural and economic strategy they practised, and is something common to most gathering and hunting peoples. The bond was further strengthened by the knowledge about the resources gained by the hundreds of years that their ancestors lived in the area. This was never considered by officials. The department, largely for the sake of administrative convenience, attempted to break that bond. Their first efforts met with comedy, their second with tragedy.

Figure 21 Inuit at Ennadai Lake in the early 1950s.

Back to Ennadai Lake

The movement of the people back to the Ennadai Lake area, from the government perspective, meant that the problem of dependency and relief remained. The Ennadai Lake Inuit 'continued to live in the close vicinity of the Radio Station and, as caribou were still plentiful in the district, they managed to eke out an existence by hunting and trapping.'[23] The radio station carried 'a small supply of staple goods so that the natives may be assisted when necessary,' and 'the R.C.M. Police [made] patrols into the area twice a year.'[24]

In the summer of 1955, these people were visited by four separate outsiders, each of whom reported on their situation. Their reports provide insight into conditions existing immediately after the return to Ennadai Lake. From mid-February to mid-March of 1955, northern service officer James Houston conducted a study of the 'Akeeamuit' and wrote a report based on his observations. From 9 August to 22 September, anthropologist Geert van den Steenhoven conducted research for his doctoral thesis on leadership and law among Keewatin Inuit. The diary notes of his visit were later published in *The Beaver*. Also, a photography crew from the popular American magazine, *Life*, visited the Ennadai Lake

Inuit in late August because they were seen as exemplary examples of 'primitive' Inuit. Finally, northern service officer W.G. Kerr also made a short visit.

Houston's ten-page report provides the most extensive description and analysis. It contains separate sections on such features as 'population,' 'clothing,' 'housing,' 'religious practices,' and so on. Houston reported that the population of the entire area was fifty-two people, adding that 'a fair number of the Ennadai population used to consider themselves Padleimuit and were born in that area. Over the past few years they have for various reasons drifted west and joined the Aheemuit because of debt, wanderlust, or argument.'[25] Houston reported that 'the extended family usually consisting of at least one inlaw and two children consider that they require 150-175 caribou per year per family if they are to have the desired food requirements.' (He noted that this meat was also used to feed dog teams.) [26]

Houston thought that 'in the average year the danger of excessive killing is greater than the possibility of obtaining too few caribou.' However, he observed that 'the killing is held in check to a major extent by the general shortage of ammunition and the ancient worn-out rifles generally in use.'[27] Still, the people seemed well off enough to him, and his main concern was 'to regulate excessive slaughter of the herd.' He thought that two members of the band, Angotilik and Hallow, were 'hunters of exceptional ability' but were not hunting the many wolves in the area, who were apparently robbing caches of food, because of a 'general lack of cartridges.'[28] This is important because later, in recounting their hunting problems, the Ennadai Lake Inuit complained about lack of ammunition.

The other important part of Houston's report was titled: 'Social Relationships and Intellectual Capacities.' In this section, Houston reported on the two camps, that of Owlijute (referred to elsewhere as Owlijoot, Oolijoot, and Owlyoot) and Boonala (probably Owliktuk and Pommela in Mowat's narrative). He also made a few comments about marriage, child relations, and so-called 'wife exchange,'[29] noting that 'at first one is inclined to believe that they are inferior to the coastal Eskimos but upon further study one realizes that they are living wisely according to the conditions and natural resources available to them.'[30] Apparently, these Inuit served an important role for the non-Natives who ran the radio station. In another section of his report, Houston wrote:

> Both the Army and the D.O.T. personnel that followed them admit that the Eskimos have been of great assistance to them. Such jobs as digging out full drums, hauling water and numerous other chores have been taken over by them, in exchange for rations. They have provided a moral support to the whites by showing them how to live in the country, how to dress for cold

weather and have provided a much needed interest beyond the cramped life within the station.[31]

The rations they got on the whole do not seem to have been welfare. They seem to have earned a good deal of it. Houston also noted that they had 'failry [sic] large trapping and family allowance credits' which, it seems, were not being paid automatically but were being held in reserve by the non-Native officials for use in times of need.

Houston's report ended with recommendations. Most interesting of these was his comment that 'the least likely solution seems to be to move them.' He explained: 'They have twice avoided such attempts by returning to their original region. They would probably do so again as they are primitive and independent people who are not yet used to accepting everything the white man tells them as wisdom.'[32] Throughout the document, 'primitiveness' is associated with resisting the influence of non-Native missionaries, traders, or government workers. In the quote above, the link between 'primitive' and 'independent' is made clear, and it seems obvious with hindsight that their non-acceptance of 'everything the white man tells them as wisdom' was probably a wise decision. Houston recommended leaving the people in the area because 'the Ennadai Lake region is splendid for caribou and vast quantities of fish can be obtained when necessary.' He thought the people's problems could be solved if somehow trade goods could be made available to them at Ennadai and if they could be encouraged to 'cache more meat and fish wisely.'[33]

The other visits made that summer confirm that the people were comparatively well off. Steenhoven's diary records a comfortable, relaxed round of successful hunting trips and drum dances. He stayed in 'Owlyoot's' camp, whom he describes as 'having the features of Rembrandt. He uses his eyes in a wonderful way and he has a fine poise in general. He says of himself that he is shy with white men. He does not impose himself at all and yet he is the camp boss here.'[34] One of his hunting trips is described as well: 'Upon rounding the hill, we saw five deer at about 120 feet distant. Owlyoot sat down, then aimed, fired and missed from that position. Apparently the deer was determined to allow itself to be killed for it remained motionless for one more minute, thus enabling Owlyoot to hit it with his second shot.'[35] Conditions in general seem to have been good: 'Nootaraloo lets us know they are doing all this [dancing] because they feel happy (*kuwuherktut*). Later this evening that statement that they feel happy is repeated, and special reference is made to the availability of tea and tobacco.'[36] Although the presence of non-Natives and the goods they brought seem to have contributed to the happiness, hunting also seems to have gone well. Steenhoven reported, for example, that on 4 September:

Figure 22 Owlijoot at Ennadai Lake in the early 1950s. Owlijoot was regarded as the elder/leader of the group which was eventually relocated to Henik Lake.

Owlyoot returns from the hunt and is noticed by the women, while he is still far away descending from the hill back of the camp. All are excited for he has tuktu, caribou, on his back. For the first time in about six days. He shot three of five. The children and young women run toward him, and some take over something from his back, such as a loose skin, or his rifle in order to carry that to camp. Quite a sight, this small triumphal march. It is always like that whenever a hunter returns with meat, but today doubly so.[37]

There are enough such descriptions from Steenhoven's short stay that the image of relative plenty, which one would expect given that this was the usual season for abundance, seems appropriate.

The other two visits confirm these impressions. Although the *Life* reporters, whose trip overlapped with Steenhoven's, 'found the Ennadai Natives in good health and well supplied with caribou meat and Fish,' the reporters 'were somewhat disappointed to find the Ennadai Eskimos using Rifles and living in canvass Tents.'[38] However, arrangements were made to have the 'Eskimos' fabricate some spears, caribou clothing, and tents for the purposes of the camera shoot. An earlier visit that same summer noted that the dogs were in excellent condition, and the northern service officer, W.G. Kerr, also wrote, 'I cannot help but admire these Eskimo who want to live their own mode of life and are confident of surviving on their own hunting ability rather than on relief rations.'[39] Kerr had come to his work as a northern service officer from the RCMP and at times perhaps found himself acting as if he were still in his old role. His tone would change dramatically a few years later.

Two Difficult Winters

Until 1955, the fall caribou hunt was relatively successful. That year, after all the outsiders were gone, the caribou hunt went poorly: 'This was, to a large extent, the fault of the Eskimos who would not move from the Radio Station to hunt.'[40] Another possibility, raised in both Steenhoven's and Houston's accounts, helps explain why caribou hunting was going poorly. The Ennadai Lake Inuit were in the process of making a transition from the older technique of spearing caribou from kayaks to using rifles to hunt. A few years later, one of the department's translators expressed the opinion that

> the Ahearmiuts didn't know how to use rifles properly and economically. He has observed at Ennadai that some members of the group were using up a whole box of shells to knock one caribou down. There [*sic*] were also seen to open fire on game before coming within reasonable range. He thought that this waste of ammunition resulted in shortages which may have had something to do with their inability finally to get what caribou may have been around at Ennadai.[41]

The Inuit themselves, when questioned about conditions at Ennadai after the tragedy at Henik Lake, revealed problems with getting enough ammunition. One couple, Yahah and Mowmik, said, 'We received only a few shells from the radio station – therefore we could not hunt much.' A second couple, Shikoak and Pallicak, reported that 'there was lots of caribou at Ennadai, but we were always short of ammunition ... If we had ammunition, we would have been alright at Ennadai.' A third, Owlijoot and Nootaraloo, reported that 'we couldn't get at the caribou because we were always short of ammunition.'[42] Interestingly, in the *Life* article based on the visit from the summer of 1955, the writers noted that 'since the ammunition supply is limited, he still resorts to the age-old method of spearing his quarry while they swim across one of the tundra's innumerable lakes.'[43] It seems quite possible that, even if the caribou were not migrating in as great numbers as in previous years, Inuit difficulties were aggravated by the fact that they were making a transition from one kind of hunting technology to another. In fact, they may have been able to sustain themselves quite well at Ennadai had they been given either enough ammunition or proper instruction and guidance in the use of their weapons.

To get them through the winter of 1955-6, rations were supplied in the form of relief. In January 1956, a report on the Ennadai Lake Inuit was made by F.G. Cunningham to Gordon Robertson, the deputy minister of northern affairs and natural resources. It was motivated by a concern that more discussion of the 'plight' of these people, stemming from the publication in 1952 of Mowat's *People of the Deer*, might take place in the House of Commons. It reveals the nature of the so-called 'relief' provided.

> On January 11 our northern service officer visited Ennadai Lake via an RCAF 'Otter,' the RCMP 'Otter' being unserviceable. They took in a capacity load of food and other supplies for the Eskimos, which had been paid for by wages due to the Eskimos by the Department of Transport for unloading aircraft at the Radio Station. All Eskimos were reported to be in good health, but apparently the main herd of caribou had not passed through the district last fall and only a few had been obtained.[44]

The relief given to these people was not in the form of social welfare, but rather wages which they were owed. In fact, what is remarkable is that throughout much of the period in question, Inuit were assisted in bad times by supplies they were owed rather than by social welfare. Family allowances were also used in this way, as the report makes clear: 'As this group has considerable Family Allowance credits, the next flight planned for February will take in Family Allowance supplies and goods purchased from the limited proceeds of the trapping. Sufficient ammunition is on hand and with the supplies they have now received, together with what will be going in, plus what they will earn during the rest of the winter, they will have little difficulty in remaining self-supporting.'[45] The considerable difficulties of the Ennadai Lake Inuit were not costing the government anything in relief payments.

By June, officials had come to the conclusion that the people should be moved. Two reasons were given for the necessity of the move. 'The impoverished condition of the natives at Ennadai Lake is attributable in no small degree to the failure of the caribou to follow their customary migratory routes, and inadequate supervision of the hunting and trading operations of these natives due largely to the remoteness of the region in relation to the established trading posts and the local administrative offices.'[46] More supervision was needed, and finding a way of placing them closer to 'local administrative offices' was the best mechanism for establishing that supervision. Cunningham wrote to P.A.C. Nichols of the Hudson's Bay Company that 'your Mr. Voisey and the representatives of the R.C.M.Police at Eskimo

Point were firmly of the opinion that suitable supervision could be given to them if these natives were removed to the Henik Lake region.'[47]

That summer, serious talks were held with the Ennadai Lake Inuit about the possibility of a move to Henik Lake. During the talks, the northern service officer, W.G. Kerr, emphasized that relief might not be so easily available in the coming year. This suggestion was clearly an attempt to influence their willingness to move. What he most likely did not mention was that the bulk, if not all, of the relief that had been provided was not really relief at all but wages or family allowances due them. Kerr reported:

> They were then shown a map of the Henick [sic] Lake district, which is within 50 Miles of the Padley [sic] Post. This district was familiar to them and they stated that this had been their home years ago. They were evidently satisfied with the place selected and immediately started to tell Mr. Voisey and myself of all the Fishing places and the good camping sites. Without exception they were all in favour of going to Henick Lake and said they would not return to Ennadai unless they talked it over with the government first.[48]

Kerr went on to note, 'I would emphasize that the conference was held in a friendly atmosphere and the decision of the Eskimo was reached by themselves and no threats or co-ercion was used.'[49] As noted later, this benign view of Inuit agreement was suspected even by officials working within the department. Kerr's claims must also be evaluated in light of other information about the perception Ennadai Lake Inuit had of the Padlei area. During the summer of 1955, when asked about the area, 'they replied that the Padlei district, where most of them had been, was a poor country for game and that they would be hungry there,' while one of the non-Native radio operators 'advanced the opinion that he thought the Natives would be discontented if moved to Padlei and would invariably drift back in a short time.'[50]

The plan had been to airlift the Ennadai Lake Inuit as soon as possible, preferably before 15 August 1956. Difficulties in finding a suitable aircraft made it impossible to do so. On 12 September, Kerr finally abandoned the project for that summer: 'The Lakes Inland are starting to freeze and it would appear that it is now to [sic] late to move the Ennadai Eskimo this year if they are to be given a fair chance to establish themselves in a new environment.'[51] Kerr also noted that the non-Natives involved would have little time to prepare and that it would be too late to start the fishing project that was essential to the success of the move. The plan was put on hold, though Ben Sivertz, then chief of the Arctic division, wrote Kerr that 'we should proceed in the understanding that the transfer of these natives to Henik Lake will be undertaken in 1957, if at all possible.'[52]

The winter of 1956-7 was also a difficult one for the Ennadai Lake Inuit. Official reports indicated that 'the caribou hunt was again a failure and, although fish was plentiful, none were cached for winter use and, as a result, most Eskimos lost their dogs through starvation.'[53] Later reports indicated that seventy of their seventy-five dogs died that winter. Government-supplied food rations and buffalo meat helped sustain the people through the winter.

The next spring, Inuit informed the northern service officer, Kerr, that 'they were willing to go to North Henik Lake (45 miles from Padley Post), as this was good hunting country and familiar to them. They also stated they were happy to be going to a place from where they could reach a trading post.'[54] Despite these claims, there is good reason to think they were not as agreeable to the move as Kerr implied.

When discussing the situation a year later, after the 1957-8 starvation, their leader/elder Owlijoot and his marriage partner, Nootaraloo, said: 'We didn't know we were moving (to Henik Lake) till just before we went. Voisey told us the day before. He didn't give us any reasons.'[55] When asked about hunting and fishing at Henik Lake, they replied: 'We don't know why the caribou didn't come – but there never was much caribou around Henik Lake.'[56] Shikoak and Pallikal, another couple, thought that 'we were moved to Henik Lake because we didn't have any ammunition.'[57]

The Move to Henik Lake

A glowing press release entitled, 'Eskimos Fly to New Hunting Grounds,' was prepared, announcing and describing the relocation. The release began: 'A community of some of Canada's most primitive citizens has moved – but they did it the modern way. Eskimo hunters and huskies left their ancient ways for a day to travel in the comfort of an aircraft to new hunting grounds.'[58] The release went on to describe the stoicism of these people in the face of the hardships of recent years, itself a result of less predictable migrations of caribou. It described the helpful efforts of the Department of Northern Affairs, which 'studied the situation' and 'searched to the surrounding country to find a place where game was more plentiful.' Such a place was found 'around Henik Lake, 125 miles to the northeast,' where 'the caribou still come ... the fishing is good, and white foxes are there to be trapped.'[59] In May 1957, the people of Ennadai were relocated to Henik Lake: 'With the co-operation of the R.C.M.P. and the Hudson's Bay Company, the move was made this month under the supervision of Northern Affairs Officer Bill Kerr. The 55 men, women, and children in the group were flown to their new home in an R.C.M.P. aircraft. Six flights were needed to complete the airlift in 24 hours. The settlers were supplied with new tents, enough ammunition for the summer, and food to last them a month.'[60]

Specific reference was made in the press release to the earlier relocations to Cornwallis and Ellesmere islands, which went on to note that 'if the success of these earlier settlers is any guide, the Ennadai Eskimos can hope to find relative prosperity in their new surroundings.'[61] The prosperity they found would be relative indeed. And the comparison may have been more apt than anyone at the time suspected.

Official reports produced later put the number of Inuit moved at fifty-eight. According to these reports, 'they were settled in a dense section of bush and equipped with new tents, ammunition fish nets and sufficient food for one month.'[62] A month later, Kerr returned to their camp 'in response to a rumour that they were hungry, and brought in another month's supply of food.'[63] On that trip, which took place on 5 June, Kerr found that the group had broken up into several campsites – which could have been expected – and that they were in generally good health. He also reported the following:

> We landed at the largest group of tents (4) and visited the Eskimos there. They reported that no Caribou had been seen in their area, but that they were obtaining Fish enough for their needs. They also reported that another group of Eskimos, camped about 5 miles away, were hungry. The Natives referred to, to my knowledge, had regularly appeared at a Camp of Prospectors for Sherrit-Gordon Mines on Bray Lake and had traded Fish for Tobacco and Tea. This Lake was about 4 miles beyond where the 'Hungry' Eskimos were camped. The Prospectors have since gone out until after the 'Break-up,' when they will probably return. It is likely that the 'Hungry' Eskimos did not want to share their source of supply with the others and so spread the story of their hunger.[64]

His estimation of the situation was drastically wrong, but he did leave food behind, as well as fishing material and ammunition. It is worth noting that at this stage, as he begins to be called on to provide relief, a note of distrust enters his reports. The report also noted that 'the late spring, prevalent throughout this area, had no doubt delayed the Northward migration of the Caribou through the Padley District.'[65] The situation at Henik Lake slowly deteriorated.

The first sign of trouble emerged over a break-in at the Sherrit-Gordon Mines camp. Sometime in June, probably on the 6th, one day after Kerr's visit, the camp was broken into while the prospectors were away for spring break-up and '$1500 worth of supplies and equipment had been stolen or wantonly destroyed.'[66] The prospectors questioned one of the Ennadai Lake Inuit, Oohootok, who was camped nearby and, although he 'had a slight knowledge of English, [he] admitted that he and other Eskimos had taken the missing supplies on 6 June. When questioned further ... he walked off and did not return.'[67] Upon hearing of this, Kerr, joined by an RCMP constable, travelled to Padlei where they found another Inuk, Karyook, who 'freely admitted that he and a Henik Lake Eskimo, Mounik, had broken the lock and the supply tent and had taken some foodstuffs. They were unaccompanied ... Corporal Gallagher placed him under arrest and he later was escorted to Eskimo point.'[68]

In reporting on these events, a tone of indignation and frustration begins to develop in Kerr's reports. He notes that the day before the theft, he 'had been at Henik Lake and had distributed a month's supply of Flour, Lard, etc, for each Family of Eskimos ... The Eskimos were therefore in no need of supplies.'[69] As a result, Kerr writes: 'I fully concur that the instigators and ringleaders should be prosecuted as an example to other Eskimos.'[70] On 7 August, Kerr, with police and interpreters, travelled to Henik Lake and visited two Inuit camps: 'At one of them Oohootuk was apprehended and at the other one Mounik.'[71] It is interesting to note that 'the other Eskimos encountered also admitted participation but stated that they did so only because Ohootuk and Munik had instigated the theft.'[72] No thought seems to have been given to the fact that the two instigators might also have been leaders or that their presence might be essential to the success or failure of the relocation project and to the survival of the small band. Oohootuk had been one of Farley Mowat's key informants, and Mounik was described later as 'a medicine man in training. Not too good a provider.'[73] The two were taken to Eskimo Point, where they were convicted, sentenced, and imprisoned until late fall. By December, they were waiting for a chance to return to their camp.

The break-ins meant that the Henik Lake band was visited with some frequency over the summer, and Kerr consistently reported on conditions. After the trip to Padlei, when Karyook was arrested, Kerr and Constable Gallagher had immediately flown to Henik Lake, but, on landing, the 'plane's pontoon struck a rock and punctured it and [we] had to leave at once.'[74] Of interest is his report that 'we had no means of getting ashore and the Eskimos had no canoe to reach us.'[75] So, although they had fishing supplies, the Inuit were expected to make their own boats and had not done so by early August. This may have contributed to the lack of success and interest in the fishing venture.

On 7 August, when the plane managed to land, they were 'equipped with a rubber raft.'[76] No mention is made of whether the Inuit had built or started building kayaks or canoes by then. Mention is made of general conditions. Kerr reports that 'the Eskimos at Henik Lake were catching sufficient Fish for their needs and shooting Caribou in small numbers. They were not hungry and in good health.'[77] The report noted that the technical officer,

Lewis Voisey, would be 'left with the Eskimos until "Freeze-up" and supervise the Caribou Hunt and Caching of the meat. He will also endeavour to have the Eskimos make proper skin clothing for themselves for the coming Winter.'[78] Voisey was described later as 'an employee of this department who has a good command of the Eskimo language. His mother is an Eskimo, and he was raised in the Padlei-Eskimo Point region. He can read and write in syllabics but is illiterate in the English language.'[79] Voisey was not left at the Inuit camps on this trip. He was left with them on the next trip in late August. Finally, Kerr made arrangements to provide for the welfare of the families of the two arrested Inuit through the HBC Post at Padlei.

The camps at Henik Lake were visited again in late August. At that time, according to Kerr, 'these Eskimos reported that Fish were being obtained and a few Caribou had been shot by them. The main herd on which they depend for their Winter meat and skin clothing had not yet appeared.'[80] Kerr goes on to report that fishnets were provided as well as a new 16-foot canoe, and that 'some Caribou skin kyaks [sic] and canoes had been made by the Inuit themselves from recently obtained hides.'[81] Ammunition and a small amount of food was also left. A note of concern about the indolence of these Inuit enters the record in connection with a proposal to relocate them again: 'If, after giving assistance and sufficient game is available, these Eskimos are unable to provide for themselves, I would suggest that it leaves us no alternative than to move them to Churchill and incorporate them in our development there.'[82]

The next news of these camps comes from the other northern service officer in the region, Doug Wilkinson (the same Wilkinson mentioned in Chapter 4, who had made a film on Idlout). Wilkinson had been asked to arrange to fly Voisey out of the Henik Lake area on 19 September. On 18 September, Wilkinson registered his concern, noting, 'If [Voisey] is out of food now then it seems quite likely that the whole group at Oftedal is out of food. If the Eskimo group was well off for food, then Mr. Voisey would not wire out to say he was out of food for he was supposed to be with the group.'[83] Wilkinson followed up with a report after Voisey's return that showed his earlier concern was well founded:

Up to the time of his departure no large kills of caribou had taken place an [sic] no winter caribou caches had been put up. Caribou in small numbers were being taken by all families enough for their day to day needs and a small reserve supply. The Eskimos were fishing but not energetically. Reports from a survey aircraft indicated that a large herd of caribou was in the region fifty miles west of Oftedal Lake and moving east towards the Eskimo camps but up until the time of Mr. Voisey's departure the caribou had not put in an appearance.[84]

The ability of the group to survive, the report went on, depended on whether the herd of caribou continued to move closer to the camps. Wilkinson also noted that as these people 'are within easy walking distance of the Padlei post there seems to be no danger of them running short of food without our knowledge,' but that, 'I would venture the prediction that they will not be able to get through the winter without assistance.'[85] Ennadai relocation number two was not working out.

Late Fall at Henik Lake

A report by northern service officer Kerr, dated 3 December, reveals not only subsequent events but a significant degree of frustration. The most important news in the report was that the Ennadai/Henik Lake Inuit had again 'broken into the buildings of the Sherrit-Gordon Mine at Bray Lake and had stolen an unknown amount of food and equipment.'[86] Although they had been released, Oohootuk and Mounik had not yet returned to Henik from Eskimo Point and had not been involved in the second break-in. Kerr reported that 'unfortunately, the Caribou did not migrate through the district last Fall in their trek south, and only a few had been previously obtained in late summer.'[87] It was obvious that these people were in trouble and the relocation had not helped them. Kerr's response at this time was to blame the Ennadai Lake Inuit for 'indolence.'

Kerr's report is worth quoting at some length.

> Lewis Voisey informed me that the Eskimos were very indolent about fishing unless he was practically standing over them and urging them on. They were scattered over the area of Ofterdahl Lake and were equipped with Caribou skin Kayaks. On visiting some of the encampments he found the fishnets washed ashore or piled up at the tents. On inquiring why they were not fishing he was informed that there were no Fish in the Lake although large Lake trout could be plainly seen breaking the surface of the Lake. On these occasions he had the Eskimos again set their nets and in a short time fish was obtained.[88]

It should have been expected that a people used to caribou hunting would have some difficulty making the transition to a subsistence economy based on fishing. One might also note that the skin kayaks to which this report refers were probably the same ones these indolent Inuit had been credited with making a few months earlier. They had been provided with a single, sixteen-foot canoe.

Voisey himself later attributed the refusal to fish to taboos among the group. He said that 'several of the Eskimos had told him they would die if they ate jackfish or certain kinds of trout. They would select the fish they considered edible out of a net and leave the others.'[89] This is contradicted by the testimony of the Inuit themselves, who when questioned later generally indicated no such problem. For example, Yahah and Sokawak said, 'We eat any kind of fish – including Jackfish. We always eat all kinds of fish. We did so even when our mothers and fathers were alive.'[90] However, Voisey, the same man responsible for encouraging them to fish, was the translator when this question was asked. Three of the four couples asked about fish indicated no difficulty. The fourth couple, Shikoak and Pallikal, said, 'We like fish but Owlijoot took our canoe and we couldn't fish. Some in our group won't eat any kind of fish – for example, jackfish. I don't know why. I would eat jackfish if I was very hungry ... We tried to fish but there were none to be had.'[91] Obviously, the availability of canoes was crucial to fishing, and canoes were not to be had for most of the summer. There is at least mixed evidence about whether fish was an acceptable part of the diet and, as noted above, one would expect Caribou hunters to have some difficulty making the transition to fishing.

The report goes on to describe an interesting incident: 'One Eskimo informed Voisey that he had shot a Caribou and assured him that he had skinned the animal and cached the meat. A few days later Voisey was walking through the area where the Eskimo had reported the shooting of the Caribou and he came upon the carcass unskinned and laying where it had been felled.'[92] It is difficult to know what to make of this. It seems a clear sign that the Ennadai Lake Inuit were in some disarray, something that could be attributed to the relocation and perhaps to the loss of some of their leaders. This behaviour is what one would expect from someone suffering severe depression. The setting is full of symbolism. Killing a caribou in a place where they are scarce, where one is far from home and a familiar landscape, and being trapped in a situation where one is forced to fish to survive, are all factors that might have contributed to this behaviour. The loss of Oohootuk and Mounik would also serve as a reminder that for this Inuit group, things were 'falling apart.' The inability to skin the animal is behaviour consistent with someone so debilitated at the moment that he does not have the psychological strength to follow through with a project he has initiated.

But if the relocation project was failing, it had to be the fault of the Inuit involved. Other rationales for Inuit behaviour in this setting were not considered. Voisey provided another possible explanation, without direct reference to this incident, a year later, when he claimed that the group 'will not butcher caribou if there are seal skin boots being worn in the vicinity.'[93]

Trapping, as well as fishing and caribou hunting, was a problem for the people who had been moved to Henik Lake.

In late November some of the Henik Lake Eskimos had come into Padley Post for supplies and, when asked if they had set out their traps, replied that they had not as they did not have a calendar. Henry Voisey, the Trading Post Manager, had previously supplied them with calendars and had marked the trapping dates on them and, when reminded of this, the Eskimos admitted that they had ignored setting a trapline. These Eskimos, as well a [sic] most others, had usually set their trapline in other years without regard for any calendar and when they thought the fox skins were marketable.[94]

Trapping in an unfamiliar area would not have been easy. It is hard to know what these people would have made of the calendars given to them, or what they understood about trapping regulations – regulations they were obviously not accustomed to being governed by. The circumstances in which the Ennadai Lake Inuit found themselves seem to have demoralized and disoriented the group.

Further evidence of the demoralizing effect relocation had on these Inuit and, perhaps, some indication of their resistance to the regimes being forced upon them, appear in the following statement by northern service officer Bill Kerr. He was obviously frustrated and inclined to see their behaviour as deficiency of character: 'While at Churchill, I visited these people practically every month and got on very well with them, but while I think I have their confidence, I do not think that I, or anyone else, could get them to shake of [sic] their lethargy about providing for themselves. They will agree to follow any program to better themselves that is suggested to them and then go back again to their former ways and blithely forget their promises.'[95] The last statement throws light on the nature of the consent to relocate obtained in the first place. Clearly, deference to people seen to be in authority was a factor in their agreeing to the move and their consent was likely a matter of 'the yes that means no.' That they were subsequently unhappy in the new location, with hindsight, is no surprise.

The same report continues: 'This is the third year in succession that these people have been unable to obtain and cache sufficient Caribou for their Winter needs (Two years at Ennadai Lake and one at Henik Lake). Their whole economy and way of life was based on the Caribou and now with the diminishing Herds, they are apparently unable to adapt themselves to the utilization of other resources within the area of their present environment.'[96] The solution to this dilemma was as obvious in late 1957 as it had been earlier the same year, as obvious as it had been in the summer of 1956 and in 1950. Move them. 'Corpl. Gallagher and myself are in agreement that these Eskimos, numbering, all told, about 55 should be moved to an area where they could be under constant supervision, but we differ as to where that place should be.'[97] Gallagher favoured the coast of Hudson Bay, somewhere north of the tree line. Kerr favoured moving them to Churchill. The crucial point is that the solution was to place the Ennadai Lake Inuit under constant supervision. If they could not meet the expectations of the northern service officer and others, then more deliberate attempts would have to be made to provide for their welfare.

The report goes on to provide further arguments supporting the proposal to relocate them to Churchill, in the context of which Kerr states: 'The Henik Lake People are very primitive and in their present belief, Pagans. As a change from their present way of life to the proposed one of semi-regimentation would be a radical one, these people would have to be handled with understanding and firmness and an understanding of their particular process of evolution.'[98] The ethnocentric benevolence of this statement is difficult to overlook. The superiority of the author's culture is taken for granted. These Inuit are 'pagans.' They have resisted all attempts to get them to behave in a manner deemed by the northern service officer and other officials as being in their best interest. Firmness was required, and this necessitated relocation to yet another setting where a watchful eye could be kept on them.[99]

January: Time to Consider Another Move
By early December, the Ennadai/Henik Lake Inuit had exhausted the patience of the northern service officer. It was obvious they would likely need assistance to get them through the winter. However, the assumption was made that their nearness to the post at Padlei would ensure that the situation could be monitored. Through December and January, although a debate emerged in the south over their future, little was done. 'While the failure of the caribou hunt was reported, it was believed the Eskimos were obtaining sufficient fish and ptarmigan to substain [sic] them. Eskimos from Henik lake were periodically visiting Padlei Post to trade and for family allowance issues and no report was made of any privations.'[100] The Inuit relocated to Henik Lake were relatively traditional. Their contacts with non-Natives had obviously involved, along with relief, lectures about self-reliance. As well, the non-Natives were constantly trying to get them to move or to undertake some activity not of their design. It therefore seems logical that they either did not realize they should report their troubles to the trading post or did not feel comfortable doing so. In any case, they did not report. And they were not visited.

In early January, Graham Rowley, secretary of the advisory committee on northern development, entered the debate about what should be done. In a detailed memorandum to the deputy minister, he wrote:

Moves have rarely been successful unless they are done with the full consent of the people concerned. To us, one part of the barrens may appear very much like another, but this is not the case with the Eskimos. The region where they have lived for many years has associations which mean a great deal to them, and detailed knowledge of any area is essential for hunters who wish to exploit its potentialities fully. In view of [the fact that] these Eskimos like the Ennadai region and did not want to leave it, it appeared unlikely that the move was really accepted by them. (It is, of course, comparatively easy to get a temporary acquiescence from the Eskimos to any suggestion put to them, and especially from this group who go to great lengths to avoid any form of conflict).[101]

Rowley also provided his views on why the Ennadai/Henik Inuit were demoralized to the point where they were resorting to break-ins and other antisocial behaviour.

It seems clear that only two years ago the Eskimos were happy and contented at Ennadai. The deterioration which appears to have set in is certainly owing in part to their being moved to unfamiliar surroundings. Another reason is probably a lack of discipline which has resulted from weakening the normal tribal procedures. Among the Eskimos in general, and specifically this tribe, decisions on moving a camp are reached after considerable discussion within the tribe ... The decision to move, to Henik Lake, initiated from the outside, cannot have failed to weaken the authority of those who usually decide these things, and may have contributed to the general despondency reported in the new area.[102]

With this in mind, the break-ins noted earlier can be interpreted as acts of defiance. However, the subsequent arrests could only have aggravated the situation and would not have contributed to the group's well-being or to its trust of non-Natives. Rowley went on to suggest that rather than moving these people to the coast or to Churchill and further disrupting them, they should be moved back to Ennadai and placed under the care or supervision of a northern service officer who would be stationed with them.

Summarizing the relocation to Henik Lake, he wrote on 22 January 1958: 'At the best, the recent move seems to have been from one depressed area to another. It was, however, from an area they liked to one of which they had unhappy memories, and one which they themselves believed to be less rich. It had therefore little or no chance to succeed.'[103] The concern here was with the break-ins, but Rowley was, in retrospect, quite perceptive about the problems. He was even more prescient about what was likely to result. A week later he wrote: 'I am concerned that this group, which is now much further away from help than before, may get into serious difficulties early this spring, possibly while trying to return to Ennadai. You might like to suggest to Mr. Sivertz that a particularly close tab should be kept on them.'[104] It did not take until spring for the group to encounter difficulties. Had a particularly close tab been kept on them, commencing 30 January, a tragedy that subsequently became the focus of international attention through the writings of Farley Mowat would probably have been avoided.

February at Henik Lake: Kikkik's Story

Two official reports are helpful in reconstructing the events that followed. A report signed by R.A.J. Phillips, dated 20 October 1958, has already been noted. It is titled: 'Re: Starvation Among the Eskimos in the Winter of 1957-58.' A more detailed report was prepared by Walter Rudnicki based on a field trip he made to Eskimo Point with Alex Stevenson. Rudnicki interviewed many of the survivors, and information from some of those interviews has already been used to reconstruct the circumstances of the move to Henik Lake. Rudnicki's report is dated March 1958 and titled: 'Report – Field Trip to Eskimo Point.'

The fall caribou hunt had been remarkably unsuccessful. All the relocated Inuit had been able to procure were about twelve caribou. Eight of these were shot by Voisey. One caribou might last a family about three days, so this was not nearly enough. According to Voisey, 'the groups broke up into four camps, each within a seven mile radius. Owlijoot, who is looked to for advice and guidance by the others lived with his large family in one camp. Ootuk and Hallow made up another camp ... each family was looking after its own needs and there seemed to be no effort at sharing.'[105] Most of the group's dogs had died the winter before. They had between four and seven dogs scattered among the four camps and as a result did not have a single dog team. Their mobility, therefore, was limited, both for caribou hunting and for going to the post at Padlei. Voisey was of the opinion that 'the Eskimos customarily did not travel further than one day's walk away from the camp on hunting forays. The expectation seemed to be that the caribou would come to them.'[106] The caribou did not, and the hunters could not go to the caribou.

Interviewed by Rudnicki later, each couple reported on the lack of success in hunting caribou and fishing at Henik Lake. Owlijoot and Nootaraloo reported that 'we never got any caribou this side of Ennadai. We had a net but could catch only one fish. There was enough ammunition but no caribou.'[107] Yahah and Howmik said, 'there was no caribou at Henik Lake. We had lots of ammunition. We did not have a boat for fishing. We get a little fish through the ice this winter. We were hungry at Henik Lake this winter.'[108] Shikoak and Pallikal told the same story: 'At Henik Lake the only caribou we got were a few in September ... After that, no more caribou. Shikoak got five caribou after September – those were his last. We had enough ammunition.'[109] They went on to say, 'We don't know about fish – the only time we fished was when Voisey was with us.'[110]

By late January, the people were in dire circumstances. The situation at Hallow and Ootuk's camp, where the most serious trouble broke out, was probably not atypical. Rudnicki reports:

As the winter progressed food became scarcer and scarcer. By February, hunger and despair filled the two igloos on the shores of Henik Lake. Hallow continued to jig for fish from early morning till late at night and managed usually to catch one or two to keep his family going. Ootuk and his family kept themselves alive by eating caribou clothing and fish bones which they got from Hallow's igloo. Soon, the children's clothing was gone and there was nothing more to eat. Not long afterwards, Igyaka, Ootuk's son died of starvation.[111]

In the other report, Igyaka's death is reported to have taken place on 8 February, the same day that trouble broke out between Ootuk and Hallow, and Igyaka is described as Ootuk's daughter, not his son. '*Igyaka* daughter of Ootuk died of malnutrition. Ootuk, through indolence, failed to provide sufficient food for family. Although he lived about 30 yards from igloo of Hallow, who provided well for his family at fishing holes about 50 yds. from both igloos.'[112] However, it seems unlikely that Hallow was providing well for his family, since the conflict between the two was probably precipitated by Hallow's desire to move his camp to find a better fishing spot. Rudnicki reports that Igyaka died on 6 February. Hallow and Kikkik were in almost as much trouble as Ootuk and Howmik, though the latter were undoubtedly worse off, possibly because Howmik was 'crippled by polio. [She] does not have use of legs and right arm. Appears to be a bright and resourceful person, however.'[113]

February 8 was a stormy, cold day. Ootuk was apparently in a foul mood, and 'struck his daughter Kooyak because she was crying for food.'[114] Telling his wife he was leaving to go to Padlei for help, he took his rifle and left the tent, but 'instead of starting for Padlei, Ootuk walked to Hallow's igloo.'[115] There he found Hallow and Kikkik 'eating strips of caribou skin and old tea leaves' and learned of Hallow's plan to move after the storm. Hallow left to try for more fish. Ootuk waited a while and left, having announced his plan to walk to Padlei.

Instead, he walked with his rifle through the storm towards Hallow's fishing hole. 'He came up behind Hallow who was crouched over the fishing hole and had not heard him approach. Ootuk stared at the huddled figure, then carefully aimed his rifle and fired. Hallow slumped forward into the water, the back of his head shattered by the force of the bullet.'[116] Ootuk then walked back to Hallow and Kikkik's igloo where Kikkik was surprised to see him return. He asked Kikkik's children to do some small tasks for him, all strange requests that were not obeyed, and then left the igloo taking Hallow's rifle. Kikkik followed, attempting to get the rifle back. Ootuk pointed the rifle at Kikkik and fired it, but she moved the barrel away just before he fired, so he missed her. The two struggled, and Kikkik yelled to her daughter to run and get Hallow. Kikkik managed to wrestle the weakened Ootuk to the ground and sit on him by the time her daughter returned with news of the murder.

> Struggling to free himself, Ootuk's reserves of strength quickly failed. Kikkik held him firmly and accused Ootuk of killing Hallow. Ootuk admitted the deed saying that Howmik, his wife, had told him to kill Hallow because he was not feeding his kin. Kikkik called to Allaymuk and asked for a knife which was quickly procured. Pleading for his life, Ootuk promised to care for Kikkik and her children now that Hallow was dead. He defended himself desperately and the knife succeeded only in tearing his face. It was too dull to inflict a fatal wound and Kikkik called to her children to bring another knife. Karlak, her nine year old son, handed her a sharp skinning knife. Before plunging the knife into Ootuk's chest, Kikkik ordered her children back into the igloo.[117]

Kikkik then covered the bodies with snow and began loading her sled, having decided to try to make the trip to Padlei. As Kikkik loaded the sled, Howmik appeared, asking after Ootuk. Kikkik said Ootuk had gone on to Padlei and that she was on her way to a new fishing camp. 'Kikkik pitied Howmik who now had no fire, no wood and no food. Kikkik didn't know what Howmik could do now to save herself and her children.'[118]

Pulling the sled, Kikkik then walked off with her children into the storm. They overnighted in a hollow she dug into the snow and continued walking the next day. Sometime on the afternoon of 9 February, Kikkik stumbled across her brother, Yahah, who was out looking for food. She told him the story and he responded by building her an igloo and leaving for Padlei himself to get help. Worried that Yahah might not actually go to Padlei, the next morning Kikkik decided to continue the journey with her children. For three more days they walked with no food or comfort. At some point the two youngest girls weakened to the point that Kikkik had to pull them in the sled. Not knowing that Yahah had reached Padlei, and rapidly losing strength, Kikkik's options continued to narrow.

During the night Kikkik thought much about what she should do. She could still manage with her oldest son and daughter and little Kokakhak who was in her hood. Annacathea and Nosha seemed very weak however and would not last much longer. The following morning, Kikkik wrapped her two daughters in two caribou skins and buried them under snow blocks. With her remaining three children, Kikkik started once more for Padlei. That noon, she stopped to rest in an abandoned cabin around fifteen miles from Padlei and it was not long before she was spotted.[119]

Kikkik was spotted by a plane carrying RCMP that had gone in search of her after Yahah reached Padlei and reported the events. Frightened by the questions the police were asking, Kikkik told them that Annacathea and Nesha 'were dead – for they surely would be by now. Kikkik and her remaining children were bundled into a plane and taken to Eskimo Point.'[120] A constable, following Kikkik's trail by dog sled to verify her story, 'heard the voice of a child calling out of the snow. He dug into the snow and found Annacatha alive and apparently unharmed. Nesha was dead.'[121] Kikkik was taken into custody and charged with murder.

On 12 February, Yahah reached the Padlei post and the HBC manager 'radioed R.C.M.Police at Eskimo Point and reported the murders of two Eskimo men at Henik Lake and other Eskimo deaths by privation. Police went to Henik Lake by their aircraft on February 13th.'[122] On the 14th, supplies were airlifted in, and on the 15th the evacuation of the Henik Lake Inuit to Eskimo Point began under the supervision of the northern service officer. The same day, in a last sweep of the area to ensure no one had been left behind, the police were reported to have 'found fish and ptarmigan fairly plentiful.'[123] This is hard to imagine. Police, sweeping the area to ensure that no one had been left behind, would hardly have taken the time to fish through the ice to see if fish were 'plentiful.' It also seems equally improbable that they could have established that there were lots of ptarmigan in the area.

While the Kikkik-Hallow and Howmik-Ootuk families were experiencing conflict and turmoil, other groups were not much better off. On 10 February, Kayai, who had frozen his toe and found decomposition setting in, died on the way to Padlei. He had tried walking, but after a day had to be pulled by sled. Ungmak 'died of exposure and exhaustion en route to Padley. His wife Tablook, discharged from Sanatorium in previous October hauled sled with no ill effects.'[124] The implication is made over and over in this report that those who died were to blame for their own misfortune. Another Inuk, Angatayok, travelled with Ungmak and Tablook but 'lagged behind and was later found dead on ice from exposure.'[125] This brought the total number of Ennadai/Henik Inuit who died in February 1957 to seven. Five others had to be evacuated to hospitals. Of the six surviving adult male family members, only three were able-bodied.

The 20 October report by R.A.J. Phillips of the department puts the blame for the incident squarely on the heads of the Inuit.

> The Coroner examined all bodies and found them all, with the exception of Igyaka, to have the appearance of well nourished persons in life. While shortage of food no doubt caused exodus of these Eskimos to Padley, there was no evidence of starvation. The failure of the caribou to appear at Henik Lake in sufficient numbers to enable the Eskimos to obtain meat was the main factor in causing the unfortunate chain of events. While the other game and fish resources were sufficient to maintain the Eskimos in food, the lack of caribou clothing prevented them from fully exploiting these resources.[126]

These observations are likely quite inaccurate and characterized by errors in judgment repeated during the investigations of Inuit deaths at Garry Lake the same winter. Starvation in the Arctic is not the same as starvation in a temperate climate. Under Arctic conditions, the loss of body fat means death from hypothermia long before the body starts to consume protein and muscle mass in an effort to sustain itself. Therefore, Inuit dying of starvation in the Arctic do not fit the stereotypical image of starvation, most commonly associated with people dying in temperate, Third World countries, whose muscle mass, by the time they die, has been severely reduced. The statement that 'there was no evidence of starvation' is, therefore, inaccurate, and the statement that 'lack of caribou clothing prevented them from fully exploiting these resources' is only partly correct. The story of Kikkik certainly indicates severe malnourishment.

The coroner's report, as a 'neutral' document, is questionable. A later memorandum, written by Northern Service Officer Kerr, commented on critical remarks found in the 20 October report that Phillips made to his director. In it, Kerr states: 'The body of Kayai did not appear undernourished when viewed by Corpl. Gallagher, Constable Laliberte and myself (As Coroner).'[127] There is no reason to believe that either Corporal Gallagher or Constable Laliberte had qualifications that would lend credibility to such an observation, and Kerr, as coroner, was himself implicated in the outcome of his own investigations.

Both Kikkik's and Howmik's families – or rather, what was left of them – were rescued and moved with the other Henik Lake Inuit to Eskimo Point. Rudnicki described them as he found them in March 1958: 'The last of the Ahearmiut are living in six igloos behind the policeman's house at Eskimo Point. They no longer have dogs, sleds, kayaks or any of the accoutrements of a way of life on the land. With no more caribou to hunt, they no longer have any aim in life. Their present existence is based on only one awareness – that they are now absolutely dependent on the white man.'[128]

Kikkik's situation was even worse:

> Kikkik is now in police custody. She has an igloo all to herself at Eskimo Point and the company of an old Eskimo woman who has been hired by the police as a matron. Annacatha is in the Churchill Military Hospital. The remaining three children are being looked after by Jimmy Gibbons the special constable at Eskimo Point. Other Eskimos do not visit her or talk to her. Though Kikkik smiles at the white men who come to see her, her eyes betray fear and bewilderment.[129]

At the time, ostracism was a form of sanction applied by members of a camp to those within their group whose behaviour was not sanctioned by the other members. When asked if they would like to have Kikkik rejoin them, most Ennadai/Henik Lake Inuit replied in the negative. Owlijoot and Nootaraloo gave the most considered opinion, stating, 'We were afraid of her at first – but she does not worry us now. Nanook (Ohootuk's wife) is very afraid of Kikkik – because she cuts up people,' while Mounik and Sokawak said, 'We are afraid of Kikkik. We would not want her to live among us again. We would accept her children,' and Yahah and Howmik said, 'We don't know about Kikkik. I don't think we would like her back again.'[130] It is important to recognize that here, as in other answers, the group may have been trying to respond in a way that would please the outsiders, who they knew were treating Kikkik as a criminal.

Under these circumstances, intensive discussion was held about what to do with the Ennadai/Henik Lake Inuit. The answer was as obvious in the spring of 1958 as it had been the year before.

What Kind of Tragedy Was This?

The Henik Lake tragedy is not a story of a people whose outdated technologies do not allow them to cope with changing ecological circumstances. The Ennadai Lake Inuit's lives were interfered with from the outside. They appear to have resisted this interference and even to have struggled back. But decisions were made for them and the power to control their future was removed from their hands. The northern service officer and others responsible for their well-being appear to have reached a point where they came to dislike and distrust them.

Kikkik's story is not told here merely for its narrative value, though it has that. Kikkik's story dramatizes, among many other things, the effects on an innocent family of decisions taken by well-meaning officials. Kikkik was clearly a very strong, and strong-willed, woman battling against incredible odds for her survival and that of her family. She was arrested, charged with murder, tried, and acquitted. In an interview years later, the Justice of the Peace, Douglas Wilkinson, indicated that he had recommended charging Kikkik to ensure that she would be looked after (by placing her in custody) and to make sure that justice was seen to be done. He indicated that not charging her would have created an issue that would have dragged on, possibly to her detriment.[131] By June of that year she had apparently remarried,[132] so the ostracism recorded by Walter Rudnicki in his investigation of the case did not last long. This raises the question of whether the ostracism was truly Inuit in origin or constructed for them by the act of incarceration.

Perhaps the best evidence that interference led to this disaster is found when one looks at what the survivors really thought of the non-Natives running their lives. This is something Walter Rudnicki examined in the spring of 1958. Rudnicki carried out a thematic apperception test with some of the Inuit survivors, showing them images he had created for the purpose and asking them to respond to these pictures with a story.[133] One of the images Rudnicki created showed a non-Native in discussion with two Inuit. Nootaraloo responded: 'The Eskimos look mad. The white man looks mad. He is the big boss ... Eskimos look like they are afraid of the white man.'[134] In response to a picture of a non-Native leaving an airplane and walking towards a group of Inuit, two of the survivors thought that the Inuit represented looked unhappy. When asked, as part of the discussion around the pictures, why they had been brought from Henik Lake to Eskimo Point, Shikoak and Pallikal said, 'We don't know why we were brought to Eskimo Point. We were told by [special constable] Jimmy that [we] were coming here and we had to come,' while Owlijoot and Nootaraloo said, 'We don't know. At Henik, we thought we were living on our own. Now we don't know anything.'[135] Both of these statements reveal that the respondents felt they had lost control of their own lives. For Owlijoot, the elder/leader, to say, 'Now we don't know anything,' reveals the profound degree of disorientation and demoralization that the Ennadai Lake Inuit were experiencing.

When asked if 'you speak among yourselves about what you would like to happen now,' they gave particularly interesting answers. Most respondents focused on the word 'speak' in the question. Mounik and Sokawak said, 'We do not talk of the future. We will do what we are told to do.' Shikoak and Pallikal said, 'We don't speak about anything. We just listen.' Yahah and Howmik responded with, 'We do not talk about the future. We just listen. Owlijoot is the "biggest one." Everyone listens to him.'[136] It is as if, having resisted and struggled for so long against the wishes of the non-Natives, the group had decided as a whole that they would now submit and obey the outsiders. Their answers are remarkably consistent. And Owlijoot, their leader, with Nootaraloo, replied: 'We do not speak about what is going to happen to us. We just listen now. We are getting food here and are not afraid any more. We do not think of the future. I [Owlijoot] was afraid at Henik Lake because I thought my family would starve.'[137] They had reached the point where they had decided to put themselves completely in the care of the outsiders who, for a decade, had been trying to control their destiny but who had also shown a disposition to provide them with food and other means of subsistence.

Rudnicki also gathered some information based on interviews with the non-Natives at Eskimo Point, including the northern service officer, RCMP, missionaries, and traders. Although he did not report the verbatim results of his interviews, he did summarize his impressions of their general attitude towards the Inuit.

> Although some concern and anxiety seemed evident about the well-being and future of the Eskimos, most references to them were couched in such terms as 'those lazy bums,' those heroes (in a sarcastic sense), the sun-burnt Irishmen, etc. Other generalizations were made about the Eskimos to the effect that they are 'unfeeling and unemotional,' that they live 'like dogs,' etc. Although these expressions suggest a generally uninformed and per-haps, an undesirable outlook on the problems of the Eskimo people, these probably reflect also a sense of resignation that anything positive will ever be done for them.[138]

A casual racism pervaded the non-Native community in this settlement. This was sustained, in part, by a lack of information and understanding on the part of southern Canadians, fuelled by images of the North that had been constructed in the 1950s around the notion of 'happy, smiling Eskimos.' There was also a general social attitude that located misfortune – in non-Native as well as Inuit society – solely in personal ineptitude and responsibility rather than in social constructs and structures. In retrospect, it is not surprising that Farley Mowat's account of these events, *The Desperate People*, received so much attention. The story it told was shocking – an anathema to what Canadians and others had come to believe was true of Inuit experience.

Bringing the Inuit and the non-Native population of Eskimo Point together seems, in retrospect, to have been a recipe for disaster. The Inuit now saw the outsiders as 'big bosses' whose orders had to be followed and whose visits meant unhappiness, while the non-Natives looked down on and distrusted the Inuit. The Ennadai Inuit were relocated twice in seven years by the outsiders, and it is vital to remember that the decision of when to move and where to move was perhaps the most important decision nomadic hunters have to make. It was clear that they had lost control of their lives. But, inexplicably, the outsiders only sporadically came with food to offer. They made decisions but did not seem to want to accept responsibility. And when Inuit took from the caches left by the non-Natives, they were arrested.

In their interviews with Rudnicki, most of the Ennadai Lake Inuit indicated never having hunted, seen, or eaten seal. When shown a picture that included a seal, for example, Pallikal said, 'They are after that thing on the ice,' while Nootaraloo said, 'What is it (indicating seal on ice-floe). It has got a tail like a fish and little legs.'[139] While some of them indicated that if no caribou were to be had they would be happy to live by the sea, Owlijoot and Nootaraloo said, 'We don't know anything about living by the sea.'[140] The Ennadai Lake people, inland caribou hunters for generations, would soon find themselves the subjects of a further relocation experiment from Eskimo Point to another coastal community created for the purpose of resettling them – Whale Cove.

6

The Garry Lake Famine

At virtually the same time as the Ennadai Lake Inuit were experiencing famine, two other more northerly groups of inland Caribou Inuit were in enormous difficulties. Those difficulties led to a famine in the Back River/Garry Lake area that officials did not become aware of until early in the spring of 1958. These famines received a great deal of media attention at the time. They reveal the difficulties the state encountered in delivering services and relief in the Far North, the impact that different non-Native agendas had on aboriginal strategies for survival, the problems created by attitudes towards relief held by government officials, and the critical impact of small errors in judgment on the part of northern officials. Once again, events at Garry Lake reveal the extent of the assumption held by government officials that relocation was the best way to alleviate a crisis.

The broad outlines of the story are quite similar to the famine experienced by the people of Ennadai Lake. Of crucial importance to both the Garry and Ennadai lakes people was their move from a nomadic lifestyle to a comparatively settled existence centred on a traditional gathering place. At Ennadai, first a trading post and then a radio station provided a focal point for Inuit. At Garry Lake, it was a Roman Catholic mission. The presence of the mission, on an island that had been a summer gathering place for the people, led the Inuit of the Garry Lake region to settle in the immediate area on a more or less permanent basis. The mission, as with the radio station, was an economic opportunity structure that Inuit used to their advantage. They seem to have adapted their traditional nomadic lifestyles in order to best exploit the presence of outsiders – in this case, the missionaries at Garry Lake. Their subsistence strategy changed from a condition of total independence and reliance on caribou and fishing, to a reliance on caribou, fishing, and relief to tide them over. In other words, the church became integrated with their subsistence economy.

The transition to a somewhat less nomadic subsistence strategy undoubtedly played some role in making it more difficult for Inuit to live off the land. Meanwhile, the government authorities were attempting to promote independence by providing as little relief as possible, while church authorities were using relief as an inducement to promote their missions.

In other words, two contradictory forces were at work. Inuit had made the most significant change possible for a nomadic people. They had become slightly more sedentary. This was only possible because of the relief they were supplied by the church in the case of Garry Lake, and by personnel at the radio station in the case of Ennadai Lake. The relief was a form of economic compensation for the lack of mobility. However, at the same time, government officials, in both cases, were trying to systematically discourage the people from relying on relief – to disperse them over the landscape in the belief that doing so would facilitate hunting and trapping and would prevent dependence on relief. The net result was that outsiders, meaning any non-Inuit who had come to the region – including missionaries, traders, police, and other government officials – sent contradictory messages to Inuit and employed contradictory strategies.

In both cases, the rudimentary facilities that enabled the outsiders to function were established inland, within the aboriginal territories of the people affected. These territories were not easily accessible to outsiders, including government officials, and made the delivery of relief and the monitoring of its delivery difficult. This was especially true about the mission at Garry Lake, which could only be reached by plane (if and when one was available) or by means of an arduous trip by dog team, north from Baker Lake over a landscape rising in elevation, windswept at temperatures as low as -45°C, and characterized by rock outcroppings and ridges.

Both groups of Inuit experienced a breakdown in the monitoring system in the winter of 1957-8, and, coupled with unsuccessful caribou hunts, this resulted in famine and the loss of life. Finally, in both cases, the solution was not to improve the monitoring infrastructure but, rather, to move Inuit from their traditional territory to a place the outsiders perceived was more economically viable and which was more accessible to the service-welfare infrastructure. Significantly, in its review of both famines, government officials placed the burden of responsibility on accident or on the negligence and indolence of the Inuit involved.

The Garry Lake Inuit

The Garry Lake Inuit were known as 'backward' or 'primitive' Inuit. They were described in a manner similar to Inuit of Ennadai Lake. Before 1950, the Garry Lake Inuit 'were nomadic and, governed by the presence and movement of the caribou, wandered throughout the general area of the Northeastern section of the Keewatin District.' Their connection with Garry

Lake was strong, however, because 'a large island in Garry Lake, and on the route of the migrating caribou herds, was the meeting place of the Eskimos during the summer. Here was the base from where they hunted the caribou for their winter food caches.'[1]

An RCMP report from January 1958 described them as the smallest of three groups of Inuit in the Baker Lake area (the other two being the Baker Lake and Back River Inuit). The report goes on: 'These Eskimos are made up of natives from the Perry River Area, some from the Back's River Delta, and even a few from Spence Bay District. These natives are the most isolated of any in this area. They live on the shores of Garry and Pelly Lakes moving inland from those lakes only when they are hunting caribou. They are poor fishermen but show signs of improving, especially if the caribou do not return in large numbers.'[2] The Garry Lake Inuit were a small band, no larger than sixty, who broke into smaller hunting units and who had, traditionally, gathered together only in the summer.

In the early 1950s, a Roman Catholic mission was established at Garry Lake, and in that decade two Catholic missionaries, Father Buliard and Father Trinel, became important figures in the lives of the Inuit in the region. A departmental memo from the fall of 1957 reported that 'there were not Eskimos in permanent residence at Garry Lake until the mission became established there. The records show that a building was erected by them at Garry Lake in August, 1949, but the mission was not established until 1952. In speaking with Father Buliard in April, 1956, I was informed that there were 15 families of natives in the region.'[3] An obituary, written by Guy Mary-Rousseliere after Father Buliard's death late in 1956, tells a slightly different story regarding the date of the mission's establishment: 'In the month of August, 1949, the plane took him to Garry Lake with all the material and provisions needed. Two fathers and a brother went along to help build a small house. One day's work took care of the essentials and they returned with the plane, leaving the father there alone for one year.'[4] The Inuit of the Back River and Baker Lake areas were nominally Protestant. The RCMP officer stationed in Baker Lake until the fall of 1956 was also Protestant and had already demonstrated some antipathy towards Catholics. The difference in the two stories might be explained, in part, by this antipathy, since the parties were likely not in close comunication. By the mid-1950s, antagonism along religious lines was a particularly important factor in the social dynamics and relationships that developed in the settlement of Baker Lake. This antipathy contributed to the events that subsequently unfolded in the winter of 1957-8.

Father Buliard single-handedly ran the Garry Lake mission from the early 1950s until his death in 1956. Given Buliard's general attitudes towards the

Figure 23 Garry Lake mission, likely taken in 1957. It was probably the most remote mission in Canada, located on an island near the west end of Garry Lake.

Inuit, it is easy to see that some of them, at least, might have found reason for hostility. He wrote that he had 'seen the Inuit living like animals and now sees them behaving like saints' and was a dedicated opponent of their beliefs and values: 'When I live with the Eskimos, stay in their houses and hear their conversations day after day, I am astonished to see how much paganism is still seeping through their hearts, pushing them to do things incompatible with their Christian life.'[5] Reading against the grain of Buliard's text, it is possible to see a strategy of 'surface conversion' on the part of the Inuit, whose 'pagan ways' might today be understood as deeply felt forms of Inuit spirituality. Buliard's feelings on these matters amounted to more than a conflict of sentiments between him and his Inuit 'flock.' His feelings had material repercussions. For example, he was strongly in favour of residential schools and was responsible for sending more than a few of the children away from their families.[6] He wrote: 'At school, you can train these good-hearted children, to become strong and capable of resisting shamanism or immorality. You will bring forth clean-living young people, zealous, pious, curbing their passions and resolved to live their Christian life without any form of pagan influence.'[7] Buliard had his share of conflict with the Inuit of his mission and proved a particularly inflexible devotee to the concept of the 'white man's burden.'

An important struggle eventually emerged over Buliard's willingness, in the interests of his mission, to provide relief to the Inuit in the area. A memorandum from 1957, revealing some of the administration's hostility towards the Catholics, reported:

> Inquiries revealed that the majority of these natives ... had been attracted to Garry Lake by the presence of the missionary who had adopted the practice of handing out miscellaneous supplies. Garry Lake abounds in fish, but the majority of the local Eskimos have been caribou hunters. They were able to fend for themselves in the course of their travels throughout the region, but since they have become established at this mission site they are no longer self-supporting. Indeed, unless these Eskimos are prepared to live on fish exclusively, they will always be in need of other supplies as long as they remain at Garry Lake.[8]

The concluding phrase, 'as long as they remain at Garry Lake,' can be interpreted in a familiar way. The prevailing attitude was that Inuit should not 'hang around' missions and trading posts – that they should be encouraged to disperse themselves (or should be dispersed) in order to hunt and trap effectively and not become 'dependent' on handouts and relief. When food was scarce and there seemed to be little possibility of Inuit living off the land, relocation took another form – that of movement to areas accessible to administrators where other plans could be made for their welfare.

It seems likely that, apart from whatever attraction (if any) the Catholic religion might have had, these Inuit were drawn to the mission by material inducements. In his obituary, Buliard's technique for saving souls was described as 'an ardent and radiant charity: all the rest came after.'[9] Buliard's mission, located in the heart of the Garry Lake Inuit's traditional territory, was an economic opportunity – enough of an economic opportunity for the people to settle down as a (nominal) Christian flock.

It is also clear that RCMP and government officials saw an obvious solution to the growing dependence on supplies provided by the mission – get Inuit to fish. For Inuit, however, fishing was not an immediately attractive activity, and when it was, the boat offered by the mission was important. Both the RCMP report and the memorandum quoted above mention the fact that the Inuit were not taking advantage of the fish perceived to be abundant in the area. The RCMP report comments on this in some detail: 'During the trips made to Garry and Pelly Lake, the writer

Figure 24 Fishing through the ice at Baker Lake in 1957.

has noticed that the natives in this area do very little fishing in the Summer. On questioning the natives it was found that they could not get out to the good fishing areas in the lake in the Summer. Only when they had possession of the R.C. Mission Canoe can they move about the lake.'[10] The report

Figure 25 Father Trinel at Cape Dorset, probably taken just before he went to Garry Lake in 1957 to replace Father Buliard.

went on to recommend providing the Inuit with two or three boats and fishing equipment to assist them.

The mission boat also seems to have become one of the drawing cards of the mission. The RCMP report stated: 'It appears that the tendency of the natives to hang around the mission at Garry Lake during the Summer probably stems from the fact that the mission has the boat to move these natives when the herds of Caribou are seen and also to help them tend nets.'[11] The mission had become important as a supplier of food in difficult times and as a source of essential equipment for the caribou hunt.

In the fall of 1956, Buliard disappeared in a blizzard on his way to check fishnets. The mission was located on an island where Back River pours into Garry Lake. The current at this point is so swift that there is open water at nearly all times of the year. However, the area was especially treacherous in the winter months, and this may have contributed to Buliard's death.[12] Father Trinel, Buliard's replacement at the mission, appears to have been confronted with Inuit accustomed to Buliard's habit of sharing with them whatever resources he had. It seems he interpreted these expectations as indicators that Garry Lake Inuit did not have enough food and were in danger of starving. He subsequently contributed to problems that developed by raising false alarms about conditions at Garry Lake. Thus, the pattern set by Buliard's 'generosity' would be a key factor in the events that unfolded over the next year and a half.

Relief and Relations at Baker Lake

By the fall of 1957, the RCMP officer posted at Baker Lake had come to view calls for help from Garry Lake, and suggestions that Inuit were experiencing food shortages and in danger of starvation, with suspicion. The missionaries had overstated their needs too many times. An official report on the starvations noted that through the 1950s, 'reports were received at Baker Lake, usually in the winter, of imminent starvation at Garry Lake from the Missionary Father residing there. In all cases the R.C.M. Police, on behalf of the Department of Northern Affairs answered the plea for help but in all cases it was found that the circumstances were exaggerated.'[13]

In January 1957, Doug Wilkinson, the newly appointed northern service officer at Baker Lake, submitted his first report on the community. Written more than a year before the tragedy at Garry Lake, it reveals in greater detail the conflict in the settlement. Both the Anglican missionary and the Hudson's Bay Company post manager, both of whom had been in the settlement for some time, were clearly at odds with the Catholic missionaries. Wilkinson noted that both men were 'completely anti-Catholic,' one of them 'outspokenly and violently so.'[14] Wilkinson also wrote about Corporal Dent, the RCMP constable prior to 1956: '[He] listened carefully to advice' from both men and 'rarely did anything to displease them.' This perhaps accounts for why he was 'not on good terms with the RC missionaries' despite being described as 'an affable person, easy with the Eskimos, ready to give assistance at the first sign of a hard luck story.'[15]

Wilkinson's report provides a good snapshot of the complex relations between the various representatives of the government and non-governmental agencies with interests and responsibilities in the area. The new northern service officers obviously had to carefully manage relations with older officials, particularly RCMP officers, as they established their mutually changing roles and responsibilities. The report is worth examining in some detail for what it tells us about these relations as well as about policies respecting the provision of relief. In the summer of 1956, the apparently affable Corporal Dent was replaced by the less affable Corporal Wilson. Wilson, in Wilkinson's view, was 'impulsive, outspoken, domineering.' He did not take the advice of the longtime non-Native residents and made it quite clear to all that he was 'handling the problems of the Eskimos in the Baker Lake area.'[16] Wilson was apparently 'on good terms' with the Catholic missionaries and his policy towards relief was to be 'harsh with the Eskimos, he [would] not issue relief food supplies unless it [was] absolutely necessary. He [spoke] disparagingly of the Eskimos as "savages." His manner with them [was] abrupt.'[17]

Wilkinson seems to have had no problems with the Catholics and no explicit biases towards or against them. He noted that he had had 'a number

Figure 26   Hudson's Bay Company buildings at Baker Lake in 1957.

of interesting talks with Father Papion' before going on to observe, 'The job of the Fathers here is not an easy one. The RC Eskimos are a minority group, one that contains quite a number of "dead-beat" types.'[18] The 'dead beats' were not exclusive to the Catholics. Although all of these descriptions pertain directly to the Baker Lake community, they certainly relate to the Garry Lake group. They are also important because they tell us something of the intergroup dynamic of the non-Natives at Baker Lake who were ultimately responsible for providing relief to Garry Lake Inuit.

Wilkinson's strategy in these circumstances was to align himself firmly with Wilson. He wrote in his report that he had 'been extra careful to maintain a very close relationship with Cpl. Wilson on all matters pertaining to Eskimo affairs.'[19] Wilkinson developed some sympathy towards Wilson, in spite of a difference of opinion over the latter's treatment of the Inuit. Wilkinson added some depth to his description of Wilson: 'He is not soft on matters of relief issues. I do not like his abrupt manner in his dealings with Eskimos; he has no patience with the idiosyncrasies of the Eskimo personality. His depreciatory manner of speaking about Eskimos is annoying at first until you realize it is not a deep feeling. He does it in much the same way as an impulsive school teacher will refer to his "little monsters."'[20] Wilkinson's own attitude seems to have been to slowly work towards the point where Inuit were 'managing their own affairs,' though this meant they 'must be encouraged to assist one another, coming to us for assistance and guidance whenever necessary, but only when necessary.'[21]

Quite complicated relations had developed by the mid-1950s among the non-Natives in the Baker Lake area. There was outright hostility between non-government workers of different Christian faiths. To varying degrees, the RCMP constables played into this, taking sides or not as their own views led them. The arrival of first Wilson, then Wilkinson, and later a male nurse named Lang provided an opportunity for shifting alliances among the small group. Wilkinson observed that

a number of attempts were made to play off Cpl. Wilson and myself one against the other. With the arrival of Mr. Lang, the nurse-in-charge of the station, he was included in these attempts. The whites in the settlement brought their problems first to one and then to the other of the government representatives in the hope that one or another of these persons would give an answer more suited to the one they wanted to hear. Eskimos were encouraged to do the same thing.[22]

It is clear that there was anything but unanimity among the non-Natives responsible for the provision of relief in the Baker Lake area. They were factious, inconsistent, mutually suspicious, and not above using Inuit to achieve their own ends. There was a deeply colonial and outright racist attitude on the part of many. While Wilkinson seems to have attempted to bring some consistency, clear direction, and unanimity to at least the government officials, he also represented a change in attitudes that may have represented another inconsistency to the Inuit.

Furthermore it is not clear how much the anti-Catholic feeling that prevailed among some may have influenced attitudes towards requests from the Garry Lake mission for relief. Wilkinson himself viewed at least some of the Catholic-allied Inuit as 'dead-beats.' While he and Wilson did not seem to have any particular anti-Catholic bias, their more strict attitude towards relief had the same effect. Wilkinson described his views on relief as follows:

I have noticed since coming to Baker Lake that there is a definite feeling among many of the Eskimos that any government agency in the area is a centre for the distribution of relief issues. During the latter part of January there has been a regular parade of Eskimos coming in to say that their fall caches of caribou meat are gone, or nearly gone, and asking for issues of food. From what I can gather here, they have been issued food under such circumstances in the past years. This year, however, they are being given no food (there are exceptions), only advice as to where caribou might be located and where the ice is still thin enough for fishing. If they have no money, we have issued cartridges or perhaps a fish net, but no food. If they have foxes to trade, they get nothing, except the advice mentioned.[23]

Wilkinson goes on to describe in detail typical conversations with Inuit who came looking to him for relief, only to be turned away. He notes that 'a few haven't been happy about not getting a relief isue [*sic*], but most have taken it as a scheme that didn't quite come off.'[24] The result of all of this is that in the winter of 1957 very little relief was issued at Baker Lake 'except for a few widows and problem personalities.'[25] What constituted a problem personality can only be the subject of conjecture at this point, although it may have coincided with anyone persistent enough in their requests to actually get relief.

The change in policy was undoubtedly resented by many Inuit and non-Inuit. In a telling comment, Wilkinson linked the importance of the provision of relief to the fur trade, noting that the new approach 'has been resented in certain quarters, particularly after the relative open hand of the past few years. Eskimos who must spend their days hunting and fishing cannot trap as energetically as would be desirable for a maximum fur return.'[26] This relationship between relief and Hudson's Bay Company profits is worthy of note. A liberal policy towards relief contributed to company profits; the more food supplied by the government, the more furs brought in by the Inuit and, perhaps, the lower the price that needed to be paid for those furs.

Of the Garry Lake Inuit in the winter of 1956-7, Wilkinson wrote: 'I do not include the Garry Lake people in this as we have no first hand information on them. They appear to be trading into Perry River this winter. As we have no reports from Perry River of any food problem in the Garry Lake area we presume these people must be getting caribou. The RCMP flight should confirm this.'[27] The capacity of the government to monitor the well-being of Garry Lake Inuit, in this case, was restricted to rumours (or the absence thereof) and the availability of an RCMP plane – something that could not be depended on given the extreme weather conditions in the area.

The actions of the non-Natives in the Baker Lake area reflected their material interests. Their attitudes towards relief were critical in this regard. The missionaries were concerned with establishing and maintaining their converts. They were quite prepared to use relief to attract potential converts and were openly hostile to one another in their efforts. The traders were allies of the missionaries in this; more relief for Inuit meant more time for the Inuit to hunt fox and, therefore, better fur returns. The HBC trader at Baker Lake was allied to the Anglican missionaries and was particularly hostile to the Catholics. The government officials may have had an objective concern to ensure that as little relief as possible was supplied, but they were subject to the pulls and pressures of their non-Native peers in the isolated posts.

Figure 27 Inuit and RCMP constable chopping up caribou meat on the shore of Baker Lake in 1957.

As a result, an inconsistent attitude had developed. For some years relief had been provided rather liberally but inconsistently to different groups. The Catholic versus Anglican attachment may have had some importance here. With the arrival of Wilkinson and Wilson, an attempt was made to implement a 'firmer,' less generous, policy. The attempt was attacked by non-government non-Natives in the area, who saw their material interests threatened. It was also difficult to implement, since there were at least some Inuit who had developed 'problem personalities.' The problem was exacerbated by the fact that the Inuit had been attracted to more stable settlements and less nomadic subsistence strategies, thereby decreasing their ability to fend for themselves.

It is difficult to read Inuit motives, feelings, and understandings in this. Inuit culture was based on generalized reciprocity and gift exchange on an everyday level (especially as pertains to food and other essentials). In this culture, kinship relations establish the most meaningful bonds (as opposed to the self-sanctioned isolation of church and state officials). Subsequently, the changing attitudes (and inconsistencies) of those who had food and encouraged them to settle down, become Christians, and trap furs – the different stories they were being told about the availability of relief, the food supplies they could see with their own eyes – all must have been cause for wonder, confusion, apprehension, and concern.

The August 1957 Scare

In January 1957, as Wilkinson was writing his first report, word was received that Father Buliard was missing. Inuit from Garry Lake had reported to Father Henry in Gjoa Haven, who in turn had passed the information on to officials in Churchill.[28] An RCMP aircraft was dispatched to Baker Lake to investigate. There were apparently suspicions of foul play, since 'rumours at Baker Lake indicated Father Buliard [was] not well liked by some Eskimos in Garry Lake area.'[29] A variety of engine and weather problems prevented the plane from leaving Baker Lake for Garry Lake until 2 April. Meanwhile, in mid-March, a report was received: 'Garry Lake Eskimos trading at Perry River and (that) they have foxes and caribou.'[30]

On 2 April, a team from Baker Lake finally managed to get in to Garry Lake to investigate the death of Father Buliard.

The R.C.M.P. aircraft flew to Garry Lake with Cpl. Wilson, Father Papion and Mr. D. Wilkinson. Mission building at Garry Lake found to be abandoned, no sign of activity. Plane proceeded.to an Eskimo camp about fifteen miles from the mission and from Eskimos at this camp the story of father Buliard's disappearance was obtained. Camp was well stocked with food; caribou carcasses on the ground and many fish in caches. Caribou were reported in the vicinity in fair numbers and all camps reported to have good food stocks.[31]

On 30 April, Inuit from Garry Lake visited Baker Lake. A meeting was held between Wilkinson, 'Cpl Wilson and Eskimos in from Garry Lake and Back River. Food conditions O.K.'[32] Buliard's replacement, Father Trinel, was flown in to the Garry Lake mission on 10 June 1957.

On 5 August, a radio message from Father Trinel sparked a flurry of activity. The message read: 'A community of 60 Eskimos menaced to starve at Garry Lake – caribou and fish scarce this spring and summer asking for government help as soon as possible.'[33] Wilkinson was suspicious of whether emergency aid was immediately needed, as his telegram to the South revealed:

FATHER TRINELL [sic] GARRY LAKE REPORTS SIXTY ESKIMO DANGER STARVATION AS CARIBOU AND FISH SCARCE ASKS GOVERNMENT AID SOONEST [STOP] HAVE WIRED KELSALL YELLOWKNIFE FOR INFORMATION ON CARIBOU HEADED FOR GARRY AND ASKED IF FLYING GARRY VICINITY TO INFORM TRINELL OF ANY CARIBOU SEEN STOP HAVE WIRED TRINELL ASKING IF ESKIMOS OKAY UNTIL WILSON GOES GARRY IN RCMP AIRCRAFT TWO TO THREE WEEKS FROM NOW [STOP] RELUCTANT TO ASK SPECIAL FLIGHT WITH RELIEF FOOD UNLESS ABSOLUTELY NECESSARY AS FISH REPORTED SWARMING IN LAKES AND RIVERS ALL OTHER AREAS [STOP] WILL KEEP YOU POSTED.[34]

In the South, R.A.J. Phillips responded with the same caution, wiring back to Wilkinson: 'Thank you for message August 5th regarding Garry Lake Eskimos. Action taken wise. Keep us advised when you obtain all facts.'[35] He wrote immediately to Ben Sivertz, quoting both telegraphs and noting that 'as we have a great deal of experience with the flying in of relief supplies to that area in the past when the situation did not warrant it, I think Mr. Wilkinson is wise to get all the facts before asking for a special flight.'[36] Sivertz, by hand, wrote on the memorandum from Phillips: 'I think Wilkinson acted well in this.'[37]

Nevertheless, there was concern that something serious was taking place. Phillips moved on 8 August to ascertain what aircraft were available and found that the RCMP aircraft was 'at Eskimo point en route to the Chesterfield Inlet area with a medical party who are carrying our X-ray surveys in that region.'[38] Phillips, the same day, sent a concerned letter to the RCMP about the incident, noting that 'we think Mr. Wilkinson is wise in getting all the facts before asking for a special flight, but, as you mentioned, the R.C.M.P. aircraft ... might be diverted to the Garry Lake region.'[39]

On 7 August, Wilson and Wilkinson managed to communicate by radio with Trinel, although the transmission was very poor. That same day, a Saskatchewan Airways Beaver aircraft, which had been carrying a prospector from Pelly Lake, landed at Baker Lake. The plane was due to return to Pelly Lake to pick up supplies, and Corporal Wilson accompanied the flight to check out conditions at Garry Lake en route. The visit and the radio communication confirmed the view that the situation was not as serious as Trinel had reported. Wilkinson then reported by radio to the South on 8 August that 'investigations reveal situation Garry Lake one of poor hunting and fishing due largely insufficient dispersion people in area stop Not critical at present.'[40] The following day he radioed to the Canadian Wildlife Service in Yellowknife, which he had contacted earlier for information on caribou movements, to advise them that Wilson had 'found food shortage but not critical at moment intend to fly food and family allowance on police plane coming week.'[41]

Meanwhile, because of the letters that had been written in the South from Phillips to the RCMP, the RCMP aircraft had been diverted up to Baker Lake, arriving on 10 August. On 11 August, Wilson brought a load of food in to Garry Lake on this aircraft, staying until the 16th. Some 1,800 pounds of food were delivered on this flight.[42] Wilson reported 'that Father Trinel had ample supplies of caribou meat at this time as he had a number of meals while he was there. All camps he visited were obtaining caribou and fish.'[43] Portions of the food were stored in an unused building in the area.

Notification of the arrival of the RCMP aircraft greatly upset Corporal Wilson, who had already determined that no real crisis was taking place and had not wired his own southern superiors to inform them of the situation. In Wilkinson's overall report of the event, dated 10 August 1957, he summarized their sense of the situation:

> We further discovered that almost all the Garry Lake Eskimos were camped on the small island around the Mission and that they had been there for some time. Here was the basic cause of the problem – sixty people trying to find food in an area that would probably support six. We advised Father Trinel to get the Eskimos scattered out a bit to the good fishing locations. If they did this they would probably be able to get sufficient food.[44]

The incident greatly exacerbated the problems among the non-Natives in the region.

Wilkinson's August 10 report illustrated the different reactions of the non-Native community to the perceived crisis. Wilson, on receipt of Trinel's initial message, 'recommended that nothing be done about the message. He had planned to visit Garry Lake towards the end of August in order to conduct a further search for clues in the disappearance of Father Bouillard [sic]. He would look into the situation at that time.'[45] Wilson did not think Wilkinson should have sent any messages to the South and was angry that the RCMP aircraft ended up being diverted to Baker Lake as a result of his communications. According to Wilkinson, '[Wilson] was angry that his unit had sent him such a wire' criticizing him for not informing them of the situation, and 'although nothing was said I know that Cpl. Wilson was also angry with me as he felt that my messages to you, although quite clear and explicit, had now only served to put him in an awkward spot with his Division.'[46] Wilson had got into trouble with his superiors and blamed Wilkinson; Wilkinson blamed his own superiors.

The incident also occasioned some conflict between the Baker Lake non-Natives and the government officials. Wilkinson reported that 'although a good deal of criticism had been heaped upon our heads by some of the local inhabitants who felt that we should have rushed in relief supplies of food immediately on receipt of the wire from Father Trinel, this had died out.'[47]

As well, relations between the Catholic Church and the government officials were strained. Wilkinson noted that 'Father Choque was extremely unhappy over the fact that the Eskimos and Father Trinel would have to get along on fish until the RCMP plane could get in.'[48] This was before the RCMP plane actually arrived in Baker Lake, en route to Garry Lake. One can only imagine how unhappy Father Trinel was. Even though supplies did reach Garry Lake sooner than anticipated, this was not due to the efforts of Wilson and Wilkinson. Rather, it arrived with their objections, the result of incomplete communications with the RCMP in the South. The priests' dissatisfaction with these two public servants probably increased as a result, further adding to tensions already present in the community.

Wilkinson was also quite unhappy with the way his messages had led to action in the South – something beyond his control. His 10 August report contains some sharp criticism of his superiors. He notes that he is 'seriously disturbed by the element of disunity introduced by the G Division action,' and that 'the prestige of our department, and of northern service officers, will hardly rise through this.'[49] He goes on to say:

> The one thing I did not want to happen, is now happening – that is, a special aircraft is being sent to Garry Lake as an emergency flight with food. This is the worst thing that could happen in this case because no such emergency action is warranted. The Eskimos at Garry Lake are not fools. The have sat around the Mission at Garry Lake most of the late spring and summer and have hoodwinked the Father into giving out most of his supplies to them and now they will be perfectly happy to take any issue of relief food that we may be able to fly in.[50]

This disrupted Wilson and Wilkinson's plan to 'let a short period of time pass so as to let the Eskimos disperse away from the Mission area so as to get food,' although the latter admits that they 'were gambling that they would move away, find food and the situation would revert to normal ... This plan has now been destroyed.'[51]

Relations between the priests, the community, and the government workers were clearly deteriorating. Of greater concern, the RCMP officer and the northern service officer had now been divided, and the latter was also critical of his superiors to the south. Some of this conflict was mirrored in relations between church and state in the South. Both Ben Sivertz and Gordon Robertson wrote in early October to representatives of the Catholic Church, saying they would not reimburse Father Trinel for providing relief to the Inuit, and explaining, in Sivertz's words, that 'on every investigation in the past year ... these reports [of starvation] have been found to be either exaggerated or unfounded.'[52] Both Robertson and Sivertz make the point that 'the continuous distribution of food in this area, whether intentionally or not, seems to us to provide an undoubted encouragement to the Eskimos to lose their interests and their skill in hunting, and to create a social and economic problem where none existed before.'[53]

The incident in August 1957 obviously sets the immediate context for what would follow in the coming winter. The government officials had found themselves red-faced, having diverted an official aircraft into an area where, in their view, relief supplies were not needed. This diversion, in the view of the officials, had the effect of encouraging 'indolence' and discouraging self-reliance. Meanwhile, relations between all the parties, in the North and in the South, had been seriously strained by the event. Officials in the North would not be inclined to look upon requests for help from Garry Lake kindly.

Prelude to Disaster

In September, Corporal Wilson apparently visited Garry Lake again, 'with an additional plane load of food supplies which was stored in the building at the airstrip.'[54] Preparations were made for the winter: 'Maneeralik [a Garry Lake Inuk] was requested to take fox skins in trade for the food but to ensure that no one went hungry. All Eskimos were encouraged to set out traps and bring in foxes which would be brought to Baker Lake on the R.C.M.P. aircraft.'[55] Furthermore, arrangements were made 'to have an Eskimo guide from Garry Lake come to Baker Lake in mid-February to accompany Cpl. Wilson on a patrol to Garry Lake.'[56]

The story of what follows can be pieced together from a number of sources. These included the comprehensive report filed by Wilkinson in December 1958, previously cited. Wilson's official RCMP reports on events include a critically important interview with Father Trinel and one with Ninayok, an Inuk woman from Garry Lake. Another report on the starvations provides some useful additional information, including the account of an Inuit hunter. Not surprisingly, each of the sources reveals a different perspective on the issues and events, with Doug Wilkinson's December 1958 report providing the broadest overview.

A statement made by Father Trinel on 18 June 1958 to Corporal Wilson, who was investigating Inuit deaths at Garry Lake, provides a useful starting point. Trinel noted that 'there were 14 families living in the Garry Lake area. Of these only 4 families are Protestant. There are no Pagans amongst the people at Garry Lake.'[57] Trinel had planned to stay the winter 'but due to the fact that the natives stole all my fish I was forced to leave.'[58] He explains:

> In November I fished with Manernaluk for a week at the rapids. I placed 6 or 7 nets & obtained 40 – 50 big fish every setting. The natives were not having hav any fish [sic]. They did not have any fish nets in the water at the rapids. They were only obtaining small fish. After I made a cache of my fish the natives all came to the rapids and took my fish leaving me short of dogfood.[59]

Manernaluk (Maneeralik), who is described by Buliard's biographer as 'a young man, an orphan, named Anthony Manernaluk, who helped him at the mission and acted as guide on the road,' is the same Inuk given responsibility for the food storehouse the previous August.[60] He retained a similar position with Father Trinel.

Trinel 'managed to get enough fish to come to Baker Lake and this I did early in December, 1957.'[61] He observed that:

> When I left Garry Lake early in December 1957 the natives were all well but were having a food shortage. There [sic] clothing was very poor as no Caribou had come in large numbers since January 1956. The storehouse at Pelly Lake contained a limited amount of food. There was a good run of foxes early in the winter and the natives took everything from the storehouse. Most of the food and supplies were taken by Teenak and his relatives. The rest of the natives only got small quantities.[62]

Trinel elaborated in some detail on this: 'After I left in December the natives continued to live off the food at the storehouse. Some of the natives at Garry Lake I believe, took too much food.' He added: 'It is natural I think that Teenak would take ample to feed himself and his family as he was in charge of the storehouse during the winter.'[63]

On 6 May, following the deaths at Garry Lake, Corporal Wilson made a trip to the area and, as well as taking in food and supplies and further investigating the deaths, evacuated two women who had survived the starvation. The statement obtained from Ninayok, one of these women, is recorded in his report on 'destitute relief' of 10 May 1958. The report notes that the two women were evacuated for medical treatment. Wilson reports that 'it appeared that Ninayook was, besides being pregnant, nearly recovered from disease of the muscles.'[64] Ninayok, the marriage partner of Sabgut, was apparently about forty-four years of age in 1958, with two children, Angotituak (a boy aged twelve) and a child listed as 'new baby' (also a boy, aged nine or ten).

Ninayok's statement provides a great deal of insight into the events of that fall and winter and illustrates the rapidly deteriorating situation of the Garry Lake Inuit. The following exchange sets some context for the events.

Q. How long have you lived at Garry Lake?
A. Three years. We used to live at Perry River.
Q. Has it been this bad a [sic] Garry Lake before?
A. It has been getting worse each year.
Q. Did the Eskimos put up any Fish caches in the Fall?
A. Sabgut put up a lot of fish during the Fall but we had to give it away to the Eskimos who were hungry.[65]

Sharing seems to have been practised by the Garry Lake Inuit in spite of the fact that the group involved Inuit from several different areas. In this context, it is not surprising that people from the group would have helped themselves to the priest's supplies or even looked at government assistance as part of the sharing network.[66] When asked 'What did the Eskimos eat at Garry Lake during the winter?' Ninayok responded with, 'They all ate fish when the [sic] could get it and Angeelik shot nine caribou. In December some of the Eskimos started to eat their dogs. After the Rolled Oats were finished at the Airstrip all the Eskimos were forced to eat their dogs.'[67]

By December, the situation seems to have been fairly drastic. If Father Trinel had reported that the Inuit were eating their dogs, this would have been a clear sign that the situation was serious. As it was, he did report that there was a food shortage but his report was not taken seriously, given the events of the past summer. Another crucial piece of information Ninayok supplied, and one that corresponded to Trinel's comments, came in answer to the question: 'Were the rest of the people living around Garry Lake?' She replied: 'The people were all fishing but they did not have warm clothing and could not stay out long.'[68] Both Trinel and Ninayok, in part, attributed the Inuit's failure to fish to a poor hunting season the year before, something none of the official reports and explanations would mention.

This observation is critical. The idea that Inuit could survive under the extreme conditions found in the interior of the Keewatin without access to a good supply of caribou contributed to problems at Garry Lake, as it had at Henik Lake. Caribou were needed for clothing, the stomach contents were an important source of vitamins and folic acid, and the red meat was a source of iron and protein essential to survival under Arctic conditions. It is doubtful that one can live entirely or even substantially on a diet of fish in such circumstances.

According to Wilkinson's later report, Father Trinel arrived at Baker Lake by sled on 10 December from Garry Lake accompanied by an Inuit whose name was deleted from the report. Trinel told Corporal Wilson that 'the Eskimos in the Garry Lake area were starving,'[69] and that 'no caribou were being taken and the fishing was poor.' The Inuk travelling with him confirmed this, although, according to Wilson, the Inuit said he 'didn't feel any undue alarm at the situation.' Wilkinson may have distrusted whether the Inuit had actually said this because he added in parentheses: 'All this information is from Cpl. Wilson.'[70] This was not something he indicated in any other reports he wrote referring to the constable's accounts.

Wilkinson was in Ottawa at the time of Trinel's visit and therefore had to rely on Wilson's reports regarding what Trinel had said. Wilkinson later noted that 'in view of previous experience with Father Trinel's reports on starvation conditions, Cpl. Wilson was doubtful that an emergency situation existed.'[71] Despite his earlier experience with Father Trinel, Wilson asked that an RCMP Otter aircraft be sent to Baker Lake to fly in supplies in case they were needed. A report written later by Corporal Wilson provides some additional information about Trinel's 10 December visit to Baker Lake: 'Fr. Trinel advised the writer that the natives at Garry Lake were again in danger of starving and would need more food. The natives [name deleted] and [name deleted] were not of the same opinion as the father but both did state that the Caribou had not been to Garry Lake and the Fishing was poor although nobody was in danger.'[72] On the surface it seems unlikely that the Inuit would contradict Father Trinel about whether relief was needed. This may explain Wilkinson's remark that 'all this information is from Cpl. Wilson.' In this context, it clearly indicates a note of distrust.

On 15 December, Wilkinson, having returned the previous day, travelled with Wilson and the Inuk guide aboard the RCMP Otter to Pelly Lake. There they found that 'the building containing the food supplies was in good shape and roughly half of the supplies which had previously been left were still inside. The additional food supplies were placed in the building and a note left on the door to the effect that the supplies had been placed inside.'[73] Presumably this note was written in syllabics. It specified that a particular individual was in charge of the food; the fox skins stored in the building 'were picked up and taken to Baker Lake where they were traded to the HBC post and a credit put on the books for the Garry Lake Eskimos concerned.'[74]

It is interesting, again, to note that what was relief, what was family allowance, and what was earned from the fur trade were all provided by the same sources, perhaps leading to an understandable confusion. It seems unlikely that the differences between relief, family allowances, emergency aid, and supplies 'earned' by the trade in furs had any significance for Garry Lake Inuit. In the end, whatever the source, food was food. They were not to get any when they most needed it.

Finally, as the three men were returning to Baker Lake on 15 December, according to Wilkinson, 'the plane made a wide sweep of the area in order to look for camps but in the failing light was unable to spot anyone. The wide sweep of the plane over the area would ensure that people in the area would hear the plane and realize that it had been to the airstrip with additional supplies.'[75] The plane's sweep was another message that may not have been received.

Wilson's report confirms most of this, though the language is slightly different. Wilson reported that 'on December 15th, 1958[76] $900 worth of Family Allowance supplies were taken into Garry Lake. This was approximately 1400 lbs the load the Otter could carry.'[77] Wilson also noted that 'there was still a fair amount of food left from the supplies taken in to Garry Lake in the Summer Months.'[78] No mention is made by Wilson of the search for camps on the return flight. Wilson also notes that another Inuk had to be found to watch over the storehouse, since '[name deleted] was leaving to become a lay brother at Gjoa Haven.'[79] This is an obvious reference to Manernaluk/Maneeralik, Father Buliard's (then Father Trinel's) assistant.

In his year-end report for 1957, dated 28 January 1958 and likely written as the situation at Garry Lake was becoming desperate, Wilson takes note of the clothing problem, writing that 'most of the natives [were] now wearing deerskin clothing several years old.' He went on to describe the general health situation as 'fair' and wrote of Garry Lake: 'During the past Winter the writer patrolled twice to Garry Lake taking in fishnets each time. It is believed that the natives have been using this equipment as there have been no Caribou in the Garry Lake district, since last summer.'[80] Mention of two visits during the past winter is confusing, since only the 15 December visit is recorded by Wilkinson's comprehensive report (although perhaps the September trip constituted a winter visit). There is no note of alarm anywhere in the report, no mention of Trinel's warnings, no worry expressed over the fact that direct contact with the Garry Lake Inuit had not been established for some time, no worry that the lack of good clothing might restrict attempts to hunt or fish. While Wilson believed that Inuit were using the fishnets he had supplied, he had no evidence that they were. On the other hand, the presence of food supplies at the airstrip hut may have been interpreted as a sign that there was no immediate fear of starvation.

The Famine: January to March 1958

The situation of the Garry Lake Inuit worsened quickly in January 1958, as revealed by reports from survivors. One Inuk hunter, located with his family at Pelly Lake on 24 April, related the following: 'Almost no caribou were obtained by the Garry Lake Eskimo during the winter but had been able to subsist on fish for some time. During January the fishing declined, but some were still being obtained. The emergency supplies, previously left at Pelly Lake, were used as a supplement to the fish obtained.'[81] A statement taken from Ninayok, another one of the survivors, confirms this story. The following exchange deals with the period immediately after Father Trinel's departure:

Q. What happened at Garry Lake after the Father left and where did the people go?

A. My husband and I stayed at the rapids between Garry & Pelly lakes with Kudloo and his family. The rest of the natives stayed around Garry Lake or Pelly Lake.

Q. Who stayed at the airstrip during the Winter?

A. Teenak and his family ...
Q. How long did the food at the airstrip last?
A. Nearly all the food was gone by the end of January. I heard that Teenak fed the Police Dogfood cache to his dogs.[82]

By late January, the situation in the camps was desperate. The stores had apparently been nearly exhausted, caribou were not being found, and fishing was difficult and providing slim returns.

In late February, the supply building containing the little food that remained to the group burned down. This crucial event is dealt with in great detail in the various documents. The unnamed hunter picked up at Pelly Lake in April related the story: 'In February 2 Eskimo men visited the food cache and lived some time in the building. It was reported that one of the Eskimos was lighting a Primus Stove when it exploded. His companion, who was sleeping and only partially clothed, were [sic] able to leave the building which became ignited and burned to the snow level, together with the food supplies inside.'[83] Ninayok's version confirms this and adds some important details.

Q. How did the storehouse at Pelly Lake burn down?
A. Akkikunga told me that he and Arnadjuak had been to the house and stayed inside. Arnadjuak made a small stove from a meat tin. When he lit it the house caught on fire and both him and Akkikunga ran outside. Akkikunga came to our camp and told us what had happened.
Q. Why did Arnadjuak stay at the airstrip?
A. He was scared because he burned the store down and thought he would wait until the Police came. Arnadjuak had also been fighting with his wife and he was scared to go home. He told Akkikunga that he would like to die.
Q. When did the building burn down?
A. About the end of February.
Q. Who was the first person to die?
A. Kadloo was the first to die sometime around the middle or the end of February but after the fire at the airstrip.[84]

The Inuk hunter's report ends with a description of what happened after the fire:

One Eskimo then left for his camp where his family was situated, and the other, lacking clothing, entered another building and crawled between some mattresses there for warmth. Here he perished from exposure. The first Eskimo returned to his camp without the food which the other members, numbering 8, were expecting. Subsequently this whole family died of starvation. Further questioning elicited that fact that 16 Eskimos in all had perished through starvation.[85]

A lengthy account of the fire is contained in a commentary by Northern Service Officer W.G. Kerr on the comprehensive report to the director about the starvations:

1. Eskimo arrives at building to get food. He stays for a day or so, eating and resting in building before returning to camp with supplies. 2. Second Eskimo arrives at building to get food. He wakens first Eskimo, who is asleep in building. Second Eskimo undresses climbs [sic] into warm sleeping bag vacated by first (this is common practice) who starts fire to make tea for first Eskimo who is very cold and hungry after walk into building from camp. 3. Stove explodes and sets building on fire. Both Eskimos get out. First Eskimo is warm and fed and is dressed, he gets out with clothes. Second Eskimo is cold and hungry and without clothes on upper body, he gets out as is. 4. First Eskimo, being well fed and dressed, is able to walk back to camp about twenty five miles from building. Second Eskimo, being hungry, cold and without adequate clothes crawls into small building and dies there.[86]

This account differs from Ninayok's. In her account, Arnadjuak, who lit the fire, is the one who stays behind and freezes.

There is also some question about how much food was in the storehouse in the first place. Documents, to be discussed later in this chapter, show that Father Trinel stayed in the storehouse in November and December, subsisting on the food there. It seems unlikely that he would have gone back to Baker Lake unless he realized that the food supplies there were running low. Kerr reports that 'at first talks between NSO and Eskimos at Garry Eskimos stated that food was in building,' but that 'following an exchange of letters between R.C. missionary at Baker and the Eskimos at Garry and later with personal contact between them, this story changed.'[87] Wilson, in his summary of events, argued that 'as the storehouse did not contain a great amount of food when it was burned it is not felt that this caused any starvation in itself.'[88]

A total of seventeen people died between late February and early March. Ironically, it was just at that crucial time, late February, that an RCMP patrol into the area had been planned. It never took place. Other events at Garry Lake continued to unfold. Another source of evidence, the autopsy reports on twelve of the dead Inuit, can be used in conjunction with Ninayok's testimony. In his summary of findings, the pathologist wrote of the twelve bodies he examined: 'All showed definite evidence of severe malnutrition as evidenced by weight loss and extreme loss of all fat from the body.'[89] This is important for two reasons. First, Corporal Wilson would initially attempt to suggest that the deaths were due to trichinosis, probably acquired from eating the dogs. Second, there were also attempts, even in the final government report, to suggest exposure as a cause of some deaths, rather than starvation. The two are clearly related. But to emphasize exposure, rather than starvation, which makes it impossible for the body to generate enough energy to protect it from the cold, is to shift the blame away from the state and onto the elements – and to explain the tragedy as an unfortunate event that could hardly have been avoided. The pathologist clearly tied malnutrition to all of the deaths and, in summary, wrote:

> It seems impossible to me under the circumstances in which the deaths occurred to completely separate the effects of starvation from those of cold and general exposure. From the information I have it seems unlikely that any of the victims had heat of any sort during the majority of the period in which the deaths occurred, and it seems likely that starvation occurring in these people might be greatly hastened by the effects of cold. This might be partially substantiated by the fact that the adults of these [sic] showed very little evidence of severe muscular wasting and their appearance suggested that death occurred rather rapidly once their fat stores were depleted.[90]

It seems clear that all the deaths at Garry Lake were due primarily to malnutrition, which in some cases contributed to exposure.

The bodies of the first two who died, Kadloo and Arnadjuak, were among the twelve examined by the pathologist. Of Kadloo, the pathologist wrote (naming him Kadluk): 'He is said to have eaten a large amount of dog meat and also some time near the end of February to have fallen in the water. He apparently escaped from this accident and got home successfully. The following day he is said to have oedema of the arms and legs but complained of no other symptoms. He died a few weeks later.'[91] The pathologist concluded, after careful examination, that 'all the findings on this body point to starvation as a cause of death.'[92] The pathologist also described Arnadjuak's death. 'He is said to have been in the warehouse when it took fire and got out but without his parka. He crawled into some mattresses in a nearby building and was later found frozen.'[93] He went on to state that 'while death may have been directly due to exposure it should be pointed out that this man showed the same signs of starvation that the other Eskimos did, weighing only 105 lbs. and being utterly devoid of any fat in his body. In addition fur was found in the gastro-intestinal tract.'[94]

Ninayok's descriptions of what happened to the Inuit who died at Garry Lake can be partly substantiated by the pathologist's report. These are particularly grim stories, which need to be retold here – without being sensationalized – to illustrate how individuals experienced the famine. Ninayok, shortly after telling of Kadloo's death, was asked about his family:

> Kadloo died first while going to Kukshouts camp. We talked to him just before he died and he told us that he was not sick but only the backs of his legs were tight and the flesh on his arms was soft and rotten. He told us that everybody was still alive at his camp. A few weeks later Kabluk came to our camp and stated that everybody was dead and that she was going to the Mission House.
>
> Q.   Was Kadluk sick or hungry?
> A.   She was just the same as Kadloo.[95]

The pathologist saw the bodies of many in Kadloo's family: Akkikunga, Kabluk, Tutiktok, Igupta, Kunnark, Putulik, Korshuk, and Pungar, the last six being children. Akkikunga had been with Arnadjuak at the warehouse fire but had managed to make it back to the camp. According to the pathologist, 'some time after this he complained of vomiting, headaches, and subconjunctival haemorrhages. He did not remain in bed but walked around staring into space. He laid down on his back which is considered unusual for an Eskimo and died approximately three weeks after the onset of these symptoms.'[96] Of Kabluk, Kadloo's wife, he wrote: 'Apparently she and the remainder of her family became split off from the rest of the group after her husband died. The entire family perished from starvation, apparently at the Roman Catholic Mission House.'[97] Tutiktok, a boy aged fifteen, 'perished with the rest of the family at the time the mother went to the Roman Catholic Mission.' Igupta, a ten-year-old girl, 'died at the time the mother moved to the Mission House.' Kunnark, listed by the pathologist as Kowatalik, and Louis Kunnar also 'died with Kabluk, the wife of Kadluk, at the Roman Catholic Mission.' Putulik, a female baby whose identity was in doubt (she may have been the younger Akkikunga, Putulik was listed by the nurse as a male infant) died because 'the mother Kabluk had insufficient milk to feed him.' Korshuck, a three-and-a-half-year-old male, 'perished from starvation at the vacated camp after their mother left.' Pungar, 'an eight year old child [female] was another of Kadluk's children who perished after being left at the vacated camp.'[98]

Ninayok's testimony becomes a similar, grim litany at this point:

> Q.   What happened to Evukluk?
> A.   He was living on a small lake North of Garry Lake. He was getting some fish everyday but he left his camp with his wife and children to go and

get a deer cache but they could not find it. He got sick while walking and could not walk. His wife left him and took the children towards our camp. On the way the youngest child died. She came to our camp and we fed her. She left after a few days and went to her father's camp. I don't know if Evukluk had been eating dog meat or not.

Q. What happened to Nearkok?

A. He was living with Kukshout during the winter and went fishing. He was found by Putooktee dead at the fish hole.

Q. What happened to Itteroyuk?

A. He was living with Puyatat south of the mission. After Puyatat moved to a different fishing place Itteroyuk was walking to Kukshout's camp. He was found frozen on the lake by Kukshouts [*sic*]. He did not have very good clothing on. I don't think he was sick from eating dogs. He died during March same day as Nearkok.[99]

Of Nearkok, the pathologist wrote: 'The male nurse's history of this man states simply that he went out fishing and that he did not return' and that 'it is uncertain from the clinical history whether this man actually froze to death or died from a combination of malnutrition and exposure.'[100] Of Itteroyuk, he wrote, 'This man who was the father of Arnadjuar who was frozen is said to have committed Eskimo suicide by walking out into the cold following the death of his son,' and 'he appeared to be suffering from definite malnutrition at this time, and of a severe degree.'[101] These two complete the list of twelve with which the pathologist's report dealt.

However, Ninayok's testimony reveals more about this tragic experience.

Q. Did you hear what happened to the two children living at Kukshout's camp. This is Kowetalik and Sibviark.

A. I heard that the children starved and couldn't move their bowels. Kukshout put Kowetalik in the Mission. Sibviark died of the same thing. I think both of the children died from starvation. Kukshout had enough fish to live on during the Winter but the children seemed to get sick from just eating fish.

Q. What happened to Akkikunga (Angalee's baby daughter)?

A. After the baby was born it couldn't get fat. It died when it was about a month old.

Q. What happened to Angnowjak the adopted daughter of Angotituak?

A. I heard that while Angotituak was at Baker Lake the baby was sick every month.

Q. Did you hear that the Adopted Mother beat the child.

A. I don't know. I heard two different stories. I know that Tamerlak likes children but I did hear that she had been beating the child. Kabloo [*sic*] told me before she died.[102]

The story that comes together from these reports – whether in the much-edited language of the Inuit hunter, the clinical vocabulary of the autopsy report, or the fatalistic replies of Ninayok to the RCMP investigator's blunt questions – is remarkably consistent. Adults in the prime of life, children, infants, and elders all starved. Families tried to help other families while fending for themselves. Individuals went mad or committed suicide or made desperate attempts to save themselves and died in the effort.

The loss of the food stored in the warehouse undoubtedly contributed to the disaster, but it is hard to place all the blame on this single event. It is by no means certain that enough food was stored there to provide for all the families through the winter. Even before Akkikunga and Arnadjuak went to the warehouse, people were in desperate trouble. The stored food would have provided relief to Kabluk and Kadloo's family, but it is hard to know for how long. In the midst of the worst of these terrible events, Kabluk led the remnants of her family to the Roman Catholic mission house in the hopes of finding help. She found none. Arnadjuak, huddled between some mattresses, waited for the RCMP to come and perhaps punish him for burning down the warehouse. No one came. And so they starved to death. Meanwhile, the relief that was so desperately needed would not arrive because those in charge of providing it hesitated and delayed and avoided at Baker Lake. No one was to reach the area until 22 March, when food was airlifted in and left behind, and the Garry Lake Inuit were not to be contacted directly until 24 April. What was happening in Baker Lake, to the south, while these events were unfolding in the Garry Lake/Back River area?

Relief Efforts: February to May, 1958
At Baker Lake, the conflict among the non-Natives continued. On 5 January, the welfare teacher, Terance Golding, wrote a letter to the chief of the education division of the Department of Northern Affairs. In it he complained that a confidential report he had submitted in November had been shared with Doug Wilkinson, the northern service officer, who in turn had discussed the contents with him and the RCMP officer, Corporal Wilson.[103] Subsequently, an 'Inter-departmental Meeting' was held at the nursing station on 13 January. The meeting discussed local matters, including what to do about the serious tuberculosis problem. No mention was made of the Garry Lake situation, but relations between Golding, Wilson, Wilkinson, and Caygill, the community nurse, seemed amiable.[104]

Wilkinson's report on this meeting left no doubt, however, that trouble was continuing to brew beneath the surface. He noted that 'although there was evidence of some ill feeling between the RCMP member and the nurse prior to the meeting, no such ill feeling crept into discussions.'[105] The report goes on to describe the developing intergroup conflicts in some detail.

> At our meeting last night I was able to ward off possible trouble by stepping in quickly to offer suggestions that I knew would be more acceptable to certain parties concerned. In searching out the middle road I often find myself lined up with Cpl. Wilson against others. This is an almost intolerable situation for, as I have explained before, although I agree with most of the end results of Cpl. Wilson's work I cannot agree with the methods used. Already I have had trouble with the teacher over this. I tried many ways to show Mr. Golding that I was forced to work with Cpl. Wilson due to circumstances beyond my control. He was not perceptive enough to realize this and I finally had to tell him outright my feelings in the Baker Lake situation. This straightened out matters with the teacher but if this information should get to Cpl. Wilson through a third party my good relations with him will be shattered.[106]

Relations were clearly deteriorating. Wilkinson described the situation as a 'powder keg.' Division between those responsible for emergency relief would play a key role in the events that unfolded. Subsequent reports from Wilson and Wilkinson complete the picture of what was transpiring in Baker Lake at the same time as Inuit at Garry Lake were starving to death. A variety of factors led to Doug Wilkinson being away from Baker Lake at crucial times when relief visits might have been made. The weather did not cooperate, and winter storms and extremely low temperatures affected travel in the region. However, the failure of Corporal Wilson to make a regular winter patrol to Garry Lake is hard to justify. It seems likely that the events of the previous summer influenced the interpretation that Wilson, Wilkinson, and others placed on Father Trinel's claims when he returned to the settlement at Christmas. There was no way of confirming the situation at Garry Lake except by travel to the area with a dog team, and while a trip was scheduled for the end of February, it never took place.

Wilkinson's schedule can be culled from his comprehensive report of 18 December 1958. In October and November 1957 he was 'in Ottawa for N.S.O. conference and annual leave,' not returning to Baker Lake until 14 December.[107] At that time he was also purchasing and learning to fly a light aircraft for use in the Keewatin. In his January report, Wilkinson noted that a number of inland Inuit, including those at Garry Lake, 'all report no caribou in their area.'[108] In February 1958, Wilkinson reported that he had conferred with Wilson on the Garry Lake situation, noting that 'Eskimo from Garry Lake had not shown up, but Cpl. Wilson stated that he was making arrangements for another Eskimo from the Back River to guide him to Garry Lake in case the Garry Lake man does not come. He expected to depart for Garry Lake February 20th-22nd.'[109]

Wilkinson's reports on Garry Lake began to show a growing sense of urgency. On 20 February, he wrote a report on the 'Garry Lake Eskimos' that noted 'without accurate, firsthand information it is difficult to make any prediction as to the present economic condition of the area.' He knew that 'no (or very few) caribou are around Garry Lake' but also that 'a fairly large stock of relief supplies was stored in the building at the Pelly Lake airstrip' so he assumed that 'the Garry Lake people are not living in luxury but neither are they starving.'[110] In this, he couldn't have been more wrong. Nevertheless, the report strongly urged a visit, noting that Wilson had planned a sled patrol and that 'if the Eskimo guide from Garry Lake fails to appear at Baker Lake, Cpl. Wilson plans to hire a guide locally and carry on with the trip.'[111] As a further contingency, which seems to reflect some doubts about Corporal Wilson's commitment to the trip, Wilkinson ended his report to the chief of the Arctic division by saying: 'If anything happens to delay Cpl. Wilson's planned patrol unduly, I shall immediately request that a flight be made to Garry Lake by the RCMP aircraft in order that we make sure no food problems exist.'[112] This was precisely the point at which such a trip was crucial. Unfortunately, Wilkinson would be called away from his post at the time when he might have ensured that the trip take place.

On 27 February, Wilkinson left for Eskimo Point, where he had been called to serve as justice of the peace in the trial of Kikkik. A day later, he left for 'Churchill en route to Ottawa to pick up his personal plane.'[113] On 1 March, while he was in Churchill, a meeting was held during which

Mr. Wilkinson met Mr. Rudnicki and Mr. Stevenson of the Arctic Division ... The Garry Lake situation was discussed with them. Mr. Wilkinson again expressed his doubts that the sled patrol would take place. It was decided to wire Cpl. Wilson suggesting that if, for any reason, the sled patrol was delayed Mr. Rudnicki and Mr. Stevenson could come to Baker Lake from Eskimo Point in the R.C.M.P. aircraft, pick up Mr. Wilson and fly to Garry Lake. Mr. Wilkinson departed for Ottawa.[114]

The situation at Henik Lake must have helped to raise some anxieties about Garry Lake. But despite taking precautionary steps to ensure that a check was made of the situation, Wilkinson's absence from Baker Lake at this crucial period clearly contributed to subsequent events. Wilkinson 'arrived back at Baker Lake in his personal aircraft' on 23 March,[115] one day after Wilson had finally managed to airlift supplies into Garry Lake.

Wilson, meanwhile, had been stationed at Baker Lake through the whole period. His report of 10 July 1958 deals quite extensively with his reasons for not making a dogsled patrol into Garry Lake as planned. Wilson begins his rationalization with a reference to the Inuk who had travelled out of Garry Lake with Father Trinel on 10 December.

Before [name deleted] left for Garry Lake he was asked by the writer if he could come to Baker Lake during the latter part of February 1958 in order to guide the writer on a patrol to Garry Lake. This [name deleted] promised to do. It was not until sometime in March that the writer heard from some of the Back's River natives to the effect that [name deleted] had told them on his trip home that he did not think he would come back down. As no other suitable guide could be found it was decided that the trip would not be done by dog team and the use of aircraft was decided upon. This matter was discussed with the Northern Service Officer Mr. Wilkinson at various times.[116]

There is a clear discrepancy between Corporal Wilson and Doug Wilkinson's accounts on whether they conferred about air travel. As noted above, on 1 March, Wilkinson reports that he conferred with Walter Rudnicki and Alex Stevenson about a sled patrol, so as of then he seems to have believed it would take place. Wilkinson also reports that on 2 March: 'Message received from Cpl. Wilson by Messrs. Rudnicki and Stevenson that sled patrol was taking place. However, no sled patrol was made.'[117] As a result, the two did not make haste to Baker Lake with the RCMP aircraft. It is also worth noting that in his July report, Wilson makes much of the fact that a number of false alarms regarding starvation had been raised in the Garry Lake area, presumably to suggest that this had some influence on his decision not to treat matters there as a crisis. Wilson also reports that 'during the middle of March Mr. Wilkinson arrived back at Baker Lake with his own personal aircraft,'[118] implying that this took place before Wilson's 22 March visit to Garry Lake, rather than after.

In any event, on 22 March, Wilson flew to Garry Lake on an RCAF Otter. Wilson reports:

Due to previous arrangements, the next patrol to Garry Lake was completed on March 22nd., 1958. As the R.C.A.F. can only carry 900 lbs in an Otter, due to large quantities of survival gear, only the writer patrolled to Garry Lake carrying in previously mentioned Family Allowances. The building was found burned to the ground and no signs of any Eskimos around. As mentioned in previous correspondence the Otter began to develop engine trouble so the patrol returned to Baker Lake.[119]

Wilson seems to have treated this discovery rather lightly. In response to the charge that 'the writer should have been somewhat concerned when the building was found burned down and the natives missing,' he replied:

> It is pointed out that the natives did not live around the airstrip. Neither were they missing. The natives in this area live scattered over Pelly Lake and Garry Lake. During the past Winter when they were starving these natives lived at various places on both of the lakes mentioned. Even if it had been known that the natives were starving it would have been almost impossible to find all of the camps. It wasn't until later in the Spring that they started to migrate toward the better known fishing holes. The airstrip at Pelly lake was only used to store a very limited amount of food.[120]

Of the same visit, Wilkinson reports that 'the ruins of the building were completely snowed in and there was no sign of life in the area. The food on the plane was placed on the ground by the burned out building and the plane returned to Baker Lake,' adding that 'some engine trouble had been experienced on the flight due to utilization of gasoline of a wrong octane rating. The plane returned to Churchill.'[121]

On 25 March, Wilson and Wilkinson again conferred over the Garry Lake situation. Wilkinson

> learned that [the] sled patrol had not taken place. Cpl. Wilson told of the trip to Garry Lake by the RCAF Otter with the additional food supplies. He reported that 'the Father's place' had burned down. This was taken to mean that the R.C. Mission had burned. Later Mr. Wilkinson discovered that the Father had moved across to the Pelly Lake airstrip in November and had been living in the building containing the food supplies until he came to Baker Lake in December and that it was this building which had burned down with the loss of everything inside. Cpl. Wilson reported that he felt no alarm at the Garry Lake situation as a good quantity of food had been left at the airstrip.[122]

One interesting detail provided here is the fact that the initial food stored in the warehouse had been used by Father Trinel through at least one month in the late fall. Although Wilkinson and Wilson decided that they should use the latter's personal aircraft for a visit to Garry Lake as soon as possible, two things created delays. Wilkinson needed further flight experience, and 'the weather, which had been excellent during early March, deteriorated badly following Mr. Wilkinson's return to Baker Lake.'[123] This was the point at which the weather intervened, preventing an early April follow-up visit into the area that might have saved lives. There seems by this point to have been no question of making a sled trip. However, in clear weather, with a guide from Baker Lake, such a trip would certainly have been feasible had enough of a sense of urgency led to its undertaking.

Although by 9 April Wilkinson had managed to get in the flight experience he thought necessary for a trip into Garry Lake and the weather had improved, on 10 April he 'received a wire from Ottawa requesting that he go to Rankin Inlet to assist at the forthcoming trial' of Kikkik. And on 13 April he 'flew to Rankin Inlet, to attend trial, in his personal aircraft.'[124] Interestingly, Wilson's report strongly implies that it was Wilkinson who was responsible for the delay and that it was Wilkinson who was not worried about the situation. 'The matter of Mr. Wilkinson making the patrol was brought up with him and he again stated that he would make the trip as soon as possible. As ample food had been taken in by the R.C.A.F. there would have been no advantage to using the larger aircraft.'[125]

On 17 April, 'Wilkinson returned to Baker Lake from Rankin Inlet. Bad weather prevented any flight to Garry Lake on the 18th although an attempt was made.'[126] Again, Wilson implies that it was Wilkinson who did not have any sense of urgency: 'The writer mentioned that a patrol should be made to Garry Lake as soon as possible but Mr. Wilkinson felt that the matter could wait until his return from Rankin Inlet.'[127] Meanwhile, Wilson could have made a sled patrol into the area had he been so inclined.

The combination of events – meetings and bad weather and lack of urgency – combined and conspired to produce a maddeningly glacial reaction to the misfortunes that were befalling Inuit at Garry Lake. Another attempt to fly to Garry Lake on 20 April was aborted due to bad weather. It persisted until 24 April, when Wilkinson and Wilson managed to fly in to the Pelly Lake airfield. Wilkinson reports:

At Pelly Lake they found two Eskimo families at airstrip. From them they learned details of deaths of Eskimos and of the fire which burned building with remaining food. Mr. Wilkinson and Cpl. Wilson returned to Baker Lake and wired for a large aircraft to come to Baker Lake to take more food supplies to Garry Lake. Eskimos remaining in Garry Lake area were living at usual fishing locations, existing on fish and supplies brought in by RCAF plane in March. They were in no immediate danger but they would require additional food supplies to see them through until late spring.[128]

The RCMP Otter reached Baker Lake on 25 April, but bad weather kept it from going on to Garry Lake until the next day.

On the 26th, when the Otter reached the Pelly Lake airfield, they found that 'about half of the Eskimos in the area had come to the airstrip and food was distributed to them for themselves and also for the people remaining at the camps in the vicinity.'[129] On 6 May, the RCMP Otter returned to Baker Lake and made three trips in to Garry Lake, ferrying in Wilkinson and Wilson as well as further supplies: 'All Eskimo camps were visited, twelve bodies located and "cached" in convenient places to await disposal instructions following consultation with Eskimos, Ottawa and Mission at Baker Lake. All camps had food and were obtaining fish and ptarmigan. No caribou had been seen in the area. Additional food supplies were left in the building at Pelly Lake in charge of the Eskimo, Teenak.'[130]

On 1 and 2 June, 'in view of desirability of having Eskimos available as witnesses for the inquest,' an 'RCAF Dakota evacuated entire Garry Lake group to Baker Lake. Group established in a tent camp near settlement.'[131] Later in July, after the inquests, the 'Garry Lake group established near the mouth of the Kazan River where good fishing existed. Men came to settlement for employment as stevedores at ship time.'[132] Their fate would parallel that of the Henik Lake Inuit. Control over their own lives was placed firmly in the hands of others.

Apportioning Responsibility
The assessments we have of the situation at Garry Lake were written largely from bureaucratic perspectives intended to ensure that blame did not fall on whoever was writing the report. However, Wilkinson's comprehensive report of 18 December 1958 is remarkable because it does not try to assign responsibility or to explain the event. But in earlier reports he does have something to say about this. In a 7 June report, he identifies three main causes for the tragedy at Garry Lake: '1. Failure of the caribou to appear in large numbers in the fall and winter of 1957-58. 2. Destruction of relief supplies of food kept in the area by fire. 3. Lack of guidance for the Eskimos in a difficult situation.'[133] Wilson, on the other hand, stresses that 'they died and the other natives starved because they lacked any form of leadership. Not one native was willing to come to Baker Lake for assistance.'[134] He also strongly implies that Wilkinson was not inclined to a sense of urgency in investigating matters, and on this point also stresses that 'nobody died between March 22nd, 1958 and April 24th, 1958,'[135] the period between his two visits to the area.

Wilkinson implies that Wilson was the one who showed little urgency. He refers to a memo he wrote on 20 February that 'expressed some doubt that the sled patrol would actually take place despite these arrangements as Cpl. Wilson had a record (at Baker Lake) of initiating projects and then never carrying them out.'[136] Clearly, had Wilson made the trip that had been planned and which Trinel's December warnings warranted, lives would have been saved. Wilkinson, on the other hand, got pulled out of the area for other reasons and could perhaps have displayed a greater sense of urgency.

But then, it is easy through the distance and comfort of archival documents to reach such conclusions. That it was far more difficult in the cold, dark winter circumstances of Baker Lake in 1958 to know where the greatest priorities should lie, especially given the events which preceded this starvation, is without doubt.

Northern Service Officer Kerr, writing about the aftermath, notes that 'many people were extremely anxious to "get" Cpl Wilson in retaliation for his bullish behaviour in the community and for his lack of concern over the plight of the interior Eskimos. This led to a rash of rumours most of which attempted to show that the administration was negligent at Garry Lake.'[137] This was clearly in the interests of both the missionaries and traders who resented Wilson's policies regarding the distribution of relief.

The overall assessment of the events at Garry Lake, written by Acting Director Hunt, places the blame, as Wilson had, on fate and the Inuit. However, perhaps Hunt follows Wilkinson's analysis most closely:

The main contributing factors to this tragic story were the failure of the caribou to arrive, and the burning of the storehouse at Pelly Lake with the emergency food stored there. Garry Lake is so isolated from the nearest post (Baker Lake) that reasonable precautions had been taken against the possible failure of the caribou to appear, even though they were expected in some numbers. Fish are abundant in this section of the country, if any serious attempt is made to obtain them during the fall. In winter they can be obtained but the operation is more arduous. The inland Eskimo trait is to base his whole economy upon the caribou and to wait hopefully for them until the winter arrives and the opportunity for a fall fishery is past. With the knowledge of this – the emergency food caches were established. If the food storehouse had not burned down, there is reason to believe that there would have been sufficient food, together with fish, to have carried the Eskimos over the intervening time between regular patrols to Garry Lake. A sworn statement by Eskimo Teenah at the subsequent Coroner's inquest showed that at the time of the fire, supplies in the building included tea, fat, and ammunition, as well as RCMP patrol supplies and dog food.[138]

This whitewash deserves close commentary. There does seem to be some doubt as to how much food was in the warehouse and its part in events. The tea, fat, and ammunition, as well as unspecified 'patrol supplies' and dog food mentioned in the statement, would not have helped, and Teenah was not the last person in the building. One wonders whether or not Nearkok, who died at a fishing hole, would agree that winter fishing, though arduous, is still possible. The 'Eskimo traits' referred to do not deserve comment.

Left out of this report is mention that the previous season's caribou hunt had not gone well enough to provide sufficient clothing stocks. Anyone who realized this in advance might have predicted problems. Caribou-skin clothing tends to wear out quickly; without a successful hunt Garry Lake Inuit were left both with inadequate food stocks and inadequate means of preparing the warm clothing they would need to be able to fish. The non-arrival of caribou and the burning of the storehouse were contributing factors. The failure of a ground patrol to follow up Trinel's warnings beyond the 15 December visit, when no Inuit were directly contacted, was also a contributing factor – fed by distrust of Trinel due to his summer exaggerations. This was the most serious of the charges that might be laid against government officials in the area.

Clearly, although some responsibility for getting into the region after 22 March falls to Wilkinson, the greatest burden lies with Wilson's failure to make a sled trip in late February or early March when lives might have been saved. Such a trip would have been no easy undertaking. The terrain is rough and the distance considerable, adding to the cold and dark that would be expected. This is a trip that Wilson blames the Inuit for not making. The fact remains that visiting the area was his responsibility and he did not do so, even though few people would have been capable of travelling into such an area under such extreme conditions. However, as noted above, it is easy from this distance to pronounce judgments on individuals and that, in the end, is not the reason for our review of these events.

The Garry Lake famine illustrates that the government of Canada had not put enough resources into monitoring and caring for Inuit who were its responsibility. It wanted a 'bare bones' commitment. This is precisely what it got. This can be contrasted with the commitment of the state to ensuring the existence of conditions that made the fur trade in the region possible and that satisfied the state's needs to keep welfare, monitoring, and the other costs of the welfare state at a minimum. As a result, there were no personnel placed at Garry Lake, no radio phones with which Inuit could communicate their need for assistance, not enough staff at Baker Lake to replace Wilkinson when he was gone, and not even enough RCMP in the area to deal with all the duties for which the Force was responsible. So people died.

The account of how these people died is not simply a sensational story. It should serve to remind us that the people referred to as 'the Eskimo Kabluk' or 'the Eskimo Teenah' were not a 'species' but individuals with friends, family, feelings, and culture – individuals who experienced the most painful of privations – the lack of food and death from starvation.

In the end, the government covered over its negligence with a whitewash report that blamed fate (the caribou did not arrive) and the Inuit themselves (their traits led them to disaster). The survivors were moved out, plans were made for them, they were moved again. Eventually, they would find themselves dispersed to coastal locations – Rankin Inlet and Whale Cove.[139]

7

The Whale Cove Relocation

'No Reasonable Alternative': Making the Decision

The Keewatin crises in the winter of 1957-8 sent shock waves through the Department of Northern Affairs. Letters to the government poured in from across the country and from other countries. The story of the deaths was to bring notoriety to the department and its Arctic staff through the writings of Farley Mowat, whose book, *The Desperate People*, documented the tragedy at Henik Lake. The Diefenbaker administration, swept to power on a platform emphasizing northern development, had reason for embarrassment; even more so when one considers the Prairie and Tory origins of John Diefenbaker and of Alvin Hamilton – his minister of northern affairs and national resources. The following letter is revealing. It was typical of the public response directed at the prime minister.

May 7, 1958

I was greatly disturbed today upon hearing over the radio, that the bodies of six or eight Eskimos who had *starved* to death, had been found. What a *great insult* and *shame* to have such a thing happen in Canada; a land of plenty, and surpluses – where farmers in Western Canada have granaries full of grain – which would greatly aid our 'starving' Eskimos.

... During the recent Election campaign, we heard a great many solutions 'proposed' to help the unemployed – a great many of whom do receive 'help' in the form of 'unemployment insurance,' etc. Why couldn't 'help' in the form of food, clothing and other necessary things be 'stocked' at 'posts' or 'outlets' for our people living in Northern Canada, in case it might be needed? Also have more such 'posts' built in Northern Canada if necessary.

... How can we stand by 'doing nothing' while our people up North starve and freeze to death, when we would think it terrible to let livestock, or other animals go through such horrors?

Yours truly,

M.J. Thomas
Milden
Saskatchewan[1]

An immediate and familiar response was required – relocation. This time, the focus would be the creation of another 'post' – the Inuit community of Whale Cove, nestled on a rocky prominence along the west coast of Hudson Bay, just south of Rankin Inlet.

Unlike the Craig Harbour and Resolute Bay relocations, sovereignty was clearly not a factor in the creation of Whale Cove. But, not unlike the creation of these far northern settlements, the development of Whale Cove was an ad hoc, hurried response to what had all the makings of a very public and politically embarrassing situation. It involved taking Inuit away from their traditional territories and setting them down in an environment completely foreign to their survival strategies. The end result might be compared to taking a steelworker from Hamilton, Ontario, and relocating him or her to northern Saskatchewan – with the expectation of producing, given a little training, a successful grain farmer. While the Whale Cove move was within the same general geographical region – the Keewatin – it involved moving inland people to a coastal area. It is also not surprising, given the public response, that the Whale Cove move involved discussion at the highest levels of government.

A memorandum to the federal cabinet, prepared by the minister of northern affairs and national resources and dated 9 May 1958, clearly laid out the options available. The memorandum was called 'Crises Among the Keewatin Eskimos' and summarized the problem as follows:

> With the sharp decline of the caribou during the past two decades or more, the situation of approximately 600 Keewatin Eskimos who depend on caribou for clothing and food has deteriorated progressively, and now is critical. During the past winter, starvation occurred in at least two camps and there are sixteen known deaths to date. These, as well as unhappy incidents as Henik Lake where murder recently occurred, are symptoms of the general situation. The disintegration of the caribou economy has led to a social breakdown, and relief issues are not an effective answer. With no prospect of an increase in the caribou herds at least for many years, the immediate and long-range future of these Eskimos has become critical.[2]

The document then outlined five choices of action: provision of government relief and assistance, introduction of Inuit to wage employment, resettlement of Inuit to other parts of the Arctic, resettlement to coastal locations, and creation of a community for rehabilitation of Keewatin Inuit. The last three options all involve relocation. On the issue of resettlement to other parts of the Arctic, the report noted that 'this measure has been applied with success' but suggested the need for wildlife surveys and the problem with depopulating 'an extremely large territory' like the Keewatin. Movement to the coast was also thought to create problems because it 'would require the inland Eskimos to be trained in hunting methods completely foreign to them and, to be successful, would demand supervision in every camp which sought to absorb them.'[3]

Clearly, it is the last option that is being recommended. While each of the other alternatives gets one paragraph, the proposal to create a rehabilitation centre gets a full page of attention, divided into six separate points, all favourable. It was noted, for example, that 'a concentration of Eskimos in one location' would make delivery of social services 'more economical and effective'; that seal, whale, and fish harvesting would provide meat and fuel; that caribou populations might slowly recover; and that 'the concentration of the Keewatin population under adequate supervision would open avenues for development of a cash economy.'[4] Furthermore, it was argued that

> the implementation of such a plan would provide a higher standard of living and a growing population. Within a generation, the Keewatin population, now the most depressed, illiterate, unhealthy, citizens of Canada, might well be a literate, healthy, self-sufficient population, equipped to contribute to the major economic developments which are certain to occur in this region. Action now is essential if achievement is to be realized in this regard through the next decade.[5]

Finally, it was determined that the projected cost would be an estimated $150,000. Arguing again for immediate action, the cabinet document proposed 'a community to be set up on the west coast of Hudson Bay, probably in the vicinity of Rankin Inlet,' and that 'simplicity, utility and self-sufficiency should be the keynotes of the proposed community.' The document concluded with a summary of this recommendation, asking for authority, funds, and a public statement.

At the ninth meeting of the Committee on Eskimo Affairs, held in Ottawa at the East Block of the Parliament Buildings on 26 May 1958, the chair, Gordon Robertson, called on R.A.J. Phillips, chief of the Arctic division, to 'outline for the Committee the Administration's proposals to alleviate the highly undesirable conditions under which a portion of the Keewatin or

Caribou Eskimos had been living in past years.'⁶ Phillips's response, as recorded in the minutes, was as follows:

> Mr Phillips referred to the recent tragedies at Henik and Garry Lakes and said these were only manifestations of a more deep-seated and lasting problem, for which a long-term solution was required. He said the administration was considering proposals to establish a community on the west coast of Hudson Bay designed to meet the needs of the Henik Lake people and of a number of coast Eskimos in the area. According to this plan, inland Eskimos, assisted by people adapted to the sea culture, would live in a permanently situated community and gain their livelihood primarily from the sea.⁷

The new community would eventually be called Whale Cove. Its population would include survivors of the Garry Lake and Henik Lake famines.

The Keewatin Committee: Planning for a Change

Within a few weeks, a Keewatin committee had been established to oversee the development of this new relocation project. The Keewatin committee, consisting of a small group of key Arctic administrators, all within government, included Don Snowden, whose area was economic development; Walter Rudnicki, who was to introduce the department to the concept of 'social planning'; and C.M. Bolger, soon to become assistant chief and then chief of the Arctic division within the department. Others who attended periodically included R.A.J. Phillips, then chief of the Arctic division, and northern service officers W.G. Kerr and D.W. Grant. The committee met six times between 23 May and 28 July 1958. It was responsible for planning the new community – from the selection of the site to the selection of Inuit. The work of the committee reveals the issues surrounding relocation in this period and provides a useful comparison to the Grise Fiord and Resolute Bay relocations.

At the first meeting of the committee, discussion focused on site selection and staff housing, with preliminary discussion of other issues, including the setting up and financing of stores and selection of personnel. There was a general sense of urgency. At one point, Walter Rudnicki urged 'that it was crucial that stores be ordered as soon as possible' and later suggested that 'personnel should be selected as soon as possible.'⁸ As for site selection, at the time, Tavani – a former Hudson's Bay Company post – was favoured. Discussion began with a review of Hudson's Bay Company buildings on the proposed site. This ranged from personal observation, such as Kerr noting that 'he had seen the dwelling from the outside and that it was modern in appearance,' to a plan to ask Kerr 'to undertake a site survey, and that the Secretary would obtain a chart of the harbour and air photographs of the site.'[9]

A second meeting of the Keewatin committee was held on 27 May, one day after the ninth meeting of the Committee on Eskimo Affairs. The Committee on Eskimo Affairs also talked about the proposed Keewatin relocations, a discussion worth reviewing. R.A.J. Phillips proposed a community on the coast that 'in its initial stage ... would have a population of about 100. Present plans called for its establishment later [that] year.' Phillips added that 'the Administration foresaw problems and had some misgivings in undertaking so radical an experiment, but there seemed to be no reasonable alternative if the problems of these people were to have any solution.'[10] In response to this, Father Ducharme, a Roman Catholic priest who had worked in the Keewatin for many years, argued against relocating inland people to the coast because he

> did not think that the Henik Lake Eskimos, being an inland people, would adapt themselves satisfactorily to taking their living from the sea. He felt they should remain inland, where they could be encouraged to hunt caribou by better methods and to harvest more efficiently the fish resources of the inland lakes. He said that if the Eskimos were supplied with proper fish nets, and taught how to use them, their situation should improve. He added that while there were reports the caribou were disappearing, he had himself seen large herds from the air a short time ago.[11]

Anecdotal information about the severity of the situation was thrown around by all sides in this discussion. Ben Sivertz responded by claiming that 'the fact remained the caribou population was sharply declining,' and this was supported by P.A.C. Nichols of the HBC, who noted that 'the Padlei trading post had received no caribou skins this year ... the caribou had apparently changed their migration routes.' Gordon Robertson, deputy minister of the department, also noted that 'it was a serious mistake to be optimistic about the caribou population.' Bishop Marsh, Anglican bishop of the Arctic, then intervened, also noting the difficulties of getting inland people to learn to live off sea resources and pointing out 'that it would be difficult to find any place on the west coast of Hudson Bay where the sea resources would be adequate to support 100 people,' suggesting 'a small pilot project before launching a settlement on a large scale.' Sivertz again responded by stressing 'the importance of bringing these people together in communities sufficiently large to permit the Administration to supervise and help them,' adding later that, 'this policy should be designed to move the people into communities where educational, health and other facilities could be properly provided.'[12] The administration had moved a long way from the early 1950s truism that any form of aid would create dependency. In reaction to the famine in the Keewatin, as well as other factors – including a growing bureaucracy concerned with welfare administration within the department – the pendulum had swung to the opposite end. A key factor in creation of this new community would be economies of scale in the delivery of social services.

Discussion about whether to proceed with planning the 'new town' was effectively closed by Robertson, who, as chair of the committee, argued that there was no other choice. His statement is poignant. Rather than the usual confidence one would expect from an administrator accustomed to backing his logic with rational arguments and the necessary facts and figures, in this case there was the simple fact that a disaster had occurred and no one was really sure what to do about it.

> The Chairman said the situation in the Keewatin was so precarious that the Administration was justified in taking a chance and going ahead to initiate the proposal for a new community. There would be risks no matter what was done, and it was certain that some action would have to be taken immediately. He added, however, that the plan would be undertaken only with adequate resources to operate it. To attempt the project without adequate financial backing would probably result only in failure.[13]

Any plan was better than no plan. Whatever response was undertaken, it would have the resources necessary to support it. This was not exactly the same rallying cry that accompanied earlier relocation projects. The die was cast. The committee, without formally approving or disapproving, merely 'noted the plans to establish a community for inland Eskimos on the west coast of Hudson Bay.' The 'rehabilitation centre' proposed to the federal cabinet in early May was, by late May, understood to be a coastal community in the making.

The next day, the second meeting of the Keewatin committee was held. Some general discussion of issues involved in relocation was initiated by D.F. Symington, head of the projects section in the Arctic division. He introduced the project as follows: 'A small community of twenty to thirty Eskimo families was to be established as soon as possible. Three or four members of the Department would be stationed there to stimulate and administer fishing, fur trapping and various cottage industries and handicrafts.'[14] P.A.C. Nichols, manager of the Arctic division of the Hudson's Bay Company, recommended 'the advantages of a site near, but not at, a settlement' and noted that the HBC 'had recognized the advantage of organizing the Eskimos into larger communities.' Symington thought 'that an advantage of an isolated location such as Tavani was that it would be possible to experiment with an educational programme suited to the needs of the Eskimos, without disruptive outside influences.'[15] This philosophical difference about the basic purpose of the community would continue to be a topic for discussion.

The third meeting took place a few days later. Talk at this point focused on site selection. During the discussion of Tavani as a possible location, the discourse turned again to the question of what basic principles would underlie the new community. An exchange between D.F. Symington and G.W. Rowley, secretary of the advisory committee on northern development, is worth following:

> Mr Symington said that an advantage of Tavani as a site would be its isolation from outside influences of all kinds.
>
> Mr. Rowley said that the objective of isolating the Eskimos seemed to contradict the policy of integrating the Eskimo into the non-Eskimo community.
>
> Mr. Symington explained that the objective of the Keewating [*sic*] Project was to establish an independent Eskimo community, socially and economically sound in relation to the resources of the country. The pilot project, if successful, would be repeated at other northern locations.[16]

The logic of escalation is clearly present here. The project might be expanded and repeated. The other locations discussed were Nunalla, Rankin Inlet, Chesterfield, and Eskimo Point. Since Nunalla was in Manitoba, it was effectively vetoed because 'the legislation of Manitoba would be in effect.' But the discussion ranged quite widely. It was mentioned that York Factory, in Ontario, was a possible site, and Graham Rowley, at one point, 'said that conditions at Nunalla would appear to the Eskimos to be the same as conditions at any location in Keewatin district. Unfamiliar conditions in a more southerly location such as Selkirk, Manitoba, would cause concern among the Eskimos.'[17]

The relative power of the churches in Canadian society during the 1950s, and their role in northern development, is revealed by the discussion about which churches – Anglican or Roman Catholic – would be situated in what location. Phillips 'suggested that in either case the other church could establish a mission if it wished to do so.' The discussion ended with agreement that Rankin Inlet and Tavani seemed the most suitable locations, and that Symington and Rudnicki would 'prepare a paper summarizing the factors to be considered' at both locales.[18]

At this meeting, the first serious discussion of recruiting Inuit took place, with Rudnicki suggesting that 'a Northern Service Officer, possibly Mr.

Wilkinson, could visit the members of these groups explaining the proposed project to them. It was expected that there would be no lack of Eskimos to volunteer to live in the community.'[19] Once again, Inuit cooperation is assumed in advance; ability to gain consent is never in doubt.

The next meeting of the Keewatin committee was on 9 June. As a first order of business, C.M. Bolger was appointed permanent chair of the committee. Most of the discussion at this meeting focused on the question of staff for the project. The committee discussed a supervisor, technical officer, teacher, resources officer, and welfare officer, suggesting specific individuals for each position. The question of selection of Inuit candidates for the project was also discussed, with Rudnicki suggesting a one-page application form and advising that 'thirty families should be selected to begin the project. While applications from the Henik Lake and Garry Lake Eskimos would be given special consideration because of the reduced circumstances of these natives, an attempt would be made to balance the destitute, demoralized and medically unfit members of the community with able, ambitious and healthy members.'[20] Thirty families would obviously lead to somewhat more than the 100 people suggested in earlier discussions. And, clearly, the success of the project was so important that it could not be seen as a project open only to the survivors of the Keewatin famine. To at least some extent, the planners seemed to have lost sight of the original purposes of the project. The fourth meeting ended with a recommendation 'to prepare immediately requisitions for supplies and materials for the project.' With the discussions of the site, personnel, and volunteers all taking shape, despite the widely different views about the basic purpose of the project, how it would work, and how it would be funded, one thing was clear. It was going ahead.

A document called 'A Project to Assist the Keewatin Eskimos,' dated 10 June 1958 and labelled 'material for Minister's book,' described the project in glowing terms. The report noted that 'the solution to this desperate problem [of the Keewatin Inuit] must be found in the skills of the people themselves, in relation to the natural resources of the various areas. Fish and marine mammals appear to be sufficiently abundant to feed all such populations.'[21] There was no comment on how people who had been exclusively caribou hunters, some of whom could not identify a seal, were to acquire these skills. Noting that 'a community will be built at Tavani,' the report went on to say that a store, run as a cooperative, would be part of the community and that 'cottage industry will be developed. Large-scale hunting and fishing will be undertaken. Trapping will be encouraged and parties may be distributed far into the interior. Cash will, at the earliest possible date, be made the medium of exchange.'[22] The skills of the people themselves would not prevent officials from developing, undertaking, and encouraging what they saw as viable activities. The incoherence of this approach is revealed by the summary paragraph: 'Relief will be pared to the absolute minimum in a major effort to introduce (for the first time in the Arctic) the consistent philosophy of "work that ye may eat." With opportunity to work with freedom from undue interference, the proposed community should become self-sufficient economically within two or three years.'[23] The idea that Inuit would be working with 'freedom from undue interference,' given the phenomenal plans being made for them, is more than ironic. Furthermore, 'working to eat' had been the only option available to Inuit for their entire history. There was nothing new about this so-called philosophy. Working to eat was simply 'life.' The contradiction between self-help and encouraging self-help was one that informed all of government policy in the period and would come to play its part in the establishment of Whale Cove.

The pace of meetings began to slow down as the practical work got under way. The fifth meeting, which took place on 20 June, began with what amounted to contract negotiations between F.J. Neville, a social worker from the welfare section, and the committee. Neville was to be hired as a community development officer. Other positions were confirmed as well, with Henry Voisey, who had assisted in the Henik Lake transfers, gaining employment as resources officer for the project. Positions for a nurse and an interpreter were also considered. By comparison with Craig Harbour and Resolute Bay, where a single RCMP officer was in charge in each settlement, in the case of Tavani, a veritable team of 'experts' was to be put in place.

This approach amounted to what Walter Rudnicki would, a few years later, call the 'Do Good' method. Selection of Inuit for the project focused on Neville's suggestion 'that the first group of Eskimos to be moved to Tavani should be a working crew of ten men.'[24] To this was added the proposal that 'the families of the Eskimo work crew members should accompany them to Tavani, thus solving the problem of keeping the men occupied after working hours. Otherwise, the supervisor might find that much of his time, and supplies as well, would be taken up with entertaining and feeding the men.'[25] Practical considerations, including the purchase of a boat, were discussed. A schedule was suggested, beginning with a 'first load of supplies and materials [which] could be transported on a ship scheduled to leave Montreal on July 2.' A work crew, Symington thought, 'should arrive at Tavani on July 15.'[26] Neville was given the task of preparing a schedule.

Site Selection: A Bureaucratic Battle

The next meeting of the Keewatin committee would not take place until 28 July. In the interim, Neville would travel to the site at Tavani with Harry Wilson and Bruce Wilson of the works research and planning division. The report Neville produced is interesting and reveals the basic considerations and approach to the selection of the physical site. The 16 July trip began with a short visit to the Tavani site. The inexpert nature of the visit is revealed by the first line describing the site. 'From what we were able to judge, we must have arrived at Tavani a [*sic*] low tide.'[27] Although he thought the site had 'ample space for the type of construction program which is envisaged,' he did 'not consider it had anything to offer, even potentially, in the way of harbour facilities.'[28] It was also noted that the old HBC house on the site was 'uninsulated and in need of considerable repair, if it was to be made habitable.'[29]

From Tavani, the team flew about twenty-five kilometres northeast, to Term Point, finding that 'from the air and from the superficial experience of beaching the aircraft there appeared to be deep water at Whale Cove, and in front of Hell's Gate, within a few feet of the shore.'[30] After landing, the team 'struck off overland in a westerly direction,' coming 'across several sites which we examined closely but which we finally decided were not well enough drained.' Then, 'from a rock promontory we sighted what appeared to be a large high bowl of land between two shoulders of rock on the west shore of Whale Cove and at the very head of the cove.'[31] At this point, Whale Cove, rather than Tavani, starts to get serious consideration as a site for the new settlement.

Neville wrote that the team 'examined this spot very carefully walking over it in every direction and checking the beach area and the fresh water supply' before going on to describe the site itself. He estimated the site as about 400 yards wide, 300 yards long, and very well drained, 'since, in fact, the entire site slopes upward from the shore,' with a small lake at the northwest end and several other small lakes further back behind the site. Neville found 'a flat, sandy beach area which could be used to unload supplies' about 150 feet to the northeast. The only question, in Neville's view, 'was whether it was large enough to handle the construction program which had been planned.' Wilson, though, 'had no misgivings about its size' and restated that opinion to the decisionmakers in the South. In summary, Neville wrote: 'In comparison to Tavani, and again relying only on my own unprofessional and superficial knowledge of the hydrography and geography of both areas I consider the Whale Cove site to be superior.' He added that 'after leaving Whale Cove, we flew westward at a low altitude, along the shore line to the mouth of the Wilson River. We did not see any further sites which we thought held equal opportunity.'[32]

Although by today's planning standards this venture looks absurd, even at the time a planned community in the South would not have been sited on the basis of such a superficial analysis. Inuit, of course, were not consulted, and factors that might have been important to them do not seem to have been on the agenda. Those factors would have included wildlife resources in the area, a very difficult thing for non-Natives to ascertain without extensive research, but a consideration about which coast-dwelling Inuit in the Keewatin might have had some knowledge. Colonial factors in site selection were the operative ones. Of these, harbour access for ships was paramount. Other considerations were the size of the site, drainage, and availability of fresh water.

At the sixth meeting, Neville's report was tabled. He gave a verbal report, noting that the Tavani site involved an unsheltered harbour and was relatively inaccessible to freighting ships. Neville then described the Whale Cove site, noting that its boundaries 'would restrict the size of the community to 25 to 30 houses.' In conclusion, he gave qualified support to the Whale Cove site. 'Mr. Neville did not wish to recommend the site at Whale Cove without stressing the limited building area available. The harbour, at any rate, was preferable to that of Tavani, and probably better than any other harbour on the west coast of the Keewatin District. He was not certain that sufficient information had been obtained to confirm the choice of Whale Cove as the site of the community.'[33] Neville suggested that a larger team visit the site. Discussion initially led to the suggestion of postponing construction until more knowledge could be gathered and 'year round conditions at the site would be known.' Members of a more qualified survey team were suggested, as well as the idea of studying aerial photographs of the area.

At this point, Alex Stevenson, then head of the administrative section, with extensive experience in 'seat of the pants' site selection through his involvement in the Craig Harbour and Resolute Bay relocations, swung the discussion in the opposite direction.

> Mr. Stevenson pointed out that it had originally been planned that the community would be no larger than twenty to thirty families and that it would be regarded as a pilot community, which, if successful, would point the way for the establishment of similar communities elsewhere. He therefore suggested that a further site survey might not be required, since in the opinion of Messrs. Wilson and Neville, based on information and opinions gathered locally, the site was suitable for a community of that size.[34]

Neville's written and verbal reports made no mention of 'opinions gathered locally,' that is, from the coastal region, unless that is taken to mean the opinions of Bruce and Harry Wilson and RCMP Corporal Gallagher, who is mentioned once. Neville did, however, talk with Inuit in Rankin Inlet about their involvement with the project and may have asked them about the site. Symington then offered to phone Wilson and confirm his opinion, while

Bolger suggested 'that the possibility of the survey team should be held in abeyance until the air photographs had been studied.' A committee was struck to examine aerial photography, talk to Wilson, and 'determine if the proposed site at Whale Cove appeared suitable.'[35]

Another interesting discussion at the sixth meeting focused on selection of Inuit. Speaking to this matter, Neville reported that there was some indication that Inuit might not be completely thrilled about the proposed new settlement.

> Mr. Neville said that it was difficult to gauge the response of the Eskimos with whom he had discussed the possibility of moving to the Keewatin Community. They had said that they would move because they did not have enough to eat, nor was there sufficient game, where they were living at present. However, he was not sure of what they really wished to do. He had not seen the Baker Lake Eskimos, who were hemmed in by ice, but the staffs of the Hudson Bay post and of the mission were of the opinion that the Eskimos wished to move.[36]

Once again, non-Natives are consulted about the views of Inuit. The discussion of family selection at this point is interesting because of the obvious disregard for kinship ties or group cohesiveness. Inuit were to be drawn from all over the Keewatin. 'The following families might also be recruited: from Eskimo Point, formerly at Henik Lake, 5; from Eskimo Point, 5; from Kazan River, formerly at Garry Lake, 8; from Baker Lake, 4; from Rankin Inlet, formerly at Eskimo Point, 2.'[37] The working crew involved a similar dispersion of Inuit from Rankin Inlet, Baker Lake, and Eskimo Point. The schedule was also discussed. The crew and supplies were projected to arrive between mid- and late August. The rest of the meeting focused on arranging the mechanics of the move, purchasing boats and materials, providing initial housing of the Inuit in tents, and arranging for dogs and *muktuk* (whale fat) and buffalo meat.

Another report on site selection was prepared by a subcommittee consisting of Vic Valentine, who had been hired by the department as a research officer, D.F. Symington, head of the projects section, and R.A. Jenness, an employee of the development section. Valentine's report was then attached to the minutes of the sixth and last meeting of the Keewatin committee. The report reviewed the nature of the Whale Cove site, as could be determined from the aerial photographs, and then goes on to state: 'In consideration of the above factors and Mr. Wilson's reiterated statement that he considers the site to be of adequate size for the proposed community, the Committee agrees that the site will be of adequate size to meet any future requirements.'[38] Each member of the subcommittee attached a note to the report. Valentine's was first and began: 'I note that this memo refers to size of the proposed settlement only and not to adequacy of harbour, snow, drifting problems, lack of airstrip, building site, etc., which I feel should be investigated by a specialist.'[39] Valentine signed the report under protest. He was concerned about the size of the site, which, he noted, 'may not be large enough to accommodate future developments'[40] and the lack of a written report from Wilson.

Symington's note was effectively a response to Valentine's. He reiterated the pilot-project nature of the venture, arguing that further expansion could take place at Rankin Inlet and noted that 'the optimum size of a resources-dependent community on subsistence level is probably not more than fifty families.' He concluded: 'I have few reservations about the site for the purpose intended or for any foreseeable contingency.'[41] Jenness wrote: 'In concurring in this memorandum, I am interpreting it as a statement of fact within the terms of reference and the severe limitations of time that this Sub-Committee was asked to work.' He agreed 'with Mr. Valentine's reservations' and thought 'a thorough on-the-spot location study should be made before, and not after, the project is launched.' However, Jenness concluded with the comment that 'in light of the exigency of getting the Keewatin community started this year, and the reports of Messrs. Wilson, Neville and Russell, I am prepared to support the Whale Cove Site.'[42]

The subcommittee meeting dealing with the site must have been interesting. Clearly it was dominated by pressure, likely from the highest levels, to get something done in the Keewatin – and quickly. The result was a site selection for a new community based on a single visit of a few hours by three officials without the combined necessary expertise to make such a judgment. The debacle that followed only underlined the degree to which hurried planning in the South, even when supported by extraordinary resources, could lead to disaster in the North.

What a Landing!

From the deliberations of the Keewatin committee, meeting in the comfortable surroundings of the Kent-Albert Building in Ottawa during the early and mid-summer of 1958, we now turn to the beach at Whale Cove. Life, as it started to unfold on the beach, was documented by reports from Northern Service Officer D.W. Grant in the late summer and fall of the same year. Much to the displeasure of Walter Rudnicki, head of the welfare section, Grant had replaced Neville, a social worker with the welfare section, as the key on-site staff. Grant's reports – lively and written in anything but bureaucratic style – begin with a description of the location and of the people on-site to create the new community. The early reports are all in the most glowing, favourable terms, and Grant's optimism continues through the subsequent series of problems.

Grant's 'Progress Report' of 29 August on Whale Cove describes the initial landing, with Grant and his 'happy little band' of Inuit joined by three members of the Voisey family from Eskimo Point, Andy Easton of the Rankin Inlet Nickel Mine, and Corporal Gallagher. 'On approaching shore two days ago, all were delighted to see a caribou grazing peacefully on what is to become our main street. This was indeed a good omen.'[43] On the 29th, 'the captains and the kings' – as Grant described them – departed, leaving him with his happy little band. As well as setting up camp, immediate activities involved hunting, which was very successful. The area seems to have been abundant in game, including caribou, whale, rabbits, and char; at least one of each was caught, and they observed 'countless seals' and 'several walrus,' though these were not hunted. The tone of Grant's report, and his approach to dealing with the Inuit, is conveyed in this description of his rationing method:

Yesterday, when it was time to hand out the rations, I tried a new wrinkle. As no scales nor proper measures were available to break down the rations correctly for each family, I issued the whole week's rations to the Eskimos to divide among themselves. To Atatlook – wife of Yahah – is issued all the flour. To Akjar – wife of Anavtilik – I issued all the tea – and so on down the line. Woe unto the family that doesn't give the proper measure to its neighbour. Next week will rotate the items. The Eskimos thought this was terrific. As I handed the week's supply to each woman, gales of laughter swept the area.[44]

The suggestion of relocating entire families – even during the construction period – had been followed. Grant's method for distributing rations is hard to evaluate. It might be considered 'progressive' as it was consistent with traditional approaches to food sharing. However, not all Inuit were from the same community, and this may have created some problems around the sharing of rations. There is no indication in later reports as to whether his approach was maintained and actually worked. As if these values had not been an intricate aspect of Inuit life already, Grant wrote, 'In each stage I am trying to foster the community and co-operative idea. They understand and seem to like it.'[45] The report noted that three Inuit, recently fired from the Rankin Inlet mine, had been delivered to the community. Grant 'put them on probation' by giving them 'the choice of working here or taking a bag of flour and going inland, never to clutter up the area again.' For the moment, the three were working hard, though Grant thought they would 'have to be pushed a little. The rest [are] first class.'[46] The report concluded on a cheerful, highly optimistic note. 'I hear shots in the distance so either our population has been decreased (we have three rivals for an attractive young widow) or were [sic] going to have fresh meat again to-morrow. This is indeed a beautiful day.'[47]

On 15 September, as well as writing a memorandum asking the department to hire seventy-eight-year-old Sam Voisey as an interpreter, Grant reported on the site in favourable terms. This topic, which had been the subject of such controversy, was obviously still a concern. Grant tried to lay the concern to rest, noting that 'this is the best area around for a building site,' that the 'harbour is tops for small craft' while 'large ships can anchor here, and have good shelter at Wilson Bay ten miles off.'[48] He also repeated the usual reports of good drainage, noted that 'a wharf can be made very easily,' and said 'there is space for expansion if necessary.' In conclusion, he reassured his southern supervisors, 'The committee can relax – I like the place and so do the Eskimos.'[49]

Grant's next report was an elaborate, hand-written memorandum to R.A.J. Phillips, chief of the Arctic division, dated 17 September. The ship carrying the bulk of building materials, furniture, and supplies, which had left Montreal in mid-August, was *The Maple Hill*, under the command of Captain Mallet. His first visit to the site was not productive. In Grant's words: 'Two days ago – I'm not sure of the date but I think it was a Monday, *The Maple Hill* arrived looked at my beach with disdain, turned up her nose and went off in a huff, her wake looking much like the flying petticoats of a miffed woman. Some people wait a lifetime for their ship to come in. Believe me, when it comes and goes like that, one could feel a touch of frustration without too much effort.'[50] Apparently, the mate of the ship did not feel the area had been suitably prepared for the cargo unloading. 'His mate came ashore with me at half tide – when any beach looks bad particularly after a three day storm – grumbled about not having welding equipment here and a bulldozer to help him in the operation, went back to the ship and instead of discussing this problem with me – the master up-anchored and sailed off into the night.'[51]

The ship moved on to Eskimo Point to unload supplies there, before returning to Whale Cove. Grant then spent the next few days using his Peterhead boat to clear the landing area of rocks and boulders to open up a wide enough channel for material to be unloaded. Grant was clearly frustrated about not being able to get even some of the supplies from *The Maple Hill*. His sarcasm is apparent. Commenting on the British Merchant Marine, he notes: 'From my experience they can land on much less favourable beaches particularly when people are shooting at them. That, I might add, could cheerfully be arranged at Whale Cove!'[52] Nevertheless, Grant was engaged in an impressive variety of activities associated with the community, and this seems to have kept him busy and cheerful.

In this one report he mentions dredging the channel, providing first aid to the Inuit for sundry ailments – including a few eye infections – repairing blown radio fuses and a battery charger, testing a mixture of clay, moss, and caribou dung 'in an effort to make adobe type bricks,' trying to repair the boat motor, as well as writing his reports. He wrote of the Inuit: 'We are also cleaning up our little band bit by bit, and the men are learning to shoot properly and care for their weapons.'[53] In this 'hectic phase' of activity, Grant recommended not 'overstaffing the operation' in response to a suggestion that he be given more assistance and 'that the families should be prepared for the move, but not moved until we give the green light from here.'[54] In closing the report he mentioned a trip to Greenland that R.A.J. Phillips, chief of the Arctic division, had made, adding, 'Perhaps some of the Greenlanders would like to visit Whale Cove and see a real community at work.'[55] He also added two postscripts with a footnote to the first of these, the excessiveness of the text matching the excessiveness of his activities.

Battle on the Beach: Unloading Supplies at Whale Cove

The next report, dated 22 September, deals with *The Maple Hill*'s second and final failed attempt to unload supplies at Whale Cove, a failure that forced a drastic change of plans. The following excerpt from the first part of Grant's report relates what happened:

On arrival of *The Maple Hill*, the weather began to deteriorate, the winds swinging to the SW-S-SE holding mainly southerly for a period of a week. This was followed by the equinoxial gales with rain and fog. To-day the winds have swung back northerly and are moving gradually to their prevailing quarter – i.e. N.N.W. or N.W. We offloaded some 50 tons of cargo and in doing so ended up with LCM and barges on the shoals. One LCM is still grounded while the other has returned to our harbour as it cannot be loaded aboard *The Maple Hill* until the seas subside. Much of the cargo discharged here has been saturated by the heavy rains. This is due to a complete lack of tarpaulins except for spare hatch covers I was able to obtain from *The Maple Hill* ... *The Maple Hill* is currently standing somewhere off Marble Island and I am not in radio contact with her ... When the weather clears *The Maple Hill* will pick-up its LCM from our harbour and proceed [to] Churchill to offload.[56]

Grant wrote a second report – over a month later – which provides a few more details about the event:

On his return to our beach, a strong southerly wind was blowing. This is the only wind that affects our beach which faces in that direction. Under normal conditions no one would attempt to land stores at such a time. Captain Gould, perhaps urged by Captain Mallet who was fretting about possible delay, gamely tried to land under what I consider very adverse conditions. His gameness bordered on the foolhardy and he himself was almost swept overboard on more than one occasion. One barge load of insulation was landed in our inner harbour. A second LCM towing a fifty ton barge and a twenty ton barge (the latter two unpowered and without rudders) came in to the main beach in complete darkness except for our burning oil drums and a few lanterns. In towing them in with a heavy following sea he obviously had no control over the last two flat barges which immediately swung onto a reef as soon as the LCM lost her forward motion. The net result was a fantastic melee of barges, spray, huge breakers and sea-faring language.[57]

Most of the material that had reached shore was damaged. Much of what was not damaged would soon become damaged in the rain. Although the weather improved after a few days, the captain had had enough: 'The Maple Hill headed for Churchill leaving us with calm seas, fifty tons of soggy stores and one useless barge.'[58]

In his evaluation of the event, Grant clearly placed much of the blame on the captain of The Maple Hill. 'In expressing my own feelings in this respect, I can only offer the subdued comment that we were badly let down.'[59] Although weather clearly played its part as well, Grant also saw that there had been problems in planning and organizing the move. In his 22 September report, written immediately after the debacle, he argued that 'out of all this grief many lessons should be learned. Among these are the need for following normal procedures of recconnoitering [sic] the area in full detail – properly equipping an advance party to prepare for the arrival of the main supplies and above all, adequate packing of materials and supplies for landing over open beach – regardless of whether inside storage accomodation [sic] is or is not available.'[60] Clearly, some were already remembering how hastily the Whale Cove site had been chosen and suggesting that it might not have been suitable in terms of its harbour. Grant, in this report, recommends 'reconnoitring the area in full detail,' which suggests he did see this as a problem.

Another detailed evaluation, written a month later, contains a more positive assessment of the Whale Cove site. In this report, Grant argues that 'to begin with, Whale Cove IS an excellent site for such a project,' adding that 'contrary to widespread belief, the landing beach is superior to many at other Arctic points. An excellent inner harbour exists which shelters small craft from any wind and any seas. The building area is spacious, sloping upwards in the shape of a giant fan. There is adequate fresh water and the community could be supplied by gravity feed during the summer months. The site is protected from prevailing winds by rocky bluffs.'[61] The fact that 'the present beach [was] cleared to a width of 150 feet and a channel 300 feet long [was] cleared to a width of sixty feet' added to the natural advantages of the location, in Grant's view. He noted that 'the area is centrally located from a point of view of collective hunting and fishing expeditions and it is very close to the floe edge for sealing in winter.'[62] Although he knew that 'a proper survey [had] not been made to assess the game population,' he nevertheless felt that 'there [were] sufficient caribou, fish, seals and whales to support a hunting and fishing community.' He added that 'foxes were particularly plentiful this year.'[63] These conclusions were based on one month's experience in the area.

In the immediate aftermath, Grant and his 'happy little band' were left with a daunting set of tasks in a climate of uncertainty. Grant reported: 'We will open and dry as many items as we can when the weather permits, oiling or greasing metal parts which are already turning rusty.'[64] The building insulation, which had been soaked, was ruined. But the most serious problem was the question of how they would get the remaining supplies, the bulk of which were not off-loaded and without which they could not begin construction. Grant still hoped to make the Whale Cove operation workable, arguing that

I have no desire to get involved with further comparisons between Whale Cove and other locations. One point to consider however, is the fact that the people I have had here since our arrival now consider this as thier [*sic*] area. They have worked hard to develop it to its present state – our beach is adequate under normal prevailing wind conditions and further improvements will enable us to off-load in the harbour in almost any conditions – they have helped stake out the locations for their own individual houses and they have considerable faith in the project.[65]

Having noted earlier in the report his sincere hope that sufficient supplies could be landed to see the people at Whale Cove through the winter, Grant recommends:

If we are unable to land sufficient materials to do much building in the short time available, they can live in tents and snow houses until next summer, given fuel and some supplies. For myself I am quite willing to either knock-up a small cabin for the winter or move into Sam Voisey's little house at Hell's Gate. Under these circumstances I will leave my family until next year. Above all we must not desert the people having gone this far. Any interim move for the winter would be, in my estimation, inadvisable. There are now two or three who speak reasonable English and I have asked their views very frankly.[66]

Unfortunately, Grant did not communicate in his written reports what those views were. An 'interim move' was exactly what would take place.

Whale Cove to Rankin Inlet: The Keewatin Re-establishment Project
The families already relocated to Whale Cove were divided between two locations. Six families totalling sixteen people ended up in a camp at Wilson River, which flowed into the inlet immediately to the south of the Whale Cove site. Twelve families, totalling thirty-seven people, were moved to a 're-establishment centre' being constructed at Melville Bay, about 1.5 kilometres south of Rankin Inlet. While Hallow and others of the Ennadai/Henik Lake people had been moved to Wilson River, Oolijoot, Howmik, and others from the same group ended up at Rankin Inlet.[67] This series of moves took place the summer and fall after the famine. While the material needs of the survivors of this famine were met, it must have been clear to them that they had lost all control over their own destinies.

Alex Stevenson outlined the status of the Rankin Inlet community:

The Keewatin Re-establishment Community which, because of circum-stances, we have established at Rankin Inlet for this winter is considered to be temporary. Originally, it was intended to organise this project at Whale Cove. Because of inclement weather, and an inexperienced (in northern navigation) ship's Captain, we could not offload our supplies at Whale Cove. Our Keewatin Community cargo was landed at Churchill, then shipped to the closest suitable site with favourable harbouring facilities near Whale Cove: Rankin Inlet.[68]

The Melville Bay site near Rankin Inlet was initially thought of as a temporary base location for the Inuit group. In fact, it would become the site of the Keewatin Re-establishment Project (KRP), while a more sponta-neous community would develop at Whale Cove.

Grant must have spent the whole of 6 November at his desk. As well as the long report on the events of September, he drafted an extensive and very revealing report on the Keewatin Project. This report begins with the note that 'since its inception, the Keewatin Project has been a controversial subject. The very mention of Whale Cove as a site for such a community is still the signal for bitter debate among persons connected with the North. In the eyes of many, the project was "doomed from the start."'[69] Noting that 'our aim was to provide security and opportunity for the depressed groups of Eskimos from the Hennik [*sic*] and Garry Lake districts,' he argued that with the establishment of a rehabilitation centre at Rankin Inlet 'this aim has been accomplished to a large extent.'[70] One marvels that anyone could gain a sense of 'security' from the events. Given that the Garry Lake group had not yet left Baker Lake, Grant's assessment seems entirely optimistic. The new 'Re-establishment Centre'[71] was described as follows:

> The new community is located on Melville Bay approximately a mile south of the present Rankin Inlet townsite. By the first of November the combined school and workshop building was complete and the three bedroom house for the Technical Officer was ready for occupancy. Two 12' x 20' insulated plywood houses had been constructed for Eskimo families and twelve more were under construction. It is expected that a total of just under thirty houses will be built for these families. Work was also underway on a one hundred foot Quonset hut which will provide a store and warehouse for the community and a plywood power house was ready for the installation of the generators.[72]

It is worth noting that a colonial social hierarchy was being planned: the technical officer gets a three-bedroom house and the Inuit families get 240-square-foot plywood houses! Thirty-nine Inuit from Ennadai Lake formed the population of the new community, and it was expected that the Garry Lake group, comprising thirty-eight Inuit evacuated to Baker Lake and then moved to the Kazan River, would soon join them. The Garry Lake group had apparently 'had a prosperous summer and they have, from all available reports, recovered largely from the hardship and ill fortune of last winter.'[73] Grant reported that 'if there is the slightest indication of deterioration in their circumstances they will be moved immediately.'[74] There was little doubt about who was making decisions.

Grant also reported on the group from Whale Cove:

> A third group who were living in depressed circumstances at Eskimo Point have been moved to a camp on the Wilson River where they are living the traditional life under the supervision of Mr. Voisey, a Technical Officer of the Department. This group, totalling nineteen in all, have a full year's supply of food, clothing material, tobacco, rifles, ammunition, traps, fishnets and fuel. Supplies are issued to them on a recoverable basis by Mr. Voisey and there is every indication that they will have a profitable winter.[75]

When it was impractical or impossible to supply people with housing, their shelter needs were met through the simple process of describing them in reports as 'living the traditional life.' What did 'living the traditional life' mean? In contrast to Inuit moved to Rankin Inlet, this group had nothing other than traditional accommodation: tents and snow houses. Other than that, it seems unlikely that their activities were very different from those Inuit relocated to Rankin Inlet. In this case, the phrase 'traditional life' seems to refer to the absence of proper housing.

Plans for the immediate future, apart from the construction of houses, included 'organized hunting and fishing ... under the guidance of Eskimos who are life-long residents of the area.' Grant's report also touched on the problem of relations with Inuit working at the Rankin Inlet Nickel Mine. The presence of the mine, as far as he was concerned, afforded an opportunity to train community residents so that they might be employed at the mine and by exploration parties doing test drilling in the region during the summer months. The dilemma the department confronted was clearly the relationship between these Inuit and modern Canadian industrial culture. Grant was not atypical of many civil servants. Liberal notions of freedom and choice, as well as a perceived need to 'guide a primitive culture' into the twentieth century, are evident from the following. These values and aspirations made for a difficult combination.

> Above all, our aim is to develop these men to a stage where they can make their own decision as to the type of life they wish to lead. When they have progressed to a point that they fully understand the responsibilities of wage employment in the mining field and also understand the possibilities of the other alternatives offered in the new community, they will make their choice.
>
> Offers of employment to certain men in this group by the mine have already been rejected on the grounds that the men do not yet fully understand the ramifications of such employment.[76]

'All in all,' wrote Grant, 'I see no reason why the project should not be a glowing success despite the difficulties of the past few months. Wisely used, the proximity of the mine can be of tremendous help in achieving this success.'[77] He concluded:

> Given additional materials, there is no reason why the establishment of a companion community at Whale Cove could not be carried out next year. Possibly the group now settled on the Wilson River would form the nucleus of such a project. Here the initial concept would be carried out, an economy based on the traditional life, aided by development of latent skills and handicraft and cottage industry. The community near Rankin could remain,

carrying on its present role with increased emphasis on the technical training required to enable the Eskimo to participate in the development of the mineral resources of the Keewatin.[78]

While mineral development in the Keewatin would bottom out in a few years (the Rankin Inlet mine would close in 1962), the main thrust of this proposal is what, in fact, would take place. The Keewatin Re-establishment Project would continue at Rankin Inlet, while in the next year, a small permanent community would finally be established at the controversial Whale Cove site.

Re-establishing Whale Cove

In the winter of 1958-9, 'approximately 130 individuals came to the community [of Rankin Inlet] from various points. They became engaged in house building, maintaining a small store, producing handicrafts and doing such hunting and trapping as the limited supply of dogs allowed.'[79] Meanwhile, 'a satellite group of six families remained on the Wilson River trapping, fishing and hunting quite successfully.'[80] By early summer, 1959, a plan was devised to give the people camped at Wilson River 'additional support so that those who desire to live closer to the land may have the opportunity to do so on a basis of financial independence,' although it was also noted that 'further construction both at the community in Rankin Inlet and at the Wilson River will be carried out this summer.'[81]

However, the decision was made to carry on with construction at the Whale Cove site during the summer of 1959. Peter Murdoch, a former Hudson's Bay Company post manager hired by the department as part of its dramatic expansion in the mid- to late 1950s, described the resulting settlement:

> The settlement consists of twenty-four families made up of fifty-two adults and thirty-seven children. Forty-four people are from the Eskimo Point area; twenty-nine from Ennadai Lake; and sixteen from Garry Lake. Ten families live in rigid frame houses and the rest, at the time of my visit, were living in tents. There is a small merchandise store which serves the community and a small school building which is at present not being used. There is also a rigid-frame building which is reserved as a stop-over house for visitors. Close to the settlement there is a small cabin which is occupied by Sam Voisey and his family.[82]

By 1960, more families, from Ennadai, Eskimo Point, and Garry Lake, had moved into the Whale Cove community. At the time Murdoch wrote this report, 'most of the people living at Whale Cove were either ill or just recovering from illness. There was a severe epidemic of flu and measles,' and tuberculosis was also present.[83]

As was apparent even at this early stage, the group was also not 'integrating' very well. Cultural distinctions among Inuit were evident.

> The various Eskimo groups at Whale Cove keep very much to themselves. Although there are cultural as well as kinship relationships between the Eskimo Point and Ennadai Lake groups, there seems to be very little co-operation between them. The Eskimo Point people have made no effort to assist the Ahermut [sic] in learning coastal hunting methods. All the groups have done some caribou hunting and these hunts have been quite successful. Only the Eskimo Point people have shown any interest in seal hunting.[84]

This is not surprising, given Rudnicki's previously mentioned observation that the Henik Lake people did not know what a seal was. In spite of this, and the people's reliance on relief, Murdoch reported that 'the people of Whale Cove appeared to be very well fed and clothed. They were pleased with the location of their camp. The Eskimo Point [people] felt they could make a very good life in this area. The inland group seemed very confused.'[85] In fact, there were two inland groups present in the community, from Garry Lake and Henik Lake, respectively. Murdoch also noted that 'since Whale Cove has been established, there have been six births, three of the babies died.'[86] Life – as Murdoch observed it, and given the indicators upon which he focused – was clearly neither easy nor entirely pleasant at the Whale Cove settlement.

At Rankin Inlet, more energy was being put into supervising and organizing the community, which, designated as the Keewatin Re-establishment Project (KRP) site, had greater official status than did Whale Cove. In spite of this, there were serious problems. Again, Peter Murdoch gives his impressions:

> There was general disorder in the settlement. Equipment and garbage littered the whole area. The people, living in the situation that has none of the conatural organization of a traditional Eskimo camp, were completely bewildered. The men spent most of their time sitting around their houses. The women visited, gossiped and spent their time loitering around the Hudson's Bay Company store. The lament, 'We are sick, we are confused.' was heard from every person interviewed. The men were not hunting – 'There are no dogs.' No crafts were being produced – 'There are no materials.' Everyone was idle – 'There is nothing to do.' Everyone was waiting. For what?[87]

The original group of KRP people had expanded somewhat. Some of the families who worked at the nickel mine had joined them, as had two families from Povungnituk. As was true in Whale Cove, the inland people were observed to be having a particularly difficult time adjusting to their new circumstances: 'Most of the inland people living here were supported by relief issues throughout the winter.'[88] Murdoch also noted that 'although the inland Eskimos have spent two winters at K.R.P., there has been little mixing between the groups either in the community or with the Rankin Inlet groups.'[89]

Murdoch also reported that 'several dances were held in the workshop at K.R.P. during the period of my visit,' something he felt was worth encouraging 'as it could lead to a better mixing of the groups.' However, 'it was noticed that the majority of dancers came from the Rankin Inlet community' and 'that most of the K.R.P. residents were excluded from the actual dancing.' Bob Williamson, who by then had replaced Grant as the northern service officer, 'noticed this and took steps to ensure that these people would be included in the dancing. We learned that the trend of excluding K.R.P. residents from participating in the dancing was an accepted practice.'[90] It is clear that the dances, far from leading to better group mixing, reproduced and re-entrenched existing divisions. In fact, Murdoch reported: 'During the dances we observed two fist fights: One between two women and one between a man and his wife. In both these fights the instigators had been drinking. We learned that fighting, especially between women, has become quite common over the past year. Several Eskimo commented that it would not be surprising if there were killings in the future if the drinking was not checked.'[91] There were obviously deep social problems and divisions in both of the newly created communities. The presence of government supervisors did little to change the situation and likely exacerbated the problems.

Murdoch's suggestions for creating leadership in the community are also revealing of the sensibilities and conflicting values that characterized the community development personnel working in the eastern Arctic during this period.

A lot has been said about the advantages to be gained by allowing the Eskimo people to develop their own leaders in their own way. On the basis of my observation in Keewatin, I am quite convinced that unless we provide a catalytic influence, these leaders will not be forthcoming. Generally, camp leaders were accepted because of their amiability and lack of aggression. This type of leader was ideal in a situation where everybody knew what to do and how to do it. But in a situation as exists at Whale Cove or Rankin Inlet, this type of leader is ineffective. If the re-settlement programme is to mean anything more than survival for these people we must begin a progressive programme of human as well as resource development.[92]

This statement condenses and conflates the basic contradiction in policy that emerged as the administration tried to deal with circumstances created by historical events whose origins more than predated the period in question. On the one hand, there was a desire to begin turning control over to Inuit to manage their own affairs, while on the other, there was the feeling that more outsider guidance was needed. Inuit had to 'fit' with a new industrial order that no longer held a place for the values associated with traditional leadership. The focus on aggression as a desired quality of leadership is entirely revealing of the values and dynamics perceived to be suitable. Under these circumstances, leaders had to be 'developed' with outside guidance. Administered self-help and controlled self-reliance were what resulted. This effectively meant no self-help and no self-reliance at all.

In Rankin Inlet, Bob Williamson had an impressive array of projects planned to foster self-reliance. These included a clothing factory, a 'home industries' craft project, a handicrafts store, a photographic service to produce black and white prints in the community, a net-making plan, organized hunts, a store, construction of dog kennels, and a men's workshop. Curiously, the building that was to be used as a craft store had 'at one time been used as a coffee shop,' and the original idea was to reopen it as a coffee shop. However, 'many adult Eskimos and white residents were opposed to this. It only offered another opportunity for the white workers to make contacts with the Eskimo girls.'[93]

The pervasive sexism that informed most of the analyses produced by field staff cannot be ignored, as it reveals the gender biases of those providing 'guided assistance' to Inuit. Many of these biases are to be found in Northern Service Officer Grant's documentation on Whale Cove. His comments about the 'attractive widow,' a hand-written note at the bottom of one of his reports in which he jokes that he is 'urgently in need of the services of the steno pool. Any volunteers? Send immediately,'[94] not to mention his use of the 'petticoats' metaphor in his description of the ship's departure lead one to be at least concerned about his attitude towards Inuit women. Not surprisingly for the 1950s, from the most senior levels in Ottawa to the fieldworkers in the North, a woman's place was clearly in the home or in performing some menial task for men. A patriarchal cultural frame of reference informed description and policy-making alike. Murdoch, for instance, noted the following in his report on Whale Cove: 'The women were for a while involved in a sewing project. Because of lack of supervision, they soon finished up all the available materials. They have made several parkas, about twenty pairs of mitts, and over four hundred pairs of duffle socks. We will probably find it difficult to dispose of this large number of socks.'[95]

Instead of observing the industriousness of these women and their determination to work without supervision, Murdoch comments on the problem created by a surplus of socks! The women's gossip in front of the HBC store in Rankin, similarly, could well be interpreted as planning, discussion, and analysis in the terms of a culture reliant on oral expression where kinship bonds – the subject of most gossip – are the determining focus of the whole worldview. And then there is the question of the fight – which today might be characterized as spousal assault – between a man and his marriage partner. While ethnocentrism, as we have pointed out at various points throughout this text, was clearly pervasive and influenced policy to the detriment of Inuit time and time again, an equally pervasive male-centred perspective determined a doubly detrimental policy towards Inuit women.

Cooperatives and Community Development

A report on Whale Cove and Rankin Inlet in the spring of 1960, by a staff member from the cooperative development group within the Arctic division, provides more information on the developing communities. It also gives another perception of how Inuit were surviving their new and, undoubtably, strange circumstances. The bulk of P. Godt's report dealt with Whale Cove. The location is noted favourably, suggesting that debates about this choice were still alive in the department.

Whale Cove is a fine location on the coast, is practically located, is easy to enter from the sea and very well protected. The big cove is surrounded by a high ridge of land with the 15-17 buildings in one row. There is very good land higher up for other buildings and for further construction of government buildings. The houses looked fine – well constructed though a coat of paint would do wonders to brighten up the place and to protect the buildings. We only entered a couple of houses as our stay was unfortunately limited to 23 hours.[96]

The purpose of Godt's visit was to begin the process of setting up a cooperative. As he was not in Whale Cove long enough to organize signing of the legal documents, he treated the visit as an information-sharing session. Godt seems to have made a serious attempt to talk to people during his short stay. He discovered that 'there are considerable differences in dialects between the Garry Lake people and the Padlei Lake people' and found, after explaining something of the purpose of his visit, that 'it was extremely difficult to get the people to talk. The only real way was the individual approach. One group of the Eskimos has a leader, the other hasn't.'[97]

After the formal part of the meeting with Whale Cove Inuit, tea was served, and, 'with Simeon's help,' Godt managed to talk to a few more people about 'what they thought of living at W.C. and the food in the area.' He reported that 'the trapping has been very poor. Only one fox was brought into the store and the best Eskimo trapper had only got four or five.' His general impression, which he was careful to qualify, was that 'the people listened well and were interested – they looked somewhat happy, but how deep that goes is extremely hard to measure. They thought a lot about a school coming in ... They looked good. Their health seems good – as Grant puts it "they better be healthy, as they live off the store."'[98] By then, Grant had been promoted to the status of area administrator and was no longer working in the community. At least Godt was not willing to settle for the usual 'happy smiling' stereotype and had the good sense to wonder how deep the happiness went.

Based on this trip and discussions with people in the area, Godt managed to discover a great deal about Whale Cove. He had an interesting description of the community's formation.

The people who are now living at Whale Cove have moved down there of their own accord. It all started with a few families making this place their winter home, because food is more plentiful in this area. Last year the Department all got involved and some build up of a community took place. 12-15 houses, mainly rigid frame were built. A small building, which was used once for a short while as a school was constructed. A warehouse and a store building were put up. This winter about 110 people have been living in these houses with fuel supplied. They have only had spasmodic supervision and assistance during this winter. They had lived at KRP since they were moved from inland.[99]

Godt felt that in his view 'some changes have to be made in the near future' because people could not be depended upon to distribute relief rations to themselves. About the residents of Whale Cove, he wrote:

There are three different groups of people who speak different dialects. Though they can understand each other, they are different. They do not marry into other groups very often. Some people are happy about living at Whale Cove, others are not. One of the largest groups is the Garry Lake people, who I am told are likely to pull out at any time. It is believed that they have stayed there this winter because of the caribou herd in the area. If they decide to move inland we will have another problem on our hands.[100]

Clearly, to Godt's way of thinking, more supervision was needed. Inuit seemed to have clear ideas of how to help themselves – ideas they had put into play in re-establishing the community. But these ideas did not necessarily suit the plans of the planners. Another move inland, for example, would make them less accessible to the training that would teach them how to help themselves. The department was clearly afraid of repeating events at Garry and Henik lakes, having concluded that Inuit could no longer survive on a trapping and hunting economy. Rather, it was felt that the resources of Hudson Bay might make commercial resource harvesting possible. At a special meeting called in November 1958, the following was agreed upon: '(a) No Eskimos be relocated in areas of poor transportation and communication; (b) Eskimo relocation would generally be within rather than across natural Arctic Areas such as northwest Quebec, Keewatin, and western Arctic; and (c) that the priority for resource studies be Keewatin, East Coast of Hudson Bay, Tuktoyaktuk-Coppermine, and North Baffin Island.'[101]

Godt was an advocate of the community development approach. He defined this 'as helping people to help themselves.' This could be done by 'having people express their needs, define their problems, plan and institute action towards solutions,' all of which would eventually lead to bigger projects. In Godt's perspective, 'the main purpose is to develop the community by developing the people along lines which they themselves agree to and are willing to work towards.'[102] The same contradiction found in Murdoch's approach to development is restated here. Inuit were to be given more control by being controlled. Outsiders were to be brought in to direct them in self-reliance. Godt wrote:

The community is presently split into different groups. If one of the groups break away new problems will be created. The first step taken should be one of bringing the community together and generate amongst the people a feeling that they belong here and that they can eventually see a future in this place. This will of course require the services of a man, who is interested in Eskimo and Eskimo welfare in general. This man must gain the confidence of the people – all of them. He must be prepared to go forward in the activities of giving leadership and guidance. This must be done in a democratic way. The people must learn all the way ... By involving the people – putting responsibility on their shoulders, results will eventually come.[103]

Effectively, Godt was articulating the new ideology that would govern Inuit affairs. The new approach was a liberal one. It was imposed with humanitarian intent and characterized by a clear (and often unconsciously assumed) set of social, economic, and political objectives.[104] While colonial thinking had previously been characterized by notions of 'civilization' versus 'savagery,' the new version set the 'modern' against the 'primitive'. Though this was justified through a language that seemed to express confidence in the people, it was still an imposition from above – albeit a different one from previous notions of what colonization was and how civilization was to be achieved.

Godt noted that 'democratic principles are important. People must learn that a majority vote is to be respected by all and also the minority groups have some rights in society. I feel strongly that such an approach is necessary if Whale Cove is going to be self-supporting.'[105] Because the people 'have not got much initiative at the moment' it was crucial, in Godt's view, to find the right kind of person to give the community direction. The most important factor in this plan was the quality of the outsider.

Godt had little to say about the Keewatin Re-establishment Project at Rankin Inlet, and admitted as much. He wrote: 'I have not too many things to say about KRP – only that I am of the opinion that a rehabilitation project could be started. The majority of the people living there now are physically handicapped. This project will need assistance for quite some time and relief measures on [sic] one kind, or another will be necessary for a long time.'[106] His general assessment of both communities, after their first full year of existence and after the people had been in the government's care for two years, is revealing. 'I am fully convinced that at present conditions in this area are not ripe for action. If anything is going to be successful and have lasting value, it will be necessary to start from scratch; then we might have a chance of building a project which will have lasting effect and value.'[107] This opinion contrasts sharply with the enthusiasm expressed by Northern Service Officer Grant two years earlier.

Later that same year, both communities were visited by 'Bud' F.J. Neville, the superintendent of welfare services, as part of his Keewatin 'welfare patrol.' His visit to Whale Cove was brief. He wrote: 'We found the Whale Cove people happy, very well fed but not particularly occupied.'[108] Neville did not write about the people at the KRP at Rankin and seems to have spent most of his time in discussions with Bob Williamson, the northern service officer, and other government officials. Their concern seems to have been matters related to lines of responsibility between different government staff and the future of the community in the event of the closing of the mine. He wrote that, 'in very general terms the situation at Rankin Inlet was very positive whether one considers it from the point of view of staff relationships, departmental activities, housing, employment opportunities and welfare services.'[109] From a planning and bureaucratic perspective, everything was fine.

Consequently, we are left to speculate on how Inuit felt about their situation. Neville did observe that 'about eight families from Repulse Bay have moved to Rankin Inlet since I left there in late March. These families are living in tents around the fringes of the community which is the usual pattern for newcomers into a settlement.'[110] Perhaps these Inuit living in tents did not feel so positive about the project. In any event, most of the men had found some form of employment and were, in Neville's view, 'managing reasonably well.'[111]

A different perspective on the Rankin project emerges from a third source of information on events developing in the Keewatin at this time: F.G. Vallee's well-known study, *Kabloona and Eskimo in the Central Keewatin.*

The KRP and Whale Cove: New Communities, New Problems

Frank Vallee, employed by the Northern Co-ordination and Research Centre of the department during the summers of 1959 and 1960, conducted fieldwork in Rankin Inlet and in Whale Cove. The Keewatin Re-establishment Project at Melville Bay, south of the mining community at Rankin Inlet, had been named 'Itavia.' Vallee confirms what Murdoch and Godt had observed about the social status of the Inuit there, noting that 'because Itavia was a rehabilitation project, the people who inhabited it came to be defined as welfare cases, and there is ample evidence that the other Eskimos in the region, namely those in the mining village, held them in low esteem.'[112] He added that 'this low esteem they shared with other Eskimos from blighted regions of the interior.' A change in the policy affecting the operation of the camp at Itavia helps explain the perceived status of Inuit living there. Vallee describes this change: 'During the second year of operation, the rehabilitation centre program became much more oriented towards the welfare of the physically and emotionally defective, leaving the "normals" to fend for themselves.'[113]

By contemporary standards, Vallee's language is anything but progressive. Nevertheless, he identifies a possible explanation for the migration from Rankin Inlet to Whale Cove in 1959 and 1960. The combination of low status in the Rankin community and a program focused on the most disadvantaged may have led many to seek residence elsewhere. According to Vallee, 'most of the rehabilitants from the Kazan ... demanded to be returned to the Baker Lake region.'[114] Others who had been relocated to Itavia from both Garry and Henik lakes found their way to Whale Cove. Vallee's description of the Whale Cove community strongly suggests that migration to Whale Cove was likely for political reasons – possibly to get away from non-Inuit interference and to reside in a community where the practice of Inuit social and cultural norms was more possible. Vallee thought that the Whale Cove project 'from a social and psychological point of view ... appears to have been quite successful so far.' He found that 'families which have always lived on the land, at least those with material resources such as rifles, boats, and motors, have demonstrated that they can adjust to a sea hunting and fishing economy.'[115] He asked people to compare their experiences at Whale Cove and Rankin Inlet, finding that 'the consensus of opinion was that Whale Cove was a much better place to live.' The two reasons given were that, first, 'the daily round of life was felt to be more like their pre-migration experience,' involving 'daily hunting and fishing,' while second, 'the feeling was expressed by several people that living was more comfortable and free in Whale Cove because it is an Eskimo community. Only one Kabloona [Qallunat] resident is settled there, a D.N.A. technical officer.'[116] Vallee found that some of the Inuit did not like living in communities with large numbers of non-Natives. When asked why, one young married man said Inuit 'feel like dogs who can't go in the tent.'[117]

Vallee noted that 'three people expressed the feeling that there were too many Kabloona "bosses" at Rankin Inlet, pointing out that one or another Kabloona was in charge of every activity other than the purely domestic.' All those government officials who were busily trying to help the Inuit help themselves had apparently not made themselves liked; the Inuit were busily trying to save themselves from being helped. In a footnote, Vallee observed that 'upon leaving the field we learned that additional Kabloona are scheduled to settle at Whale cove.' These included 'missionaries from two denominations, a school teacher, and another government official.' He commented somewhat wryly, 'It will be interesting to observe how relations between this and the Eskimo element develop and what effect the Kabloona invasion will have on the morale of the inhabitants.'[118]

Vallee, like Murdoch and Godt, noticed the divisions among the Inuit that existed in the community of Whale Cove. He writes that 'some social distance was maintained between groups from different regions of the Arctic,' and he adds later that 'the immigrants from the Baker Lake region who were our informants admitted that there were tensions and conflict between some households.'[119] Another report, written at about the same time, also confirms this view:

> The various Eskimo groups at Whale Cove keep very much to themselves. Although there are crucial cultural as well as kinship relationships between the Eskimo Point and Ennadai Lake groups, there seems to be very little co-operation between them. The Eskimo Point people have made no effort to assist the Ahermut [*sic*] in learning coastal hunting methods. All the groups have done some caribou hunting and these hunts have been quite successful. Only the Eskimo Point people have shown any interest in seal hunting.[120]

Vallee's observations contrast with those of Peter Murdoch and P. Godt, noted earlier. Vallee stated that 'we have never been in an Arctic community where we saw more friendly interaction and spontaneous play than at Whale Cove.'[121] These included 'daily football games' and frequent square dances.[122] He also found that 'when asked whether or not they would care to return to their region of origin, they claimed that they were "too well off" at Whale Cove to think of such a move.'[123] The 'invasion' of government employees that followed, civil servants whose job was to help the Inuit help themselves, may have changed these attitudes.

The Whale Cove experience was, like its predecessors in the high Arctic, a planning disaster. Northern circumstances confounded southern organizers – something exacerbated by the urgency with which the plans had to be made. Inuit were shuffled around like cards – moved from one place to another. In the case of voluntary moves between Itavia/Rankin Inlet and Whale Cove, it appears that Inuit were trying to get away from their benign, helpful overseers. The spontaneous move down to Whale Cove, although supported by government infrastructures and relief, may have been pulled by the feeling Grant had promoted in the month or so he had with Inuit workers that this site would belong to them, but it was undoubtedly also pushed by what Vallee calls the 'caste' system at Rankin Inlet, a caste system that left the relocatees at the bottom and at the mercy of the overly helpful outsiders. But even Vallee, reflecting on all he had seen and on his overall analysis of the economic situation in the Keewatin, would write: 'It will have been gathered from what has been said so far about the economy that some planned relocation is necessary.'[124]

8

Relocation and Responsibility, 1955-63

> Mr. Ayaruark called attention to the need to permit Eskimos to make their own decisions in matters directly affecting them. He said that sometimes Eskimos were overshadowed by those in authority and this had been evident in cases where they had been moved from one area to another when they did not want to go. They had agreed to move only because they were 'overawed.'
>
> – comments made by John Ayaruark of Rankin Inlet to tenth meeting of the Committee on Eskimo Affairs

By the time of the famines at Garry and Henik lakes, two opposing directions affecting the relationship of the state to the Inuit could be identified within the northern administration. The resolution of this policy conflict led to significant changes in the way the North was governed. On the one hand, the well-established practice of using relocation to solve welfare and related problems continued. This was a geographical solution to what were defined as geographical problems. The creation of Whale Cove – virtually out of thin air – is an illustration of this policy at work.

On the other hand, it was slowly recognized that Inuit should have a greater say in their own lives. Inuit community councils began to give an Inuit voice to decisions that profoundly affected Inuit lives. This is not to imply that a policy of developing Inuit community councils supplanted the policy of relocation; the relocation of aboriginal Canadians persisted into the 1960s and '70s.[1] However, in the 1950s, two themes dominated policy: relocation and guided self-determination. Both were seen to lead to integration with the dominant liberal democratic structures of Canadian society. 'Guided self-determination' took two forms: direct intervention, with guidance provided by non-Inuit experts, and a second form that was less heavy-handed. Both attempted to move Inuit from one culture to another using a step-by-step incremental approach.

These themes of relocation and self-determination can be identified from a significant debate that took place as the social and economic problems of the 1950s escalated into major concerns for the northern administration. The subject of the debate was whether, and to what degree, Inuit should be relocated to southern Canada. The seriousness of this proposal is emphasized by the creation of a committee to examine it.

This chapter examines five facets of government policy in the eastern Arctic in the late 1950s and early '60s. First, the arguments and proposals surrounding relocation to the South are considered. Second, proposals to expand relocations into the high Arctic are discussed. Third, the expansion of social welfare administration and the norms and precepts that accompanied it are noted. Fourth, a specific instance of this expansion and of changing values in the administration of the North – the debate over how family allowances were to be paid to Inuit recipients – is considered. Finally, the emergence of community councils and of an Inuit role in policymaking is discussed.

The review of these discussions returns us to the question of the dynamic between totalization and resistance referred to in the introduction. Significantly, throughout the period examined in this chapter, administration of Inuit affairs grew increasingly bureaucratized; the instrumental logic took a form characteristic of late modern states, replacing the 'northern frontier' mentality that dominated early decades of this century. Hence, calls for more research, more committees, and the establishment of policy frameworks creep into the discussion. The process of totalization could envisage drastically different policy options – wholescale relocation to the South or to the high Arctic – as mechanisms for incorporating Inuit into the logic of the established order. Regardless of what policy was consciously adopted, the state almost inexorably expanded its regulatory and surveillance apparatus into the North. More employees are hired and sent north, more 'services' are offered to Inuit. A period of neglect is swiftly replaced by a period of intense activity. Fitting Inuit into the rational exigencies of the established order proves difficult, as the debate on family allowance payments shows. And throughout, there is Inuit intransigence and resistance: to being moved, to changing their values and life ways, and finally to being spoken for. We conclude with the establishment of Inuit community councils and the first phase of a new period in which totalization becomes a process that must address a situation where Inuit speak directly for themselves.

The events and discussions surrounding the establishment of Whale Cove in the late 1950s make it clear relocation had not been discredited as a policy option. In fact, planners and administrators were contemplating expanding the scope and scale of their relocation projects and using relocation in entirely new ways. Within the administration, it had become an orthodoxy that the Grise Fiord and Resolute Bay relocations were a complete success. Minutes from the fifth meeting of the Committee on Eskimo Affairs, held 29 November 1954, include the report that 'the Eskimos who had been transferred to Banks, Cornwallis and Ellesmere Islands have continued to make a very satisfactory living. They have been able to obtain all the food they need and have also had quite substantial earnings from their trapping activities.'[2]

Consistently favourable reports on past relocation projects contributed to the belief that relocation to areas where Inuit could supposedly make a better living, and where social services ('relief,' family allowances, rehabilitation, etc.) could be more easily delivered, made sense. With the traditional trapping economy in shambles, the population growing, caribou and other resources believed to be in decline, limited opportunities for wage employment, and the costs of northern administration rising, a small step in logic was all that was required for the administration to begin contemplating a desperate 'solution' – wholescale relocation to the South.

Rehabilitation Centres in Southern Canada
The proposal to relocate Inuit to southern Canada developed slowly through the 1950s. However, concerns over welfare, the collapse of fur prices – despite some modest recovery through the 1950s – alternative employment possibilities, and access to medical and educational facilities were predicated on another social objective: integrating or assimilating Inuit with the dominant Canadian culture. For some, assimilation was the key to solving the welfare and medical problems. For others, the medical and welfare problems provided an opportunity to achieve assimilation.

It was generally believed that many Inuit hospitalized in the South as a result of epidemics of tuberculosis, polio, and other debilitating conditions were unable to readjust to northern conditions. Something had to be done for them. In the early 1950s, the Committee on Eskimo Affairs had been established to coordinate the activities of the various government and non-government agencies dealing with Inuit. Commencing in 1954, the committee was chaired by Gordon Robertson, the deputy minister of the newly created Department of Northern Affairs and Natural Resources. The committee also included representatives from the RCMP – usually the commissioner – the Anglican and Catholic churches, the Hudson's Bay Company, and other appropriate government departments such as National Health and Welfare.

By the committee's fifth meeting in November 1954, the response to the tuberculosis epidemic in the North was in full swing. Dr. P.E. Moore, the director of Indian Health Services, Department of National Health and

Welfare, reported that 'there are about 450 Eskimos under treatment at southern sanatoria and 150 in mission hospitals in the Northwest Territories.' Although Moore thought that the rate of hospitalization would 'gradually decline' over the following years, little thought had been given about what to do with Inuit after their hospitalization. Stopgap measures were taken: 'It was agreed, however, that everything possible should be done to improve communications between patients in hospitals and their relatives at home, and to provide means of educating and preparing patients to rehabilitate themselves after their discharge from hospital.'[3]

In 1954, there was still no one with overall responsibility for social welfare working with the Arctic division of the Department of Northern Affairs and Natural Resources. At the committee's fifth meeting, there was some discussion of welfare concerns.

> The suggestion was made that centres should be set up where aged Eskimos and others incapable of providing for themselves could be cared for. Coupled with this, was a proposal that a community centre for Eskimos could be set up at a place near a hospital, such as Hamilton, where Eskimos, because of inability or lack of inclination to return to the native life, could be trained after discharge from hospital to take up other employment either in the Arctic or elsewhere.[4]

By the seventh meeting, Walter Rudnicki had been hired as chief of the welfare section of the Arctic division, a new section that would grow by leaps and bounds in coming years. During this meeting, RCMP Commissioner Nicholson thought it necessary to review the original goals and objectives of the committee. One of these had been stated in the negative: 'To do nothing to encourage the Eskimos to leave the north.'[5] As the meeting progressed, there was extensive discussion of the problems associated with rehabilitating Inuit patients discharged from hospitals. Walter Rudnicki outlined 'some of the Department's plans and programs relating to field social welfare rehabilitation for Eskimo patients and the medico-social welfare work among Eskimos in hospitals.' Anglican Bishop Donald Marsh asked whether whole families were going to be moved to northern rehabilitation centres to be with their relatives. Rudnicki responded by noting that there were really two groups, those 'who will recover to stay in the rehabilitation centre as transients' and those 'who are permanently disabled.' In the case of the former, families would not be moved, while in the case of the latter, 'their families will be brought to the centre.'[6]

The conversation then swiftly escalated into a discussion of large-scale relocation. This began with a statement by Dr. Moore, who reported that: 'Forty-five people were going back to the north [that] summer from Hamilton and that he thought [the administration] needed an escape hatch for the Eskimos from the north. He recommended that they be rehabilitated in the south in areas where they [could] take employment.'[7] After more discussion, Moore went on to be 'quite emphatic that in a place where the economic future is good, they would integrate completely.' He added that the administration 'could overcome the break-up of family ties by bringing out the whole group.'[8] The discussion sparked by this comment is worth following in its entirety:

> The Chairman [Robertson] asked how we could get over the problem of the current generation. He said it might mean the support of a large group while the children were being educated.
> Dr. Moore said they will have to be supported by a straight subsidy; they will need to be sorted out by religion; nursing and school services will have to be provided.
> The Chairman said, would the group be established from adults incapable of returning.
> Dr. Moore replied yes, there are examples already out.
> Mr. Cunningham said that it was our understanding from reports from hospitals, none of the Eskimos wanted to stay in the south and asked what Dr. Moore thought of this.
> Dr. Moore said that this is a matter of education.[9]

The problems the committee was examining were relatively small ones. These were defined as 'the many problems associated with rehabilitation, the need for educating and giving these Eskimos in question some skills.' That is, it was a problem of logistics – how to return hospitalized Inuit to the North – and of education and job training – how to take advantage of the presence of these Inuit by giving them job skills. However, Dr. Moore quickly shifted the discussion, seeing an opportunity to also assimilate Inuit more completely into Canadian society. When F.J.G. Cunningham, the director of the Northern Administration and Lands Branch, stopped for a moment to suggest that the Inuit might not be in favour of the proposal, Moore's rebuttal was firm. Education would change their minds. A stronger statement about education's role in the new liberal and humanitarian approach to integrating Inuit into another culture is hard to imagine.

This suggestion resulted in a smaller subcommittee being established, which was to report back to the Eskimo Affairs Committee at a later date. The subcommittee met on 1 June 1956 and included Commissioner Nicholson of the RCMP, F.J. Cunningham, Dr. Moore, Inspector W.J. Fitzsimmons of the RCMP, Walter Rudnicki, and Dr. J.S. Willis, also with the Indian and Northern Health Service of National Health and Welfare.

Members again addressed the subject of resettling families in the South and the need for an 'experimental project ... a sort of escape hatch ... to drain of [*sic*] surplus population from the north. The observation was made that increasing numbers of Eskimos are not fit to return to Arctic conditions of life. One alternative would be to subsidise such persons until they are re-established in the south.'[10] What Inuit were 'escaping' from was never made clear. Cunningham's earlier comments suggested that, if anything, Inuit patients looked forward to escaping hospitalization in the South and to returning home. Moore's assumptions were more than a little ethnocentric. Why would anyone, he seems to be saying, want to return to such a hostile climate and to such primitive conditions?

Again, escalation was the order of the day: 'The family unit was the nucleus around which the experiment would be built. Ten families was regarded as a good start.'[11] But families – even ten families – might not be enough. The suggestion was made that 'chances for recruitment would be greater on a group basis. The opinion was that Eskimos would not co-operate singly in a resettlement project and might not even do so as families. Selection might have to be made on the basis of a group of families from a given area.'[12] Having come to the conclusion that something of a grand scale was needed, cautions were introduced: for instance, that 'the successful Eskimos in the north would probably not be interested in moving south,' and that, 'as a general policy, Eskimos should be kept as far north as possible in preference to urban settlement.' A case was cited of a resettlement project involving 'Indians which resulted in a group of indigents. It was agreed that, if integration is the goal, it certainly would not be wise to circumscribe a group of people.'[13]

The committee quickly began to speculate about other aspects of such a project. When it came to occupations for Inuit resettled in the South, the suggestion was made that 'something like lumbering would be better than agriculture.' The question of jurisdiction had to be addressed because, in the view of the subcommittee, 'Eskimos who might be self-supporting in a province for one year would become provincial responsibilities.'[14] A working group of this subcommittee, consisting of Fitzsimmons, Rudnicki, and Willis, was struck to prepare a more detailed report.

This was completed in time for the eighth meeting of the Committee on Eskimo Affairs, 13 May 1957. The subcommittee's report, entitled 'Report on Proposed Eskimo Resettlement in Southern Canada,' began with the assertion that 'the fact has to be faced that the traditional relationship between Eskimos and their physical environment has ceased to exist.'[15] The report makes a familiar reference to Inuit use of modern consumer goods and to economic and cultural linkages with the rest of Canada. In other words, Inuit were already on their way to becoming ordinary Canadians.

The rationale for the policy recommendations made later in the report was threefold:

(1) Eskimos have over the past decades been conditioned to an economic existence qualitatively different from the absolute self-sufficiency of their forefathers. The clock can't be turned back in their case any more than it can in ours. (2) Economic interdependence has meant that during periods of depression in the fur trade, relief rations have had to serve as a stop gap. (3) Depopulation through starvation and disease no longer is significant because of such measures as relief rations and medical care. The result is a gradually increasing population.[16]

For the authors, the conclusion was 'fairly obvious:' 'If the population of the north increases at a rate in excess of its capacity to support the population, a serious human problem will result.' Since 'it would be unwise to assume that the capacity of the country will at all times keep pace with the increased Eskimo population,' the report endorses the idea 'that consideration should be given to the possibility, as a pilot operation, of some limited resettlement of Eskimo families on a trial basis.'[17]

By resettlement is meant the transfer of Eskimo family groups from areas which are chronically depressed to locations where they are able to support themselves. This is not a new concept in the department. Over the past few years, highly successful resettlement projects have been carried out. The most notable are the group of Port Harrison and Pond Inlet Eskimos who moved to better hunting grounds at Resolute and Craig Harbour, and the Fort Chimo Eskimos who moved to Churchill and are now established workers and tradesmen.[18]

The resettlement contemplated here is defined on much broader terms than the notion of 'rehabilitation centres' for outpatients from southern sanatoriums. Transfers of 'family groups' from 'chronically depressed areas' had changed the original rehabilitation scheme to something much more expansive and followed the same logic of escalation that took place in the meetings where the plan was initially proposed.

With this rationale and definition, the practicalities of southern resettlement, the various factors to be considered, and the next immediate steps to be taken were outlined. The question was asked: 'Is Southern Resettlement Practical?' A positive response was assumed. Rather than addressing the question, the report focused on whether Inuit subjects could be found for the project. A titular nod is given to the rights of Inuit as Canadian citizens: 'In principle, few would deny that as Canadian citizens, Eskimos have the right to live and work anywhere in Canada.'[19] This observation was made in passing. The problem of recruitment, on the other hand, received serious consideration: 'The subjects for this pilot project (for such it is) would need to be Eskimos who have had some significant contact with southern civilization and who are already well on their way to cultural integration. Above all, candidates for resettlement in the south would have to be *willing* to make such a move because of the knowledge that benefits would accrue to them and the certainty that the Arctic, in their case, has nothing to offer them.'[20] While the original purpose for the plan was to find a way around the problems associated with rehabilitating hospital patients, in the framework of the report, the hospital patients are treated as a target population in a larger scheme whose purpose is to alleviate a much deeper problem: northern 'surplus population.'[21] Thus, 'the most logical recruiting places seem to be sanatoria in the south.'[22]

It was conceded that 'it is common knowledge that many Eskimos have refused to entertain any possibility of remaining in the South in instances where such an approach has been made in the past.' However, it was assumed that such opposition could easily be overcome, since 'most Eskimos find a concrete proposal outlined in comprehensible terms a more acceptable thing than a vague offer which cannot tell him where he will live, what he will do, and what there is in it for him and his family. Finally, an Eskimo who is aware that his hospitalization has made him a misfit for the Arctic is a far more likely person to approach than someone who is managing well in the north.'[23] The report also suggests that other advantages could 'spin off' from the project, including the possibility that some southern, resettled Inuit might eventually return to the North as 'clerks, stenographers, technicians, policemen, teachers, doctors, dentists, nurses, welfare workers, administrators.' As well, 'resettled Eskimos in the south ... could facilitate the integration of newcomers arriving from the north subsequently to take up a new life.'[24] This theme – that Inuit might eventually be coaxed out of the North – reoccurs many times throughout this and subsequent documents dealing with relocation.

The next section of the report, 'Factors to be Considered in Resettlement,' takes the question of expanding the project even further:

There might be other sources of Eskimos for southern resettlement. There are large groups of Eskimo trainees just starting to come down to various urban centres for vocational training ... There may be others who have never been out of the Arctic but who may want to emulate friends or relatives by following them south. If resettlement gathers momentum in this way over the next few years, it would be neither possible nor desirable to confine it to any particular category of Eskimos or even to a specific program.[25]

In effect, this modest pilot project was intended to carry the seed for a massive change, possibly leading to the relocation of a sizable portion of the Inuit population and integration or assimilation into life in southern Canada.

The idea of such a massive relocation was not unique to government officials. Not only did it have currency among many southern Canadians, but, as the following letter to John Diefenbaker illustrates, the idea made sense to others who had never even seen the Canadian Arctic.

Sir –

Kindly hand this letter to the Department which it concerns.

I have been reading Dr. Moody's book on his experiences among the Eskimos. If there are only 9,000 of them, as he says, would it not be economical to move them south where they could work on the farms and in the factories? Thus they would be an asset to the country.

This is just a kindly suggestion from a well wisher of yours and requires no answer.

Sincerely yours,
(sgd) David Cole
Port Antonio
Jamaica, B.W.I.

Sept. 4, 1957[26]

The suggestion certainly required an answer and the answer was a serious one. Two approaches were suggested for accomplishing such a relocation. The first approach, 'Method A,' involved the establishment of 'Integration Centres' for outpatients and their families where 'there would be a gradual introduction to city life, breadwinners would be established in vocational training courses, the housewife would be taught the elements of housekeeping and children would be enroled in local schools.'[27] What the report contemplates is the construction of Inuit suburban, nuclear, patriarchal families, with male breadwinners, female housewives, and children as students.

'Method B' – obviously a kind of 'straw dog' – involved training outpatients on an individual basis in existing programs and finding them some kind of work. Furthermore, 'any dependents would be brought south at the point where the Eskimo has become more or less settled in a job.' There would be no integration centres in this method, and 'the dependents would be expected to learn about their new environment and about the demands of a different culture from their newly-established relative.'[28] The second method is seen as generally less likely to be successful and is given more cursory treatment in the report.

The practical question of where to establish the pilot project was tackled next. This was based on the presumption that the first method would be adopted. The areas discussed were: Fort Smith or Great Slave Lake, Northwest Territories; Edmonton, Alberta; Selkirk or Churchill, Manitoba; and Hamilton, Ontario. A preliminary costing of the proposals was also developed.

The subcommittee's report was circulated to members of the Committee on Eskimo Affairs on 3 May 1957 and discussed at the eighth meeting on 13 May. Commissioner Nicholson immediately expressed concern over the idea of depopulating the North. The minutes record that

> Commissioner Nicholson thought nothing should be done to depopulate the north of the people most fitted to live in it, and said that he would not wish to encourage any plans to a hurried mass movement of Eskimos to the south. It seemed reasonable to move some people who could be productive in the south, but who could only remain on relief it they continued to live in the north. It was also reasonable that former patients who were not fit for northern life should be settled in southern Canada. Those Eskimos who must be moved should be kept together after their arrival in the south, to help them preserve their identity.[29]

Gordon Robertson tried to reassure Nicholson by explaining that 'the proposals before the Committee were not meant to suggest that Eskimos should be moved south in large numbers. The present proposal called for a small pilot project in which Eskimos already in southern hospitals would take part.' However, Robertson added: 'If in future it became necessary to carry out large-scale movements of Eskimos to the south, the experience gained in a pilot project should be very valuable.'[30]

Nevertheless, opinions about the wisdom of resettlement in the South varied widely. Dr. H.A. Proctor, representing Dr. Moore, noted that 'any resettlement should be carried out on a strictly voluntary basis.' Walter Rudnicki echoed this concern, stating that 'the Sub-Committee felt that only volunteers should be resettled and that it should be up to the Eskimos concerned to decide whether or not they wished to remain in their own communities after they had become integrated in city life.' On the other hand, Bishop Marsh disagreed with this perspective, noting that 'many Eskimos had distorted ideas about the south' and that 'the Eskimo should be advised as to what he should do, and should not be left to decide as fancy dictated.'[31]

Deputy Minister Robertson responded by emphasizing, again, the relatively small scale of the pilot project. He argued 'that no more than a modest experiment should be attempted until all the problems that might be involved had been brought to light. Eskimos who would take part in any resettlement program would have to be carefully selected.'[32] Robertson's emphasis on careful selection of participants rather than willingness of volunteers suggests that getting candidates who seemed suitable to the planners was more important than getting candidates who were willing or enthusiastic.

The one voice of outright disapproval for the scheme came from Father Piche of the Indian Welfare Training Oblate Commission. Piche stated that 'he was expressing the missionary's point of view when he expressed opposition to a policy of Eskimo resettlement. He said that of the Eskimos who had come out of the Arctic in the past, ninety-eight percent had decided in the long run that they wanted to return. He thought that the same situation would arise if organized resettlement were begun.'[33] Again, it was Robertson who responded, arguing that 'something had to be done for people who were no longer fit to stand the Arctic environment. It was better for Eskimos to be supporting themselves in the south than dependent on relief in the north.'[34] Again, the important role of welfare – of rising bills for 'relief' – can be seen as a crucial factor driving the policy of relocation. Robertson effectively collapsed the two issues – resettlement of outpatients and resettlement of so-called 'surplus population' – using the first to justify the pilot project and the second as an opening for possible expansion. After this relatively short discussion and debate, the committee 'recommended institution of a limited experimental resettlement project along the lines of the Sub-Committee's method.'[35]

The minutes do not specify which method was to be adopted. However, a memorandum written the next day by Gordon Robertson to Ben Sivertz makes it clear. 'We secured agreement yesterday that we should go ahead with something along the lines of method (A), as recommended by the Committee in their report and that it should be initially on the limited basis suggested.'[36] Eventually the Dynevor Indian Hospital in Selkirk, Manitoba, was chosen as the site for the resettlement scheme. In the end, however, the plan was not implemented, and seems to have fizzled out.[37]

In his brief examination of this plan in *The Road to Nunavut*, Richard Diubaldo argues that 'what is important about the plan is that, with hindsight, it is indicative of the lengths to which those well-meaning civil servants, responsible for the handling of Inuit affairs, would go in their attempts to find solutions to the "Eskimo problem."'[38] Although this is certainly true, the plan reveals much more. Following its development, it becomes clear that relatively small problems could lead to grandiose solutions. A logic of escalation operated throughout the development of this

Relocation and Responsibility 317

proposal, a logic that went virtually unchecked. Despite almost all of the actors in this mini-drama being aware that Inuit did not want to stay in the South, they took for granted that cooperation could be secured.

The substance of this plan echoes a proposal made by anthropologist Diamond Jenness to the joint Senate and House of Commons committee that had been established in 1946 to examine Indian affairs. Jenness had effectively recommended wholesale relocation of Inuit to southern camps. Some in the bureaucracy, whether they were influenced by Jenness directly or not, had the same idea. The plan was based on profoundly ethnocentric assumptions: in particular the notion that Inuit could ultimately be educated to prefer a life in the South to that in the North, and the correlative notion that life in the South was inherently better. These assumptions were held by both progressive and conservative factions within the department as well as by others. Control of Inuit was necessary to change Inuit culture, to 'help' Inuit fit better with Canadian social norms and practices. Since control could be best achieved by having Inuit populations in settlements where they were accessible to state representatives, the proposal to move Inuit to the South was a logical extension of existing policies and practices.

Finally, the degree to which Inuit themselves may have been responsible for the failure of this plan through lack of cooperation and lack of enthusiasm is worthy of note. The Inuit who would have been asked to volunteer were in hospitals in the South, isolated from friends and families, weakened by sickness, treatment, changed diet, loneliness, and so on. In spite of their illness, in spite of determined encouragement by doggedly cheerful non-Native authorities who had a great deal of power over them, they knew one thing and held fast to it: they wanted to return to the North. The few copies of their letters that remain in archival files testify eloquently to this. One letter reads: 'I have come to the whiteman's land because I thought it would be nice here, but sometimes I am very unhappy here ... when one doesn't belong to this land it is not very pleasant.' Another Inuk writes: 'I am worrying about my home. I want to go home so badly that I don't care, don't give a hoot, if I'm not quite cured so please speak to the doctor ... I want to stay here no longer; I am really fed up ... While I am here it is awful in this lousy white-man's land.'[39] This attitude can be understood as one form of implicit resistance and opposition to government policy, a resistance to what might have become a strategically valuable tool in the government's arsenal of assimilationist policies: southern 'integration centres.'

Expanding 'Colonization' in the High Arctic

At roughly the same time as the scheme to move Inuit to the South had been conceived, plans were afoot to expand the movement of Inuit further

north. Because the relocations to Grise Fiord and Resolute Bay were perceived as resounding successes, it was suggested that these experiments be
emulated and expanded to the point of a systematic, planned migration
similar in scope to the southern movement. But not only was the geographical direction entirely opposite, the rationale was also completely reversed.
The northward move would assist Inuit in their existing and traditional
activities by moving them to regions reputedly well stocked in wildlife. The
idea was to help Inuit regain self-sufficiency and to reduce the financial and
personal costs of welfare dependency.

By the summer of 1958, Ben Sivertz was writing Vic Valentine of the
Northern Research Coordination Centre to suggest establishing a research
project on high Arctic resources, a first step in a plan to expand the
movement of Inuit northward. He noted that 'there is a growing pressure
from Eskimos on the east coast of Hudson Bay to move to the high Arctic.
Most of them wish to join relatives at Resolute Bay or Grise Fiord, who have
given them enthusiastic reports of life there.'[40] He continued:

> We think that the success of the two new communities in the high Arctic
> more than justifies a continuation of such movement. We have continued
> to postpone it, however, because we think it unwise to engage in any further
> relocation plans without a thorough knowledge of the remaining resources
> in the new areas. As a temporary measure, we are letting three families go
> from Port Harrison to Grise Fiord this year, since they are close relatives of
> people already there.[41]

The memorandum goes on to note that 'it is becoming more and more
urgent for us to look for more efficient places where Eskimos can hunt and
for more efficient ways for them to do it' and that 'the study of local food
resources in possible relocation areas requires the highest priority for
1959.'[42] Walter Rudnicki was quick to respond with enthusiastic support for
the northward movement of additional families.

> The Povungnituk region has never provided more than a meagre existence
> and much relief has been needed every year. There are good reasons then
> why this move should receive our blessings.
>
> It is very likely that the Hudson [sic] Bay Company will protest any attempt
> to shift the families to a new location. The factor at Harrison has already
> complained to the R.C.M.P. that the area will be depleted of hunters and
> no doubt the missionary will have his own suggestions.[43]

Rudnicki suggested immediate approval so that there would be no surprises
come shipping season.

Despite this enthusiasm among departmental officials, there were some doubts about the wisdom of moving more families north, far from medical services and into an area where it had not been confirmed by proper studies that game populations would support more hunting. It was June of 1958. The starvations at Garry Lake and Henik Lake were on everyone's minds. Sivertz recommended setting up a committee to discuss and possibly coordinate the necessary studies.

On 18 November 1958, a meeting was held to 'discuss resource studies for the proposed relocation of Eskimos.' The meeting included R.A.J. Phillips, chief of the Arctic division, Alex Stevenson, chief of the administration section of the Arctic division, Walter Rudnicki, chief of the welfare section, D.F. Symington, chief of the projects section, Vic Valentine of the Northern Research Co-ordination Centre, and John Tener of the Canadian Wildlife Service. Ben Sivertz, director of the Northern Administration and Lands Branch, was not present.

Phillips began the meeting 'by commenting on the successful relocation of Eskimos at both Grise Fiord and Resolute, and mentioned that these moves had been accomplished without the aid of resource studies – a risky procedure. These studies were desirable before any future relocation of Eskimos.' Alex Stevenson reiterated that, 'the Eskimos who had been relocated at Resolute and Grise Fiord were extremely satisfied in their adopted communities, and from time to time their relatives from Eastern Hudson Bay joined them.' Tener and Valentine reported on studies that had already been undertaken, acknowledging that 'information on resources in these islands was far from complete.'[44]

After some discussion of various problems associated with relocation, the committee arrived at three recommendations: '(1) no Eskimos be relocated in areas of poor transportation and communication; (2) Eskimo relocation would generally be within rather than across natural Arctic areas such as northwest Quebec, Keewatin, and western Arctic; and (3) that the priority for resource studies be Keewatin, East Coast of Hudson Bay, Tuktoyaktuk-Coppermine, and North Baffin Island.'[45] Relocation to the central Arctic and Queen Elizabeth Islands was specifically thought to be unfeasible. From a discussion of relocation to the high Arctic, the committee had come around to proposing studies that would support a system of relocations within each of the broad Arctic regions. Of four targeted areas, only North Baffin Island fell within the scope of the idea that had provided initial impetus for the meeting.

On 7 December, Sivertz wrote to Deputy Minister Gordon Robertson, communicating the committee's three recommendations. Sivertz's memorandum contains the stamp 'approved,' with Robertson's signature underneath. Above that is a hand-written note: 'I agree, except that # 2 is too

narrow. I would prefer to substitute "eastern Arctic" for "Keewatin" otherwise you would not use Franklin, which has some good relocation areas.
Note that Franklin is included in # 3.'[46] A systematic survey of regional
resources was not undertaken, however, though the idea of relocating Inuit
to the high Arctic continued to have currency in the department.

In the fall and winter of 1960-1, a series of memorandums were exchanged
within the department about the subject. The first of these was a confidential memorandum to Sivertz from C.M. Bolger, administrator of the Arctic.
It begins: 'Recently you discussed with me the possibility of establishing
additional groups of Eskimos in the High Arctic, particularly in the vicinity
of the joint Arctic weather stations at Eureka, Alert, Isachsen and Mould
Bay.'[47] Bolger's seven-page analysis reviewed the Resolute and Grise Fiord
moves in glowing terms and made recommendations for further relocations.
In it, he states: 'The outcome of these ventures has been more successful
and satisfactory than had ever been anticipated.'[48] Bolger went on to say
that 'although the Eskimos at Grise Fiord have not had the opportunities of
employment, they have, however, obtained a good livelihood from the
country and this community also serves a distinctly useful purpose in
confirming, in a tangible manner, Canada's sovereignty over this vast region
of the Arctic.'[49] While the purpose of any new relocations would primarily
be to alleviate economic hardship, Bolger felt that, regarding employment
of Eskimos at weather stations, 'again the matter of sovereignty would be
another aspect of such employment.' He noted that resource surveys had
been planned in the past but 'because of staff limitations it has never been
possible to make the survey required.'[50]

Sovereignty, as noted in previous chapters, was a familiar theme in the
occupation of the Arctic islands. By 1960, the matter had taken a different
turn. Sovereignty over the Arctic islands was apparently still a relevant
consideration in departmental discussions about high Arctic settlement. But
the matter of sovereignty over Arctic waters and whether the fabled Northwest Passage constituted an international waterway added a new dimension
to the issue and was prompted by a new and non-military concern: the
growing realization that the Arctic islands might be the repository of reserves
of oil and gas. In recognition of this possibility, cabinet had requested, and
received, in 1959, a paper on sovereignty over Arctic waters.[51] On 8 March
1960, cabinet requested additional information from the advisory committee on northern development about Canadian sovereignty over the Arctic
islands. A paper was prepared and submitted on 27 June 1960 by Alvin
Hamilton, just prior to his departure as minister of the Department of
Northern Affairs and National Resources.[52] In this climate of concern for
Arctic sovereignty, the department had a familiar response.

In a confidential memo to Sivertz, Bolger endorsed the notion of more high Arctic relocations centred on weather stations: 'We have had some problems at Grise Fiord in respect of supply and medical services and I believe we should not duplicate such communities at other isolated locations. My understanding is that you would prefer that any new colonies be established in the vicinity of existing weather stations such as Mould Bay, Isachsen and Eureka. I am in general agreement with this principle.' He added: 'However, I think that many Eskimos will want to make a livelihood from the country for some time to come, provided of course the resources are available. Therefore I do not think we should eliminate entirely in any study the setting up of communities away from established stations.'[53] He suggested that 'the logical development would be to start these colonies as satellites of the Resolute Bay community' and recommended reconvening meetings of the various agencies that would have to be involved to discuss the matter further. He characterized 'the Eskimos at Resolute Bay and Grise Fiord [as] an invaluable human resource in the northern economic development taking place on Cornwallis Island and adjacent islands' and also, once again, reminded Sivertz that 'the occupation of these northern islands by Canada's first Arctic citizens only enhances our claims to sovereignty of these regions.'[54] As of 1960, departmental officials still thought relocation of Inuit would be a contributing factor to Canadian Arctic sovereignty. In this case, at least one official envisaged a dramatic expansion of high Arctic relocations, even to such forbidding locations as Eureka and Alert on the northern tip of Ellesmere Island.

Sivertz responded to Bolger's memo in a generally approving manner ten days later. He thought that Bolger had written 'a very good review of a situation that is not entirely unsatisfactory' and expressed disappointment 'to learn that the surveys of wildlife on land and in the sea were not carried out as planned in 1956.' Sivertz had a few thoughts to contribute to Bolger's detailed proposals, but he was generally supportive of a new high Arctic relocation scheme:

The thing for you to concentrate on right now is the possibility of establishing new colonies in the high Arctic in the vicinity of existing weather stations. I would not be averse to adding to the list of Mold [*sic*] Bay, Isaacson [*sic*], Eureka, Alert, at least tentatively, such places as hold promise of becoming centres of activity, e.g. Radstock Bay, Little Cornwallis Island and some of the oil and gas sites that the Resources Division might be able to indicate, perhaps after the 1961 exploration season. You say you do not think we should eliminate entirely in our study the setting up of communities away from established radio stations. I agree. Keep the possibility always in your studies and do not hesitate to recommend such locations if you have reason to do so.[55]

This exchange of memorandums sparked something of a debate within the administration, with Rudnicki and Snowden, chief of the industrial division, staking out opposing views on how new communities could be created. Relocation itself, however, was never challenged as a mechanism for solving problems. Relocation to the high Arctic in particular – and despite the recommendations made at the November 1958 relocation committee meeting to study relocations within rather than between regions – was once again, given the larger political context, seen as a viable policy option.

Writing about the proposal to relocate Inuit to the high Arctic, Walter Rudnicki responded with, 'This is a proposal which I support wholeheartedly.' He saw a broad potential for the idea, noting:

> It offers both a means of alleviating population pressures in the more established areas and a way of bringing some of the further reaches of the north within the sphere of human habitation. The potential import of such a project is such, however, that it might well be referred to not as a proposal to relocate Eskimos, but rather as a plan to create new northern communities. This, in effect, would be the result of a well-conceived resettlement program.[56]

Rudnicki's six-page memorandum suggested a variety of alternative methods for creating new communities. He identified a 'laissez-faire' approach similar to what had been done in the Grise Fiord and Resolute Bay relocations, a 'do-good' approach where significant outside staff would be employed to manage and organize the Inuit during a specified transition period, and a 'self-help' approach – obviously the preferred tactic – where a 'step-by-step process marked by ever-increasing ability of the Eskimos concerned to run their own affairs' is roughly mapped out.[57] The 'self-help' and 'management of their own affairs' aspects of this last strategy were to be controlled and managed by the administrators.

Rudnicki noted that 'this third approach has been discussed frequently in the Branch though until now there has been no real opportunity to give it a proper trial.'[58] He then proceeded to discuss 'Sociological Factors.' This section of the text is of interest because it contains the criticisms of the earlier high Arctic relocations noted in Chapter 4. Rudnicki's recommendations were largely administrative: responsibility for relocation should be assigned to one specific branch within the department, a 'Committee on Eskimo Resettlement' should be created to coordinate activities in the area, and a 'Resettlement Plan' should be developed 'which would indicate in general the policy framework for carrying out resettlement projects, the fiscal relationship between the Government and the Eskimos involved in this process, and the minimum material and staff requirements for each project.'[59]

Rudnicki wanted to view relocation as a process of community develop-ment leading to self-sufficiency. However, the contradiction, that relocation was still the underlying reality that would initiate this process, remained. Nevertheless, Rudnicki's approach can be distinguished, quite sharply, from that of his co-workers.

One of these co-workers, D. Snowden, responded with some strong criticisms of Rudnicki. Snowden's reply begins with the by now common rhetoric about the value of relocation: 'We, of course, agree that many Eskimos now living in areas which are relatively over-populated in relation to the available resources should be encouraged to move elsewhere.'[60] He then proceeds to re-emphasize what he sees as the 'fundamental principles' involved in relocation. These were: the need for area resource surveys during the planning stages; that 'the Eskimos moved should never be without easy access either to a white official or to a radio post'; 'above all else, the Eskimos should be given guidance at the new area of settlement ... to enable them to live much more self-sufficiently and efficiently on the land'; and, finally, after the first year, 'a school would command our next priority.'[61] Snowden was advocating much more intervention and guidance from 'technically qualified and sympathetic' outsiders at all stages of the process.

Snowden recognized that this put him in opposition to Rudnicki. While he affirmed a general solidarity with both Rudnicki's and Bolger's sugges-tions, he did not 'share Mr. Rudnicki's apprehensions about "Do-Good" settlements where white staff members undertake to organize a community for the Eskimos.' For Snowden, it was the 'character of the officials' involved that was the crucial factor in whether relocation led to dependence or not. Snowden was concerned about the possibility that 'Eskimos may be brought south, at considerable expense, to learn skills, including a lot of miscella-neous information, which they may never apply, or know how to apply, back home.' He therefore recommended 'training by experience with ade-quate instruction given right on the job, so to speak,' noting 'the willingness of people to adopt new methods and new outlooks on the job, provided these are properly explained by technical experts who work directly with the people.' He added, in a hand-written note: 'In due course, the assistance will be completely withdrawn.'[62]

Rudnicki's comments about social problems in the high Arctic communi-ties of Grise Fiord and Resolute Bay – the same comments noted in Chapter 4 – drew Snowden's concluding fire:

There is no question that mutual hostility, suspicion and bickering occur in many communities where there are people drawn from different locations in the Arctic. It is significant, however, that these are most prevalent where there has never been a well-developed resource harvesting programme or a co-operative or community scheme involving all groups equally. We can never prevent human animosity, although many anthropologists and sociologists would like it otherwise, and these are normally things which people work out best themselves. A positive community programme leading to better harvests, housing, etc., together with adult education and a growing familiarity with their new environment, will go a long way to overcome internecine rifts.[63]

Snowden and Rudnicki effectively articulated two different approaches to creating settlements and to community development. Snowden's can be characterized as interventionist, while Rudnicki's might be described as incrementalist.

Ultimately, no Inuit communities were created at the weather stations at Alert, Eureka, Isachsen, and Mould Bay. That this could even be the subject of passing speculation on the part of senior officials is startling. Although Eureka is situated in a reasonably resource-rich area, the other stations are extremely forbidding and sparse in resources. And, of course, resupply of a settlement at Eureka and the other locations would have been a serious proposition. That such a proposal could be seriously contemplated is a sign of just how separated southern planners were from northern social and environmental realities.

Discussion of high Arctic relocations was indicative of two different tendencies that subsequently developed in the department and that are the subject of much of the rest of this chapter. One tendency, a logical conclusion of the interventionist approach, led to a massive expansion of departmental personnel – especially northern service officers and welfare officials. The other tendency, which reflects the incrementalist approach, led to creation of community councils and greater Inuit representation on decision-making bodies. With these structures, Inuit resistance would eventually move beyond its implicit forms to an explicit, organized level. The division between these approaches was not so clear in practice. The same actors could occupy different positions. For example, Walter Rudnicki was responsible for a significant expansion of interventionist personnel in the form of welfare workers. The community development workers employed in the 1960s occupied positions that embodied both tendencies.

The initial steps at turning control over to Inuit can be found in this dynamic tension. Ironically, these were occurring while the state's capacity to interfere in Inuit lives was being dramatically expanded. This tension is most evident in debates about relocation and in the creation of communities

– of which the development of Whale Cove, documented in Chapter 7, is illustrative.

Helping Inuit to Help Themselves

During the late '50s and early '60s, an 'invasion' – to borrow Vallee's apt description – took place in the Arctic. Why did such an invasion take place? Why were Inuit not left to their own devices? The answers to these and related questions are not to be found exclusively in the sincere belief of state officials that they were doing something genuine to help people in serious trouble. Nor are they to be found in the fact that the misfortunes of Inuit might have embarrassed a supposedly progressive nation on a world stage where Canada was increasingly seen as advocating global human rights and playing an increasingly important role in international development, though this too played its role.

The answer perhaps lies more in embedded notions of development and progress. Diefenbaker had been elected in 1957 on a platform of northern development: the exploitation of a northern frontier to accomplish a modern-day version of the nation-building associated with Sir John A. Macdonald's settlement of the Prairies. And with development came the 'problem' of aboriginal people, Inuit in this case, and their assimilation into the dominant society. This sentiment is succinctly captured by the following article from the *Edmonton Journal*, published after Diefenbaker's election as prime minister.

OTTAWA (CP) – The Progressive Conservative government plans to review the old Liberal administration's policy toward Canada's Eskimo population.

Generally speaking, the Liberal policy was aimed at introducing the Eskimo gradually to the 20th century so that he would eventually be able to fit into the white man's civilization.

... However, privately, some authorities on the Arctic argue that this policy is only destroying the Eskimo's self-reliance so that he will eventually become dependent almost entirely on the government.

... The objective might have been worthy, the dissenters say, but the method was wrong.

Instead, the Eskimos could have been brought south, especially the school-age ones. They could have been placed in schools in such a place as Churchill, Man., saving the large amounts of money spent on new schools in the Arctic.

In a generation, most of the Eskimo population could have been integrated into the Canadian scene. The United States was accomplishing just such a policy in Alaska.

The sooner he is integrated into the white population, the faster he can advance socially and economically. Otherwise, he will only remain on the fringes of the white man's northern camps doing menial jobs and being held in unhappy suspension between one world he does not understand and another in which he has lost his old skills to survive.[64]

Unlike earlier invasions, which involved largely coercive forces – whaling captains, fur traders, missionaries, led by soldiers and policemen – this invasion came directly from what might be called the 'ideological arm of the state.' It was an invasion of northern service officers (NSOs), welfare workers, and community development workers. With them would come state-employed teachers and medical staff. These people were hired to help the Inuit; preferably to help Inuit help themselves. People may have tried to escape this help – as appears to have been the case in the migrations to Whale Cove from Rankin Inlet and other attempts by scattered groups to return to the land – but buildings, medical aid, and food kept coming. These tied Inuit to specific locales. Furthermore, this material help was tied to helpers whose norms, precepts, and expectations were an obvious interference with Inuit ways of doing things.

Two groups of officials initiated the process of expanded intervention. One was the northern service officers, hired to coordinate government activities in northern communities. The others were welfare officers and social workers. A 1959 report described their roles in the following terms: 'Changes in their [Inuit] way of life are inevitably bringing problems to many Eskimo people. The task of guiding Eskimos during this difficult transition period falls upon an increasing staff of Northern Service Officers and trained Social Workers.'[65] The first group of six northern services officers were appointed by the Arctic division in February 1955. By December 1956, there were eleven NSOs, among them James Houston and Doug Wilkinson. By 1958-9, there were nineteen NSOs, with plans to add eight more in 1959-60.

In material prepared for the minister, the duties of the NSOs were described as follows:

> The Northern Service Officer takes a stand somewhere between the two societies to act as an interpreter of one culture to the other. Moving among the Eskimo people, he is expected to get to know them, to gain their confidence, respect, friendship and co-operation and to help them to help themselves. To accomplish this he assists the Eskimos in social and political development by organizing group effort and community life, encouraging broad participation in local decision and action and working toward responsible and articulate pulbic [*sic*] opinion.[66]

The role of northern service officers was consistent with a liberal humanitarian view that Inuit were entitled to and should have the same rights, privileges (and status) as non-Inuit Canadians, and to gain those rights they should adopt the values of non-Inuit citizens. In short, that they should be assimilated into the dominant Canadian society.

> We are confident that as the native people come to participate more actively in the economic development of their country, they will attain increasingly a sense of personal responsibility. Northern Service Officers can help these people adjust their thoughts and lives to the changes their culture is undergoing. Everyone with some knowledge of the situation agrees that the problems affecting the Eskimos are many and their solution is not simple. The objective of Government policy, however, is relatively easy to define: – to give the Eskimos the same rights, pribilegs [sic], opportunities and responsibilities as all other Canadians – in short, to enable them to play a real part in the national life of Canada.[67]

While economic development had initially been the rationale for the creation of NSO positions, it is apparent from the above quotation that political development came to be the major consideration. They were to control the process of developing Inuit control. An advertisement for the NSO positions in 1958 described them as offering 'a rare kind of challenge,' and noted that 'personal suitability was perhaps the most important qualification.' However, the job description clearly stressed leadership: 'a good mind, tact, patience, good judgement, backbone and spirit – all of these qualities will stand the NSO in good stead, but of all, leadership is possibly the most important to work amongst Eskimos and non-Eskimos alike.'[68] The NSOs were to foster leadership by being leaders.

Obviously, a great deal was expected of NSOs. Like Indian Agents, they had wide-ranging responsibilities. Unlike Indian Agents, however, they were not so closely tied to a specific legislative framework where land, and responsibility for Indian land in particular, defined much of the scope of activity. The NSO needed to have a variety of practical and human skills and be willing to endure what for most non-Natives would likely be seen as hardship and isolation.

The NSO was also expected to be an on-site coordinator of activities. Northern service officers were to 'endeavour to co-ordinate the activities of all field organizations with a view to making the greatest possible use of all resources available and to improving economic and living conditions among the Eskimos in the areas to which they are assigned.' The activities specifically mentioned were 'education, health measures, vocational

CIVIL SERVICE OF CANADA REQUIRES

NORTHERN SERVICE OFFICERS

for the
DEPARTMENT OF NORTHERN AFFAIRS AND NATIONAL RESOURCES

SALARY $4,500 TO $5,100

PLUS NORTHERN ALLOWANCE UP TO $2,100

IN NORTHERN ESKIMO COMMUNITIES TO:

- ADMINISTER ESKIMO AFFAIRS
- PROMOTE ECONOMIC AND SOCIAL DEVELOPMENT
- STIMULATE COMMUNITY ACTION

- UNIVERSITY GRADUATES PREFERRED
- PREVIOUS NORTHERN EXPERIENCE DESIRABLE BUT NOT ESSENTIAL

FOR DETAILS AND APPLICATIONS WRITE TO
CIVIL SERVICE COMMISSION, OTTAWA
QUOTING COMPETITION NO. 56-573
CLOSING DATE FOR ENQUIRIES APRIL 16, 1956

13/3/56

Figure 28 Advertisement for northern service officers in 1956. They were to coordinate development of newly emerging Inuit settlements. Their role, as described by the deputy minister at the time, was comparable to that of Canadian diplomats sent abroad.

training and direction in community living,' and it was noted that 'all of these require interest and active participation on the part of the Eskimos.' However, political development was, again, seen as crucial.

> It has been asked whether there are not already too many white men issuing orders to the Eskimos and whether the Northern Service Officer will be just one more. The remedy, however, does not lie in confining this kind of authority to one or two but rather in returning local authority and responsibility to the people. It would be rash to offer a blueprint. It will doubtless be necessary to proceed from trial to revision repeatedly, looking not to the day when the pattern will be set for all time, but to the time when revisions will be suggested by the Eskimos.[69]

Remember that this statement, 'It would be rash to offer a blueprint,' was being made as plans to relocate Inuit both further north and to the south were under way.

The initial concern around the position of northern service officer was the degree to which responsibilities would overlap with the RCMP, which was already responsible for coordinating and delivering the meagre social services available in the early 1950s. At the time the position was created in 1954, problems of jurisdiction arose. It was decided that 'responsibility for decisions in administrative matters which are the business of this department, rests with the Director of this branch or his local representative where there is one of the rank of northern service officer, sub-district administrator or district administrator. This applies to relief, welfare matters, Eskimo loans, family allowances, vocational training and employment of Eskimos etc.'[70]

Furthermore, the RCMP was to 'investigate and report upon all persons who may be in need of relief and make recommendations thereon to the appropriate officer as mentioned above for his decision. On patrol or in other emergency circumstances, the R.C.M.P. will naturally issue such relief as in their judgement is required.'[71] Despite its intentions, this left open the possibility of conflicts between northern service officers, social workers, and the RCMP, which was very much the case during the Baker Lake situation discussed in Chapter 6. Furthermore, as more field staff from various departments were placed in the North, and as the NSOs gained some northern experience, the vagueness of their role began to be felt.

During an 'Arctic Conference' in 1957, NSOs were the subject of much discussion. On the first day, the theme of which was 'Who's Who in the Arctic,' R.A.J. Phillips made the following remarks:

> The Northern Service Officer's job ... involved much more than Eskimo welfare. It included community development, responsibility for ethnic

relationships, and liaison with outside organizations contributing to economic expansion ... The Northern Service Officer should know everything going on in his community in order than [*sic*] he could report in a full and comprehensive way on the activities of his locality ... Specialists, such as the welfare officer, teacher, the Works and Services Officer, were responsible for their own particular spheres, but the Northern Service Officer was responsible for general problems.[72]

Much stress was placed on coordination of different staff. Though these other staff did not report through the NSO, they were expected to keep NSOs informed just as NSOs were expected to keep them informed. Doug Wilkinson, one of the most vocal of the NSOs, noted 'that the ideal of co-operation as expressed by earlier speakers was quite contrary to actual trends of thought now in many Arctic communities, where there was a tendency for individual officers to pursue their own interests without referring them to other departmental officers.'[73] Clearly, the old divisions between missionaries, traders, and police were being reproduced, only now they were between different factions and representatives within the state.

The second day of the conference was organized around the theme 'What's Wrong with the Division?' and the day began with another discussion of the NSO. In the opening address, Phillips summarized some of Gordon Robertson's views on the 'concept of the Northern Service Officer in relation to his colleagues.' Robertson, who had experience in both External Affairs and Citizenship and Immigration, 'used the analogy of a Canadian Diplomatic Mission abroad,' where there might be 'specialist officers' who were not part of External Affairs but nevertheless 'were part of the Mission, and bore certain responsibilities to the Head of the Mission.' This involved a change in the way NSOs were to be viewed and used. As Phillips described it:

> Mr. Robertson had said that he considered this analogy an almost exact one for the Arctic, and he thought it desirable now to define it in those terms ...
> It was essential, the Deputy Minister said, to have one representative of the department in each area finally responsible for all departmental activities and of departmental staff. This was a role he now wished to have Northern Service Officers or the designated departmental representative, play in the Arctic.[74]

This ideal was never quite realized. NSOs continued as one of many personnel in a rapidly expanding northern service. In some communities, they would exercise an overseeing authority, while in others they found themselves in conflict with other officers.

Figure 29 The first Arctic Conference of Northern Service Officers in 1957.
Seated (left to right) are A.J. Baker, R.L. Kennedy, D.B. Wilkinson, O.W.P. Farley,
J.J. Bond, W.G. Kerr, R.A. Hodgkinson, and A.F. Flucke. Standing (left to right) are
J.G. Walton, J.W. Evans, R.J. Green, B.J. Saunders. Northern service officers were
hired, commencing in 1956, by the Arctic division of the Department of Northern
Affairs and National Resources.

The talk through these papers is of NSOs as 'men,' and men occupied all
of the NSO positions in this period. The 1958 advertisement was quite
specific on this point: 'The competition to select NSO's is open to male
applicants.'[75] A letter written in 1957 by R.A.J. Phillips to fourteen field
staff, titled 'The Ladies,' deals with the question of spousal roles. It begins,
'A wise man would probably not seek to define the role of ladies in the
north, or particularly the wives of our officers. There are, however, some
general considerations which seem to be fairly well established.' The letter
goes on:

Whether or not we have made it clear in the past – and we probably haven't
– we really do expect the ladies to make a contribution to our work ... From
all we have read of Dorothy Dix, we understand that the role of wives is to
help their husbands in their work and we are also hopeful that in the north
the ladies themselves will be so caught up in the enthusiasm and sense of
mission of the task, that they themselves will wish to help. And the ladies

do help. It is not just through long hours of studying cook books that they are able to keep their mates happy, and it is not just through memorization of the principles of Dale Carnegie that they have been able to master that certain smile when a husband returns from his long day at the office, or with a sick friend.[76]

Clearly, Phillips and other staff within the Arctic division accepted a dominant patriarchal cultural bias. Of concern here is not so much how this led them to subordinate their own spousal partners, a subject of concern to broader feminist history and social analysis, but how this image or construction of gender roles informed the projects they developed for Inuit, who had another cultural frame and a vastly different conception of the gender division of labour. Although there was a clear division of labour – though Inuit valued flexibility and the division may not have been unyeilding – it is arguable that Inuit had far more egalitarian gender relations than Western societies. Regarding the southern administrator's views, one example among many: A report on plans for 1959 notes that 'increasing emphasis has been placed on training Eskimo girls in domestic sciences and household economics.'[77] The attitude towards non-Native female spousal partners was extended and applied to Inuit women.

The NSO – always a man – was paid for his work. His wife, it appears, was expected to assist him in ways beyond 'mastering that certain smile' for no remuneration. The letter from Phillips to his field staff continues:

They actively help in a community. This is what we like to see and, if you will forgive us for being frank, this is what we have come to expect. For example, wives sometimes take an active part in developing a project such as sewing handicrafts for Eskimo women. In many places this sort of thing does not apply, but they may do excellent work merely by having the women of the community in for tea and gossip. Real progress in the development of satisfactory ethnological relations can be made by such simple devices.[78]

One wonders how Phillips might have defined 'satisfactory ethnological relations.' The women's reward for such work, other than through 'the provision of housing, as well as by those frightfully generous allowances'[79] – which were, incidentally, provided to single men as well – was to be relatively intangible.

Sometimes – not necessarily in our service – wives have had crashing ideas for work that they would like to do, and the people back in Ottawa are very pleased until they notice the price tag. So perhaps we had better clear up this matter of price tags now. Clear departmental policy on which we have recently sought and been given written instructions does not allow us to pay wives for the work which they might do in the Arctic except in a few rather rare and clearly defined circumstances.[80]

These circumstances are, effectively, 'when we ask her, for the sake of the service, to accept an established position which would otherwise have to be filled. The only such positions which have ever occurred, and which are likely to occur, are jobs as teachers and nurses.' Fortunately, Phillips noted, the wives could depend on other compensations for their work: 'It will make their life more interesting. It will give them a feeling of satisfaction, and it may well help their husbands in their work and in their careers.' Noting that 'we are not trying to recruit slave labour,' Phillips concluded with the memorable lines, 'next payday when we Ottawa bureaucrats can enjoy our semi-monthly glass of beer, we shall drink a toast to the previously unsung ladies who are helping the north and us. God bless them.'[81] Patriarchy, in its 1950s suburban modality, was the order of the day, and it was entrenched in the values of the social actors as well as in the administrative and social structures those actors were constructing and were placed in.

With the election of the Diefenbaker government in 1957 and the expansion of the northern administration, NSOs were increasingly joined by social workers and welfare officers. As noted, this process was started with the appointment of Walter Rudnicki, late in 1955, as chief of the welfare section of the Arctic division. By December of that year, he had a staff of two in addition to two social workers. The welfare section 'alone or in collaboration with other organizations, as required, develops and administers welfare programs for Eskimos. Welfare establishments at selected northern sites are operating or planned as one step in the overall program to help the Eskimo people, whenever necessary, to adjust to a changed existence.'[82] At the first meeting of the Committee on Eskimo Affairs he attended in May 1956, Rudnicki tabled a report explaining the field of social welfare. The report discussed the different activities of the welfare section and the role of welfare in general.

Many of the problems that are now being handled in our own communities by means of welfare programs are beginning to emerge in the north. Eskimos particularly are vulnerable to the impact our civilization is having on them. They need many of the welfare services which we now take for granted in our own communities. These services are needed to ensure as much as possible their continuing physical well-being, their adjustment to changing times, and to contribute to any plan or project which will keep them self-supporting and contented.[83]

Rudnicki's definition, given the focus in the department on 'relief' and its fatal result – 'indigence' – is both enlightened and expansive. The most dramatic difference was the equation of Inuit welfare with the welfare needs of society in general: it was not some inherent laziness on the part of Inuit that led to a reliance of social support. Rather, this was part of a need 'which we now take for granted in our own communities.'

Much of the early work of the welfare section was focused on Inuit patients in southern sanatoriums. Contrary to Dr. Moore's opinion that the 450 Inuit patients in southern Canada in 1954 represented a peak in numbers and that these rates of hospitalization would decline thereafter, the rate of hospitalization continued to increase. In 1958, Rudnicki reported that 'from 800 to 1,000 Eskimo patients were admitted yearly to southern hospitals, mostly in Ontario, Manitoba and Alberta.'[84] A report by Phillips in 1959 noted that 'roughly 8% of the Eskimo population [is] now in tuberculosis sanatoria in southern Canada.'[85] By 1961, the death rate from tuberculosis – with the help of Western medical practices – had declined from 173 per 100,000 population to 76 per 100,000, but the number of new active cases continued to climb.[86] In many cases, this reflected the terrible housing conditions experienced by Inuit who were being moved into settlements and who were taking up residence in one-room prefabricated plywood 'boxes' – known, in fact, as 'matchboxes.' Without running water, proper ventilation, or windows, they exacerbated the serious problem of tuberculosis already present in Arctic settlements. Thus, the move to settlements was actually accompanied by a rise in the rate of occurrence of the disease. The decline in those being hospitalized in southern sanatoriums, projected by Dr. Moore in 1954, would finally take place almost a decade later: 'In 1956, 1,600 Eskimos were in hospitals in southern Canada. Now [1962] there are only about 350.'[87]

In his first report to the Committee on Eskimo Affairs in 1956, Rudnicki dwelt at length on services provided to Inuit patients. These included everything from organizing correspondence between family and friends to establishing rehabilitation centres at Frobisher Bay and Aklavik for Inuit considered 'too disabled to return to the rigours of their former life in the Arctic.'[88] The ideology of helping Inuit to help themselves extended to these rehabilitation centres, where 'the programme will encourage qualities of self-determination and self-help in the Eskimo and it will condition them to a new set of social and economic relationships.'[89] Given Rudnicki's perception that 'there are two aspects to any welfare programme: the economic, which is aimed at man's physical well-being, and the social, which is directed at man's personal adjustment,'[90] problems of jurisdiction were inevitable. The NSOs had a broad but vague field of concern; the social workers and welfare officers had overlapping concerns.

An exchange of memoranda in October 1958 illustrates how factious and divisive the conflicts that emerged could be. On 9 October, R.A.J. Phillips wrote to Sivertz to complain about Rudnicki's perceptions of the northern welfare service. Rudnicki responded directly to Phillips the next day. Each memorandum provides a detailed analysis of the role of welfare services. Phillips took particular umbrage at Rudnicki's suggestion that one of the functions of the Northern Welfare Service (NWS) was 'facilitating the transition of groups of Eskimos to a wage economy.' Phillips argued that the policy of the Arctic division had never been to 'delegate to the welfare service the responsibility for diversification of the Eskimo economy, for introducing cash income, for facilitating the transition to a wage economy.'[91] As will become clear, this was the basic difference between Phillips and Rudnicki.

One of the practical difference they discussed in this exchange focused on roles and responsibility for the Keewatin Re-establishment Project.[92] On the broader issue, Phillips wrote:

The NWS is an advisory body designed to provide the administration with counsel on the treatment of group and individual social problems under the general lines of policy which the administration must set. Within the lines of accepted policy, to the NWS is delegated direct responsibility for the administration of a number of services, e.g. rehabilitation of the handicapped through institutions or individually, family guidance, child placement, casework services, certain workshop facilities; this list is not exclusive. In addition, the NWS will be asked to give advice on major plans involving social and economic readjustment of groups and individuals, and it may, on an ad hoc basis, be asked to assume direct administrative responsibility for certain aspects of such programmes. On the other hand, the NWS will emphatically not be made responsible for the future treatment of all social problems in the north, nor will it be responsible for all social and economic readjustment in the north. The role of the northern administration will not be confined to the provision of clerical services to the NWS.[93]

Clearly, the expansion of the welfare service had touched a nerve.

In an interview with Rudnicki in 1990, he spoke in general terms about how his efforts to meet the enormous social welfare challenges in the North were perceived by some in the administration as bureaucratic empire-building. This exchange of memorandums must have been one of the incidents he had on his mind.

At the time of these events, he provided a detailed response to Phillips that contains more than one memorable metaphor: 'We are now somewhat in the position of a man on the street being reprimanded by the fire department for putting out a fire before they got there with their shiny new equipment.'[94] He also gave a fairly substantial analysis of the role of his section in October 1958. On the question of economic responsibilities, Rudnicki noted that 'over the past year, Northern Welfare Services have organized and are operating a marketing arrangement and a network of cottage industries in the eastern Arctic was well as a number of Eskimo-operated enterprises,' adding that 'the impact of this programme has been to do those very things that you say we should not be doing. Do we pack up shop now?'[95] He also pointed to the activities of the welfare departments in Newfoundland and Saskatchewan, noting that they were also involved in economic affairs. On Phillips's suggestion that welfare services take an advisory role, Rudnicki wrote:

> The treatment of group and individual social problems is recognized by the [Civil Service] Commission, by the Professional Institute of the Civil Service, and by professional organizations in this country and abroad as being within the competence of persons who have earned degrees in social work. If the Department relegates Northern Welfare Services to the role of an advisory body to administration and takes away from it responsibility for treatment, it follows logically that the same principle would hold for teachers, doctors and others concerned with particular areas of endeavour in the north. It will be very difficult to recruit persons from jobs where they have treatment responsibilities to a job where this role is denied them.[96]

Rudnicki goes on to list some of the activities of the NWS at the time, which included a hospital services program, establishment of transit centres across the Arctic, creation of an 'Eskimo Index,' a correspondence system, a child welfare program, a program of case finding and job placement, a pilot rehabilitation program, and the introduction of medical social services to accompany the medical survey.

He concludes by noting that 'at this early stage in the evolution of the Department's role in the north, there is a formidable amount of sorting out to be done in functions, responsibilities and policies.' A note of resentment crept in: 'I very much regret what appears to be an attempt to play down the value and deny recognition to an organization which has aspired to excellence in the service it has provided to the Department which created it.' Still in a very bitter tone, Rudnicki went on to recognize the limitations of his profession: 'If we sometimes speak with certainty, we do so not out of arrogance but with the security of a profession which has given us some knowledge and a few tools to understand and handle the complex social problems you refer to.' He adds, 'We are not infallible and, unlike doctors, we cannot bury our mistakes.'[97]

This exchange illustrates the degree to which the expansion of the Arctic division was creating conflict, along with mutual suspicions and jealousies. In fact, the power of southern bureaucrats was commensurate with the number of personnel in each section. It is not surprising that social workers and northern service officers stumbled into each other at the community level: their superiors were firing memorandums across each other's desks as if they were cannon shots. Rudnicki's role in these expanding services is contradictory. He played a generally progressive role in developing an enlightened welfare policy that ended an era of neglect. His endorsement of the misguided southern relocation scheme is more in tune with the assimilationist attitudes that dominated Canadian culture at the time and are still a crucial part of Canadian culture and government policy. Two attitudes came to dominate northern adminstration: those of a traditional colonial elite and those of a new generation who had placed the friendly face of liberal reform on older patterns of colonialism and assimilation. The extraordinary expansion of the bureaucracy that took place in the late 1950s only served to exacerbate the tensions between them.

Some insight into how the new field staff, NSOs, and social workers were going about helping Inuit to help themselves is provided by an undated (probably 1959) document titled 'Common Eskimo Phrases.' These were the expressions, translated into Inuktitut, that fieldworkers were most in need of in their work with Inuit. Of the thirty-five phrases translated, thirty-four are direct commands. The first phrase and only non-command is, 'I want to see the Doctor because I am sick,' a phrase of great utility given that there were almost no doctors in any Arctic communities at that time. The next few phrases are 'wash the floor,' 'sweep the floor,' 'fill up the oil tanks,' 'clear the snow away from the porches,' followed by 'haul some gas,' 'see your supervisor,' 'clean out the basins,' 'fill the barrel,' 'remove the rocks from the road,' 'your help is needed,' 'make some urinals out of snow,' 'wait here,' 'ask your supervisor,' and the like.[98] This was hardly a list designed to promote self-sufficiency and leadership skills, the stated goals of the northern field staff. Questions like 'What do you think?' are noticeably absent.

An interesting exchange took place at the Arctic Conference of 1957 during a discussion lead by Rudnicki on Welfare in the New Economy. The subject for the day – the fifth session of the conference – was The Future of the North, and the particular exchange dealt with some of the possible side-effects of expanding the mechanisms for delivering social services. The exchange began with Rudnicki noting that 'at present the Welfare Officer was a generalist, concerned with a wide variety of activities. In future he would become more of a specialist in such things as child welfare.' Northern Service Officer Doug Wilkinson responded: 'During this period of massive government activity, it is easy to forget the many other agencies which have carried out welfare work in the past and will continue to do so.' An exchange followed between Ruth Lor, a guest attendee from the Student Christian Movement, J.J. Bond, another northern service officer, and R.J. Green, superintendent of the rehabilitation centre at Frobisher Bay.

Miss Lor asked how the Eskimos had taken care of their welfare problems before the advent of the white man. Mr. Bond replied that this had been done on a kinship basis. Miss Lor said that we might be destroying this kind of community responsibility by providing an alternative. Mr. Green said that the changing economy and society was of course breaking down the solidarity of kinship associations and that this was inevitable. The Eskimos were being faced with new problems and we must provide help and guidance to him in his efforts to solve them. At Frobisher, families do not know about each other, even if they are closely related. In areas or situations where there is any possibility of community solutions we should not offer help. Miss Lor asked if they don't come to us merely because there is now an alternative to community solution. Mr. Green said that the policy of giving something for nothing was not an aspect of modern work and that at no time should we provide easy solutions to difficult problems. The Eskimo was entitled to face his problems and solve them with help.[99]

This last statement from Green embodies all of the contradictions of the new policies. Inuit would be 'allowed' to 'face their own problems and solve them with help.' The 'inevitability' of historical processes leading to the breakdown of kinship relations was taken for granted. Meanwhile, as Lor pointed out, those employed to mitigate the effects of this breakdown were, in most cases with the best of intentions, actively contributing to that inevitability. The legacy of neglect from the 1940s had been discredited; any policy of enlightened non-interference could not be contemplated. It had been replaced by policies with their own implications for the health and welfare of northern people and Inuit culture.

Green continued the discussion, with Northern Service Officer Kerr, D.E. De Bow from the Department of Transport, and Dr. J.S. Willis of National Health and Welfare adding their comments.

This was a necessary part of social maturing. This course was difficult for the Eskimo and for the persons engaged in helping him. An easier solution was for the white man to make the decision. However, this course was the only means by which the Eskimo can come into full participation in the affairs of the community and country. Mr. De Bow asked if the normal culture of the camps was breaking down, due to the effects of economic change and the presence of Northern Service Officers and others in the government service. Mr. Kerr replied that adjacent to DEW Line sites and other areas of economic development and change the normal patterns were breaking down, but that in areas less touched the traditional patterns were being maintained to a considerable degree. Dr. Willis added that there was a general tendency away from nomadism and into consolidated communities.[100]

This was a general tendency being promoted through almost every fibre of government policy. Furthermore, many non-Native 'helpers' were doing exactly as Green suggested: making crucial decisions for Inuit.

The northern service officers, welfare officers, and social workers – like the teachers, nurses, community development workers, researchers, and students to follow in the early 1960s – did address terrible problems the Inuit had inherited from a long and troubled history of association with the trapping economy, missionary activity, militarism, and the introduction of non-Native diseases. At the same time, their generally assimilationist attitudes did much to confuse Inuit cultural practices, family traditions, and cosmologies. And their very presence meant a whole new layer of outside interference in the lives of Inuit. That is to say, the presence of these 'experts,' dominated by the idea that integration with the dominant values and practices of Canadian culture was inevitable and essential, placed a colonial (or neo-colonial) non-Inuit decision-making elite on the ground in virtually each Inuit community. However, the expanded intervention, combined with the tenacity with which Inuit continued to express their cultural preferences, eventually contributed to the creation of new structures that gave Inuit a voice – even if it was not always a voice the state wanted to hear.

Finishing the Feud over Family Allowances
The conflicts and contradictions that emerged in this period are also illustrated by the ongoing feud over family allowances and how they were to be paid to Inuit recipients – in goods or by cheque. This particular conflict was a long-standing one, dating back to debates held at the time the policy was initiated in 1945. By the mid-1950s, the battle was still proving to be long and difficult. At a meeting of the Committee on Eskimo Affairs on 29 November 1954, Ben Sivertz advanced the idea that payment of family allowances be made to all Inuit in the Northwest Territories by cheque.[101] No agreement was reached on whether this was a good idea, and the committee referred the matter for further study. The battle to get family allowance paid to Inuit in the same form it was paid to other Canadians was to be a persistent cause of both Ben Sivertz and Walter Rudnicki throughout their tenure with the department.

By 1956, the matter was still unresolved. Some in the department, like

Sivertz and Rudnicki, argued that the practice of making payment in kind was paternalistic and not likely to assist Inuit in managing their own affairs. Others had different ideas. At the seventh meeting of the Committee on Eskimo Affairs, a Mr. Blais, the assistant national director of the family allowances and old age security division of National Health and Welfare, spoke strongly against any move to make a payment by cheque.

> Mr. Blais reminded the Committee that the main purpose of family allowances was for assistance to the children. It should be used wisely, he said, and not be used as a means for Eskimos to learn to handle their own money. He went on to say that when paying it in kind, we can be sure it is used for milk and baby foods. He preferred that no cheques should be issued for family allowances but credit given at posts, which gave us greater control of the issues.[102]

F.J. Cunningham, the director of the Northern Administration and Lands Branch, clearly did not share Sivertz's ideas about payment by cheque. He indicated his full support for Blais's position. Thus it appears that while National Health and Welfare was initially not enthusiastic about family allowances being used as a means-tested welfare system, they had no objections to it being issued in kind so the government could keep track of what Inuit were receiving for their money.

By 1958, things had changed. Cunningham was gone as director of the Northern Administration and Lands Branch and had been replaced by Sivertz. Between them, Sivertz and Rudnicki moved quickly to change the department's policies respecting family allowances. At the ninth meeting of the Committee on Eskimo Affairs in May 1958, Rudnicki noted that family allowances were being paid by cheque to some families at Aklavik, Churchill, Rankin Inlet, and Frobisher Bay. He stated the intention of the department to introduce, as quickly as possible, a system for paying all family allowances by cheque.[103]

In a meeting with National Health and Welfare in October 1958, Walter Rudnicki indicated that the department wished to have family allowances paid to Inuit by cheque effective 1 April 1959.[104] When asked by Health and Welfare for his opinion on how family allowances should be handled, Henry Larsen, the RCMP's commanding officer in the Arctic division, responded by producing field officers' reports that dealt with some of the problems they reportedly encountered in administering the allowance system. Larsen was definitely of the 'old school,' and this was well known to those within the department.

Knowing that Larsen had warned Health and Welfare not to make family allowance payments by cheque, Ben Sivertz sent a memo to his deputy minister on 19 June 1959 warning him of Larsen's attitude and pointing out the mindset the administration was up against.

> As you know, the thinking in 'G' Division which thoroughly permeates the RCMP, both in Ottawa and in the field, is based on passive resistance to change and a devotion to a rather idyllic picture of Eskimo life as it once existed. Although Superintendent Larsen is one of the main authors of this outlook, it is far deeper than any single person. It arises from Police training and outlook and it would be wrong of us to assume that there will be any rapid change in it until the RCMP makes it the main requirement in the recruitment of Police to have administrators and social scientists, with a broad background in human and community problems.
>
> ... Rarely are there cases of direct sabotage of Government policy, but there is a widespread passive resistance which, from time to time, becomes vocal in the communities concerned. The result is confusion, misdirection and lack of confidence in Government policies.[105]

Sivertz went on to suggest that the police be relieved of their administrative responsibilities and that these be handed over to people with the education, training, and experience to accept them.[106]

On 18 June 1959, Gordon Robertson, deputy minister of northern affairs and national resources, took it upon himself to write Dr. G.F. Davidson, deputy minister of national health and welfare, inquiring about the delay in dealing with the issue. He commented on the presence of four Inuit at the recently held Committee on Eskimo Affairs meeting, discussed in detail below, and said he was 'especially struck with the two-fold impression that Eskimos want to have a voice in deciding their own destinies, and they want no avoidable delay in education and other opportunity for their people. They were particularly vocal on laws and administrative decisions which tended to set the Eskimos apart and suggested a special – and inferior – citizenship for them.'[107] Not to be outdone, Davidson replied that he had perused the minutes of the meeting to which Robertson referred and could find no reference to any comments about discrimination and the administration of family allowances. He stated: 'This might suggest that those concerned with Eskimo affairs in your Department are somewhat more concerned about the discrimination involved in the present family allowance arrangements than are the spokesmen of the Eskimo themselves.'[108]

The position taken by National Health and Welfare was based, in part, on information they had received from the RCMP in the field and from Henry Larsen. These sources were cited by a 'Miss N. O'Brian,' the regional director of family allowances, in an exhaustive memo sent to Blais, the national director, on 29 October 1959. In it she expressed admiration for Henry

Larsen and his opinions on what should be done about the allowances.[109]

The issue of payment was finally resolved in 1960 by a compromise. At Walter Rudnicki's suggestion, a triage system was put in place whereby family allowance administrators in each community would deal with the payment of the allowance. The system involved categorizing families receiving cheques. In the first instance, cheques were to be mailed directly to recipients. In the second category, cheques were to be mailed to the administrator who would then hand them over to the family. In the third instance, the cheque would be paid to the administrator who would manage the funds in trust for the child in question.

The system was devised to get around fears expressed by Health and Welfare, and confirmed by the RCMP, that Inuit were, in many cases, incapable of managing their own affairs; that simply handing over the money would result in the purchase of useless 'luxury items' and that children would not benefit. In countering these arguments, Rudnicki advanced his idea of 'guided integration' or administered self-reliance.

> There is even more alarming evidence in the growth of attitudes amongst non-Eskimos in the North that the Eskimo cannot be trusted to handle his own affairs. Perhaps one of the greatest problems of the north is the prevalence of those who want to *do* things for the Eskimo. The tuktu (caribou) may be diminishing, but the do-gooder flourishes. They scrutinize his savings (without his permission), they arrange his spending (without his understanding), they control his Family Allowances (without his help). The tragedy of all this is, of course, that the Eskimo takes less and less part in his own affairs and becomes more and more dependent upon the help we thrust upon him.
>
> ... Guidance is indeed required. But guidance and control are not synonymous. We can guide, and thus prepare the Eskimo to administer his own responsibilities. We cannot control his affairs and expect other than complete dependence.[110]

From the colonial isolationism that dominated federal policy in the early 1940s, the Arctic administration had moved towards a policy of guided integration of Inuit into Canadian society and economy. In case there was any doubt, the notice sent to parents about the change in family allowance policy made it clear: 'Remember that the changes have been made because the people have shown themselves to be wise when they spend money. Guard this wisdom and you will guard your children.'[111]

Towards Inuit Control of Inuit Affairs

The tenth meeting of the Committee on Eskimo Affairs was a watershed in

Arctic history. In attendance, along with the usual representatives of various government departments and non-governmental agencies in the North, were Prime Minister John Diefenbaker and Alvin Hamilton, minister of northern affairs and renewable resources. This signalled the importance that the Conservative government was attaching to northern development, as expressed by its Roads to Resources policy. More important, for the first time, Inuit delegates were present: Abraham Okpik from Aklavik, George Koneak from Fort Chimo, and John Ayaruark and Shingituk, both from Rankin Inlet. Virtually all the key actors in Arctic affairs in the 1950s, Robertson, Sivertz, Phillips, Bolger, Stevenson, Rudnicki, Snowden, Rowley, and Valentine, were present for the occasion. Rudnicki's team from the welfare division included Inuit staff members Mary Panegoosho and Elijah Menarik. The meeting was open to the public, and Farley Mowat had a ring-side seat.

Minutes from this meeting reveal all the previously outlined contradictions and conflicts embodied in government policy. The presence of Inuit delegates indicated the tensions and dynamics that would govern policy over the next decade. The meeting began with ceremonial speeches by Diefenbaker and Hamilton. Hamilton began his introductory remarks 'with a greeting in the Eskimo language,' while Diefenbaker, calling the meeting 'an historic occasion,' welcomed the Eskimo delegation and said it was 'his firm hope that this would be only the beginning of developments that would see the Eskimo people participating more and more in everything connected with their affairs.'[112]

The Inuit delegates took quite different approaches to their involvement. Okpik was the most outspoken, intervening at some point on almost every issue of discussion. Koneak and Shingituk confined themselves to short statements on specific community needs. Ayaruark spoke only twice, both times when asked, but his second speech was very long (slightly over one full page of the thirteen-page minutes is devoted to it) and dealt with broad issues. Ayaruark also sent a substantial list of corrections to the speech as it was recorded in the minutes, which was then appended to them.

The first order of business was 'The Voice of the Eskimo' and focused on the creation of community councils. Deputy Minister Robertson began by commenting 'on the potential usefulness of the continuing attendance of Eskimo representatives at Eskimo Affairs Committee meetings in the years ahead' and added that 'just as important as their participation in this meeting was the participation by Eskimos in many Arctic settlements in the affairs of their own communities.'[113] Bolger, administrator of the Arctic, reported that the community councils were 'giving opportunities for the Eskimo voice at the local level ... Two of these objectives were to stimulate among the Eskimos an awareness of their Canadian citizenship and to help a sense of initiative among the people.' He continued:

> With the encouragement of the Northern Service Officers, effective Eskimo councils had been set up in several Arctic communities, including Baker Lake, Cape Dorset, Sugluk, and Cambridge Bay. In several other communities such as Great Whale River, Eskimo councils were being either established or reorganized. The organization of the councils had varied to meet local conditions, but everywhere the aim had been to bring together the people of the community to discuss mutual problems. In areas relatively unaffected by civilization, the councillors, with the aid of local Northern Service Officers, had discussed such matters as game conservation and techniques for the better harvesting of country resources. Where the effects of southern civilization were more evident, matters pertaining to employment and to adjustment to a new way of life were more likely to be discussed.[114]

Bolger thought that 'the response from Eskimos to the idea of councils had been encouraging and in general the experiment had been a success.' He also 'stressed that Northern Service Officers were encouraged to withdraw as soon as possible from a leading part in Eskimo councils; where possible, the members were encouraged to conduct their own meetings.'

Interestingly, both Inuit members who responded at this point were not so glowing; in fact, they were decidedly lukewarm in their reactions. Koneak, 'who had participated in the official visit of Canadian Eskimos to Greenland in 1958, agreed that council meetings were worthwhile to Canadian Eskimos in this and other respects; he considered Greenland was far in advance of the Canadian Arctic.' Danish policy probably represented the most viable, practical alternative to Canadian policy in the area of Inuit affairs and, in stark contrast to the Canadian approach, led to the relatively rapid development of Greenlandic self-governing institutions.

Okpik said 'he was familiar with the work of the Eskimo council at Aklavik, but he felt that it was not accomplishing much. He pointed out that from time to time council members had written letters to the Department outlining problems faced by the council, but without results.' Sivertz responded to this, saying that 'the Department would look into the matter of whether or not it had failed to assist the Aklavik Council with its requests. He wondered if there were not problems in Aklavik which the local council might solve locally.'[115] In their first comments, the Inuit representatives had quickly cut through the atmosphere of ceremonial goodwill and cordial self-congratulation, putting the department on the defensive.

This exchange sparked a discussion of whether the councils were to deal with local matters or whether they were to lobby government. Bishop Marsh thought that 'Eskimo councils should be designed to permit Eskimos to think out their own problems on their own time,' while Robertson observed that 'it was hoped that councils would act on local problems, but they were also free to refer matters to Ottawa.' Father Renaud, OMI, 'thought that if Eskimo councillors were to learn to manage their own affairs, then this learning process would be largely the responsibility of Northern Service Officers and other non-Eskimos in Arctic communities.' He added 'that instead of purely Eskimo councils, it might be advisable to have Eskimos and non-Eskimos serving together on community councils.' Robertson responded to this by pointing 'out that the problems faced by Eskimo councils are often complex and therefore, the councillors needed some guidance. At the same time, he agreed care must be taken not to push councillors to decisions.'[116] These discussions make it clear that Inuit were to be guided towards a point at which they could exercise control, but that the structures created along the way – not to mention the values exercised within those structures – were to correspond to the non-Inuit ideal of liberal democratic and responsible government. Thus, as soon as Inuit mastered the workings of a non-Inuit system, they could take it over.

Okpik responded to Robertson's comments by stressing education: 'If Eskimos were to conduct their council meetings in accordance with the accepted ways of the white man, then they must first be educated to understand and use them.' The phrase 'accepted ways of the white man' is key here: Okpik presumably understood that Inuit could run councils in Inuit fashion without difficulty. Sivertz agreed with Okpik that education was 'of prime importance, but did not think it was necessary to wait until the Eskimos were educated before going ahead with the formation of councils.' He also agreed with Father Renaud that 'mixed community councils composed of Eskimo and non-Eskimo members were desirable.' Okpik again responded, noting that 'progress in council work could be made at the present educational level. He went on to say that at joint meetings of Eskimos and non-Eskimos at Aklavik, Eskimo representatives were often obliged to sit back and listen to others.'[117] This is a telling remark, emphasizing the degree to which Inuit voices were being actively silenced in the structures being developed to promote them. The discussion of Inuit councils ended on a benign note. Robertson reiterated that 'while Eskimo councils should be encouraged to refer problems to Ottawa when necessary, the main object of councils should be the encouragement of local initiative and local action' and the committee 'agreed that the continuation of Eskimo councils should be encouraged.'[118] Inuit issues and concerns remained unaddressed.

A discussion of 'The Changing Economy' followed, during which

Figure 30 Rankin Inlet in 1962. The mining shaft can be seen in the background, and housing for the mine employees appears in the foreground.

Ayaruark and Shingituk commented that 'the Eskimo workmen were pleased with conditions at the [Rankin Inlet Nickel] mine,' though Shingituk would return to this topic later. A. Easton, manager of the Rankin Inlet Nickel Mine, was present. Both Okpik and Koneak, at different points, stressed the need for better vocational and agricultural training. Okpik responded to some comments about relief with this statement:

> The last thing the Eskimo people wanted was relief. They wanted work and not handouts. Eskimos were willing to try their hand at projects if the government would help them get started. In the Aklavik area, there was room for projects in such fields as handicrafts, mink farming, lumber and fishing. Too often in the past Eskimos who wanted to work had been obliged to go on relief. If relief became necessary, then work relief projects should be initiated. As the Eskimo population increased, the incidents of relief seemed likewise to increase, and Mr. Okpik asked whether it was intended to make idlers out of the Eskimo people or to make them productive citizens.[119]

This probably warmed the hearts of many within and outside of the Arctic administration. But Okpik's more important point seems to be that he was not in the South to demand more relief. Inuit wanted to be contributors to whatever development would be taking place in their homeland.

Discussion turned to housing before coming to the next item on the agenda, 'The Changing Society.' Rudnicki began with a report on rehabilitation centres in the North, and Robertson called on Ayaruark 'to comment on social problems.' Ayaruark responded with a lengthy speech. He began 'by thanking the Government for the help it had given his people.' He then expressed concern over hospitalization, noting that 'frequently families were worried because they received no news of their loved ones for long periods of time. He added that it was unfortunate that sick persons were obliged to travel so far for treatment. His comments quoted at the outset of this chapter, about being 'over-shadowed' by those in authority, followed, and he expressed more thoughts on the same question, which significantly linked political control to relocation.

It happens sometimes that Eskimos agreed to be transferred elsewhere not because they want to but because destitution forces them to accept the offer made to them of transferring them elsewhere. Referring specifically to Rankin Inlet, Mr. Ayaruark described it as a settlement populated by people from many scattered places, speaking different dialects, some of whom, particularly from inland Keewatin, were confused and unsettled by their new environment. He pointed out that, like the white man, the Eskimo had his own ideas about what he wanted to do with his life and his homeland, and the wishes of the Eskimo people should be respected. Many people, like himself, had come to Rankin Inlet of their own accord and had come to feel at home there.[120]

The message in this statement is clear. Relocation was something about which Inuit were concerned. The Inuit perspective on relocation was based on paying more than lip service to an Inuit right of self-determination. Ayaruark had raised the issue of the right of Inuit to exercise control over their own destiny, revealing that relocation and political control, at least for Ayaruark, were linked.

Ayaruark went on to comment on how Inuit 'now were obliged to eat strange foods from southern Canada,' some of which 'had no strength in it.' At this point he made an interesting practical suggestion for the integration of wage and traditional economies.

He called for an organization to be set up along co-operative lines whereby people of the community who were free to hunt would be able to provide food for the wage-employed. At the same time, the skills of the employed could in turn produce goods for the benefit of the hunters. This would call for some form of two way marketing arrangement. At the present time, wage-employed Eskimos were sometimes absent from their jobs while hunting for country food. This disturbed their employers. The people wanted to know how to organize their lives in order both to hunt and to work. Now some of the people were confused and despondent simply because they did not know what was expected of them. This despondency was sometimes mistaken for laziness but it could be removed by a practical arrangement whereby men of the community could live together and decide who should play what part in providing 'those things considered good.'[121]

Inuit did not seem to need the lessons on how to live cooperatively that NSOs were so eager to provide. Ayaruark's plan was for a much closer, cooperative community than anything contemplated by southern planners and northern fieldworkers. Of course, crucial to this plan was a need to have Inuit 'decide who should play what part,' something the overanxious intervenors felt better qualified to determine. Inuit apparently had to be taught how to make decisions first.

The rest of Ayaruark's speech dealt with a variety of social problems. On education, he suggested 'that teachers should exercise patience and understanding in dealing with the children, for they could not learn if they lived in fear of the teachers' anger.' He also spoke about drinking problems, suggesting 'if Eskimos are to be allowed to drink, only one place should be selected for this purpose and it should be absolutely prohibited to bring liquor home.' Ayaruark was concerned about 'the desirability of reuniting families that had been separated for one reason or another' and suggested that 'if some way could be found to bring such families together the men would do better work because their minds would be free from worry about their families.' He talked about 'the vanishing caribou,' noting that 'Eskimos who still followed the old ways believed that they could not do so much longer. They believed that the old ways must go and a new kind of life must be found.' He observed 'that since he had come to Ottawa he had seen how people lived in the south and believed the Eskimo people were capable of living in this same way, for it was not a way of life reserved exclusively for the white man,' adding 'the time had come for a change, and it could not be a slow change because there was nothing to support the people while the change took place. The change must be made now.'[122]

He concluded by discussing his own community, Rankin Inlet. He was concerned 'with the need for better facilities for hunting in the Rankin Inlet area. He said the hunters needed a larger boat because while there was game, the distances to be travelled to find it were very great. He said that with the help of the Administration the hunters at Rankin Inlet could work out a successful way of life.'[123] Thus, while he talked of adopting southern standards, in practical terms he recommended measures for improving life on the land. On the whole, this speech could be read as a virtual manifesto, showing a clear sense of the basic problems and both practically oriented as well as philosophically reflective suggestions about what had to be done. The other Inuit delegates who subsequently spoke argued in favour of Inuit 'old ways.'

Robertson responded primarily to the narrow issues raised by Ayaruark, focusing on liquor ordinances and the development of 'new and improved procedures' for helping families communicate with hospitalized members. Discussion then turned to other topics raised by Inuit delegates. One of these was raised by Shingituk, who 'wanted to know what would happen to the people of Rankin Inlet if the mine closed down.' In response, Easton of Rankin Inlet Nickel Mine 'pointed out that any mine could run out of ore, but that the people who had received training in the mine ... would probably be able to use their skills in work elsewhere,' while Robertson 'said there were prospects of more mines opening elsewhere in the Arctic and he did not think the Eskimos as at Rankin Inlet needed to worry.'[124]

But Shingituk's worries were well founded. Within a few short years, the closing of the Rankin Inlet mine would cause major headaches for the northern administration and serious problems for dislocated Inuit workers. No other mines would open in the Keewatin, attempts to relocate Inuit miners to Yellowknife would fail miserably, and the wage economy in the area would be devastated. In fact, Gordon Robertson himself would be writing to his minister in April 1962 outlining the disastrous situation created by the closing of the mine at Rankin Inlet under the heading 'Keewatin Region Crisis.'[125] Other questions by Shingituk were more specific: he wanted to know when Rankin Inlet would get a freezer, and what the policy was on returning mine workers to home communities for visits. Okpik's concern was with discrimination in liquor laws; he felt 'that while Eskimos were forbidden to drink there was discrimination against his people.'[126] Discussion of this was deferred until the next meeting.

The comments of the Inuit delegates at this meeting are historically significant. The prime minister had been in attendance, as had many important Arctic administrators. Major policy issues were discussed. Despite the pleasantries and formalities, the Inuit delegates were clearly not entirely pleased with developments in the eastern Arctic. Okpik's interventions and Ayaruark's speech, in particular, make it clear that Inuit were fully aware of the challenges that faced them, quite capable of standing up to the colonizers when they had to, and that they had a coherent set of policy alternatives. Koneak was prepared to recommend the Greenland approach, which involved a greater degree of self-government. Okpik stressed a need for education. Ayaruark had a proposal for integrating wage labour and traditional life on the land through cooperatives, which would make these efforts mutually supportive. Shingituk knew enough to worry well ahead of time about the problems that would come when the mine closed. Practically speaking, each of the Inuit delegates proposed more Inuit control over Inuit affairs in meaningful ways, rather than through the exercise of limited formal responsibilities. The government, which had solicited Inuit delegates for its showcase meeting, got more than it bargained for. A process had been started that could not easily be stopped.

Evidence of this is to be found in the aftermath of this meeting. Ayaruark and other Inuit had their own ideas about how things should be run and were increasingly unwilling to be the objects of northern administration. On the matter of medical care at Rankin Inlet, Ayaruark and other Inuit decided to petition the minister of northern affairs and national resources for changes. The following is a translation from Inuktitut.

> This is Jean Ayaruak [*sic*] writing to the big boss in Ottawa. I don't have the thoughts of a white man and neither do I write English because I am an Eskimo, but I certainly do have thoughts.
>
> Why is it that, every summer when they are building all the houses, there is no one working in the hospital? Some say that the house of the worker in the hospital is too small and noisy. Also, those who want medical attention are asked to come during only three hours, between 2 p.m. and 5 p.m. Whenever those who want medical attention are numerous, some of them just have to go away without attention. It would also be more satisfactory all around if the doctor had a real interpreter with him ...
>
> That is all I have to write about. Goodbye.[127]

In addition to Ayaruark, the letter was signed by nineteen other residents of Rankin Inlet. The phrase: 'I am an Eskimo, but I certainly do have thoughts' is entirely revealing of Inuit perceptions and experience. The inference is that Ayaruark felt he was treated as barely human and took this occasion to remind 'the boss' that he was as capable of thinking as any white man.

F.L. 'Bud' Neville's response to this correspondence is more than a little interesting. Neville was the civil servant largely responsible for the Hickling Report, commissioned by the government in 1990 in response to the high Arctic relocations discussed in Chapters 3 and 4. At the time, Neville was the superintendent of welfare for the region. Neville was apparently 'miffed' that the Inuit in question would not refer the matter first to those responsible for 'helping them to help themselves.'

> Before beginning to comment on the various points which Mr. Ayaruark has raised I want to say first of all that I am at a loss to know why the petition

was directed to the Minister instead of to our Area Administrator at Rankin Inlet or to you. One cannot challenge the right of any Eskimo or group of Eskimos to petition or to write to a member of Cabinet any more than one could in the case of any other Canadian. However it has been the practice up to this point for Eskimos to direct problems of local concern to local government representatives, such as Area Administrators, social workers or teachers depending upon the nature of the problem. Canadians in the south are expected to follow a similar course of action.[128]

Clearly, Inuit at Rankin Inlet were, in fact, organized and, unlike many Canadians in the South, had decided to go right to 'the top' in getting their concerns addressed. It also seems highly likely that they had already frustrated other channels and had got nowhere with local officials who were not taking the advice of their 'wards' seriously. Not surprisingly, Neville defends the arrangements about which the petitioners were complaining, although not entirely. His response is also revealing of the problems of depending on private sector interests for the provision of health care at the time. The infirmary was provided for the community by North Rankin Nickel Mines, and it appears that the Indian and Northern Health Service was constantly pressuring the mining company to upgrade the facility. However, Neville was conciliatory: 'All in all, then, I would certainly consider that while N. Rankin Infirmary has certain limitations it does nevertheless provide a mudh [sic] needed medical service at a level that could probably be considered adequate, if one takes into consideration the very definite future of N.R. Nickel Mines.'[129] As had been true of their experiences with the Hudson's Bay Company, under these arrangements, the health of Inuit at Rankin Inlet was subject to corporate interests.

This self-definition and self-advocacy in settlements that were themselves not of Inuit making, to some extent, had its origins in the formation of community councils. They became the initial vehicles for dealing with the many problems that plagued the communities forming in the 1950s and 1960s. The first council was apparently established by Northern Service Officer Doug Wilkinson at Baker Lake. It had its first meeting on 26 February 1957. At the Arctic Conference in the fall of that year, Wilkinson reported in some detail on its creation.

On his arrival at this post he was impressed by the passive attitude of the local Eskimos. Things were done by rote, day by day. He called the Eskimos together in the school for the purpose of explaining his role in the community. This initial meeting was the forerunner of weekly meetings during the winter and a single one in summer, and became the Eskimo Council. The Council solved only one or two problems during the year but the results were: 1. The Eskimos took more interest in their own economic position. 2. The Council had a disquieting effect on the non-Eskimo residents and started them thinking about their community, albeit in a negative way, as they never had before.[130]

Wilkinson's comments on the disquieting effect of the council on non-Inuit community members are interesting and point to the potential of the council to upset the established power structure in the community.

Wilkinson went on to report that 'the Council was made up of about 30 members with a "hard core" of 10-15. Members were not elected although the Eskimo Chairman and Secretary were elected from the group.' Another NSO, J.J. Bond, then described the council in the community of Cambridge Bay, noting that it was

similar to the Baker Lake group with the difference that it was elected. It formed a communicating link between the administration and the community. Mr. Bond was impressed by the consultative ability of the Eskimo people. The consensus comes out easily. He thought that the Council cultivated this ability of the Eskimo to express themselves in a group. The Chairman [Symington] suggested that the flow of communication should be from the Eskimos to the Government as well as from the Government to the Eskimos.[131]

Bond's recognition of the consultative abilities of Inuit in Cambridge Bay is somewhat ironic. The Arctic administration had, for nearly a decade, been running things in the North with hardly any consultation with those towards whom it had a responsibility. Symington's comment reveals that much of the speaking at these meetings may have consisted of NSO announcements.

An interesting discussion developed after the reports from Wilkinson and Bond.

Mr. Wilkinson introduced a note of caution. We should not build the Eskimos up with the prospect of solving every problem through the Eskimo Council. Mr. Kerr asked Mr. Wilkinson whether individuals tended to monopolize the meeting. Mr. Wilkinson replied that the role of the Northern Service Officer was to keep a finger on the proceedings. He should find ways of broadening the discussions but should not hinder the proceedings.

The councils were clearly to be guided by the barely hidden hand of the northern service officer.

The Chairman wondered when the whites would be admitted to Community Councils. Mr. Wilkinson could see no reason why they should not, except that at present they were conducted in the Eskimo language. They could, however, be bi-lingual provided adequate interpreters were available. Mr. Snowden asked whether there was any indication that Eskimos discussed Council Meetings when they went home afterwards. He also wanted to know how we make them feel part of the national community. Mr. Wilkinson did not know if they discussed proceedings at home. He did think, however, that the meetings had a profound effect on the community. He went on to explain that the first two thirds of the meeting was devoted to community matters. The last part was devoted to showing slides, when available, and giving talks on such topics as the national government and the United Nations.[132]

Clearly, councils were to serve two purposes. Consistent with ideas of the day about assimilation, integration, and citizenship, they were to give Inuit a voice but were also to serve the distinct purpose of integrating Inuit into the national fabric, of instilling citizenship.

A policy directive, written in the fall of 1961, shows that there was much confusion in the Arctic administration about the purposes of these community councils. Noting that 'in Arctic areas we have placed a heavy emphasis on encouragement to local councils,' the directive adds: 'We have laid down no forms and printed no blueprints for local community organization.'[133] The advantages of this in terms of flexibility were noted, but the problem – 'a committee will wither if it has nothing to do' – was also becoming apparent. The solution was obvious – give people real control. It is at this point that the historical reluctance of the Canadian state in developing anything other than representative liberal democratic structures becomes obvious.[134] In fact, in this case, even representative structures were a problem. The logic of Inuit – supposedly citizens of Canada – spending other people's money, was invoked to support the argument that they could, at best, have only an advisory role:

We must start from the assumption that no body of people, at any level of government, can exercise authority without responsibility. This is fundamental to Canadian political theory at every level and it is a truism which must be taken without dispute. For example, one can simply not assign to a local group decision-making in the expenditure of substantial Federal funds as long as the Federal Government must take responsibility for the wise use of those funds.

... it is also clearly impossible to give to any local group powers greater

than those enjoyed by a local improvement district ... A local organization
... can only be advisory in character when it comes to the spending of others
money [*sic*].[135]

In the case of Inuit, real power was to be held by the federal government.
The directive dealt with this conclusion by offering some practical advice
and guidance. A small sample of this is worth considering.

> The strength of a local council may be damaged by too great a reliance upon
> it. The sincere administrator, anxious to get local views, may ask the council,
> in the hope that not only will he get the views but that he will prove that
> he has asked for them. In this case, formal machinery may become a moral
> excuse for true consultation. There may be many community settings which
> do not lend themselves to frank expression of views in front of a group ...
> The second fundamental problem is the choice of people who make deci-
> sions. There is no point in saying that community leaders must be banded
> together to form local councils unless there is in the community a reason-
> able idea of who the local leaders are ... many local citizens probably have
> as little idea as we have of what constitutes a local leader in a rapidly
> changing northern community. The prestige of a hunter may linger long
> after his direct influence on a community has waned with the disappearance
> of the old way. Those who have entered new paths and who come closest
> to understanding them are frequently the young whose age alone weakens
> their effectiveness as community spokesmen.[136]

The incoherence of the first few sentences reflects the incoherence of the
policy directive, which actually provides no direction. Traditional Inuit
leaders, who might not be favourable to government's policies, were not
desired, as the last few sentences make apparent. However, one thing
seemed clear: in the latest stage of northern development, local consultation
was beginning to have a purpose. The directive continues:

> Until now it has been unrealistic to consider asking local people to take even
> an advisory role in most of the programmes which have determined the
> shapes of communities ... We are, however, entering a new phase with our
> attempt to bring community facilities in the north more in line with those
> in the south, in kind if not in degree ... The operation of some of these
> facilities may provide new opportunities for genuine local consultation ...
> There are services which affect the daily lives of local residents, and as in
> any southern community, excite local opinions. We must now take a new
> look at the extent to which local advisory groups can participate in the

operation of community facilities. Our general model in this respect must be the typical southern community.[137]

The directive concluded with a call for information from the administrator of the Mackenzie and from the administrator of the Arctic on the experiences of the local organization to date and for suggestions for future directions.[138]

Although everyone seemed to think they were a good idea, development of Inuit councils was a relatively slow process. The fact that no real power was given to these councils undoubtedly contributed to a lack of interest on the part of Inuit. A report filed on the Keewatin Region in late 1961 in response to the directive showed active councils at Baker Lake and Rankin Inlet, while at Resolute Bay 'the business meetings associated with the Co-op are equivalent to community council meetings.'[139] A council was being planned for Whale Cove.

A more detailed response in early 1962 showed councils, or other significant forms of local organization, at Frobisher Bay, Cape Dorset, Baker Lake, Rankin Inlet, Resolute Bay, Fort Chimo, Great Whale River, Sugluk, Inukjuak, and Povungnetuk. Matters dealt with by the councils included dog control, housing, community clean-up, morality, employment practices, and home-brew making. Other topics it was thought could be added to this list included relief allowance, assignment of housing, community planning, and settlement services. This report included an elaborate analysis of community leadership:

Regarding the question of community leadership and how this is developing, no clear cut pattern has emerged yet from the limited Council operations available for study. In the more permanent communities the family patriarchs control opinion and action within their own groups but they do not necessarily influence community thinking and are merely spokesmen for their own interests. Those Eskimos with some mixed blood seem to be more aggressive and readier to speak up at group meetings but this is often countered by the resentful attitude of the more conservative older hunters determined to be uninfluenced by the white men. There is no doubt in some settlements the younger better educated Eskimo with a more advanced understanding of the changing world expresses views carrying weight and acts in some ways as a bridge uniting the old and the new. Generally, it appears that few Eskimos go beyond the role of spokesman for the interests they represent and in no way shape community opinion. Perhaps, however, John Ayaryak [sic] at Rankin Inlet can be cited as an exception to this generalization and has personally progressed somewhat farther than his fellows towards being a real leader of this people.[140]

There was clearly little recognition that Inuit might have a different model of decision-making – that leadership might be defined using different criteria, that a spokesperson might be expected to represent and respect the views of others and to build consensus rather than direct and order people, or make decisions without first achieving consensus. Administrators had very definite ideas about what a 'real' leader was, and the traditional, 'conservative' spokesman did not meet that culturally constructed standard. In promoting Inuit leadership, administrators were also actively promoting an ideology of 'advancement' against one that looked to traditions. Leadership would have to come in non-Inuit terms.

A basic lack of respect for traditional leaders and political values generally informed the judgments and approaches of government staff in Arctic administration. A discussion on the 'Political Status of the Eskimos,' which took place in the last session of the Arctic Conference of 1957, illustrates this clearly. Northern Service Officer W.G. Kerr remarked that 'the Eskimos were confused by elections, that some in his area thought that the government "had always been there" and that the candidates were merely looking for jobs.' The statement characterizes the whole tone of the discussion.[141] Administrators sometimes had a hard time accepting the judgment of local Inuit, as this report on an election to chose a delegate to the Committee on Eskimo Affairs reveals. Reporting that 'Johnnie Inukpuk was elected by an overwhelming majority,' R.D. Evans, the administrator, adds: 'I had rather hoped that Lazarusie Epoo, President of the Council, would be elected as he would be more outspoken than Johnnie who is rather quiet and shy. However, Lazarusie came a poor second and there is no doubt that the people want Johnnie to go.'[142] Some of the unhappiness with Inukpuk as a delegate undoubtedly stems from the fact that 'Johnnie is the leader of a group of Eskimos who are still living in the traditional way,' although 'under Johnnie's leadership [his camp] is one of the most progressive camps in this Area.'[143] Evans recognized that 'in this respect Johnnie is truly representative of the majority of the inhabitants of the Port Harrison area, since the majority are still camp dwellers,'[144] but this is acknowledged grudgingly and clearly Inukpuk does not meet Evans's standards for a delegate to the committee.

In spite of the best efforts of the bureaucrats to prevent it, traditionally minded Inuit leaders did get elected to councils and as delegates to the southern conferences. The record of such meetings through the early part of the 1960s contains their statements with increasing frequency as more opportunities were made available. The northern administrators were left trying to placate, accommodate, and rationalize their way around voices they did not always see as legitimate, reasonable, or knowledgable. One of these voices belonged to Kilikavioyak who, at the eleventh meeting of the Committee on Eskimo Affairs in 1960, stated that

> he had been asked by the people in Coppermine to say that many Eskimos there, particularly the older people, regarded the old way of life as still best for them. Only a minority of the people in Coppermine wanted to change their old way of life and the rest wanted to be left alone to make a living. Many people thought that if they were to take part in large scale organized hunting they would eventually kill off all the game resources in the area and no game would be left for the future.[145]

As structures were being developed that allowed them to speak to those who administered their lives, Inuit began to say things that did not accord with the policymaker's views. Such perspectives were not appreciated and were attributed to Inuit who were too old, uneducated, or unknowledgeable to get on with 'fitting' with the modern era being introduced to the North.

However, it is possible to read in the words of these Inuit leaders the origins of the contemporary movement for self-government in the eastern Arctic. Inuit were not prepared to be assimilated or integrated. They were fighting for cultural survival and, contrary to the image held by many Canadians of Inuit as demoralized and confused children, were increasingly stating their opposition to the totalizing processes being directed by the state.

> We the Eskimo people, where do we come from and how did we get here? This is a big question to us all even in the white man's way of thinking or learning. We are still a mystery to them, but our ancestors are the ones who we give praise to for all that they have achieved, to live, to feel, to survive for centuries before the white people came. Some of the kablonat came with good intentions to teach us a better way to live, some came to destroy our livelihood and our culture ...
>
> Let us think back even fifty years ago and compare our people's living conditions then, with our present living environment. We have gained very little to add to what our forefathers have left us.
>
> ... We must remember this, where no other people could have survived, our ancestors did, with a hope that some day we would be known to the other parts of the world, not as the people of present new day, but as the people of old who had great determination to live, to survive, and to learn the daily needs. Today if we can think like our ancestors and put to use what

they have achieved for us, and adopt the white man's way of learning, at the same time, and keep our own, we will be further ahead. We should learn as much as we can from this new culture, but we must not forget our own culture which is important to all of us.

The survival of the Eskimo people depends on the survival of the language. When people meet Eskimos, they are disappointed if they cannot show their knowledge of Eskimo ways ... If the Eskimos themselves don't use their language more, it will be forgotten, and very soon the Eskimo too will be a forgotten people ...

There are only very few Eskimos, but millions of whites, just like mosquitoes. It is something very special and wonderful to be an Eskimo – they are like the snow geese. If an Eskimo forgets his language and Eskimo ways, he will be nothing but just another mosquito.[146]

A more eloquent declaration is hard to imagine. The year was 1962. And Inuit had good reason for noting that living conditions were not better than those experienced by their forefathers. At Keewatin communities along the west coast of Hudson Bay – Rankin Inlet, Camp 20 at Churchill, Whale Cove, and especially Eskimo Point – conditions were appalling. In Eskimo Point, eighty-two Inuit households were crowded into sixty-four wooden and snow houses. Late in 1962 and early in 1963, an epidemic of tuberculosis affected 55 per cent of these households, half the children in the community, and 24 per cent of the adult population.[147] The following account of conditions at Eskimo Point – laced with all the ethnocentrism and stereotyping of the time – was printed by the *Winnipeg Free Press* in November 1962.

I found a settlement of 240 white and Eskimo souls – and 150 dogs: a village where despair is slowly evolving into hope, a cold crucible where dedicated people, aided by government funds, are forging a new race of people out of the most malleable of material, the Padleirmuit [sic] children ...

The Padleirmuit [sic] live in snow covered tents and foul smelling igloos. They wear store-bought clothing which an old Arctic 'hand' said is entirely unsuited for this kind of life. To keep warm, they operate their primus stoves continually, melting their igloos' snow blocks. The result: colds, pneumonia and other respiratory aliments.

When they lived in the wilds, they abandoned their tents or igloos when they became dirty. Now, through sheer inertia or the wasting influence of 'civilization,' they let the dirt accumulate, creating ideal breeding places for impetigo and other chronic skin diseases.

Many of the Padleirmuit resist the government's feeble efforts to turn them into fishermen or fox hunters. They wait patiently for the return of the mighty rivers of caribou which gave their lives meaning and dignity. In so doing, they evoke the disgust of the old Arctic 'hands.'[148]

At Whale Cove there were food shortages, and problems created by the earlier relocations were persistent: 'The very sad part of the people at Whale Cove is that most of the population is made up of inlanders and these people are not partial to seal meat but would rather have caribou which has been their main staple diet inland. In talking to some of these people they mention that they get enough flour and grain products to eat but are hungry. When questioning them as to what they are hungry for their reply is caribou meat.'[149]

And so people suffered and they struggled. And it is no surprise that they increasingly began to say things that did not accord with the views of the social workers, teachers, and northern service officers sent to integrate them with Canadian society. Their claim that what Canadian society offered was no improvement on what their forefathers had provided was easily substantiated. That such a thing was true was difficult, if not impossible, to believe for helpers who thought that theirs was a culture of 'progress.'

Despite representing new levels of intervention, the northern service officers and social workers did, here and there, promote the creation of bodies that would begin to challenge the status quo. This was the basic contradiction that was to characterize the dynamic of community development in the next decade. The program of administered self-reliance would lead at one and the same time to greater interference and the seeds of self-government. By 1960, a rapidly expanding bureaucracy was changing all the rules in the North. A new level of formality entered into decision-making processes: statistics were developed, massive research energies were expended, consultation procedures began to be put into place. The slogan 'community development' came to embody all of these contradictory tendencies, the hopes and plans of many administrators and Inuit leaders alike. The advisory councils that emerged out of the muddle of the late 1950s also embodied these contradictions, not least because of their circumscribed status as advisory and the potential they would offer for subversion and for a meaningful role in transferring decision-making power to communities.

Totalization, and resistance to it, became an even more nuanced dynamic. Resistance could be felt within the state, in the debates and struggles that occurred between policy tendencies. Totalization could be carried forward by Inuit themselves. The state as the embodiment of a form of decision-making and as a constitutor of social subjects remained the guarantor of totalization, and a new generation of Inuit leaders became its fiercest opponents in the Arctic. But the arguments made within the state, discussed in this chapter, and the debates within Inuit communities made for an even more complex struggle. The terms of this struggle can be found implicitly in the archival record of the late 1950s and early 1960s.

Conclusion

The narratives of the North are most frequently epic narratives of progress. After all, where there were no permanent settlements a mere 100 years ago, now there are many. Where there were no buildings, nursing stations, schools, airstrips, permanent houses, now they abound. Where virtually nothing was spent on social welfare, education, health, economic development, now there is significant financial investment. Where once Arctic affairs was a backwater bureaucracy employing few, now it is a veritable beehive of activity. But we have shown that any close reading of the historical record must acknowledge another story, as episodic as it is epic. Southern plans were often so incongruent with northern conditions that it would be laughable, were it not for the lives that hung in the balance in some instances. There were as many, if not more, planning disasters as there were successes. There was utter blindness to real needs. An era of neglect within the space of a few short years lead to an era of massive control. The importance of asking the Inuit people affected by decisions what they thought of them did not occur to planners for a long, long time, and then, when it did, they asked in a half-hearted and confused fashion. People were moved. And moved again to solve the problems that moving them had created. And split up and moved again. And some were taken South. And many never saw their loved ones again. In the late 1980s, the government of the Northwest Territories sponsored a research program to assist aboriginal northerners in tracking down relatives and loved ones who were taken from the North in the 1950s and never returned. The vast majority of these searches lead to graveyards. Was this an era of progress?

A close reading of the historical record must acknowledge a story other than that of the 'great men,' 'great events,' and inexorable improvements that have become a staple of Canadian northern history. What southern 'experts' regarded as successes were questioned by Inuit whose experiences were at odds with the images held by their benefactors. Inuit experienced disease, starvation, separation from family and community – and death. Things did not always improve. Many of the social impacts of the changes brought about with the guidance of well-intentioned administrators have come to dominate the modern Canadian experience of the eastern Arctic – a region of high unemployment, plagued by persistent social problems.

But even this image can be challenged. The efforts of Inuit to retain their art, language, and culture, to translate these into modern forms – television as well as print media – are as significant as their move towards Nunavut and Inuit self-government. The postwar history of the eastern Arctic not only suggests that absolute and universal approaches to the assessment of human needs are suspect, it highlights the dangers of failing to seek, and to recognize as legitimate, self-definition in the articulation of those needs. The attempted totalization of Inuit society by the Canadian state produced not only serious problems for Inuit communities, but new and ongoing forms of struggle. Inuit self-government is in large part about self-definition. It is perhaps the necessary outcome of a history of relocation, the administration of 'relief' – in all its forms – and attempts by the state to exercise responsibility for those who now choose to be responsible for themselves.

Notes

Introduction

1 See Arthur Ray, 'Periodic Shortages, Native Welfare, and the Hudson's Bay Company 1670-1930,' in *The Subarctic Fur Trade: Native Social and Economic Adaptations*, ed. Shepard Krech III (Vancouver: University of British Columbia Press 1984).

2 Jean-Paul Sartre, *Critique of Dialectical Reason*, vol. 1, trans. Alan Sheridan-Smith (London: Verso 1982), 45, 46.

3 Inuktitut for a person of other than Inuit origin.

4 Sartre, *Critique of Dialectical Reason*, 266.

5 Marshall Sahlins, *Culture and Practical Reason* (Chicago: University of Chicago Press 1976), 211.

6 Michel de Certeau, *The Practice of Everyday Life* (Berkeley: University of California Press 1984), xxi.

Chapter 1: Are Inuit Indians?

1 Morris Zaslow, *The Opening of the Canadian North: 1870-1914* (Toronto: McClelland & Stewart 1971), 255.

2 Mark O. Dickerson, *Whose North? Political Change, Political Development, and Self-Government in the Northwest Territories* (Vancouver: UBC Press 1992), 29.

3 Morris Zaslow, *The Opening of the Canadian North*, 257.

4 Shelagh Grant, *Sovereignty or Security? Government Policy in the Canadian North, 1936-1950* (Vancouver: University of British Columbia Press 1988), 10.

5 Diamond Jenness, *Eskimo Administration: II. Canada* (Montreal: Arctic Institute of North America 1964), 18-19.

6 William R. Morrison, *Showing the Flag: The Mounted Police and Canadian Sovereignty in the North, 1894-1925* (Vancouver: University of British Columbia Press 1985), 39.

7 Ibid., 39-40.

8 Diamond Jenness, *Eskimo Administration: II*, 17.

9 Ibid., 32.

10 Ibid.

11 R. Quinn Duffy, *The Road to Nunavut: The Progress of the Eastern Arctic Inuit since the Second World War* (Montreal and Kingston: McGill-Queen's University Press 1988), 4.

12 The activities of the council and of the Northwest Territories administration during the 1920s and 1930s are discussed by Zaslow in *The Northward Expansion of Canada* (Toronto: McClelland & Stewart 1988), 199-202.

13 Writing in *The Government of Canada and the Inuit, 1900-1967* (Ottawa: Research Branch, Corporate Policy, Department of Indian and Northern Affairs Canada 1985), Richard Diubaldo gives the impression that the pattern of the deputy minister serving as commissioner commenced in 1931 when Finnie's branch was eliminated (p. 53). However, W.W. Cory, who was commissioner from 1921 until 1931 was also at the time the deputy minister of the Department of the Interior. Sivertz indicates that the decision to make him commissioner followed from the argument put forth by Deputy Minister Gordon Robertson that the two responsibilities had become too much for the deputy minister to perform (Ben Sivertz, personal communication, 11 August 1992).

14 For example, in 1930, the commissioner was W.W. Cory, deputy minister of the Department of

the Interior, and the deputy commissioner was R.A. Gibson, the assistant deputy minister. Council members included Dr. Charles Camsell, deputy minister of the Department of Mines, O.S. Finnie, the director of the Northwest Territories and Yukon Branch of the department, Duncan Campbell Scott, deputy superintendent general of Indian Affairs, H.H. Rowatt of the Dominion Lands Board, Colonel Starnes, commissioner of the RCMP, and D.L. McKeand as secretary.

15 Mark Dickerson, *Whose North?*, 46.

16 Shelagh Grant, *Sovereignty or Security?*, 14.

17 Ibid., 17.

18 Diamond Jenness, *Eskimo Administration: II*, 30.

19 Treaties and Historical Research Centre, *Indian Acts and Amendments*, 2nd ed. (Ottawa: Research Branch, Corporate Policy, Department of Indian and Northern Affairs Canada 1981), 140.

20 Quoted by Diubaldo in *The Government of Canada and the Inuit*, 33.

21 Quoted by R. Quinn Duffy in *The Road to Nunavut*, 6.

22 Quoted by Diubaldo in *The Government of Canada and the Inuit*, 34.

23 Richard Diubaldo, *The Government of Canada and the Inuit*, 36. Jenness (*Eskimo Administration: II*, 33) gives 31 March 1928 as the date for this, but see National Archives of Canada (hereafter NAC), RG 85, vol. 2081, file 1012-4, pt. 3, for a copy of the order (PC 709) with the former date.

24 See Arthur Ray, 'Periodic Shortages, Native Welfare, and the Hudson's Bay Company 1670-1930' in *The Subarctic Fur Trade: Native Social and Economic Adaptations*, ed. Shepard Krech III (Vancouver: University of British Columbia Press 1984), 16-17.

25 NAC, RG 85, vol. 786, file 5997, pt. 2, 'Memorandum, – Mr. Scott, [from] G.C. Canku, Inspector, Ottawa,' 6 October 1922, p. 1.

26 NAC, RG 85, vol. 786, file 5997-C, letter to the 'Officer Commanding, Royal Canadian Mounted Police, Headquarters Division, Ottawa, ONT:. Re; – Eskimos Edineyah, Pannikpah and Koud-noo and their wives and families Starved to death on Admiralty Inlet., (sgd) A.W. Joy, S/Sergt: I/C Detachment, Pond Inlet,' 26 May 1923, p. 1.

27 NAC, RG 85, vol. 786, file 5997-B, letter to the 'Officer Commanding, Hdqrs. Divn., R.C.M.Police, Ottawa Ont., re: Contagious Diseases amongst the Eskimos., [from] C.E. Wilcox, Inspr., Commanding Eastern Arctic Sub-Dist.,' 23 September 1926,' pp. 1-2.

28 NAC, RG 85, vol. 786, file 5997, pt. 3, 'Memorandum, – Mr. Scott [from] G.C. Canku, Inspector, Ottawa,' 6 October 1922, p. 3.

29 Ibid., 4.

30 Ibid.

31 NAC, RG 85, vol. 786, file 5997, pt. D, letter to the 'Officer Commanding, R.C.M.Police, Headquarters Division, OTTAWA, Re: Clothing received from Indian Department in possession of Hudson's Bay Coy., [from] O.G. Petty, Cpl. #5718, In charge Chesterfield Inlet Detachment, Chesterfield Inlet, NWT,' 31 January 1926.

32 NAC, RG 85, vol. 828, file 7257, pt. 2, quoted in 'Memorandum: Mr. Gibson, [from] D.L. McKeand, Ottawa,' 10 November 1938, p. 1.

33 Ibid.

34 NAC, RG 85, vol. 786, file 5997, pt. D, letter to the 'Department of Indian Affairs, OTTAWA, [from] Donald B. Marsh, ANGLICAN MISSION, ESKIMO POINT, NWT.,' 28 March 1927.

35 NAC, RG 85, vol. 28, file 7257, pt. 2, extract from an undated personal letter addressed to 'Major McKeand [from] the Reverend R.W. Wenham, Fort Chimo, Ungava Bay, Que.' The letter came by dog sled via 'Fort McKenzie, Seven Islands and Quebec City, Que., and Hamilton, Ont.,' 7 June 1938, p. 1.

36 NAC, RG 85, vol. 786, file 5997, pt. D, letter to 'Bishop Dewdney, D.D., Bishop of Keewatin, Bishopstowe, Kenora, Ont., [from] Duncan C. Scott, Deputy Superintendent General,' 14 June 1927, p. 1.

37 Ibid., 1-2.

38 NAC, RG 85, vol. 786, file 5997, pt. D, Sergeant Clay, as quoted in letter to 'Mr. Moodie, Deputy Superintendent General, Department of Indian Affairs, OTTAWA, Ont., [from] Cortlandt Starnes, Commissioner, Royal Canadian Mounted Police,' 28 April 1925.

39 On homeguard Indians see Arthur Ray, *Indians in the Fur Trade: Their Role as Trappers, Hunters and Middlemen in the Lands Southwest of Hudson Bay, 1660-1870* (Toronto and Buffalo: University of Toronto Press 1974).

40 On this, see Daniel Francis and Toby Morantz, *Partners in Furs: A History of the Fur Trade in Eastern James Bay, 1600-1870* (Montreal and Kingston: McGill-Queen's University Press 1983).

41 NAC, RG 85, vol. 828, file 7257, pt. 2, extracts from the 'Minutes of the Sixty-fifth Session of the Northwest Territories Council held on February 9th, 1937 (item 5. Relief).'
42 NAC, RG 85, vol. 828, file 7257, pt. 2, 'Memorandum: – Mr Gibson, [from] D.L. McKeand,' 17 March 1937, p. 1.
43 NAC, RG 85, vol. 828, file 7257, pt. 2, extract from an undated personal letter addressed to 'Major McKeand [from] the Reverend R.W. Wenham, Fort Chimo, Ungava Bay, Que.' The letter came by dog sled via 'Fort McKenzie, Seven Islands and Quebec City, Que., and Hamilton, Ont.,' 7 June 1938,' p. 1.
44 NAC, RG 85, vol. 825, file 7257, pt. 2, letter to the 'Officer Commanding, R.C.M. Police, Toronto. Ontario., [from] E.S. Covell, Reg. No. 9510, i/c Moose Factory Detachment, Moose Factory. Ont.,' 25 September 1932, p. 2.
45 Ibid., 2.
46 NAC, RG 85, vol. 828, file 7257, pt. 2, 'Memorandum: J. Lorne Turner, Esq., Acting Chairman, Dominion Land Board., [from] Commissioner of Dominion Lands, Department of the Interior, Ottawa,' 12 June 1934, p. 1.
47 Ibid., 2.
48 Ibid.
49 NAC, RG 85, vol. 828, file 7257, pt. 2, 'Memorandum. – J. Lorne Turner, Esq., Acting Chairman, Dominion Lands Board., [from] D.L. McKeand, Commissioner of Dominion Lands, Ottawa,' 26 December 1933, p. 2.
50 NAC, RG 85, vol. 825, file 7257, pt. 2, letter to 'Charles Lanctot, Deputy Attorney General, Quebec, P.Q., [from] the Deputy Minister,' 29 March 1933, p. 1.
51 Quoted in ibid., 3.
52 Ibid.
53 Ibid., 3-4.
54 Ibid., 4.
55 Ibid.
56 Ibid.
57 Ibid.
58 Ibid., 5.
59 Ibid., 6.
60 Ibid., 7.
61 NAC, RG 85, vol. 825, file 7257, pt. 2, 'Acting Minister of Finance,' quoted in 'Memorandum., to H.H. Rowatt, Esq., Deputy Minister of the Interior, Ottawa, "Destitute Eskimos in Northern Quebec," [from] Chairman, Dominion Lands Board,' 26 July 1933, p. 2.
62 NAC, RG 85, vol. 825, file 7257, pt. 2, quoted in letter to 'Honourable L.A. Taschereau, Premier and Attorney General of Quebec, QUEBEC, P.Q., (Sgd.) H. Guthrie, Minister of Justice,' 29 July 1933, p. 1.
63 NAC, RG 85, vol. 825, file 7257, pt. 2, 'Memorandum., to H.H. Rowatt, Esq., Deputy Minister of the Interior, Ottawa, "Destitute Eskimos in Northern Quebec," [from] Chairman, Dominion Lands Board,' 26 July 1933, p. 1.
64 Ibid.
65 Ibid.
66 Ibid., 1-2.
67 Ibid., 2, emphasis added.
68 Supreme Court of Canada, *Supreme Court Registry (SCR)*, 'In the Matter of a Reference as to Whether "Indians" in S. 91(24) of the B.N.A. Act includes Eskimo inhabitants of the Province of Quebec, 1939,' p. 105.
69 *Montreal Daily Star*, 'Expert Declares Eskimo is Indian,' 25 November 1937.
70 Supreme Court of Canada, *SCR*, 'In the Matter of a Reference as to Whether "Indians" in S. 91(24) of the B.N.A. Act includes Eskimo inhabitants of the Province of Quebec, 1939,' p. 109.
71 Ibid., 110.
72 Ibid., 115.
73 Ibid., 116.
74 Ibid., 114.
75 Ibid., 105, 117, 119.
76 NAC, RG 85, vol. 2081, file 1012-4, pt. 3, letter to 'Mr. Gibson., Reference re Indians and Eskimos, [from] T.L. Cory,' 17 June 1946. The letter summarizes earlier events.

77 NAC, RG 85, vol. 2081, file 1012-4, pt. 3, 'STATUS OF ESKIMO, [document signed by] J.G. Wright,' n.d., p. 2.
78 NAC, RG 85, vol. 2081, file 1012-4, pt. 3, letter to 'Mr. Nason, [from] Deputy Commissioner, Administration of the Northwest Territories,' 4 December 1946.
79 NAC, RG 85, vol. 2081, file 1012-4, pt. 3, 'STATUS OF ESKIMO, [document signed by] J.G. Wright,' p. 3.
80 NAC, RG 85, vol. 2081, file 1012-4, pt. 3, 'MEMORANDUM, to Mr. Wright, [from] J.W.K. Lock, Ottawa,' 25 June 1947.
81 NWT Archives, Alex Stevenson Collection, N92-023, 'Memorandum [from] James Cantley, Arctic Division, to Mr. Sivertz,' 16 August 1954, p. 1.
82 Ibid., 2.
83 Ibid.
84 Ibid.
85 NAC, RG 85, vol. 1900, file 1006-8, pt. 5 'MEMORANDUM TO CABINET, "Quebec Eskimos – Financial Arrangements," CONFIDENTIAL, [from] Arthur Laing, Minister of Northern Affairs and National Resources,' 16 March 1964, p. 2.
86 NAC, RG 85, vol. 1900, file 1006-8, pt. 5, letter from 'Arthur Laing to The Right Honourable Lester B. Person, Prime Minister of Canada, OTTAWA, Canada, CONFIDENTIAL, Re: Eskimos of New Quebec,' 17 April 1964, p. 1. Interestingly, a note typed beside this paragraph reads, 'O.K. but when did we state this publicly?'
87 See Sally M. Weaver, *Making Canadian Indian Policy: The Hidden Agenda, 1968-70* (Toronto: University of Toronto Press 1981).
88 NAC, RG 85, vol. 1962, file A-1006-8, pt. 1, memo 'to REGIONAL ADMINISTRATOR, Arctic QUEBEC, [from] P.J. Gillespie, Northern Administrator, CONFIDENTIAL, Great Whale River, Quebec,' 19 April 1966, p. 5.
89 Ibid., 6.
90 NAC, RG 85, vol. 1962, file A-1006-8, pt. 1, 'REPORT ON THE QUEBEC PROVINCIAL ANNUAL ESKIMO CONFERENCE HELD AT FORT CHIMO ON MARCH 24th AND 25th, 1966., [from] J.D. Furneauz, Northern Administrator, Povungnituk,' 28 April 1966, pp. 5-6.
91 NAC, RG 85, vol. 1962, file A-1006-8, pt. 1, letter to 'THE MINISTER, Department of Indian Affairs and Northern Development, Quebec Eskimo Affairs, from the Deputy Minister, (signed J.H.G.), Ottawa 4,' 25 October 1966, p. 3.
92 R. Quinn Duffy, *The Road to Nunavut*, 7.

Chapter 2: Social Welfare and Social Crisis in the Eastern Arctic
1 Two significant studies conducted in the 1960s deal with this transformation and its profound implications for Inuit culture. See F.G Vallee, *Kabloona and Eskimo in the Central Keewatin* (Ottawa: St. Paul University, Canadian Research Centre for Anthropology 1967); and John and Irma Honigmann, *Arctic Townsmen: Ethnic Background and Modernization* (Ottawa: St. Paul University, Canadian Research Centre for Anthropology 1970).
2 Despite the presence of schools and medical facilities and, subsequently, considerable pressure to relocate to settlements, in some parts of the Arctic the resistance to relocate was considerable. For example, notes made by Dr. Otto Schaefer aboard the Eastern Arctic Patrol in 1965, indicate that, in the Cumberland Sound area of Baffin Island, approximately 30-40 per cent of the population was still living in hunting camps. His observations also indicate that, in 1964, half of Inuit trading into Clyde River, Arctic Bay, and Pond Inlet were still living in hunting camps. For these areas, the move to settlements was virtually complete by the late 1960s (personal communication, Dr. Otto Schaefer, Edmonton, Alberta, 5 October 1992).
3 Dennis Guest, *The Emergence of Social Security in Canada* (Vancouver: University of British Columbia Press 1980), 75-6.
4 Desmond Morton, *Working People: An Illustrated History of the Canadian Labour Movement* (Ottawa: Deneau 1980), 183.
5 Writing in *The Liberal Party* (Toronto: McClelland & Stewart 1962), former Liberal cabinet minister Jack Pickersgill – one of the key 'reform Liberals' in the administration of Mackenzie King during the 1940s – makes it clear that the welfare reforms introduced by the Liberals were a deliberate attempt to address the rising popularity of labour and farm movements without capitulating to CCF calls for higher prices for farm products and higher wages. In particular, the family allowance scheme (which was to present major logistical and administrative problems in the eastern Arctic

and to have a significant impact on the Inuit) as well as other welfare reforms were based on the analysis that 'a large part of the pressure both from farmers and from labour arises not from discontent with their present situations, but from fear of a postwar depression with ruinously low prices and mass unemployment' (p. 33).

6 Not only was the party divided internally between 'welfare liberals' and 'business liberals,' the latter committed to minimal government intervention in the economy. The same divisions were evident at all levels in the civil service of the day.

7 NWT Archives, Alex Stevenson Collection, N92-023, R.T. Flanagan, 'A History of the Department of Northern Affairs and National Resources,' Northern Administration Branch, n.d., pp. 51-2.

8 Ibid., 47.

9 *Calgary Albertan*, 'Find Eskimos Are Healthy,' 7 November 1946.

10 *Ottawa Citizen*, 'Daily Paper Only Thing Missed in the Arctic: Life among Eskimos More Pleasurable and Placid than South's "Civilization,"' 10 October 1946.

11 *Calgary Albertan*, 'All Possible Done for Stricken Eskimos, Official Denies Calgary Expert's Charge of Neglect,' 13 February 1946.

12 *American Weekly*, 'Eskimos Sitting on Top of the World,' 19 May 1946. The article is written by Charles Lynch, using the ghost name of 'Homer Croy.' Lynch was brazen enough to send a copy to Roy Gibson, director of the Lands, Parks and Forest Branch. To his credit, Gibson was not impressed.

13 The account given here is derived primarily from two sources: NAC, RG 85, vol. 855, file 8012, pt. 3, report of RCMP Inspector H.H. Cronkite, officer commanding 'G' Division, Eastern Arctic, Chesterfield Division, 'Re: EPIDEMIC POLIOMYELITIS AMONG NATIVES CHESTERFIELD INLET SETTLEMENT FEBRUARY 1949,' 10 March 1949, and an article by J.D. Adamson et al. entitled 'Poliomyelitis in the Arctic,' in the *Canadian Medical Association Journal* 61 (October 1949):339-48.

14 Curiously, these deaths are not reported in the RCMP report of 10 March 1949 from the officer commanding 'G' Division, who summarized the situation. They are also not reported in the *Canadian Medical Association Journal* article which appears to be based largely on the RCMP report. However, they are reported in a letter to the 'Commissioner, R.C.M.Police, OTTAWA, Ontario, [from] H.H. Cronkhite, Insp., Officer Commanding "G" Division, December 6th, 1948, Re: Death of Five Eskimos, unnamed (from unstated cause) Chesterfield Inlet District, Northwest Territories.' See NAC, RG 85, vol. 855, file 8012, pt. 3.

15 While it is possible that Father Dionne was a carrier of the disease, it is also possible that it was brought to Chesterfield by Inuit coming to Chesterfield to trade between the beginning of November and early February. The incubation time for the enteric virus causing polio is between three and forty days, but for the paralytic variety it is believed to be between nine and twenty days. Therefore, while Father Dionne may have been a carrier, and while the outbreak corresponds to a period immediately following his visit, other routes of transmission are possible.

16 NAC, RG 85, vol. 855, file 8012, pt. 3, NAC, RG 85, vol. 855, file 8012, pt. 3, report of RCMP Inspector H.H. Cronkite, officer commanding 'G' Division, Eastern Arctic, Chesterfield Division, 'Re: EPIDEMIC POLIOMYELITIS AMONG NATIVES CHESTERFIELD INLET SETTLEMENT FEBRUARY 1949,' 10 March 1949, p. 2.

17 The following Inuit, many of them well-known residents of the Keewatin, were evacuated to hospital in Winnipeg: Simon Kolit, Pierre Karlik, Thomas Sammurtok, Augustin Sudlutor, Leonie Pikteusar, Thomas Tudlik, Simon Aklunark, Maurice Tinnuadluk, Georges Tanuyark, Melanie Milluk, Simeon Yerak, and Philemon Tigumiar.

18 *Toronto Globe and Mail*, 'Germ-Carrying Eskimo Blamed for Death Toll, Paralysis in Northland,' 9 March 1949.

19 NAC, RG 85, vol. 855, file 8012, pt. 3, report of RCMP Inspector H.H. Cronkite, officer commanding 'G' Division, Eastern Arctic, Chesterfield Division, 'Re: EPIDEMIC POLIOMYELITIS AMONG NATIVES CHESTERFIELD INLET SETTLEMENT FEBRUARY 1949,' 10 March 1949, pp. 3-4.

20 J.D. Adamson et al., 'Poliomyelitis in the Arctic,' 340.

21 These have been extensively dealt with by Shelagh Grant in *Sovereignty or Security? Government Policy in the Canadian North, 1936-1950* (Vancouver: UBC Press 1988).

22 NAC, RG 85, vol. 229, file 630/153-3, report from 'RCMP Detachment, Eskimo Point, 24 August 1942, Re: Rev. Paul Dionne and Rev. Thibert, Eskimo Point, N.W.T.'

23 General Synod Archives, Anglican Church of Canada, Toronto Ontario, Diocese of the Arctic, M71-4, Bishop Marsh, Miscellaneous, Ili, 'Notes for New Workers by Archdeacon Marsh,' Eskimo Point N.W.T., n.d.

24 NAC, RG 85, vol. 984, file 10593, RCMP report from 'R.W. Hamilton, Reg. No. 10196, i/c Baker Lake Detachment, Re: Rev. Father T. Choque, Baker Lake, N.W.T. – Common Assault – Sec. 291, C.C.C.,' 26 October 1944.
25 Data provided by Dr. Otto Schaefer, Edmonton, Alberta, 5 October 1992.
26 J. Lewis Robinson, 'Eskimo Population in the Canadian Eastern Arctic: Distribution, Numbers and Trends,' *Canadian Geographical Journal* 29 (1944):131.
27 House of Commons, *Debates*, 1953, p. 698.
28 Hugh L. Keenleyside, *On the Bridge of Time*, vol. 2 of *Memoirs of Hugh L. Keenleyside* (Toronto: McCelland & Stewart 1981), 271.
29 Morris Zaslow, *The Northward Expansion of Canada, 1914-1967* (Toronto: McClelland & Stewart 1988), 309.
30 Hugh Keenleyside, *On the Bridge of Time*, 289.
31 On numerous occasions both prior to 1940 and in his report on the Eastern Arctic Patrol for 1942, McKeand warned his superiors, especially Deputy Commissioner Gibson, of the grossly inadequate way in which the government was handling health and welfare issues in the Arctic. His warnings produced little action. In *Sovereignty or Security?* (UBC Press 1988), Shelagh Grant reports that after Keenleyside was appointed deputy minister in 1945, he inquired as to whether or not the Northwest Territories Council could take over responsibility for educational and health services. Gibson reportedly replied that these matters were better left to the missions as it was less costly and 'hospitalization was synonymous with the advancement of civilization and Christianity' (p. 88).
32 Morris Zaslow, *The Northward Expansion of Canada*, 308.
33 NWT Archives, Alex Stevenson Collection, N92-023, R.T. Flanagan, Northern Administration Branch, 'A History of the Department of Northern Affairs and National Resources,' n.d., pp. 46-8.
34 Ibid., 49-50.
35 The other ministers responsible for the Department of Mines and Resources between 1945 and 1950 were James Glen, C.D. Howe as acting minister, James MacKinnon, and Colin Gibson. Glen's tenure as minister was cut short by a heart attack in the summer of 1947.
36 Hugh Keenleyside, *On the Bridge of Time*, 357.
37 Ben Sivertz, personal communication, 6 August 1992.
38 R.T. Flanagan, 'A History of the Department of Northern Affairs and National Resources,' p. 55.
39 In *The Government of Canada and the Inuit, 1900-1967* (1985) Richard Diubaldo notes that Lesage, in an article published in *The Beaver* in March 1955, admits to the chaotic nature of northern administration and both proposes and defends a remedy which included the appointment of northern service officers and the greater involvement of Inuit in local decision-making (pp. 113-14).
40 R.T. Flanagan, 'A History of the Department of Northern Affairs and National Resources,' 59.
41 It is interesting to note the presence of social-democratic and Tory perspectives within the Arctic administration as it developed in the late 1940s and 1950s. Different, yet complementary, these views were often mutually reinforcing, making possible initiatives which might otherwise have gone nowhere. This observation is consistent with those made by Gad Horowitz in *Canadian Labour in Politics* (Toronto: University of Toronto Press 1969). Horowitz notes how the Tory tradition of intervention for philanthropic purposes has reinforced social democratic ideals in Canada and given socialists a voice that might otherwise not have been heard.
42 NAC, RG 85, vol. 1069, file 251-1, pt. 1A, 'Extracts from the Minutes of Special Meeting of the Northwest Territories Council held on 27-10-49.'
43 NWT Archives, Alex Stevenson Collection, N92-023, extract from letter to R. Parsons from H.H. Rowatt, 13 July 1933.
44 R. Quinn Duffy, *The Road to Nunavut: The Progress of the Eastern Arctic Inuit since the Second World War* (Montreal and Kingston: McGill-Queen's University Press 1988), 140-1.
45 Relief paid out must also be understood in relation to the sales at HBC posts. For example, in 1947-8 and in 1948-9, sales at Inukjuak were $29,012 and $44,908, respectively. At George's River, also in Arctic Quebec, sales were $10,184 in 1947-8 and $10,414 in 1948-9. Therefore, in 1947-8, relief payments in Inukjuak were 11.3 per cent of merchandise sales and 7.5 per cent in 1948-9. At George's River they were also considerably higher than other Arctic posts, at 5.6 per cent in 1947-8 and 8.0 per cent in 1948-9.
46 In the summer of 1949, James Cantley travelled aboard the *Rupertsland*, the HBC ship chartered by the government to supply part of the eastern Arctic after the sinking of the *Nascopie* at Cape

Dorset the previous summer. Cantley handed over his Baffin Trading Company posts to the Hudson's Bay Company. As Alex Stevenson noted: 'Once again the Hudson's Bay Company reigned supreme in the Eastern Arctic!' (NWT Archives, N84-006, Alex Stevenson, letter to 'Mr. S.G. Ford, 7 British Square, St. John's Newfoundland,' 27 October 1949).

47 NAC, RG 85, vol. 786, file 5997, pt. 2, 'Report from R.N. Yates, Cst., Reg. No. 11234, I/C Detachment, "G" Division, N.W.T., Coppermine, 14-8-40,' emphasis added.

48 NAC, RG 85, vol. 786, file 5997, pt. 2, 'Report from H.A. McBeth, Reg. No. 7850. I/C Baker Lake Detachment. Re: Destitution amongst the natives of Baker Lake District, N.W.T.,' 1 July 1940, p. 2.

49 Ibid., 3.

50 NAC, RG 85, vol. 786, file 5997, pt. 2, 'Memorandum from A.L. Cumming, Bureau of Northwest Territories and Yukon Affairs, [to] R.A. Gibson, Esq., Deputy Commissioner, Ottawa,' 18 September 1940.

51 Peter C. Newman, *Merchant Princes* (Toronto: Viking 1991), 213-14.

52 NAC, RG85, vol. 786, file 5997, pt. 2, letter from 'J. Cantley, Manager, Baffin Trading Co. Ltd., [to] R.A. Gibson, Esq., Deputy Commissioner, Department of Mines and Resources, Northwest Territories Branch, Norlite Building, Ottawa,' 25 November 1940.

53 James Cantley (1896-1969) arrived in Labrador in 1913 aboard the last HBC sailing ship, the *Pelican*. In 1914 he established the first HBC post at Ward Inlet, Frobisher Bay, not far from the present site of Iqaluit. He advanced through the ranks of The Company to become, in 1930, assistant fur trade commissioner, based in Winnipeg. In 1939 he left and organized the Baffin Trading Company. This company was dissolved in 1949 as fur prices collapsed, and Cantley joined the Department of Resources and Development in 1950 when he was asked to carry out a survey of economic conditions in the Arctic. He retired in 1956.

54 NAC, RG 85, vol. 786, file 5997, pt. 2, letter from 'James Cantley, Manager, Baffin Trading Co. Ltd. [to] R.A. Gibson, Esq., Deputy Commissioner, Administration of the Northwest Territories, Norlite Building, Ottawa, Ont.,' 28 December 1940.

55 NWT Archives, Alex Stevenson Collection, N92-023, letter from 'R.H. Chesshire, Manager, Fur Trade Department, Hudson's Bay Company [to] R.A. Gibson, Deputy Commissioner, Northwest Territories, Department of Mines and Resources, OTTAWA,' 10 June 1943.

56 NWT Archives, Alex Stevenson Collection, N92-023, 'Memorandum of Instructions to District Managers Concerned, From Manager, Fur Trade Department, Winnipeg,' 13 July 1944.

57 Ibid.

58 R. Quinn Duffy, *The Road to Nunavut*, 140.

59 NWT Archives, Alex Stevenson Collection, N92-023, circular letter to 'Traders, R.C.M.Police, Missionaries and Doctors in the Eastern Arctic,' issued by Roy Gibson, deputy commissioner of the Northwest Territories, Ottawa, Ontario, 21 July 1947.

60 NWT Archives, Alex Stevenson Collection, N92-023, 'Circular Letter to Traders, R.C.M.Police, Missionaries and Doctors respecting the Issue of Relief and Rations to Eskimos,' from Roy Gibson, deputy commissioner, Northwest Territories Administration, Department of Mines and Resources, Ottawa, 22 March 1948.

61 NAC, RG 85, vol. 1069, file 251-1, pt. 1A, memo from 'J.G. Wright, [to] Mr. Sinclair, Department of Resources and Development, Northern Administration,' 9 October 1951, p. 3.

62 House of Commons, *Family Allowances Act* (1944), section 5.

63 Ibid., section 11(d).

64 The regulations and policy circulars governing family allowances were consolidated in a single document, a copy of which was found in GNWT Archives, Alex Stevenson Collection, N92-023.

65 GNWT Archives, Alex Stevenson Collection, N92-023, draft, 'Eskimo Adoption Procedure,' Ottawa, 7 July 1950.

66 Ibid.

67 House of Commons, *Family Allowances Act* (1944), section 4(2).

68 NAC, RG 85, vol. 1125, file 163-1, pt. 1, letter from 'George F. Davidson, Deputy Minister of Welfare, [to] R.A. Gibson, Esq., Deputy Commissioner, Northwest Territories, Department of Mines and Resources, Norlite Bldg., OTTAWA, Ont.,' 13 July 1945.

69 J. Lewis Robinson, 'Eskimo Population in the Canadian Eastern Arctic: Distribution, Numbers and Trends,' *Canadian Geographical Journal* 29 (1944):142. An infant death is defined as one which occurs before the child is one year old. Another source reports the Inuit infant mortality rate for the period 1951-4 as 164.5 per thousand live births. By comparison, for all Canadians the infant

mortality rate in 1950 was 42 per thousand live births. Some measure of the upheaval experienced by Inuit in the 1950s is evidenced by the infant mortality rate during the period of DEW Line construction. Between 1955 and 1958, the rate climbed to 231.5 per thousand. By comparison, the rate for Canadians had dropped to 27 per thousand by 1960 (see O. Schaefer, 'The Unmet Needs of Canadian Children,' in *Report of the First Canadian Ross Conference of Paediatric Research,* ed. H.G. Dunn et al. [Montreal: Ross Laboratories 1974], 382-8). It is interesting to speculate on the relative contributions of the conditions created by DEW Line construction and the medicalization of Inuit birthing to this statistic.

70 NWT Archives, Alex Stevenson Collection, N92-023, 'Regulations under the Family Allowance Act, 1944, Policy Circulars, 4K, No. 1, Issue of Milk and Pablum on Family Allowances Credits,' p. 1.

71 Ibid.

72 NAC, RG 85, vol. 1125, file 163-1, pt. 1A, 'MEMORANDUM [from] S.J. Bailey, Regional Director, Family Allowances for the Yukon and Northwest Territories, to Mr. R.B. Curry, National Director of F.A.'s, Re: Holding Up of Credits For Eskimos,' 24 March 1947, p. 4. It was noted that mixing water with powdered milk did not produce anything particularly palatable unless it was beaten. Consideration was given to supplying Inuit with beaters before the idea of providing a whip, costing about 15 cents, was finally agreed upon. The room was full of men. One bright soul among them suggested actually testing a wire whipper to see if it would work.

73 NWT Archives, Alex Stevenson Collection, N92-023, 'Regulations under The Family Allowance Act, 1944, Policy Circulars, No. 7, Nursing and Expectant Mothers,' 3 July 1950, p. 6.

74 *Vancouver Sun,* 'Headaches in New Child Allowances,' 26 January 1945

75 NAC, RG 85, vol. 1125, file 163-1, pt. 1, letter from 'R.H. Cheshire, Manager, Fur Trade Department [to] R.A. Gibson, Deputy Commissioner, Administration of the Northwest Territories, OTTAWA, Ont.,' 21 May 1945.

76 Ibid.

77 NAC, RG 85, vol. 1125, file 163-1, pt. 1, 'The Family Allowances Regulations,' section 36, July 1945.

78 NAC, RG 85, vol. 1125, file 163-1, pt. 1, letter from 'R.H. Chesshire, General Manager, Fur Trade Department [to] R.A. Gibson, Esq., Deputy Commissioner, Administration of the Northwest Territories, OTTAWA, Ont.,' 18 June 1945.

79 Ibid.

80 NAC, RG 85, vol. 1125, file 163-1, pt. 1A, 'ESKIMO FAMILY ALLOWANCES, ADMINISTRATION AND ACCOUNTING PROCEDURES, [from] Manager's Office, Fur Trade Department, Winnipeg, Man.,' 20 June 1945.

81 NAC, RG 85, vol. 1125, file 163-1, pt. 1A, 'Progress Report, Payment of Family Allowances to ESKIMOS and NOMADS in the Northwest Territories and Northern Quebec.' The document is undated, although it is clear from the content that it was reporting on the situation as of 21 March 1946.

82 NAC, RG 85, vol. 1175, file 163-1, pt. 1A, 'Progress Report, PAYMENT OF FAMILY ALLOWANCES as at October 31, 1946.'

83 NAC, RG 85, vol. 1125, file 163-1, pt. 1A, 'Eastern Arctic Patrol, to the O.C. "G" Div. R.C.M.P., Ottawa, Ont., Re: Family Allowances for Eskimos. Eastern Arctic District., [from] Insp. J.A. Peacock, Inspecting Officer,' 1 October 1946.

84 NAC, RG 85, vol. 1125, file 163-1, pt. 1A, 'Progress Report, Payment of Family Allowances to ESKIMOS and NOMADS in the Northwest Territories and Northern Quebec.' The document is undated, although it is clear from the content that it was reporting on the situation as of 21 March 1946.

85 *Vancouver Sun,* 'Girls Welcome in Igloo Now: Eskimos Get "Baby Bonuses,"' 30 April 1946.

86 Ibid.

87 NAC, RG 85, vol. 1125, file 163-1, pt. 1A, letter from 'R.A. Gibson, Deputy Commissioner [to] R.H. Chesshire, Esq., Manager, Fur Trade Department, Hudson's Bay Company, Winnipeg, Manitoba,' 7 May 1946.

88 NAC, RG 85, vol. 1125, file 163-1, pt. 1A, letter from 'R.A. Gibson, Deputy Commissioner, to J.D. Cantley, Manager, Baffin Trading Company Ltd., 1501 Royal Bank Building, 360 St. James Street West, Montreal 1, Quebec.'

89 Ibid.

90 NAC, RG 85, vol. 1125, file 163-1, pt. 1A, confidential report from 'Cpl. W.J.G. Stewart, Reg. No.

10416, i/c Port Harrison Detachment, 'REQUEST OF NATIVES IN DISTRICT No. E-9, PORT HARRISON, P.Q. REGARDING FAMILY ALLOWANCE CREDITS,' 27 December 1946.
91 Ibid.
92 NAC, RG 85, vol. 1125, file 163-1, pt. 1A, memorandum to 'Mr. Gibson from J.G. Wright,' Ottawa, 21 March 1947.
93 NAC, RG 85, vol. 1125, file 163-1, pt. 1A, letter from 'R.B. Curry, National Director, Family Allowances to Mr. T.F. Phillips, Chief Treasury Officer, Dept. National Health and Welfare, OTTAWA, Ontario,' 12 February 1947.
94 NAC, RG 85, vol. 1125, file 163-1, pt. 1A, memo from 'R. Gibson, Deputy Commissioner to Mr. Wright,' 24 March 1947.
95 NAC, RG 85, vol. 1125, file 163-1, 'MEMORANDUM To: Mr. R.B. Curry, National Director of F.A.'s., [from] S.J. Bailey, Regional Director, Family Allowances for the Yukon & Northwest Territories, Re: Holding Up of Credits for Eskimos, File 10/2-3,' 24 March 1947.
96 Ibid., 1.
97 Ibid., 2.
98 The invocation of 'education' as an answer to social problems is a characteristically liberal solution, which was increasingly employed following the Second World War as a response to social and economic crises. It was evoked here for the first time in the eastern Arctic. Education as a solution avoids the necessity of looking at structural considerations as the source of social problems and, while appearing to be an enlightened response, shifts responsibility for addressing issues onto individuals. If, in the presence of education, people continue to eat the wrong foods or purchase the wrong goods, then clearly they are at fault. The roles of coercion, necessity, and other circumstances in explaining human behaviour are conveniently overlooked.
99 NAC, RG 85, vol. 1125, file 163-1, 'MEMORANDUM To: Mr. R.B. Curry, National Director of F.A.'s., [from] S.J. Bailey, Regional Director, Family Allowances for the Yukon & Northwest Territories, Re: Holding Up of Credits for Eskimos, File 10/2-3,' 24 March 1947, p. 3.
100 NWT Archives, Alex Stevenson Collection, N84-006, draft, 'The Book of Wisdom,' Bureau of Northwest Territories and Yukon Affairs, Lands, Parks and Forests Branch, Department of Mines and Resources, Ottawa, 1947.
101 NAC, RG 85, vol. 1072, file 254-1, pt. 2A, letter from 'Marjorie Hinds, Welfare Teacher, Port Harrison P.Q., [to] R.A. Gibson, Esq., Deputy Commissioner, Northwest Territories Administration, Norlite Building, Ottawa,' 9 September 1950.
102 Ibid., 19-29.
103 NWT Archives, Alex Stevenson Collection, N84-006, memo to 'Mr. Wright [from] Alex Stevenson, Ottawa,' 6 June 1959.
104 NAC, RG 85, vol. 1125, file 163-1, pt. 1A, letter from 'R.H. Chesshire, General Manager, Fur Trade Department, Hudson's Bay Company, [to] R.A. Gibson, Esq., Deputy Commissioner, Administration of the Northwest Territories, OTTAWA, Ont.,' 26 March 1947.
105 NAC, RG 85, vol. 1125, file 163-1, pt. 1B, letter from 'R.A. Gibson [to] R.H. Chesshire, Esq., General Manager, Fur Trade Department, Hudson's Bay Company, Winnipeg Manitoba,' 16 April 1947.
106 NAC, RG 85, vol. 1125, file 163-1, pt. 1B, 'SUPPLEMENTARY REPORT OF THE FIELD MATRON, FT. MCPHERSON N.W.T. for the month of July 1947, (signed) Mrs. A.S. Dewdney, Field Matron,' 26 July 1947.
107 NAC, RG 85, vol. 1125, file 163-1, pt. 1-B, report of 'D.J. Martin, Supt., Officer Commanding "G" Division, [to] The Commissioner, R.C.M.Police, OTTAWA, Re: Family Allowances in the N.W.T. – Report of Mr. S.J. Bailey – Regional Director, OTTAWA,' 3 October 1947, p. 2
108 NAC, RG 85, vol. 1125, file 163-1, pt. 1B, 'Eskimo – Administration of Eskimo Family Allowance Credits by R.C.M.P.' This document is untitled but, in the context of other papers contained in the same file, is clearly a section taken from Bailey's report of his investigation. The last statement reveals that Bailey had not yet recognized that Mines and Resources, as a trustee, had the right to withhold family allowances and had chosen to do so. Therefore, his observation that withholding payment was beyond their jurisdiction is incorrect.
109 NWT Archives, Alex Stevenson Collection, N92-023, 'INSTRUCTIONS TO DISTRICT AND SUB-DISTRICT REGISTRARS FOR FAMILY ALLOWANCES AND VITAL STATISTICS, [from] R.A. Gibson, Deputy Commissioner, Northwest Territories, Ottawa,' 20 March 1948.
110 NAC, RG 85, vol. 1069, file 251-1, pt. 1A, extract from S.J. Bailey's Report dated at Churchill, 13 August 1948.
111 NAC, RG 85, vol. 1069, file 251-1, pt. 1A, letter from 'R.A. Gibson, Deputy Commissioner [to] R.H.

372 Notes to pp. 89-98

Cheshire, Esq., General Manager, Fur Trade Department, Hudson's Bay Company, WINNIPEG,' 2 February 1949.
112 NAC, RG 85, vol. 79, file 201-1-1, letter from 'R.A. Gibson, Deputy Commissioner, [to] Mr. R.B. Curry, National Director, Family Allowances, Department of National Health & Welfare, Jackson Building, Ottawa,' 24 June 1949, p. 3.
113 NAC, RG 85, vol. 1507, file 600-3, pt. 1, RCMP report by 'E.J. Ard, #15059, I/c Tuktoyaktuk Detachment, 26-6-50, Miss ROBINSON – Tuktoyaktuk, N.W.T., compl. re: – School Attendance.'
114 Ibid., 2.
115 NAC, RG 85, vol. 1068, file 163-1, pt. 5, 'Eskimo Council Meeting Held at Reindeer Station (Nov. 26 1952).'
116 Ibid.
117 That this idea had been first suggested by Inuit at Aklavik is revealed in a memo dated 25 April 1953 from F. Fraser of the department to Mr. Wright in which he addressed the concerns raised by the Inuit council. Fraser was less than enthusiastic about the idea of a cooperative, suggesting that it would be patronized in hard times but that in good times, when money was plentiful, 'the natives would be inclined to leave the cooperative and deal with the traders.' See NAC, RG 85, vol. 1068, file 163-1, Pt. 5, 'Memorandum for Mr. Wright, [from] F. Fraser, Ottawa,' 25 April 1953.
118 Ibid.
119 NAC, RG 85, vol. 1068, file 163-1, pt. 5, letter from 'George F. Davidson, Deputy Minister of Welfare [to] Right Reverend Donald Marsh, Anglican Bishop of the Arctic, Church House, 604 Jarvis Street, TORONTO, Canada,' 20 January 1953, p. 2
120 Ibid.
121 By this time the Northwest Territories and Yukon Services had been reorganized. Arctic adminis-tration was now located within the Northern Administration and Lands Branch of the newly created Department of Northern Affairs and National Resources.
122 NAC, RG 85, vol. 1068, file 163-1, pt. 5, RCMP report from 'R.A. White, #15940, AKLAVIK DETACHMENT, [to] The Director, Northern Administration and Lands Branch, Department of Resources and Development, OTTAWA, Ontario,' 21 November 1953.
123 NAC, RG 85, vol. 1068, file 163-1, pt. 5, 'PORT HARRISON, P.Q., AN INTERVIEW WITH JIMMY KOODLOOALLOK OF BELCHER ISLANDS AUGUST 20, 1953 AT 7 p.m. IN THE WELFARE TEACHER'S KITCHEN,' pp. 1-2.
124 Ibid.
125 NAC, RG 85, vol. 1103, file 565-1, pt. 2, 'PRECIS FOR THE NORTHWEST TERRITORIES COUNCIL, Old Age Allowances to Eskimos,' 21 June 1950.
126 Ibid.
127 Ibid.
128 NAC, RG 85, vol. 1103, file 565-1, pt. 2, 'Extracts from the Minutes of Special Meeting of the Northwest Territories Council held on June 23, 1950.'
129 Ibid.
130 NAC, RG 85, vol. 1103, file 565-1, pt. 2, 'DRAFT, INSTRUCTION TO DISTRICT REGISTRARS OF VITAL STATISTICS, ESKIMOS – OLD AGE PENSIONS,' n.d., p. 2.
131 NAC, RG 85, vol. 1103, file 565-1, vol. 2, 'MEMORANDUM FOR THE COMMISSIONER OF THE NORTHWEST TERRITORIES, [from] Frank J.G. Cunningham, Deputy Commissioner,' 3 August 1951, p. 1.
132 NAC, RG 85, vol. 1103, file 565-1, vol. 2, letter from 'J.W. MacFarlane, Director of Old Age Pensions, National Health and Welfare, [to] Mr. G.E.B. Sinclair, Director, Northern Administration & Lands Branch, Department of Resources and Development, Ottawa, Ontario,' 5 July 1951.
133 Dennis Guest, The Emergence of Social Security in Canada, 145.
134 NAC, RG 85, vol. 1068, file 163-1, pt. 5, letter from 'George F. Davidson, Deputy Minister of Welfare [to] Right Reverend Donald Marsh, Anglican Bishop of the Arctic, Church House, 604 Jarvis Street, TORONTO, Canada,' 20 January 1953.
135 NWT Archives, Alex Stevenson Collection, N92-023, memorandum for 'Mr. Wright [from] J. Cantley, Arctic Services,' 12 February 1951.
136 NWT Archives, Alex Stevenson Collection, N92-023, 'The Fur Trade,' n.d. While undated, this document appears to be a collection of statistics on the fur trade worked up for James Cantley's report on economic conditions in the Northwest Territories.
137 NWT Archives, Alex Stevenson Collection, N92-023, 'Family Allowance Credits Including Trans-fers by Financial Years to Date.,' n.d.

138 NWT Archives, Alex Stevenson Collection, N92-023, data from the 'Fur Trade Department, Hudson's Bay Company, Winnipeg,' 2 January 1950.
139 James Cantley, *The Cantley Economic Report on Eskimo Affairs* (Ottawa: Department of Resources and Development 1950), 48.
140 Ibid.
141 NAC, RG 85, vol. 1070, file 251-4, pt. 1, memo from 'H.A. Larsen, Insp., Officer Commanding, "G" Division, [to] The Commissioner, R.C.M.Police, OTTAWA, Ontario, Responsibility, Care and Supervision of Eskimos,' 30 October 1951, p. 1.
142 Ibid., 1-2.
143 NAC, RG 85, vol. 1070, file 251-4, pt. 1, 'MEMORANDUM FOR MR. WRIGHT, [from] J. Cantley, Arctic Services,' 29 November 1951,' pp. 1-2 (emphasis from the original text).
144 NAC, RG 85, vol. 1513, file 1012-1, pt. 1, 'SUMMARY OF THE PROCEEDINGS AT A MEETING ON ESKIMO AFFAIRS HELD MAY 19 AND 20, 1952, IN THE BOARD ROOM OF THE CONFEDERATION BUILDING, OTTAWA,' p. 8.
145 See reviews by A.E. Porsild in *The Beaver* (June 1952):47-9, and by Douglas Leechman in the *Canadian Geographical Journal* (August 1952):v-vi.

Chapter 3: Planning for Relocation to the High Arctic

1 Indian and Northern Affairs Canada, 'Government to Return Inuit To Inukjouak,' *Communique*, 19 November 1990, p. 2. The spelling of Inukjuak is highly variable on maps, in papers, and in government reports and includes: Inukjouac, Inukjuak, Inoucdjouac, and Inukjouak.
2 Shelagh Grant, 'A Case of Compounded Error: The Inuit Resettlement Project, 1953, and the Government Response, 1990,' *Northern Perspectives* 19 (Spring 1991):12. Grant suggests that the second motive – welfare concerns – were of 'little significance in determining time or place, but of primary importance in defining who would participate and what form the projects would take.' At the time of the relocation, welfare conditions in Arctic Quebec were a problem the federal administration felt it had to address. The need to locate RCMP in the high Arctic for sovereignty reasons corresponded with the need to find a solution to the welfare problem which had become critical in Arctic Quebec. Otherwise, it is likely that the RCMP would have used Inuit from Baffin Island to meet their needs for travel and other assistance. Welfare concerns appear to be relevant to both the timing of the relocation and the matter of who participated in the move.
3 *Toronto Star*, editorial, 'Arctic Self-Exiles Canada's Shame,' 2 July 1991.
4 D. Soberman, 'Report to the Canadian Human Rights Commission on the Complaints of the Inuit People Relocated from Inukjouak and Pond Inlet, to Grise Fiord and Resolute Bay in 1953 and 1955,' Kingston, ON, 11 December 1991, p. 55.
5 Ibid., 56.
6 Magnus Gunther, 'The 1953 Relocations of the Inukjuak Inuit to the High Arctic: A Documentary Analysis and Evaluation,' Trent University, Peterborough, ON, 1992.
7 Shelagh Grant, 'A Case of Compounded Error,' 12.
8 Keith Lowther, 'An Exercise in Sovereignty: The Government of Canada and the Inuit Relocation of 1953,' M.A. thesis, University of Calgary, 1989.
9 Andrew Orkin, 'Immersion in the High Arctic: An Examination of the Relocation of Canadian Inuit in 1953 from the Perspective of the Law on Experimentation Involving Human Subjects,' paper submitted to the Canadian Arctic Resources Committee, June 1991. A CBC edition of *Quirks and Quarks*, broadcast 28 September 1991, was based on Orkin's use of the Nuremberg Code to evaluate what he claimed was the 'experimental' nature of the relocation. Although Orkin, in both his unpublished paper and the CBC program, stated that he did not intend a comparison with the Nuremberg experiments conducted by the Nazis on Jews during the Second World War, the comparison was difficult to avoid.
10 Alan Marcus, 'Out in the Cold: Canada's Experimental Inuit Relocation to Grise Fiord and Resolute Bay,' *Polar Record* 27, no. 163 (1991):285-96.
11 *Vancouver Sun*, 'Ottawa Won't Apologize to Inuit It Moved in '50s,' 21 November 1992.
12 Many of the families relocated from Inukjuak returned to the community in the mid-1980s.
13 Resolute Bay was named after the *Resolute*, a 410-ton vessel which was the flagship of a British squadron under a Captain Austin. The *Resolute* sailed from England on 3 May 1850 in search of the Franklin expedition, which had left England in 1845. The squadron consisted of four ships. They wintered in 1850-1 on the ice between Griffith and Cornwallis islands. The squadron returned to England in the fall of 1851.

The *Resolute* returned to the Arctic in 1852 and wintered at Dealey Island off the south shore of Melville Island. She was abandoned in 1854, and her crew returned to England aboard another vessel. The ship drifted in the ice 900 miles from where she was abandoned to a point near Cumberland Sound on the east coast of Baffin Island. There, she was picked up by an American whaler, James Buddington, on 10 September 1855. She was returned to New London, Connecticut, and purchased by the U.S. government, which after repairing and refitting the vessel, returned her to the British government as a goodwill gesture.

14 Diamond Jenness, *Eskimo Administration: II. Canada* (Montreal: Arctic Institute of North America 1964), 29.

15 Ibid., 30.

16 See Morris Zaslow, *The Northward Expansion of Canada, 1914-1967* (Toronto: McClelland & Stewart 1988), 200-1.

17 Government of Canada, Order-in-Council No. 1146, 19 July 1926, *Canadian Gazette*, no. 5, vol. IX (Ottawa: King's Printer), pp. 382-3.

18 'Memorandum to the Cabinet: Canadian Sovereignty Over the Arctic Archipelago,' 27 June 1960, Ottawa, Department of Northern Affairs and National Resources, p. 4. The memorandum was presented to cabinet by the then minister, Alvin Hamilton.

19 Government of Canada, Order-in-Council No. 1925, 5 August 1939, *Canadian Gazette*, no. 6, vol. LXXIII (Ottawa: King's Printer), 351-8.

20 Diamond Jenness, *Eskimo Administration: II. Canada*, 56.

21 This is the same Frederick Banting credited, along with his assistant Charles Best, with the isolation of the hormone insulin at the University of Toronto in 1921.

22 NWT Archives, Alex Stevenson Collection, N92-023, 'Canadian Arctic Expedition – 1927,' p. 5.

23 Writing in *The Government of Canada and the Inuit, 1900-1967* (Ottawa: Research Branch, Corporate Policy, Department of Indian and Northern Affairs Canada 1985), Richard Diubaldo indicates that Banting made his trip in 1928 (p. 71). However, from the dates on Banting's reports to Finnie, it appears that the trip was made in the summer of 1927.

24 NWT Archives, Alex Stevenson Collection, N92-023, 'Medical Investigation Among Eskimo,' p. 1.

25 NAC, RG 85, vol. 2081, file 1012-4, pt. 3A, 'memorandum for Mr. Gibson, Bureau of Northwest Territories and Yukon Affairs [from] D.L. McKeand,' 9 March 1945.

26 NAC, RG 85, vol. 2081, file 1012-4, pt. 3A, 'Private and confidential report to Mr. O.S. Finnie, Department of the Interior, North West Territories and Yukon Branch, Ottawa [from] F.G. Banting,' 8 November 1927, p. 2. This report is an elaboration of a report submitted on 14 September of the same year.

27 Ibid., 2.

28 Morris Zaslow, *The Northward Expansion of Canada*, 137.

29 Diamond Jenness, *Eskimo Administration: II. Canada*, 36.

30 These prices are reported in 'The Far North: Back to Self-Sufficiency,' *Time Magazine*, 8 December 1952. The article focuses on the appointment of James Wright, a long-time civil servant with the Northern Affairs and Lands Branch of Northern Affairs and National Resources, to head an 'Eskimo Research Unit,' which was to focus on diversifying the economic base of Inuit. In *Merchant Princes*, volume 3 of his examination of the history of the Hudson's Bay Company (Viking 1991), Peter Newman reports the decline in prices as being even more dramatic. He claims prices declined from $35 to $3 between 1946 and 1948 (p. 244). The most accurate record is likely provided in a report done for the Council of the Northwest Territories by James Cantley in 1950, cited in the previous chapter. Jenness notes that in 1948-9 the average price of white fox fur was $8.88 and that at one point, in 1949-50, it fell as low as $3.50 (see Jenness, Diamond, *Eskimo Administration: II. Canada*, 79, n. 4).

31 For examples of how the RCMP regarded Hudson's Bay Company traders, see Richard Diubaldo, *The Government of Canada and the Inuit*, 62-8.

32 The ship, launched from North Vancouver in April 1928, left Vancouver on 28 June and reached Herschel Island by 27 July. It wintered over until breakup on 24 June 1929 and returned to Vancouver by October of the same year. Larsen took the ship north again in June 1930. See Henry Larsen, Frank R. Sheer, and Evard Omholt-Jensen, *The Big Ship: An Autobiography* (Toronto: McClelland & Stewart 1967), 39, 42, 57-8, and The *St. Roch*, Ship's Log, *Daily Journal*, Vancouver, St. Roch National Historic Site, entries for 26 June-10 November, 1928, and 1 May-23 September, 1929.

33 The first cooperatives were organized at Ungava Bay, Port Burwell, George River, and Cape Dorset

in 1959. See Morris Zaslow, *The Northward Expansion of Canada*, 277.
34 A classic example can be found in J. Lewis Robinson, 'Eskimo Population in the Canadian Eastern Arctic,' *Canadian Geographical Journal* 29 (September 1944):129-42. Robinson goes to great lengths to calculate the number of Inuit per mile of coastline and per unit area in different regions of the eastern Arctic, coming to the conclusion that the density of population in Arctic Quebec explains the high costs of relief in the region (p. 133).
35 Diamond Jenness, *Eskimo Administration: II. Canada*, 57.
36 Morris Zaslow states that 'when [the] experiment failed, the company returned most of the natives to their Baffin Island homes and some to the newly opened Fort Ross' (see Zaslow, *The Northward Expansion of Canada*, 137). While some Inuit were returned to the areas from which they had been taken, many, as evidenced by contemporary claims made by residents of Spence Bay, were not.
37 At the time, the only transportation over long distances between communities was once a year on the Eastern Arctic Patrol vessel which then was the Hudson's Bay Company vessel the *Nascopie*. Cape Dorset Inuit therefore had no means of returning to their home community without the assistance of the government or the HBC. Even the advent of air travel didn't solve the problem. With established relationships with other Cape Dorset migrants in the community, and family and relatives still in Cape Dorset, the individual or family was faced with the dilemma of trying to decide whether to leave or stay.
38 As quoted in Diamond Jenness, *Eskimo Administration: II. Canada*, 57.
39 NWT Archives, Alex Stevenson Collection, N92-023, 'The Arctic and Some of Its Problems,' Dr. D. Jenness, lecture given at Staff College, Armour Heights, Toronto, 9 December 1944 and 5 December 1945, p. 9.
40 Diamond Jenness, *Eskimo Administration: II. Canada*, 58.
41 Henry Larsen, 'Patrolling the Arctic and the Northwest Passage in the R.C.M.P. ship St. Roch – 1944' (Ottawa: Department of Northern Affairs and National Resources), p. 2.
42 NWT Archives, Alex Stevenson Collection, N92-023, 'British Sovereignty in the Arctic,' letter from S.T. Wood, commissioner, to the deputy minister, Department of Mines and Resources, 24 November 1944.
43 Makavik Corporation, Inuit Tapirisat of Canada, Kativik Regional Government, 'Position Paper Regarding Grise Fiord/Resolute Bay Relocation Issue,' 20 January 1987, p. 3.
44 'Inuit "Internal Exiles" Want Ottawa to Pay $10 Million Compensation,' *Globe and Mail*, 2 January 1987.
45 For example, see Shelagh Grant, *Sovereignty or Security? Government Policy in the Canadian North, 1936-1950* (Vancouver: UBC Press 1988)
46 Andrew Orkin, 'Immersion in the High Arctic: An Examination of the Relocation of Canadian Inuit in 1953 from the Perspective of the Law on Experimentation Involving Human Subjects.' The paper was submitted to the Canadian Arctic Resources Committee, who decided not to publish it. Following the publication of the report by Magnus Gunther in 1992, Orkin wrote an editorial for the *Globe and Mail*, 'Using the Inuit as Human Flagpoles' (4 December 1992), in which he reiterated that no comparison with the experiments done by the Nazis on Jews during the Second World War was intended and noted that he had made this clear in both his paper and on the CBC special edition of *Quirks and Quarks* of 28 September 1991. Orkin argued that the motives of officials were irrelevant to the conclusion that the relocation was improper. However, in order to make such a claim, the case must first be made that a social 'experiment' was being conducted and not the execution of a policy intended to address a number of problems facing the administration. The claim that this was a 'social experiment' of a type eligible for evaluation by the Nuremberg Code seems to be the weakest aspect of Orkin's claim.
47 Mr. Jacques Gerin, deputy minister of Indian Affairs and Northern Development, as quoted in 'Inuit "Internal Exiles" Want Ottawa to Pay $10 Million Compensation,' *Globe and Mail*, 2 January 1987.
48 Readers familiar with the field of international development will note that commitments to the notion of 'modernization' and the development of 'primitive people' were not, at the time, restricted to Canadian relations with Native people. These concepts guided attempts to develop the former colonies of Africa and other countries of the so-called 'Third World' following the Second World War. The Canadian government played a significant role in these initiatives with Lester Pearson, secretary of state for external affairs, playing a key part in developing an important Canadian role in attempts by the United States, Britain, and their European allies to modernize the so-called 'primitive' cultures of the Third World.

49 W.L.M. King, diary, 29 March 1943, as cited by C. Nordman, 'The Army of Occupation,' in *The Alaska Highway: Papers of the 40th Anniversary Symposium*, ed. Kenneth Coates (Vancouver: UBC Press 1985), and quoted in Shelagh Grant, *Sovereignty or Security?*, 111.
50 Grant Shelagh, *Sovereignty or Security?*, 132.
51 NAC, RG 2/18, vol. 57, file A25-5, report from Captain W.W. Bean to the Chiefs of Staff Committee, 13 November 1947, cited in Shelagh Grant, *Sovereignty or Security?*, 215.
52 NAC, RG 85, vol. 300, file 1009-3, pt. 1, Privy Council Office, 20 December 1949, 'SECRET, Fifth Meeting Advisory Committee on Northern Development, December 19th, 1949, Proposed Itinerary: C.D. Howe.'
53 Ibid.
54 *Journal of Commerce*, 'Ownership of Land in Arctic Sought,' 9 March 1944, as cited in Shelagh Grant, *Sovereignty or Security?*, 133.
55 Ibid., 230.
56 Peter C. Newman, *Merchant Princes*, vol. 3 (Toronto: Viking 1991), 213.
57 Canada, *Report of the Department of Resources and Development*, Ottawa, 1950. p. 12; *Report of the Department of Resources and Development*, Ottawa, 1951, p. 80. In 1949 the Northwest Territories Council was chaired by Hugh Keenleyside and in 1950 by his replacement as deputy minister of the department, Major-General Hugh Young. In October of 1950, F.J.G. Cunningham succeeded Roy Gibson as deputy commissioner.
58 NAC, RG 85, vol. 2085, file 20996, pt. 3, 'Memorandum for Mr. J.G. Wright, Chief, Arctic Division [from] Mr. J.W. Burton,' 13 October 1950.
59 NAC, RG 85, vol. 2085, file 20996, pt. 3. 'Memorandum for Mr. Burton [from] J.G. Wright, Chief, Arctic Division,' 21 October 1950.
60 'Eskimos Advised to Go Northward,' *Montreal Gazette*, 20 October 1943.
61 Oblate Fathers of Hudson Bay Vicarate, 'The Boarding School at Chesterfield and the Education of the Eskimo,' *Eskimo*, December 1955, p. 12.
62 NAC, RG 85, vol. 79, file 201-1-1, pt. 25A, 'Extracts from Report of A. Stevenson, Officer-in-charge, Eastern Arctic Patrol, 1950.'
63 In writing his report, 'The 1953 Relocations of the Inukjuak Inuit to the High Arctic,' for the minister of Indian affairs and northern development, Professor Gunther gets drawn into addressing the issue of sovereignty as a 'high level conspiracy' and, not surprisingly, finds no evidence to support such a claim. However, the statements from those in the field, aware of the larger political context and military developments taking place at the time, and having personal feelings about Canadian Arctic sovereignty, make it clear that the impetus for addressing sovereignty by relocating Inuit came from the field – from the lower ranks of the civil service, not the top.
    When the concept – articulated by knowledgeable men in the field – met with the threat to what Gunther calls de facto sovereignty, with which Deputy Minister Hugh Young was faced (documented later in the text), it is not hard to see how relocating Inuit conveniently served two purposes at the same time: making a statement about Canadian sovereignty and dealing with the Quebec welfare problem. In other words, Inuit did not merely contribute to Canadian sovereignty once relocated – there was clearly a perception within the department, *before* they were moved, that they could make such a contribution.
64 Ibid., 27.
65 NAC, RG 85, vol. 294, file 1005-7 pt. 5, confidential letter to the 'Commissioner, R.C.M.Police, Ottawa, Ontario, [from] H.A. Larsen, Insp., Officer Commanding, "G" Division,' 11 October 1950.
66 NAC, RG 85, vol. 294, file 1005-7, pt. 5, confidential letter from 'S.T. Wood, Commissioner, RCMP, [to] Deputy Commissioner Northwest Territories, Department of Resources and Development, Norlite Building, Ottawa,' 13 October 1950.
67 NAC, RG 85, vol. 1127, file 201-1-8, vol. 2A, telegram from the 'C.D. Howe, Sept. 2, 1951, 230PM from STEVENSON to J G WRIGHT OTTAWA.'
68 NAC, RG 22, vol. 176, file 40-2-20, pt. 3. 'DRAFT PRESS RELEASE,' 2 September 1951.
69 NAC, RG 85, vol. 294, file 1005-7, pt. 5, letter from 'H.A. Larsen, Insp., Officer Commanding, "G" Division, [to] The Commissioner, RCMP. Ottawa,' 7 November 1951.
70 Frank Cunningham was a Saskatchewan magistrate who headed an inquiry into the 1935 'On-to-Ottawa' march. He had acted as a judge for war crimes trials in Singapore at the end of the Second World War, prior to joining the civil service. He died in 1964.

71 NAC, RG 85, vol. 294, file 1005-7, pt. 5, letter from 'J.A. Peacock, Commissioner, [to] the Deputy Commissioner, Administration of the Northwest Territories, Ottawa,' 16 November 1950. (The letter is dated 1950, but it is obvious from the sequence of events and the content that the date was actually 1951.)

72 NAC, RG 85, vol. 294, file 1005-7, pt. 5, memorandum from 'J.G. Wright [to] Mr. Sinclair, Director, Northern Administration Division,' 18 January 1952, and from 'G.E.B. Sinclair, Director, to The Commissioner, RCMP,' 26 January 1952.

73 NAC, RG 85, vol. 1070, file 251-4, pt. 1, letter from 'L.H. Nicholson, Commissioner, [to] Major General H.A. Young, Deputy Minister,' 11 February 1952.

74 Ibid.

75 NAC, RG 85, vol. 79, file 201-1-1, pt. 25A, 'Extracts from Report of A. Stevenson, Officer-in-charge, Eastern Arctic Patrol, 1950.'

76 Personal communication, interview with Constable Ross Gibson, Victoria, BC, 9 February 1992.

77 NAC, RG 85, vol. 1070, file 251-4, pt. 1, letter from 'L.H. Nicholson, Commissioner, [to] Major General H.A. Young, Deputy Minister,' 11 February 1952.

78 D. Barry, ed., 'Note from Privy Council Office to Clerk of Privy Council,' 29 December 1952, in *Documents on Canada's External Relations, 1952* (Ottawa: Department of External Affairs and International Trade 1990, vol. 18, p. 1194. Our attention was first directed to this source by Shelagh Grant, Department of History, Trent University, Peterborough, Ontario.

79 Ibid., 'Extract from Attachment to Memorandum,' p. 1195.

80 Ibid.

81 NAC, RG 85, vol. 2085, file 20996, pt. 12, letter from 'H.A. Young, Deputy Minister [to] A.D.P. Heeney, Esq., Q.C., Under-Secretary of State for External Affairs, Ottawa,' 28 March 1952.

82 NAC, RG 22, vol. 176, file 40-2-20, pt. 3, 'Report On Eastern Arctic Patrol, Churchill to Quebec, 1952,' p. 9.

83 D. Barry, ed., 'Memorandum from Privy Council Office to Clerk of Privy Council,' 1952, *Documents on Canada's External Relations*, p. 1199.

84 NAC, RG 22, vol. 176, file 40-2-20, pt. 3, 'MEMORANDUM FOR THE ACTING DIRECTOR, [from] J.G. Wright, Chief, Eskimo Research Section, Ottawa,' 25 November 1952.

85 D. Barry, ed., 'Memorandum from Privy Council Office to clerk of Privy Council,' 1952, *Documents on Canada's External Relations*, p. 1197.

86 Ibid.

87 Ibid., 1198.

88 Ibid., 1199.

89 NAC, RG 22, vol. 176, file 40-2-20, pt. 3., 'Report On Eastern Arctic Patrol, Churchill to Quebec, 1952,' p. 8.

90 D. Barry, ed., 'Memorandum from Under-Secretary of State for External Affairs to Secretary of State for External Affairs,' 1952, *Documents on Canada's External Relations*, pp. 1201-2.

91 Ibid.

92 NAC, RG 85, vol. 294, file 1005-7, pt. 5, letter from 'H.A. Larsen, Insp., Officer Commanding "G" Division [to] The Commissioner, RCMPolice, Ottawa,' 14 October 1952.

93 NAC, RG 22, vol. 254, file 40-8-1, pt. 3, 'Minutes of the First Meeting of Special Committee on Eskimo Affairs held Thursday, October 16, 1952, in Room 304, Langevin Block, Ottawa,' p. 4.

94 NAC, RG 85, vol. 2085, file 20996, pt. 36, letter from 'L.D. Wilgress [to] General Young, CONFIDENTIAL,' 14 January 1953.

95 NAC, MG 30 E 133, vol. 294, file ACND, vol. 1, 'Minutes of the 6th meeting of the ACND,' 16 February 1953, pp. 2-3, cited in Shelagh Grant, 'A Case of Compounded Error,' 10.

96 Ibid., 2.

97 Ibid., 3.

98 Ibid.

99 Ibid., 4.

100 Ibid.

101 Magnus Gunther, 'The 1953 Relocations of the Inukjuak Inuit to the High Arctic,' 54-5.

102 Ibid., 55.

103 NAC, MG 30 E 133, vol. 294, file ACND, vol. 1, 'Minutes of the 6th meeting of the ACND,' 16 February 1953, p. 4.

104 NWT Archives, Alex Stevenson Collection, N92-023, 'Secret Memorandum, Eskimos – Importance to the National Defence of Canada,' 7 January 1950. The memo is addressed to AMOT (Thru DASS)

which is code. At this time, the military was using code for all documents related to the Arctic. Other departments of government were supposed to do the same, although it was a practice that was seldom followed.

105   Ibid., 1-2.
106   Ibid., 2.
107   NAC, MG 30 E 133, vol. 294, file ACND, vol. 1, 'Minutes of the 6th meeting of the ACND,' 16 February 1953, p. 5.
108   It seems unlikely that such directives exist. In researching the subject, we uncovered thirty-six volumes of material donated to the NWT Archives by the widow of Alex Stevenson, and we had the opportunity to go through the collection before it had been officially catalogued. This impressive collection had been in storage since it was donated in the early 1980s. Despite containing many interesting confidential and otherwise secret documents – including some from the period in question – no such directives were found, although many documents relating to the relocation were present. Given the nature of the collection, Alex Stevenson's obvious ability to amass an impressive collection of important documents, and his relationship to these events, it seems likely that, were it to exist, such documentation would have been present in the files.

Chapter 4: Recolonizing the Arctic Islands

1   NAC, RG 22, vol. 254, file 40-8-1, pt. 3, 'MEMORANDUM FOR THE DEPUTY MINISTER, Ottawa,' 16 March 1953.
2   NAC, RG 85, vol. 294, file 1005-7-5, letter from 'H.A. Young, Deputy Minister [to] L.D. Wilgress, Esq., Under-Secretary of State for External Affairs, East Block, Ottawa,' 2 April 1953.
3   Reference to this inquiry is found in a memo to the commissioner of the RCMP, Ottawa, by H.A. Larsen, officer commanding 'G' Division. He notes: 'In his letter of May 13th 1953, to you, Major-General H.A. Young says: "we have been exploring this angle with the Air Force and are awaiting their reply as to what number, if any, they could give full time employment to"'(NAC, RG 85, vol. 1070, file 251-4, pt. 1).
4   NAC, RG 85, vol. 1070, file 251-4, pt. 1, letter from 'F.J.G. Cunningham, Director, [to] S/Inspector J.J. Atherton, Officer in Charge, Criminal Investigation Branch, Royal Canadian Mounted Police, Ottawa, Ontario,' 7 May 1953.
5   Hickling Corporation, 'Assessment of the Factual Basis of Certain Allegations Made Before the Standing Committee on Aboriginal Affairs Concerning the Relocation of Inukjuak Inuit Families in the 1950s,' report submitted to the Department of Indian Affairs and Northern Development, Northern Program, September 1990, p. 27.
6   Much of the attention on the choice of which Inuit would go north focuses on the written records, which attribute the process to Corporal Webster, who was in charge at Port Harrison at the time. However, it was Ross Gibson who was responsible for identifying Inuit to go north. Webster was a chronic alcoholic – to the point where he was often unable to perform his duties and even to the point where he reportedly placed not only his, but the lives of others in the community, at risk.
7   Tommy Pallisser was an employee of the Hudson's Bay Company in Port Harrison. Originally from Nain, Labrador, he was the interpreter used in relating the idea of the move to Inuit. Roop Ploughman was the manager of the HBC in Port Harrison, and Willya was an Inuk special constable, the brother of 'Fatty,' one of the relocatees to Grise Fiord.
8   Personal communication, interview with Ross Gibson, former RCMP constable, Victoria, BC, 9 February 1992.
9   Personal communication, interview with Ross Gibson, Victoria, BC, 22 April 1992. The reference to records is to the welfare and the trading records of the Hudson's Bay Company, which would have revealed who was trapping, who was a successful trapper, and who was receiving large amounts of social assistance.
10   However, as noted, the decision to send Inuit to Resolute Bay clearly had already been made in March in submitting appropriations for the Eskimo Loan Fund. Therefore, the impression that Constable Gibson was working under was incorrect. However, he confirmed the fact that he did not know that he or Inuit were to be located to Resolute Bay until the *C.D. Howe* reached Craig Harbour. This corroborates Inuit testimony before the House of Commons Standing Committee on Aboriginal Affairs that Inuit did not know they were going to be split into two groups until they arrived in the high Arctic. Apparently they were not the only ones who were unclear about their destination. The telegram to which Constable Gibson refers in this interview is dated 14

April 1953. The trip made to recruit volunteers occurred at the end of April, by which time weather conditions for travel by dog team in the area were deteriorating.

11 NAC, RG 85, vol. 1072, file 252-3, pt. 4, 'Teletype Message [from] Henry Larsen, Insp., O.C. "G" Division, to THE N.C.O. IN CHARGE, R.C.M.P., PORT HARRISON, P.Q.,' 14 April 1953.

12 Ibid.

13 NAC, RG 85, vol. 1072, file 252-3, pt. 4, letter from 'H.A. Larsen, Insp., Officer Commanding, "G" Division, [to] The Director, Northern Administration and Lands Branch, Department of Resources and Development, Ottawa, Ontario,' 14 April 1953.

14 Translation of testimony of Mr. Markoosie Patsauq before the House of Commons Standing Committee on Aboriginal Affairs, *Minutes of Proceedings and Evidence of the Standing Committee on Aboriginal Affairs*, 19 March 1990, Issue No. 22 (Ottawa: Queen's Printer 1990), p. 6.

15 Hickling Corporation, *Assessment of the Factual Basis of Certain Allegations Made Before the Standing Committee on Aboriginal Affairs Concerning The Relocation Of Inukjuak Inuit Families in the 1950s*, pp. 37-43.

16 House of Commons Standing Committee on Aboriginal Affairs, *Minutes of Proceedings and Evidence*, 19 March 1990, p. 5.

17 Ibid., 6.

18 NAC, RG 85, vol. 1070, file 251-4, pt. 1, 'Minutes of a Meeting Held at 10:00 A.M. August 10, 1953 ... to Discuss the Transfer of Certain Eskimo Families from Northern Quebec to Cornwallis and Ellesmere Islands.' Despite the intention not to separate families, it would appear that officials had only nuclear families in mind. According to Inuit testimony before the House of Commons Standing Committee on Aboriginal Affairs, families were separated.

19 House of Commons Standing Committee on Aboriginal Affairs, *Minutes of Proceedings and Evidence*, 19 March 1990, p. 14.

20 *Arctic Circular* 6, no. 5 (1953):53. The *Arctic Circular* was a news bulletin published for the benefit of civil servants working for the department.

21 NAC, RG 85, vol. 80, file 201-1 (28). 'Department of Transport, Ottawa, Press Release #435,' 26 June 1953.

22 In addition to being featured in Wilkinson's 1953 film *Land of the Long Day*, the story of Idlout was told in a 1990 film produced by Investigative Productions entitled *Between Two Worlds*. The film focuses on Idlout's experiences subsequent to being featured in *Land of the Long Day*. It provides further insight into the social conditions experienced by Inuit living in the community of Resolute Bay.

23 NAC, RG 85, vol. 1070, file 251-4, pt. 1, letter to 'G.W. Rowley, Secretary, Advisory Committee on Northern Development [from] F.J.G. Cunningham, Director,' 15 December 1953, p. 3.

24 Wilfred Doucette, 'Cape Herschel, the Post Office That Never Was,' *Postal History Society of Canada Journal* 46 (1986):20. Curiously, after the issue of why the Inuit were relocated had resurfaced in 1990-1, Doucette wrote a letter to the *Globe and Mail* in which he claimed that sovereignty had nothing to do with the move and that Inuit were moved 'for humanitarian reasons – to find a better life for themselves and their families' (*Globe and Mail*, 23 October 1991).

25 NAC, RG 85, vol. 1446, file 1000/133, pt. 1, RCMP report 'Re: Eskimo conditions, CRAIG HARBOUR, area, Period ending December 31st, 1953 [from] A/Cpl., (G.K. Sargent) # 14756 I/c Craig Harbour Detachment,' 31 December 1953, pp. 1-2.

26 NAC, RG 85, vol. 461, file 630/123-1, pt. 1, report entitled 'Resolute Bay, Cornwallis Island, N.W.T.,' written as part of an inspection and survey of educational facilities in the eastern Arctic. This survey was conducted as part of the Eastern Arctic Patrol in the summer of 1953, by E.N. Grantham.

27 Personal communication, interview with Douglas Wilkinson, Kingston, Ontario, September 1991.

28 This information was taken from police reports on the relocated families and confirmed with the assistance of former RCMP Constable Ross Gibson, as well as by conversations with Dr. Otto Schaefer, formerly with Health and Welfare Canada, who treated the infant whose death is noted below.

29 NAC, RG 85, vol. 1446, file 1000/133, pt. 1, RCMP Division file no. 31-17/181, 'Re: Assistance to Eskimo Native Camp on Establishment Craig Harbour, District,' 30 November 1953.

30 There is some disagreement over whether or not the boat was offloaded or had been left at Resolute Bay by the detachment in 1950. Ross Gibson, the constable in charge at Resolute, claims that the boat was offloaded from the *d'Iberville* – minus the propeller.

31 This sentence is a reference to the statements by Inuit before the House of Commons Standing Committee that they were starving on the beach in Resolute Bay during the first winter. This was

something that Ross Gibson found difficult to believe. There are many potential problems here. What does 'starving' mean? Does it mean that Inuit were hungry? Is it possible that Constable Gibson failed to recognize that even though there was non-country food available, Inuit might still be hungry, finding that these supplies did not satisfy them, etc?

32 Personal communication, interview with Ross Gibson, 9 February 1992.

33 But Inuit do eat polar bear. Asked to elaborate, Gibson explained that the Inukjuak Inuit, who had not previously hunted polar bear, would not eat it initially as it was not part of their normal diet.

34 Personal communicaton, interview with Ross Gibson, 9 February 1992.

35 NAC, RG 22, vol. 176, file 40-2-20, pt. 3, 'Memorandum for the Deputy Minister, [from] Ben Sivertz, Administrative Officer,' 23 September 1953.

36 John Amagoalik is not the son of Amagoalik from Pond Inlet referred to above in the description from Ross Gibson. John and his family came from Inukjuak. This highlights the problem that non-Native people had in keeping track of Inuit names and families and the rationale for assigning 'E numbers' in the early 1940s.

37 House of Commons Standing Committee on Aboriginal Affairs, *Minutes of Proceedings and Evidence*, 19 March 1990, p. 15.

38 The suggestion and Sivertz's continued interest in education is not surprising considering that he was a teacher in British Columbia after a stint as a seaman during the 1930s and prior to taking up a position teaching navigation at the Royal Military College at Kingston during the Second World War. After the war, he joined the Department of External Affairs and helped to streamline the passport office and establish Canadian consulates in the United States. In the early 1950s, he accepted a transfer to work in the Department of Resources and Development as a special assistant to Deputy Minister Hugh Keenleyside.

39 NAC, RG 22, vol. 176, file 40-2-20, pt. 3, 'CONFIDENTIAL, REPORT ON TOUR OF THE Arctic ISLANDS, SEPTEMBER 8-12, 1953, G.W. Stead,' 29 September 1953, p. 6.

40 Ibid., 13.

41 NAC, RG 85, vol. 1042, file 22341, 'Memorandum for the Director [from] James Cantley, Arctic Services,' 13 October 1953, pp. 2-3.

42 Ibid.

43 Personal communication, interview with Ross Gibson, 9 February 1992. The problems with oral and written reports on game in the period in question are many. RCMP reports often covered huge areas. For example, in November of 1953, Constable Webster at Inukjuak filed a report on the Richmond Gulf area stating that 'the Richmond Gulf is an excellent area for country food' (NAC, RG 85, vol. 1269, file 1000/304, vol. 3, 'Conditions Amongst Eskimos – Generally Richmond Gulf Area, Nov. 13th, 1953'). However, the Richmond Gulf is far south of Inukjuak at the tree line and Webster's comments cannot be taken as implying anything about conditions at Inukjuak. Populations of birds and mammals vary from year to year. Therefore, a report for one year or season does not necessarily say anything about subsequent years. These observations are particularly relevant to reports of game conditions from the police based at Inukjuak, who covered a huge area from Great Whale River to the south to as far north as Sugluk.

44 NAC, RG 85, vol. 1446, file 1000/133, pt. 1, RCMP report 'Re: Eskimo conditions, CRAIG HARBOUR, area, Period ending December 31st, 1953 [from] A/Cpl., (G.K. Sargent) # 14756 l/c Craig Harbour Detachment,' 31 December 1953, pp. 1-2. Twenty caribou do not constitute much food. There were seven Inuit families living on the Lindstrom Peninsula. A caribou will last a family of five approximately three days. In other words, the twenty caribou represented not more than approximately nine days' worth of food for the community. Similarly, a seal might feed a family of five for one day. This does not take into consideration feed for dogs. In other words, in both the case of Craig Harbour and Resolute Bay, the amount of country food harvested is not as impressive as police reports would have us believe.

45 Personal communication, interview with Ross Gibson, 8 December 1992.

46 NAC, RG 85, vol. 1510, file 1000/123, pt. 1, RCMP report, 'Re: ESKIMO PROJECT – Resolute Bay, North-west Territories,' 14 October 1953.

47 NAC, RG 85, vol. 1269, file 1000/133, pt. 1, RCMP, 'Re: Annual Report on Game Conditions, Craig Harbour Detachment Area,' 21 August 1954. Writing in *Polar Record*, Alan Marcus suggests that conditions in Resolute and at Grise Fiord were similar: 'At Grise Fiord and Resolute Bay there were few birds or caribou or fish' ('Out in the Cold: Canada's Experimental Inuit Relocation to Grise Fiord and Resolute Bay,' *Polar Record* 27, no. 163 (1991):288). However, the region accessible to

Inuit on the Lindstrom Peninsula was plentiful in seals, walruses, and polar bears and was, generally, an area richer in mammals and birds than Resolute Bay.

48 House of Commons Standing Committee on Aboriginal Affairs, *Minutes of Proceedings and Evidence,* 19 March 1990, p. 16.

49 NAC, RG 85, vol. 1510, file 1000/123, pt. 1, RCMP report 'Re: ESKIMO PROJECT – Resolute Bay, North-west Territories,' 14 October 1953.

50 NAC, RG 85, vol. 1072, file 252-3, pt. 4, letter from 'F.J.G. Cunningham, Director, [to] Commissioner L.H. Nicholson, RCMP,' 8 April 1953.

51 Personal communication, interview with Doug Wilkinson, September 1991.

52 For example, the maximum January low for Port Harrison (Inukjuak) in January of 1953 was -12°F. The maximum low for Resolute Bay was -25°F. There is a difference in long-term average minimum and maximum January temperatures for Resolute Bay and Inukjuak, with the latter being about seven or eight degrees warmer (Environment Canada, *Canadian Climate Normals,* 1982, pp. 47, 73).

53 NAC, RG 85, vol. 1446, file 1000/133, pt. 1, RCMP report 'Re: Eskimo conditions, CRAIG HARBOUR, area, Period ending December 31st, 1953 [from] A/Cpl., (G.K. Sargent) # 14756 I/c Craig Harbour Detachment,' 31 December 1953, pp. 1-2. Buffalo hides and reindeer skins were air-dropped to Craig Harbour in September after a request was sent to Ottawa by the RCMP.

54 Ibid., 1.

55 House of Commons Standing Committee on Aboriginal Affairs, *Minutes of Proceedings and Evidence,* testimony of Martha Flaherty, 19 March 1990, p. 12.

56 NAC, RG 85, vol. 1070, file 251-4, pt. 2, Gibson, as cited in a letter from 'L.H. Nicholson, Commissioner, [to] Mr. R.G. Robertson, Deputy Minister, Department of Northern Affairs and National Resources,' 20 April 1954.

57 NAC, RG 85, vol. 1510, file 1000/123, pt. 1, RCMP report 'Re: ESKIMO PROJECT – Resolute Bay, North-west Territories,' 14 October 1953, p. 1.

58 NAC, RG 85, vol. 1446, file 1000/133, pt. 1, RCMP report 'Re: Eskimo conditions, CRAIG HARBOUR, area, Period ending December 31st, 1953 [from] A/Cpl., (G.K. Sargent) # 14756 I/c Craig Harbour Detachment,' 31 December 1953, p. 2.

59 Ibid.

60 Frank J. Tester, *Socio-economic and Environmental Impacts of the Proposed Polar Gas Pipeline – Keewatin District,* Vol. 2, Northern Pipelines Branch, Indian and Northern Affairs Canada, Ottawa, 1978, p. 270.

61 House of Commons Standing Committee on Aboriginal Affairs, *Minutes of Proceedings and Evidence,* 19 March 1990, p. 15.

62 NWT Archives, Alex Stevenson Collection, N92-023, 'Property Return Dept Resources and Development, Articles in possession of Thomassie E9-1589 Trading Store at Craig Harbour, N.W.T. the year ending December 31st, 1955.'

63 L. Amagoalik, *Makivik News* 15 (1989):15-17, cited in Alan Marcus, 'Out in the Cold,' 288.

64 Ibid., 3-4.

65 NAC, RG 85, vol. 1510, file 1000/123, vol. 1, report on 'ESKIMO PROJECT – Resolute Bay, Northwest Territories, 10-2-54.'

66 NAC, RG 85, vol. 1446, file 1000/133, pt. 1, RCMP report 'Re: Eskimo conditions, CRAIG HARBOUR, area, Period ending December 31st, 1953 [from] A/Cpl., (G.K. Sargent) # 14756 I/c Craig Harbour Detachment,' 31 December 1953, pp. 1-2.

67 Ibid., 5.

68 Ibid.

69 House of Commons Standing Committee on Aboriginal Affairs, *Minutes of Proceedings and Evidence,* 19 March 1990, p. 8.

70 NAC, RG 85, vol. 1070, 251-4, pt. 1, 'Report by C.J. Marshall, Secretariat A.C.N.D., Eskimo Settlement at Resolute,' 9 November 1953, p. 6.

71 NAC, RG 85, vol. 80, file 201-1 (28), 'Memorandum for Mr. Stevenson [from] J. Cantley, Arctic Services,' 8 June 1953. Not only was Alex Stevenson aboard the *C.D. Howe* on the trip north, he was accompanied by the Danish governor of Greenland, Mr. Christensen (personal communication, Ross Gibson, 5 January 1993).

72 NAC, RG 85, vol. 1070, file 251-4, pt. 1, 'Memorandum for Mr. Fraser, [from] J. Cantley, Arctic Services,' 19 November 1953, p. 5.

73 NAC, RG 85, vol. 1070, file 251-4, pt. 1, 'Memorandum for Mr. Fraser, [from] J. Cantley, Arctic

Services,' 19 November 1953, pp. 4-5.
74 In 'A Case of Compounded Error: The Inuit Resettlement Project, 1953, and the Government Response, 1990,' *Northern Perspectives* 19, no. 1 (Spring 1991):20, Grant states: 'Admittedly, freight problems might be expected, but the officials responsible should have had sufficient knowledge of probable delays, site conditions, and shipping problems, and should have taken steps to avoid such incidents ... As a result of the haste and bureaucratic bumbling, the ill-conceived plan was off to a very dubious start.'
75 Personal communications, interview with Ross Gibson, 9 February 1992, and Ben Sivertz, Victoria, BC, 16 June 1992.
76 Personal communication, interview with Ross Gibson, 9 February 1992.
77 Personal communication, interview with Ben Sivertz, 16 June 1992.
78 NAC, RG 85, vol. 1070, file 251-4, pt. 1, draft of a letter from 'F.J.G. Cunningham, Director, [to] Colonel G.W. Rowley, Secretary, Advisory Committee on Northern Development, Department of Resources and Development, Ottawa,' 14 December 1953, p. 4. James Cantley drafted this reply. His overly defensive response is evident in the editing that was done to the draft before the final version was forwarded to Graham Rowley.
79 Ibid., 1-2.
80 Ibid., 5.
81 Ibid., 4.
82 Ibid., 5.
83 NAC, RG 85, vol. 1446, file 1000/133, pt. 1, letter to the 'Director, Northern Administration and Lands Branch, Dept. of Northern Affairs and National Resources [from] H.A. Larsen, Supt. Officer Commanding, "G" Division,' 19 December 1953.
84 NAC, RG 85, vol. 1070, file 254-4, pt. 1, letter to 'Colonel G.W. Rowley, Secretary, Advisory Committee on Northern Development, Department of Resources and Development, Ottawa, [from] F.J.G. Cunningham, Director, Ottawa,' 15 December 1953, p. 5.
85 NAC, RG 85, vol. 1510, file 1000/123, pt. 1, letter from 'Ben Sivertz [to] Superintendent H.A. Larsen, Officer Commanding, "G" Division, Royal Canadian Mounted Police,' 14 June 1954.
86 NWT Archives, Alex Stevenson Collection, N92-023, 'Memorandum for the Director, [from] J. Cantley, Arctic Services,' 27 November 1953, p. 2.
87 NAC, RG 85, vol. 1070, file 251-4, pt. 1, 'Report by C.J. Marshall, Secretariat A.C.N.D., Eskimo Settlement at Resolute,' 9 November 1953, p. 5.
88 NAC, RG 85, vol. 1510, file 1000/123, pt. 1, 'ESKIMO PROJECT – Resolute Bay, Northwest Territories,' [report submitted by] Cst. Ross Gibson, #16593, Resolute Bay Detachment, 24 April 1954.
89 NWT Archives, Alex Stevenson Collection, N92-023, 'EXTRACT from the minutes of a meeting of the Honourable the Treasury Board, held at Ottawa, on June 24, 1953,' p. 1.
90 Ibid.
91 Fraser, as quoted in Alan Marcus, 'Out in the Cold,' 290.
92 Warner, as cited in Shelagh Grant, 'A Case of Compounded Error.'
93 NWT Archives, Alex Stevenson Collection, N92-023, letter to 'Superintendent H.A. Larsen, Officer Commanding "G" Division Royal Canadian Mounted Police, Ottawa, Ontario, [from] F.J.G. Cunningham,' 23 November 1954.
94 Ibid.
95 Ibid.
96 NWT Archives, Alex Stevenson Collection, N92-023, 'THE ROYAL CANADIAN MOUNTED POLICE, File No. 31-20/181, DIVISION H.Q. OTTAWA, December 23, 1954, [report from] H. Kearney, #10368, "G" Division C.I.B.'
97 Ibid.
98 NWT Archives, Alex Stevenson Collection, N92-023, 'MEMORANDUM FOR MR. B.G. SIVERTZ: Aboard C.G.S. *C.D. Howe* At Resolute Bay, N.W.T.,' 23 August 1954, p. 4.
99 NWT Archives, Alex Stevenson Collection, N92-023, letter from 'B.G. Sivertz, Chief, Arctic Division, [to] Cst. F.R. Gibson, Royal Canadian Mounted Police Detachment, Resolute Bay, N.W.T.,' 24 February 1956.
100 NWT Archives, Alex Stevenson Collection, N92-023, report to 'OFFICER COMMANDING R.C.M.Police, "G" Division, Ottawa, [from] EASTERN Arctic SUB/DIVISION, Resolute Bay Detachment, April 6th, 1956, Re: SUDLAVENICK'S E9-1765 Trading Store, – RESOLUTE BAY, N.W.T.'
101 Ibid., 2. In another situation, Inuit working for the Geological Survey of Canada were credited for

their work. The Inuit, employed with Operation Franklin, operated by the Geological Survey of Canada, Department of Mines and Technical Surveys, were hired at $10 a day plus board and dog feed. The women, fabricating stockings, were paid one dollar per pair with duffle supplied to them. The total earned by five Inuit men over periods ranging from eighteen to twenty-nine days was $1,230. The total earned by three women, who among them sewed a total of fifty pair of duffle socks, was $50.

102 House of Commons Standing Committee on Aboriginal Affairs, *Minutes of Proceedings and Evidence,* 19 March 1990, pp. 14-15.

103 'RCMP Internal Investigation into Allegations of RCMP Misconduct, Grise Fiord and Resolute Bay, ca. 1953,' July 1991, report submitted to the House of Commons Standing Committee on Aboriginal Affairs, 22 January 1992, pp. 4-5.

104 Ibid., 5.

105 NAC, RG 85, vol. 1510, file 1000/123, pt. 1, RCMP report 'Re: ESKIMO PROJECT – Resolute Bay, Northwest Territories, [filed by] Cst. F.R. Gibson, # 16593,' 10 February 1954.

106 Ibid., 7.

107 NWT Archives, Alex Stevenson Collection, N92-023, 'MEMORANDUM FOR THE DIRECTOR, "ESKIMO LOAN FUND – TRADING LOANS," [from] Ben Sivertz, Chief, Arctic Division, Ottawa,' 28 May 1956.

108 Ibid.

109 Personal communication, interview with Ben Sivertz, 16 June 1992.

110 NWT Archives, Alex Stevenson Collection, N92-023, letter to the 'Cst. In Charge, R.C.M.Police, RESOLUTE BAY, N.W.T., Re: Supervision of Eskimo Trading – Resolute Bay, N.W.T., [from] W.J. Fitzsimmons, Insp., I/C "G" Division, C.I.B.,' 17 April 1957.

111 NAC, RG 85, vol. 1050, file A-251-2-3, 'MEMORANDUM FOR MR. GODT, "Transfer of Eskimo Trading Store (Eskimo Loan Fund #3) Resolute Bay to the Resolute Bay Eskimo Co-operative Limited," [from] A. Sprule, Co-operative Development Officer, Ottawa,' 14 December 1960, p. 7.

112 NAC, RG 85, vol. 1934, file A-251-7, pt. 2, 'Development of Eskimo Co-operatives,' July 1962, p. 2.

113 NAC, RG 85, vol. 1072, file 251-4, pt. 1, letter from 'H.A. Young, Deputy Minister, [to] Brigadier G.M. Drury, C.B.E., D.S.O., B.C.L., Deputy Minister, Department of National Defence, Ottawa, Ontario,' 15 June 1953.

114 NAC, RG 85, vol. 1070, file 251-4, pt. 1, letter from 'Robt. C. Ripley A/C, Air Officer Commanding, RCAF Air Transport Command, [to] The Chief of the Air Staff, Air Force Headquarters, Ottawa, Ontario,' 6 July 1953.

115 NAC, RG 85, vol. 1070, file 251-4, pt. 1, letter from 'James Sharpe, A.D.M., Department of National Defence, [to] Major General Hugh Young, Deputy Minister, Department of Resources and Development, Ottawa, Ont.,' 30 July 1953.

116 NAC, RG 85, vol. 1070, file 251-4, pt. 1, 'Minutes of a Meeting Held at 10:00 A.M. August 10, 1953, in Room 304, Langevin Block, to Discuss the Transfer of Certain Eskimo Families from Northern Quebec to Cornwallis and Ellesmere Islands,' p. 3.

117 Ibid.

118 Ibid.

119 'MEMORANDUM FOR THE MEMBERS OF THE A.C.N.D.: "FUTURE OF THE JOINT WEATHER STATIONS," Confidential Document ND-69-A, [from] G.W. Rowley, Secretary, A.C.N.D., Department of Resources and Development,' 19 November 1953, pp. 2-3. (This document was provided by Professor Shelagh Grant, Department of History, Trent University.)

120 Ibid., 3.

121 According to Ben Sivertz, Hugh Young, the previous deputy minister, had not found favour with the Roman Catholic or with the Anglican church hierarchy which, at this time, still had considerable influence on government policy. Young was committed to making all schools in the Northwest Territories public, rather than church-run institutions. These sentiments did not find favour with the church or with Prime Minister Louis St. Laurent, who was a committed Catholic. Young was subsequently moved to the Department of Public Works, and Robertson became deputy minister of the new department (personal communication, interview with Ben Sivertz, Victoria, BC, 16 June 1992).

122 NAC, RG 85, vol. 1070, file 251-4, pt. 2, letter from 'James A. Sharpe, Department of National Defense, Office of the Deputy Minister, Ottawa, to Mr. Robertson, Department of Northern Affairs and National Resources, Langevin Block, Ottawa, Ontario,' 2 February 1954.

123 Personal communication, interview with Ross Gibson, 9 February 1992.
124 NAC, RG 85, vol. 1070, file 251-4, pt. 2, letter from 'R.G. Robertson, [to] C.M. Drury, Deputy Minister of National Defense, Ottawa Ontario,' 18 February 1954.
125 Ibid.
126 NAC, RG 85, vol. 1070, file 251-4, pt. 2, letter from 'L.H. Nicholson, Commissioner RCMP, [to] Mr. Gordon Robertson, Deputy Minister, Department of Northern Affairs and National Resources, Ottawa, Ontario,' 20 April 1954.
127 NAC, RG 85, vol. 1070, file 251-4, pt. 2, letter from 'R.G. Robertson, [to] C.M. Drury, Deputy Minister of National Defense, Ottawa Ontario,' 18 February 1954, p. 2.
128 NAC, RG 85, vol. 1510, file 1000/123, pt. 1, RCMP report, 'Re: Eskimo Project – Resolute Bay, Northwest Territories,' 10 February 1954.
129 NAC, RG 85, vol. 1510, file 1000/123, pt. 1, 'Memorandum For Mr. Sivertz [from] G.W.R., Ottawa,' 3 June 1954.
130 NAC, RG 85, vol. 1269, file 1000/133, pt. 1, contained in a 'Memorandum for Mr. Doyle, [from] B.G. Sivertz, Chief – Arctic Division, Ottawa,' 26 August 1954.
131 NAC, RG 85, vol. 1269, file 1000/133, pt. 1, 'Memorandum for Mr. Sivertz: Mr. Cantley:, "Re. Eskimo Loan Fund – Craig Harbour, Resolute Bay," [from] A. Stevenson, Arctic Division, Ottawa,' 17 September 1954.
132 NAC, RG 85, vol. 1510, file 1000/123, pt. 1, RCMP, 'CONDITIONS AMONGST ESKIMOS – RESOLUTE BAY, N.W.T., Sgd. Cst. F.R. Gibson, #16593, Resolute Bay Detachment, 14-11-56,' pp. 1-2.
133 House of Commons Standing Committee on Aboriginal Affairs, *Minutes of Proceedings and Evidence of the Standing Committee on Aboriginal Affairs*, 18 June 1990, Issue No. 40 (Ottawa: Queen's Printer 1990), p. 51.
134 In actual fact, it appears that they were unable to build igloos until much later in the winter than was usual at Inukjuak, because the snow conditions in Resolute were unsuitable for igloos until quite late in the season (personal communication, interview with Ross Gibson, 9 February 1992).
135 House of Commons Standing Committee on Aboriginal Affairs, *Minutes of Proceedings and Evidence*, 19 March 1990, p. 32.
136 NAC, RG 85, vol. 1510, file 1000/123, pt. 1, letter from 'B.G. Sivertz, Chief, Arctic Division [to] Constable R. Gibson, RCMP, Resolute Bay, Ottawa,' 28 December 1954.
137 NAC, RG 85, vol. 1510, file 1000/123, pt. 1, RCMP report, 'Conditions Amongst Eskimos – Resolute Bay, N.W.T.,' 29 December 1954, p. 1.
138 Ibid., 2.
139 NAC, RG 22, vol. 176, file 40-2-20, pt. 3, letter from 'R.G. Robertson [to] C.W. West, Esq., Deputy Minister of Transport, Ottawa,' 7 May 1954.
140 NAC, RG 85, vol. 1510, file 1000/123, pt. 1, letter from 'F.J.G. Cunningham, Director, [to] Superintendent H.A. Larsen, Officer Commanding "G" Division, RCMP,' 10 May 1954.
141 NAC, RG 85, vol. 1070, file 251-4, pt. 2, RCMP report, 'Re: Eskimo Conditions at Resolute Bay, N.W.T. – Proposed Move of Eskimo Idlout from Pond Inlet to Resolute Bay,' 5 May 1954.
142 NAC, RG 85, vol. 1510, file 1000/123, pt. 1, letter from 'F.J.G. Cunningham, Director, [to] Superintendent H.A. Larsen, Officer Commanding "G" Division, RCMP,' 10 May 1954.
143 NAC, RG 85, vol. 1070, file 251-4, pt. 2, letter from 'B.G. Sivertz, Chief, Arctic Division, [to] MR. P.A.C. Nichols, Manager, Arctic Division, Hudson's Bay Company, Hudson's Bay House, Winnipeg, Manitoba, Ottawa,' 16 May, 1955, pp. 1-2.
144 NAC, RG 85, vol. 1070, file 251-4, pt. 2, letter from 'B.G. Sivertz, Chief, Arctic Division, [to] Superintendent H.A. Larsen, Officer Commanding, "G" Division, Royal Canadian Mounted Police, Ottawa, Ontario,' 16 May 1955.
145 NAC, RG 85, vol. 1070, file 251-4, pt. 2, letter to 'B.G. Sivertz, Chief, Arctic Division, Department of Northern Affairs and National Resources [from] P.A.C. Nichols, Manager, Arctic Division, Hudson's Bay Company, Winnipeg,' 24 May 1955. Sugluk is an area of Arctic Quebec where it is evident that the government also had concerns about the relationship between population and the resources and where the Hudson's Bay Company saw some possibility of relocating Inuit north to Baffin Island to take advantage of its unexploited trapping potential.
146 NWT Archives, Alex Stevenson Collection, N92-023, 'MEMORANDUM FOR MR. B.G. SIVERTZ, [from] Alex Stevenson, Aboard C.G.S. *C.D. Howe* At Resolute Bay, N.W.T.,' 23 August 1955.
147 Personal communication, interview with Dr. Otto Schaefer, Edmonton, Alberta, 11 January 1993. Dr. Schaefer was on the *C.D. Howe* at the time and indicated that he did not hear about the incident

until some time later, something he confirmed in subsequent conversations with Inuit in Pond Inlet and Arctic Bay.

148 Personal communication, interview with Ross Gibson, 9 February 1992.

149 NAC, RG 85 vol. 1510, file 1000/123, pt. 1, letter commencing 'Hello Kingmerk' from Idlout, 16 December 1955. It is difficult to make out all the words in this letter. It was written without punctuation and it is therefore difficult to tell where one sentence ends and another begins.

150 NAC, RG 85, vol. 1510, file 1000/123, pt. 1, 'MEMORANDUM FOR MR. WILKINSON, [from] J. Cantley, A/Chief, Arctic Division,' 10 January 1956, pp. 1-2.

151 NAC, RG 85, vol. 1510, file 1000/123, pt. 1, letter from 'W.J. Fitzsimmons, Insp., I/C "G" Division, C.I.B. [to] The Director, Northern Administration and Lands Branch, Dept. of Northern Affairs and National Resources, OTTAWA, Ontario,' 21 September 1956.

152 NAC, RG 85, vol. 461, file 630/123-1, pt. 1, 'MEMORANDUM FOR MR. J.V. JACOBSON, [from] B.G. Sivertz, Chief, Arctic Division, Ottawa,' 12 October 1956. The design was called a '512' as this was the number of square feet it contained.

153 Paniloo is referred to as 'Panilook' in the archival documents relating to this period.

154 NAC, RG 85, vol. 1510, file 1000/123, pt. 1, RCMP report, Spence Bay Detachment, 'Enquiry Re: Eskimo Panilook, Spence Bay, N.W.T.' [from] 'Cpl. A.C. Fryer, #15273, i/c Spence Bay Detachment,' 10 November 1956, p. 1.

155 Ibid.

156 NAC, RG 85, vol. 1510, file 1000/123, pt. 1, letter from 'Idlouk [to] B.G. Sivertz, Resolute Bay, N.W.T.,' 18 December 1956.

157 It is also rather humorous to note that when asked to send money from Resolute to Churchill to cover Idlout's purchases, constable Moodie of the Resolute detachment – who had replaced Ross Gibson the previous fall – was unable to do so as the store in Resolute operated on a barter system. Instead, Constable Moodie sent fox skins to cover the cost. See NAC, RG 85, vol. 1070, file 251-4, pt. 3, 'MEMORANDUM FOR THE CHIEF OF THE Arctic DIVISION, Churchill Manitoba, 28 February 1958 [from] R.L. Kennedy, Northern Service Officer.'

158 Ibid.

159 Idlout was needed that summer. Eight Inuit were employed by the Department of National Defence, organized into two groups working in alternating weeks so as to permit hunting. The groups worked ten hours a day, six days a week at $1.55/hour and were charged 70 cents per meal for a noonday and evening meal.

160 NAC, RG 85, vol. 1070, file 251-4, pt. 3, RCMP report, 'Re: Idlouk, Resolute Bay, N.W.T., Cpl. (D.S. Moodie) Reg. No. 14888 I/C Resolute Bay Detachment,' 3 May 1958.

161 NAC, RG 85 vol. 1070, file 251-4, pt. 3, 'MEMORANDUM TO THE CHIEF, Arctic DIVISION, "Purchase of Boat by the Resolute Bay Group," Resolute Bay, N.W.T., [signed] R.G.H. Williamson,' 3 March 1958.

162 NAC, RG 85, vol. 1070, file 251-4, pt. 3 letter to 'Superintendent H.A. Larsen, Officer Commanding, "G" Division, Royal Canadian Mounted Police, Ottawa, Ontario, [from] B.G. Sivertz, Director, Ottawa,' 11 April 1958.

163 The details of Idlout's demise, recounted here, are the subject of *Between Two Worlds*, a film produced by Investigative Productions, Toronto, 1990.

164 NAC, RG 85, vol. 1269, file 1000/133, pt. 1, RCMP report, 'Re: Native Trading Store, Craig Harbour, N.W.T., to THE DIRECTOR, NORTHERN ADMINISTRATION AND LANDS BRANCH, DEPT. OF NORTHERN AFFAIRS AND NATIONAL RESOURCES, OTTAWA, ONTARIO [from] H.A. Larsen, Supt., Officer Commanding, "G" Division, Ottawa,' 14 January 1955.

165 The Canadian Wildlife Service was not much help. Their opinions on whether or not the wildlife resources in a given area could support a population were guarded and indefinite. In their attempts at an 'exact science,' the service could only guess what sort of hunting pressures populations could support and, knowing this, appears to have contributed little to the policy matters facing the department. This is evident from a 30 May 1962 memo to the deputy commissioner of the NWT based on research conducted on the Queen Elizabeth Islands by Dr. John Tener. The service was unable to answer the department's question as to whether or not the Inuit populations of Grise Fiord and Resolute were too large for the game available. See NAC, RG 85, vol. 1070, file 251-4, pt. 3, 'MEMORANDUM FOR THE DEPUTY COMMISSIONER, "Queen Elizabeth Islands Game Survey – 1961," [from] C.M. Bolger, Administrator of the Arctic, Ottawa,' 30 May 1962.

166 NAC, RG 85, vol. 1070, file 251-4, pt. 2, letter from 'B.G. Sivertz, Chief, Arctic Division, [to] Superintendent H.A. Larsen, Officer Commanding, "G" Division, Royal Canadian Mounted

Police, Ottawa, Ontario, Ottawa,' 16 May 1955.
167 NWT Archives, Alex Stevenson Collection, N92-023, 'MEMORANDUM FOR MR. B.G. SIVERTZ: [from] A. Stevenson, Officer in Charge, Eastern Arctic Patrol, Aboard C.G.S. "C.D. Howe" At Resolute Bay, N.W.T.,' 23 August 1955.
168 NAC, RG 85, vol. 461, file 630/123-1, pt. 1, 'MEMORANDUM FOR MR. JACOBSON: from J. Cantley, Arctic Division,' 6 September 1955.
169 NAC, RG 85, vol. 1269, file 1000/133 pt. 1, RCMP report, 'Re: Eskimo Conditions, Craig Harbour Area, Period ending December 31st, 1955, [from] Cpl. G.R. Sargent, #14756, I/c Craig Harbour Detachment,' p. 2. It is curious to note that Alex Stevenson reported from Resolute that this family was put ashore with its dogs and equipment, none of which seems to have made it to Craig Harbour. Furthermore, Rynee Flaherty, interviewed in Grise Fiord in the summer of 1991, indicates that Josephie worked at the weather station in Inukjuak and was not a hunter and therefore should not have been expected to have the equipment which Glen Sargent thought he would have upon his arrival (personal communication, interview with Rynee Flaherty, Grise Fiord, 30 June 1991).
170 NAC, RG 85, vol. 1070, file 251-4, pt. 2, 'Memorandum from J. Cantley, A/Chief, Arctic Division, [to] Mr. Sivertz, Acting Director, Ottawa,' 28 March 1956.
171 NAC, RG 85, vol. 1070, file 251-4, pt. 2, letter from 'R.G. Robertson, Deputy Minister, [to] Commissioner L.H. Nicholson, Royal Canadian Mounted Police, Ottawa, Ontario, Ottawa,' 10 May 1956.
172 Ibid.
173 NAC, RG 85, vol. 1070, file 251-4, pt. 2, 'MEMORANDUM FOR THE DEPUTY MINISTER: "ESTABLISHMENT OF NEW ESKIMO SETTLEMENT IN THE HIGH Arctic," [from] G.W.R.,' 31 May 1956.
174 NAC, RG 18, acc 85-86/048, vol. 55, file TA 500-8-1-1, letter to 'THE DIRECTOR, NORTHERN ADMINISTRATION AND LANDS BRANCH, DEPARTMENT OF NORTHERN AFFAIRS AND NATIONAL RESOURCES, OTTAWA ONTARIO, Re: Proposed Transfer of Eskimos to Alexandra Fiord District, Ellesmere Island, N.W.T., [from] W.J. Fitzsimmons, Insp., I/C "G" Division C.I.B.,' 21 August 1956. (This document provided by Shelagh Grant, Department of History, Trent University.)
175 NWT Archives, Alex Stevenson Collection, N92-023, 'MEMORANDUM FOR THE DIRECTOR: "ESKIMO SETTLEMENTS AT RESOLUTE AND CRAIG HARBOUR," [from] B.G. Sivertz, Chief, Arctic Division, Ottawa,' 22 October 1956.
176 NAC, RG 85 vol. 1070, file 251-4, pt. 3, report to OFFICER COMMANDING, R.C.M. Police, "G" Division, Ottawa, Re: Eskimo Movements – Grise Fiord., [from] Cpl. G.K. Sargent, I/c Grise Fiord Detachment,' 19 February 1957.
177 NAC, RG 85, vol. 1269, file 1000/133, pt. 1, RCMP report, 'Eskimo Conditions, GRISE FIORD Area, Period ending December 31st, 1957, [from] Cpl. (G.K. Sargent) #14756, I/c Grise Fiord Detachment,' 31 December 1957.
178 NAC, RG 85, vol. 1269, file 1000/133, pt. 1, letter to 'Inspector Fitzsimmons, I/C "G" Division, C.I.B., R.C.M.P., Ottawa, [from] R.A.J. Phillips, Chief of the Arctic Division, Ottawa,' 30 May 1957.
179 NWT Archives, Alex Stevenson Collection, N92-023, 'MEMORANDUM FOR MR. PHILLIPS, Re: Situation at Resolute Bay, Confidential, (sgd.) F.J. Neville, Welfare Officer, Resolute Bay, N.W.T.,' 28 August 1957. F.J. (Bud) Neville is the same person who was the principle author of the Hickling Report, commissioned by the minister of Indian and northern affairs in 1990 and which found that sovereignty was not a major consideration in the relocations.
180 NAC, RG 85, vol. 1510, file 1000/123, pt. 1, letter from 'B.G. Sivertz, Director, [to] Dr. P.E. Moore, Director, Indian and Northern Health Services, Ottawa, Ont.,' 22 November 1957.
181 NAC, RG 85, vol. 1269, file 1000/133, pt. 1, RCMP report, 'Eskimo Conditions, GRISE FIORD Area, Period ending December 31st, 1957, [from] Cpl. (G.K. Sargent) #14756, I/c Grise Fiord Detachment,' 31 December 1957, p. 3.
182 NAC, RG 85, vol. 1070, file 251-4, pt. 3, 'MEMORANDUM TO THE CHIEF, Arctic DIVISION, "Port Harrison Migrant Families at Resolute Bay en Route to Grise Fiord," from R.G.H. Williamson, Resolute Bay, Cornwallis Island, N.W.T.,' 4 March 1958.
183 NAC, RG 85, vol. 1070, file 251-4, pt. 3, letter to 'THE DIRECTOR, NORTHERN ADMINISTRATION AND LANDS BRANCH, DEPT. OF NORTHERN AFFAIRS AND NATIONAL RESOURCES, KENT-ALBERT BUILDING, OTTAWA, ONT., [from] H.A. Larsen, Supt., Officer Commanding "G" Division., OTTAWA, ONT.,' 16 April 1958.

184 NAC, RG 85, vol. 1070, file 251-4, pt. 3, 'MEMORANDUM FOR THE DEPUTY MINISTER, "Re-location of Eskimos," [from] B.G. Sivertz, Director, Ottawa,' 6 June 1958.
185 NWT Archives, Alex Stevenson Collection, N92-023, 'Grise Fiord – August 27, 1958.' This document consists of four pages extracted from what appears to be the report of the Eastern Arctic Patrol for the year 1958. The author is not indicated.
186 NAC, RG 85, vol. 1269, file 1000/133, pt. 1, RCMP report, 'Conditions Amongst Eskimoes Generally – Annual Report – GRISE FIORD AREA, N.W.T., Year Ending December 31, 1958., Cst. (R.S. Pilot) Reg. #17873. I/c Grise Fiord Detachment,' 19 January 1959, p. 4. Thomassie's children drowned while playing on ice at the flow edge.
187 Ibid.
188 NAC, RG 85, vol. 1510, file 1000/123, pt. 1., 'MEMORANDUM FOR THE REGIONAL ADMINIS-TRATOR – Churchill, Manitoba, "Relocation of Eskimos – Resolute Bay," C.M. Bolger, Administrator of the Arctic, Ottawa,' 7 March 1960.
189 NAC, RG 85, vol. 1948, file A 571-1, pt. 1, letter to 'Superintendent W.G. Fraser, Officer Commanding "G" Division, Royal Canadian Mounted Police, Ottawa, Ontario., [from] C.M. Bolger, Administrator of the Arctic, Ottawa,' 27 June 1960.
190 NAC, RG 85, vol. 1948, file A-571-1, pt. 1, letter to the 'Officer Commanding, "G" Division, R.C.M. Police, OTTAWA, Ontario., [from] Cst. (T.C. Jenkins) Reg. 18653. I/c. Resolute Bay Detach., Resolute Bay, N.W.T.,' 28 July 1960, p. 4.
191 NAC, RG 85, vol. 1050, file A-251-2-2, pt. 2, 'MEMORANDUM FOR THE DIRECTOR, "Eskimo Trading Store – Grise Fiord," from C.M. Bolger, Administrator of the Arctic,' 4 October 1960.
192 NAC, RG 85, vol. 1947, file A560-1, pt. 1, 'MEMORANDUM FOR THE DEPUTY MINISTER, "Epidemic – Grise Fiord," [from] B.G. Sivertz, Director, Ottawa,' 18 November 1960.
193 NWT Archives, Alex Stevenson Collection, N92-023, 'Eskimo Correspondence Record,' letter written by Willya, Special Constable, Port Harrison, Quebec, received 5 November 1957, translated by Leo Manning. Other correspondence from Peter Kasadluak of Inukjuak (dated 5 November 1957) makes similar claims and also requests Constable Gibson's replacement. A letter from 'Jacka' (dated 14 January 1958), found in the same file, requests that he and his family be sent north and emphasizes that the family is 'three families here in three snowhouses. We are inseparable as a group.' In regard to his stepfather, the writer states: 'He is an old man and the whites at Port Harrison are not much interested in his welfare, even though he is an old man and has no sons to take care of him.' And: 'Also our police here are not very nice – they are the cause of the children being hungry ... Another thing – the trader steals some of the Eskimos trapping money. He never pays the same prices and since Christmas he has paid less for some and more for others.'
194 NAC, RG 85, vol. 1382, file 1012-13, pt. 5, 'MEMORANDUM FOR THE DEPUTY MINISTER, "RELOCATION OF ESKIMOS," [from] B.G. Sivertz, Director, Ottawa,' 7 December 1958.
195 These are summarized by Magnus Gunther, 'The 1953 Relocations of the Inukjuak Inuit to the High Arctic: A Documentary Analysis and Evaluation,' Trent University, Peterborough, ON, 1992, 255-65. However, in his report on the controversies surrounding the establishment and history of these communities, Gunther, while acknowledging that difficulties were reported, appears to downplay the problems faced by the two groups from Inukjuak and Pond Inlet in order to portray the outcome of the 'experiment' in the best light. The divisions in these communities were evident from visits to Resolute Bay in 1973 and 1974 and subsequent visits to Resolute and Grise Fiord in the summer of 1991. However, the archival evidence makes it clear that these divisions were present from the founding of the communities.
196 NAC, RG 85, vol. 1382, file 1012-13, Pt. 5, 'MEMORANDUM FOR THE DIRECTOR, "Creating New Communities," [from] W. Rudnicki, Chief, Welfare Division, Ottawa,' 13 December 1960, p. 4.
197 Ibid., 6.
198 Ibid.
199 Ibid.

Chapter 5: The Ennadai Lake Relocations

1 NAC, RG 85, vol. 1267, file 1000/179 pt. 1, p. 2, letter to 'Mr. P.A.C. Nichols, Manager, Arctic Division, Hudson's Bay Company, Hudson's Bay House, Winnipeg, Manitoba, "ESKIMOS – ENNADAI LAKE," [from] F.J.G. Cunningham, Director, Ottawa,' 25 June 1956, p. 2.
2 NAC, RG 22, vol. 254, file 40-8-1, vol. 2, report, 'ESKIMOS LIVING IN THE NUELTIN LAKE – KAZAN RIVER AREAS OF THE DISTRICT OF KEEWATIN, N.W.T.,' 16 April 1952, p. 1.
3 NAC, RG 85, vol. 1267, file 1000/179, pt. 1, 'PROPOSED TRANSFER OF ENNADAI LAKE NATIVES,

J.P. Richards, Ottawa,' 4 June 1956, p. 2.
4 NAC, RG 22, vol. 254, file 40-8-1, vol. 2, report, 'ESKIMOS LIVING IN THE NUELTIN LAKE –
   KAZAN RIVER AREAS OF THE DISTRICT OF KEEWATIN, N.W.T.,' 16 April 1952, p. 1.
5 NWT Archives, Alex Stevenson Collection, N92-023, 'MEMORANDUM FOR THE DIRECTOR, RE:
   STARVATION AMONG THE ESKIMOS IN THE WINTER OF 1957-58, [from] R.A.J.P. [Phillips],
   Ottawa,' 20 October 1958, p. 1.
6 Personal correspondence from Wilkinson to the authors, 24 February 1993, p. 1. Wilkinson goes
   on to note that 'some of these white trappers were men who had worked on the Hudson Bay
   Railway construction then decided to head north instead of south when construction finished,
   mainly because the Depression had settled in by that time and there was little prospect of work
   in the south.'
7 Ibid., 1.
8 The basic premise is inspired by Arthur Ray's analysis of the fur trade credit system. See Arthur
   Ray, 'Periodic Shortages, Native Welfare, and the Hudson's Bay Company 1670-1930' in *The
   Subarctic Fur Trade: Native Social and Economic Adaptations*, ed. Shepard Krech III (Vancouver:
   University of British Columbia Press 1984).
9 NAC, RG 22, vol. 254, file 40-8-1, vol. 2, report, 'ESKIMOS LIVING IN THE NUELTIN LAKE –
   KAZAN RIVER AREAS OF THE DISTRICT OF KEEWATIN, N.W.T.,' 16 April 1952, p. 1.
10 Ibid.
11 Ibid.
12 Ibid.
13 Ibid.
14 NAC, RG 22, vol. 545, file Rowley ACND 1956, 'MEMORANDUM FOR THE DEPUTY MINISTER:
   FISHING EXPERIMENT AT NUELTIN LAKE, G.W.R. [Rowley],' 1 November 1956, p. 1.
15 Ibid.
16 NAC, RG 22, vol. 254, file 40-8-1, vol. 2, report, 'ESKIMOS LIVING IN THE NUELTIN LAKE –
   KAZAN RIVER AREAS OF THE DISTRICT OF KEEWATIN, N.W.T.,' 16 April 1952, p. 3.
17 Ibid.
18 NAC, RG 22, vol. 545, file Rowley ACND 1956, 'MEMORANDUM FOR THE DEPUTY MINISTER:
   FISHING EXPERIMENT AT NUELTIN LAKE,' 1 November 1956, p. 2.
19 Ibid.
20 NAC, RG 22, vol. 254, file 40-8-1, vol. 2, report 'ESKIMOS LIVING IN THE NUELTIN LAKE –
   KAZAN RIVER AREAS OF THE DISTRICT OF KEEWATIN, N.W.T.,' 16 April 1952, p. 1.
21 NAC, RG 22, vol. 545, file Rowley ACND 1956, 'MEMORANDUM FOR THE DEPUTY MINISTER:
   FISHING EXPERIMENT AT NUELTIN LAKE,' 1 November 1956, p. 2.
22 Ibid. The report goes on: 'I think the report should stand as it is. If we added any further
   explanation it might only tend to draw attention to the incident, which I do not think would be
   useful.'
23 NAC, RG 22, vol. 254, file 40-8-1, vol. 2, report, 'ESKIMOS LIVING IN THE NUELTIN LAKE –
   KAZAN RIVER AREAS OF THE DISTRICT OF KEEWATIN, N.W.T.,' 16 April 1952, p. 1.
24 Ibid., 4.
25 NWT Archives, Alex Stevenson Collection, N92-023, 'Report on: ENNADAI LAKE NORTHWEST
   TERRITORIES – 1955, by James A. Houston, Arctic Division,' p. 2.
26 Ibid., 3. Later in the report he estimates that 'the Akkeeamuit probably kill about 1000 caribou
   per year' (p. 4).
27 Ibid., 3.
28 Ibid., 5.
29 He wrote: 'Wife changing which seems to have decreased in many areas due to missionary
   influence is rampant among the Ennadai people and it is not uncommon for a hunter to boast of
   his child being fathered by his wife and friend. This practice does not seem to disturb their social
   structure' (p. 6). This observation is made from an ethnocentric and patriarchal frame: wife
   changing could as easily be characterized as husband sharing. Rather than 'disturbing their social
   structure' the practice might in fact be a ground of the social structure, constantly working to
   undermine paternal ownership of children and other interconnected social structures that
   constitute patriarchy; hence the 'pride of the hunter' who does not own his children and is
   therefore not the generative centre, possessive owner, or hierarchical leader of the familial matrix.
30 Ibid., 6.
31 Ibid., 9.

32 Ibid.
33 Ibid., 10.
34 Geert van den Steenhoven, 'Ennadai Lake People, 1955,' *The Beaver* (Spring 1968):13.
35 Ibid., 14.
36 Ibid., 16.
37 Ibid., 17-18.
38 NAC, RG 85, vol. 1513, file 1000/500, pt. 3, 'Memorandum to the chief of the Arctic Division Re: "Time-Life" Expedition to Ennadai Lake, N.W.T., [from] W.G. Kerr, Northern Service Officer – Churchill, Man.,' 7 August 1955, p. 1.
39 NAC, RG 85, vol. 1513, file 1000/500, pt. 3, 'Memorandum to the Chief of the Arctic Division, [from] (W.G. Kerr), Northern Service Officer, Churchill, Man.,' 4 July 1955, p. 3.
40 NAC, RG 22, vol. 254, file 40-8-1, vol. 2, report, 'ESKIMOS LIVING IN THE NUELTIN LAKE – KAZAN RIVER AREAS OF THE DISTRICT OF KEEWATIN, N.W.T.,' 16 April 1952, p. 2.
41 Walter Rudnicki, 'Report: Field Trip to Eskimo Point,' March 1958, Appendix B, p. 15 (document supplied by Walter Rudnicki, Ottawa, Ontario, 14 May 1991).
42 Quoted in Walter Rudnicki, 'Report: Field Trip to Eskimo Point,' Appendix B, p. 4.
43 'A Mesolithic Age Today: Caribou Eskimos Illustrate Its Culture,' *Life*, 27 February 1956, 86.
44 NWT Archives, Alex Stevenson Collection, N92-023, 'MEMORANDUM FOR THE DEPUTY MINISTER: "Conditions Among Eskimos in the District of Keewatin," [from] F.J.G. Cunningham, Ottawa,' 31 January 1956, p. 2.
45 Ibid.
46 NAC, RG 85, vol. 1267, file 1000/179 pt. 1, p. 2, letter to 'Mr. P.A.C. Nichols, Manager, Arctic Division, Hudson's Bay Company, Hudson's Bay House, Winnipeg, Manitoba, "ESKIMOS – ENNADAI LAKE," [from] F.J.G. Cunningham, Director, Ottawa,' 25 June 1956, p. 1.
47 Ibid.
48 NAC, RG 85, vol. 1267, file 1000/179, pt. 1, 'Memorandum to the Chief of the Arctic Division, Re: Eskimos – Ennadai Lake, N.W.T., [from] (W.G. Kerr), Northern Service Officer – Churchill, Man.,' 3 August 1956, p. 2.
49 Ibid.
50 NAC, RG 85, vol. 1513, file 1000/500, pt. 3, 'Memorandum to the Chief of the Arctic Division, [from] (W.G. Kerr), Northern Service Officer, Churchill, Man.,' 4 July 1955, p. 2.
51 NAC, RG 85, vol. 1267, file 1000/179, pt. 1, 'Memorandum to the Chief of the Arctic Division, Re: Eskimo – Ennadai Lake, N.W.T., [from] (W.G. Kerr), Northern Service Officer – Churchill Man.,' 12 September 1956, p. 1.
52 NWT Archives, Alex Stevenson Collection, N92-O23, 'MEMORANDUM FOR MR. W.G. KERR, Re: Eskimo – Ennadai Lake, N.W.T., [from] B.G. Sivertz, Chief, Arctic Division, Ottawa,' 28 September 1956, p. 2.
53 NAC, RG 22, vol. 254, file 40-8-1, vol. 2, report, 'ESKIMOS LIVING IN THE NUELTIN LAKE – KAZAN RIVER AREAS OF THE DISTRICT OF KEEWATIN, N.W.T.,' 16 April 1952, p. 2.
54 Ibid.
55 Quoted in Walter Rudnicki, 'Report: Field Trip to Eskimo Point,' Appendix B, p. 15.
56 Ibid., 5.
57 Ibid., 4.
58 NAC, RG 85, vol. 1267, file 1000-179, pt. 1, 'DEPARTMENT OF NORTHERN AFFAIRS AND NATIONAL RESOURCES, EDITORIAL AND INFORMATION DIVISION, Press release, ESKIMOS FLY TO NEW HUNTING GROUNDS,' 24 May 1957, p. 1.
59 Ibid.
60 Ibid., 2.
61 Ibid.
62 NAC, RG 22, vol. 254, file 40-8-1, vol. 2, report, 'ESKIMOS LIVING IN THE NUELTIN LAKE – KAZAN RIVER AREAS OF THE DISTRICT OF KEEWATIN, N.W.T.,' 16 April 1952, p. 2.
63 Ibid.
64 NAC, RG 85, vol. 1511, file 1000/179, pt. 2, 'Memorandum to the Chief of the Arctic Division, Re: Eskimos – Ennadai Lake, N.W.T., [from] (W.G. Kerr), Northern Service Officer – Churchill, Man.,' 6 June 1957, p. 1.
65 Ibid., 2.
66 NAC, RG 85, vol. 1511, file 1000/179, 'Memorandum to the Chief of the Arctic Division, Re: Eskimos – Henik Lake, N.W.T. (Formerly of Ennadai Lake), [from] (W.G. Kerr), Northern Service

Officer, Churchill, Man.,' 4 August 1957, p. 1.
67 Ibid.
68 Ibid.
69 Ibid., 2.
70 Ibid., 1.
71 NAC, RG 85, vol. 1511, file 1000/197, 'Memorandum to the Chief of the Arctic Division Re: Eskimos – Henik Lake, N.W.T. (Formerly of Ennadai Lake), [from] (W.G. Kerr), Churchill, Man.,' 8 August 1957, p. 1.
72 Ibid.
73 Walter Rudnicki, 'Report: Field Trip to Eskimo Point,' Appendix A, p. 6.
74 NAC, RG 85, vol. 1511, file 1000/179, 'Memorandum to the Chief of the Arctic Division, Re: Eskimos – Henik Lake, N.W.T. (Formerly of Ennadai Lake), [from] (W.G. Kerr), Northern Service Officer, Churchill, Man.,' 4 August 1957, p. 1.
75 Ibid.
76 NAC, RG 85, vol. 1511, file 1000/197, 'Memorandum to the Chief of the Arctic Division Re: Eskimos – Henik Lake, N.W.T. (Formerly of Ennadai Lake), [from] (W.G. Kerr), Churchill, Man.,' 8 August 1957, p. 1.
77 Ibid.
78 Ibid.
79 Walter Rudnicki, 'Report: Field Trip to Eskimo Point,' Appendix B, p. 14.
80 NAC, RG 85, vol. 1511, file 1000/179, 'Memorandum to the Chief of the Arctic Division, Re: Eskimos – Henik Lake, N.W.T., (W.G. Kerr) – Churchill, Man.,' 1 September 1957, p. 1.
81 Ibid.
82 Ibid.
83 NAC, RG 85, vol. 1511, file 1000/179, 'MEMORANDUM FOR CHIEF, Arctic DIVISION. Ennadai Eskimos at Oftedal Lake, [from] D.E. Wilkinson, N.S.O., Churchill, Man.,' 18 September 1957, p. 1.
84 NAC, RG 85, vol. 1511, file 1000/179, 'MEMORANDUM FOR CHIEF, Arctic DIVISION. Ennadai Eskimos at Oftedal Lake, [from] D.E. Wilkinson, N.S.O.,' 25 September 1957, p. 1.
85 Ibid., 2.
86 NAC, RG 85, vol. 1511, file 1000/179, 'Memorandum to the Chief of the Arctic Division, Re: Eskimos – Henik Lake, N.W.T., [from] (W.G. Kerr), Rankin Inlet, N.W.T.,' 3 December 1957, p. 1.
87 Ibid.
88 Ibid., 2.
89 Walter Rudnicki, 'Report: Field Trip to Eskimo Point,' Appendix B, p. 15.
90 Ibid., 6.
91 Ibid.
92 Ibid., 2.
93 Ibid., 15.
94 Ibid., 2.
95 Ibid.
96 Ibid., 3.
97 Ibid.
98 Ibid., 4.
99 There is considerable frustration evident in Kerr's documentation. However, his frustration and impatience may have been due, in part, to general problems he was having at the time. In an interview with Frank Tester (20 September 1991), Doug Wilkinson revealed that Kerr was, by this time, working extremely long hours, was thoroughly exhausted, and had to be eased out of his responsibilities for a badly needed rest.
100 NAC, RG 22, vol. 254, file 40-8-1, vol. 2, report, 'ESKIMOS LIVING IN THE NUELTIN LAKE – KAZAN RIVER AREAS OF THE DISTRICT OF KEEWATIN, N.W.T.,' 16 April 1952, p. 3.
101 NAC, RG 22, vol. 545, file ACND 1958, 'MEMORANDUM FOR THE DEPUTY MINISTER: ENNADAI ESKIMOS, [from] G.W. Rowley, CONFIDENTIAL, Ottawa,' 22 January 1958, p. 2.
102 Ibid.
103 Ibid., 1.
104 NAC, RG 22, vol. 545, file ACND 1958, 'MEMORANDUM FOR THE DEPUTY MINISTER: [from] G.W.R. [Rowley], CONFIDENTIAL,' 29 January 1958, p. 1.
105 Walter Rudnicki, 'Report: Field Trip to Eskimo Point,' Appendix B, p. 15.

106 Ibid.
107 Ibid., 5.
108 Ibid.
109 Ibid.
110 Ibid.
111 Ibid., Appendix D, p. 1.
112 NAC, RG 22, vol. 254, file 40-8-1, vol. 2, report, 'ESKIMOS LIVING IN THE NUELTIN LAKE – KAZAN RIVER AREAS OF THE DISTRICT OF KEEWATIN, N.W.T.,' 16 April 1952, p. 4.
113 Walter Rudnicki, 'Report: Field Trip to Eskimo Point,' Appendix A, p. 3.
114 Ibid., Appendix D, p. 2.
115 Ibid.
116 Ibid.
117 Ibid., Appendix B, p. 3.
118 Ibid., Appendix D, p. 3.
119 Ibid., 4.
120 Ibid., 3.
121 Ibid.
122 NWT Archives, Alex Stevenson Collection, N92-023, 'MEMORANDUM FOR THE DIRECTOR, RE: STARVATION AMONG THE ESKIMOS IN THE WINTER OF 1957-58, [from] R.A.J.P. [Phillips], Ottawa,' 20 October 1958, p. 3.
123 Ibid.
124 Ibid., 4.
125 Ibid.
126 Ibid.
127 NAC, RG 85, vol. 1511, file 1000/179, 'Memorandum for Mr. Stevenson, Arctic Division, [from] (W.G. Kerr), Northern Service Officer, Rankin Inlet,' 17 November 1958, p. 2.
128 Walter Rudnicki, 'Report: Field Trip to Eskimo Point,' Findings, p. 1.
129 Ibid., Appendix D, p. 5.
130 Ibid., Appendix B, p. 13.
131 Personal communication, interview with Doug Wilkinson, Kingston, Ontario, 20 September 1991.
132 NAC, RG 22, vol. 545, file ACND 1958, letter to 'Geert van den Steenhoven, Esq., Fazantplein 14, The Hague, Holland, [from] (G.W. Rowley),' 2 June 1958, p. 1.
133 A thematic apperception test is carried out by showing the respondent a picture in which what is happening is not inherently obvious. The picture leaves room for interpretation and the respondent is asked to tell his or her own story about what is taking place. The results are held to reveal the thought patterns and inclinations of the person telling the story. Walter Rudnicki, head of the welfare division of the northern administration, was an amateur artist and cartoonist. He drew pictures which had relevance to the situation and used these drawings in a manner similar to those used in this psychological test – a particularly interesting and innovative technique, given the circumstances.
134 Walter Rudnicki, 'Report: Field Trip to Eskimo Point,' Appendix C, picture no. 3.
135 Ibid., Appendix B, p. 8.
136 Ibid., Appendix B, p. 11.
137 Ibid.
138 Ibid., Appendix B, p. 17.
139 Ibid., Appendix C, picture no. 9.
140 Ibid., Appendix B, p. 12.

Chapter 6: The Garry Lake Famine
1 NAC, RG 85, vol. 1349, file 1000/179, pt. 3, 'R.A.J.P [Phillips], MEMORANDUM FOR THE DIRECTOR, RE: STARVATION AMONG THE ESKIMOS IN THE WINTER OF 1957-58, Ottawa,' 20 October 1958, p. 4.
2 NAC, RG 85, vol. 1269, file 1000/133, pt. 1, 'RCMP Division "G," Report [from] Cpl. V.D.R. Wilson, i/c Baker Lake Detachment, RE: Conditions Amongst the Eskimos – General, Annual Report, Period Ending Dec. 31st, 1957, Baker Lake, N.W.T.,' 28 January 1958, p. 1.
3 NAC, RG 85, vol. 1447, file 1000/159, vol. 2, 'Memorandum for Mr. Phillips, Account – Sustenance Eskimos Garry Lake, [from] J.P. Richards, Ottawa,' 30 September 1957, p. 1.
4 NAC, RG 85, vol. 478, file 630-189-3, Guy Mary-Rousseliere, *Eskimo*, June 1957, p. 13. Wilkinson

recalls that 'actually Father Buliard was flown in to Garry Lake in the autumn of 1948 ... The second flight [with building supplies] was never made and Father Buliard was left at Garry Lake on his own with only the supplies he had on that first and only flight. He lived that winter with Inuit at their camps. In April of 1949, after a winter with no word from him, [pilot] Gunnar [Ingabritson] flew in to Garry Lake with the Norseman, found Father Buliard and flew him to Churchill. I was in Churchill at the time and I met Father Buliard at that time. So the flight in August of 1949 was the second attempt to establish the mission at Garry Lake' (personal communication with authors, correspondence, 24 February 1993, p. 3).

5   Quoted by Charles Choque in *Joseph Buliard: Fisher of Men* (Churchill, Manitoba: Roman Catholic Episcopal Corporation 1987), 173-4. There are many examples of similar sentiments. In one letter he wrote: 'Everything raises one's soul toward God, the disgusting moral decay on the one hand and on the other the wonderful effects of divine grace' (p. 185).

6   A report submitted as part of the central and western Arctic air patrol of 1956 stated that four children from the Garry Lake area were attending the boarding school at Chesterfield Inlet, another two had been taken out in 1955, and there were plans to remove six more in 1957. Chesterfield Inlet was not accessible to Garry Lake Inuit, and the loss of their children undoubtably created hardship and emotional strain. See NAC, RG 85, vol. 478, file 630-189-3, 'Garry Lake, N.W.T., April 16th, 1956,' p. 1.

7   Charles Choque, *Joseph Buliard*, 212.

8   NAC, RG 85, vol. 1447, file 1000/159, vol. 2., 'Memorandum for Mr. Phillips, Account – Sustenance Eskimos Garry Lake, [from] J.P. Richards, Ottawa,' 30 September 1957, p. 1.

9   NAC, RG 85, vol. 478, file 630-189-3, Guy Mary-Rousseliere, *Eskimo*, June 1957, p. 19.

10 NAC, RG 85, vol. 1269, file 1000/133, pt. 1, 'RCMP Division "G," [report from] Cpl. V.D.R. Wilson, i/c Baker Lake Detachment, RE: Conditions Amongst the Eskimos – General, Annual Report, Period Ending Dec. 31st, 1957, Baker Lake, N.W.T.,' 28 January 1958, p. 3.

11 Ibid.

12 Buliard's biography, *Joseph Buliard: Fisher of Men*, contains an extensive evaluation of Buliard's disappearance and the theories around his death. See pp. 247-53.

13 NAC, RG 85 vol. 1349, file 1000/179, pt. 3, 'MEMORANDUM FOR MR. CUNNINGHAM: STARVATION AMONG THE KEEWATIN ESKIMOS IN THE WINTER OF 1957-58, [from] L.A.C. Hunt, Acting Director, Ottawa,' 26 January 1959, p. 4. Hunt was acting director of the Northern Administration and Lands Branch at the time. The director, Ben Sivertz, was absent due to the death of his father.

14 NAC, RG 85, vol. 623, file A-205-4/159, pt. 1, 'MONTHLY REPORT – JANUARY 1957, [to the] Chief, Arctic Division, Department of Northern Affairs and National Resources, Kent-Albert Building, OTTAWA, [from] D.E. Wilkinson, NSO, Baker Lake,' 8 February 1957, p. 4.

15 Ibid.

16 Ibid., 5.

17 Ibid.

18 Ibid., 4.

19 Ibid., 6.

20 Ibid., 7.

21 Ibid., 7-8.

22 Ibid.

23 Ibid., 8. Wilson's attitude, as expressed in his report of January 1958, very closely parallels Wilkinson's. Wilson wrote: 'The hardest thing the white man has to do in the North is refuse to help these people. The native has come to realize that he does not have to worry about the future or his health or his prosperity. The white man is willing to do this for him. The writer believes that these people could, if left alone, solve most of their problems. It is believed that more emphasis should be placed on making the native solve his own problems and only give assistance in the form of equipment rather than food.' See NAC, RG 85, vol. 1269, file 1000/133, pt. 1, 'RCMP Division "G," Report from Cpl. V.D.R. Wilson, i/c Baker Lake Detachment, RE: Conditions Amongst the Eskimos – General, Annual Report, Period Ending Dec. 31st, 1957, Baker Lake, N.W.T.,' 28 January 1958, p. 5.

24 Ibid., 9. In describing one such encounter Wilkinson wrote: 'We parted friends, I think. I just hope I don't run into trouble on the trail sometime in the near future and turn up at his camp looking for food. It may be quite a joke to him' (p. 10).

25 Ibid., 10.

26 Ibid.

27 Ibid., 13.
28 NAC, RG 85, vol. 1447, file 1000/159, vol. 3, 'MEMORANDUM FOR MR. PHILLIPS, GARRY LAKE CHRONOLOGY 1957-58, [from] Doug Wilkinson, CONFIDENTIAL, Ottawa,' 18 December 1958, p. 1.
29 Ibid.
30 Ibid., 2.
31 Ibid.
32 Ibid.
33 NAC, RG 85, vol. 1447, file 1000/159, vol. 2, copy of radio message received from Pelly Lake, 5 August 1957, Trinel to Wilkinson.
34 NAC, RG 85 vol. 1447, file 1000/159, vol. 2, telegraph, 'WILKINSON TO Arctic NORADMIN KENT ALBERT OTTAWA,' 6 August 1957, 2:31 A.M.
35 NAC, RG 85, vol. 1447, file 1000/159, vol. 2, 'MEMORANDUM FOR MR. SIVERTZ, [signed by] A. Stevenson for R.A.J.P. [Bob Phillips], Ottawa,' 6 August 1957.
36 Ibid.
37 Ibid. (handwritten note on memo addressed to Mr. Stevenson from Ben Sivertz).
38 NAC, RG 85, vol. 1447, file 1000/159, vol. 2, 'MEMORANDUM FOR MR. SIVERTZ, GARRY LAKE – REPORTED STARVATION, [signed by] A.S. (Alex Stevenson) from R.A.J.P. (Bob Phillips), Ottawa,' 8 August 1957.
39 NAC, RG 85, vol. 1447, file 1000/159, vol. 2, letter signed by 'A.S. (Alex Stevenson) [for] R.A.J. Phillips, Chief of the Arctic Division, to Inspector W.J. Fitzsimmons, Officer in Charge, C.I.B., "G" Division, Royal Canadian Mounted Police, Ottawa, Ontario,' 8 August 1957, p. 1.
40 NAC, RG 85, vol. 1447, file 1000/159, vol. 2, radio message, 'WILKINSON to Arctic NORTHERN AFFAIRS KENT-ALBERT OTTAWA,' 8 August 1957.
41 NAC, RG 85, vol. 1447, file 1000/159, vol. 2, radio message, 'WILKINSON to J.P. Kelsall, Wildlife Service, Yellowknife, N.W.T.,' 9 August 1957.
42 NAC, RG 85, vol. 1447, file 1000/159, vol. 2, 'Memorandum for Mr. Phillips, Account – Sustenance Eskimos Garry Lake, [from] J.P. Richards, Ottawa,' 30 September 1957, p. 3.
43 NAC, RG 85, vol. 1447, file 1000/159, vol. 3, 'MEMORANDUM FOR MR. PHILLIPS, GARRY LAKE CHRONOLOGY 1957-58, [from] Doug Wilkinson, CONFIDENTIAL, Ottawa,' 18 December 1958, p. 4.
44 NAC, RG 85, vol. 1447, file 1000/159, vol. 2, 'MEMORANDUM FOR CHIEF, Arctic DIVISION. Starvation report – Garry Lake Eskimos, [from] D.E. Wilkinson, N.S.O., Baker Lake, N.W.T.,' 10 August 1957, p. 3.
45 Ibid., 1-2.
46 Ibid., 4.
47 Ibid.
48 Ibid.
49 Ibid., 5.
50 Ibid., 6.
51 Ibid.
52 NAC, RG 85, vol. 1447, file 1000/159, vol. 2, letter from 'B.G. Sivertz, Director, [to] Father Rene Belair, O.M.I., Vicariate Apostolic, Hudson Bay, Churchill, Manitoba, Ottawa,' 2 October 1957, p. 1.
53 Ibid., 2.
54 NAC, RG 85, vol. 1447, file 1000/159, vol. 2, 'MEMORANDUM FOR MR. PHILLIPS, GARRY LAKE CHRONOLOGY 1957-58, [from] Doug Wilkinson, CONFIDENTIAL, Ottawa,' 18 December 1958, p. 4.
55 Ibid.
56 Ibid.
57 NAC, RG 85, vol. 1447, file 1000/159, vol. 3, 'RCMP Report, Re: E2-326 KADLUK, (Eskimo Male) (D.O.B. 1910), et al, Baker Lake, N.W.T., Accidental Death at Garry Lake District, N.W.T., [from] V.D.R. Wilson, #15337 i/c Baker Lake Detachment, Baker Lake,' 19 June 1958, p. 3.
58 Ibid.
59 Ibid.
60 NAC, RG 85, vol. 478, file 630-189-3, Guy Mary-Rousseliere, *Eskimo*, June 1957, p. 13.
61 NAC, RG 85, vol. 1447, file 1000/159, vol. 3, 'RCMP Report, Re: E2-326 KADLUK, (Eskimo Male) (D.O.B. 1910), et al, Baker Lake, N.W.T., Accidental Death at Garry Lake District, N.W.T., [from]

V.D.R. Wilson, #15337 i/c Baker Lake Detachment, Baker Lake,' 19 June 1958, p. 3.
62 Ibid.
63 Ibid.
64 NAC, RG 85, vol. 1447, file 1000/159, vol. 3, 'RCMP Report, Re: Destitute Relief and Issues of Family Allowances to Garry Lake Eskimos, N.W.T., [by] V.D.R. Wilson, #15337, i/c Baker Lake Detachment, Baker Lake,' 10 May 1958, p. 3. Another woman, Papaloo, 'was placed in the nursing station for treatment of the same disease' (p. 3). Of her, Wilson later wrote: 'The girl Papaloo was questioned by the writer some time ago but nothing was learned. The girl will state anything that comes into her head.' See NAC, RG 85, vol. 1447, file 1000/159, vol. 3, 'RCMP Report, Re: E2-326 KADLUK, (Eskimo Male) (D.O.B. 1910), et al, Baker Lake, N.W.T., Accidental Death at Garry Lake District, N.W.T., [from] V.D.R. Wilson, #15337 i/c Baker Lake Detachment, Baker Lake,' 19 June 1958, p. 4.
65 Ibid., 6.
66 Although there is also evidence that Inuit showed extraordinary respect for other people's food caches. For example, Doug Wilkinson passed along the following report of a pilot who talked with Buliard: 'I could see by signs in the snow that Eskimos had been around the building that winter but nothing had been touched, not even the garbage we'd left behind ... Father Buliard ... told a sad story of a very cold winter with few caribou to hunt. He said that all the people in the region were very hungry. I asked him why they didn't take some of the food we had stored in the building. He replied that neither he nor they would take it as it wasn't their's to have. I couldn't get over this' (personal communication with authors, correspondence, 25 February 1993, p. 1).
67 NAC, RG 85, vol. 1447, file 1000/159, vol. 3, 'RCMP Report, Re: Destitute Relief and Issues of Family Allowances to Garry Lake Eskimos, N.W.T., [by] V.D.R. Wilson, #15337, i/c Baker Lake Detachment, Baker Lake,' 10 May 1958, p. 5.
68 Ibid.
69 NAC, RG 85, vol. 1447, file 1000/159, vol. 2, 'MEMORANDUM FOR MR. PHILLIPS, GARRY LAKE CHRONOLOGY 1957-58, [from] Doug Wilkinson, CONFIDENTIAL, Ottawa,' 18 December 1958, p. 5.
70 Ibid.
71 Ibid.
72 NAC, RG 85, vol. 1447, file 1000/159, vol. 3, 'RCMP Report, Re: E2-326 KADLUK, (Eskimo Male) (D.O.B. 1910), et al, Baker Lake, N.W.T., Accidental Death at Garry Lake District, N.W.T., [from] V.D.R. Wilson, #15337 i/c Baker Lake Detachment, Baker Lake,' 19 June 1958, p. 2.
73 NAC, RG 85, vol. 1447, file 1000/159, vol. 2, 'MEMORANDUM FOR MR. PHILLIPS, GARRY LAKE CHRONOLOGY 1957-58, [from] Doug Wilkinson, CONFIDENTIAL, Ottawa,' 18 December 1958, p. 5.
74 Ibid.
75 Ibid.
76 This date is clearly in error and should read '1957.'
77 NAC, RG 85, vol. 1447, file 1000/159, vol. 3, 'RCMP Report, Re. E2-326 KADLUK, (Age 50) et al, Baker Lake, N.W.T. Accidental Death at Garry Lake District, N.W.T., [from] V.D.R. Wilson, Cpl. #15337 I/C Baker Lake Detachment,' 10 July 1958, p. 2.
78 Ibid.
79 Ibid.
80 NAC, RG 85, vol. 1269, file 1000/133, pt. 1, 'RCMP Report, Re., conditions Amongst the Eskimos – General, Annual Report, Period ending Dec. 31st., 1957 Baker Lake, N.W.T. [from] V.D.R. Wilson, #15337 i/c Baker Lake Detachment,' p. 4.
81 NAC, RG 85, vol. 1349, file 1000/179, pt. 3, 'MEMORANDUM FOR THE DIRECTOR RE: STARVA-TION AMONG THE ESKIMOS IN THE WINTER of 1957-58, [from] R.A.J.P. (Bob Phillips) Ottawa,' 20 October 1958, p. 6.
82 NAC, RG 85, vol. 1447, file 1000/159, vol. 3, 'RCMP Report, Re., Destitute Relief and Issues of Family Allowances to Garry Lake Eskimos, N.W.T., [from] V.D.R. Wilson, #15337, i/c Baker Lake Detachment, 10 May 1958, p. 5.
83 NAC, RG 85, vol. 1349, file 1000/179, pt. 3, 'MEMORANDUM FOR THE DIRECTOR RE: STARVA-TION AMONG THE ESKIMOS IN THE WINTER of 1957-58, [from] R.A.J.P. (Bob Phillips) Ottawa,' 20 October 1958, p. 6.
84 NAC, RG 85, vol. 1447, file 1000/159, vol. 3, 'RCMP Report, Re., Destitute Relief and Issues of

Family Allowances to Garry Lake Eskimos, N.W.T., [from] V.D.R. Wilson, #15337, i/c Baker Lake Detachment, 10 May 1958, p. 5.

85 NAC, RG 85, vol. 1349, file 1000/179, pt. 3, 'MEMORANDUM FOR THE DIRECTOR RE: STARVA-TION AMONG THE ESKIMOS IN THE WINTER of 1957-58, [from] R.A.J.P. (Bob Phillips) Ottawa,' 20 October 1958, p. 6.

86 NAC, RG 85, vol. 1349, file 1000/179, pt. 3, 'COMMENTS ON COMMENTS ON KERR REPORT TO DIRECTOR RE STARVATION, [by] W.G. Kerr, Northern Service Officer,' n.d., p. 1.

87 Ibid.

88 NAC, RG 85, vol. 1447, file 1000/159, vol. 3, 'RCMP Report, Re. E2-326 KADLUK, (Age 50) et al, Baker Lake, N.W.T. Accidental Death at Garry Lake District, N.W.T., [from] V.D.R. Wilson, Cpl. #15337 I/C Baker Lake Detachment,' 10 July 1958, p. 4.

89 NAC, RG 85, vol. 1447, file 1000/159, vol. 3, 'REPORT ON AUTOPSIES PERFORMED ON THE ESKIMOS AT BAKER LAKE ON June 4, 1958,' no author, p. 28.

90 Ibid.

91 Ibid., 3.

92 Ibid., 7.

93 Ibid., 21.

94 Ibid., 22.

95 NAC, RG 85, vol. 1447, file 1000/159, vol. 3, 'RCMP Report, Re., Destitute Relief and Issues of Family Allowances to Garry Lake Eskimos, N.W.T., [from] V.D.R. Wilson, #15337, i/c Baker Lake Detachment, 10 May 1958, p. 6.

96 NAC, RG 85, vol. 1447, file 1000/159, vol. 3, 'REPORT ON AUTOPSIES PERFORMED ON THE ESKIMOS AT BAKER LAKE ON June 4, 1958,' no author, p. 8.

97 Ibid., 17.

98 Ibid., 27, 23, 26, 24, 25, 26.

99 NAC, RG 85, vol. 1447, file 1000/159, vol. 3, 'RCMP Report, Re., Destitute Relief and Issues of Family Allowances to Garry Lake Eskimos, N.W.T., [from] V.D.R. Wilson, #15337, i/c Baker Lake Detachment, 10 May 1958, p. 6.

100 NAC, RG 85, vol. 1447, file 1000/159, vol. 3, 'REPORT ON AUTOPSIES PERFORMED ON THE ESKIMOS AT BAKER LAKE ON June 4, 1958,' no author, pp. 12, 16.

101 Ibid., 22, 23.

102 NAC, RG 85, vol. 1447, file 1000/159, vol. 3, 'RCMP Report, Re., Destitute Relief and Issues of Family Allowances to Garry Lake Eskimos, N.W.T., [from] V.D.R. Wilson, #15337, i/c Baker Lake Detachment, 10 May 1958, p. 6.

103 NAC, RG 85, vol. 1447, file 1000/159, vol. 3, letter from 'Terence Golding, Federal Day School, Baker Lake, [to] The Chief – Education Division, Department of Northern Affairs,' 5 January 1958, p. 1.

104 NAC, RG 85, vol. 1447, file 1000/159, vol. 3, 'MINUTES OF INTER-DEPARTMENTAL MEETING, BAKER LAKE, N.W.T. January 13/58, [taken by] D.E. Wilkinson, N.S.O.'

105 NAC, RG 85, vol. 1447, file 1000/159, vol. 3, 'MEMORANDUM FOR CHIEF, Arctic DIVISION. INTERDEPARTMENTAL MEETINGS, [from] D.E. Wilkinson, N.S.O., Baker Lake, N.W.T.,' 16 January 1958, p. 1.

106 Ibid., 2.

107 NAC, RG 85, vol. 1447, file 1000/159, vol. 3, 'MEMORANDUM FOR MR. PHILLIPS, GARRY LAKE CHRONOLOGY 1957-58, [from] Doug Wilkinson, CONFIDENTIAL, Ottawa,' 18 December 1958, pp. 4-5.

108 NAC, RG 85, vol. 1447, file 1000/159, vol. 3, 'MONTHLY REPORT – NORTHERN SERVICE OFFICER – JANUARY 1958, Baker Lake, N.W.T.,' 31 January 1958, p. 1.

109 Ibid., 5-6.

110 NAC, RG 85, vol. 1447, file 1000/159, vol. 3, 'MEMORANDUM FOR CHIEF, Arctic DIVISION. Garry Lake Eskimos, [from] D.E. Wilkinson, N.S.O., Baker Lake, N.W.T.,' 20 February 1958, p. 1.

111 Ibid., 2.

112 Ibid.

113 Ibid., 6.

114 Ibid.

115 Ibid., 7.

116 NAC, RG 85, vol. 1447, file 1000/159, vol. 3, 'RCMP Report, Re. E2-326 KADLUK, (Age 50) et al, Baker Lake, N.W.T. Accidental Death at Garry Lake District, N.W.T., [from] V.D.R. Wilson, Cpl.

396 Notes to pp. 267-77

#15337 I/C Baker Lake Detachment,' 10 July 1958, p. 2.
117 NAC, RG 85, vol. 1447, file 1000/159, vol. 3, 'MEMORANDUM FOR MR. PHILLIPS, GARRY LAKE CHRONOLOGY 1957-58, [from] Doug Wilkinson, CONFIDENTIAL, Ottawa,' 18 December 1958, p. 6.
118 NAC, RG 85, vol. 1447, file 1000/159, vol. 3, 'RCMP Report, Re. E2-326 KADLUK, (Age 50) et al, Baker Lake, N.W.T. Accidental Death at Garry Lake District, N.W.T., [from] V.D.R. Wilson, Cpl. #15337 I/C Baker Lake Detachment,' 10 July 1958, p. 2.
119 Ibid.
120 Ibid., 3.
121 NAC, RG 85, vol. 1447, file 1000/159, vol. 3, 'MEMORANDUM FOR MR. PHILLIPS, GARRY LAKE CHRONOLOGY 1957-58, [from] Doug Wilkinson, CONFIDENTIAL, Ottawa,' 18 December 1958, p. 7.
122 Ibid.
123 Ibid.
124 Ibid., 7-8.
125 NAC, RG 85, vol. 1447, file 1000/159, vol. 3, 'RCMP Report, Re. E2-326 KADLUK, (Age 50) et al, Baker Lake, N.W.T. Accidental Death at Garry Lake District, N.W.T., [from] V.D.R. Wilson, Cpl. #15337 I/C Baker Lake Detachment,' 10 July 1958, p. 3.
126 NAC, RG 85, vol. 1447, file 1000/159, vol. 3, 'MEMORANDUM FOR MR. PHILLIPS, GARRY LAKE CHRONOLOGY 1957-58, [from] Doug Wilkinson, CONFIDENTIAL, Ottawa,' 18 December 1958, p. 8.
127 NAC, RG 85, vol. 1447, file 1000/159, vol. 3, 'RCMP Report, Re. E2-326 KADLUK, (Age 50) et al, Baker Lake, N.W.T. Accidental Death at Garry Lake District, N.W.T., [from] V.D.R. Wilson, Cpl. #15337 I/C Baker Lake Detachment,' 10 July 1958, p. 3.
128 NAC, RG 85, vol. 1447, file 1000/159, vol. 3, 'MEMORANDUM FOR MR. PHILLIPS, GARRY LAKE CHRONOLOGY 1957-58, [from] Doug Wilkinson, CONFIDENTIAL, Ottawa,' 18 December 1958, p. 8.
129 Ibid.
130 Ibid., 9.
131 Ibid.
132 Ibid.
133 NAC, RG 85, vol. 1447, file 1000/159, vol. 3, 'MEMORANDUM FOR CHIEF, Arctic DIVISION, Garry Lake Eskimos, [from] D.E. Wilkinson, N.S.O., Baker lake, N.W.T.,' 7 June 1958, p. 2.
134 NAC, RG 85, vol. 1447, file 1000/159, vol. 3, 'RCMP Report, Re. E2-326 KADLUK, (Age 50) et al, Baker Lake, N.W.T. Accidental Death at Garry Lake District, N.W.T., [from] V.D.R. Wilson, Cpl. #15337 I/C Baker Lake Detachment,' 10 July 1958, p. 4.
135 Ibid.
136 NAC, RG 85, vol. 1447, file 1000/159, vol. 3, 'MEMORANDUM FOR MR. PHILLIPS, GARRY LAKE CHRONOLOGY 1957-58, [from] Doug Wilkinson, CONFIDENTIAL, Ottawa,' 18 December 1958, p. 6.
137 NAC, RG 85, vol. 1349, file 1000/179, pt. 3, 'COMMENTS ON COMMENTS ON KERR REPORT TO DIRECTOR RE STARVATION, [by] W.G. Kerr, Northern Service Officer,' n.d., p. 1.
138 NAC, RG 85, vol. 1349, file 1000/179, pt. 3, 'MEMORANDUM FOR MR. CUNNINGHAM: STARVATION AMONG THE KEEWATIN ESKIMOS IN THE WINTER OF 1957-58, [report by] L.A.C.O. Hunt, Acting Director, Ottawa,' 26 January 1959, pp. 6-7.
139 See F.G. Vallee, *Kabloona and Eskimo in the Central Keewatin* (Ottawa: St. Paul University, Canadian Research Centre for Anthropology 1967), 49.

Chapter 7: Whale Cove Relocation
1 NAC, RG 85, vol. 1447, file 1000/159, vol. 3, letter to 'Prime Minister John Diefenbaker, Government of Canada, Ottawa, Ont. Can. [from] M.J. Thomas, Milden, Saskatchewan,' 7 May 1958, pp. 1-2.
2 NWT Archives, Alex Stevenson Collection, N92-023, 'MEMORANDUM TO THE CABINET,' 9 May 1958, p. 1.
3 Ibid., 1-2.
4 Ibid., 2.
5 Ibid., 3.
6 NWT Archives, Alex Stevenson Collection, N92-023, 'Minutes of the Ninth Meeting of the

Committee on Eskimo Affairs,' 26 May 1958, p. 10.
7 Ibid.
8 NAC, RG 85, vol. 1659, file NR 4-2-4, 'KEEWATIN COMMITTEE, Minutes of the First Meeting, Room 315; Kent-Albert Building at 4.00 p.m., Friday, May 23, 1958,' p. 3.
9 Ibid., 1-2.
10 NWT Archives, Alex Stevenson Collection, N92-023, 'Minutes of the Ninth Meeting of the Committee on Eskimo Affairs,' 26 May 1958, p. 10.
11 Ibid., 10-11.
12 Ibid., 11.
13 Ibid.
14 NAC, RG 85, vol. 1659, file NR 4-2-4, 'KEEWATIN COMMITTEE, Minutes of the Second Meeting held at 4.00 p.m., Tuesday, May 27, 1958, in Room 315, Kent-Albert Building,' p. 2.
15 Ibid.
16 NAC, RG 85, vol. 1659, file NR 4-2-4, 'KEEWATIN COMMITTEE, Minutes of the Third Meeting, held in Room 315, Kent-Albert Building at 3.00 p.m., Friday May 30, 1958,' p. 2.
17 Ibid., 1-2.
18 Ibid., 3.
19 Ibid., 4.
20 NAC, RG 85, vol. 1659, file NR 4-2-4, 'KEEWATIN COMMITTEE, Minutes of the Fourth Meeting held in Room 315, Kent-Albert Building at 9:00 a.m., Monday, June 9, 1958,' p. 3.
21 NWT Archives, Alex Stevenson Collection, N92-023, 'A Project to Assist the Keewatin Eskimos' 10 June 1958, p. 1.
22 Ibid., 1-2.
23 Ibid., 2.
24 NAC, RG 85, vol. 1659, file NR 4-2-4, 'KEEWATIN COMMITTEE, Minutes of the Fifth Meeting, held in Room 315, Kent-Albert Building at 9.00 a.m., on Friday, June 20, 1958,' p. 3.
25 Ibid.
26 Ibid.
27 NWT Archives, Alex Stevenson Collection, N92-023, 'MEMORANDUM FOR MEMBERS OF KEEWATIN COMMITTEE, REPORT ON PROPOSED STIES FOR KEEWATIN COMMUNITY AT TAVANI AND WHALE COVE, [from] F.J. Neville,' 11 August 1958, p. 1.
28 Ibid.
29 Ibid.
30 Ibid.
31 Ibid.
32 Ibid., 2.
33 NWT Archives, Alex Stevenson Collection, N92-023, 'KEEWATIN COMMITTEE, Minutes of the Sixth Meeting, held in Room 313, Kent-Albert Building, at 3.00 p.m., Monday, July 28, 1958,' p. 3.
34 Ibid.
35 Ibid., 4.
36 Ibid., 1.
37 Ibid.
38 NWT Archives, Alex Stevenson Collection, N92-023, 'MEMORANDUM FOR MEMBERS OF KEEWATIN COMMITTEE, ADEQUACY OF WHALE COVE AS SITE FOR NEW COMMUNITY,' n.d., p. 1.
39 Ibid.
40 Ibid.
41 Ibid., 2.
42 Ibid.
43 NAC, RG 85, vol. 1071, file 251-6, pt. 2, 'MEMORANDUM FOR THE CHIEF – Arctic DIVISION, Progress Report – Whale Cove, [from] D.W. Grant, Whale Cove, N.W.T.,' 29 August 1958, p. 1.
44 Ibid., 2-3.
45 Ibid., 3.
46 Ibid.
47 Ibid., 4.
48 NAC, RG 85, vol. 1071, file 251-6, pt. 2, 'MEMORANDUM FOR THE CHIEF – Arctic DIVISION, Sam Voisy, [from] D.W. Grant, Ottawa,' 15 September 1958, p. 1.

49 Ibid.
50 NAC, RG 85, vol. 1071, file 251-6, pt. 2, 'Memo for the Chief, Arctic Division, Progress Report –
    Whale Cove [signed] 'Sayanara,' doug grant, Whale Cove, N.W.T.,' 17 September 1958, p. 1.
51 Ibid., 3.
52 Ibid., 5.
53 Ibid., 8.
54 Ibid., 9.
55 Ibid., 10.
56 NAC, RG 85, vol. 1071, file 251-6, pt. 2, 'Memorandum for Chief, Arctic Division, Whale Cove
    Project, [from] D.W. Grant, Whale Cove, N.W.T.,' 22 September 1958, pp. 1-3.
57 NAC, RG 85, vol. 1071, file 251-6, pt. 2, 'MEMORANDUM FOR THE CHIEF, Arctic DIVISION,
    Whale Cove vs M.V. "Maple Hill," [from] D.W. Grant, Northern Service Officer, Rankin Inlet,' 6
    November 1958, p. 2.
58 Ibid.
59 Ibid., 3. In his 17 September report, Grant had written: 'The master has never been in Arctic waters
    before and he's extremely cautious' (p. 5); while in a 6 November report, entitled 'The Keewatin
    Project,' he wrote: 'The reason for abandoning Whale Cove lies purely and simply with the refusal
    of the master of the *Maple Hill* to remain there long enough to discharge his cargo' (p. 4).
60 NAC, RG 85, vol. 1071, file 251-6, pt. 2, 'Memorandum for Chief, Arctic Division, Whale Cove
    Project, [from] D.W. Grant, Whale Cove, N.W.T.,' 22 September 1958, p. 4.
61 NAC, RG 85, vol. 1071, file 251-6, pt. 2, 'THE KEEWATIN PROJECT, D.W. Grant, N.S.O., Rankin
    Inlet,' 6 November 1958, pp. 3-4.
62 Ibid., 4.
63 Ibid.
64 Ibid., 5.
65 Ibid., 10-11.
66 Ibid., 7-8.
67 NAC, RG 85, vol. 1071, file 251-6, pt. 2, 'DISTRIBUTION OF WHALE COVE FAMILIES AS OF
    OCTOBER 1st, 1958,' [signed by] D.W. Grant, NSO, Whale Cove Community.
68 NAC, RG 85, vol. 1071, file 251-6, pt. 2, 'MEMORANDUM FOR MR. WALTON – GREAT WHALE
    RIVER, WHALE COVE, [from] A. Stevenson, Chief, Administrative Section, Arctic Division,
    Ottawa,' 30 October 1958, p. 1.
69 NAC, RG 85, vol. 1071, file 251-6, pt. 2, 'THE KEEWATIN PROJECT, D.W. Grant, N.S.O., Rankin
    Inlet,' 6 November 1958, p. 1.
70 Ibid.
71 The K.R.P. project, as it came to be known, is variously referred to in the archival documents as
    the Keewatin Rehabilitation Project, the Keewatin Relocation Project, and the Keewatin Re-estab-
    lishment Project. The later seems to be the correct title for the undertaking.
72 NAC, RG 85, vol. 1071, file 251-6, pt. 2, 'THE KEEWATIN PROJECT, D.W. Grant, N.S.O., Rankin
    Inlet,' 6 November 1958, p. 1.
73 Ibid., 2.
74 Ibid.
75 Ibid., 2.
76 Ibid., 3.
77 Ibid., 4.
78 Ibid., 4-5.
79 NWT Archives, Alex Stevenson Collection, N92-023, 'Keewatin Re-establishment Project,' 14 July
    1959, p. 1.
80 Ibid.
81 Ibid., 2.
82 NAC, RG 85, vol. 1349, file 1000/184, pt. 4, 'REPORT ON RANKIN INLET – WHALE COVE, [by]
    P.E. Murdoch,' n.d., p. 2. While undated, this report seems to have been written in the summer
    of 1960.
83 Ibid., 2.
84 Ibid.
85 Ibid., 3.
86 Ibid.
87 Ibid., 1.

88 Ibid.
89 Ibid.
90 Ibid., 2-3.
91 Ibid., 2.
92 Ibid., 4.
93 Ibid., 5.
94 NAC, RG 85, vol. 1071, file 251-6, pt. 2, 'Memo for the Chief, Arctic Division, Progress Report – Whale Cove [signed] "Sayanara," doug grant, Whale Cove, N.W.T.,' 17 September 1958, p. 10.
95 NAC, RG 85, vol. 1349, file 1000/187, pt. 4, 'REPORT ON RANKIN INLET – WHALE COVE, [by] P.E. Murdoch,' n.d., p. 2.
96 NAC, RG 85, vol. 1349, file 1000/184, pt. 4, 'Memorandum for the Chief, Industrial Division, Rankin Inlet Trip, P. Godt, A/C Co-op Development Group, Ottawa,' 8 March 1960, p. 2.
97 Ibid., 3.
98 Ibid., 3-4.
99 Ibid., 7.
100 Ibid.
101 NAC, RG 85, vol. 1382, file 1012-13, 'MINUTES OF THE MEETING HELD NOVEMBER 18, AT 10:30 a.m., IN THE CONFERENCE ROOM TO DISCUSS RESOURCE STUDIES FOR THE PROPOSED RELOCATION OF ESKIMOS, Arctic Division,' 24 November 1958, p. 2. The meeting was chaired by Bob Phillips, chief of the Arctic division. He opened it by commenting on the successful relocations to Resolute Bay and Grise Fiord. His comments were followed by a claim from Alex Stevenson that these relocations had been so successful that the relocatees were asking that their relatives join them in the high Arctic. However, the recommendation that people not be relocated across geographical areas seems a little strange in light of these claims. The minutes of this meeting are extremely brief and obviously more dialogue took place than was actually recorded. It is known from other sources that Walter Rudnicki, who was also present, was not as blindly enthusiastic about the outcome of the high Arctic relocations and this may account for the second point agreed upon.
102 NAC, RG 85, vol. 1349, file 1000/184, pt. 4, 'Memorandum for the Chief, Industrial Division, Rankin Inlet Trip, P. Godt, A/C Co-op Development Group, Ottawa,' 8 March 1960, p. 7.
103 Ibid.
104 Inuit were to come into closer contact with liberal democratic ideals in the next few years – a regime dominated by what the internationally renowned Canadian political scientist, the late C.B. MacPherson, has called 'possessive individualism.' MacPherson traces the origins of this ideal in *The Political Theory of Possessive Individualism: Hobbes to Locke* (Toronto: Oxford University Press 1962).
105 NAC, RG 85, vol. 1349, file 1000/184, pt. 4, 'Memorandum for the Chief, Industrial Division, Rankin Inlet Trip, P. Godt, A/C Co-op Development Group, Ottawa,' 8 March 1960, p. 8.
106 Ibid., 6.
107 Ibid., 8.
108 NAC, RG 85, vol. 1961, file A-1011-1, vol. 2, 'KEEWATIN WELFARE PATROL, August 29 to September 9, 1960, DRAFT, F.J. Neville,' p. 5. 'Bud' Neville is the same person who, in 1990, was responsible for the 'Hickling Report,' the federal government's investigation into the controversy surrounding the relocation of Inuit to the high Arctic in 1953, documented in Chapters 3 and 4.
109 Ibid., 7
110 Ibid., 8.
111 Ibid.
112 F.G. Vallee, *Kabloona and Eskimo in the Central Keewatin* (Ottawa: St. Paul University, Canadian Research Centre for Anthropology 1967), 51.
113 Ibid., 52.
114 Ibid., 51.
115 Ibid., 53.
116 Ibid., 54.
117 Ibid., 54.
118 Ibid., 54n.
119 Ibid., 54-5.
120 NAC, RG 85, vol. 1952, file A-1000/184, 'REPORT ON RANKIN INLET – WHALE COVE, [by] P.E. Murdoch,' n.d., p. 2.

121 F.G. Vallee, *Kabloona and Eskimo in the Central Keewatin*, 54.
122 Ibid.
123 Ibid., 55.
124 Ibid., 49.

Chapter 8: Relocation and Responsibility
1 In 1993, the conditions and social circumstances faced by the Mushuau Innu (not to be confused with Inuit) of Davis Inlet, Labrador, received world-wide attention. Davis Inlet is the story of a community which, until the Innu were convinced by the government and a local priest to relocate from the mainland to an island in Davis Inlet in 1967, was a functional culture whose livelihood depended on the caribou hunt. The relocation isolated the Innu from the mainland and seriously limited the traditional hunt. The destruction of cultural practices and norms which followed is undoubtably the most significant consideration in explaining the alcoholism, physical abuse, and solvent use which was subsequently sensationalized by the Canadian and international press.
  In the summer of 1962, Inuit from West Ungava were relocated to Port Burwell, NWT, where the government had decided to operate a fishery. In other words, the policy of relocation continued in different forms beyond the period of developing community councils and more liberal democratic institutions for aboriginal people in the North.
2 NAC, RG 85, vol. 1514, file 1012, vol. 3, 'MINUTES OF THE FIFTH MEETING OF THE COMMITTEE ON ESKIMO AFFAIRS,' 29 November 1954, p. 6.
3 Ibid., 5.
4 Ibid., 6.
5 NAC, RG 85, vol. 1514, file 1012-1, pt. 6, 'MINUTES OF THE SEVENTH MEETING OF THE COMMITTEE ON ESKIMO AFFAIRS,' 28 May 1956, p. 7.
6 Ibid., 9.
7 Ibid.
8 Ibid.
9 Ibid., 9-10.
10 Ibid.
11 Ibid.
12 Ibid.
13 Ibid.
14 Ibid., 2.
15 NAC, RG 85, vol. 1660, file NR4/3-3, pt. 1, 'TO THE COMMITTEE ON ESKIMO AFFAIRS: REPORT ON PROPOSED ESKIMO RESETTLEMENT IN SOUTHERN CANADA,' n.d., p. 1.
16 Ibid., 2.
17 Ibid., 2-3.
18 Ibid., 3.
19 Ibid.
20 Ibid.
21 By the 1990s, this use of hospital patients as subjects for various social 'experiments' had acquired a certain notoriety in Canada as a result of revelations about the use of psychiatric patients for CIA-funded experiments in Montreal in the 1960s.
22 NAC, RG 85, vol. 1660, file NR4/3-3, pt. 1, 'TO THE COMMITTEE ON ESKIMO AFFAIRS: REPORT ON PROPOSED ESKIMO RESETTLEMENT IN SOUTHERN CANADA,' n.d., p. 4.
23 Ibid.
24 Ibid., 5.
25 Ibid., 7.
26 NAC, RG 85, vol. 1070, file 251-4, pt. 3, letter to 'Prime Minister, Ottawa, Canada, [from] David Cole, Port Antonio, Jamaica, B.W.I.,' 4 September 1957.
27 Ibid., 9.
28 Ibid., 12.
29 NAC, RG 85, vol. 1514, vol. 1012-1, pt. 6, 'MINUTES OF THE EIGHTH MEETING OF THE COMMITTEE ON ESKIMO AFFAIRS, HELD ON MAY 13, 1957 IN ROOM 304, LANGEVIN BLOCK, OTTAWA,' p. 11.
30 Ibid.
31 Ibid
32 Ibid., 11-12.

33 Ibid., 12.
34 Ibid.
35 Ibid.
36 NAC, RG 85, vol. 1514, file 1012-1, pt. 6, 'MEMORANDUM FOR MR. SIVERTZ ESKIMO RESET-TLEMENT IN SOUTHERN CANADA, [from] R.G.R. Ottawa,' 14 May 1957, p. 1.
37 Richard Diubaldo, *The Government of Canada and the Inuit, 1900-1967* (Ottawa: Research Branch, Corporate Policy, Department of Indian and Northern Affairs Canada 1985), 129. Ben Sivertz has suggested that the proposal died from lack of enthusiasm within the department and a recognition that such a scheme would ultimately be controversial in many ways. He noted the opposition of the church but also suggested that other factors were relevant. The racial tensions and problems that would likely be created by trying to integrate Inuit into southern Canada in the 1950s were noted. He also indicated that, with few exceptions, employers were not likely to be favourably disposed to hiring a Native person (personal communication, interview with Ben Sivertz, Victoria, BC, 27 February 1993).
38 Richard Diubaldo, *The Government of Canada and the Inuit*, 129-30.
39 NAC, RG 85, vol. 314, file 1012-8, vol. 3, letter by Rosie, p. 1, and Tommy, p. 1.
40 The department had in its possession many letters from residents of Resolute and Grise Fiord who talked favourably about these communities and who asked that relatives be sent to join them. On the surface, such letters appear to indicate that the relocations were a success. However, there are good reasons to doubt this interpretation. Inuit deference to authority has already been noted. Inuit were aware that if they wanted to get something from officials, it was important to tell them what they wanted to hear and to do so in a manner which gave officials the respect they were supposed to deserve. In a situation where Inuit did not see how they could return to Inukjuak, and given the importance of numbers in community politics in a community divided along lines of origin, asking relatives to join them made sense. In rare circumstances, such as those noted earlier in the case of correspondence from southern sanitoriums, Inuit felt free to express their true feelings.
41 NAC, RG 85, vol. 1659, file NR4/2-3, pt. 1, 'MEMORANDUM FOR V.F. VALENTINE, NORTHERN RESEARCH CO-ORDINATION CENTRE, [from] B.G. Sivertz,' 16 July 1958, p. 1.
42 Ibid., 1-2.
43 NAC, RG 85, vol. 1070, file 251-4, pt. 3, 'MEMORANDUM FOR MR. PHILLIPS, RELOCATION OF ESKIMOS IN NORTHERN CANADA, [from] W. Rudnicki, Chief, Welfare Section,' 26 May 1958.
44 NAC, RG 85, vol. 1382, file 1012-13, pt. 5, 'MINUTES OF THE MEETING HELD NOVEMBER 18, AT 10:30 a.m., IN THE CONFERENCE ROOM TO DISCUSS RESOURCE STUDIES FOR THE PROPOSED RELOCATION OF ESKIMOS,' p. 1.
45 Ibid., 2.
46 NAC, RG 85, vol. 1382, file 1012-13, pt. 5, 'MEMORANDUM FOR THE DEPUTY MINISTER, RELOCATION OF ESKIMOS, [from] B.G. Sivertz, Director,' 7 December 1958, p. 2.
47 NAC, RG 85, vol. 1382, file 1012-13, pt. 5, 'MEMORANDUM FOR THE DIRECTOR, Relocation of Eskimo Groups in the High Arctic, C.M. Bolger, Administrator of the Arctic, Confidential,' 15 November 1960, p. 1.
48 Ibid., 2.
49 Ibid., 3.
50 Ibid., 4.
51 NWT Archives, Alex Stevenson Collection, N92-023, 'MEMORANDUM FOR THE ADVISORY COMMITTEE ON NORTHERN DEVELOPMENT: CANADIAN SOVEREIGNTY OVER Arctic WATERS, [from] G.W. Rowley, Secretary, DOCUMENT ND-314, SECRET,' 9 November 1960.
52 NWT Archives, Alex Stevenson Collection, N92-023, 'MEMORANDUM TO THE CABINET: CANADIAN SOVEREIGNTY OVER THE Arctic ARCHIPELAGO, CONFIDENTIAL,' 27 June 1960.
53 NAC, RG 85, vol. 1382, file 1012-13, pt. 5, 'MEMORANDUM FOR THE DIRECTOR, Relocation of Eskimo Groups in the High Arctic, C.M. Bolger, Administrator of the Arctic, Confidential,' 15 November 1960, p. 5. The timing of Bolger's memo relative to Cabinet concerns is a little too obvious to be coincidental. Again, while it appears that no high-level directives were involved, clearly departmental bureaucrats still saw themselves as having a role to play in addressing these concerns – hence the wording of Bolger's confidential memo.
54 Ibid., 6.
55 NAC, RG 85, vol. 1382, file 1012-13, pt. 5, 'MEMORANDUM FOR MR. BOLGER, ADMINISTRATOR OF THE Arctic, Relocation of Eskimo Groups in the High Arctic, [from] B.G. Sivertz, Director,' 25

November 1960, p. 1.
56 NAC, RG 85, vol. 1382, file 1012-13, pt. 5, 'MEMORANDUM FOR THE DIRECTOR, Creating New Communities, W. Rudnicki, Chief, Welfare Division, Ottawa, 13 December 1960, p. 1.
57 Ibid., 2-3.
58 Ibid., 3.
59 Ibid., 6.
60 NAC, RG 85, vol. 1382, file 1012-13, pt. 5, 'MEMORANDUM FOR THE DIRECTOR, Relocation of Eskimo Groups and Creating of New Communities., D. Snowden, Chief, Industrial Division, Ottawa,' 9 February 1961, p. 1.
61 Ibid., 1-2.
62 Ibid., 2.
63 Ibid., 3.
64 NAC, RG 85, vol. 652, file 1010-68, pt. 1, 'TORIES PLAN TO REVIEW ESKIMO POLICY,' *Edmonton Journal*, 27 June 1957.
65 NWT Archives, Alex Stevenson Collection, N92-023. This item has the handwritten title, 'Mr. Stevenson's copy, Arctic Administration Activities and Plans for 1959,' and is signed, 'Arctic Administration, April 17 1959,' p. 1.
66 NWT Archives, Alex Stevenson Collection, N92-023, 'MATERIAL FROM Arctic DIVISION FOR THE MINISTER'S USE,' 28 December 1956, pp. 3-4.
67 Ibid., 4.
68 NWT Archives, Alex Steven Collection, N92-023, 'Competition Number 58-526,' signed by R.A.J. Phillips, p. 2.
69 NWT Archives, Alex Stevenson Collection, N92-023, 'NORTHERN SERVICE OFFICERS,' 26 December 1956, p. 1.
70 NWT Archives, Alex Stevenson Collection, N92-023, 'MEMORANDUM FOR MR. HUNT, POLICY GOVERNING ADMINISTRATIVE WORK PERFORMED BY THE R.C.M.P. ON BEHALF OF THIS DEPARTMENT, [from] F.J.G. Cunningham, Director, Ottawa,' 19 July 1955, p. 1.
71 Ibid., attachment.
72 NAC, RG 85, vol. 1660, file NR4-3-1, 'DEPARTMENT OF NORTHERN AFFAIRS AND NATIONAL RESOURCES, Arctic CONFERENCE, 1957, REPORT OF THE OPENING SESSION,' 28 October 1957, p. 4.
73 Ibid., 4.
74 NAC, RG 85, vol. 1660, file NR4-3-1, 'DEPARTMENT OF NORTHERN AFFAIRS AND NATIONAL RESOURCES, Arctic CONFERENCE, 1957, REPORT OF THE SECOND SESSION,' 28 October 1957, pp. 1-2.
75 NWT Archives, Alex Stevenson Collection, N92-023, 'Competition Number 58-526,' [signed by] R.A.J. Phillips, p. 2.
76 NWT Archives, Alex Stevenson Collection, N92-023, 'MEMORANDUM FOR FIELD STAFF, THE LADIES, [from] R.A.J. Phillips, Chief of the Arctic Division, Ottawa,' 24 June 1957, p. 1.
77 NWT Archives, Alex Stevenson Collection, N92-023, 'Arctic Administration Activities and Plans for 1959,' 17 April 1959, p. 5.
78 NWT Archives, Alex Stevenson Collection, N92-023, 'MEMORANDUM FOR FIELD STAFF, THE LADIES, [from] R.A.J. Phillips, Chief of the Arctic Division, Ottawa,' 24 June 1957, pp. 1-2.
79 Ibid., 1.
80 Ibid., 2.
81 Ibid., 3.
82 NWT Archives, Alex Stevenson Collection, N92-023, 'MATERIAL FROM Arctic DIVISION FOR THE MINISTER'S USE,' 28 December 1956, p. 2.
83 NAC, RG 85, vol. 1514, file 1012-1, pt. 6, 'Notes for the Seventh Meeting of the Committee on Eskimo Affairs,' 28 May 1956, p. 1.
84 NAC, RG 85, vol. 1514, file 1012-1, pt. 7, 'MINUTES OF THE NINTH MEETING OF THE COMMITTEE ON ESKIMO AFFAIRS HELD ON MAY 26, 1958, IN THE LARGE CONFERENCE ROOM, EAST BLOCK, PARLIAMENT BUILDINGS, OTTAWA,' p. 14.
85 NWT Archives, Alex Stevenson Collection, N92-023, 'THE ADMINISTRATION OF NORTHERN CANADA, [by] R.A.J. Phillips,' 6 January 1959, p. 4.
86 NWT Archives, Alex Stevenson Collection, N92-023, 'REPORT OF SUBCOMMITTEE ON ESKIMO HOUSING PROGRAMMES, Ottawa,' Table 1, (no label), 25 June 1964, and 'TUBERCULOSIS N.W.T., NEW ACTIVE CASES & DEATHS' (appended).

87 NWT Archives, Alex Stevenson Collection, N92-023, 'COMMITTEE TO EXAMINE RISING SOCIAL ASSISTANCE EXPENDITURES,' Northern Administration Branch, 27 February 1963. Appended document headed by: 'The increase in relief expenditures over the five-year period 1957-1962, is due to a number of inter-related social and economic factors,' 31 October 1962, p. 2.
88 NAC, RG 85, vol. 1514, file 1012-1, pt. 6, 'Notes for the Seventh Meeting of the Committee on Eskimo Affairs,' 28 May 1956, p. 3. Notes are appended to the minutes of the meeting.
89 Ibid., 4.
90 Ibid., 1.
91 NWT Archives, Alex Stevenson Collection, N92-023, 'MEMORANDUM FOR THE DIRECTOR: Rehabilitation Services in the North, from R.A.J.P., Restricted,' 9 October 1958, p. 1.
92 Phillips wrote: 'Mr. Rudnicki notes that the NWS has been given no significant part in the implementation of the Keewatin Re-establishment Programme. This is not true. The NWS took an important and useful part in the committee through which the plans were implemented; to a member of the NWS (Mr. Neville) was delegated responsibility for the entire task of selecting members for the community ... I particularly regret the suggestion in this section that the NWS was alone responsible for the formulation of the Resettlement Project idea' (p. 2). Rudnicki responded: 'Northern Welfare Service has had no significant part to play in doing something for the cripples and widows that make up the Ahearmiuts. By significant I do not mean selecting members for a new community. It was fairly obvious who would have to go to the new community. By significant I mean the direct participation of a welfare officer on the ground, i.e. living with these people, earning their trust and confidence ... and guiding them in the adjustments they will have to a new mode of life.' He added that although he believed in 'the view that team work is important ... the contributions of individual officers should be recognized ... I lay claim to being the sole officer of the Eskimo Point report ... Granted that the idea of the Resettlement Project is neither new nor the invention of any single individual. Flying has also been discussed since the days of Leonardo da Vinci, but surely the Wright brothers deserve a little bit of credit.' See NWT Archives, Alex Stevenson Collection, N92-023, 'MEMORANDUM FOR THE CHIEF, Arctic DIVISION, REHABILITATION SERVICES IN THE NORTH, [from] W. Rudnicki, Chief, Northern Welfare Services, RESTRICTED, Ottawa,' 10 October 1958, p. 4.
93 NWT Archives, Alex Stevenson Collection, N92-023, 'MEMORANDUM FOR THE DIRECTOR: Rehabilitation Services in the North, [from] R.A.J.P., Restricted,' 9 October 1958, p. 3.
94 NWT Archives, Alex Stevenson Collection, N92-023, 'MEMORANDUM FOR THE CHIEF, Arctic DIVISION, REHABILITATION SERVICES IN THE NORTH, [from] W. Rudnicki, Chief, Northern Welfare Services, RESTRICTED, Ottawa,' 10 October 1958, p. 2.
95 Ibid.
96 Ibid., 4-5.
97 Ibid., 7.
98 NAC, RG 85, vol. 314, file 1012-8, vol. 3, 'COMMON ESKIMO PHRASES,' pp. 1-2.
99 NAC, RG 85, vol. 1660, file NR4-3-1, 'DEPARTMENT OF NORTHERN AFFAIRS AND NATIONAL RESOURCES, Arctic CONFERENCE 1957, REPORT OF THE FIFTH SESSION,' 1 November 1957, p. 9.
100 Ibid.
101 NAC, RG 85, vol. 1514, file 1012, vol. 3, 'MINUTES OF THE FIFTH MEETING OF THE COMMITTEE ON ESKIMO AFFAIRS HELD ON NOVEMBER 29th, 1954, IN ROOM 304, LANGEVIN BLOCK, OTTAWA,' p. 4.
102 NAC, RG 85, vol. 1514, file 1012-1, pt. 6, 'MINUTES OF THE SEVENTH MEETING OF THE COMMITTEE ON ESKIMO AFFAIRS HELD ON MAY 28, 1956, IN ROOM 304, LANGEVIN BLOCK, OTTAWA,' p. 10.
103 NAC, RG 85, vol. 1514, file 1012-1, pt. 7, 'MINUTES OF THE NINTH MEETING OF THE COMMITTEE ON ESKIMO AFFAIRS HELD ON MAY 26, 1958, IN THE LARGE CONFERENCE ROOM, EAST BLOCK, PARLIAMENT BUILDINGS, OTTAWA,' p. 14.
104 NAC, RG 85, vol. 1472, file 163-1-1, vol. 1, 'MEMORANDUM FOR MR. R.A.J. PHILLIPS, FAMILY ALLOWANCES, [from] W. Rudnicki, Chief, Welfare Division, Ottawa,' 17 April 1959.
105 NAC, RG 85, vol. 1472, file 163-1-1, vol. 1, 'MEMORANDUM FOR THE DEPUTY MINISTER: ADMINISTRATION OF FAMILY ALLOWANCES, [from] B.G. Sivertz, Director,' 19 June 1959, p. 2.
106 Ibid.
107 NAC, RG 85, vol. 1472, file 163-1-1, vol. 1, letter from 'R.G. Robertson, Deputy Minister [to] Dr. G.F. Davidson, Deputy Minister of National Health and Welfare, Ottawa, Ontario,' 18 June 1959.

108 NAC, RG 85, vol. 1472, file 163-1-1, vol. 1, letter from 'George F. Davidson, Deputy Minister of Welfare, [to] R.G. Robertson, Esq., Deputy Minister, Department of Northern Affairs and National Resources, OTTAWA, Canada,' 24 June 1959.
109 NAC, RG 85, vol. 1472, file 163-1-1, vol. 1, interdepartmental correspondence from 'Miss N. O'Brian, Regional Director, Family Allowances, Yukon and Northwest Territories, [to] Mr. J. Albert Blais, National Director, Family Allowances,' 29 October 1959, p. 6.
110 NAC, RG 85, vol. 1472, file 163-1-1, vol. 1, 'FAMILY ALLOWANCE PAYMENTS TO ESKIMOS,' 1 March 1960, pp. 14-15. The author of the document is not indicated. However, it is obvious from the style and content that the author was Walter Rudnicki, the chief of Northern Welfare Services.
111 NAC, RG 85, vol. 1472, file 163-1-1, vol. 1, 'NOTICE TO PARENTS RECEIVING FAMILY ALLOWANCES.'
112 NWT Archives, Alex Stevenson Collection, N92-023, 'MINUTES OF THE TENTH MEETING OF THE COMMITTEE ON ESKIMO AFFAIRS HELD ON MAY 25, 1959 IN THE LARGE CONFERENCE ROOM, EAST BLOCK, PARLIAMENT BUILDINGS, OTTAWA,' p. 1.
113 Ibid.
114 Ibid.
115 Ibid., 2.
116 Ibid.
117 Ibid., 2-3.
118 Ibid., 3.
119 Ibid., 4.
120 Ibid., 7. The first sentence of this quotation is in Ayaruark's list of additions to the minutes, which are contained in a 'MEMORANDUM FOR MR. V. VALENTINE,' entitled 'TENTH MEETING OF THE COMMITTEE ON ESKIMO AFFAIRS,' Ottawa, 25 September 1959, p. 2.
121 NWT Archives, Alex Stevenson Collection, N92-023, 'MINUTES OF THE TENTH MEETING OF THE COMMITTEE ON ESKIMO AFFAIRS HELD ON MAY 25, 1959 IN THE LARGE CONFERENCE ROOM, EAST BLOCK, PARLIAMENT BUILDINGS, OTTAWA,' pp. 7-8.
122 Ibid., 9-10.
123 Ibid., 8.
124 Ibid., 9.
125 NAC, RG 85, vol. 1448, file 1000/184, vol. 6, 'MEMORANDUM FOR THE MINISTER, Keewatin Region Crisis, R.G. Robertson, Deputy Minister, Ottawa,' 19 April 1962.
126 Ibid., 10.
127 NAC, RG 85, vol. 1360, file 252-5/500, pt. 1, letter signed by 'Jean Ayaruaq, Michel Angutituak, Thomas Uyaq, Pierre Nipisaq, Arsene Isaq, Vilisi Quppaq, Simon Quliq, Joseph Nattat, Celestine Iqujjuk, Michel Tulugaq, Lucien Tapassi, Donat Anaruaq, Thomas Tuugaq, Rupert Tati, Louis Aggalik, Antony Uttu, Paul Kablalik, Alurniq, Vasisi Auttut, Joachim Urilik,' attached to, 'MEMORANDUM FOR THE DEPUTY MINISTER Petition of Jean Ayaruaq and Others Addressed to the Minister, [from] B.G. Sivertz, Director, Ottawa,' 2 December 1960.
128 NAC, RG 85, vol. 678, file A-252-5/184, vol. 1, 'Memorandum [by] F.L. Neville,' 5 December 1960, pp. 2-3.
129 Ibid., 3.
130 NAC, RG 85, vol. 1660 File NR4-3-1, 'DEPARTMENT OF NORTHERN AFFAIRS AND NATIONAL RESOURCES Arctic CONFERENCE 1957, REPORT OF THE FOURTH SESSION, Subjects: The Changing Arctic (Continued) THE INDIANS, THE ESKIMOS AND US, OTTAWA,' 31 October 1957, p. 5.
131 Ibid., 5.
132 Ibid., 6.
133 NAC, RG 85, vol. 1962, file A-1012-9, vol. 2, 'NORTHERN ADMINISTRATION BRANCH, Branch Policy Directive no. 13, Community Development and Local Organization,' 25 October 1961, p. 1.
134 For a discussion of this history see Frank Tester, 'Reflections on Tin Wis: Environmentalism and the Evolution of Citizen Participation in Canada,' *Alternatives: Perspectives on Society, Technology and Environment* 19, no. 1 (1992):34-41.
135 NAC, RG 85, vol. 1962, file A-1012-9, vol. 2, 'NORTHERN ADMINISTRATION BRANCH, Branch Policy Directive no. 13, Community Development and Local Organization,' 25 October 1961, p. 2.
136 Ibid., 3.

137 Ibid., 4.
138 By this time, the administration of the Arctic had been divided between an administrator for the western Arctic (the MacKenzie) and one for the eastern Arctic.
139 NAC, RG 85, vol. 1962, file A 1012-9, vol. 2, 'MEMORANDUM FOR THE ADMINISTRATOR OF THE Arctic, COMMUNITY COUNCILS, [from] R.L. Kennedy, Regional Administrator, CHUR-CHILL, Manitoba,' 12 December 1961, p. 1.
140 NAC, RG 85, vol. 1948, file A 560-1-5, pt. 1, 'MEMORANDUM FOR THE DIRECTOR, Community Development and Local Organization, [from] C.M. Bolger, Administrator of the Arctic,' 5 January 1962, p. 6.
141 NAC, RG 85, vol. 1660, file NR4-3-1, 'DEPARTMENT OF NORTHERN AFFAIRS AND NATIONAL RESOURCES, Arctic CONFERENCE 1957, REPORT OF THE FIFTH SESSION,' 1 November 1957, p. 10.
142 NWT Archives, Alex Stevenson Collection, N92-023, 'MEMORANDUM FOR THE REGIONAL ADMINISTRATOR FOR Arctic QUEBEC, [from] R.O. Evans, Area Administrator, Port Harrison, P.Q.,' 31 January 1962, p. 1.
143 Ibid., 2.
144 Ibid., 3. Inukpuk actually spoke quite frequently at the Thirteenth Meeting of the Committee on Eskimo Affairs, primarily raising matters of local concern and speaking clearly from a 'traditionalist perspective.' For example, during the discussion on education, he said 'that if the children kept going to school and staying in hostels they would forget how to hunt and will not be able to hunt with their fathers.' See NAC, RG 85, vol. 1470, file 1012-9, vol. 8, 'MINUTES OF THE THIRTEENTH MEETING OF THE COMMITTEE ON ESKIMO AFFAIRS, April 2 and 3rd, 1962,' p. 10.
145 NWT Archives, Alex Stevenson Collection, N92-023, 'MINUTES OF THE ELEVENTH MEETING OF THE COMMITTEE ON ESKIMO AFFAIRS HELD ON MARCH 28 AND 29, 1960, IN THE LARGE CONFERENCE ROOM, EAST BLOCK, PARLIAMENT BUILDINGS, OTTAWA,' p. 6.
146 Abraham Okpik, 'What Does It Mean to Be an Eskimo?' *North* 9 (March-April 1962):26-8, translated from Inuktitut.
147 NAC, RG 85, vol. 1446, file 1000/153, vol. 2, 'PUWALLUTTUQ: An Epidemic of Tuberculosis at Eskimo Point, Northwest Territories' by P.E. Moore, M.D., D.P.H., Director, Medical Services, Department of National Health and Welfare, Ottawa, Canada, 1963, pp. 1-2.
148 Ray Tulloch, 'Hope and Despair at Eskimo Point,' *Winnipeg Free Press*, Saturday Magazine Section, Winnipeg, Saturday, 17 November 1962, p. 21.
149 NAC, RG 85, vol. 1952, file A1000/184, 'MEMORANDUM FOR THE AREA ADMINISTRATOR RANKIN INLET N.W.T., WHALE COVE GENERAL, [from] R.B. Tinling. T.O.2., Rankin Inlet N.W.T.,' 9 March 1961, p. 1.

Bibliography

Archives

National Archives of Canada, Ottawa

Federal Archives Division
Department of Indian Affairs and Northern Development Records, RG 22
Department of National Health and Welfare Records, RG 29
Department of Transport Records, RG 12
Northern Affairs Programme Records, RG 85
Royal Canadian Mounted Police Records, RG 18

Manuscript Division
Arnold Heeney Papers, MG 30 E 133
Brooke Claxton Papers, MG 32 B 5

Prince of Wales Northern Heritage Centre, Archives, Yellowknife
Alex Stevenson Collection, N92-023
Minnie Allakariallak Photos, N91-053
Letia and Herodier Kalluk Photos, N91-054
Sarah Amagoalik Photos, N91-055

General Synod Archives, Anglican Church of Canada, Toronto
Diocese of the Arctic, M71-4, Bishop Marsh

St. Roch National Historic Site, Vancouver
St. Roch, Ship's Log, *Daily Journal*

Government Documents and Reports
Barry, D., ed. *Documents on Canadian External Relations, 1952.* Ottawa: Department of External Affairs and International Trade 1990
Canada. Department of Northern Affairs and National Resources. *Annual Reports.* Fiscal years 1953-4, 1954-5, 1955-6, 1956-7, 1957-8, 1958-9, 1959-60, 1960-1, 1961-2, 1962-3
–. Department of Northern Affairs and National Resources. *Arctic Circular,* vol. VI, no. 5, 1953
–. Department of Resources and Development. *Report of the Department of Resources and Development.* Ottawa: King's Printer, 1950-1, 1951-2
–. Environment Canada. *Canadian Climate Normals.* Ottawa, 1982
–. House of Commons. *Debates,* 1953
–. House of Commons. *Family Allowances Act,* 1944
–. House of Commons. Standing Committee on Aboriginal Affairs. *Minutes of Proceedings and Evidence of the Standing Committee on Aboriginal Affairs,* 19 March 1990, Issue No. 22. Ottawa: Queen's Printer 1990

–. House of Commons. Standing Committee on Aboriginal Affairs. *Minutes of Proceedings and Evidence of the Standing Committee on Aboriginal Affairs*, 18 June 1990, Issue No. 40. Ottawa: Queen's Printer 1990

–. Order-in-Council No. 1925, 5 August 1939. *Canadian Gazette*, no. 6, vol. LXXIII. Ottawa: King's Printer, 351-8

–. Order in Council No. 1146, 19 July 1926, *Canadian Gazette*, no. 5, vol. IX. Ottawa: King's Printer, 382-3

Cantley, James. *The Cantley Economic Report on Eskimo Affairs*. Ottawa: Department of Resources and Development 1950

Diubaldo, Richard. *The Government of Canada and the Inuit, 1900-1967*. Ottawa: Research Branch, Corporate Policy, Department of Indian and Northern Affairs Canada 1985

Gunther, Magnus. 'The 1953 Relocations of the Inukjuak Inuit to the High Arctic: A Documentary Analysis and Evaluation.' Trent University, Peterborough, ON, 1992

Hickling Corporation. 'Assessment of the Factual Basis of Certain Allegations Made Before the Standing Committee on Aboriginal Affairs Concerning the Relocation of Inukjuak Inuit Families in the 1950s.' Report submitted to the Department of Indian Affairs and Northern Development, Northern Programme, Ottawa, September 1990

Larsen, Henry. 'Patrolling the Arctic and the Northwest Passage in the R.C.M.P. ship St. Roch – 1944.' Ottawa: Department of Northern Affairs and National Resources 1944

Makavik Corporation, Inuit Tapirisat of Canada, Kativik Regional Government. 'Position Paper Regarding Grise Fiord/Resolute Bay Relocation Issue.' Ottawa, 20 January 1987

Rudnicki, Walter. 'Report: Field Trip to Eskimo Point.' Ottawa, March 1958. Report prepared for the Department of Northern Affairs but not located in National Archives. Supplied by Walter Rudnicki, Ottawa, 1991

Schaefer, O. 'The Unmet Needs of Canadian Children.' In *Report of the First Canadian Ross Conference of Paediatric Research*, ed. H.G. Dunn et al. Montreal: Ross Laboratories 1974:382-8

Smith, Gordon W. *Territorial Sovereignty in the Canadian North: A Historical Outline of the Problem*, Ottawa: Northern Co-ordination and Research Centre, Department of Northern Affairs and National Resources 1963

Soberman, D. 'Report to the Canadian Human Rights Commission on the Complaints of the Inuit People Relocated from Inukjouak and Pond Inlet, to Grise Fiord and Resolute Bay in 1953 and 1955.' Kingston, ON, 1991

Supreme Court of Canada. *Supreme Court Registry*. 'In the Matter of a Reference as to Whether "Indians" in S.91(24) of the B.N.A. Act includes Eskimo inhabitants of the Province of Quebec, 1939'

Tester, Frank J. *Socio-economic and Environmental Impacts of the Proposed Polar Gas Pipeline – Keewatin District*. Vol. 2. Ottawa: Northern Pipelines Branch, Indian and Northern Affairs Canada 1978

Treaties and Historical Research Centre. *Indian Acts and Amendments*. 2nd ed. Ottawa: Research Branch, Corporate Policy, Department of Indian and Northern Affairs Canada 1981

Books and Manuscripts

Ashlee, Jette Elsebeth. 'Inuit Integration with Denmark and Canada: A Comparative Study of Colonialism in Greenland and the Northwest Territories.' Doctoral thesis, Wolfson College, Cambridge University, 1984

Choque, Charles. *Joseph Buliard: Fisher of Men*. Churchill: Roman Catholic Espiscopal Corporation 1987

–. *The Grey Nuns of Chesterfield Inlet, N.W.T., Health Services and Education, 1931-1988*. Churchill: Hudson Bay Diocese 1989

de Certeau, Michel. *The Practice of Everyday Life*. Berkeley: University of California Press 1984

Dickerson, Mark. *Whose North? Political Change, Political Development, and Self-Government in the Northwest Territories*. Vancouver: UBC Press 1992

Duffy, R. Quinn. *The Road to Nunavut: The Progress of the Eastern Arctic Inuit since the Second World War*. Montreal and Kingston: McGill-Queen's University Press 1988

Francis, Daniel and Toby Morantz. *Partners in Furs: A History of the Fur Trade in Eastern James Bay, 1600-1870*. Montreal and Kingston: McGill-Queen's University Press 1983

Grant, Shelagh. *Sovereignty or Security? Government Policy in the Canadian North, 1936-1950*. Vancouver: University of British Columbia Press 1988

Guest, Dennis. *The Emergence of Social Security in Canada.* Vancouver: University of British Columbia Press 1980
Honigmann, John and Irma. *Arctic Townsmen: Ethnic Background and Modernization.* Ottawa: St. Paul University, Canadian Research Centre for Anthropology 1970
Horowitz, Gad. *Canadian Labour in Politics.* Toronto: University of Toronto Press 1969
Jenness, Diamond. *Eskimo Administration: II. Canada.* Montreal: Arctic Institute of North America 1964
Keenleyside, Hugh L. *On The Bridge of Time.* Vol. 2 of *Memoirs of Hugh L. Keenleyside.* Toronto: McClelland & Stewart 1981
Krech, Shepard, III, ed. *The Subarctic Fur Trade: Native Social and Economic Adaptations.* Vancouver: University of British Columbia Press 1984
Larsen, Henry A., Frank R. Sheer, and Evard Omholt-Jensen. *The Big Ship: An Autobiography.* Toronto: McClelland & Stewart 1967
Lloyd, Trevor. 'The Political Geography of the Arctic.' In *The Changing World: Studies in Political Geography,* ed. W. Gordon East and A.E. Moodie. London: George G. Harrap 1956
Lowther, Keith. 'An Exercise in Sovereignty: The Government of Canada and the Inuit Relocation of 1953.' M.A. thesis, University of Calgary, 1989
MacPherson, C.B. *The Political Theory of Possessive Individualism: Hobbes to Locke.* Toronto: Oxford University Press 1962
Mallet, Captain Thierry. *Glimpses of the Barren Lands.* New York: Revillon Freres 1930
Morrison, William R. *Showing the Flag: The Mounted Police and Canadian Sovereignty in the North, 1894-1925.* Vancouver: University of British Columbia Press 1985
Morton, Desmond. *Working People: An Illustrated History of the Canadian Labour Movement.* Ottawa: Deneau 1980
Mowat, Farley, *People of the Deer,* New York: Pyramid Books 1968
Newman, Peter C. *Merchant Princes.* Toronto: Viking 1991
Pickersgill, Jack. *The Liberal Party.* Toronto: McClelland & Stewart 1962
Ray, Arthur. *Indians In The Fur Trade: Their Role as Trappers, Hunters and Middlemen in the Lands Southwest of Hudson Bay, 1660-1870.* Toronto and Buffalo: University of Toronto Press 1974
Sahlins, Marshall. *Culture and Practical Reason.* Chicago: University of Chicago Press 1976
Sartre, Jean-Paul. *Critique of Dialectic Reason.* Vol. 1. Trans. Alan Sheridan-Smith. London: Verso 1982
Vallee, F.G. *Kabloona and Eskimo in the Central Keewatin.* Ottawa: St. Paul University, Canadian Research Centre for Anthropology 1967
Weaver, Sally, M. *Making Canadian Indian Policy: The Hidden Agenda, 1968-70.* Toronto: University of Toronto Press 1981
Zaslow, Morris. *The Opening of the Canadian North: 1870-1914.* Toronto: McClelland & Stewart 1971
–. *The Northward Expansion of Canada, 1914-1967.* Toronto: McClelland & Stewart 1988

Articles
Adamson, J.D., J.P. Moody, A.F.W. Peart, J.C. Wilt, and W.J. Wood, 'Poliomyelitis in the Arctic.' *Canadian Medical Association Journal* (October 1949):339-48
Baird, Irene. 'The Eskimo Woman: Her Changing World.' *The Beaver* (Spring 1959):48-55
Barnett, Lincoln. 'A Mesolithic Age Today: Caribou Eskimos Illustrate Its Culture.' *Life,* 27 February 1956, pp. 80-7
Bruemmer, Fred. 'Eskimos of Grise Fiord.' *Canadian Geographical Journal* 77, no. 2 (1968):64-71
Croft, Frank. 'The Changeling Eskimos of the Mountain San.' *Maclean's,* 1 February 1958, pp. 22-3, 28, 30-1
Doucette, Fred. 'Cape Hershel, The Post Office That Never Was,' *Postal History Society of Canada Journal* 46 (1986):20-4
Flucke, A.F. 'Wither the Eskimo?' *North* 10, no. 1 (1963):17-23
Fryer, Cst. A.C. 'Eskimo Rehabilitation Program at Craig Harbour.' *RCMP Quarterly* 20, no. 2 (1954):139-42
Gimpel, Charles. 'Journey From The Igloo.' *The Beaver* (Spring 1957):12-19
Grant, Shelagh. 'A Case of Compounded Error: The Inuit Resettlement Project, 1953, and the Government Response, 1990.' *Northern Perspectives* 19, no. 1 (1991):3-29
Harrington, Richard. 'The Padleimiuts.' *Canadian Geographical Journal* 44, no. 1 (1952):2-15

Harrison, Phyllis. 'Social Work Goes North.' *Canadian Welfare* 35, no. 3 (May 1959):110-15
Haygood, Wil. 'The Lie at the Top of the World.' *Boston Globe Magazine*, 9 August 1992, pp. 13-43
Hewetson, H.W. 'What Are the Possibilities of Settlement in Canada's North Land?' *Public Affairs* 10 (1946):20-5
Hildes, J.A. 'Health Problems in the Arctic.' *Canadian Medical Association Journal* 83 (1960):1255-7
Hughes, Charles C. 'Observations on Community Change in the North: An Attempt at Summary.' *Anthropologica*, n.s., 5, no. 1 (1963):69-79
LaCroix, Marc. 'Integration or disintegration?' *The Beaver* (Spring 1959):37-40
Lantis, Margaret. 'Problems of Human Ecology in the North American Arctic.' *Arctic* 7, nos. 3-4 (1954-5):307-20
Leechman, Douglas. Review of *People of the Deer*, by Farley Mowat. *Canadian Geographical Journal* (August 1952):v-vi
Lesage, Hon. Jean. 'Education of Eskimos.' *Canadian Education* 12, no. 3 (1957):44-8
Marcus, Alan. 'Out in the Cold: Canada's Experimental Inuit Relocation to Grise Fiord and Resolute Bay.' *Polar Record* 27, no. 163 (1991):285-96
Marsh, Donald B. 'Canada's Caribou Eskimo.' *National Geographic Magazine* 91, no. 1 (1947):87-104
Marshall, C.J. 'North America's Distant Early Warning Line.' *Geographical Magazine* 29, no. 12 (1957):616-28
Michie, George H. and Eric M. Neil. 'Cultural Conflict in the Canadian Arctic.' *Canadian Geographer* 5 (1955):33-41
Nicholson, L.H. 'The Problem of the People.' *The Beaver* (Spring 1959):20-4
Oblate Fathers of Hudson Bay Vicarate. 'The Boarding School at Chesterfield and the Education of the Eskimo.' *Eskimo*, December 1955
Okpik, Abraham. 'What Does It Mean to Be an Eskimo?' *North* 9, no. 2 (1962):26-8
Orkin, Andrew. 'Immersion in the High Arctic: An Examination of the Relocation of Canadian Inuit in 1953 from the Perspective of the Law on Experimentation Involving Human Subjects.' Unpublished paper submitted to the Canadian Arctic Resources Committee, 1991
Oswalt, Wendell H. and James W. VanStone. 'The Future of the Caribou Eskimos,' *Anthropologica*, n.s., 2, no. 2 (1960):154-76
Phillips, R.A.J. 'The Growing North in the Growing World,' *External Affairs* 7, no. 12 (1955):310-16
–. 'The Future of the North.' *Canadian Architect* 1, no. 11 (November 1956):37-40
Porsild, A.E. Review of *People of the Deer*, by Farley Mowat. *The Beaver* (June 1952):47-9
Robertson, R.G. 'Administration for Development in Northern Canada: The Growth and Evolution of Government.' *Canadian Public Administration* 3, no. 4 (1960):354-62
–. 'The Future of the North.' *North* 8, no. 2 (1961):1-13
Robinson, J. Lewis. 'Eskimo Population in the Canadian Eastern Arctic: Distribution, Numbers and Trends.' *Canadian Geographical Journal* 29 (1944):129-42
–. 'Mineral Resources and Mining Activity in the Canadian Eastern Arctic.' *Canadian Geographical Journal* 29 (1944):55-75
Sivertz, B.G. 'Administration for Development in Northern Canada: Development of Material and Human Resources.' *Canadian Public Administration* 3, no. 4 (1960):363-6
Stefansson, Vilhjalmur. 'The Arctic.' *Air Affairs* 3, no. 2 (1950):391-402
Tester, Frank. 'Reflections on Tin Wis: Environmentalism and the Evolution of Citizen Participation in Canada.' *Alternatives: Perspectives on Society, Technology and Environment* 19, no. 1 (1992):34-41
–. 'Serializing Inuit Culture: The Administration of "Relief" in the Eastern Arctic, 1940-1953.' *Canadian Social Work Review* 1 (1993):109-23
Tulloch, Ray, 'Northern Report: Squalor and Hope at Eskimo Point.' *Maclean's*, 19 May 1962, p. 77
Tuu'lug, Marion. 'A Story of Starvation.' *Inuit Today* 6, no. 9 (1977):26-31, 56
van den Steenhoven, Geert. 'Ennadai Lake People, 1955.' *The Beaver* (Spring 1968):12-18
Van Norman, Sgt. R.D. 'Resources of the Northland.' *RCMP Quarterly* 24, no. 4 (1959):268-78. Continued in 25, no. 1 (1959):11-20; 25, no. 2 (1960):121-5; and 25, no. 3 (1960):191-202
White, Gavin. 'Canadian Apartheid.' *Canadian Forum* 31 (1951):102-3

Wilkinson, Doug. 'A Vanishing Canadian.' *The Beaver* (Spring 1959):25-8, 62
Willmot, W.E. 'The Flexibility of Eskimo Organization.' *Anthropologica*, n.s., 2, no. 1 (1960):48-59
Wonders, William. 'Our Northward Course.' *Canadian Geographer* VI, nos. 3-4 (1962):96-105
Young, Major-General H.A. 'Natural Resources of the Northwest Territories and the Yukon.' *Engineering Journal* 36, no. 6 (1953):703-6

Interviews and Correspondence
Titus Allooloo, Yellowknife, NWT
Ellen Bielawaski, Sidney, British Columbia
Father Charles Choque, Ottawa, Ontario
Dr. H. Ewart, Ancaster, Ontario
Ross Gibson, Victoria, British Columbia
Professor Shelagh Grant, Peterborough, Ontario
Geoff Hattersley-Smith, Kent, England
Jack Hicks, Ottawa, Ontario
Alan Marcus, Cambridge, England
Hon. Paul Martin, Windsor, Ontario
Graham Rowley, Ottawa, Ontario
Walter Rudnicki, Ottawa, Ontario
Harold Sersen, Brentwood Bay, British Columbia
Ben Sivertz, Victoria, British Columbia
Dr. Otto Schaefer, Edmonton, Alberta
Hon. Tom Siddon, Ottawa, Ontario
Prof. Daniel Soberman, Kingston, Ontario
Harold and Kathy Welch, Resolute Bay, NWT
Nigel Wilford, Ottawa, Ontario
Douglas Wilkinson, Kingston, Ontario
Inuit interviewed at Resolute Bay and Grise Fiord are listed in the Preface

Newspapers and Magazines
American Weekly
The Beaver
Boston Globe
Calgary Albertan
Globe and Mail
Makivik News
Maclean's
Montreal Gazette
Ottawa Citizen
Time
Toronto Star
Vancouver Sun
Winnipeg Free Press

Index

292-3, 296, 304; and starvation, 209-37
Epoo, Lazarusie, 356
Eskimo Loan Fund, 136, 138, 165-7, 170
Eureka, 119, 130, 320-1, 324
Evukluk, 262-3

Family Allowance Act (1944), 46, 71, 73, 78;
form of payment, 339-42; and Garry Lake
starvations, 257, 267; and high Arctic
relocations, 126, 137, 166, 203; and
Hudson's Bay Company, 69; and
schooling, 73
Family Allowances, 11, 44, 48-9, 71-94, 98,
205, 307-8, 329; administration of, 70;
and Ennadai Lake Inuit, 210, 215, 219
Fatty and Mary, 149, 173
Finnie, O.S., 16, 19, 20, 106-7. *See also*
Department of the Interior
Fitzsimmons, W.J., 195, 310-11
Fort Chimo, 39, 44, 52, 138, 312, 343, 355
Fort George, 24
Fort Macpherson, 87
Fort Ross, 111, 119
Fournier, Captain Paul, 149
Fraser, W.G., 168
Fur Trade, 19-20, 25, 110, 166, 272; at Arctic
Bay (1927), 107-8; and Chesshire, R.H., 77;
collapse of, 7, 44, 48, 98, 101, 308, 312;
dependency on, 41, 54, 76, 83, 339; and
Ennadai Lake Inuit, 207-9, 218, 220; and
family allowances, 86; and fur prices, 61-2,
209; in 1920s and 1930s, 3-4; and 'post
Eskimos,' 25; and relief, 248; at Resolute
Bay and Craig Harbour, 168-70, 192-3;
and sales of fur, 92; as a welfare system, 20

Gallagher, Corporal, 222, 226-7, 233, 284,
287
Garry Lake, 12, 86, 205-6, 238-40, 242-5,
247-8, 250-8, 260-2, 264-72, 277, 301, 306,
319
Garry Lake Inuit, 239-45, 306, 319; and
Father Joseph Buliard, 86, 242-5; and
Father Trinel, 252-3; images of, 246; and
re-establishment centres at Itavia and
Whale Cove, 46, 247-8, 252-3, 277, 281,
295-6, 299, 300-1, 303; 306; and Roman
Catholic Mission, 238-40; starvation of,
12, 205-6, 250-8, 260-2, 264-72
Gerin, Jacques, 115, 197
Gibbons, Jimmy, 50, 234
Gibson, Ross, 148, 198, 200, 202; and
condition of Inuit women and children at
Resolute, 158; and conditions at Inukjuak,
155-6; and conditions at Resolute, 151,
162, 181-4, 192; and government store at
Resolute, 167, 169-72; and Joseph Idlout,
188-9; and the military at Resolute, 177;

and 'volunteers' for high Arctic, 139-40
Gibson, Roy, 26, 57-9, 67-9, 77-8, 80-2, 86,
88, 98
Giddens, Anthony, 5-6
Gillespie, P.J., 39
Gjoa Haven, 250, 258
Godhaven (Greenland), 107
Godt, P., 299-302, 304-5
Golding, Terance, 264-5
Gould, Captain, 290
Government of Canada and the Inuit, The. See
Diubaldo, Richard.
Government stores, 126, 166-74, 189, 191;
at Craig Harbour, 198-201; and Keewatin
Committee, 277; responsibility for, 204;
supplies for, Resolute Bay, 162-3. *See also*
Gibson, Ross
Grant, D.W., 277, 286-94, 300, 302, 305. *See
also* Northern service officers
Grant, Shelagh, 102-3, 116, 118, 163, 168
Great Whale River, 27, 31, 39, 194, 344, 355
Green, R.J., 338
Grise Fiord, 7, 147, 151, 164, 168, 180-1,
277, 308; conditions at, 159, 161,
192-204; government store at, 173; and
sovereignty, 102, 318-23
Gunther, Magnus, 103, 122, 131
Guthrie, H., 31

Hallow, 214, 229-32, 292
Hamilton, Alvin, 173-4, 274, 320, 343
Heagerty Report, 46
Heaps, A.A., 45
Heeney, Arnold, 60
Henik Lake, 256, 266, 274-5, 277, 301;
conditions at, 225-9; and relocation to
Whale Cove, 303; and relocation from
Ennadai Lake, 205-7, 219-23; deaths at,
12, 232, 234, 306, 319
Herschel Island, 14-15
Hickling Report, 102-3, 139, 142
Hinds, Marjorie, 85-6, 93, 139, 164
House of Commons Standing Committee
on Aboriginal Affairs, 141-2, 144, 152,
171-2, 181-2, 199, 204, 218
Houston, James, 174, 184, 326; and Ennadai
Lake, 213-14, 217. *See also* Northern
service officers
Howmik (Mownik), 217, 229, 232-5, 292
Hudson's Bay Company, 104-5, 134, 204,
318, 351; at Arctic Bay, 107-9; at Baker
Lake, 245, 257; and Committee on Eskimo
Affairs, 308; and competition from Baffin
Trading Company, 119; and dependency,
54; and Ennadai Lake Inuit, 218; and
family allowances, 74, 76-82, 84, 86-7, 89;
and fur prices, 98-9; and Henry Larsen,
126; and high Arctic relocations, 193,

197-8; and Inuit relocation to Dundas Harbour, 44-5, 111-12; and James Cantley, 60, 163; and the *Nascopie*, 117; at Nueltin Lake, 208; and O.S. Finnie, 16; at Padlei Post, 220; and Quebec Inuit, 31; at Rankin Inlet, 295-6, 299; and relief, 20, 25-6, 31, 41, 63-4, 67-9, 71, 109, 248; relocations to Arctic Bay, Fort Ross, and Spence Bay, 141; responsibility for Inuit, 34, 56; rivalry with Revillon Frères, 119; and Tavani, 277-9, 283

Idlout, Joseph, 146, 157, 184-92
Idlout, Leah, 188-9, 190, 196
Idlout, Paniloo, 189-90
Igloolik, 21, 185
Impetigo. *See* Diseases
Indian Act, 78; amendment to (1924), 19; amendment to (1952), 36; and application to Inuit, 33; of 1867, 13; and Old Age Pensions Act, 96
Influenza. *See* Diseases
Inglis, Peter, 127
Intrepid Bay, 183
Inuit, and Greenland, 14-15, 105, 121-2, 124-5, 128, 130, 136, 138, 195, 289
Inuit, images of, 21-3, 35, 47-9, 54, 115, 132, 166, 180, 182-3, 200, 206, 214-17, 220, 227-8, 236, 241, 300, 360
Inuit affairs, 4, 7, 37, 41, 47, 51, 60, 98, 100
Inuit children, 71-4, 76-8, 80-3, 85, 89, 152, 158, 178, 183, 197, 200, 216, 220, 336-7, 340; adoption of, 72-3, 335; education of, 84, 89, 120, 314, 348, 360; of Kikkik, 231-2, 234, 262-4; starvation of, 230; and Inuit citizenship, 7, 15, 30, 33, 37, 96, 220, 312-13, 327, 344, 353
Inuit councils, 306-7, 343-5, 353-6, 359; at Baker Lake, 351-2, 355; at Cambridge Bay, 352; at Mackenzie Delta, 90-1
Inuit culture, 5, 8, 22, 43-5, 52-3, 72, 154, 212, 226; survival strategies of, 22, 209; of Ennadai Lake Inuit, 207, 209, 215-16, 225
Inuit dependency (indolence) (indigence), 7, 19-20, 24, 180, 205; at Chesterfield Inlet, 23; and Ennadai Lake Inuit, 210, 213, 223, 224; and family allowances, 72, 88, 98-9, 342; and Hudson's Bay Company, 23, 26, 41, 107-8; and relief, 54, 91, 98-9, 113, 166, 200, 334; and relocation, 323
Inuit elders, 91, 94-7, 160, 195, 309, 357
Inuit families, 3, 8, 44, 64, 67, 72-3, 82, 143-4, 193, 196, 206, 285, 309-12, 338, 348
Inuit health, 16, 46-51, 58, 99, 338, 351; and *Book of Wisdom*, 86; conditions of, in Arctic Bay (1927), 107-8; and Ennadai Lake Inuit, 218, 221-2; and epidemics and

evacuation to the south, 43, 308; and family allowances, 74, 76, 82; and Hudson's Bay Company, 77; and Indian and Northern Health Services, 39; and Inuit women, 84; and medical services at Grise Fiord, 321; Quebec, responsibility for, 38; at Whale Cove, 300
Inuit history, 4, 207, 360
Inuit policy, 4, 8, 10, 13, 19, 37-8, 40-2, 45, 104
Inuit population, 28, 54, 110, 312-15, 322-3, 334, 346; of Ennadai Lake Inuit, 221, 226
Inuit resistance, 3, 8, 10, 44-5, 60, 104, 187, 307, 317, 324, 359, 361; and Ennadai Lake Inuit, 212, 215, 226, 228, 234
Inuit self-government, 6, 60, 357, 359, 361
Inuit women: assimilation of, 314, 332; and child care, 76, 83-4; at Ennadai Lake, 216, 220; and family allowances, 304; at Garry Lake, 255; at Grise Fiord, 200; and high Arctic relocations, 145, 154, 158-9; and isolation at Resolute, 178, 183; Leah Idlout, 196; and pensions, 96; at Rankin Inlet, 296-9; at Whale Cove, 287-8. *See also* Kikkik
Inukjuak (Port Harrison): Baffin Trading Company at, 109; conditions at, 155; and family allowances, 78, 81; health services at, 115, 197; Hudson's Bay Company at, 198; Inuit council at, 355; and Marjorie Hinds, 85, 93; and relief, 31, 68-9, 98; and relocation to high Arctic, 60, 64, 101-5, 128, 138, 140-8, 153, 156-9, 162, 164, 175, 180-1, 184-93, 196, 201-4, 312, 318
Inukpuk, Johnnie, 356
Iqaluit (Frobisher Bay), 10, 175, 190, 334, 338, 340, 355
Isachsen, 320-1, 324
Itteroyuk, 263

Jackson, A.Y., 106. *See also* Banting, Dr. Frederick
James, Reverend, 53
Jasse, R.F., 128
Jaybeddie, 149, 169, 172
Jenkins, Constable, 200-1
Jenness, Diamond, 15, 33, 105-6, 111-12, 317
Jenness, R.A., 285-6
Josephie and Rynee, 193

Kabluk, 262, 264, 272
Kanayook, Annie, 189
Karyook, 222
Kayai, 232
Kazan River, 50, 206, 211, 270
Kearney, H., 169-70
Keenleyside, Hugh, 57-8, 60

Set in Stone by Vancouver Desktop Publishing Centre

Printed and bound in Canada by D.W. Friesen & Sons Ltd.

Copy-editor: Carolyn Bateman

Proofreader: Joanne Richardson

Cartographer: Eric Leinberger